METHODS OF
RHETORICAL CRITICISM

METHODS OF
RHETORICAL CRITICISM

A TWENTIETH-CENTURY PERSPECTIVE

Second edition, revised
Edited by
Bernard L. Brock, *Wayne State University, and*
Robert L. Scott, *University of Minnesota*

Wayne State University Press
Detroit,

Library of Congress Cataloging in Publication Data
Main entry under title:

Methods of rhetorical criticism.   P N
   Edition for 1972 entered under R. L. Scott.   4061
   Bibliography: p.   S37
   Includes index.   1980
   1. Oratory—Addresses, essays, lectures.
2. Criticism—Addresses, essays, lectures.
I. Brock, Bernard L. II. Scott, Robert Lee,
1928–   comp. Methods of rhetorical criticism.
PN4061.S37   1980   801'.955   80-11422
ISBN 0-8143-1648-4

About the cover photos
Left to right:
   first row—Dwight D. Eisenhower, Richard M. Nixon,
      Barry Goldwater, Hubert Humphrey
   second row—Ted Kennedy, Nikita Khrushchev,
      Franklin D. Roosevelt, Martin Luther King
   third row—Edmund Muskie, Abraham Lincoln, "Rocky,"
      Jimmy Carter
   fourth row—William Buckley, Jr., George McGovern,
      Fidel Castro, George Wallace

Cover art and design by Mary Primeau.

CONTENTS

PREFACE TO FIRST EDITION

The criticism of rhetorical discourse is steadily assuming a more vital role in American life. So pervasive and varied are the efforts of some to influence the beliefs and actions of others that our very environment is taking on a rather distinctly rhetorical character. Coming to some understanding of these efforts in various media of communication has energized critics in such academic departments as English, political science, sociology, journalism, and history to describe and evaluate the flow of public address. Popular journalism is becoming increasingly filled with what we would call rhetorical criticism.

The increased use and diversity of criticism has resulted in such a proliferation of terms and methods that the field of rhetorical criticism appears chaotic to the novice. One is apt to be driven either to oversimplify critical form so as to include all methods or to make criticism so individual as virtually to exclude any method. We would hope that this book responds to the current confusion in criticism by hitting between these two extremes. No one should believe that his favorite nomenclature or method for dealing with those phenomena is apt to be universally adopted. We certainly have no such illusion that ours will be so adopted— not even in that fraction of consciousness of humanity and its ways that we know as academic departments of speech-communication. We do believe, however, that there has been a rather strong and useful tradition of rhetorical criticism in such departments. Moreover, we believe that that tradition has been affected by some important evolutionary forces.

In order to describe those forces and to make possible a way of looking at them that may prove useful for many interested in rhetorical criticism, we have undertaken to assemble this book. A key assumption is that Thomas S. Kuhn is right in arguing that modes of thought dominate the structures scientists find in the reality they describe and manipulate. He calls these modes "paradigms." We believe that Kuhn's concept is useful in considering the regularities in what rhetorical criticism has been in departments like ours and, more importantly, in understanding the situation that critics are in regarding their tradition and present inclinations. We have argued that rhetorical criticism has taken certain shapes in the past and that the present indicates certain potentials for the future. Those arguments will have to stand as readers use and scrutinize this book. We hope that even if many are inclined to reject the way we have typified the reality presented to us by critical activity that these readers will find their rejections meaningful acts in reformulating the reality.

In addition to our describing the abstract forms, we have gathered together two sorts of illustrative materials: essays stating what criticism is or should be and essays actually undertaking the criticism of rhetorical discourse. These essays have been selected from among scores of others that we might have included. If we have chosen well, then the substance of our arguments depends most heavily on these two sorts of illustrations. Clearly we owe a great debt to those scholars who have allowed us to use their writing for our purposes. They should not be held responsible for the purposes that we have brought to them. But we do thank them again for their kind permissions.

Arguments with our colleagues have been instrumental in forming our thought, but these have been too numerous to mention with justice. We hope that some of our friends will see reflected here some influences that they might approve. If they do not see some that make them uneasy, we shall feel that we have not done our job well.

We are most in debt to the tradition that we have mentioned, even though both of us believe that substantially we reject that tradition. We know, however, that no one can say sensibly that he has rejected a tradition unless he has been strongly influenced by it. Only then can a rejection be meaningful. As labels go, Mr. Scott sees himself operating from an "experiential" perspective and Mr. Brock from one of the "new rhetorics."

R. L. S.
B. L. B.
Minneapolis
October 1971

PREFACE TO SECOND EDITION

In preparing the second edition of *Methods of Rhetorical Criticism: A Twentieth Century Perspective* we noted that rhetorical criticism has grown even more diverse than when we prepared the first edition. More than before some sort of overview may be helpful to students who must deal with the diversity that contemporary criticism offers. Although the terminology we extented has not been universally accepted by rhetorical critics (we scarcely expected it to be), it apparently has proved useful enough to warrant a second edition of the book. We have in this edition retained the basic pattern of the first: identifying major perspectives on rhetorical criticism and then presenting essays illustrating theoretical approaches and their application.

If anything, rhetorical criticism seems to have become not only more diverse but more vigorous during the 1970s. That vigor is difficult to express and impossible to contain in a set of covers; it lies rather in the work of numerous colleagues appearing in a variety of journals. We can scarcely recognize properly all those to whom we allude. Clearly a book such as this must be a transient device for studying the broad sweep of criticism.

In this edition we have modified some of the terminology and updated some illustrative essays, but the major change has been an attempt to account for almost a decade's development in rhetorical criticism. In the constant change we note two minor consistencies: Mr. Scott still calls himself an "experientialist" and Mr. Brock a "new rhetorician."

B. L. B.
R. L. S.
April 1979

1
AN INTRODUCTION TO RHETORICAL CRITICISM

"Can President Carter Cope?" "U.S. Mideast Effort Falters," and "Pot of '80 Hopefuls Simmering for GOP" are titles that virtually leap out at us as we leaf through newspapers or magazines. In response we may feel a mixture of curiosity, disdain, or any number of emotions. But if we focus even momentarily on what is written, we are apt to respond in some way.

Not all our responses are critical. Nor are all the articles we glance at critical. But many are. Every day our experiences make us aware of circumstances that seem to cry out for explanations. What we feel moving within us at these moments of special questioning may be called "the critical impulse." But what is this impulse? It is difficult to pinpoint. Perhaps it is a queasy feeling or the urge to run or to strike out. Often it manifests itself by verbalizing agreement or disagreement. At other times the critical impulse is formed into a guarded intellectual statement.

The Province of Criticism

Although what we call the critical impulse is a vague feeling that cannot be defined with precision, man sets some boundaries for himself as critic. Of the phenomena that surround him, he does not undertake to criticize those that might be called natural. If he were to say, "I am a critic of the rocks and hills, of bees and flowers," the statement would strike us as whimsy. He might well find himself puzzled when confronting the objects of nature and raise questions to pursue in hope of finding answers, but we do not think of such work as criticism. Rather, it is to the work of man himself that we turn when moved by the critical impulse.

The vibrations of the air may be considered to be an aspect of the physics of sound. The phenomena of pitch and overtone may be taken to be constituents of harmony and counterpoint. But it is to musical composition and performance that the critic turns.

One can quite readily compose a list of works that are relevant to criticism: theater and literature, sculpture and music, cinema and dance. These we tend to call "art." And although we are not so likely to list them initially, we commonly find references to the art of war (or, less often, the art of peace), to the art of government, or even to the art of marriage. These human relationships in which we find ourselves involved, although unique as particular occurrences, partake of traditions, of institutions, of plans; they are, in short, human productions.

The distinction we tend to make between "fine art" and "practical art" is beguiling. Notice that although we may criticize the practice of the art of government or the performance of a musical composition, in the former case we are less likely to think of ourselves as critics or our product as criticism. Our feeling is that, like natural phenomena, which are not subject to criticism, the practical arts are instruments to aid man's living, whereas the fine arts express man's humanity. Right here, however, the line between the fine and the practical begins to fade as one asks, "What is *living*? Is it simply staying alive?" The line becomes even more obscure if one inserts the term good, as in "What is a good life?"

Clearly, we cannot settle such questions here, but we may point out that the critical impulse has again manifested itself in our responses, and, we trust, in those of our readers. Man does not simply live in an environment; he creates instruments and institutions for living, which he uses, discards, and re-creates. And he sees and assesses what he does. In fact, he seems scarcely able to keep himself from "sizing it up."

But how does one size up in a critical sense? If we simply see a piece of copper, we do not criticize it. As metallurgists, we may question its properties and determine, for example, that it is copper of a certain purity. We begin to size up critically when we see in something a purpose for human use. We may perceive that a particular piece of copper in a peculiar shape is useful for plumbing. Given our interests and abilities, we may say, "He certainly sweats a nice joint."

To speak of "sweating a joint" may be quite foreign to some readers. "I wouldn't think of criticizing one; in fact, I wouldn't know one if I saw one," might be a possible response, and one that helps us make a point. The more we know about some human enterprise, and the more salient it is to our interests, the more likely we are to feel the critical impulse. In fact, consciously or unconsciously we often repress the critical impulse, saying, in effect, "Let me know more about it first."

This observation raises the question, Can't one just know about something without criticizing it? Our position is that (1) knowing about something and (2) recognizing that the object of interest has in some respect become entwined with human purposes in the creation of a human product will lead to criticism. But this position does not preclude answering the question positively. In fact, the impulse to know things in-and-of-themselves may be referred to as the scientific impulse.

We may make several assertions about the scientific impulse with a fair degree of confidence. First, the impulse predates what nearly everyone today calls "science." Ways of knowing things-in-and-of-themselves and the knowledge that scientific procedures presuppose were both so rudimentary and sketchy until the last few centuries that science in a contemporary sense was scarcely possible. Another way of saying all of this is that science itself has a history and preconditions. A second assertion we can make is that designating something as a science, or even as an object for scientific scrutiny, entails an arbitrary narrowing of focus. Thomas H. Huxley recognized this problem when he was explaining the Darwinian theory of natural selection in accounting for the evolution of species. The idea of "nature" (another way of saying things-in-and-of-themselves) must be restricted to those parts of the phenomenal world in which man does not play "the part of immediate cause."[1]

The scientific impulse has become science, then, both historically and operationally, through a series of limitations. The power of science lies in large part in these limitations. If we remember this fact, we shall not go wrong in asking, "Can't we just know about something without criticizing it?" Nor shall we go wrong in believing that finding out about things-as-they-are may be a useful predisposition to criticism.

Too often, however, we believe that we can dispose of all important questions by "scientific" procedures. "The scientist is one of the cultural heroes of our age." With this sentence Edwin Black begins his important book on rhetorical criticism.[2] However, with the crises of war, race, and environment, the accomplishments of science seem a little less heroic. Of course, scientists as scientists have not sought the role of heroes, although some of them as politicians may have done so.

Even now some scientists are in revolt and are arguing that the bulk of their research is not relevant to the most serious problems facing humanity.[3] Such revolts do not indicate a new science as much as a fresh political conscience for the men of science. These revolts may also indicate the critical impulse.

We have no formulary solution to the problem that C. P. Snow popularized as "the two cultures,"[4] but we do believe that the ground for *rapprochement* is being prepared by a contemporary awareness of the inevitability of man's participation in whatever it is he takes to be the facts of the matter.[5]

[1] Thomas H. Huxley, "The Struggle for Existence in Human Society," Evolution and Ethics, New York, Appleton-Century-Crofts, 1899, p. 202.

[2] Edwin Black, Rhetorical Criticism: A Study in Method, New York, Macmillan, 1965, p. 1.

[3] See, for example, "Scientists' 'Relevant' Study Asked," Minneapolis Star (July 22, 1970), p. 5A.

[4] C. P. Snow, The Two Cultures and a Second Look, Cambridge, Cambridge University Press, 1964.

[5] For a discussion from another point of view of some of the problems of the interaction of science and criticism, see Robert L. Scott, "A Rhetoric of Facts: Arthur Larson's Stance as a Persuader," Speech Monographs, XXXV, 2 (June 1968), 109–121. Edwin Black, in the source cited previously, begins his book on criticism with a comparison of science and criticism.

If we are correct in saying that a new humanism is evident in man's capacity to look critically at his own creations, including what he has created as scientist, then the critical impulse seems central to humaneness. But our perception of the welter of activity around us may be wrong and, surely, is biased. The bias is a commitment to criticism, but such commitment should not blind us to the contributions of science, nor to the humaneness of the scientific impulse. If recent history has witnessed a blindness to the limits of science, surely there must be a contrary possibility of a blindness to the limits of criticism. If our analysis suggests that there must be a balance between these impulses, then that balance will result from continuing interactions that will constantly threaten imbalance.

Rather than define "criticism," we have discussed the vague notion of a critical impulse, arguing that such an impulse manifests itself naturally as a man becomes knowledgeable about any human activity and as he sees that this activity is salient to his purposes as a fully functioning man. We would argue that man cannot completely repress the critical impulse because it is a part of learning how to act toward something or someone. Knowing about something necessarily includes knowing how to behave toward it. We recognize, moreover, that although we claim the impulse is natural, it is difficult to imagine a common set of circumstances in which a man depends on that impulse alone. Traditions of criticism surround him and direct his attention and help him formulate methods of dealing critically with the objects of his interest.

Rhetoric as an Object of Criticism

Rhetoric may be defined as the human effort to induce cooperation through the use of symbols. Most definitions tend to give rise to troublesome questions of inclusion and exclusion; this definition is no exception.

First, the limits of rhetoric are imprecise. The simple request, "Please pass the salt," is an example of the use of symbols to induce cooperation. On the other hand, such requests, if repeatedly ignored, may be reinforced with angry shouts and kicks. Although normally we would exclude simple, conventional requests and physical coercion from the concept of rhetoric, no one can draw the boundaries easily. If the notion of voluntary cooperation, that is, that which involves choice on the part of those responding to symbolic inducements, is necessary to define rhetoric, then certainly the everyday conventions that groups respond to are germane; moreover, threats of coercion are much more common than coercion itself, and often succeed. The question, Has one *really* cooperated if he accedes to conventional requests or to threats? calls attention to the difficulty of making distinctions and also to the need for criticism.[6]

Second, an ambiguity of this sort appears in the question, Does rhetoric refer to the process of inducing cooperation or to the product of that process? The obvious answer is that it refers to both, but the answer does not reduce the ambiguity. Historically and currently, the word has been and is used in both senses.

Traditionally, one thinks of criticism in terms of the products of human creation. One is used to thinking of criticism in regard to paintings, novels, and speeches. "Rhetorical criticism" and "speech criticism" are often taken as synonymous. When the living voice was the only practical public means to induce cooperation, speeches nearly exhausted the possibilities of rhetoric. The printing press ended that circumstance. Although the marvels of electronic media have again brought the living voice and visage back to prominence, the forms of presentation stagger the capacity of speeches to contain them. The spot commercial and the Presidential press conference both seem designed to induce cooperation through the use of symbols.

The products of rhetoric, then, are multitudinous. Part of the task of rhetorical criticism is to find a focus, to pick products that will be fruitful to criticize.

But the very idea of product, as traditional as it is for the critic, may be detrimental to the deepest fulfillment of the critical impulse if it is taken as a limit. This conclusion is especially apparent if one follows carefully the implications of the existence of any product, say an ordinary public speech. Where does the speech start? Where does it end? Does it start in the mind of the speaker as he interacts with his social and physical environment? Immediately we are likely to see relationships between his thought, its formation and expression, and similar thoughts, formations, and expressions. We are apt to become aware that the context in which the speech occurs is a rhetorical context. The critic may find himself less interested in commenting on specific speeches as speeches than in typifying the verbal, and perhaps the nonverbal, forms that permeate many speeches and seem to constitute some discernible phenomena.[7] Our effort here is not to typify a par-

---

[6] An exceedingly interesting piece of criticism focuses on a specific case illustrative of the interaction of persuasion and coercion. See James R. Andrews, "The Rhetoric of Coercion and Persuasion: The Reform Bill of 1832," The Quarterly Journal of Speech, LVI, 2 (April 1970), 187–195.

[7] See, for example Franklyn Haiman, "The Rhetoric of the Streets: Some Legal and Ethical Considerations," The Quarterly Journal of Speech, LIII, 2 (April 1967), 99–114; Robert L. Scott and Donald K. Smith, "The Rhetoric of Confrontation," The Quarterly Journal of Speech, LV, 1 (February 1969), 1–8; and Parke G. Burgess, "The Rhetoric of Black Power: A Moral Demand?" The Quarterly Journal of Speech, LV, 2 (April 1969), 122–133.

ticular kind of criticism but rather to point out that ones focus may easily shift from a distinct product toward the process that apparently brings the product into being.

The rhetorical critic may be concerned with such traditional objects as speeches and editorials,[8] or he may be interested in scrutinizing less traditional objects, such as novels and plays,[9] from a rhetorical point of view. He may sense that some event or campaign or movement formed of congeries of rhetorical products will yield to his efforts.[10] Whatever his endeavor, however, it is aroused by his sense of the importance of man's effort to induce cooperation through the use of symbols. Since the critic will wish to bring his audience closer to his own point of view regarding some phenomena, his communication will probably display a deeply rhetorical characteristic. To say that critical comment on rhetoric will likely be rhetorical itself, however, leads to the question: What are the purposes of rhetorical criticism?

Purposes of Rhetorical Criticism

The rhetorical impulse reveals its own purposes. In one sense, the plural *purposes* must be used; in another, when the critic works well, the purposes of rhetorical criticism tend to merge into a unique whole, all present, and yet all subordinate to the purpose of that instance.

The critic's attention is drawn to a certain phenomenon. He sees, but he perceives that his experience is not universally shared. In part, his function is to indicate, to point out, to draw the attention of others to the phenomenon. Since he is not working with something that is simply there, he must show the phenomenal aspects of whatever object he focuses on. In this first respect, his purpose is descriptive.

With more or less awareness of the implications of his activity, the critic endows with meaning the phenomenon to which he attends. We say that he endows it because the meaning shaped in his descriptions is one among several possibilities. In the very act of singling out from among the welter of his experiences those aspects he will set forth as constituting a phenomenon—the impact of a single speech, the career of a speaker, the outlines of a campaign, the sort of argument that typifies a repeated phenomenon in like circumstances, and so on—he

---

[8] For an interesting rhetorical case study of newspaper reporting, see Meredith W. Berg and David M. Berg, "The Rhetoric of War Preparation: The New York Press in 1898," Journalism Quarterly, XLV, 4 (Winter 1968), 653–660.

[9] See, for example, Ray Lynn Anderson, "The Rhetoric of Science Fiction," unpublished Ph.D. dissertation, Minneapolis, University of Minnesota, 1968.

[10] See, for example, James R. Andrews, "Confrontation at Columbia: A Case Study in Coercive Rhetoric," The Quarterly Journal of Speech, LV, 1 (February 1969), 9–16; Leland Griffith, "The Anti-Masonic Persuasion," unpublished Ph.D. dissertation, Ithaca, N.Y., Cornell University, 1950.

begins to shape the meaning of the phenomenon for anyone who attends to his critique. In taking responsibility for his shapings, the critic's purpose becomes interpretive.

Finally, the critic judges. In some way or another, implicitly or explicitly, he says that the rhetoric, product or process, is well done or ill. On what basis does he judge? We shall turn to that question shortly.

Many rhetorical critics would like to ignore the evaluative purpose of criticism. Some pointedly exclude evaluation by labeling their efforts "descriptive," as if to say that this is their sole purpose. Although we can understand some of the motivations for such limitations, we believe that evaluation cannot be excluded entirely. The descriptive act, in and of itself, implies that the phenomenon as described is worth attending to.

The primary purposes of rhetorical criticism are to describe, to interpret, and to evaluate. These purposes tend to merge into one another. One purpose prepares for the next; the one that follows reflects back on the one that has been explicated.

The process of calling attention to a phenomenon, interpreting it, and judging it, will inevitably result in a product that is designed, more or less consciously, to be persuasive. The critic says implicitly, "See as I see, know as I know, value as I value." If we are correct in our interpretation of the critical act, then when that act is directed toward rhetorical objects, which are themselves potentially persuasive, the critic enters into the arena of argument inhabited by the object he criticizes.

Just as the critic may choose to deemphasize the evaluative function of criticism, he may wish to minimize the persuasive potential of his work. Nevertheless, he should be prepared to recognize the possible social consequences, for if rhetoric seeks to induce the cooperation of others, then the seeking and the cooperation achieved will have consequences.

Criticism is a potent social force. Although academic critics seem quite chary of it, popular critics are much less cautious. For example, those who criticize Presidential speaking, formally or informally, whether or not they call themselves rhetorical critics, usually embrace vigorously the possibility of a persuasive impact of their acts.

In addition to the primary purposes of description, interpretation, evaluation, and, we would add, persuasion, rhetorical criticism may have a number of secondary purposes. Primary purposes include those that seem to adhere to the act of criticism itself; secondary purposes are any others that the act may be made to serve.

Clearly in the critical impulse lies the motivation to learn about things. The pedagogical function of rhetorical criticism stretches back to antiquity. Choosing model speeches for the students to imitate was an early critical act. The question was, What speeches are worth saving and studying? In addition to the basic evaluation necessary, interpretation was needed, that is, the schoolboy had to understand the speech in his own way, if imitation of it was not simply to be slavish.[11]

Closely allied to the pedagogical function is the theoretical. Criticism may serve theoretical motivations in two ways: First, it may give rise to insights that can then be phrased as principles for further use or hypotheses for further testing. Second, criticism may serve as a test. If conventional principles are sound, then they should be confirmed in the practice of good speakers. Again, descriptive, interpretative, and evaluative functions are necessary to serve adequately these secondary purposes.[12]

In addition to learning about rhetoric, one may undertake the study of rhetorical criticism to learn about other matters, such as those involved in speaking, writing, or other symbolic actions. One's motivation may be historical, biographical, or cultural. Indeed, rhetorical materials are artifacts, and, therefore, are the evidence for reconstructing the lives and ways of the people who produced these materials.

Criteria for Rhetorical Criticism

If evaluation continually manifests itself in criticism, then the question, On what grounds shall I evaluate? is inevitable. The question is difficult to deal with.

The difficulty first arises out of the multiplicity of purposes that criticism can serve. If, at its best, a piece of criticism subordinates the ordinary purposes to a unique whole, then the criteria appropriate to the critical act may be unique. But if we leave the matter at this point, we have simply refused to answer an honest question: Is there no standard common to all acts of rhetorical criticism?

The most common standard asserted is that of effect. Since rhetorical acts are normally viewed as instrumental, as indeed the phrase "inducing cooperation" may be taken, then is not success in using the instrument the final measure? If, for example, the purpose of a Presidential campaign is to elect the candidate, then the candidate elected has mounted a good campaign.

As tempting as this pragmatic evaluation may be, the critic who invokes it so simply is likely to find himself in some embarrassing positions. May not the success in a campaign, for example, be attributed

---

[11] For an excellent discussion of the classical notion of imitatio, see Donald Leman Clark, Rhetoric in Greco-Roman Education, New York, Columbia University Press, 1957, chap. 6.

[12] For a vigorous criticism of the contention that rhetorical criticism can serve these purposes well, see Phillip K. Tompkins, "Rhetorical Criticism: Wrong Medium?" Central States Speech Journal, XIII, 1 (Winter 1962), 90–95.

more to the ineptness of the opposition than to the adequacy of the winner? Long before the New Left was arguing that neither American political party gives the citizens an adequate choice, some people on the political right were saying almost the same thing. Hence, one of the slogans of the 1964 campaign: "A choice, not an echo." Are not some of the most successful persuaders, on the face of what they say, disreputable, and some of the best unsuccessful? Would the criterion of effect lead us to conclude that Adolph Hitler was one of the finest speakers of history and Demosthenes among the poorest? Was Martin Luther King, Jr., successful?

The answers to these questions are not simple, but two conclusions are indicated. First, we tend to shift our perspective. For example, we can say that Hitler was good in one respect and bad in another, or that Martin Luther King, Jr., was overwhelmingly successful, given the circumstances within which his rhetoric worked. Second, in spite of the difficulties that the criterion of effect entails, it is impossible to do without this criterion altogether. Although the question, Is one success as good as another? indicates the ultimate shortcoming of that criterion, the very question assumes some weight when applied to the notion of effect.

We have scarcely discussed all of the difficulties. Some of these arise from traditional uncertainties, such as linking causes with effects in any circumstance. Again the difficulties are compounded by the necessity to focus on a few effects among many, since it is an impossible task to be aware of all the possible effects of any complex, human action. The shifting of perspective mentioned in the last paragraph may be one of turning from immediate effects to long-run effects.

Motivated in part by the difficulties of assessing effect and in part by their concept of rhetoric, some critics examine the process of persuasion and then appeal to artistic criteria to evaluate. Such an appeal may be thought of as the doctrine of effectiveness in contrast to the doctrine of effect. Authority for this doctrine is drawn from Aristotle, who defines rhetoric as "the faculty of observing in any given case the available means of persuasion." Focusing on the means, not the ends, the point of rhetoric is "not simply to succeed in persuading, but rather to discover the means of coming as near such success as the circumstances of each particular case allow."[13]

Appealing to artistic criteria assumes that there are well-recognized principles that can be embodied concretely in particular works. Today many critics might question such an assumption. Indeed, because of such an inclination to question the notion that there are clearly recog-

---

[13] *Aristotle,* Rhetoric (*W. Rhys Roberts trans.*) 1355^{b}26; 1355^{b}10.

nized, artistic principles to which the critic may appeal, we have undertaken to compile this book.

If a critic is to appeal to the doctrine of effectiveness, what will be the source of his critical criteria? The very assumption of principles that are used in such a way that they can be appealed to as criteria suggests that authority or tradition will be their source. But why should a critic follow a particular tradition or authority? Two reasons are given as possible explanations, although they are not always clearly distinct from one another. The first is that the authority or tradition seems consistent with practice, which may be a way of appealing obliquely to the doctrine of effect. The second is that the authority or tradition seems internally consistent and the principles are coherent with one another and with the sense of good practice with which the critic and his immediate culture feel comfortable.

In considering traditional criteria, whatever the theoretical vocabulary may be, one senses the potential interactions of product and process in the doctrines of effect and effectiveness. We do not mean to suggest the comfortable compromise of a platitudinous "at best all work together," which is obviously true but not helpful. What we see is a circularity in which the appeal to good practice helps to establish principle and the appeal to principle helps to determine good practice. Often the observation of circularity is offered as a refutation of the efficacy of whatever exhibits that characteristic. We do not offer our observation in a refutative sense, however. We believe that such circularity is inevitably a part of building a tradition. If the critic rejects a tradition, he will probably do so either because it fails to do what it promises or because he appeals to standards that are outside the tradition.

Often rhetorical critics appeal to standards that are outside rhetoric. The tendency to make ethical judgments about the goodness of rhetoric is often such an appeal; perhaps it is inevitably such an appeal. In any case, critics often do submit rhetoric to ethical or moral judgments.

The doctrine of effect leads to the judgment of rhetoric as good pragmatically; that is, whatever the given ends, the rhetorical means seem causally important in reaching them. The doctrine of effectiveness leads to the judgment of rhetoric as a qualified good, that is, given a sense of good means, the rhetoric in question is an embodiment of such means. To make a moral judgment of rhetoric may be to extend the doctrine of effect—to argue that some ultimate goals are or are not enhanced by the rhetoric in question. On the other hand, such a judgment may be focused on means, on the assumption that some means are per se valuable whereas others are destructive to human value.

Recently some critics have argued that although most ethical evaluations of rhetoric have indeed been an appeal beyond the rhetorical itself to nonrhetorical standards, the critic may find an intrinsically rhetorical ethic. We cannot argue the questions raised by such a potentiality in this introduction, but the notion, as it is now being worked out, is one of the most exciting problems in contemporary rhetorical theory.[14]

The State of the Art of Rhetorical Criticism

We have raised many more questions than we have answered. Nevertheless, we have made a number of assertions that might be argued at some length. In short, looking at rhetorical criticism as it is revealed in practice, the nature of the art seems uncertain and unclear. Issues to be settled are basic ones, not ones of application of accepted procedures to commonly perceived problems.

Probably the most important recent book to be published on rhetorical criticism is Edwin Black's *Rhetorical Criticism: A Study in Method.*[15] In it he identified and objected to a tradition that appeared to have been well accepted for more than thirty years. This tradition he called neo-Aristotelian criticism.

We believe that Professor Black was astoundingly accurate in his assessment. Although we may disagree in some details, in our opinion his descriptions of and arguments about the insufficiency of neo-Aristotelianism are penetrating.[16] But Professor Black's voice was not so lonely as it seemed when he first raised it. Although he drew together, better than any other single person, feelings that the old assumptions were not adequate for the tasks at hand, he was scarcely alone in his convictions.

We are in the midst of a disintegrating tradition. Perhaps rhetorical criticism now is transitional; from it will grow a fresh tradition. Of the latter point, we cannot be certain; of the former we are convinced.

Thomas S. Kuhn's picture of *The Structure of Scientific Revolutions*[17] may be instructive in understanding the state of rhetorical criticism at this moment. Kuhn's own thought is revolutionary. He rejects the well-established notion that scientific knowledge grows by a gradual accu-

[14] *For an excellent idea of the potentialities now envisioned, see Parke G. Burgess,* "The Rhetoric of Moral Conflict," The Quarterly Journal of Speech, *LVI, 2 (April 1970), 120–130.*

[15] *Edwin Black,* Rhetorical Criticism: A Study in Method, *New York, Macmillan, 1965.*

[16] *Our fundamental disagreement with Professor Black stems from his argument that in a time of crisis in values the lack of shared values makes* logos *(in the sense of enthymemes based on culturally assumed premises) impossible. For a critique of the book see Robert L. Scott,* The Quarterly Journal of Speech, LI, 3 (October 1965), 333–338.

[17] *Thomas S. Kuhn,* The Structure of Scientific Revolutions, *Chicago, University of Chicago Press, 1962. (The book is also available in a paperback Phoenix edition from the University of Chicago Press.)*

mulation of knowledge; in such a process errors are sifted out and replaced by fresh hypotheses, which are verified and developed into an
orderly, unified pattern. If the unified pattern does not exist, this view
contends, the hypothesis is assumed to be the goal of a progression
proceeding from the engrained ignorance and misinformation of prescientific culture to the full explanation of nature in-and-of-itself.

Kuhn argues that science grows by fits and starts. That fundamental to
change, which may not be progress at all, is the construction of a fresh
"paradigm." By paradigm he means an imaginative picture of what reality
is like. Rather than being noncultural, scientists form a community, or
community of interests. When a number are convinced of the efficacy of a
particular paradigm, usually resulting from the insight of an unusually creative thinker, the work of "ordinary science" begins. Ordinary science is
the clarifying and testing of innumerable hypotheses implied by the paradigm. As this work progresses, the inadequacies, the lacunae, and the
contradictions of the paradigm become more apparent and more bother-
some. At first these are simply ignored—for they can be ignored until
scientists have worked out other problems from among the myriad hypotheses that can be stated in the various branches of science. Finally,
however, the old paradigm breaks down from the weight of its inadequacies, which are really the dissatisfactions (one might almost say "the lack
of faith") of scientists in it. Other paradigms compete for the loyalties of
scientific workers—for working to the pattern of a paradigm is an excellent
definition of such loyalty.

Whether or not the sort of rhetorical criticism that grew up in the speech
departments of American colleges and universities during the past fifty
years would qualify as *paradigmatic* is probably arguable. But a strong
tradition, the roots of which are best revealed by Herbert Wichelns's 1925
essay, "The Literary Criticism of Oratory," did grow (see Chapter 2). The
inadequacies of the tradition were undoubtedly always apparent, but they
began to impress themselves on more and more rhetorical critics in the
1960s. Searching for alternative frames of reference, critics have turned in
a number of directions. By gathering together both theoretical essays
about criticism and examples of criticism, we shall try to indicate some of
the most promising of these directions, letting the critics who take them
speak for themselves.

The Pattern of the Book
We believe that the efforts we shall try to describe are pre-paradigmatic.
Whether or not any of the critical probings now apparent will build into a
fresh paradigm is not clear. Therefore, our dividing the book into four
general sections—traditional, experiential, and "New Rhetorics" perspectives, and the meta-critical approaches—should not be taken as an attempt to fix the outlines along which criticism must proceed.

Within the traditional perspective we have identified two approaches: the dominant neo-Aristotelian, and the historical. The former emphasizes that the speaker's role determines the choices that make speeches. Historical effects seem best explained in terms of the choices of dominant individuals who interpret and express the circumstances in which people struggle in such a way as to demonstrate leadership. People who speak out in a time of crisis arouse the interest of the traditional critic.

We have observed three general tendencies to break from the traditional perspective: First, a move to reorient the critique from the speaker to the critic; second, an attempt to replace Aristotelian rhetorical theory as the starting point for criticism; and third, a transcendence of isolated theoretical perspectives in favor of an overarching framework that allows critics to work from various perspectives within the whole.

Criticism that has a critic's orientation we have called the "experiential" perspective. The experiences of critics—the rhetorical standards that they have established throughout years of extensive reading and varied contacts—are drawn on creatively as starting points for their rhetorical criticism. Experiential criticism is probably more diverse than any other perspective, but two approaches that stand out within this perspective are those we call "eclectic" and "social reality."

Criticism that attempts to replace Aristotelian theory will be referred to as the "New Rhetorics" perspective. The critics who embrace the views of the New Rhetorics believe that there is an underlying theory capable of informing criticism generally, although they do not agree on what that theory should be. We shall refer to two tendencies within this perspective: the "language-action" approach and the "dramatistic" approach. Although we believe this latter tendency, which we have called "meta-criticism," might take many forms, we have noted two potent frames: movement studies and generic criticism.

In each section of this anthology we shall endeavor, first, to explain the critical perspective; second, to represent it with theoretical essays; and third, to illustrate it with criticism embodying the relevant theory.

We believe that agreement was complete enough and practice consistent enough to justify our referring to the traditional perspective of rhetorical criticism as a paradigm. But, in organizing the breaks from tradition into three categories, we do not mean to imply that these are clearly unified counter traditions. We do think that the nature of these tendencies, the assumptions underlying them, and their theoretical implications are well enough formed to warrant the categories and sub-categories that we shall make. But we also believe that the circumstance of criticism is quite fluid and that the tendencies involved may form themselves in ways that we can scarcely predict.

The critic, of course, must form his or her own discourse. We are particularly interested in writing and include essays here. Although the world of publication is a rapidly shifting, electronic one, we believe that essays are apt to remain important to the substance of rhetorical criticism into the foreseeable future.

As Edwin Black argues tellingly, the critic's own style will be essential in forming the critique.[18] The rhetorical critic should gather reference books which deal with such details of writing as style and usage. This book, however, is not intended to be a handbook on the mechanics of writing critical essays. Our final chapter, "Decisions in Rhetorical Criticism," should not be taken in that vein. Rather we hope to raise some important questions about junctures at which the critic must make decisions that will shape specific pieces of criticism.

There are a number of essays that are similar to our final chapter in their intent. Especially worthy of the student's attention are James W. Chesebro and Caroline D. Hamsher's "Rhetorical Criticism: A Message-Centered Procedure"[19] and Wayne Brockriede's "Rhetorical Criticism as Argument."[20]

We hope this text goes behind the mechanics of writing criticism to the theory and methods involved. At the same time we have included essays by critics which should stand as illustrations not only of each method but of critical writing.

For other general orientations toward criticism, students may want to study one or more recent books listed at the end of this chapter. The bibliography at the end of the book offers a more complete listing.

Some Recent Books on Rhetorical Criticism

Arnold, Carroll C. *Criticism of Oral Rhetoric*. Columbus, Ohio: Charles E. Merrill, 1974.

Black, Edwin. *Rhetorical Criticism: A Study in Method*. New York: Macmillan, 1965 (Reprinted by the University of Wisconsin Press, 1978).

Campbell, Karlyn Kohrs. *Critiques of Contemporary Rhetoric*. Belmont, California: Wadsworth, 1972.

Hillbruner, Anthony. *Critical Dimensions: The Art of Public Address Criticism*. New York: Random House, 1966.

Nichols, Marie Hochmuth. *Rhetoric and Criticism*. Baton Rouge, Louisiana: Louisiana State University Press, 1963.

---

[18] *This argument seems to us one of the main thrusts of Black's "Foreword" to the 1978 edition of* Rhetorical Criticism: A Study in Method. *See especially p. xiv.*

[19] *"Rhetorical Criticism: A Message-Centered Procedure,"* The Speech Teacher, *XXII, 4 (November 1973), 282–90.*

[20] *"Rhetorical Criticism as Argument,"* The Quarterly Journal of Speech, *LX, 2 (April 1974), 165–74.*

Nilsen, Thomas R., ed. *Essays on Rhetorical Criticism.* New York: Random House, 1968.

Stewart, Charles J.; Ochs, Donovan J.; Mohrmann, Gerald P.; eds. *Explorations in Rhetorical Criticism.* University Park, Pennsylvania: Pennsylvania State University Press, 1973.

Thonssen, Lester, and Baird, A. Craig. *Speech Criticism: The Development of Standards for Rhetorical Appraisal.* New York: Ronald Press, 1948 (2d ed. with Waldo Braden, 1970).

2
THE TRADITIONAL PERSPECTIVE

We have discussed a "critical impulse," suggesting that it inheres in the process of making some phenomena a part of human experience; in fact, the critical impulse is central to the human experience. The impulse can be studied because people continually formalize and institutionalize it to serve their needs.

In the academic work of speech-communication departments, the "critical impulse" was formalized into a traditional perspective for rhetorical criticism during the first half of the twentieth century. Herbert Wichelns laid the cornerstone with his essay, "The Literary Criticism of Oratory."[1] The basic outlines Wichelns laid down were given the fullest detail by Lester Thonssen and A. Craig Baird in *Speech Criticism.*[2] Essays representative of the sort of criticism that drew on this tradition are in the three-volume series, *A History and Criticism of American Public Address,* sponsored by the Speech Association of America.[3]

The traditional perspective solidified into a paradigm during the ferment of departmentalization of American higher education. In the late nineteenth and early twentieth centuries some of the traditional, broad disciplines began to splinter, and new fields such as psychology, sociology, and political science sought to establish unique identities. Speech-communication, or what some people called oratory and drama, became a part of that process. In 1898 Brander Matthews wrote that "an oration or a drama, shall be judged not as literature only, but also in accordance with the principles of its own art."[4] Matthews accepted a basic link between speech and literature and attempted to establish, in addition, some unique characteristics for oratory and drama. The drive for differentiation was intensified as the discipline of speech-communication became increasingly separate from English departments. The separation was symbolized by the formation of the National Association of Academic Teachers of Public Address in 1915 (renamed the Speech Association of America in 1946, and the Speech Communication Association in 1970).

[1] *"The Literary Criticism of Oratory," in A. M. Drummond (ed.),* Rhetoric and Public Speaking in Honor of James A. Winans, *New York, Century, 1925.*

[2] Speech Criticism, *New York, Ronald Press, 1948, 2d ed., Waldo Braden, 1970.*

[3] *W. Norwood Brigance (ed.),* A History and Criticism of American Public Address, *vols. I and II, New York, McGraw-Hill, 1943; and Marie Hochmuth Nichols (ed.),* A History and Criticism of American Public Address, vol. III, *London, Longmans, Green, 1955.*

[4] *"The Relation of Drama to Literature," Forum (January 1898), 630–40 in Thomas R. Nilsen (ed.),* Essays on Rhetorical Criticism, *New York, Random House, 1968, p. 4.*

In his formative essay, after exhaustively reviewing available work, Herbert Wichelns concluded that "we have not much serious criticism of oratory." He sought to establish a framework for such criticism. For two reasons we believe that it is fair to cite Wichelns's essay as the beginning of the paradigm that has since dominated. First, he sets forth a difference between literature and rhetoric that is still generally accepted—rhetoric is concerned with effect and literature with permanence. Second, his fundamental outline for criticism was accepted by most critics for at least thirty years.

In *Speech Criticism,* the first book in the field devoted solely to the theory and methods of criticizing speeches, Lester Thonssen and A. Craig Baird extended the traditional perspective as defined by Wichelns. Although the authors surveyed much of the history of rhetoric and drew examples from twentieth-century criticism, essentially they took the Aristotelian rhetorical theory and historical method suggested by Wichelns and developed them into a more complex series of patterns.

Finally, in 1955 Marie Hochmuth Nichols published the third volume of *History and Criticism of American Public Address,* supplementing William Norwood Brigance's two volumes released in 1943. These works include the critical efforts of forty scholars in the field of speech-communication and demonstrate the application of the basic patterns to traditional criticism. However, the application was uneven and at times deviated significantly from the ideal. Wichelns, and later Thonssen and Baird, stressed making judgments about the effects of rhetoric, but these critical essays tended to stress description, stopping shy of evaluation. The thrust of traditional criticism apparently brought many critics to look upon their art as that of identifying conventional rhetorical strategies and presenting an account of the speaker and the times.

Within the traditional perspective two approaches to criticism stand out: the neo-Aristotelian and the historical. Some critics weave the two approaches into a unified work, but often they stand quite separately. The roots of these approaches can be found in Wichelns's discussion of three types of criticism. The first is "predominantly personal or biographical" and "goes behind the work to the man" [historical]. The second "attempts to hold the scales even between the biographical and the literary [rhetorical] interest. . . . The third is occupied with the work and tends to ignore the man" [neo-Aristotelian].

Neo-Aristotelian Approach

The nomenclature common to traditional criticism is derived from Aristotle's *Rhetoric.* To stress that the pattern is derived from the ancient source, Edwin Black labels it "neo-Aristotelian."[5]

---

[5] Rhetorical Criticism: A Study in Method, *New York, Macmillan, 1965, passim, esp. p. 31. This book was reprinted in 1978 by the University of Wisconsin Press, Madison, Wisconsin.*

In his 1925 essay, Herbert Wichelns listed the necessary elements for neo-Aristotelian criticism: "The speaker's personality as a conditioning factor . . . the public character of the man . . . a description of the speaker's audience . . . the leading ideas with which he plied his hearers—his topics, the motives to which he appealed, the nature of the proofs he offered . . . the surviving texts to what was actually uttered . . . the speaker's mode of arrangement and his mode of expression . . . his habit of preparation and his manner of delivery . . . diction and sentence movement . . . the effect of the discourse on its immediate hearers." This impressive list of Aristotelian topics became the rhetorical ideal for the neo-Aristotelian critic, who, after 1948, drew from the heavily detailed Aristotelianism of Thonssen and Baird's *Speech Criticism*.[6]

The ideal prescribed by Wichelns was quite ambitious because its method, essentially, required the critic to describe and analyze in depth all aspects of the historical and rhetorical elements that surround a rhetorical act. In practice few critics were able to achieve the ideal, even though the neo-Aristotelian approach dominated the literature of rhetorical criticism for thirty years. In studying the three volumes of *History and Criticism of American Public Address,* Black concluded that fifteen of the fifty essays employ this pattern and that the neo-Aristotelian influence significantly affected many of the remaining twenty-five essays.[7]

Following our pattern for including essays in this anthology—one setting forth and another applying theory—we have chosen two essays to illustrate neo-Aristotelian criticism: Herbert Wichelns's "The Literary Criticism of Oratory" and Marie Hochmuth Nichols's "Abraham Lincoln's First Inaugural Address." We have already commented on the significance of Wichelns's work. Professor Nichols's essay represents the neo-Aristotelian tradition at its best. She does an excellent job of discussing all of the elements initially set forth by Wichelns, weaving history and rhetorical analysis together quite effectively. In the process the essay typifies the common neo-Aristotelian bent, stressing description and interpretation rather than evaluation.

Historical Approach
Wichelns's three types of criticism describe a continuum of emphasis, one end of which is "predominantly personal or biographical." We label this emphasis "historical." The neo-Aristotelian perspective tends to shortcut the demanding traditional criticism by focusing on the *work* from an Aristotelian point of view; the historical approach tends to reduce the

---

[6] *Walter Fisher, "Method in Rhetorical Criticism,"* Southern Speech Communication Journal, XXXV, 2 (Winter 1969), 101–9, reads Wichelns in much the same way we do.

[7] *Black, p. 28.*

complete traditional pattern by concentrating on the *historical elements* of the person and the times. The historical approach assumes a causal relation between events in history and public address. Viewing public address as both formed by and formative of the events of history, the historical critic analyzes the interrelationship of rhetoric and its times as essential to his study. Ernest Wrage, an historical critic, believed that American public address should be approached as a study in the history of ideas. From his perspective the critical act is viewed as "tracing out an American intellectual pattern." We offer his essay "Public Address: A Study in Social and Intellectual History" as representative of the *theory* of the historical approach and, as an application of that approach, "The Little World of Barry Goldwater." Wrage contrasts his approach to neo-Aristotelian criticism, "One focuses mainly upon the speaker and the speaking activity [neo-Aristotelian], the other upon the speech and its content [intellectual history]. One seeks to explain factors which contributed to personal persuasion; the other yields knowledge of more general interest in terms of man's cultural strivings and heritage." Wrage then unites the rhetorical perspective and the historical approach, "To adopt the rhetorical perspective is actually to approximate more closely a genuinely historical point of view when analyzing and interpreting speeches as documents of ideas in social history."

Characteristics of the Traditional Perspective

In spite of their different emphasis, the neo-Aristotelian and the historical approaches share a common heritage, perspective, and several assumptions. Their common heritage starts with the dictates of the classical rhetoricians, especially Aristotle's famous definition of rhetoric as "the faculty of observing in any given case the available means of persuasion."[8] In its subsequent development, rhetorical criticism served as an illustration and refinement of what has become known as the "classical canon." The point of departure for traditional criticism is well indicated by Wichelns, "One must conceive of the public man as influencing the men of his own times by the power of his discourse." It is in this light that the neo-Aristotelian critic studies the progress of any identifiable influence that originates with the speaker, while the historical critic studies the ideas presented by the speaker as an integral part of their times. We refer to the traditional perspective with its focus on the speaker as the center of interest as a *speaker orientation*. The traditional critic is likely to see the historical ap-

---

[8] *1355^{b}26. Aristotle's* Rhetoric *is readily available in several editions. We are citing the translation by W. Rhys Roberts which may be found in an inexpensive Modern Library edition by Random House.*

proach as posing problems that can be represented by such questions as: What strategies or rhetorical principles or ideas does the speaker employ in his message? How did the speaker adapt to the audience? How did his times, background, and training influence the speaker? How did the speaker take advantage of the historical setting and occasion? It is not simply that the traditional perspective examines the interaction among the speaker, message, occasion, setting, and audience, but that the interaction is consistently viewed through the speaker's eyes. Aristotle's principles are taken as choices that a speaker must make. If the question, Is the rhetoric good for society? evolves, the critic is likely to put it aside as not relevant since the approach itself "gives the speaker his purposes." Thus, the traditional perspective tends to be amoral, attempting to raise and answer technical problems.

The traditional approach, with its speaker orientation, seems to assume that society is highly stable and that people, circumstances, and rhetorical principles remain fundamentally unchanged throughout history. It further assumes that rhetoricians have discovered the essential principles of public persuasion, and that the critic's primary concern should be to describe the use of the traditional principles in conjunction with modern variations in the ongoing public address.

The traditional critic is apt to scrutinize historical rather than contemporary public address because greater objectivity can be attained and the details of the events better documented.[9] If he strives for objectivity and believes that rhetorical principles reflect a relatively stable reality, it follows that an accurate reconstruction of history is his goal.

The orientation, assumptions, and consensus that describe the traditional perspective are summarized in the following outline:

1. Orientation. The critic concentrates on the speaker (or the apparent source of discourse). His purpose is to consider the speaker's response to the rhetorical problems that the speaking situation poses.

2. Assumptions.

a. Society is stable; people, circumstances, and rhetorical principles are fundamentally the same throughout history.

b. Rhetoricians have discovered the essential principles of public discourse.

c. Rhetorical concepts are reasonably discrete and can be studied apart from one another in the process of analyzing rhetorical discourse.

---

[9] As one well-known traditional critic warned, though one may suspect with at least a touch of humorous hyperbole, any speaker studied should "be safely dead and buried, the principal reason being the prime necessity of critical perspective." Loren Reid, "The Perils of Rhetorical Criticism," The Quarterly Journal of Speech, XXX, 4 (December 1944), 419.

   d. A reasonably close word-thought-thing relationship exists. Rhetorical concepts accurately describe an assumed reality.

   3. Consensus. Rhetoricians generally agree that Aristotle identified the ideal rhetorical process.

   All dividing and labeling of human activity must be suspected of being arbitrary to some degree, but we believe that a traditional perspective is observable in much twentieth-century rhetorical criticism. This perspective was dominant and unchallenged for nearly twenty-five years; so well established was it that we have chosen to call it "paradigmatic" in that its norms circumscribed acceptable critical activity. The subordinate approaches, which we call the neo-Aristotelian and the historical, are often separate but sometimes merged as critics approach the ideal set by Wichelns.

   Students interested in additional examples of traditional criticism should study applications in the three volumes of *A History and Criticism of American Public Address* as convenient sources. Almost any essay published consciously as rhetorical criticism from 1925 until 1960 will probably illustrate the paradigm.

   One should not conclude that the elements that made the traditional perspective vigorous are by any means moribund, either in theory or in practice. A brilliant application of neo-Aristotelian principles and a discussion of the relevancy of these principles may be studied in a pair of essays by G. P. Mohrmann and Michael Leff.[10] Few would deny that their reading of Abraham Lincoln's "Cooper Union Address" quickens interest and insight into this highly significant speech. The theoretical discussion in their analysis of the text reinvigorates the tradition and relates it to the growing interest in what is being called "generic criticism," a term we discuss and illustrate later in this book.

   Nor are Mohrmann and Leff the only persons drawing imaginatively from neo-Aristotelianism. In 1972, Forbes Hill applied those principles in criticizing a speech by Richard Nixon with an aim, in part, of providing a sharp contrast with the readings made by several other critics.[11] The existence of those varied critiques and the ensuing exchange between Forbes Hill and Karlyn Kohrs Campbell over the contrasting readings and the efficacy of

---

[10] *"Lincoln at Cooper Union: A Rationale for Neo-Classical Criticism,"* The Quarterly Journal of Speech, *LX, 4 (December 1974), 459–67; and "Lincoln at Cooper Union: A Rhetorical Analysis of the Text,"* The Quarterly Journal of Speech, *LX, 3 (October 1974), 346–58. (Notice that Mohrmann and Leff use "neo-classical" rather than "neo-Aristotelian." They seem to make this move to distinguish their analysis from that of Edwin Black who used the latter term. One or both of these parties might well object to our having collapsed their efforts into a unit.)*

[11] *"Conventional Wisdom—Traditional Form: The President's Message of November 3, 1969,"* The Quarterly Journal of Speech, *LVIII, 4 (December 1972), 373–86.*

the methods offer a stimulating case study for students of rhetorical criticism.[12]

Finally, students should not miss Barnet Baskerville's argument for the significance and the integrity of an historical reading of rhetorical materials.[13] Our analysis leads us to present this historical impulse as one of two approaches within a more complete tradition. We recognize that this position can be taken as a negative judgment even though we intend to describe what critics actually do.[14] Baskerville argues that historical essays are as fully useful as rhetorical essays on any subject and, therefore, are not offshoots of anything,[15] but are capable of standing alone.

The traditional perspective is far from dead. It represents a special formalizing of the critical impulse, which came to be questioned as other forms of the impulse took shape. To study the breaks from tradition, however, we believe that the dominant mode must be understood and appreciated. As a means of gaining that understanding and appreciation, we present the theory and its application in the following selections which illustrate the traditional perspective. And we also present the selections as useful in themselves.

[12] Campbell and Hill, " 'Conventional Wisdom—Traditional Form': A Rejoinder," The Quarterly Journal of Speech, LVIII, 4 (December 1972), 415–60. Campbell's critique of the speech appears in her book, Critiques of Contemporary Rhetoric, California, Wadsworth, 1972, pp. 39–49. See the footnotes of essays cited here for other readings to fill in a fascinating picture of differing ways of working.

[13] "Must We All Be 'Rhetorical Critics'?" The Quarterly Journal of Speech, LXIII, 2 (April 1977), 107–16.

[14] See Bernard L. Brock, "Brock on Baskerville," The Quarterly Journal of Speech [The Forum], LXIV, 1 (February 1978), 97–98, with a reply by Baskerville, pp. 99–100.

[15] The problem of presenting compatible yet contrasting views of "history" and "criticism" has stimulated a number of writers. We believe that an especially worthy effort is that of Bruce E. Gronbeck, "Rhetorical History and Rhetorical Criticism; A Distinction," The Speech Teacher, XXIV, 4 (November 1975), 309–20.

THE NEO-ARISTOTELIAN APPROACH

The Literary Criticism of Oratory
by Herbert A. Wichelns

1

Samuel Johnson once projected a history of criticism "as it relates to judging of authors." Had the great eighteenth-century critic ever carried out his intention, he would have included some interesting comments on the orators and their judges. Histories of criticism, in whole or in part, we now have, and histories of orators. But that section of the history of criticism which deals with judging of orators is still unwritten. Yet the problem is an interesting one, and one which involves some important conceptions. Oratory—the waning influence of which is often discussed in current periodicals—has definitely lost the established place in literature that it once had. Demosthenes and Cicero, Bossuet and Burke, all hold their places in literary histories. But Webster inspires more than one modern critic to ponder the question whether oratory is literature; and if we may judge by the emphasis of literary historians generally, both in England and in America, oratory is either an outcast or a poor relation. What are the reasons for this change? It is a question not easily answered. Involved in it is some shift in the conception of oratory or of literature, or of both; nor can these conceptions have changed except in response to the life of which oratory, as well as literature, is part.

This essay, it should be said, is merely an attempt to spy out the land, to see what some critics have said of some orators, to discover what their mode of criticism has been. The discussion is limited in the main to Burke and a few nineteenth-century figures—Webster, Lincoln, Gladstone, Bright, Cobden—and to the verdicts on these found in the surveys of literary history, in critical essays, in histories of oratory, and in biographies.

Of course, we are not here concerned with the disparagement of oratory. With that, John Morley once dealt in a phrase: "Yet, after all, to disparage eloquence is to depreciate mankind."[1] Nor is the praise of eloquence of moment here. What interests us is the method of the critic: his standards, his categories of judgment, what he regards as important. These will show, not so much what he thinks of a great and

From *Studies in Rhetoric and Public Speaking in Honor of James Albert Winans*, by Pupils and Colleagues. Copyright © 1925, by The Century Company. Dr. Wichelns was Professor Emeritus of Speech, Cornell University.

[1] Life of William Ewart Gladstone, *New York, 1903, II, 593.*

ancient literary type, as how he thinks in dealing with that type. The chief aim is to know how critics have spoken of orators.

We have not much serious criticism of oratory. The reasons are patent. Oratory is intimately associated with statecraft; it is bound up with the things of the moment; its occasion, its terms, its background, can often be understood only by the careful student of history. Again, the publication of orations as pamphlets leaves us free to regard any speech merely as an essay, as a literary effort deposited at the shrine of the muses in hope of being blessed with immortality. This view is encouraged by the difficulty of reconstructing the conditions under which the speech was delivered; by the doubt, often, whether the printed text of the speech represents what was actually said, or what the orator elaborated afterwards. Burke's corrections are said to have been the despair of his printers.[2] Some of Chatham's speeches, by a paradox of fate, have been reported to us by Samuel Johnson, whose style is as remote as possible from that of the Great Commoner, and who wrote without even having heard the speeches pronounced.[3] Only in comparatively recent times has parliamentary reporting pretended to give full records of what was actually said; and even now speeches are published for literary or political purposes which justify the corrector's pencil in changes both great and small. Under such conditions the historical study of speech making is far from easy.

Yet the conditions of democracy necessitate both the making of speeches and the study of the art. It is true that other ways of influencing opinion have long been practiced, that oratory is no longer the chief means of communicating ideas to the masses. And the change is emphasized by the fact that the newer methods are now beginning to be investigated, sometimes from the point of view of the political student, sometimes from that of the "publicity expert." But, human nature being what it is, there is no likelihood that face to face persuasion will cease to be a principal mode of exerting influence, whether in courts, in senate-houses, or on the platform. It follows that the critical study of oratorical method is the study, not of a mode outworn, but of a permanent and important human activity.

Upon the great figures of the past who have used the art of public address, countless judgments have been given. These judgments have varied with the bias and preoccupation of the critics, who have been historians, biographers, or literary men, and have written accordingly. The context in which we find criticism of speeches, we must, for the purposes of this essay at least, both note and set aside. For though the aim of the critic conditions his approach to our more limited problem—

[2] Select Works, ed. E. J. Payne, Oxford, 1892, I, xxxviii.
[3] Basil Williams, Life of William Pitt, New York, 1913, II, 335–337.

the method of dealing with oratory—still we find that an historian may view an orator in the same light as does a biographer or an essayist. The literary form in which criticism of oratory is set does not afford a classification of the critics.

"There are," says a critic of literary critics, "three definite points, on one of which, or all of which, criticism must base itself. There is the date, and the author, and the work."[4] The points on which writers base their judgments of orators do afford a classification. The man, his work, his times, are the necessary common topics of criticism; no one of them can be wholly disregarded by any critic. But mere difference in emphasis on one or another of them is important enough to suggest a rough grouping. The writers with whom this essay deals give but a subordinate position to the date; they are interested chiefly in the man or in his works. Accordingly, we have as the first type of criticism that which is predominantly personal or biographical, is occupied with the character and the mind of the orator, goes behind the work to the man. The second type attempts to hold the scales even between the biographical and the literary interest. The third is occupied with the work and tends to ignore the man. These three classes, then, seem to represent the practice of modern writers in dealing with orators. Each merits a more detailed examination.

II

We may begin with that type of critic whose interest is in personality, who seeks the man behind the work. Critics of this type furnish forth the appreciative essays and the occasional addresses on the orators. They are as the sands of the sea. Lord Rosebery's two speeches on Burke, Whitelaw Reid's on Lincoln and on Burke, may stand as examples of the character sketch.[5] The second part of Birrell's essay on Burke will serve for the mental character sketch (the first half of the essay is biographical); other examples are Sir Walter Raleigh's essay on Burke and that by Robert Lynd.[6] All these emphasize the concrete nature of Burke's thought, the realism of his imagination, his peculiar combination of breadth of vision with intensity; they pass to the guiding principles of his thought: his hatred of abstraction, his love of order and of settled ways. But they do not occupy themselves with Burke as a speaker, nor even with him as a writer; their first and their last concern is with the man rather than with his works; and their method is to fuse

---

[4] D. Nichol Smith, Functions of Criticism, Oxford, 1909, p. 15.

[5] See Rosebery, Appreciations and Addresses, London, 1899, and Whitelaw Reid, American and English Studies, New York, 1913, II.

[6] See Augustine Birrell, Obiter Dicta, New York, 1887, II; Walter Raleigh, Some Authors, Oxford, 1923; Robert Lynd, Books and Authors. London, 1922.

into a single impression whatever of knowledge or opinion they may have of the orator's life and works. These critics, in dealing with the public speaker, think of him as something other than a speaker. Since this type of writing makes but an indirect contribution to our judgment of the orator, there is no need of a more extended account of the method, except as we find it combined with a discussion of the orator's works.

III

Embedded in biographies and histories of literature, we find another type of criticism, that which combines the sketch of mind and character with some discussion of style. Of the general interest of such essays there can be no doubt. Nine-tenths of so-called literary criticism deals with the lives and personalities of authors, and for the obvious reason that every one is interested in them, whereas few will follow a technical study, however broadly based. At its best, the type of study that starts with the orator's mind and character is justified by the fact that nothing can better illuminate his work as a persuader of men. But when not at its best, the description of a man's general cast of mind stands utterly unrelated to his art: the critic fails to fuse his comment on the individual with his comment on the artist; and as a result we get some statements about the man, and some statements about the orator, but neither casts light on the other. Almost any of the literary histories will supply examples of the gulf that may yawn between a stylistic study and a study of personality.

The best example of the successful combination of the two strains is Grierson's essay on Burke in the *Cambridge History of English Literature.* In this, Burke's style, though in largest outline only, is seen to emerge from the essential nature of the man. Yet of this essay, too, it must be said that the analysis of the orator is incomplete, being overshadowed by the treatment of Burke as a writer, though, as we shall see, the passages on style have the rare virtue of keeping to the high road of criticism. The majority of critics who use the mixed method, however, do not make their study of personality fruitful for a study of style, do not separate literary style from oratorical style even to the extent that Grierson does, and do conceive of literary style as a matter of details. In fact, most of the critics of this group tend to supply a discussion of style by jotting down what has occurred to them about the author's management of words; and in the main, they notice the lesser strokes of literary art, but not its broader aspects. They have an eye for tactics, but not for strategy. This is the more strange, as these same writers habitually take large views of the orator himself, considered as a personality, and because they often remark the speaker's great themes and his leading ideas. The management of ideas—what the

Romans called invention and disposition—the critics do not observe; their practice is the *salto mortale* from the largest to the smallest considerations. And it needs no mention that a critic who does not observe the management of ideas even from the point of view of structure and arrangement can have nothing to say of the adaptation of ideas to the orator's audience.

It is thus with Professor McLaughlin in his chapter in the *Cambridge History of American Literature* on Clay and Calhoun and some lesser lights. The pages are covered with such expressions as diffuse, florid, diction restrained and strong, neatly phrased, power of attack, invective, gracious persuasiveness. Of the structure of the speeches by which Clay and Calhoun exercised their influence—nothing. The drive of ideas is not represented. The background of habitual feeling which the orators at times appealed to and at times modified, is hinted at in a passage about Clay's awakening the spirit of nationalism, and in another passage contrasting the full-blooded oratory of Benton with the more polished speech of Quincy and Everett; but these are the merest hints. In the main, style for McLaughlin is neither the expression of personality nor the order and movement given to thought, but a thing of shreds and patches. It is thus, too, with Morley's pages on Burke's style in his life of the orator, and with Lodge's treatment of Webster in his life of the great American. A rather better analysis, though on the same plane of detail, may be used as an example. Oliver Elton says of Burke:

He embodies, more powerfully than any one, the mental tendencies and changes that are seen gathering force through the eighteenth century. A volume of positive knowledge, critically sifted and ascertained; a constructive vision of the past and its institutions; the imagination, under this guidance, everywhere at play; all these elements unite in Burke. His main field is political philosophy. . . . His favorite form is oratory, uttered or written. His medium is prose, and the work of his later years, alone, outweighs all contemporary prose in power. . . . His whole body of production has the unity of some large cathedral, whose successive accretions reveal the natural growth of a single mind, without any change or essential break. . . .

Already [in the Thoughts *and in the* Observations*] the characteristics of Burke's thought and style appear, as well as his profound conversance with constitutional history, finance, and affairs. There is a constant reference to general principles, as in the famous defence of Party. The maxims that come into play go far beyond the occasion. There is a perpetual ground-swell of passion, embanked and held in check, but ever breaking out into sombre irony and sometimes into figure; but metaphors and other tropes are not yet very frequent. . . .*

In the art of unfolding and amplifying, Burke is the rival of the ancients. . . .

In the speech on Conciliation the [oft-repeated] key-word is peace. . . . This iteration makes us see the stubborn faces on the opposite benches. There is contempt in it; their ears must be dinned, they must remember the word peace through the long intricate survey that is to follow. . . .

Often he has a turn that would have aroused the fervor of the great appreciator known to us by the name of Longinus. In his speech on Economical Reform (1780) Burke risks an appeal, in the face of the Commons, to the example of the enemy. He has described . . . the reforms of the French revenue. He says: "The French have imitated us; let us, through them, imitate ourselves, ourselves in our better and happier days." A speaker who was willing to offend for the sake of startling, and to defeat his purpose, would simply have said, "The French have imitated us; let us imitate them." Burke comes to the verge of this imprudence, but he sees the outcry on the lips of the adversary, and silences them by the word ourselves; and then, seizing the moment of bewilderment, repeats it and explains it by the noble past; he does not say when those days were; the days of Elizabeth or of Cromwell? Let the House choose! This is true oratory, honest diplomacy.[7]

Here, in some twenty pages, we have but two hints that Burke had to put his ideas in a form adapted to his audience; only the reiterated *peace* in all Burke's writings reminds the critic of Burke's hearers; only one stroke of tact draws his attention. Most of his account is devoted to Burke's style in the limited use of the term: to his power of amplification—his conduct of the paragraph, his use of clauses now long, now short—to his figures, comparisons, and metaphors, to his management of the sentence pattern, and to his rhythms. For Professor Elton, evidently, Burke was a man, and a mind, and an artist in prose; but he was not an orator. Interest in the minutiae of style has kept Elton from bringing his view of Burke the man to bear on his view of Burke's writings. The fusing point evidently is in the strategic purpose of the works, in their function as speeches. By holding steadily to the conception of Burke as a public man, one could make the analysis of mind and the analysis of art more illuminating for each other than Elton does.

It cannot be said that in all respects Stephenson's chapter on Lincoln in the *Cambridge History of American Literature* is more successful than Elton's treatment of Burke; but it is a better interweaving of the biographical and the literary strands of interest. Stephenson's study of the

[7] *Oliver Elton, Survey of English Literature, 1780–1830, I, 234–53, published by The Macmillan Company.*

personality of Lincoln is directly and persistently used in the study of Lincoln's style:

> *Is it fanciful to find a connection between the way in which his mysticism develops—its atmospheric, non-dogmatic pervasiveness—and the way in which his style develops? Certainly the literary part of him works into all the portions of his utterance with the gradualness of daylight through a shadowy wood. . . . And it is to be noted that the literary quality . . . is of the whole, not of the detail. It does not appear as a gift of phrases. Rather it is the slow unfolding of those two original characteristics, taste and rhythm. What is growing is the degree of both things. The man is becoming deeper, and as he does so he imposes himself, in this atmospheric way, more steadily on his language.*[8]

The psychology of mystical experience may appear a poor support for the study of style. It is but one factor of many, and Stephenson may justly be reproached for leaning too heavily upon it. Compared to Grierson's subtler analysis of Burke's mind and art, the essay of Stephenson seems forced and one-sided. Yet he illuminates his subject more than many of the writers so far mentioned, because he begins with a vigorous effort to bring his knowledge of the man to bear upon his interpretation of the work. But though we find in Stephenson's pages a suggestive study of Lincoln as literary man, we find no special regard for Lincoln as orator. The qualities of style that Stephenson mentions are the qualities of prose generally:

> *At last he has his second manner, a manner quite his own. It is not his final manner, the one that was to give him his assured place in literature. However, in a wonderful blend of simplicity, directness, candor, joined with a clearness beyond praise, and a delightful cadence, it has outstripped every other politician of the hour. And back of its words, subtly affecting its phrases, . . . is that brooding sadness which was to be with him to the end.*[9]

The final manner, it appears, is a sublimation of the qualities of the earlier, which was "keen, powerful, full of character, melodious, impressive";[10] and it is a sublimation which has the power to awaken the imagination by its flexibility, directness, pregnancy, wealth.

In this we have nothing new, unless it be the choice of stylistic categories that emphasize the larger pattern of ideas rather than the minute

---

[8] Cambridge History of American Literature, *New York, 1921, III, 374–5.*
[9] Cambridge History of American Literature, *III, 378.*
[10] Ibid., *pp. 381–2.*

pattern of grammatical units, such as we have found in Elton and to some extent shall find in Saintsbury; it must be granted, too, that Stephenson has dispensed with detail and gained his larger view at the cost of no little vagueness. "Two things," says Stephenson of the Lincoln of 1849–1858, "grew upon him. The first was his understanding of men, the generality of men. . . . The other thing that grew upon him was his power to reach and influence them through words."[11] We have here the text for any study of Lincoln as orator; but the study itself this critic does not give us.

Elton's characterization of Burke's style stands out from the usual run of superficial comment by the closeness of its analysis and its regard for the architectonic element. Stephenson's characterization of Lincoln's style is distinguished by a vigorous if forced effort to unite the study of the man and of the work. With both we may contrast a better essay, by a critic of greater insight. Grierson says of Burke:

What Burke has of the deeper spirit of that movement [the romantic revival] is seen not so much in the poetic imagery of his finest prose as in the philosophical imagination which informs his conception of the state, in virtue of which he transcends the rationalism of the century. . . . This temper of Burke's mind is reflected in his prose. . . . To the direct, conversational prose of Dryden and Swift, changed social circumstances and the influence of Johnson had given a more oratorical cast, more dignity and weight, but, also, more of heaviness and conventional elegance. From the latter faults, Burke is saved by his passionate temperament, his ardent imagination, and the fact that he was a speaker conscious always of his audience. . . . [Burke] could delight, astound, and convince an audience. He did not easily conciliate and win them over. He lacked the first essential and index of the conciliatory speaker, lenitas vocis; his voice was harsh and unmusical, his gesture ungainly. . . . And, even in the text of his speeches there is a strain of irony and scorn which is not well fitted to conciliate. . . . We have evidence that he could do both things on which Cicero lays stress—move his audience to tears and delight them by his wit. . . . Yet, neither pathos nor humor is Burke's forte. . . . Burke's unique power as an orator lies in the peculiar interpenetration of thought and passion. Like the poet and the prophet, he thinks most profoundly when he thinks most passionately. When he is not deeply moved, his oratory verges toward the turgid; when he indulges feeling for his own sake, as in parts of Letters on a Regicide Peace, it becomes hysterical. But, in his greatest speeches and pamphlets, the passion of Burke's mind shows itself in the luminous thoughts which it emits, in the imagery which at once

[11] Ibid., p. 377.

moves and *teaches, throwing a flood of light not only on the point in question, but on the whole neighboring sphere of man's moral and political nature.*[12]

The most notable feature of these passages is not their recognition that Burke was a speaker, but their recognition that his being a speaker conditioned his style, and that he is to be judged in part at least as one who attempted to influence men by the spoken word. Grierson, like Elton, attends to the element of structure and has something to say of the nature of Burke's prose; but, unlike Elton, he distinguishes this from the description of Burke's oratory—although without maintaining the distinction: he illustrates Burke's peculiar oratorical power from a pamphlet as readily as from a speech. His categories seem less mechanical than those of Elton, who is more concerned with the development of the paragraph than with the general cast of Burke's style; nor is his judgment warped, as is Stephenson's, by having a theory to market. Each has suffered from the necessity of compression. Yet, all told, Grierson realizes better than the others that Burke's task was not merely to express his thoughts and his feelings in distinguished prose, but to communicate his thoughts and his feelings effectively. It is hardly true, however, that Grierson has in mind the actual audience of Burke; the audience of Grierson's vision seems to be universalized, to consist of the judicious listeners or readers of any age. Those judicious listeners have no practical interest in the situation; they have only a philosophical and æsthetic interest.

Of Taine in his description of Burke it cannot be said that he descends to the minutiæ of style. He deals with his author's character and ideas, as do all the critics of this group, but his comments on style are simply a single impression, vivid and picturesque:

Burke had one of those fertile and precise imaginations which believes that finished knowledge is an inner view, which never quits a subject without having clothed it in its colors and forms. . . . To all these powers of mind, which constitute a man of system, he added all those energies of heart which constitute an enthusiast. . . . He brought to politics a horror of crime, a vivacity and sincerity of conscience, a sensibility, which seem suitable only to a young man.

. . . The vast amount of his works rolls impetuously in a current of eloquence. Sometimes a spoken or written discourse needs a whole volume to unfold the train of his multiplied proofs and courageous

[12] *From H. J. C. Grierson in* Cambridge History of English Literature, *XI, 30– 35 by Cambridge University Press (1914). Abridgements by permission of the publisher.*

*anger. It is either the exposé of a ministry, or the whole history of Brit-
ish India, or the complete theory of revolutions . . . which comes
down like a vast overflowing stream. . . . Doubtless there is foam on
its eddies, mud in its bed; thousands of strange creatures sport wildly
on its surface: he does not select, he lavishes. . . . Nothing strikes
him as in excess. . . . He continues half a barbarian, battening in exaggeration and violence; but his fire is so sustained, his conviction so
strong, his emotion so warm and abundant, that we suffer him to go on,
forget our repugnance, see in his irregularities and his trespasses only
the outpourings of a great heart and a deep mind, too open and too
full.*[13]

This is brilliant writing, unencumbered by the subaltern's interest in
tactics, but it is strategy as described by a war-correspondent, not by
a general. We get from it little light on how Burke solved the problem
that confronts every orator: so to present ideas as to bring them into
the consciousness of his hearers.

Where the critic divides his interest between the man and the work,
without allowing either interest to predominate, he is often compelled
to consider the work *in toto,* and we get only observations so generalized as not to include consideration of the form of the work. The speech
is not thought of as essentially a means of influence; it is regarded as
a specimen of prose, or as an example of philosophic thought. The
date, the historical interest, the orator's own intention, are often lost
from view; and criticism suffers in consequence.

IV

We have seen that the critic who is occupied chiefly with the orator
as a man can contribute, although indirectly, to the study of the orator
as such, and that the critic who divides his attention between the man
and the work must effect a fusion of the two interests if he is to help
materially in the understanding of the orator. We come now to critics
more distinctly literary in aim. Within this group several classes may be
discriminated: the first comprises the judicial critics; the second includes the interpretative critics who take the point of view of literary
style generally, regarding the speech as an essay, or as a specimen of
prose; the third and last group is composed of the writers who tend to
regard the speech as a special literary form.

The type of criticism that attempts a judicial evaluation of the literary
merits of the work—of the orator's "literary remains"—tends to center
the inquiry on the question: Is this literature? The futility of the question

[13] *H. A. Taine,* History of English Literature, *tr. H. Van Laun, London, 1878,
II, 81–3.*

appears equally in the affirmative and in the negative replies to it. The fault is less with the query, however, than with the hastiness of the answers generally given. For the most part, the critics who raise this problem are not disposed really to consider it: they formulate no conception either of literature or of oratory; they will not consider their own literary standards critically and comprehensively. In short, the question is employed as a way to dispose briefly of the subject of a lecture or of a short essay in a survey of a national literature.

Thus Phelps, in his treatment of Webster and Lincoln in *Some Makers of American Literature*,[14] tells us that they have a place in literature by virtue of their style, gives us some excerpts from Lincoln and some comments on Webster's politics, but offers no reasoned criticism. St. Peter swings wide the gates of the literary heaven, but does not explain his action. We may suspect that the solemn award of a "place in literature" sometimes conceals the absence of any real principle of judgment.

Professor Trent is less easily satisfied that Webster deserves a "place in literature." He grants Webster's power to stimulate patriotism, his sonorous dignity and massiveness, his clearness and strength of style, his powers of dramatic description. But he finds only occasional splendor of imagination, discovers no soaring quality of intelligence, and is not dazzled by his philosophy or his grasp of history. Mr. Trent would like more vivacity and humor and color in Webster's style.[15] This mode of deciding Webster's place in or out of literature is important to us only as it reveals the critic's method of judging. Trent looks for clearness and strength, imagination, philosophic grasp, vivacity, humor, color in style. This is excellent so far as it goes, but goes no further than to suggest some qualities which are to be sought in any and all works of literary art in dramas, in essays, in lyric poems, as well as in speeches.

Let us take a third judge. Gosse will not allow Burke to be a complete master of English prose: "Notwithstanding all its magnificence, it appears to me that the prose of Burke lacks the variety, the delicacy, the modulated music of the very finest writers."[16] Gosse adds that Burke lacks flexibility, humor, and pathos. As critical method, this is one with that of Trent.

Gosse, with his question about mastery of prose, does not directly ask, "Is this literature?" Henry Cabot Lodge does, and his treatment of Webster (in the *Cambridge History of American Literature*) is curious.

[14] *Boston, 1923.*

[15] *W. P. Trent,* History of American Literature, 1607–1865, *New York, 1917, pp. 576–7.*

[16] *Edmund Gosse,* History of Eighteenth Century English Literature, 1660–1780, *London, 1889, pp. 365–6.*

Lodge is concerned to show that Webster belongs to literature, and to explain the quality in his work that gives him a place among the best makers of literature. The test applied is permanence: Is Webster still read? The answer is, yes, for he is part of every schoolboy's education, and is the most quoted author in Congress. The sight of a literary critic resigning the judicial bench to the schoolmaster and the Congressman is an enjoyable one; as enjoyable as Mr. H. L. Mencken's reaction to it would be; but one could wish for grounds more relative than this. Mr. Lodge goes on to account for Webster's permanence: it lies in his power to impart to rhetoric the literary touch. The distinction between rhetoric and literature is not explained, but apparently the matter lies thus: rhetorical verse may be poetry; Byron is an example. Rhetorical prose is not literature until there is added the literary touch. We get a clue as to how the literary touch may be added: put in something imaginative, something that strikes the hearer at once. The example chosen by Lodge is a passage from Webster in which the imaginative or literary touch is given by the single word "mildew."[17] This method of criticism, too, we may reduce to that of Trent, with the exception that only one quality—imagination—is requisite for admission to the literary Valhalla.

Whether the critic's standard be imagination, or this together with other qualities such as intelligence, vivacity, humor, or whether it be merely "style," undefined and unexplained, the point of view is always that of the printed page. The oration is lost from view, and becomes an exercise in prose, musical, colorful, varied, and delicate, but, so far as the critic is concerned, formless and purposeless. Distinctions of literary type or kind are erased; the architectonic element is neglected; and the speech is regarded as a musical meditation might be regarded: as a kind of harmonious musing that drifts pleasantly along, with little of inner form and nothing of objective purpose. This, it should be recognized, is not the result of judicial criticism so much as the result of the attempt to decide too hastily whether a given work is to be admitted into the canon of literature.

V

It is, perhaps, natural for the historian of literature to reduce all literary production to one standard, and thus to discuss only the common elements in all prose. One can understand also that the biographer, when in the course of his task he must turn literary critic, finds himself often inadequately equipped and his judgment of little value, except on the scale of literature generally rather than of oratory or of any given type. More is to be expected, however, of those who set up

[17] Cambridge History of American Literature, New York, 1918, II, 101.

as literary critics in the first instance: those who deal directly with Webster's style, or with Lincoln as man of letters. We shall find such critics as Whipple, Hazlitt, and Saintsbury devoting themselves to the description of literary style in the orators whom they discuss. Like the summary judicial critics we have mentioned, their center of interest is the work; but they are less hurried than Gosse and Lodge and Phelps and Trent; and their aim is not judgment so much as understanding. Yet their interpretations, in the main, take the point of view of the printed page, of the prose essay. Only to a slight degree is there a shift to another point of view, that of the orator in relation to the audience on whom he exerts his influence; the immediate public begins to loom a little larger; the essential nature of the oration as a type begins to be suggested.

Saintsbury has a procedure which much resembles that of Elton, though we must note the fact that the former omits consideration of Burke as a personality and centers attention on his work. We saw that Elton, in his passages on Burke's style, attends both to the larger elements of structure and to such relatively minute points as the management of the sentence and the clause. In Saintsbury the range of considerations is the same. At times, indeed, the juxtaposition of large and small ideas is ludicrous, as when one sentence ends by awarding to Burke literary immortality, and the next describes the sentences of an early work as "short and crisp, arranged with succinct antithetic parallels, which seldom exceed a single pair of clauses."[18] The award of immortality is not, it should be said, based entirely on the shortness of Burke's sentences in his earliest works. Indeed much of Saintsbury's comment is of decided interest:

The style of Burke is necessarily to be considered throughout as conditioned by oratory. . . . In other words, he was first of all a rhetorician, and probably the greatest that modern times have ever produced. But his rhetoric always inclined much more to the written than to the spoken form, with results annoying perhaps to him at the time, but even to him satisfactory afterwards, and an inestimable gain to the world. . . .

The most important of these properties of Burke's style, in so far as it is possible to enumerate them here, are as follows. First of all, and most distinctive, so much so as to have escaped no competent critic, is a very curious and, until his example made it imitable, nearly unique faculty of building up an argument or a picture by a succession of complementary strokes, not added at haphazard but growing out of and

[18] G. E. B. Saintsbury, Short History of English Literature, *New York, 1915,* p. 630.

onto one another. No one has ever been such a master of the best and grandest kind of the figure called . . . Amplification, and this . . . is the direct implement by which he achieves his greatest effects.

. . . The piece [Present Discontents] may be said to consist of a certain number of specially labored paragraphs in which the arguments or pictures just spoken of are put as forcibly as the author can put them, and as a rule in a succession of shortish sentences, built up and glued together with the strength and flexibility of a newly fashioned fishing-rod. In the intervals the texts thus given are turned about, commented on, justified, or discussed in detail, in a rhetoric for the most part, though not always, rather less serried, less evidently burnished, and in less full dress. And this general arrangement proceeds through the rest of his works.[19]

After a number of comments on Burke's skill in handling various kinds of ornament, such as humor, epigram, simile, Saintsbury returns to the idea that Burke's special and definite weapon was "imaginative argument, and the marshalling of vast masses of complicated detail into properly rhetorical battalions or (to alter the image) mosaic pictures of enduring beauty."[20] Saintsbury's attitude toward the communicative, impulsive nature of the orator's task is indicated in a passage on the well-known description of Windsor Castle. This description the critic terms "at once . . . a perfect harmonic chord, a complete visual picture, and a forcible argument."[21] It is significant that he adds, "The minor rhetoric, the suasive purpose [presumably the argumentative intent] must be kept in view; if it be left out the thing loses"; and holds Burke "far below Browne, who had no needs of purpose."[22] It is less important that a critic think well of the suasive purpose than that he reckon with it, and of Saintsbury at least it must be said that he recognizes it, although grudgingly; but it cannot be said that Saintsbury has a clear conception of rhetoric as the art of communication: sometimes it means the art of prose, sometimes that of suasion.

Hazlitt's method of dealing with Burke resembles Taine's as Saintsbury's resembles that of Elton. In Hazlitt we have a critic who deals with style in the large; details of rhythm, of sentence pattern, of imagery, are ignored. His principal criticism of Burke as orator is contained in the well-known contrast with Chatham, really a contrast of mind and temperament in relation to oratorical style. He follows this with some excellent comment on Burke's prose style; nothing more is said of his

[19] Ibid., *pp. 629–30.*
[20] Ibid., *p. 631.*
[21] Ibid.
[22] Ibid.

oratory; only in a few passages do we get a flash of light on the relation of Burke to his audience, as in the remark about his eagerness to impress his reader, and in the description of his conversational quality. It is notable too that Hazlitt finds those works which never had the form of speeches the most significant and most typical of Burke's style.

Burke was so far from being a gaudy or flowery writer, that he was one of the severest writers we have. His words are the most like things; his style is the most strictly limited to the subject. He unites every extreme and every variety of composition; the lowest and the meanest words and descriptions with the highest. . . . He had no other object but to produce the strongest impression on his reader, by giving the truest, the most characteristic, the fullest, and most forcible description of things, trusting to the power of his own mind to mold them into grace and beauty. . . . Burke most frequently produced an effect by the remoteness and novelty of his combinations, by the force of contrast, by the striking manner in which the most opposite and unpromising materials were harmoniously blended together; not by laying his hands on all the fine things he could think of, but by bringing together those things which he knew would blaze out into glorious light by their collision.[23]

Twelve years after writing the essay from which we have quoted, Hazlitt had occasion to revise his estimate of Burke as a statesman; but his sketch of Burke's style is essentially unaltered.[24] In Hazlitt we find a sense of style as an instrument of communication; that sense is no stronger in dealing with Burke's speeches than in dealing with his pamphlets, but it gives to Hazlitt's criticisms a reality not often found. What is lacking is a clear sense of Burke's communicative impulse, of his persuasive purpose, as operating in a concrete situation. Hazlitt does not suggest the background of Burke's speeches, ignores the events that called them forth. He views his subject, in a sense, as Grierson does: as speaking to the judicious but disinterested hearer of any age other than Burke's own. But the problem of the speaker, as well as of the pamphleteer, is to interest men here and now; the understanding of that problem requires, on the part of the critic, a strong historical sense for the ideas and attitudes of the people (not merely of their leaders), and a full knowledge of the public opinion of the times in which the orator spoke. This we do not find in Hazlitt.

Two recent writers on Lincoln commit the opposite error: they devote

[23] Sketches and Essays, *ed. W. C. Hazlitt, London, 1872, II, 420–1.*
[24] Political Essays with Sketches of Public Characters, *London, 1819, pp. 264–79.*

themselves so completely to description of the situation in which Lincoln wrote as to leave no room for criticism. L. E. Robinson's *Lincoln as Man of Letters*[25] is a biography rewritten around Lincoln's writings. It is nothing more. Instead of giving us a criticism, Professor Robinson has furnished us with some of the materials of the critic; his own judgments are too largely laudatory to cast much light. The book, therefore, is not all that its title implies. A single chapter of accurate summary and evaluation would do much to increase our understanding of Lincoln as man of letters, even though it said nothing of Lincoln as speaker. A chapter or two on Lincoln's work in various kinds—letters, state papers, speeches—would help us to a finer discrimination than Professor Robinson's book offers. Again, the proper estimate of style in any satisfactory sense requires us to do more than to weigh the soundness of an author's thought and to notice the isolated beauties of his expression. Something should be said of structure, something of adaptation to the immediate audience, whose convictions and habits of thought, whose literary usages, and whose general cultural background all condition the work both of writer and speaker. Mr. Robinson has given us the political situation as a problem in controlling political forces, with little regard to the force even of public opinion, and with almost none to the cultural background. Lincoln's works, therefore, emerge as items in a political sequence, but not as resultants of the life of his time.

Some of the deficiencies of Robinson's volume are supplied by Dodge's essay, *Lincoln as Master of Words.*[26] Dodge considers, more definitely than Robinson, the types in which Lincoln worked: he separates messages from campaign speeches, letters from occasional addresses. He has an eye on Lincoln's relation to his audience, but this manifests itself chiefly in an account of the immediate reception of a work. Reports of newspaper comments on the speeches may be a notable addition to Lincolniana; supported by more political information and more insight than Mr. Dodge's short book reveals, they might become an aid to the critical evaluation of the speeches. But in themselves they are neither a criticism nor an interpretation of Lincoln's mastery of words.

Robinson and Dodge, then, stand at opposite poles to Saintsbury and Hazlitt. The date is put in opposition to the work as a center of critical interest. If the two writers on Lincoln lack a full perception of their author's background, they do not lack a sense of its importance. If the critics of Burke do not produce a complete and rounded criticism, neither do they lose themselves in preparatory studies. Each method is incomplete; each should supplement the other.

[25] *New York, 1923.*
[26] *New York, 1924.*

We turn now to a critic who neglects the contribution of history to the study of oratory, but who has two compensating merits: the merit of recognizing the types in which his subject worked, and the merit of remembering that an orator has as his audience, not posterity, but certain classes of his own contemporaries. Whipple's essay on Webster is open to attack from various directions: it is padded, it "dates," it is overlaudatory, it is overpatriotic, it lacks distinction of style. But there is wheat in the chaff. Scattered through the customary discussion of Webster's choice of words, his power of epithet, his compactness of statement, his images, the development of his style, are definite suggestions of a new point of view. It is the point of view of the actual audience. To Whipple, at times at least, Webster was not a writer, but a speaker; the critic tries to imagine the man, and also his hearers; he thinks of the speech as a communication to a certain body of auditors. A phrase often betrays a mental attitude; Whipple alone of the critics we have mentioned would have written of "the eloquence, the moral power, he infused into his reasoning, so as to make the dullest citation of legal authority *tell* on the minds he addressed."[27] Nor would any other writer of this group have attempted to distinguish the types of audience Webster met. That Whipple's effort is a rambling and incoherent one, is not here in point. Nor is it pertinent that the critic goes completely astray in explaining why Webster's speeches have the nature of "organic formations, or at least of skilful engineering or architectural constructions"; though to say that the art of giving objective reality to a speech consists only of "a happy collocation and combination of words"[28] is certainly as far as possible from explaining Webster's sense of structure. What is significant in Whipple's essay is the occasional indication of a point of view that includes the audience. Such an indication is the passage in which the critic explains the source of Webster's influence:

What gave Webster his immense influence over the opinion of the people of New England, was first, his power of so "putting things" that everybody could understand his statements; secondly, his power of so framing his arguments that all the steps, from one point to another, in a logical series, could be clearly apprehended by every intelligent farmer or mechanic who had a thoughtful interest in the affairs of the country; and thirdly, his power of inflaming the sentiment of patriotism in all honest and well-intentioned men by overwhelming appeals to that sen-

---

[27] E. P. Whipple, *"Daniel Webster as a Master of English Style,"* in American Literature, *Boston, 1887, p. 157.*
[28] Ibid., *p. 208.*

timent, so that after convincing their understandings, he clinched the matter by sweeping away their wills.

Perhaps to these sources of influence may be added . . . a genuine respect for the intellect, as well as for the manhood, of average men.[29]

In various ways the descriptive critics recognize the orator's function. In some, that recognition takes the form of a regard to the background of the speeches; in others, it takes the form of a regard to the effectiveness of the work, though that effectiveness is often construed as for the reader rather than for the listener. The "minor rhetoric, the suasive purpose" is beginning to be felt, though not always recognized and never fully taken into account.

VI

The distinction involved in the presence of a persuasive purpose is clearly recognized by some of those who have written on oratory, and by some biographers and historians. The writers now to be mentioned are aware, more keenly than any of those we have so far met, of the speech as a literary form—or if not as a literary form, then as a form of power; they tend accordingly to deal with the orator's work as limited by the conditions of the platform and the occasion, and to summon history to the aid of criticism.

The method of approach of the critics of oratory as oratory is well put by Lord Curzon at the beginning of his essay, *Modern Parliamentary Eloquence:*

In dealing with the Parliamentary speakers of our time I shall, accordingly, confine myself to those whom I have myself heard, or for whom I can quote the testimony of others who heard them; and I shall not regard them as prose writers or literary men, still less as purveyors of instruction to their own or to future generations, but as men who produced, by the exercise of certain talents of speech, a definite impression upon contemporary audiences, and whose reputation for eloquence must be judged by that test, and that test alone.[30]

The last phrase, "that test alone," would be scanned; the judgment of orators is not solely to be determined by the impression of contemporary audiences. For the present it will be enough to note the topics touched in Curzon's anecdotes and reminiscences—his lecture is far from a systematic or searching inquiry into the subject, and is of interest rather for its method of approach than for any considered study

[29] *Ibid., p. 144.*
[30] *London, 1914, p. 7.*

of an orator or of a period. We value him for his promises rather than for his performance. Curzon deals with the relative rank of speakers, with the comparative value of various speeches by a single man, with the orator's appearance and demeanor, with his mode of preparation and of delivery, with his mastery of epigram or image. Skill in seizing upon the dominant characteristics of each of his subjects saves the author from the worst triviality of reminiscence. Throughout, the point of view is that of the man experienced in public life discussing the eloquence of other public men, most of whom he had known and actually heard. That this is not the point of view of criticism in any strict sense, is of course true; but the *naïveté* and directness of this observer correct forcibly some of the extravagances we have been examining.

The lecture on Chatham as an orator by H. M. Butler exemplifies a very different method arising from a different subject and purpose. The lecturer is thinking, he tells us, "of Oratory partly as an art, partly as a branch of literature, partly as a power of making history."[31] His method is first to touch lightly upon Chatham's early training and upon his mode of preparing and delivering his speeches; next, to present some of the general judgments upon the Great Commoner, whether of contemporaries or of later historians; then to re-create a few of the most important speeches, partly by picturing the historical setting, partly by quotation, partly by the comments of contemporary writers. The purpose of the essay is "to reawaken, however faintly, some echoes of the kingly voice of a genuine Patriot, of whom his country is still justly proud."[32] The patriotic purpose we may ignore, but the wish to reconstruct the *mise en scène* of Chatham's speeches, to put the modern Oxford audience at the point of view of those who listened to the voice of Pitt, saw the flash of his eye and felt the force of his noble bearing, this is a purpose different from that of the critics whom we have examined. It may be objected that Butler's lecture has the defects of its method: the amenities observed by a Cambridge don delivering a formal lecture at Oxford keeps us from getting on with the subject; the brevity of the discourse prevents anything like a full treatment; the aim, revivification of the past, must be very broadly interpreted if it is to be really critical. Let us admit these things; it still is true that in a few pages the essential features of Pitt's eloquence are brought vividly before us, and that this is accomplished by thinking of the speech as originally delivered to its first audience rather than as read by the modern reader.

The same sense of the speaker in his relation to his audience appears in Lecky's account of Burke. This account, too, is marked by the

---

[31] Lord Chatham as an Orator, *Oxford, 1912, p. 5.*
[32] Ibid., *pp. 39–40.*

use of contemporary witnesses, and of comparisons with Burke's great rivals. But let Lecky's method speak in part for itself:

He spoke too often, too vehemently, and much too long; and his elo-quence, though in the highest degree intellectual, powerful, various, and original, was not well adapted to a popular audience. He had little or nothing of that fire and majesty of declamation with which Chatham thrilled his hearers, and often almost overawed opposition; and as a par-liamentary debater he was far inferior to Charles Fox. . . . Burke was not inferior to Fox in readiness, and in the power of clear and cogent reasoning. His wit, though not of the highest order, was only equalled by that of Townshend, Sheridan, and perhaps North, and it rarely failed in its effect upon the House. He far surpassed every other speaker in the copiousness and correctness of his diction, in the range of knowl-edge he brought to bear on every subject of debate, in the richness and variety of his imagination, in the gorgeous beauty of his descriptive passages, in the depth of the philosophical reflections and the felicity of the personal sketches which he delighted in scattering over his speeches. But these gifts were frequently marred by a strange want of judgment, measure, and self-control. His speeches were full of epi-sodes and digressions, of excessive ornamentation and illustration, of dissertations on general principles of politics, which were invaluable in themselves, but very unpalatable to a tired or excited House waiting eagerly for a division.[33]

These sentences suggest, and the pages from which they are ex-cerpted show, that historical imagination has led Lecky to regard Burke as primarily a speaker, both limited and formed by the conditions of his platform; and they exemplify, too, a happier use of stylistic cate-gories than do the essays of Curzon and Butler. The requirements of the historian's art have fused the character sketch and the literary criti-cism; the fusing agent has been the conception of Burke as a public man, and of his work as public address. Both Lecky's biographical in-terpretation and his literary criticism are less subtle than that of Grier-son; but Lecky is more definitely guided in his treatment of Burke by the conception of oratory as a special form of the literature of power and as a form molded always by the pressure of the time.

The merits of Lecky are contained, in ampler form, in Morley's bi-ography of Gladstone. The long and varied career of the great parlia-mentarian makes a general summary and final judgment difficult and perhaps inadvisable; Morley does not attempt them. But his running

---

[33] W. E. H. Lecky, History of England in the Eighteenth Century, *New York, 1888, III,* 203–4.

account of Gladstone as orator, if assembled from his thousand pages, is an admirable example of what can be done by one who has the point of view of the public man, sympathy with his subject, and understanding of the speaker's art. Morley gives us much contemporary reporting: the descriptions and judgments of journalists at various stages in Gladstone's career, the impression made by the speeches upon delivery, comparison with other speakers of the time. Here history is contemporary: the biographer was himself the witness of much that he describes, and has the experienced parliamentarian's flair for the scene and the situation. Gladstone's temperament and physical equipment for the platform, his training in the art of speaking, the nature of his chief appeals, the factor of character and personality, these are some of the topics repeatedly touched. There is added a sense for the permanent results of Gladstone's speaking: not the votes in the House merely, but the changed state of public opinion brought about by the speeches.

Mr. Gladstone conquered the House, because he was saturated with a subject and its arguments; because he could state and enforce his case; because he plainly believed every word he said, and earnestly wished to press the same belief into the minds of his hearers; finally because he was from the first an eager and a powerful athlete. . . . Yet with this inborn readiness for combat, nobody was less addicted to aggression or provocation. . . .

In finance, the most important of all the many fields of his activity, Mr. Gladstone had the signal distinction of creating the public opinion by which he worked, and warming the climate in which his projects throve. . . . Nobody denies that he was often declamatory and discursive, that he often overargued and overrefined; [but] he nowhere exerted greater influence than in that department of affairs where words out of relation to fact are most surely exposed. If he often carried the proper rhetorical arts of amplification and development to excess, yet the basis of fact was both sound and clear. . . . Just as Macaulay made thousands read history, who before had turned from it as dry and repulsive, so Mr. Gladstone made thousands eager to follow the public balance-sheet, and the whole nation became his audience. . . .

[In the Midlothian campaign] it was the orator of concrete detail, of inductive instances, of energetic and immediate object; the orator confidently and by sure touch startling into watchfulness the whole spirit of civil duty in man; elastic and supple, pressing fact and figure with a fervid insistence that was known from his career and character to be neither forced nor feigned, but to be himself. In a word, it was a man— a man impressing himself upon the kindled throngs by the breadth of

his survey of great affairs of life and nations, by the depth of his vision, by the power of his stroke.[34]

Objections may be made to Morley's method, chiefly on the ground of omissions. Though much is done to re-create the scene, though ample use is made of the date and the man, there is little formal analysis of the work. It is as if one had come from the House of Commons after hearing the speeches, stirred to enthusiasm but a little confused by the wealth of argument; not as if one came from a calm study of the speeches; not even as if one had corrected personal impressions by such a study. Of the structure of the speeches, little is said; but a few perorations are quoted; the details of style, one feels, although noticed at too great length by some critics, might well receive a modicum of attention here.

Although these deficiencies of Morley's treatment are not supplied by Bryce in his short and popular sketch of Gladstone, there is a summary which well supplements the running account offered by Morley. It has the merit of dealing explicitly with the orator as orator, and it offers more analysis and an adequate judgment by a qualified critic.

Twenty years hence Mr. Gladstone's [speeches] will not be read, except of course by historians. They are too long, too diffuse, too minute in their handling of details, too elaborately qualified in their enunciation of general principles. They contain few epigrams and few . . . weighty thoughts put into telling phrases. . . . The style, in short, is not sufficiently rich or finished to give a perpetual interest to matters whose practical importance has vanished. . . .

If, on the other hand, Mr. Gladstone be judged by the impression he made on his own time, his place will be high in the front rank. . . . His oratory had many conspicuous merits. There was a lively imagination, which enabled him to relieve even dull matter by pleasing figures, together with a large command of quotations and illustrations. . . . There was admirable lucidity and accuracy in exposition. There was great skill in the disposition and marshalling of his arguments, and finally . . . there was a wonderful variety and grace of appropriate gesture. But above and beyond everything else which enthralled the listener, there were four qualities, two specially conspicuous in the substance of his eloquence—inventiveness and elevation; two not less remarkable in his manner—force in the delivery, expressive modulation in the voice.[35]

[34] Life of William Ewart Gladstone, *I, 193–4; II, 54–5, 593.*
[35] Gladstone, his Characteristics as Man and Statesman, *New York, 1898,* pp. 41–4.

One is tempted to say that Morley has provided the historical setting, Bryce the critical verdict. The statement would be only partially true, for Morley does much more than set the scene. He enacts the drama; and thus he conveys his judgment—not, it is true, in the form of a critical estimate, but in the course of his narrative. The difference between these two excellent accounts is a difference in emphasis. The one lays stress on the setting; the other takes it for granted. The one tries to suggest his judgment by description; the other employs the formal categories of criticism.

Less full and rounded than either of these descriptions of an orator's style is Trevelyan's estimate of Bright. Yet in a few pages the biographer has indicated clearly the two distinguishing features of Bright's eloquence—the moral weight he carried with his audience, the persuasiveness of his visible earnestness and of his reputation for integrity, and his "sense for the value of words and for the rhythm of words and sentences";[36] has drawn a contrast between Bright and Gladstone; and has added a description of Bright's mode of work, together with some comments on the permanence of the speeches and various examples of details of his style. Only the mass and weight of that style are not represented.

If we leave the biographers and return to those who, like Curzon and Butler, have written directly upon eloquence, we find little of importance. Of the two general histories of oratory that we have in English, Hardwicke's[37] is so ill organized and so ill written as to be negligible; that by Sears[38] may deserve mention. It is uneven and inaccurate. It is rather a popular handbook which strings together the great names than a history: the author does not seriously consider the evolution of oratory. His sketches are of unequal merit; some give way to the interest in mere anecdote; some yield too large a place to biographical detail; others are given over to moralizing. Sears touches most of the topics of rhetorical criticism without making the point of view of public address dominant; his work is too episodic for that. And any given criticism shows marked defects in execution. It would not be fair to compare Sears's show-piece, his chapter on Webster, with Morley or Bryce on Gladstone; but compare it with Trevelyan's few pages on Bright. With far greater economy, Trevelyan tells us more of Bright as a speaker than Sears can of Webster. The *History of Oratory* gives us little more than hints and suggestions of a good method.

With a single exception, the collections of eloquence have no criti-

---

[36] G. M. Trevelyan, Life of John Bright, *Boston, 1913, p. 384.*
[37] *Henry Hardwicke,* History of Oratory and Orators, *New York, 1896.*
[38] *Lorenzo Sears,* History of Oratory, *Chicago, 1896.*

cal significance. The exception is *Select British Eloquence,*[39] edited by Chauncey A. Goodrich, who prefaced the works of each of his orators with a sketch partly biographical and partly critical. The criticisms of Goodrich, like those of Sears, are of unequal value; some are slight, yet none descends to mere anecdote, and at his best, as in the characterizations of the eloquence of Chatham, Fox, and Burke, Goodrich reveals a more powerful grasp and a more comprehensive view of his problem than does Sears, as well as a more consistent view of his subject as a speaker. Sears at times takes the point of view of the printed page; Goodrich consistently thinks of the speeches he discusses as intended for oral delivery.

Goodrich's topics of criticism are: the orator's training, mode of work, personal (physical) qualifications, character as known to his audience, range of powers, dominant traits as a speaker. He deals too, of course, with those topics to which certain of the critics we have noticed confine themselves: illustration, ornament, gift of phrase, diction, wit, imagination, arrangement. But these he does not overemphasize, nor view as independent of their effect upon an audience. Thus he can say of Chatham's sentence structure: "The sentences are not rounded or balanced periods, but are made up of short clauses, which flash themselves upon the mind with all the vividness of distinct ideas, and yet are closely connected together as tending to the same point, and uniting to form larger masses of thought."[40] Perhaps the best brief indication of Goodrich's quality is his statement of Fox's "leading peculiarities."[41] According to Goodrich, Fox had a luminous simplicity, which combined unity of impression with irregular arrangement; he took everything in the concrete; he struck instantly at the heart of his subject, going to the issue at once; he did not amplify, he repeated; he rarely employed a preconceived order of argument; reasoning was his *forte,* but it was the reasoning of the debater; he abounded in *hits*—abrupt and startling turns of thought—and in side-blows delivered in passing; he was often dramatic; he had astonishing skill in turning the course of debate to his own advantage. Here is the point of view of public address, expressed as clearly as in Morley or in Curzon, though in a different idiom, and without the biographer's fulness of treatment.

But probably the best single specimen of the kind of criticism now under discussion is Morley's chapter on Cobden as an agitator. This is as admirable a summary sketch as the same writer's account of Gladstone is a detailed historical picture. Bryce's brief essay on Gladstone is inferior to it both in the range of its technical criticisms and in

---

[39] *New York, 1852.*
[40] *P. 75.*
[41] *P. 461.*

the extent to which the critic realizes the situation in which his subject was an actor. In a few pages Morley has drawn the physical character- istics of his subject, his bent of mind, temperament, idiosyncrasies; has compared and contrasted Cobden with his great associate, Bright; has given us contemporary judgments; has sketched out the dominant quality of his style, its variety and range; has noted Cobden's attitude to his hearers, his view of human nature; and has dealt with the impres- sion given by Cobden's printed speeches and the total impression of his personality on the platform. The method, the angle of approach, the categories of description or of criticism, are the same as those em- ployed in the great life of Gladstone; but we find them here condensed into twenty pages. It will be worth while to present the most interesting parts of Morley's criticism, if only for comparison with some of the passages already given:

I have asked many scores of those who knew him, Conservatives as well as Liberals, what this secret [of his oratorical success] was, and in no single case did my interlocutor fail to begin, and in nearly every case he ended as he had begun, with the word persuasiveness. *Cob- den made his way to men's hearts by the union which they saw in him of simplicity, earnestness, and conviction, with a singular facility of exposition. This facility consisted in a remarkable power of apt and homely illustration, and a curious ingenuity in framing the argument that happened to be wanted. Besides his skill in thus hitting on the right argument, Cobden had the oratorical art of presenting it in the way that made its admission to the understanding of a listener easy and un- denied. He always seemed to have made exactly the right degree of al- lowance for the difficulty with which men follow a speech, as compared with the ease of following the same argument on a printed page. . . .*

Though he abounded in matter, Cobden can hardly be described as copious. He is neat and pointed, nor is his argument ever left un- clinched; but he permits himself no large excursions. What he was thinking of was the matter immediately in hand, the audience before his eyes, the point that would tell best then and there, and would be most likely to remain in men's recollections. . . . What is remarkable is, that while he kept close to the matter and substance of his case, and resorted comparatively little to sarcasm, humor, invective, pathos, or the other elements that are catalogued in manuals of rhetoric, yet no speaker was ever further removed from prosiness, or came into more real and sympathetic contact with his audience. . . .

After all, it is not tropes and perorations that make the popular speaker; it is the whole impression of his personality. We who only read them can discern certain admirable qualities in Cobden's speeches; aptness in choosing topics, lucidity in presenting them, buoyant con-

fidence in pressing them home. But those who listened to them felt much more than all this. They were delighted by mingled vivacity and ease, by directness, by spontaneousness and reality, by the charm . . . of personal friendliness and undisguised cordiality.[42]

These passages are written in the spirit of the critic of public speaking. They have the point of view that is but faintly suggested in Elton and Grierson, that Saintsbury recognizes but does not use, and Hazlitt uses but does not recognize, and that Whipple, however irregularly, both understands and employs. But such critics as Curzon and Butler, Sears and Goodrich, Trevelyan and Bryce, think differently of their problem; they take the point of view of public address consistently and without question. Morley's superiority is not in conception, but in execution. In all the writers of this group, whether historians, biographers, or professed students of oratory, there is a consciousness that oratory is partly an art, partly a power of making history, and occasionally a branch of literature. Style is less considered for its own sake than for its effect in a given situation. The question of literary immortality is regarded as beside the mark, or else, as in Bryce, as a separate question requiring separate consideration. There are, of course, differences of emphasis. Some of the biographers may be thought to deal too lightly with style. Sears perhaps thinks too little of the time, of the drama of the situation, and too much of style. But we have arrived at a different attitude towards the orator; his function is recognized for what it is: the art of influencing men in some concrete situation. Neither the personal nor the literary evaluation is the primary object. The critic speaks of the orator as a public man whose function it is to exert his influence by speech.

VII

Any attempt to sum up the results of this casual survey of what some writers have said of some public speakers must deal with the differences between literary criticism as represented by Gosse and Trent, by Elton and Grierson, and rhetorical criticism as represented by Curzon, Morley, Bryce, and Trevelyan. The literary critics seem at first to have no common point of view and no agreement as to the categories of judgment or description. But by reading between their lines and searching for the main endeavor of these critics, one can discover at least a unity of purpose. Different in method as are Gosse, Elton, Saintsbury, Whipple, Hazlitt, the ends they have in view are not different.

[42] Life of Richard Cobden, *Boston, 1881, pp. 130–2.*

Coupled with almost every description of the excellences of prose and with every attempt to describe the man in connection with his work, is the same effort as we find clearly and even arbitrarily expressed by those whom we have termed judicial critics. All the literary critics unite in the attempt to interpret the permanent value that they find in the work under consideration. That permanent value is not precisely indicated by the term beauty, but the two strands of æsthetic excellence and permanence are clearly found, not only in the avowed judicial criticism but in those writers who emphasize description rather than judgment. Thus Grierson says of Burke:

His preoccupation at every juncture with the fundamental issues of wise government, and the splendor of the eloquence in which he set forth these principles, an eloquence in which the wisdom of his thought and the felicity of his language and imagery seem inseparable from one another . . . have made his speeches and pamphlets a source of perennial freshness and interest.[43]

Perhaps a critic of temper different from Grierson's—Saintsbury, for example—would turn from the wisdom of Burke's thought to the felicity of his language and imagery. But always there is implicit in the critic's mind the absolute standard of a timeless world: the wisdom of Burke's thought (found in the principles to which his mind always gravitates rather than in his decisions on points of policy) and the felicity of his language are not considered as of an age, but for all time. Whether the critic considers the technical excellence merely, or both technique and substance, his preoccupation is with that which age cannot wither nor custom stale. (From this point of view, the distinction between the speech and the pamphlet is of no moment, and Elton wisely speaks of Burke's favorite form as "oratory, uttered or written";[44] for a speech cannot be the subject of a permanent evaluation unless it is preserved in print.)

This is the implied attitude of all the literary critics. On this common ground their differences disappear or become merely differences of method or of competence. They are all, in various ways, interpreters of the permanent and universal values they find in the works of which they treat. Nor can there be any quarrel with this attitude—unless all standards be swept away. The impressionist and the historian of the evolution of literature as a self-contained activity may deny the utility or the possibility of a truly judicial criticism. But the human mind insists upon

---

[43] Cambridge History of English Literature, *New York, 1914, XI, 8.*
[44] *Oliver Elton,* Survey of English Literature, 1780–1830, *London, 1912, I, 234.*

judgment *sub specie æternitatis.* The motive often appears as a merely practical one: the reader wishes to be apprised of the best that has been said and thought in all ages; he is less concerned with the descent of literary species or with the critic's adventures among masterpieces than with the perennial freshness and interest those masterpieces may hold for him. There is, of course, much more than a practical motive to justify the interest in permanent values; but this is not the place to raise a moot question of general critical theory. We wished only to note the common ground of literary criticism in its preoccupation with the thought and the eloquence which is permanent.

If now we turn to rhetorical criticism as we found it exemplified in the preceding section, we find that its point of view is patently single. It is not concerned with permanence, nor yet with beauty. It is concerned with effect. It regards a speech as a communication to a specific audience, and holds its business to be the analysis and appreciation of the orator's method of imparting his ideas to his hearers.

Rhetoric, however, is a word that requires explanation; its use in connection with criticism is neither general nor consistent. The merely deprecatory sense in which it is often applied to bombast or false ornament need not delay us. The limited meaning which confines the term to the devices of a correct and even of an elegant prose style—in the sense of manner of writing and speaking—may also be eliminated, as likewise the broad interpretation which makes rhetoric inclusive of all style whether in prose or in poetry. There remain some definitions which have greater promise. We may mention first that of Aristotle: "the faculty of observing in any given case the available means of persuasion";[45] this readily turns into the art of persuasion, as the editors of the *New English Dictionary* recognize when they define rhetoric as "the art of using language so as to persuade or influence others." The gloss on "persuade" afforded by the additional term "influence" is worthy of note. Jebb achieves the same result by defining rhetoric as "the art of using language in such a way as to produce a desired impression upon the hearer or reader."[46] There is yet a fourth definition, one which serves to illuminate the others as well as to emphasize their essential agreement: "taken broadly [rhetoric is] the science and art of communication in language";[47] the framers of this definition add that to throw the emphasis on communication is to emphasize prose, poetry being regarded as more distinctly expressive than communicative. A German writer has made a similar distinction between poetic as the art

---

[45] Rhetoric, *ii, 2, tr. W. Rhys Roberts in* The Works of Aristotle, *XI, Oxford, 1924.*
[46] Article "Rhetoric" in the Encyclopaedia Britannica, *9th and 11th editions.*
[47] *J. L. Gerig and F. N. Scott, article "Rhetoric" in the* New International Encyclopaedia.

of poetry and rhetoric as the art of prose, but rather on the basis that prose is of the intellect, poetry of the imagination.[48] Wackernagel's basis for the distinction will hardly stand in face of the attitude of modern psychology to the "faculties"; yet the distinction itself is suggestive, and it does not contravene the more significant opposition of expression and communication. That opposition has been well stated, though with some exaggeration, by Professor Hudson:

> The writer in pure literature has his eye on his subject; his subject has filled his mind and engaged his interest, and he must tell about it; his task is expression; his form and style are organic with his subject. The writer of rhetorical discourse has his eye upon the audience and occasion; his task is persuasion; his form and style are organic with the occasion.[49]

The element of the author's personality should not be lost from sight in the case of the writer of pure literature; nor may the critic think of the audience and the occasion as alone conditioning the work of the composer of rhetorical discourse, unless indeed he include in the occasion both the personality of the speaker and the subject. The distinction is better put by Professor Baldwin:

> Rhetoric meant to the ancient world the art of instructing and moving men in their affairs; poetic the art of sharpening and expanding their vision. . . . The one is composition of ideas; the other, composition of images. In the one field life is discussed; in the other it is presented. The type of the one is a public address, moving us to assent and action; the type of the other is a play, showing us [an] action moving to an end of character. The one argues and urges; the other represents. Though both appeal to imagination, the method of rhetoric is logical; the method of poetic, as well as its detail, is imaginative.[50]

It is noteworthy that in this passage there is nothing to oppose poetry, in its common acceptation of verse, to prose. Indeed, in discussing the four forms of discourse usually treated in textbooks, Baldwin explicitly classes exposition and argument under rhetoric, leaving narrative and description to the other field. But rhetoric has been applied to the art of prose by some who include under the term even non-

---

[48] K. H. W. Wackernagel, Poetik, Rhetorik und Stilistik, ed. L. Sieber, Halle, 1873, p. 11.

[49] H. H. Hudson, "The Field of Rhetoric," Quarterly Journal of Speech Education, IX (1923), 177. See also the same writer's "Rhetoric and Poetry," ibid., X (1924), 143 ff.

[50] C. S. Baldwin, Ancient Rhetoric and Poetic, New York, 1924, p. 134.

metrical works of fiction. This is the attitude of Wackernagel, already mentioned, and of Saintsbury, who observes that Aristotle's *Rhetoric* holds, "if not intentionally, yet actually, something of the same position towards Prose as that which the *Poetics* holds towards verse."[51] In Saintsbury's view, the *Rhetoric* achieves this position in virtue of its third book, that on style and arrangement: the first two books contain "a great deal of matter which has either the faintest connection with literary criticism or else no connection with it at all."[52] Saintsbury finds it objectionable in Aristotle that to him, "prose as prose is merely and avowedly a secondary consideration: it is always in the main, and sometimes wholly, a mere necessary instrument of divers practical purposes,"[53] and that "he does not *wish* to consider a piece of prose as a work of art destined, first of all, if not finally, to fulfil its own laws on the one hand, and to give pleasure on the other."[54] The distinction between verse and prose has often troubled the waters of criticism. The explanation is probably that the outer form of a work is more easily understood and more constantly present to the mind than is the real form. Yet it is strange that those who find the distinction between verse and prose important should parallel this with a distinction between imagination and intellect, as if a novel had more affinities with a speech than with an epic. It is strange, too, that Saintsbury's own phrase about the right way to consider a "piece of prose"—as a work of art destined "to fulfil its own laws"—did not suggest to him the fundamental importance of a distinction between what he terms the minor or suasive rhetoric on the one hand, and on the other poetic, whether or not in verse. For poetry always is free to fulfil its own law, but the writer of rhetorical discourse is, in a sense, perpetually in bondage to the occasion and the audience; and in that fact we find the line of cleavage between rhetoric and poetic.

The distinction between rhetoric as theory of public address and poetic as theory of pure literature, says Professor Baldwin, "seems not to have controlled any consecutive movement of modern criticism."[55] That it has not controlled the procedure of critics in dealing with orators is indicated in the foregoing pages; yet we have found, too, many suggestions of a better method, and some few critical performances against which the only charge is overcondensation.

Rhetorical criticism is necessarily analytical. The scheme of a rhetorical study includes the element of the speaker's personality as a conditioning factor; it includes also the public character of the man—not

---

[51] G. E. B. *Saintsbury*, History of Criticism and Literary Taste in Europe, *New York, 1900, I, 39.*

[52] Ibid., *p. 42.*

[53] History of Criticism and Literary Taste in Europe, *p. 48.*

[54] Ibid., *p. 52.*

[55] Op. cit., *p. 4.*

what he was, but what he was thought to be. It requires a description of
the speaker's audience, and of the leading ideas with which he plied
his hearers—his topics, the motives to which he appealed, the nature
of the proofs he offered. These will reveal his own judgment of human
nature in his audiences, and also his judgment on the questions which
he discussed. Attention must be paid, too, to the relation of the surviving texts to what was actually uttered: in case the nature of the
changes is known, there may be occasion to consider adaptation to
two audiences—that which heard and that which read. Nor can rhetorical criticism omit the speaker's mode of arrangement and his mode of
expression, nor his habit of preparation and his manner of delivery from
the platform; though the last two are perhaps less significant. "Style"
—in the sense which corresponds to diction and sentence movement—
must receive attention, but only as one among various means that secure for the speaker ready access to the minds of his auditors. Finally,
the effect of the discourse on its immediate hearers is not to be ignored,
neither in the testimony of witnesses, nor in the record of events. And
throughout such a study one must conceive of the public man as influencing the men of his own times by the power of his discourse.

VIII

What is the relation of rhetorical criticism, so understood, to literary
criticism? The latter is at once broader and more limited than rhetorical
criticism. It is broader because of its concern with permanent values;
because it takes no account of special purpose nor of immediate effect;
because it views a literary work as the voice of a human spirit addressing itself to men of all ages and times; because the critic speaks as the
spectator of all time and all existence. But this universalizing of attitude
brings its own limits with it: the influence of the period is necessarily
relegated to the background; interpretation in the light of the writer's
intention and of his situation may be ignored or slighted; and the
speaker who directed his words to a definite and limited group of hearers may be made to address a universal audience. The result can only
be confusion. In short, the point of view of literary criticism is proper
only to its own objects, the permanent works. Upon such as are found
to lie without the pale, the verdict of literary criticism is of negative
value merely, and its interpretation is false and misleading, because it
proceeds upon a wrong assumption. If Henry Clay and Charles Fox are
to be dealt with at all, it must not be on the assumption that their works,
in respect of wisdom and eloquence, are or ought to be sources of
perennial freshness and interest. Morley has put the matter well:

*The statesman who makes or dominates a crisis, who has to rouse
and mold the mind of senate or nation, has something else to think
about than the production of literary masterpieces. The great political*

*speech, which for that matter is a sort of drama, is not made by pas-
sages for elegant extract or anthologies, but by personality, movement,
climax, spectacle, and the action of the time.*[56]

But we cannot always divorce rhetorical criticism from literary. In
the case of Fox or Clay or Cobden, as opposed to Fielding or Addison
or De Quincy, it is proper to do so; the fact that language is a common
medium to the writer of rhetorical discourse and to the writer in pure
literature will give to the critics of each a common vocabulary of
stylistic terms, but not a common standard. In the case of Burke the
relation of the two points of view is more complex. Burke belongs to
literature; but in all his important works he was a practitioner of public
address written or uttered. Since his approach to *belles-lettres* was
through rhetoric, it follows that rhetorical criticism is at least a preliminary to literary criticism, for it will erect the factual basis for the understanding of the works: will not merely explain allusions and establish
dates, but recall the setting, reconstruct the author's own intention, and
analyze his method. But the rhetorical inquiry is more than a mere preliminary; it permeates and governs all subsequent interpretation and
criticism. For the statesman in letters is a statesman still: compare
Burke to Charles Lamb, or even to Montaigne, and it is clear that the
public man is in a sense inseparable from his audience. A statesman's
wisdom and eloquence are not to be read without some share of his
own sense of the body politic, and of the body politic not merely as a
construct of thought, but as a living human society. A speech, like a
satire, like a comedy of manners, grows directly out of a social situation; it is a man's response to a condition in human affairs. However
broadly typical the situation may be when its essential elements are
laid bare, it never appears without its coverings. On no plane of
thought—philosophical, literary, political—is Burke to be understood
without reference to the great events in America, India, France, which
evoked his eloquence; nor is he to be understood without reference to
the state of English society. (It is this last that is lacking in Grierson's
essay: the page of comment on Burke's qualities in actual debate wants
its supplement in some account of the House of Commons and the national life it represented. Perhaps the latter is the more needful to a
full understanding of the abiding excellence in Burke's pages.) Something of the spirit of Morley's chapter on Cobden, and more of the
spirit of the social historian (which Morley has in other parts of the
biography) is necessary to the literary critic in dealing with the statesman who is also a man of letters.

In the case of Burke, then, one of the functions of rhetorical criticism

[56] Life of William Ewart Gladstone, *II, 589–90.*

is as a preliminary, but an essential and governing preliminary, to the literary criticism which occupies itself with the permanent values of wisdom and of eloquence, of thought and of beauty, that are found in the works of the orator.

Rhetorical criticism may also be regarded as an end in itself. Even Burke may be studied from that point of view alone. Fox and Cobden and the majority of public speakers are not to be regarded from any other. No one will offer Cobden's works a place in pure literature. Yet the method of the great agitator has a place in the history of his times. That place is not in the history of *belles-lettres;* nor is it in the literary history which is a "survey of the life of a people as expressed in their writings." The idea of "writings" is a merely mechanical one; it does not really provide a point of view or a method; it is a book-maker's cloak for many and diverse points of view. Such a compilation as the *Cambridge History of American Literature,* for example, in spite of the excellence of single essays, may not unjustly be characterized as an uneven commentary on the literary life of the country and as a still more uneven commentary on its social and political life. It may be questioned whether the scant treatment of public men in such a compilation throws light either on the creators of pure literature, or on the makers of rhetorical discourse, or on the life of the times.

Rhetorical criticism lies at the boundary of politics (in the broadest sense) and literature; its atmosphere is that of the public life,[57] its tools are those of literature, its concern is with the ideas of the people as influenced by their leaders. The effective wielder of public discourse, like the military man, belongs to social and political history because he is one of its makers. Like the soldier, he has an art of his own which is the source of his power; but the soldier's art is distinct from the life which his conquests affect. The rhetorician's art represents a natural and normal process within that life. It includes the work of the speaker, of the pamphleteer, of the writer of editorials, and of the sermon maker. It is to be thought of as the art of popularization. Its practitioners are the Huxleys, not the Darwins, of science; the Jeffersons, not the Lockes and the Rousseaus, of politics.

Of late years the art of popularization has received a degree of attention: propaganda and publicity have been words much used; the influence of the press has been discussed; there have been some studies of public opinion. Professor Robinson's *Humanizing of Knowledge*[58] is a cogent statement of the need for popularization by the instructed element in the state, and of the need for a technique in doing

---

[57] *For a popular but suggestive presentation of the background of rhetorical discourse, see J. A. Spender,* The Public Life, *New York, 1925.*
[58] *New York, 1923.*

so. But the book indicates, too, how little is known of the methods its author so earnestly desires to see put to use. Yet ever since Homer's day men have woven the web of words and counsel in the face of all. And ever since Aristotle's day there has been a mode of analysis of public address. Perhaps the preoccupation of literary criticism with "style" rather than with composition in the large has diverted interest from the more significant problem. Perhaps the conventional categories of historical thought have helped to obscure the problem: the history of thought, for example, is generally interpreted as the history of invention and discovery, both physical and intellectual. Yet the history of the thought of the people is at least as potent a factor in the progress of the race. True, the popular thought may often represent a resisting force, and we need not marvel that the many movements of a poet's mind more readily capture the critic's attention than the few and uncertain movements of that Leviathan, the public mind. Nor is it surprising that the historians tend to be occupied with the acts and the motives of leaders. But those historians who find the spirit of an age in the total mass of its literary productions, as well as all who would tame Leviathan to the end that he shall not threaten civilization, must examine more thoroughly than they as yet have done the interactions of the inventive genius, the popularizing talent, and the public mind.

Lincoln's First Inaugural
by Marie Hochmuth Nichols

Part I
"Spring comes gently to Washington always," observed the poet-historian, Carl Sandburg. "In early March the green of the grass brightens, the magnolia softens. Elms and chestnuts burgeon. Redbud and lilac carry on preparations soon to bloom. The lovemaking and birthing in many sunny corners go on no matter what or who the blue-prints and personages behind the discreet bureau and departmental walls."[1] Spring of 1861 was little different from other springs in physical aspect. March 4th dawned as other March 4th's, no doubt, wavering between clearness and cloudiness. At daylight clouds hung dark and heavy in the sky. Early in the morning a few drops of rain fell, but scarcely enough to lay the dust. A northwest wind swept down the cross streets to Pennsylvania Avenue. The weather was cool and bracing, and on the

---

From *American Speeches* by Wayland Maxfield Parrish and Marie Hochmuth Nichols (New York: 1954). Used by permission of the David McKay Company, Inc. Dr. Nichols was professor of speech at the University of Illinois.

[1] *Carl Sandburg,* Abraham Lincoln: The War Years (*Harcourt, Brace and Co., 1939*), *I, 120.*

whole, "favorable to the ceremonies of the day."[2] The sun had come out.

But if, on the whole, spring had come "gently" as usual, there was little else that bespoke the same rhythm. Out of the deep of winter had come the somewhat bewildered voice of President Buchanan asking, "Why is it . . . that discontent now so extensively prevails, and the union of the States, which is the source of all these blessings is threatened with destruction?"[3] Spiritually and morally, the city, indeed the nation, were out of tune, cacophonous, discordant.

Would there be a harmonizing voice today from the gaunt "orator of the West," about to take the helm of the nation? "Behind the cloud the sun is shining still," Abraham Lincoln had said three weeks before, as his train meandered across the Illinois prairies taking him on an "errand of national importance, attended . . . with considerable difficulties."[4] Trouble had not come suddenly to the nation, of course. Only a year previously the country had been "eminently prosperous in all its material interests."[5] Harvests had been abundant, and plenty smiled throughout the land. But for forty years there had been an undercurrent of restlessness. As early as 1820, an occasional voice had urged the necessity for secession. Again in 1850, with somewhat greater vehemence, voices were raised as the distribution of newly acquired Mexican territory took place. Then came the repeal of the Missouri Compromise in 1854, the civil war in Kansas and the Sumner-Brooks combat in the Senate in 1856, the Dred Scott decision in 1857, and the spectacular John Brown's raid at Harper's Ferry in 1859, all giving rise to disorder, unrest, and threats of secession as abolition sentiment mounted. Finally, came the election of 1860, and the North appeared to have "capped the mighty pyramid of unfraternal enormities by electing Abraham Lincoln to the Chief Magistracy, on a platform and by a system which indicates nothing but the subjugation of the South and the complete ruin of her social, political and industrial institutions."[6] It was not merely that Lincoln had been elected president, but the "majorities" by which he was elected were "more significant and suggestive than anything else—more so than the election itself—for they unmistakably indicate the hatred to the South which animates and controls the

[2] New York Times, March 5, 1861, p. 1, col. 1.

[3] James Buchanan, "Fourth Annual Message, December 3, 1860," The Works of James Buchanan, collected and edited by John Bassett Moore (Philadelphia: J. B. Lippincott Co., 1910), XI, 7.

[4] Speech at Tolono, Illinois, February 11, 1861, as reported in New York Daily Tribune, February 12, 1861, p. 5, col. 3.

[5] Buchanan, loc. cit.

[6] New Orleans Daily Crescent, November 13, 1860, as quoted in Southern Editorials on Secession, edited by Dwight Lowell Dumond (New York and London: The Century Co., 1931), p. 237.

masses of the numerically strongest section of the Confederacy."[7]
Senator Clingman of North Carolina found the election a "great, remarkable and dangerous fact that has filled my section with alarm and
dread for the future," since Lincoln was elected *"because he was
known to be a dangerous man,"* avowing the principle of the "irrepressible conflict."[8] Richmond observers commented that a party "founded
on the single sentiment, the exclusive feeling of hatred of African slavery," was "now the controlling power in this Confederacy," and noted
that the question "What is to be done . . . presses on every man."[9]
In Charleston, South Carolina, the news of Lincoln's election was met
with great rejoicing and "long continued cheering for a Southern Confederacy."[10]

Scarcely more than a month had passed when South Carolina led
off in the secession movement. Her two senators resigned their seats
in the United States Senate on November 10, 1860, and on December
20 an Ordinance of Secession was adopted,[11] bringing in its wake
secessionist demonstrations throughout the South.[12] By the first of
February of the new year, Mississippi, Florida, Alabama, Louisiana,
Texas, and Georgia had "repealed, rescinded, and abrogated" their
membership in the Union by adopting secession ordinances, standing
"prepared to resist by force any attempt to maintain the supremacy of
the Constitution of the United States."[13] The other slaveholding states
held a position of "quasi neutrality," declaring that their adhesion to the
Union could be secured only by affording guarantees against wrongs
of which they complained, and dangers which they apprehended.[14]
Already by the end of 1860, secessionists at Charleston were in possession of the post office, the federal courts, the customhouses, and
forts Castle Pinckney and Moultrie.[15]

It was not without clamor and fanfare that senators took their leave
from familiar places. When, on December 31, Senator Judah Benjamin

[7] New Orleans Daily Crescent, *November 12, 1860, as quoted in* Southern
Editorials on Secession, *p. 228.*

[8] *Speech of Senator Thomas L. Clingman of North Carolina in the Senate,
December 3, 1860,* The Congressional Globe, *Second Session, 36th Congress,
Vol. 30, p. 3.*

[9] Richmond Semi-Weekly Examiner, *November 9, 1860, as quoted in* Southern
Editorials on Secession, *p. 223.*

[10] The Daily Herald, *Wilmington, N. C., November 9, 1860, as quoted in*
Southern Editorials on Secession, *p. 226.*

[11] *Daniel Wait Howe,* Political History of Secession (*New York: G. P. Putnam's
Sons, 1914*), *p. 449.*

[12] *J. G. Randall,* Lincoln the President (*New York: Dodd, Mead and Co.,
1945*), *I, 215.*

[13] New York Times, *February 11, 1861, p. 4, col. 2.*

[14] Ibid.

[15] *Randall,* loc. cit.

of Louisiana reported that he would make a parting secession speech, "every corner was crowded"[16] in the Senate galleries. His closing declaration that "you can never subjugate us; you never can convert the free sons of the soil into vassals . . . never, never can degrade them to the level of an inferior and servile race. Never! Never!"[17] was greeted by the galleries with "disgraceful applause, screams and uproar."[18] As the galleries were cleared because of misbehavior, people murmured in departing, "Now we will have war," "D—n the Abolitionists," "Abe Lincoln will never come here."[19] Critics observing the national scene remarked, "The President . . . enters upon one of the most momentous and difficult duties ever devolved upon any man, in this country or any other. No one of his predecessors was ever called upon to confront dangers half as great, or to render a public service half as difficult, as those which will challenge his attention at the very outset of his Administration."[20]

January of 1861 came without hope, and with little possibility of the cessation of unrest. Occasionally the newspapers scoffed at the recommendation of the *Richmond Inquirer* that an armed force proceeding from Virginia or Maryland should invade the District of Columbia and prevent the peaceful inauguration of Abraham Lincoln, dismissing it as the "exaggeration of political rhetoric."[21] The capital of the nation was beset by rumor, clamor, occasional attempts at compromise, and general misbehavior. "I passed a part of last week in Washington," observed a Baltimore reporter, "and never, since the days of Jerico [sic], has there been such a blowing of rams' horns as may now be heard in that distracted city. If sound and clamor could overthrow the Constitution, one might well expect to see it go down before the windy suspirations of forced breath that shock and vibrate on all sides." Almost everywhere he met "intemperate and alarming disciples of discord and confusion." "War, secession, and disunion are on every lip; and no hope of compromise or adjustment is held out by any one. The prevailing sentiment in Washington is with the South."[22]

As secession went on apace in the South, Wendell Phillips declared in Boston's Music Hall that he hoped that all the slave states would leave the Union.[23] Horace Greeley, impatient after forty years of Southern threat, disclaimed a "union of force,—a union held together by

[16] New York Times, *January 1, 1861, p. 1, col. 1.*
[17] Congressional Globe, *Second Session, 36th Congress, Vol. 30, p. 217.*
[18] New York Times, *January 1, 1861, p. 1, col. 1.*
[19] Ibid.
[20] New York Times, *February 11, 1861, p. 4, col. 2.*
[21] The National Intelligencer (*Washington*), *January 3, 1861, p. 3, col. 2.*
[22] New York Times, *January 15, 1861, p. 1, col. 5.*
[23] New York Times, *January 21, 1861, p. 1, col. 4; see also, complete text of speech in ibid., p. 8, cols. 5, 6 and p. 5, cols. 1, 2.*

bayonets," and would interpose "no obstacle to their peaceful withdrawal."[24] Meanwhile, however, a few held out for compromise. On
December 18, Senator Crittenden of Kentucky introduced a series of
compromises in the Senate,[25] but action seemed unlikely. And when,
on January 7, Senator Toombs of Georgia made a "noisy and ranting
secession speech, and at the close was greeted with a storm of hisses
and applause, which was continued some time," Crittenden's "appeal
to save the country," presented in "good taste," created "little or no
additional favor for his compromise measure."[26] While Crittenden appealed in the Senate, a peace conference met in Washington at the
invitation of Virginia, with its announced purpose "to afford to the people of the slaveholding States adequate guarantees for the security of
their rights."[27] Although delegates assembled and conducted business,
ultimately submitting to the Senate a series of resolutions, it appeared
from the beginning that "no substantial results would be gained."[28]
It was clear that the sympathies of the border states which had not yet
seceded "were with those which had already done so."[29] Ultimately,
the propositions were rejected by the Senate, just as were the Crittenden resolutions, in the closing days of the Congress. In all, it appeared
to be an era of "much talk and small performance," a dreary season
of debate, with "clouds of dusty and sheety showers of rhetoric," a nation trying to live by "prattle alone," a "miserably betalked nation."[30]

When Lincoln left Springfield, February 11, to wend his way toward
Washington, another President, Jefferson Davis, elected on February 9
to head the newly organized Southern Confederacy, was traveling from
Mississippi to the Montgomery Convention of slaveholding states to
help complete the act of secession, his trip being "one continuous
ovation."[31] "The time for compromise is past," observed Davis, as he
paused at the depot at Montgomery to address the crowd, "and we are
now determined to maintain our position, and make all who oppose us
smell Southern powder, feel Southern steel."[32] Clearly, people could
agree that Lincoln was to inherit "a thorny wilderness of perplexities."[33]
Would he "coerce" the seceded states and ask for the restoration of

[24] *Horace Greeley,* Recollections of a Busy Life *(New York: J. B. Ford and
Co., 1868), p. 398.*
[25] Congressional Globe, *Second Session, 36th Congress, Part I, Vol. 30, pp.
112–14.*
[26] New York Times, *January 8, 1861, p. 1, col. 1; see also,* Congressional
Globe, *Second Session, 36th Congress, Part I, Vol. 30, pp. 264–71.*
[27] *Howe, op. cit., p. 465.*
[28] Ibid., *p. 467.*
[29] Ibid., *p. 467.*
[30] New York Daily Tribune, *March 13, 1861, p. 4, col. 4.*
[31] New York Daily Tribune, *February 18, 1861, p. 5, col. 6.*
[32] Ibid., *p. 5, col. 6.*
[33] Ibid., *March 4, 1861, p. 4, col. 2.*

federal properties in possession of the secessionists? Would he respond to pressure "from all sides" and from a "fraction of his own party" to consent to "extension" of slavery, particularly below the line 36° 30'? Would he listen to "compromise" Republicans in Congress and only *"seem"* to compromise, "so as not to appear obstinate or insensible to the complaints of the Slaveholders"?[34] Would he stand by the Chicago Republican platform, severe in its strictures on the incumbent Democratic administration's acceptance of the principle that the personal relation between master and slave involved "an unqualified property in persons"?[35] Would he stand by the part of the platform which pledged "the maintenance inviolate of the rights of the States, and especially the right of each State to order and control its own domestic institutions according to its own judgment exclusively"?[36] Was the belief that he had so often uttered representative of the true Lincoln: "A house divided against itself cannot stand"?[37]

On March 4 as the newspapers gave advance notice of what was to transpire during the day, there was a note of fear and uncertainty in regard to the safety of the President-elect, along with the general eagerness about the outlines of Lincoln's course of action to be announced in the Inaugural. "The great event to which so many have been looking forward with anxiety—which has excited the hopes and fears of the country to an extent unparalleled in its comparatively brief history—will take place to-day," observed the *New York Times*. "The occasion has drawn to the Federal Capital a greater crowd, probably, than has ever been assembled there on any similar occasion. . . . Whether the ceremonies will be marred by any untoward event is, of course, a matter of conjecture, though grave fears are expressed on the subject."[38] While visitors to Washington were seeking to get a glimpse of the tumultuous Senate in all-night session, General Scott and his advisers were together planning to take the "greatest precaution" for preventing "any attack upon the procession or demonstration against Mr. Lincoln's person."[39] Rumors of the presence of a "large gang of 'Plug Uglies' who are here from Baltimore,"[40] circulated freely. Whether they were in Washington to make an attack on the person of the Presi-

---

[34] New York Daily Tribune, *February 18, 1861, p. 6, col. 1.*

[35] *M. Halstead,* A History of the National Political Conventions of the Current Presidential Campaign *(Columbus, Ohio: Follett, Foster and Co., 1860); p. 138.*
[36] Ibid.

[37] *"A House Divided: Speech Delivered at Springfield, Illinois, at the Close of the Republican State Convention, June 16, 1858," in* Abraham Lincoln: His Speeches and Writings, *edited with critical and analytical notes by Roy P. Basler (Cleveland, Ohio: The World Publishing Co., 1946), p. 372.*

[38] New York Times, *March 4, 1861, p. 4, col. 1.*
[39] New York Times, *March 4, 1861, p. 1, col. 2.*
[40] Ibid.

dent or to "create a disturbance, and plunder private persons"[41] was a matter for general speculation. Whatever the purpose, General Scott and his advisers had decided to leave nothing undone to secure the safety of the President-elect. Riflemen in squads were to be placed in hiding on the roofs commanding buildings along Pennsylvania Avenue. Orders were given to fire in the event of a threat to the presidential carriages. There were cavalry regulars to guard the side-street crossings, moving from one to another as the procession passed. From the windows of the Capitol wings riflemen were to watch the inauguration platform. General Scott would oversee the ceremonies from the top of a slope commanding the north entrance to the Capitol, ready to take personal charge of a battery of flying artillery stationed there. District militia in three ranks were to surround the platform to keep back the crowd. Armed detectives in citizen's clothing were to be scattered through the great audience.[42]

The occasion must have seemed strange to the man who had been accustomed to being carried on the shoulders of admirers on speaking occasions in his years as a stump orator in the West, and to being the idol of many a torchlight procession during the combats with the "Little Giant" in the tumultuous debates of 1858. Even the Capitol grounds where the crowds had begun to assemble had a strangely unfamiliar look in contrast to its fixity during his years as congressman in 1847 and 1848. "The old dome familiar to Congressman Lincoln in 1848 had been knocked loose and hauled down," noted Sandburg. "The iron-wrought material on the Capitol grounds, the hammers, jacks, screws, scaffolds, derricks, ladders, props, ropes, told that they were rebuilding, extending, embellishing the structure on March 4, 1861." "On the slope of lawn fronting the Capitol building stood a bronze statue of Liberty shaped as a massive, fertile woman holding a sword in one hand for power and a wreath of flowers in the other hand for glory. Not yet raised to her pedestal, she looked out of place. She was to be lifted and set on top of the Capitol dome, overlooking the Potomac Valley, when the dome itself should be prepared for her."[43] The carpenters had set up a temporary platform fronting the Senate wing for the occasion, with a small wooden canopy covering the speaker's

[41] Ibid.

[42] Ibid.; see also, Sandburg, The War Years, I, 120–21; Randall, Lincoln the President, I, 293, 294; William E. Baringer, A House Dividing (Springfield, Ill.: Abraham Lincoln Association, 1945), pp. 331–34; The Diary of a Public Man, Prefatory notes by F. Lauriston Bullard, Foreword by Carl Sandburg (Chicago: Privately printed for Abraham Lincoln Book Shop, 1945), pp. 73, 74; Clark E. Carr, Stephen A. Douglas, His Life and Public Services, Speeches and Patriotism (Chicago: A. C. McClurg and Co., 1909), p. 123.

[43] Sandburg, The War Years, I, 120.

table.[44] "The crowd swarmed about all the approaches leading to the capitol grounds," observed a witness, "while the spacious level extending from the east front of the capitol was one vast black sea of heads."[45] There were between 25,000 and 50,000 people there, waiting with expectancy.[46] "Every window in the north front of the Capitol was filled with ladies. Every tree top bore its burden of eager eyes. Every fence and staging, and pile of building material, for the Capitol extension was made a 'coyn of vantage' for its full complement of spectators."[47] It was noticeable that "scarce a Southern face is to be seen"[48] in the crowd, "judging from the lack of long-haired men."[49] While the crowd waited for the administration of the oath of the Vice-President, which took place in the Senate chambers, it was entertained with martial music, and "by the antics of a lunatic, who had climbed a tall tree in front of the capitol and made a long political speech, claiming to be the rightful President of the United States." Policemen were detached to bring him down, but he merely climbed higher and "stood rocking in the wind, and made another speech."[50] The ceremonies over indoors, the major figures of the occasion were seen emerging, Abraham Lincoln with James Buchanan by his side.

As Lincoln and Buchanan took places on the right side of the speaker's stand, Chief Justice Taney, who soon would administer the oath of office, took a seat upon the left. Many in the audience were seeing Lincoln for the first time. "Honest Abe Lincoln," the folks back home called him, or just "Old Abe" was the affectionate cry at the Chicago "Wigwam" as thousands cheered and shook the rafters "like the rush of a great wind, in the van of a storm,"[51] when he was nominated. Walt Whitman thought "four sorts of genius, four mighty and primal hands, will be needed to the complete limning of this man's future portrait—the eyes and brains and finger-touch of Plutarch and Eschylus and Michel Angelo, assisted by Rabelais."[52] "If any personal description of me is thought desirable," Lincoln had written two years before, "it may be said I am, in height, six feet four inches, nearly; lean in flesh, weighing on an average one hundred and eighty pounds;

[44] Baringer, op. cit., p. 333.
[45] Correspondence of the Cincinnati Commercial, as quoted in The Chicago Daily Tribune, March 8, 1861, p. 2, col. 4.
[46] New York Daily Tribune, March 5, 1861, p. 5, col. 4.
[47] Chicago Daily Tribune, March 9, 1861, p. 3, col. 2.
[48] New York Times, March 4, 1861, p. 1, col. 2.
[49] Chicago Daily Tribune, March 5, 1861, p. 1, col. 2.
[50] Correspondence of the Cincinnati Commercial, as quoted in The Chicago Daily Tribune, March 8, 1861, p. 2, col. 4.
[51] Halstead, op. cit., pp. 149–51.
[52] The Complete Writings of Walt Whitman (New York: G. P. Putnam's Sons, 1902), II, 244.

dark complexion, with coarse black hair and gray eyes. No other marks or brands recollected."[53] He was "not a pretty man," his law partner, Herndon, thought, "nor was he an ugly one: he was a homely man, careless of his looks, plain looking and plain acting." But he had that "inner quality which distinguishes one person from another."[54] "I never saw a more thoughtful face," observed David Locke, "I never saw a more dignified face, I never saw so sad a face."[55] Emerson had found in him the "grandeur and strength of absolute simplicity," when, on occasion, he had heard him speak, seen his small gray eyes kindle, heard his voice ring, and observed his face shine and seem "to light up a whole assembly."[56] "Abraham Lincoln: one of nature's noblemen," he was sometimes toasted.[57]

"It was unfortunate," says the noted Lincoln scholar, J. G. Randall, "that Lincoln was not better known, North and South, in March of 1861. Had people more fully understood his pondering on government, reverence for law, peaceful intent and complete lack of sectional bitterness, much tragedy might have been avoided."[58] "Gentle, and merciful and just!"[59] William Cullen Bryant was eventually to write. But now, in 1861, there was something unknown about Lincoln to many. It is true that after the Lincoln-Douglas debates he had gained recognition beyond the limits of his state. The Chicago *Democrat* called attention to the fact that "Mr. Lincoln's name has been used by newspapers and public meetings outside the State in connection with the Presidency and Vice Presidency, so that it is not only in his own State that Honest Old Abe is respected." "Even his opponents profess to love the man, though they hate his principles," it observed.[60] Again the *Illinois State Journal* took pride in reporting his growing fame. In "other states," it said, he had been found "not only . . . an unrivalled orator, strong in debate, keen in his logic and wit, with admirable powers of statement, and a fertility of resources which are equal to every occasion; but his truthfulness, his candor, his honesty of purpose, his magnanimity . . . have stamped him as a statesman whom the Republicans throughout the

---

[53] *Lincoln to J. W. Fell, Springfield, Illinois, December 20, 1859,* Complete Works of Abraham Lincoln, *edited by John G. Nicolay and John Hay (New York: The Tandy-Thomas Co., 1905), V, 288, 289.*

[54] *Herndon MS fragment, quoted in Randall, op. cit., p. 28.*

[55] Remembrances of Abraham Lincoln by Distinguished Men of His Time, *collected and edited by Allen Thorndike Rice (8th ed.; New York: Published by the* North American Review, *1889), p. 442.*

[56] *John Wesley Hill,* Abraham Lincoln, Man of God *(4th ed.; New York: G. P. Putnam's Sons, 1930), p. 306.*

[57] *Carl Sandburg,* Abraham Linclon, The Prairie Years *(New York: Harcourt, Brace and Co., 1926), 1, 199, 200.*

[58] New York Times Magazine, *February 6, 1949, p. 11.*

[59] *"Abraham Lincoln," in* The Poetical Works of William Cullen Bryant, *edited by Parke Godwin (New York: D. Appleton and Co., 1883), II, 151.*

[60] *Quoted in* Daily Illinois State Journal, *November 15, 1858, p. 1, col. 1.*

Union may be proud of."[61] In 1860, in New York, the "announcement that Hon. Abraham Lincoln, of Illinois, would deliver an address in Cooper Institute . . . drew thither a large and enthusiastic assemblage," and William Cullen Bryant thought that he had only "to pronounce the name of Abraham Lincoln" who had previously been known "only by fame" in order to secure the "profoundest attention."[62] Lincoln had faced thousands of people along the way to Washington, at Indianapolis, Cleveland, Philadelphia, Albany, Harrisburg, and elsewhere, being greeted enthusiastically. Still, "in general," observed Randall, "it cannot be said that he had a 'good press' at the threshold of office. Showmanship failed to make capital of his rugged origin, and there faced the country a strange man from Illinois who was dubbed a 'Simple Susan,' a 'baboon,' or a 'gorilla.' "[63] "Our Presidential Merryman," *Harper's Weekly* had labeled him,[64] later carrying a caricature recounting the fabricated story of his incognito entry into Washington. "He wore a Scotch plaid Cap and a very long Military Cloak, so that he was entirely unrecognizable," the caption read.[65] Men like Stanton thought of him as a "low, cunning clown."[66] And the Associated Press reporter, Henry Villard, remembered his "fondness for low talk," and could not have persuaded himself "that the man might possibly possess true greatness of mind and nobility of heart," admitting to a feeling of "disgust and humiliation that such a person should have been called upon to direct the destinies of a great nation."[67]

In the South, there had been little willingness to know the Lincoln they "should have known," the Lincoln who "intended to be fair to the Southern people, and, as he had said at the Cooper Union in February of 1860, 'do nothing through passion and ill-temper,' 'calmly consider their demands, and yield to them' where possible."[68] The South had made up its mind that whatever the North did to ingratiate Lincoln with them was done in deceit. "Since the election of Lincoln most of the leading Northern Abolition papers have essayed the herculean task of reconciling the Southern People to his Presidential rule," observed the *New Orleans Daily Crescent.* "Having succeeded to their heart's content in electing him—having vilified and maligned the South through a long canvass, without measure or excuse—they now tell us that Mr. Lincoln is a very good man, a very amiable man; that he is not at all violent in his prejudices or partialities; that, on the contrary, he is a

[61] Ibid., *November 12, 1858, p. 2, col. 1.*
[62] New York Times, *February 28, 1860, p. 1, col. 1.*
[63] *Randall, op. cit., I, 292.*
[64] *Vol. V (March 2, 1861), p. 144.*
[65] Ibid. *(March 9, 1861), p. 160.*
[66] The Diary of a Public Man, *pp. 48, 49.*
[67] Memoirs of Henry Villard *(Boston: Houghton, Mifflin Co., 1904), I, 144.*
[68] *J. G. Randall, "Lincoln's Greatest Declaration of Faith,"* New York Times Magazine, *February 6, 1949, p. 11.*

moderate, kindly-tempered, conservative man, and if we will only submit to his administration for a time, we will ascertain that he will make one of the best Presidents the South or the country ever had! 'Will you walk into my parlor said the spider to the fly.' " "Mr. Lincoln may be all that these Abolition journals say he is. But, we do not believe a word they say," the *Crescent* continued. "We are clearly convinced that they are telling falsehoods to deceive the people of the South, in order to carry out their own selfish and unpatriotic purposes the more easily. They know that, although Lincoln is elected to the Presidency, he is not yet President of the United States, and they are shrewd enough to know that grave doubts exist whether he ever will be. The chances are that he will not, unless the South is quieted. . . ."[69]

The South found it easier to view Lincoln as a stereotype, a "radical Abolitionist," an "Illinois ape," a "traitor to his country." Then, too, the escape through Baltimore by night could "not fail to excite a most mischievous feeling of contempt for the personal character of Mr. Lincoln throughout the country, especially at the South."[70]

Thus appeared Lincoln, who "without mock modesty" had described himself en route to Washington as "the humblest of all individuals that have ever been elevated to the presidency."[71]

Senator Baker of Oregon advanced to the platform and announced, "Fellow-Citizens: I introduce to you Abraham Lincoln, the President-elect of the United States of America."[72]

Mr. Lincoln had the crowd "matched"[73] in sartorial perfection. He was wearing a new tall hat, new black suit of clothes and black boots, expansive white shirt bosom. He carried an ebony cane with a gold head the size of a hen's egg. He arose, "walked deliberately and composedly to the table, and bent low in honor of the repeated and enthusiastic cheering of the countless host before him. Having put on his spectacles, he arranged his manuscript on the small table, keeping the paper thereon by the aid of his cane."[74] In a clear voice he began:[75]

Fellow-citizens of the United States:

In compliance with a custom as old as the government itself, I appear before you to address you briefly, and to take, in your presence, the oath prescribed by the Constitution of the United States, to be taken by the President "before he enters on the execution of his office."

[69] Southern Editorials on Secession, *p. 229.*

[70] The Diary of a Public Man, *p. 46.*

[71] *"Address to the Legislature of New York, at Albany, February 18, 1861,"* in Complete Works of Abraham Lincoln, *VI, 140.*

[72] New York Times, *March 5, 1861, p. 1, col. 3.*

[73] *Sandburg,* The War Years, *I, 122.*

[74] New York Times, *March 5, 1861, p. 1, col. 3.*

[75] *The text of the Inaugural being used is that contained in* Abraham Lincoln: His Speeches and Writings, *edited by Roy P. Basler, pp. 579–90.*

I do not consider it necessary at present for me to discuss those matters of administration about which there is no special anxiety or excitement.

Apprehension seems to exist among the people of the Southern States, that by the accession of a Republican Administration, their property, and their peace, and personal security, are to be endangered. There has never been any reasonable cause for such apprehension. Indeed, the most ample evidence to the contrary has all the while existed, and been open to their inspection. It is found in nearly all the published speeches of him who now addresses you. I do but quote from one of those speeches when I declare that "I have no purpose, directly or indirectly, to interfere with the institution of slavery in the States where it exists. I believe I have no lawful right to do so, and I have no inclination to do so." Those who nominated and elected me did so with full knowledge that I had made this, and many similar declarations, and had never recanted them. And more than this, they placed in the platform, for my acceptance, and as a law to themselves, and to me, the clear and emphatic resolution which I now read:

"Resolved, That the maintenance inviolate of the rights of the States, and especially the right of each State to order and control its own domestic institutions according to its own judgment exclusively, is essential to that balance of power on which the perfection and endurance of our political fabric depend; and we denounce the lawless invasion by armed force of the soil of any State or Territory, no matter under what pretext, as among the gravest of crimes."

I now reiterate these sentiments: and in doing so, I only press upon the public attention. the most conclusive evidence of which the case is susceptible, that the property, peace and security of no section are to be in any wise endangered by the now incoming Administration. I add too, that all the protection which, consistently with the Constitution and the laws, can be given, will be cheerfully given to all the States when lawfully demanded, for whatever cause—as cheerfully to one section as to another.

There is much controversy about the delivering up of fugitives from service or labor. The clause I now read is as plainly written in the Constitution as any other of its provisions:

"No person held to service or labor in one State, under the laws thereof, escaping into another, shall, in consequence of any law or regulation therein, be discharged from such service or labor, but shall be delivered up on claim of the party to whom such service or labor may be due."

It is scarcely questioned that this provision was intended by those who made it, for the reclaiming of what we call fugitive slaves; and the intention of the law-giver is the law. All members of Congress swear their support to the whole Constitution—to this provision as much as to any other. To the proposition, then, that slaves whose cases come within the terms of this clause, "shall be delivered up," their oaths are unanimous. Now, if they would make the effort in good temper, could they not, with nearly equal unanimity, frame and pass a law, by means of which to keep good that unanimous oath?

There is some difference of opinion whether this clause should be enforced by national or by state authority; but surely that difference is not a very material one. If the slave is to be surrendered, it can be of but little consequence to him, or to others, by which authority it is done. And should any one, in any case, be content that his oath shall go unkept, on a merely unsubstantial controversy as to how it shall be kept?

Again, in any law upon this subject, ought not all the safeguards of liberty known in civilized and humane jurisprudence to be introduced, so that a free man be not, in any case, surrendered as a slave? And might it not be well, at the same time to provide by law for the enforcements of that clause in the Constitution which guarantees that "the citizens of each State shall be entitled to all privileges and immunities of citizens in the several States"?

I take the official oath to-day, with no mental reservations, and with no purpose to construe the Constitution or laws, by any hypercritical rules. And while I do not choose now to specify particular acts of Congress as proper to be enforced, I do suggest that it will be much safer for all, both in official and private stations, to conform to, and abide by, all those acts which stand unrepealed, than to violate any of them, trusting to find impunity in having them held to be unconstitutional.

It is seventy-two years since the first inauguration of a President under our national Constitution. During that period fifteen different and greatly distinguished citizens, have, in succession, administered the executive branch of the government. They have conducted it through many perils; and, generally, with great success. Yet, with all this scope for [of] precedent, I now enter upon the same task for the brief constitutional term of four years, under great and peculiar difficulty. A disruption of the Federal Union, heretofore only menaced, is now formidably attempted.

I hold, that in contemplation of universal law, and of the Constitution, the Union of these States is perpetual. Perpetuity is implied, if not expressed, in the fundamental law of all national governments. It is safe to assert that no government proper, ever had a provision in its organic law for its own termination. Continue to execute all the express provisions of our national Constitution, and the Union will endure forever—it being impossible to destroy it, except by some action not provided for in the instrument itself.

Again, if the United States be not a government proper, but an association of States in the nature of contract merely, can it, as a contract, be peaceably unmade, by less than all the parties who made it? One party to a contract may violate it—break it, so to speak; but does it not require all to lawfully rescind it?

Descending from these general principles, we find the proposition that, in legal contemplation, the Union is perpetual, confirmed by the history of the Union itself. The Union is much older than the Constitution. It was formed in fact, by the Articles of Association in 1774. It was matured and continued by the Declaration of Independence in 1776. It was further matured and the faith of all the then thirteen States expressly plighted and engaged that it should be perpetual, by the Articles of Confederation in 1778. And finally, in 1787, one of the declared objects for ordaining and establishing the Constitution, was "to form a more perfect Union."

But if [the] destruction of the Union, by one, or by a part only, of the States, be lawfully possible, the Union is less perfect than before the Constitution, having lost the vital element of perpetuity.

It follows from these views that no State, upon its own mere motion, can lawfully get out of the Union,—that resolves and ordinances to that effect are legally void, and that acts of violence, within any State or States, against the authority of the United States, are insurrectionary or revolutionary, according to the circumstances.

I therefore consider that in view of the Constitution and the laws, the Union is unbroken; and to the extent of my ability I shall take care, as the Constitution itself expressly enjoins upon me, that the laws of the Union be faithfully executed in all the States. Doing this I deem to be only a simple duty on my part; and I shall perform it, so far as practicable, unless my rightful masters, the American people, shall withhold the requisite means, or, in some authoritative manner, direct the contrary. I trust this will not be regarded as a menace, but only as the declared purpose of the Union that it will constitutionally defend and maintain itself.

In doing this there needs to be no bloodshed or violence; and there shall be none, unless it be forced upon the national authority. The power confided to me will be used to hold, occupy, and possess the property and places belonging to the government, and to collect the duties and imposts; but beyond what may be necessary for these objects, there will be no invasion—no using of force against or among the people anywhere. Where hostility to the United States, in any interior locality, shall be so great and so universal, as to prevent competent resident citizens from holding the Federal offices, there will be no attempt to force obnoxious strangers among the people for that object. While the strict legal right may exist in the government to enforce the exercise of these offices, the attempt to do so would be so irritating, *and so nearly impracticable with all, that I deem it better to forego, for the time, the uses of such offices.*

The mails, unless repelled, will continue to be furnished in all parts of the Union. So far as possible, the people everywhere shall have that sense of perfect security which is most favorable to calm thought and reflection. The course here indicated will be followed, unless current events and experience shall show a modification or change to be proper; and in every case and exigency my best discretion will be exercised according to circumstances actually existing, and with a view and a hope of a peaceful solution of the national troubles, and the restoration of fraternal sympathies and affections.

That there are persons in one section or another who seek to destroy the Union at all events, and are glad of any pretext to do it, I will neither affirm nor deny; but if there be such, I need address no word to them. To those, however, who really love the Union, may I not speak?

Before entering upon so grave a matter as the destruction of our national fabric, with all its benefits, its memories and its hopes, would it not be wise to ascertain precisely why we do it? Will you hazard so desperate a step, while there is any possibility that any portion of the ills you fly from have no real existence? Will you, while the certain ills you fly to, are greater than all the real ones you fly from? Will you risk the commission of so fearful a mistake?

All profess to be content in the Union, if all constitutional rights can be maintained. Is it true, then, that any right, plainly written in the Constitution, has been denied? I think not. Happily the human mind is so constituted, that no party can reach to the audacity of doing this. Think, if you can, of a single instance in which a plainly written provision of the Constitution has ever been denied. If, by the mere force of numbers, a majority should deprive a minority of any clearly written constitutional right, it might, in a moral point of view, justify revolution—certainly would, if such a right were a vital one. But such is not our case. All the vital rights of minorities, and of individuals, are so plainly assured to them, by affirmations and negations, guarantees and prohibitions, in the Constitution, that controversies never arise concerning them. But no organic law can ever be framed with a provision specifically applicable to every question which may occur in practical administration. No foresight can anticipate, nor any document of reasonable length contain express provisions for, all possible questions. Shall fugitives from labor be surrendered by national or by State authority? The Constitution does not expressly say. May Congress prohibit slavery in the territories? The Constitution does not expressly say. Must Congress protect slavery in the territories? The Constitution does not expressly say.

From questions of this class spring all our constitutional controversies, and we divide upon them into majorities and minorities. If the minority will not acquiesce, the majority must, or the government must cease. There is no other alternative; for continuing the government, is acquiescence on one side or the other. If a minority, in such case, will secede rather than acquiesce, they make a precedent which, in turn, will divide and ruin them; for a minority of their own will secede from them whenever a majority refuses to be controlled by such minority. For instance, why may not any portion of a new confederacy, a year or two hence, arbitrarily secede again, precisely as portions of the present Union now claim to secede from it? All who cherish disunion senti- ments, are now being educated to the exact temper of doing this.

Is there such perfect identity of interests among the States to com- pose a new Union, as to produce harmony only, and prevent renewed secession?

Plainly, the central idea of secession, is the essence of anarchy. A majority, held in restraint by constitutional checks and limitations, and always changing easily with deliberate changes of popular opinions and sentiments is the only true sovereign of a free people. Whoever rejects it, does, of necessity, fly to anarchy or to despotism. Unanimity is im- possible; the rule of a minority, as a permanent arrangement, is wholly inadmissible; so that, rejecting the majority principle, anarchy or despo- tism in some form is all that is left.

I do not forget the position assumed by some, that constitutional questions are to be decided by the Supreme Court; nor do I deny that such decisions must be binding in any case, upon the parties to a suit, as to the object of that suit, while they are also entitled to very high respect and consideration in all parallel cases by all other departments of the government. And while it is obviously possible that such decision may be erroneous in any given case, still the evil effect following it, be- ing limited to that particular case, with the chance that it may be over- ruled, and never become a precedent for other cases, can better be borne than could the evils of a different practice. At the same time, the candid citizen must confess that if the policy of the government upon vital questions, affecting the whole people, is to be irrevocably fixed by decisions of the Supreme Court, the instant they are made, in ordinary litigation between parties, in personal actions, the people will have ceased to be their own rulers, having to that extent practically resigned their government into the hands of that eminent tribunal. Nor is there in this view any assault upon the court or the judges. It is a duty from which they may not shrink, to decide cases properly brought before them; and it is no fault of theirs if others seek to turn their decisions to political purposes.

One section of our country believes slavery is right, and ought to be extended, while the other believes it is wrong, and ought not to be ex- tended. This is the only substantial dispute. The fugitive slave clause of the Constitution, and the law for the suppression of the foreign slave trade, are each as well enforced, perhaps, as any law can ever be in a community where the moral sense of the people imperfectly supports the law itself. The great body of the people abide by the dry legal obligation in both cases, and a few break over in each. This, I think, cannot be perfectly cured; and it would be worse in both cases after the separation of the sections, than before. The foreign slave trade, now imperfectly suppressed, would be ultimately revived without restriction, in one section; while fugitive slaves, now only partially surrendered, would not be surrendered at all, by the other.

Physically speaking, we cannot separate. We cannot remove our respective sections from each other, nor build an impassable wall between them. A husband and wife may be divorced, and go out of the presence, and beyond the reach of each other; but the different parts of our country cannot do this. They cannot but remain face to face; and intercourse, either amicable or hostile, must continue between them. Is it possible, then, to make that intercourse more advantageous or more satisfactory, after separation than before? Can aliens make treaties easier than friends can make laws? Can treaties be more faithfully enforced between aliens than laws can among friends? Suppose you go to war, you cannot fight always; and when, after much loss on both sides, and no gain on either, you cease fighting, the identical old questions, as to terms of intercourse, are again upon you.

This country, with its institutions, belongs to the people who inhabit it. Whenever they shall grow weary of the existing government, they can exercise their constitutional right of amending it, or their revolutionary right to dismember or overthrow it. I cannot be ignorant of the fact that many worthy and patriotic citizens are desirous of having the national Constitution amended. While I make no recommendation of amendments, I fully recognize the rightful authority of the people over the whole subject to be exercised in either of the modes prescribed in the instrument itself; and I should under existing circumstances favor rather than oppose a fair opportunity being afforded the people to act upon it.

I will venture to add that to me the Convention mode seems preferable, in that it allows amendments to originate with the people themselves, instead of only permitting them to take or reject propositions, originated by others, not especially chosen for the purpose, and which might not be precisely such as they would wish to either accept or refuse. I understand a proposed amendment to the Constitution, which amendment, however, I have not seen, has passed Congress, to the effect that the federal government shall never interfere with the domestic institutions of the States, including that of persons held to service. To avoid misconstruction of what I have said, I depart from my purpose not to speak of particular amendments, so far as to say that holding such a provision to now be implied constitutional law, I have no objection to its being made express and irrevocable.

The Chief Magistrate derives all his authority from the people, and they have conferred none upon him to fix terms for the separation of the States. The people themselves can do this also if they choose; but the executive, as such, has nothing to do with it. His duty is to administer the present government, as it came to his hands, and to transmit it, unimpaired by him, to his successor.

Why should there not be a patient confidence in the ultimate justice of the people? Is there any better or equal hope, in the world? In our present differences, is either party without faith of being in the right? If the Almighty Ruler of nations, with his eternal truth and justice, be on your side of the North or on yours of the South, that truth, and that justice, will surely prevail, by the judgment of this great tribunal, the American people.

By the frame of the government under which we live, this same people have wisely given their public servants but little power for mischief; and have, with equal wisdom, provided for the return of that little to their own hands at very short intervals.

While the people retain their virtue and vigilance, no administration, by any extreme of wickedness or folly, can very seriously injure the government in the short space of four years.

My countrymen, one and all, think calmly and well, upon this whole subject. Nothing valuable can be lost by taking time. If there be an object to hurry any of you, in hot haste, to a step which you would never take deliberately, that object will be frustrated by taking time; but no good object can be frustrated by it. Such of you as are now dissatisfied, still have the old Constitution unimpaired, and, on the sensitive point, the laws of your own framing under it; while the new administration will have no immediate power, if it would, to change either. If it were admitted that you who are dissatisfied, hold the right side in the dispute, there still is no single good reason for precipitate action. Intelligence, patriotism, Christianity, and a firm reliance on Him, who has never yet forsaken this favored land, are still competent to adjust, in the best way, all our present difficulty.

In your hands, my dissatisfied fellow countrymen, and not in mine, is the momentous issue of civil war. The government will not assail you. You can have no conflict, without being yourselves the aggressors. You have no oath registered in Heaven to destroy the government, while I shall have the most solemn one to "preserve, protect and defend" it.

I am loth to close. We are not enemies, but friends. We must not be enemies. Though passion may have strained, it must not break our bonds of affection. The mystic chords of memory, stretching from every battle-field, and patriot grave, to every living heart and hearth-stone, all over this broad land, will yet swell the chorus of the Union, when again touched, as surely they will be, by the better angels of our nature.

With "more of Euclid than of Demosthenes"[76] in him, his delivery was not that of the spellbinder, agitator, or demagogue. His voice was a tenor that "carried song-tunes poorly but had clear and appealing modulations."[77] Habitually a little "scared"[78] when he spoke, he was "pale and very nervous"[79] on this occasion, but his "cheerfulness was marked."[80] "Compelled by nature, to speak slowly,"[81] his manner was "deliberate and impressive"[82] and his voice "remarkably clear and penetrating."[83] There was little evidence in his voice of the fear that might have come as the result of knowing that there were "heavy bets" about his safety.[84] Some of the spectators noted a "loud, and distinct voice, quite intelligible by at least ten thousand persons below him";[85] others found it a "clear, ringing voice, that was easily heard by those on the outer limits of the crowd";[86] still others noted his "firm tones of voice," his "great deliberation and precision of emphasis."[87] Sandburg might have remarked that it gave out "echoes and values."[88]

As Lincoln read on, the audience listened respectfully, with "intense interest, amid a stillness almost oppressive."[89] In the crowd behind the speaker sat Horace Greeley, momentarily expecting the crack of rifle fire.[90] At one point he thought it had come. The speaker stopped. But it was only a spectator crashing down through a tree.[91] Otherwise, the

---

[76] Randall, op. cit., I, 49.

[77] Sandburg, The Prairie Years, I, 305.

[78] [W. H. Herndon and J. W. Weik], Herndon's Life of Lincoln, with an intro-duction and notes by Paul M. Angle (Cleveland: The World Publishing Co., 1949), p. 220.

[79] The Diary of a Public Man, p. 74.

[80] Correspondence of the Cincinnati Commercial, as quoted in Chicago Daily Tribune, March 8, 1861, p. 2, col. 4.

[81] Herndon and Weik, op. cit., p. 273.

[82] New York Tribune, March 5, 1861, p. 5, col. 4.

[83] Ibid.

[84] New York Times, March 4, 1861, p. 1, col. 2.

[85] National Intelligencer, March 5, 1861, p. 3, col. 3.

[86] New York Times, March 5, 1861, p. 1, col. 3.

[87] Correspondence of the Cincinnati Commercial, quoted in Chicago Daily Tribune, March 8, 1861, p. 2, col. 4.

[88] Sandburg, The Prairie Years, I, 306.

[89] Frederick W. Seward, Seward at Washington, as Senator and Secretary of State (New York: Derby and Miller, 1891), I, 516.

[90] Greeley, op. cit., p. 404.

[91] Diary of a Public Man, p. 74.

crowd in the grounds "behaved very well."[92] Buchanan sat listening, and "looking as straight as he could at the toe of his right boot."[93] Douglas, close by on Lincoln's right, listened "attentively," showing that he was "apparently satisfied" as he "exclaimed, *sotto voce*, 'Good,' 'That's so,' 'No coercion,' and 'Good again.'"[94]Chief Justice Taney "did not remove his eyes from Mr. Lincoln during the entire delivery."[95] Mr. Cameron stood with his back to the President, on the opposite side to Mr. Douglas, "peering off into the crowd."[96] Senator Seward and the other Cabinet officers-elect "kept themselves in the background."[97] Senator Wigfall of Texas, with folded arms "leaned conspicuously in a Capitol doorway," listening to the Inaugural, plainly wearing "contempt, defiance, derision, on his face, his pantomimic posture saying what he had said in the Senate, that the old Union was a corpse and the question was how to embalm it and conduct the funeral decently."[98] Thurlow Weed moved away from the crowd, reporting to General Scott at the top of the slope "The Inaugural is a success," as the old general exclaimed, "God be praised! God in his goodness be praised."[99] To a newspaper reporter surveying the scene, there was a "propriety and becoming interest which pervaded the vast assembly" and "impressed every spectator who had the opportunity of overlooking it."[100] The crowd "applauded repeatedly" and "at times, rapturously,"[101] particularly at points where he "announced his inflexible purpose to execute the laws and discharge his whole constitutional duty."[102] When Lincoln declared, "I hold that in the contemplation of international law, and of the Constitution, the Union of these States is perpetual," the "cheers were hearty and prolonged."[103] When he said, "I shall take care that the laws of the Union be faithfully executed in all the States," he was met with a "tremendous shout of approval."[104] But the "greatest impression of all was produced by the final appeal,"[105] noted one of the

[92] Ibid.

[93] New York Times, *March 5, 1861, p. 1, col. 3.*

[94] Ibid.

[95] Ibid.

[96] *Correspondence of the* Cincinnati Commercial, *as quoted in* Chicago Daily Tribune, *March 8, 1861, p. 2, col. 4.*

[97] Ibid.

[98] *Sandburg,* The War Years, *I, 123.*

[99] *Seward, op. cit., pp. 516, 517.*

[100] New York Daily Tribune, *March 5, 1861, p. 5, col. 4.*

[101] Chicago Daily Tribune, *March 8, 1861, p. 2, col. 4, quoted from Cincinnati Commercial.*

[102] New York Daily Tribune, *March 5, 1861, p. 5, col. 4.*

[103] Chicago Daily Tribune, *March 8, 1861, p. 2, col. 4, quoted from Cincinnati Commercial.*

[104] Chicago Daily Tribune, *March 8, 1861, p. 2, col. 4, quoted from Cincinnati Commercial.*

[105] Ibid.

reporters. "With great solemnity of emphasis, using his gestures to add significance to his words," Lincoln remarked "You have no oath registered in Heaven to destroy this Government, while I shall have the most solemn one to preserve, protect and defend it," and the crowd responded with "round after round of cheering."[106] Finally, after Lincoln had addressed his "words of affection" to the audience, ending his address, "men waved their hats, and broke forth in the heartiest manifestations of delight. The extraordinary clearness [sic], straight-forwardness and lofty spirit of patriotism which pervaded the whole address, impressed every listener, while the evident earnestness, sincerity and manliness of Mr. Lincoln extorted the praise even of his enemies."[107] "The effect of the Inaugural on the country at large remains to be awaited and to be gathered from many sources," observed a reporter, "but it is conceded on all hands that its effect, already noticeable on the vast gathering here, upon the city, and the tone of feeling here is eminently happy, and the source of great gratulation on every side."[108]

Chief Justice Taney stepped forward, shrunken, old, his hands trembling with emotion, and held out an open Bible. Lincoln laid his left hand upon it, raised his right hand, and repeated with a "firm but modest voice"[109] the oath: "I do solemnly swear that I will faithfully execute the office of President of the United States, and will, to the best of my ability, preserve, protect, and defend the Constitution of the United States." Lincoln was now President. Below, the crowd "tossed their hats, wiped their eyes, cheered at the tops of their voices, hurrahed themselves hoarse," and "had the crowd not been so very dense, they would have demonstrated in more lively ways, their joy, satisfaction and delight."[110] Over on the slope the artillery boomed a salute to the sixteenth President of the United States.[111] The crowd ebbed away, and Lincoln rode down Pennsylvania Avenue with Buchanan, bidding him good-bye at the Presidential mansion.[112]

The address had taken thirty-five minutes in delivery, and now it was all over, at least until the nation in general turned in its response. Lincoln had spent six weeks in preparing it—six weeks and many years of lonely thought, along with his active experience on the circuit and the stump. Like the "House Divided Speech" and the "Cooper Union Address" it was deliberately and cautiously prepared, undergoing revision up to the moment of delivery. "Late in January," he told his law

[106] Ibid.
[107] Chicago Daily Tribune, *March 8, 1861, p. 2, col. 4, quoted from* Cincinnati Commercial.
[108] Chicago Daily Tribune, *March 9, 1861, p. 3, col. 2.*
[109] New York Times, *March 5, 1861, p. 1, col. 3.*
[110] Ibid.
[111] *Sandburg,* The War Years, *I, 122.*
[112] *Baringer,* op. cit., *p. 334.*

partner, Herndon, that he was "ready to begin"[113] the preparation of the Inaugural. In a room over a store, across the street from the State House, cut off from all intrusion and outside communication, he began the preparation. He had told Herndon what works he wanted to consult and asked to be furnished "Henry Clay's great speech delivered in 1850; Andrew Jackson's proclamation against Nullification; and a copy of the Constitution." He "afterwards" called for a copy of Webster's reply to Hayne, a speech which he regarded as "the grandest specimen of American oratory."[114] "With these few 'volumes,' and no further sources of reference,"[115] he began his work on the address.

On February 2, 1861, he wrote a friend, George D. Prentice,[116] editor of the *Louisville Journal,* "I have the document blocked out; but in the now rapidly shifting scenes I shall have to hold it subject to revision up to the time of delivery."[117] He had an original draft printed by one of the proprietors of the *Illinois State Journal* to whom he entrusted the manuscript.[118] "No one else seems to have been taken into the confidence of Mr. Lincoln as to its contents until after he started for Washington on February 11."[119] Upon reaching Indianapolis, he presented a copy to O. H. Browning who had accompanied him from Springfield. According to Browning, "before parting with Mr. Lincoln at Indianapolis, Tuesday, he gave me a copy of his inaugural address, and requested me to read it, and give him my opinion, which I did. I thought it able, well considered, and appropriate, and so informed him. It is, in my judgment, a very admirable document. He permitted me to retain a copy, under promise not to show it except to Mrs. Browning."[120]

Upon arriving in Washington, Lincoln submitted a copy to Secretary Seward with the same invitation to criticize it.[121] According to Louis A. Warren, "As far as we know these two men are the only ones who made any suggestions about certain revisions in the original copy,"[122] even though a few others may have seen it.[123]

Reporters showed an avid interest in the preparation of the Inaugural,

[113] *Herndon and Weik,* op. cit., *p. 386.*
[114] Ibid.
[115] Ibid.
[116] Lincoln Lore, *No. 308 (March 4, 1935).*
[117] *Louis A. Warren, "Original Draft of the First Inaugural,"* Lincoln Lore, *No. 358 (February 17, 1936).*
[118] Ibid.
[119] Ibid.
[120] The Diary of Orville Hickman Browning, *edited with an introduction and notes by Theodore Calvin Pease and James G. Randall (Springfield, Ill.: Illinois State Historical Library, 1925), I, 1850–1864, 455, 456.*
[121] *Seward,* op. cit., *p. 512.*
[122] Lincoln Lore, *No. 358.*
[123] *John G. Nicolay and John Hay,* Abraham Lincoln, A History *(New York: The Century Co., 1914), III, 319. Nicolay and Hay observe that "Judge David Davis read it while in Springfield," and "Francis P. Blair, Sr., read it in Washington, and highly commended it, suggesting no changes."*

sometimes reporting inaccurately on the various stages of its preparation. Recording the activities of the President on Saturday night,
March 2, one reporter erroneously observed: "Mr. Lincoln sent for
Senator Seward, and at 11½ o'clock that gentleman reached the
hotel. Mr. Lincoln read to him the Inaugural for the first time, and then
asked his advice. Senator Seward took it up section after section and
concurred heartily in a great part of it. He suggested a few modifications, an occasional emendation and a few additional paragraphs, all
of which were adopted by Mr. Lincoln, and the Inaugural was declared
complete and perfect by Senator Seward, who then retired."[124] On
Sunday, the reporter remarked, "Mr. Lincoln stated this evening that
the Inaugural could not be printed, as some points might require modifying or extending, according to the action of the Senate to-night. His
son is now writing copies of what is finished, one of which will be
given to the Associated Press when he commences reading it."[125] On
the same day there were "reports of efforts in high quarters to induce
the president to tone down his inaugural, but it is not affirmed that they
were successful."[126]

A final report on the preparation of the Inaugural records the activities on the morning of March 4th: "Mr. Lincoln rose at 5 o'clock. After
an early breakfast, the Inaugural was read aloud to him by his son
Robert, and the completing touches were added, including the beautiful and impassioned closing paragraph."[127]

As J. G. Randall has observed, "if one would justly appraise Lincoln's
first presidential state paper, this inaugural of 1861 deserves to be read
as delivered and to be set over against the alternative statements that
Lincoln avoided or struck out in revision. Statements pledging maintenance of Federal authority were toned down and shorn of truculence,
while promises of conciliation were emotionally underlined."[128] Mr.
Browning advised "but one change," supposed by some authorities to
be "the most important one in the entire document."[129] "Mr. Seward
made thirty-three suggestions for improving the document and nine-
teen of them were adopted, eight were used after Mr. Lincoln had modified them, and six were discarded in toto."[130] Finally, Lincoln, "without
suggestion from any one made sixteen changes in the original draft."[131]

And so, however much the country might criticize as it scanned the

[124] New York Times, March 4, 1861, p. 1, col. 1.
[125] New York Times, March 4, 1861, p. 1, col. 2.
[126] New York Daily Tribune, March 4, 1861, p. 5, col. 1.
[127] New York Times, March 5, 1861, p. 1, col. 1.
[128] Randall, op. cit., I, 309.
[129] Warren, loc. cit.
[130] Ibid.
[131] Ibid.

Inaugural, Lincoln could respond, as he did to the Douglas taunt in 1858, that the "House Divided Speech" had been "evidently well prepared and carefully written."[132] "I admit that it was. I am not master of language; I have not a fine education; . . . I know what I meant, and I will not leave this crowd in doubt. . . ."[133]

Lincoln did not have to wait long for a response from the country at large. As he delivered the address, little audiences unseen by the speaker dotted the land, clustering around newspaper offices and waiting for telegraphic reports of what was in the Inaugural. Between Washington and New York, the American Telegraph Company had placed at the disposal of the Associated Press three wires for the communication of the address.[134] Similar arrangements had been made with other key cities. The delivery of the Inaugural commenced at 1:30 P.M., Washington time, and the "telegraphers promptly to the minute" began its transmission. "The first words of the Message were received by the agents of the Press at 1:45, and the last about 3:30," observed the *New York Times*.[135] "Such rapidity in telegraphic communication has never before been reached in this country."[136] By four o'clock, "the entire document was furnished to the different newspapers,"[137] and special editions of the press were in the hands of readers within an hour. "People of all parties in this city, as elsewhere, were on tip-toe all day to know what was going on at Washington, and especially to hear what President Lincoln would say in his Inaugural," observed the *New York Times*.[138] "At length it was announced that the procession had reached the Capitol, and then, while the President was delivering his speech and the reporters were transmitting it by telegraph, there was a long period of unalloyed expectancy. Meantime, men given to talking, in the many crowds, discussed all sorts of topics, connected with the questions of the day, before little groups of gaping listeners. There was many a prophet among them, not without honor, before the Message was received, who knew exactly what it was going to contain, and foretold with marvelous preciseness the points which Mr. Lincoln would dwell on.

"It was nearly 5 o'clock when the eloquence of these worthies was

---

[132] *Speech of Senator Douglas, delivered in Chicago, July 9, 1858, in* The Political Debates between Abraham Lincoln and Stephen A. Douglas, *with an introduction by George Haven Putnam (New York: G. P. Putnam's Sons, 1913), p. 24.*

[133] *Speech in reply to Douglas at Chicago, Illinois, July 10, 1858, in* Abraham Lincoln, His Speeches and Writings, *edited by Roy P. Basler, p. 392.*

[134] New York Times, *March 5, 1861, p. 8, col. 5.*

[135] Ibid.

[136] Ibid.

[137] Ibid.

[138] New York Times, *March 5, 1861, p. 8, cols. 4, 5.*

suddenly quenched as by a wet blanket, and the wet sheets of the latest edition, with the President's Inaugural in black and white, leaped forth from the presses into the hands of all who could get copies. Then there was wild scrambling around the counters in publication offices, a laying down of pennies and a rape of newspapers, and the crowds began to disperse, each man hastening to some place remote from public haunt, where he might peruse the document in peace. The newsboys rushed through the city crying with stentorian lungs 'The President's Message!' 'Lincoln's Speech!' 'Ex-tray Times!' 'Get Lincoln's Inau-gu-ra-a-a-il!' And an hour later everybody had read the Message and everybody was talking about it."[139]

Out in Mattoon, Illinois, a similar scene was being enacted. A roving reporter, heading south from Chicago to observe the reactions of the crowds, made a "tour of the town" and stopped at hotel lobbies, where the speech, fresh from the press, was being "read and re-read, silently and aloud, to groups of ardent listeners . . . As the reading in a crowd progresses, when the reader comes to the place where Mr. Lincoln 'puts his foot down,' down goes likewise every foot in the circle."[140]

The home folks whom Lincoln had bade an affectionate farewell three weeks before were among the most anxious of the unseen audiences. Whereas they spoke only for themselves at the time of the tearful departure, they were now ready to speak for the nation. "The Inaugural Address of our noble Chief Magistrate has electrified the whole country," they said. "It has satisfied people of all parties who love the Union and desire its preservation. In this city it gives almost universal satisfaction."[141] In Quincy, the scene of one of the debates of 1858, the address was received with "much enthusiasm," and the Republican Gun Squad fired thirty-four guns;[142] in Peoria, "so great was the anxiety felt to see what Mr. Lincoln said, that people came forty miles to get copies of the message,"[143] reading it with "much enthusiasm."[144]

But occasionally there was a dissenting voice back home, particularly in the Democratic press, as there was generally throughout the North. While the *Chicago Daily Tribune* was "quite sure that no document can be found among American state papers embodying sounder wisdom and higher patriotism,—breathing kindlier feelings to all sections of the country,"[145] the Chicago *Times* denounced the Inaugural as "a loose, disjointed, rambling affair," concluding that the Union was

[139] Ibid.
[140] Chicago Daily Tribune, *March 8, 1861, p. 2, col. 3.*
[141] Illinois State Journal, *March 6, 1861, p. 2.*
[142] Chicago Daily Tribune, *March 6, 1861, p. 1, col. 3.*
[143] Ibid.
[144] Ibid.
[145] Chicago Daily Tribune, *March 5, 1861, p. 1, col. 1.*

now "lost beyond hope."[146] While the New York Times observed that "conservative people are in raptures over the Inaugural," and that "Its conciliatory tone, and frank, outspoken declaration of loyalty to the whole country, captured the hearts of many heretofore opposed to Mr. Lincoln,"[147] the New York Herald found that "the inaugural is not a crude performance—it abounds in traits of craft and cunning. It bears marks of indecision, and yet of strong coercion proclivities . . . It is neither candid nor statesmanlike; nor does it possess any essential dignity or patriotism. It would have caused a Washington to mourn, and would have inspired a Jefferson, Madison, or Jackson with contempt."[148] There were those in Maine who found it a "poor, weak, trashy affair, a standing disgrace to the country, and a fit commentary on the fanaticism and unreasonableness which made him President."[149] Some in Pennsylvania found it "one of the most awkwardly constructed official documents we have ever inspected," and "pitiably apological for the uprising of the Republican party, and his own election to the Presidency, by it."[150] And there were those in Ohio "who never expected to see a Black Republican peaceably inaugurated in this White Republican country . . . but now the Rubicon is passed," and the Inaugural, "like its distinguished author," is "flat-footed. It is more magazinish in sound than in style, smelling strongly of gunpowder, and is 'coercion' all over, as the South understands that word."[151]

"It is an interesting study" said a Douglas journal, the Peoria Daily Democratic Union, on March 7th, "to look over the various journals that have come to our table since the delivery of President Lincoln's Inaugural Address, and notice the different manner in which they speak of it." "All of these criticisms of the Address cannot be correct, for they clash materially; and that fact demonstrates very plainly that some of them were either the offspring of prejudice, or were written by men incapable of judging of the merits of this first state paper of President Lincoln."[152]

Whereas there was difference of opinion in the North, much of it stopped short of vehement denunciation. However, the South saw little hope from Lincoln, and expressed itself accordingly. "Mr. Lincoln's

[146] Quoted in Randall, op. cit., p. 306.

[147] New York Times, March 5, 1861, p. 1, col. 4.

[148] Quoted in the New York Daily Tribune, March 7, 1861, p. 6, col. 6.

[149] The Bangor Union, as quoted in New York Daily Tribune, March 8, 1861, p. 6, col. 5.

[150] The Philadelphia Evening Journal, as quoted in New York Daily Tribune, March 7, 1861, p. 7, col. 3.

[151] Cleveland Plaindealer, as quoted in Chicago Daily Tribune, March 9, 1861, p. 1, col. 3.

[152] Quoted in Northern Editorials on Secession, edited by Howard Cecil Perkins (New York: D. Appleton-Century Co., 1942), II, 643.

Inaugural Address is before our readers," observed the *Richmond Enquirer,* "couched in the cool, unimpassioned, deliberate language of the fanatic, with the purpose of pursuing the promptings of fanaticism even to the dismemberment of the Government with the horrors of civil war . . . Civil war must now come. Sectional war, declared by Mr. Lincoln, awaits only the signal gun from the insulted Southern Confederacy, to light its horrid fires all along the borders of Virginia."[153] The *Richmond Dispatch* was equally strong: "The Inaugural Address of Abraham Lincoln inaugurates civil war, as we have predicted it would from the beginning . . . The sword is drawn and the scabbard thrown away . . . ere long Virginia may be engaged in a life and death struggle. . . ."[154] The *Baltimore Sun* observed, "The Inaugural, as a whole, breathes the spirit of mischief," and found "no Union spirit in the address."[155] "We presume nobody is astonished to hear that Secessionists regard the Inaugural as a 'declaration of war,'" noted one observer. "Before the Inaugural has been read in a single Southern State, it is denounced, through the telegraph, from every Southern point, as a declaration of war."[156] "I have heard but one construction of Mr. Lincoln's declaration of his intention to 'hold, occupy, and possess the property and places belonging to the Government, and to collect the duties and imposts,'" observed a special correspondent in Richmond. The Inaugural "is received with much disfavor," and "is regarded, if not as a declaration of war, as at least the expression of a determination to coerce the seceding States into compliance with the demands of the Federal Government."[157] Reporting from Charleston, South Carolina, another correspondent observed, "The part which, of course, attracted most attention and was read and re-read with deep interest, was that wherein Mr. Lincoln declares that to the best of his ability, he will take care, according to his oath and the Constitution, that 'the laws of the Union are faithfully executed in all the States,' and that he will use the power confided to him to 'hold, occupy and possess the property and places belonging to the Government, and to collect the duties and imposts.'" The verdict was, according to this correspondent, "that rebellion would not be treated tenderly by Mr. Lincoln, and that he was quite another sort of man from James Buchanan."[158]

At least a minority of the people of the South responded less vehemently. Occasionally a roving reporter, mingling among the crowds in

---

153 *Quoted in* New York Daily Tribune, *March 7, 1861, p. 7, col. 2. See also,* Southern Editorials on Secession, *pp. 474, 475.*
154 Southern Editorials on Secession, *p. 475.*
155 *Quoted in* New York Daily Tribune, *March 7, 1861, p. 7, col. 1.*
156 New York Times, *March 7, 1861, p. 4, col. 2.*
157 New York Daily Tribune, *March 9, 1861, p. 6, col. 2.*
158 New York Daily Tribune, *March 9, 1861, p. 6, col. 1.*

Southern cities, reported less fury. From Montgomery came word that Alexander Stevens had found the Inaugural "the most *adroit* State paper ever published on the Continent," and "a great moral impression has been produced"[159] in both Charleston and Montgomery. In Savannah, Georgia, "Not a word have we yet heard uttered against its tone," observed a reporter, predicting "a powerful and sweeping effect at the South."[160] Now and then a reporter noticed "a pretty general disappointment that the document contained so little 'blood and thunder.' "[161] "That the document should be calm and dignified in tone and style, logical in its conclusions, and plain and kind in its treatment of the great topic of the day, was annoying to the Rebels, who hoped to find in the address a provocation for extreme action."[162]

While the country at large read the speech and responded both favorably and unfavorably, Senator Clingman of North Carolina and Stephen A. Douglas engaged in debate over its meaning in the United States Senate. "If I understand it aright, all that is direct in it, I mean, at least, that purpose which seems to stand out clearly and directly, is one which I think must lead to war—war against the confederate or seceding State"[163] remarked Clingman. Douglas, on the other hand, who had "read it carefully" could not "assent to the construction" of the senator from North Carolina, believing he could "demonstrate that there is no foundation for the apprehension which has been spread throughout the country, that this message is equivalent to a declaration of war."[164]

Just as the country searched the Inaugural for the sentiments it contained, it also examined and appraised the language and style in which it was couched. The Toronto *Leader* could not admire the "tawdry and corrupt schoolboy style," even as it gave "credit" for its "good sense."[165] An Albany, New York, observer found it "useless to criticize the style of the President's Inaugural when the policy it declares is fraught with consequences so momentous." Nevertheless, he paused to describe it as a "rambling, discursive, questioning, loose-jointed stump speech." It consisted of "feeble rhetorical stuff."[166] While papers unfriendly to Lincoln were finding it "inferior in point of elegance, perspicuity, vigor, talent, and all the graces of composition to any other

[159] New York Daily Tribune, *March 12, 1861, p. 6, col. 1.*
[160] New York Daily Tribune, *March 11, 1861, p. 6, col. 2.*
[161] New York Daily Tribune, *March 9, 1861, p. 6, col. 1.*
[162] Ibid.
[163] Congressional Globe, *Second Session, 36th Congress, Vol. 30, Part II, p. 1436.*
[164] Ibid.
[165] *Quoted in* New York Daily Tribune, *March 7, 1861, p. 7, col. 3.*
[166] Albany Atlas and Argus, *as quoted in* Northern Editorials on Secession, *II, 628.*

paper of a like character which has ever emanated from a President of the Republic,"[167] papers that were friendly found the contrary to be the case. "It is clear as a mountain brook," commented a Detroit reporter. "The depth and flow of it are apparent at a glance."[168] In Boston, the *Transcript* reporter commented at length. "The style of the Address is as characteristic as its temper. 'Right words in their right places'; this is the requirement of good rhetoric. Right words at the right times, should be the test by which we try the speech of statesmen; and this test Mr. Lincoln's address will bear. It has not one flaming expression in the whole course of its firm and explicit statements. The language is level to the popular mind,—the plain homespun language of a man accustomed to talk with 'the folks' and 'the neighbors,' the language of a man of vital common sense, whose words exactly fit his facts and thoughts."[169] Occasionally, the concluding paragraph was singled out for praise. In Indianapolis, the reporter of the *Daily Journal* remarked: "The closing sentence, the only attempt at rhetorical display in the whole address, is singularly and almost poetically beautiful."[170]

Part II

Given the circumstances that brought forth the Inaugural Address, and removed in time from the passions which agitated the country, what may one say of Lincoln's address on March 4, 1861? The historian has often examined it for its effects, and has concluded that "Though not fully appreciated then, this was one of the great American inaugurals."[171] And the literary critic has sometimes observed its final passage, finding in it poetic beauty and enduring worth. Unlike the historian, we are not concerned merely with the Inaugural as a force in the shaping of American culture; nor are we concerned with its enduring worth as literature. The Inaugural was a speech, "meant to be heard and intended to exert an influence of some kind on those who heard it,"[172] or those who read it. We must, therefore, be concerned with evaluating the Inaugural as a speech, a medium distinct from other media, and with methods peculiarly its own. We must be concerned with discovering in this particular case "the available means of persuasion" and with evaluating their worth.

[167] Jersey City American Standard, *as quoted in* Northern Editorials on Secession, *II, 625.*

[168] Detroit Daily Tribune, *as quoted in* Northern Editorials on Secession, *II, 623.*

[169] *Quoted in* New York Daily Tribune, *March 7, 1861, p. 7, col. 1.*

[170] *Quoted in* Northern Editorials on Secession, *II, 619.*

[171] *J. G. Randall, "Lincoln's Great Declarations of Faith,"* New York Times Magazine, *February 6, 1949, p. 23.*

[172] *Wayland M. Parrish and Marie Hochmuth Nichols,* American Speeches, *New York, David McKay, 1954, p. 3.*

Let us view the Inaugural as a communication, with a purpose, and a content presumably designed to aid in the accomplishment of that purpose, further supported by skillful composition in words, and ultimately unified by the character and manner of the person who presented it.

We must not casually assume that Lincoln's purpose is easily discernible in the occasion itself. It is true, of course, that this was an inaugural ceremony, with a ritual fairly well established by fifteen predecessors, "Yet, with all this scope for [of] precedent," Lincoln was keenly aware that he entered upon the same task "under great and peculiar difficulty. A disruption of the Federal Union, heretofore only menaced, is now formidably attempted." If we are to discern the purpose that Lincoln had when he addressed the American people on March 4, 1861, we must recall the experiences of the nation between his election as President and the day of his inauguration. During that time, he had been made keenly aware of Southern resentment to a "sectional" President. The rapid movement of the Secessionists followed closely on the announcement of his election, and of the ascendancy of the Republican party to a position of power. The South viewed the Republican platform as an instrument for its "subjugation" and the "complete ruin of her social, political and industrial institutions."[173] By its acts of secession, and its establishment of a provisional government of its own, the lower South raised the very practical question: What is the authority of the federal government in regard to maintaining itself and in regard to reclaiming those federal properties possessed by retiring members?

Lincoln had also been made keenly aware of the doubts and skepticism that prevailed regarding his ability to lead his party and the nation. "I cannot but know what you all know," he had observed on his way to Washington, "that without a name, perhaps without a reason why I should have a name, there has fallen upon me a task such as did not rest even upon the Father of this Country . . ."[174] In addition, he was keenly aware of both Northern and Southern distrust of his moral character and integrity. Even to members of his party, he was a "funny man," given to stories in bad taste, and an Illinois wag. And to the South, he was at best thought to be as radical as the most rabid of the left-wing Republicans, hence a "dangerous man."[175] That he was aware of the prevailing sentiments regarding him as a man is reflected in his casual remark en route to Washington when, for a moment, his

[173] New Orleans Daily Crescent, *November 13, 1860, as quoted in* Southern Editorials on Secession, *p. 237.*

[174] *"Address to the Legislature of Ohio at Columbus, February 13, 1861,"* Complete Works, VI, 121.

[175] *Speech of Senator Clingman of North Carolina in the Senate, December 3, 1860,* The Congressional Globe, *Second Session, 36th Congress, Vol. 30, p. 3.*

address was misplaced. In a worried search, he described the Inaugural as. "my certificate of moral character, written by myself."[176]

Although from the time of his election he was urged to state his views on the passing events, Lincoln had remained silent. That his silence was not due to a lack of anxiety is easily apparent. "Allusion has been made," he noted on his way to Washington, "to the interest felt in relation to the policy of the new administration. In this I have received from some a degree of credit for having kept silence, and from others some deprecation. I still think that I was right . . .

"In the varying and repeatedly shifting scenes of the present, and without a precedent which could enable me to judge by the past, it has seemed fitting that before speaking upon the difficulties of the country I should have gained a view of the whole field, being at liberty to modify and change the course of policy as future events may make a change necessary.

"I have not maintained silence from any want of real anxiety."[177]

What, then, was Lincoln's purpose? Clearly, he intended to take the occasion of the inauguration to declare the position of the Republican party in regard to the South, to announce his considered judgment in regard to the practical questions raised by the movement of secession, and, in all, to give what assurance he could of his personal integrity.

In evaluating the Inaugural, we must keep in mind its purpose, for the purpose of the speech controlled Lincoln's selection of materials, his arrangement, his style, and his manner.

Let us turn to the speech itself in order to note the materials and methods he employed to sustain his purpose. Considering the general predisposition of the South to view the incoming administration with suspicion, and considering the fact that Lincoln had not spoken for his own party since his nomination, he found it necessary to take a moment to "press upon the public attention the most conclusive evidence of which the case is susceptible," the idea of the integrity of the Republican party and his own integrity as its helmsman. Wise judgment could scarcely have dictated otherwise, for the lower South had gone out of the Union partly on the grounds that it expected no fair consideration from the newly born party, and the border states were contemplating similar measures. Lincoln attempted to conciliate his audience by assuring the country that "the property, peace and security of no section are to be in any wise endangered by the now incoming Administration." In order to do this he called attention to the fact that

[176] Ward Hill Lamon, Recollections of Abraham Lincoln, 1847–1865, edited by Dorothy Lamon Teillard (Washington, D.C.: Published by the editor, 1911), p. 36.
[177] "Address to the Legislature of Ohio at Columbus, February 13, 1861," Complete Works, VI, 121, 122.

he was taking a solemn oath in "your presence"; he committed himself again to previously spoken words[178] that have "all the while existed, and been open to their inspection"; to the Republican platform pertaining to the "maintenance inviolate of the rights of the States, and especially the right of each State to order and control its own domestic institutions according to its own judgment exclusively";[179] and to the clause "plainly written in the Constitution," pertaining to delivering up "on claim of the party to whom such service or labor may be due"[180] the escaping fugitive. He concluded his opening remarks with a reiteration of the avowal that he took the "official oath to-day, with no mental reservations, and with no purpose to construe the Constitution or laws, by any hypercritical rules." This was neither the material nor the method of a "deceitful" or "dangerous" man. By it, Lincoln was attempting to touch off those favorable responses that accrue to the appearance of honesty, straightforwardness, and obedience to the Constitution. One must remember that Lincoln's pledge of faith could not have given satisfaction to the Abolitionist group within his own party with whom he was constantly identified by the South; it did, however, serve to differentiate him from the radical element and hence to reassure the states yet within the Union. From the standpoint of persuasiveness Lincoln was undoubtedly wise in taking the advice of Seward to omit the two paragraphs immediately following his opening statement in the original draft of the Inaugural:

The more modern custom of electing a Chief Magistrate upon a previously declared platform of principles, supercedes, in a great measure, the necessity of restating those principles in an address of this sort. Upon the plainest grounds of good faith, one so elected is not at liberty to shift his position. It is necessarily implied, if not expressed, that, in his judgment, the platform which he thus accepts, binds him to nothing either unconstitutional or inexpedient.

Having been so elected upon the Chicago Platform, and while I would repeat nothing in it, of aspersion or epithet or question of motive against any man or party, I hold myself bound by duty, as well as impelled by inclination to follow, within the executive sphere, the principles therein declared. By no other course could I meet the reasonable expectations of the country.[181]

[178] *"Mr. Lincoln's Reply," First Joint Debate, at Ottawa, August 21, 1858,* The Political Debates between Abraham Lincoln and Stephen A. Douglas, *p. 209.*

[179] *Halstead, op. cit., p. 138.*

[180] *Article IV, Sec. 2.*

[181] *For changes in the Inaugural, see MS of early printed version with secretarial reproductions of the changes, and accompanying letter of John Hay to Charles Eliot Norton, dated March 25, 1899, explaining the nature of the revi-*

To have used the paragraphs would undoubtedly have incited anew the suspicion that he was merely a "sectional" President and an "abolitionist" or "party man."

Having spent time in an attempt to gain a fair hearing for the rest of his address, Lincoln next took up the question for which the whole country awaited an answer, namely, What is the duty and the policy of the Republican administration in regard to Secession? Without delay, he laid down the proposition, "I hold, that in contemplation of universal law, and of the Constitution, the Union of these States is perpetual. Perpetuity is implied, if not expressed, in the fundamental law of all national governments"; hence "no State, upon its own mere motion, can lawfully get out of the Union,—that *resolves* and *ordinances* to that effect are legally void, and that acts of violence, within any State or States, against the authority of the United States, are insurrectionary or revolutionary, according to circumstances." Furthermore, "if the United States be not a government proper, but an association of States in the nature of contract merely, can it, as a contract, be peaceably unmade, by less than all the parties who made it?"

To the North, the mere assertion of the principle of perpetuity would have been sufficient; no further proof would have been necessary. But to the lower South, already out of the Union, and to the border states and upper South contemplating similar action, clearly assertion was not sufficient. Therefore, Lincoln found his proposition "confirmed by the history of the Union itself." The Union, he pointed out, was "much older than the Constitution"; it was "formed in fact, by the Articles of Association in 1774"; it was "matured and continued by the Declaration of Independence in 1776"; it was "further matured and the faith of all the then thirteen States expressly plighted and engaged that it should be perpetual, by the Articles of Confederation in 1778"; finally "in 1787, one of the declared objects for ordaining and establishing the Constitution, was *'to form a more perfect Union.'*" Although Lincoln's support of his proposition was factual, the facts themselves carried with them the respect and loyalty that had always attached to the founding fathers who were held in esteem for their vision and their wisdom.

Having stated the principle that guided him, Lincoln continued logically with its application, holding that "to the extent of my ability I

---

sions, in Widener Library of Harvard University. See also, John G. Nicolay and John Hay, Abraham Lincoln, *III, 327–344;* Louis A. Warren, *"Original Draft of the First Inaugural,"* Lincoln Lore, *No. 358 (February 17, 1936) and No. 359 (February 24, 1936). See,* The Robert Todd Lincoln Collection of the Papers of Abraham Lincoln, *Library of Congress. Microfilm in University of Illinois Library. This collection contains the most important source for the various working sheets of the Inaugural.*

shall take care, as the Constitution itself expressly enjoins upon me, that the laws of the Union be faithfully executed in all the States." In discussing the policy of the government in enforcing the laws of the Union, Lincoln does not speak as the master or the mere advocate handing down a bloodless decision, but as a servant performing a "simple duty," the "American people" being "my rightful masters." As a skilled persuader, he was undoubtedly aware that lines of argument will often meet with varied responses according to whether they are put forward by those toward whom one feels sympathetic or antagonistic.[182] Nowhere in the Inaugural does Lincoln seek more earnestly to be conciliating and mild. He was aware that legalism alone would not sustain his purpose. He could have used the bold and confident assertion that appeared in the original draft of the Inaugural:

All the power at my disposal will be used to reclaim the public property and places which have fallen; to hold, occupy and possess these, and all other property and places belonging to the government and to collect the duties and imposts; but beyond what may be necessary for these objects, there will be no invasion of any State.

Even in the original draft, Lincoln had avoided the use of the names of specific forts to which he had reference. Pickens and Sumter were in a precarious position and were peculiarly explosive topics of discussion. However, Lincoln yielded even further in tempering his remarks, accepting the suggestion of O. H. Browning, and finally choosing only to say:

The power confided to me will be used to hold, occupy, and possess the property and places belonging to the Government, and to collect the duties and imposts; but, beyond what may be necessary for these objects, there will be no invasion, no using of force against or among the people anywhere.

Furthermore, "Where hostility to the United States, in any interior locality, shall be so great and so universal, as to prevent competent resident citizens from holding the Federal offices," he would make "no attempt to force obnoxious strangers among the people for that object," even though the "strict legal right may exist." And, the mails "unless repelled" would continue to be furnished. In doing this, "there needs to be no bloodshed or violence," he assured the country, and promised that "there shall be none, unless it be forced upon the na-

[182] *Robert K. Merton,* Mass Persuasion (*New York: Harper and Brothers, 1946*), *p. 109.*

tional authority." Nowhere did Lincoln assert a power or a practice that he believed impossible of enforcement, or that he believed could be interpreted as "coercion" in its baldest and most belligerent form.

Having announced his specific policy, Lincoln turned to those "who really love the Union," neither affirming nor denying that there were those "who seek to destroy the Union at all events," being "glad of any pretext to do it." In his original draft, he had intended pointedly to observe "Before entering upon so grave a matter as the destruction of our national Union, would it not be wise to ascertain precisely why we do it?" In his final draft, however, he blotted out the word "Union" and substituted for it the unifying and figurative word "fabric," further inserting the words "with all its benefits, its memories and its hopes," thereby seeking to heighten feeling by suggesting appropriate attitudes.

Having passed the climax of his remarks, Lincoln moved, in the last half of the Inaugural, to a reasoned discussion of related topics. He denied that any right plainly written in the Constitution had been violated, observing that majorities and minorities arise as a result of that class of questions for which no specific constitutional answer has been provided. The alternative to accepting the "majority principle" was always either "anarchy or depotism." Not even the Supreme Court could serve as the final arbiter on questions "affecting the whole people," for unless it limited its activity to making decisions on specific "cases properly brought before them," the "people will have ceased to be their own rulers." He argued the impracticability of secession, contrasting it with the simple act of divorce between husband and wife who may remain "beyond the reach of each other," and concluded that "Physically speaking, we cannot separate." Not even war was a satisfactory solution to difficulties, for "you cannot fight always," and after much "loss on both sides, and no gain on either," the "identical old questions" are again to be settled. "This country, with its institutions, belongs to the people who inhabit it," he insisted, urging that when the whole people "shall grow weary of the existing government, they can exercise their *constitutional* right of amending it, or their *revolutionary* right to dismember or overthrow it."

Lincoln's appeal throughout was to the "patient confidence in the ultimate justice of the people." "Is there any better or equal hope, in the world?" he asked, even as he noted the human tendency of parties in dispute to insist with equal confidence on being in the "right." Rising to the position of impartial leader, he sought faith in a higher law, and in a disinterested Ruler: "If the Almighty Ruler of nations, with his eternal truth and justice, be on your side of the North or on yours of the South, that truth, and that justice, will surely prevail, by the judgment of this great tribunal, the American people."

Lincoln ended his address with both a challenge and a declaration of faith. "In *your* hands, my dissatisfied fellow countrymen, and not in *mine,* is the momentous issue of civil war. The government will not assail *you.*" He was just about to take an oath, and to him an oath was a solemn pledge, not only in word, but in truth. It was an avowal of morality, binding him not only to duty to the people but to God, "the Almighty Ruler of nations." "*You* have no oath registered in Heaven to destroy the government," he pleaded in an attempt to secure the cooperation of all those who could help him in fulfilling the pledge he was to take, "while *I* shall have the most solemn one to 'preserve, protect and defend' it." His final appeal was to feeling rather than to reason. He undoubtedly realized that when men cannot achieve common ground through reason, they may achieve it through the medium of feeling. "I am loth to close," he observed. "We are not enemies, but friends. We must not be enemies. Though passion may have strained, it must not break our bonds of affection." No longer the advocate, or even the President performing official duties, Lincoln, taking the advice of Seward, became the affectionate father, the benevolent and hopeful counselor, trusting not only in reason, but calling on "memory," the "patriot grave," the "heart and hearth-stone," "the better angels of our nature" to "swell the chorus of the Union."

Whereas the disgruntled may have "found too much argumentative discussion of the question at issue, as was to have been expected from a man whose whole career has been that of an advocate,"[183] obviously others could not have failed to notice that Lincoln sought valiantly to employ all the "available means of persuasion." He had sought to reach his audience not only through reason, but through feeling and through the force of his own ethical ideals.

Any fair-minded critic, removed from the passions of the times, must find himself much more in agreement with those observers of the day who believed the Inaugural met the "requirements of good rhetoric" by having "right words in their right places" and "right words at the right times,"[184] than with those who labeled it "feeble rhetorical stuff," and found it "inferior in point of elegance, perspicuity, vigor, talent, and all the graces of composition to any other paper of a like character from a President of the Republic."[185] One who studies the revisions in phrase and word in the various drafts of the Inaugural must become aware that Lincoln was concerned not only with using the right argument, but with using words cautiously, and purposefully, to obtain a desired effect from his listeners and from his potential readers. To the

[183] The Diary of a Public Man, *p. 75.*

[184] The Boston Transcript, *as quoted in* New York Daily Tribune, *March 7, 1861, p. 7, col. 1.*

[185] Jersey City Standard, *as quoted in* Northern Editorials on Secession, *II, 625.*

rhetorician, style is not an aspect of language which can be viewed in isolation or judged merely by the well-attuned ear. Nor is it sufficient to apply such rubrics as clarity, vividness, elegance as absolute values, or as an adequate description of style. Words are an "available means of persuasion," and the only legitimate question is: Did Lincoln use words effectively to achieve his specific purpose?

Although Lincoln may have lamented that he did not have a "fine education" or that he was not a "master of language,"[186] he had a keen sensitiveness for language. He "studied to see the subject matter clearly," said an early teacher, "and to express it truly and strongly. I have known him to study for hours the best way of three to express an idea."[187] And when his partner, Herndon, attempted the grandiose in expression, Lincoln sometimes remarked, "Billy, don't shoot too high —aim lower and the common people will understand you. They are the ones you want to reach—at least they are the ones you ought to reach. The educated and refined people will understand you any way. If you aim too high your ideas will go over the heads of the masses, and only hit those who need no hitting."[188] Lincoln had become adept at stump speaking, and knew how to use language to make himself clear and to make a point. That he knew the power of language to fire passions and to cloud understanding is amply demonstrated in his remarks at Indianapolis when he was en route to Washington. "Solomon says there is 'a time to keep silence,' " he observed, "and when men wrangle by the month with no certainty that they mean the same thing, while using the same word, it perhaps were as well if they would keep silence. The words 'coercion' and 'invasion' are much used in these days, and often with some temper and hot blood. Let us make sure, if we can, that we do not misunderstand the meaning of those who use them. Let us get exact definitions of these words, not from dictionaries, but from the men themselves, who certainly deprecate the things they would represent by the use of words."[189] Lincoln was keenly aware that words themselves were often grounds for argument, systems of attitudes suggesting courses of action.[190] Then, too, Lincoln knew that his "friends feared" and "those who were not his friends hoped, that, forgetting the dignity of his position, and the occasion, he would descend

---

[186] *Speech in reply to Douglas at Chicago, Illinois, July 10, 1858, in* Abraham Lincoln: His Speeches and Writings, *edited by Roy P. Basler, p. 393.*

[187] *Herndon and Weik,* op. cit., *p. 99.*

[188] Ibid., *p. 262.*

[189] *"Address to the Legislature of Indiana at Indianapolis, February 12, 1861,"* Complete Works, *VI, 112, 113.*

[190] *Kenneth Burke, "Two Functions of Speech,"* The Language of Wisdom and Folly, *edited and with an introduction by Irving J. Lee (New York: Harper and Brothers, 1949), p. 40.*

to the practices of the story-teller, and fail to rise to the level of a statesman."[191]

The desire for clearness, the desire to subdue passion, the desire to manifest the integrity and dignity befitting a statesman in a responsible position—these are the factors that influenced Lincoln in his composition of the Inaugural, and to appraise his style without constant awareness of them is likely to lead the critic far afield. Let us consider Lincoln's style, then, as a system of symbols designed to evoke certain images favorable to the accomplishment of his purpose and, in so far as he could, to prevent certain other images from arising.

One of the most marked characteristics of Lincoln's style is its directness. By it he attempts to achieve the appearance of candor and honesty, traits that were eminently significant to the success of the Inaugural, considering the doubts and suspicions that were prevalent regarding his integrity. From the opening sentence to the conclusion one notes the unmistakable honesty and straightforwardness that reside in direct address. "I appear before you," he remarks, "to address you briefly, and to take, in your presence, the oath prescribed by the Constitution of the United States . . . ." Again, he observes, "I have no purpose, directly or indirectly, to interfere with the institution of slavery in the States where it exists"; "I now reiterate these sentiments"; "I take the official oath to-day, with no mental reservations"; *"You* have no oath registered in Heaven to destroy the government, while *I* shall have the most solemn one to 'preserve, protect and defend' it." Direct and forthright throughout, he could scarcely have used words to better advantage in emphasizing his honesty and integrity.

What doubts there were pertaining to inadequacies traceable to his humble origins and his lack of formal education must in some wise have been dispelled by his clearness, his accuracy, and his freedom from the awkward expression or the simple idiom of the Western stump speaker. Lincoln had felt his inadequacies when he addressed an Eastern audience of educated men at Cooper Union and was uncomfortable. In his Inaugural, prepared for an audience representative of the whole country, he had been cautious and careful to use language that was sustained in its dignity. Seward, sometimes known for his polished expression, had given him some aid in the choice of the proper word. Lincoln accepted advice in such word changes as "acquiesce" instead of "submit," "constituted" instead of "constructed," "void" instead of "nothing," "repelled" instead of "refused," and he also accepted such a change of phrase as "imperfectly supports the law itself" for "is against the law itself." Although the changes are minor, they reflect Lin-

---

[191] *L. E. Chittenden,* Recollections of President Lincoln and His Administration *(New York: Harper and Brothers, 1904), p. 88.*

coln's desire for correctness and conciseness. On his own better judgment, he deleted the one extended metaphor that appeared in the
original draft. "I am, rather for the old ship, and the chart of the old
pilots," he had originally written, with some of the tang and flavor of
his speech in addressing popular Western audiences. "If, however, the
people desire a new, or an altered vessel, the matter is exclusively their
own, and they can move in the premises, as well without as with an
executive recommendation." The figure was not equal in elevation to
the rest of his remarks. His final draft read simply, "I cannot be ignorant of the fact that many worthy and patriotic citizens are desirous of
having the national Constitution amended. While I make no recommendation of amendments, I fully recognize the rightful authority of the
people over the whole subject . . ." Such phrasing, simple in its dignity, undoubtedly was more appropriate and suited to his needs.

That Lincoln sought to control the behavior of his audience and the
reader through the appropriately affective word is apparent throughout
his address. There are times when even the level of specificity and
concreteness, usually thought to be virtues of style, is altered in favor
of the more general word or allusion. For instance, Lincoln had originally intended to say, "why may not South Carolina, a year or two
hence, arbitrarily, secede from a new Southern Confederacy . . . ?"
Finally, however, he avoided being specific, altering his remarks to
read "why may not any portion of a new confederacy, a year or two
hence, arbitrarily secede again . . . ?" Again, the ridicule in his assertion, "The Union is less perfect than before, which contradicts the
Constitution, and therefore is absurd," is eliminated and reason is
substituted: "The Union is *less perfect* than before the Constitution,
having lost the vital element of its perpetuity." Lincoln sometimes chose
the longer statement in preference to the sharp, pointed word or
phrase, if by a longer expression he could avoid truculence or the
pointing of an accusing finger. Such a phrase as "be on your side of
the North or on yours of the South," aided considerably in creating an
image of impartiality, and was to be preferred for the shorter, but divisive phrase, "be on our side or yours." The changes that Lincoln
made in the direction of fullness rather than compression were designed to aid in clearness, exactness, and completeness, for the country expected him to express himself fully on the disturbing problems of
the time.

The close of Lincoln's address, often cited for its poetic beauty, reflects not only his aesthetic sense, but perhaps more importantly, his
power of using words to evoke images conducive to controlling response. As is very well known, Lincoln was not merely trying to be
eloquent when he closed the address. He achieved eloquence and
cadenced beauty through his direct attempt to be "affectionate,"

Seward having reminded him that perhaps feeling should supplement reason, and having suggested a possible conclusion:

I close. We are not we must not be aliens or enemies but ~~countrym~~ fellow countrymen and brethren. Although passion has strained our bonds of affection too hardly they must not ~~be broken they will not~~ I am sure they will not be broken. The mystic chords of memory which proceeding from ~~every ba~~ so many battle fields and ~~patriot~~ so many patriot graves ~~or~~ pass through all the hearts and hearths all the hearths in this broad continent of ours will yet ~~harmo~~ again harmonize in their ancient music when ~~touched as they surely~~ breathed upon ~~again~~ by the ~~better angel~~ guardian angel of the nation.[192]

An image of great-heartedness, great humility, and great faith resulted when Lincoln rephrased Seward's suggestion in his own style. It was his final declaration of faith and had in it the emotional intensity that often accompanies the hoped-for but unknown. It was his final plea for a course of action befitting "friends."

Let us conclude our remarks on Lincoln's style by emphasizing that it reflected the same purposefulness that was characteristic of the arguments contained in the address. Through directness, clearness, dignity, and appropriately affective words, he sought to aid himself in achieving his ends.

One further means of persuasion may be noted, namely, that of his manner in oral presentation. Lincoln's delivery, of course, was significant chiefly to those who composed his immediate audience, and not to any great extent to the much larger audience throughout the country, except in so far as eyewitnesses and newspaper reports conveyed impressions pertaining to the character and personality of the speaker. It is undoubtedly true that Lincoln's manner contributed heavily to his effectiveness on this particular occasion. It may even be true that, had the whole country been immediately present, it would have found further grounds for trust. Ethical stature often shows itself not only in the selection of argument or the composition of words, but in those "echoes and values" that emanate from physical presence alone. "If I were to make the shortest list of the qualifications of the orator," Emerson once remarked, "I should begin with *manliness;* and perhaps it means here presence of mind."[193] It must be remembered that when Lincoln advanced to the platform to deliver his Inaugural, he did so in

[192] *Facsimile of the original suggestion of Seward as reprinted in* Abraham Lincoln: His Speeches and Writings, *edited by Roy P. Basler, pp. 589, 590.*
[193] *"Eloquence,"* The Complete Works of Ralph Waldo Emerson (*New York: Sully and Kleinteich, 1875*), VIII, 123.

face of threats on his life. That he manifested little fear is apparent from practically all of the newspaper accounts of the day. The most usual observation indicated that "the great heart and kindly nature of the man were apparent in his opening sentence, in the tone of his voice, the expression of his face, in his whole manner and bearing."[194] In the judgment of many, he "gained the confidence of his hearers and secured their respect and affection."[195] Lincoln appears to have had a sense of communication, a complete awareness of what he was saying when he was saying it. His thought emerged clearly and appeared to be in no way obstructed by affectation or peculiarities of manner. With dignity and firmness coupled with mildness and humility he sought to enforce his plea by those powers that reside in personality. That they have stimulus value one can scarcely question.

Thirty-nine days after Lincoln delivered his Inaugural Address, Fort Sumter was fired upon. Civil war had begun. Lincoln had sought to save the Union by carefully reasoned argument, by regard for the feelings and rights of all the people, and by a solemn avowal of justice and integrity. That the Inaugural alone could not prevent the war is surely insufficient ground to condemn it for ineptness. "In speechmaking, as in life, not failure, but low aim, is crime."[196] There were many divisive forces, and these had gained great momentum by the time Lincoln addressed the American people. The South accepted the burden of his challenge, "In *your* hands, my dissatisfied fellow countrymen, and not in *mine,* is the momentous issue of civil war."

[194] *Chittenden,* loc. cit.
[195] Ibid., *p. 90.*
[196] *Parrish and Nichols,* op. cit., *p. 12.*

THE HISTORICAL APPROACH

Public Address: A Study in Social and Intellectual History
by Ernest J. Wrage

In the title of a book, *Ideas are Weapons,* Max Lerner gives to ideas a twentieth century connotation, for in this century all of the resources of man have twice comprised actual or potential materiel of warfare. The merit of the title lies in the emphasis it places upon function, although one must read beyond it to grasp the diversity of function which ideas perform. Man's capacities for thought somewhat resemble modern industrial plants which are capable of converting raw materials into either soap or bullets, of refining sugar into nutritive food or into alcohol for the manufacture of explosives. Similarly, from the biochemical processes of individual minds responding to environment may emerge ideas which serve to promote social conflict, while there are yet others, fortunately, which contribute to resolution of differences. Man's intellectual activities may result in ideas which clarify his relationships with his fellow men and to the cosmos, or in ideas which close minds against further exploration in favor of blind conformity to tradition and authority. It is axiomatic that the extant records of man's responses to the social and physical world as expressed in formulations of thought provide one approach to a study of the history of his culture. Whether we seek explanations for an overt act of human behavior in the genesis and moral compulsion of an idea, or whether we accept the view that men seek out ideas which promote their interests and justify their activities, the illuminating fact is that in either case the study of ideas provides an index to the history of man's values and goals, his hopes and fears, his aspirations and negations, to what he considers expedient or inapplicable.

The word *ideas,* therefore, is not restricted here to a description of the great and noble thoughts uttered by accredited spokesmen for the edification of old and young. It is employed in a more inclusive sense and refers widely to formulations of thought as the product and expression of social incentives, which give rise and importance now to one idea, then to another. They are viewed as the product of social environment, as arising from many levels of life, and as possessing social utility. Ideas are not here treated as entities which enjoy an independent existence and which serve as objects of contemplation by the self-avowed or occasional ascetic. While the history of ideas is un-

From *The Quarterly Journal of Speech,* XXXIII, 4 (December 1947), 451–457. Used by permission of Mrs. Naomi Wrage and the Speech Communication Association. Dr. Wrage was professor of speech at Northwestern University.

deniably concerned with major works in systematized thought, and with the influence of thinker upon thinker, exclusive devotion to monumental works is hopelessly inadequate as a way of discovering and assessing those ideas which find expression in the market place. Subtle intellectual fare may be very well for stomachs accustomed to large helpings of ideational substances rich in concentration; but there also is nutritional value in the aphoristic crumbs which fall into stomachs unaccustomed and unconditioned to large helpings of such fare, and the life sustained by the crumbs is not without historical interest. The force of Emerson's ideas upon the popular mind of his time, and even later, derives less from his intricate elaborations upon man and the cosmos than from his dicta on self-reliance. Moreover, ideas arise at many levels of human life and find expression in and attain force through casual opinion as well as learned discourse; and while the life span of many popularly-held ideas is admittedly short, often these "out-of-the-way" ideas thrive and emerge at higher levels of development. This extension in the conception of the history of ideas which includes more than monumental distillations of thought in philosophy, religion, literature, and science may be offensive to those of fastidious intellectual tastes, but there is increasing awareness that adequate social and intellectual history cannot be written without accounting for popular opinions, beliefs, constellations of attitudes, and the like.

I

Ideas attain history in process, which includes transmission. The reach of an idea, its viability within a setting of time and place, and its modifications are expressed in a vast quantity of documentary sources. Man's conscious declarations of thought are embodied in a mosaic of documents, in constitutions and laws, literature and song, scientific treatises and folklore, in lectures, sermons, and speeches. Of these, not the least either in quantity or value, as Curti points out, are the lectures, sermons, and speeches:

Historians of ideas in America have too largely based their conclusions on the study of formal treatises. But formal treatises do not tell the whole story. In fact, they sometimes give a quite false impression, for such writings are only a fraction of the records of intellectual history. For every person who laboriously wrote a systematic treatise, dozens touched the subject in a more or less casual fashion. Sometimes the fugitive essays of relatively obscure writers influenced the systematizers and formal writers quite as much as the works of better-known men. The influence of a thinker does not pass from one major writer to another without frequently being transformed or dissipated, or compressed in the hands of a whole series of people who responded to the

*thinker and his ideas. It is reasonably certain, moreover, that in the
America of the early nineteenth century ephemeral writings, widely
scattered as they were in pamphlets, tracts, and essays, reached a
much wider audience and are often more reliable evidence of the climate of opinion than the more familiar works to which historians of
ideas have naturally turned. The student of the vitality and modification
of ideas may well direct his attention, then, toward out-of-the-way sermons, academic addresses, Fourth of July orations, and casual guides
and essays.*[1]

As a parenthetical comment, one recent study which makes extensive
use of fugitive literature, particularly speeches, is Merle Curti's *The
Roots Of American Loyalty,* published in 1946. But in the main, the rich
vein of literature in speaking has hardly been tapped for this purpose
except by the occasional prospector.

Curti's observations have germinal significance for the student of
public address. They suggest an approach which is interesting for its
freshness and fruitful in intellectual promise. If American life, to adopt
his point of reference, is viewed through ideas historically viable, then
ideas are to be studied as a body of intricate tissues, of differentiated
yet related thought. While the establishment of macroscopic relationships provides the ultimate reasons for tracing out an American intellectual pattern, explorations of the parts is a necessary preliminary to
this achievement. As an enterprise in scholarship, then, the first operation is one of collecting and classifying data within limited areas amen-
able to description and analysis. This accomplished, generalizations
from the data become at once permissible and desirable, and provide
a basis from which further exploration may be conducted.

It is at once apparent that the delineation of an American intellectual
tradition calls for division of labor. It is not only the magnitude in task
but diversity in data and in media of expression which invites spe-
cialization and varied technical skills in scholarship. There are, after
all, appreciable and striking differences between the materials of hymn-
ology and constitutional law. While students of philosophy, history, and
literature are traditionally accredited as the official custodians and interpreters of intellectual history, it is the thesis of this paper that students
of public address may contribute in substantial ways to the history of
ideas. They possess credentials worthy of acknowledgment and interest in a type of materials germane to the object.

It has been amply treated and clearly said by others that the rhetoric

---

[1] *Merle Curti, "The Great Mr. Locke: America's Philosopher, 1783–1861,"*
The Huntington Library Bulletin, *April, 1937, pp. 108–109.*

of public address does not exist for its own sake, that its value is instrumental, and that its meaning apart from an application to something is sterile. An endorsement of this doctrine leads us to an immediate recognition that the basic ingredient of a speech is its content. The transmission of this content is its legitimate function. It is a vehicle for the conveyance of ideas. It is a mode of communication by means of which something of the thought of the speaker is incorporated and expressed in language in ways which make for ready comprehension and acceptance by one or more audiences. It is for the very reason that public speeches and lectures are prepared with a listening audience in mind that they serve so admirably in a study of social thought. The full import of this point is disclosed by some comparisons.

When reporting the results of work to members of his guild, the physical scientist may confine himself to an exclusive concern with data, intricate operations, and complex thought. In preparation and presentation neither detail nor comprehensiveness needs to be sacrificed, for his discourse is not prepared with an eye to the limiting factors present in the differentiated audience. As distinguished from this highly specialized form of reporting, a public speech is a more distinctly popular medium which is useful for explaining the essence of an idea, for explaining the applicability of a particular, for establishing impressions and evoking attitudes, for direction in the more or less common affairs of men. Because speeches are instruments of utility designed in the main for the popular mind, conversely and in significant ways they bear the impress of the popular mind. It is because they are pitched to levels of information, to take account of prevalent beliefs, and to mirror tone and temper of audiences that they serve as useful indices to the popular mind.

This interaction between the individual mind of the speaker and the collective mind of the audience has long been appreciated, but for the most part this interaction has been considered in terms of its relationship to the speaker's techniques. What has happened to the ideas themselves under the impact of this interaction remains a field which is relatively unexplored in any systematic sense by students of public address. The techniques of the speakers are often highly individualized and perish with their bones; their ideas live after them. From the study of speeches may be gained additional knowledge about the growth of ideas, their currency and vitality, their modifications under the impress of social requirements, and their eclipse by other ideas with different values. Such a study of speeches belongs to what Max Lerner calls the "naturalistic approach" to the history of ideas, one which includes "not only the conditions of the creation of ideas but also the conditions of their reception, not only the impulsions behind the ideas, but also the uses to which they are put, not only the thinkers but also the popularizers, the propagandists, the opinion skill-groups, the final audience that believes or disbelieves and acts accordingly.''[2]

Is not such scholarship properly confined to the professional historian? The question is dated and should be so treated. Squabbles over contested rights are hang-overs from an age of academic primogeniture. A study is to be judged by its merits, not by the writer's union card. But a more convincing argument for participation in scholarship of the history of ideas by students of public address is made apparent when we take another step in our thinking. The very nature and character of ideas in transmission is dependent upon configurations of language. The interpretation of a speech calls for complete understanding of what goes into a speech, the purpose of the speech and the interplay of factors which comprise the public speaking situation, of nuances of meaning which emerge only from the reading of a speech in the light of its setting. At this juncture a special kind of skill becomes useful, for the problem now relates directly to the craftsmanship of the rhetorician. The student who is sensitized to rhetoric, who is schooled in its principles and techniques, brings an interest, insight, discernment, and essential skill which are assets for scholarship in the history of ideas, as that history is portrayed in public speeches.

II

The prevailing approach to the history and criticism of public address appears to consist of a study of individual speakers for their influence upon history. If one may judge from studies available through publication, they fall short of that ambitious goal for reasons which are painfully apparent to anyone who has attempted to assess influence in history. Nevertheless, they do provide a defensible pattern in research which has yielded highly interesting data about prominent speakers, their speechmaking and speaking careers. Reference is made to this standard approach to public address simply as a means of establishing and clarifying some distinctions between it and the proposed method of study which concentrates upon the ideas in speeches. The differences are those of focus, of knowledge to be gained, and of procedure to be followed in investigation. While one approach is "speaker centered," the other is "idea centered." One focuses mainly upon the speaker and the speaking activity, the other upon the speech and its content. One seeks to explain factors which contributed to personal persuasion; the other yields knowledge of more general interest in terms of man's cultural strivings and heritage.

In point of procedure it should be at once apparent that there are differences involved in a study which centers, let us say, upon Henry

[2] *Max Lerner,* Ideas Are Weapons *(1940), p. 6.*

Clay as an orator and in a study which centers upon the ideas embodied in his speeches on the American System. To pursue the example, a study of the ideas in Clay's speeches is not committed to searching out the sources of his personal power with an audience, but is concerned with the doctrine of a self-contained economy as portrayed in his speeches in the perspective of that doctrine's history, from Hamilton to Matthew Carey's *Olive Branch,* to the congenial, nascent nationalism of Clay and contemporary speakers. Inasmuch as the American System is compounded of political and economic ideas, competence in handling the data of history is necessary; but it is also to be remembered that inasmuch as the ideas are projected through speeches, they are also the province of the rhetorician; that inasmuch as they are employed in speeches with the object of reaching and affecting a wide audience, the ideas are framed in a context of rhetorical necessities and possibilities. To adopt the rhetorical perspective is actually to approximate more closely a genuinely historical point of view when analyzing and interpreting speeches as documents of ideas in social history.

The possibilities for analysis in the rhetoric of ideas is illustrated in Roy P. Basler's essay on "Lincoln's Development As A Writer." The title of the essay should properly have included "And Speaker," for much of the brilliance of Basler's commentary arises from the treatment he gives the speeches.[3] Basler sets forth the basic ideas which are the essence of Lincoln's philosophy and links them to the dominant intellectual currents of Lincoln's age. He analyzes the rhetoric of Lincoln, not because he is interested in rhetoric *per se,* but because Lincoln's ideas were framed by his rhetoric, which, in turn, was profoundly affected by the exigencies present in the totality of social factors bearing upon the speaking situation. From an analysis of his rhetoric in this relationship, it is possible to come into a closer understanding of Lincoln's thought patterns and of the ideas he sought to lodge in the minds of his audiences. For instance, Basler recounts how the theme in the "House Divided" speech was carried through many stages of inference, that it underwent many modifications in order to achieve the nuances and implications which Lincoln desired. Basler concludes that "It would be difficult to find in all history a precise instance in which rhetoric played a more important role in human destiny than it did in Lincoln's speeches of 1858."[4] He speaks, of course, of the instrumental role of rhetoric as it served to crystallize the meanings which

---

[3] *Roy P. Basler,* Abraham Lincoln; His Speeches and Writings (*Cleveland and New York, 1946*), *pp. 1–49.*

[4] Ibid., *p. 28.*

Lincoln sought to convey. Through a masterful analysis of the rhetoric in the Gettysburg Address, Basler presents the underlying pattern of Lincoln's thought, as is suggested by a short excerpt from his treatment:

Lincoln's problem at Gettysburg was to do two things: to commemorate the past and to prophesy for the future. To do these things he took the theme dearest to his audience, honor for the heroic dead sons and fathers, and combined it with the theme nearest to his own heart, the preservation of democracy. Out of this double theme grew his poetic metaphor of birth, death, and spiritual rebirth, of the life of man and the life of the nation. To it he brought the fervor of devoutly religious belief. Democracy was to Lincoln a religion, and he wanted it to be in a real sense the religion of his audience. Thus he combined an elegiac theme with a patriotic theme, skillfully blending the hope of eternal life with the hope of eternal democracy.[5]

A speech is an agency of its time, one whose surviving record provides a repository of themes and their elaborations from which we may gain insight into the life of an era as well as into the mind of a man. From the study of speeches given by many men, then, it is possible to observe the reflections of prevailing social ideas and attitudes. Just as the speeches of Schwab and Barton, of Coolidge and Dawes (accompanied by the latter's broom-sweeping histrionics) portray the ethos of business and a negative view toward government intervention in social affairs, so do the speeches of Roosevelt and other New Dealers mark the break from the attitudes and conceptions which dominated the twenties. Both schools of thought express the social and economic values of the times. Both mirror the dominant moods of their respective audiences. The very structure, idiom, and tone of the speeches, moreover, play their parts in the delineation of those ideas. For example, the full import of Roosevelt's First Inaugural Address is not perceived without reference to the many nuances and imperatives of his rhetoric. It is in the metaphor of war and the image of the religious crusade, as well as in argument and statements of intention, that the speech articulates the inchoate feelings of the people on government's social responsibility. Similarly, from a wide investigation of sermons, lectures, and speeches related to issues, movements, and periods, might we not extend and refine our knowledge of social ideas portrayed in history? Such an attempt would constitute a kind of anthropological approach to a segment of cultural history.

[5] Ibid., *p. 42.*

III

Let the final argument be a practical one. Specifically, what applications may be made of this approach to public address in a university classroom? Experience has made it apparent to the writer that a course consisting only of successive case histories of individual speakers and speech-making leaves much to be desired. It certainly is open to question if an accidental chronology or arbitrary selection of orators provides a satisfactory focus and basic framework to warrant the label, "history of public address," or if it provides adequate intellectual and educational outcomes for the time expended. Interesting in its way as may be the study for its own sake of the personality, platform virtuosity, and career of an individual speaker, a mere progression of such more or less independent treatments is likely to be without secure linkage to historical processes. It is likely to result in an assortment of isolated, episodical, or even esoteric information which can make little claim to the advancement of the student's general culture.

There is more than a suggestion of antiquarianism in the whole business. We need, therefore, to provide a more solid intellectual residual. This may be realized when the focus of a course consists in the ideas communicated, in the ascertainable sources of those ideas, the historical vitality and force of the ideas, and of demonstrable refractions, modifications, or substitutions. As an adjunct to the materials of such a course, the study of the speaking careers and skills of individual speakers makes a valuable contribution. Such studies have supplementary value; but even more important is the study of the speeches themselves against a backdrop of history. Naturally, the exclusive study of speeches would result in historical distortion unless related to a larger framework of life and thought, to allied and competing ideas in the intellectual market place.

Seen against a broad and organized body of materials in intellectual and social history, the study of speeches both gives and takes on meaning in ways which contribute substantially to educational experience. Especially helpful as leads in providing background are such familiar works as Vernon L. Parrington, *Main Currents in American Thought;* Merle Curti, *The Growth of American Thought;* and Ralph H. Gabriel, *The Course of American Democratic Thought,* to mention but a few. Such literature supplies references and guidance to the main lines of thought which underlie movements and problems in American life; it brings into view not only tributaries which fed the main streams, but also rivulets of ideas which had a kind of independent existence. Speeches may be studied in relation to these movements. For example, intellectual turmoil and diluvial expression were provoked by the slavery controversy. Antislavery appeals, historians tell us, were couched in the language of personal liberty and Christian humanitarianism. Pro-slavery speakers, forced to compete upon an equally elevated plane, advanced arguments which derived from similar or equivalent ethical bases but which were interpreted in ways congenial to Southern insti-tutional life and practice. True, the rhetoric of ideas fails to account for all the forces at work; yet a wide reading in sermons, lectures, and speeches does bring one into a deeper understanding of the basic ideational themes, variations upon the themes, and the dissonance which were a part of the controversy and contributed to ultimate settle-ment. When seen against a contextual backdrop, speeches become at once a means of illustrating and testing, of verifying or revising gen-eralizations offered by other workers in social and intellectual history.

There is an implied recognition in what has been said, of a deficiency in the scholarship of public address. There is need for an organized body of literature which places speeches and speaking in proper rela-tionship to the history of ideas. Quite apart from reasons of classroom utility, research in the ideas communicated through speeches needs doing as a means of contributing to knowledge and understanding gen-erally. Adequate social and intellectual history cannot be written without reference to public speaking as it contributed to the ideas injected into public consciousness. But if research is to move forward, perhaps the time has arrived to explore in our individual and joint capacities the rationale, procedures, and materials by which it may be carried on. To this end, a symposium of papers which deals with these problems would help to clarify and stimulate research in public address in its relation to social and intellectual history.

The Little World of Barry Goldwater
by Ernest J. Wrage

You may wonder if this is a program on the rhetoric of contemporary politics or on the politics of contemporary rhetoricians. However pro-vocative, I submit that my title for this paper is descriptively appropriate. For well over two years now, Barry Goldwater has made national news by riding the circuit, crying in the wilderness of contemporary com-plexity, recalling errant countrymen to the lost innocence of William McKinley—to a littler world spinning on a shortened axis of local gov-ernment, a self-regulating economy, and a no-nonsense foreign policy that spells victory in big letters. All this for the enlargement of freedom which, he contends, has been whittled down by the welfare state and one-worldism.

From *Western Speech*, XXVII, 4 (Fall 1963), 207–215. Used by permission of Mrs. Naomi Wrage and the Western Speech Communication Association. Dr. Wrage was professor of speech at Northwestern University.

In his biography of the Senator, Stephen Shadegg—the Senator's absolute alter-ego and ghoster—uses a subtitle to forge linkage between Goldwater and modernity. "Freedom is his flight-plan," says Shadegg,[1] to which I must add, into *unreality*. For surely, Barry Goldwater's world is Utopia fashioned out of nostalgia. It reminds me of a pertinent malapropism attributed to Mayor Richard Daley, hard-boiled Democratic boss of Chicago, who once exclaimed perfervidly, "What we have to do for Chicago is to restore to Chicago all those good things it never had!"[2]

Since November 6, 1962, Goldwater's little world seems to have become smaller, but for the moment, at least, he remains the most authentic popular spokesman for self-conscious conservatism in America. He must be accounted for as part of a renaissance of conservatism.

In 1949, in his presidential address to the Speech Association of America, Dean James H. McBurney, himself confessing a conservative bias, spoke critically of the disinclination of conservatives to test their credo in public forums, contenting themselves with "ceremonial chanting and cries of distress."[3] The same year, in his preface to *The Liberal Imagination,* Lionel Trilling remarked that ". . . Liberalism is not only the dominant but even the sole intellectual tradition." The impulses toward conservatism are strong, he acknowledged, but they express themselves not in ideas but in "irritable mental gestures." This is bad, he admonished prophetically for "it is just when a movement despairs of having ideas that it turns to force, which it masks in ideology."[4] Trilling wrote in December, 1949. Less than three months later, in a Lincoln Day speech at Wheeling, West Virginia, Joseph McCarthy exploited this despair by uncorking a demonology from which flowed the greatest witch hunt of our age.

The pleas of McBurney, Trilling, Clarence Randall and others, late in the 1940's, for well-articulated and responsible conservatism remain timely. But no longer does the voice of conservatism die in the throat, though it speaks in many accents. A thousand organizations promote the cause.[5] Its journals range from the scurrilous *The Cross and The Flag* to the popular *National Review* to *Modern Age* for the high-brows.

[1] *Stephen Shadegg,* Barry Goldwater: Freedom Is His Flight Plan (*New York, 1962*).

[2] *"Politician in Trouble: Richard Joseph Daley,"* The New York Times, *January 30, 1960, p. 11.*

[3] *James H. McBurney, "The Plight of the Conservative in Public Discussion,"* Vital Speeches of the Day, *XVI (March 1950), 343–345.*

[4] *Lionel Trilling,* The Liberal Imagination (*New York, 1950*).

[5] *Ralph E. Ellsworth and Sarah M. Harris,* The American Right Wing (*Washington, D.C.: Public Affairs Press, 1962), p. 2. This pamphlet, a report to the Fund for the Republic, contains a wealth of information about contemporary conservative groups.*

It enlists sophisticated writers such as Russell Kirk, Richard Weaver, Peter Vierek, Clinton Rossiter and others, and they have, seemingly, a guaranteed publishing outlet in the Regnery press. Frequently their thinking seems untouched by the Industrial Revolution and widespread democratization. They draw heavily on 18th Century archetypal conservatives such as Edmund Burke and John Adams and their doctrine, borrowing Burke's belief in the Divine Tactic or Providential Hand in History, ultimately turns into a mystique, largely unintelligible to a modern mind that is essentially secular and pragmatic. Even so, they are undeniably thinkers intent on fashioning a respectable conservative doctrine. But these are not the conservatives who command the Great Audience. That award goes to the politicos and pulpit pitchmen.

And what a variety on the popular spectrum! As classified by Clinton Rossiter, himself a worthy conservative, we have Robert Welch, the maladjusted conservative; Barry Goldwater, the non-adjusted; Eisenhower, the adjusted; and Rockefeller, the over-adjusted type.[6] You may play the game for yourself, pegging such names as Richard Nixon, George Romney, Ayn Rand, John Tower, Clarence Manion, J. Bracken Lee, John Flynn, Carl McIntire, Fred Schwarz, William F. Buckley, Jr., Ev and Charley of show fame, and others that come to mind.

How may we account for this flowering, or, in many instances, rank growth? The full explanation is complicated, to be sure, but I suggest three points that underscore a rhetoric of frustration.

1. For a generation, conservatives have stood largely discredited before the bar of public opinion. During the New Deal Era their cherished abstractions such as the Constitution, sanctity of contract, and the American way of life fell on deaf ears, and though they organized as "The American Liberty League," they were thumpingly rejected. Why? Before the touted "forgotten man" of the Hoover era stepped into the polling booth, FDR had only to take to the air waves and invite him to make the empirical test: "Are you better off than you were last year?" Roosevelt asked in his best man-to-man tones. "Have you lost any of your rights or Constitutional freedom of action and choice?"[7] The empiricism of these two questions goes far to explain both New Deal and Fair Deal successes and therefore the impotency of conservative inducements and rhetoric.

2. Two revolutions within a generation, from rugged individualism to the welfare state, from isolation to planetary involvements, have en-

---

[6] *Quoted on "Thunder on the Right," a CBS television documentary, February 22, 1962.*

[7] *For example, see Franklin D. Roosevelt, "Fireside Chat on the Accomplishments of the New Deal," in Ernest J. Wrage and Barnet Baskerville, eds., Contemporary Forum (New York, 1962), pp. 162–167.*

gulfed us. Both were responses to shock—to crisis in capitalism and to World War II and its aftermath. It's not easy to abandon deep-set convictions, values, and myths and to supplant them with improvisation as as a mode of life, particularly when a not-so-brave world keeps on trembling in ever deepening shadows of violence and extinction. Unrelieved tension and the inability of conservatives to achieve the power that confers responsibility made plausible the devil theory of history. Thus McCarthy exploited the moment, and with his theory of the great conspiracy—the twenty years of treason he so loudly alleged—succeeded for half a decade in misdirecting conservatism.

3. Contemporary conservatives remain perplexed on how to regain power. They regard the Republican Party, though not perfect, as the best vehicle for the return trip. But under whose theory of propulsion? Under Landon and his "New Frontier" (Landon's use of the caption antedated by a quarter of a century Kennedy's apparently unwitting appropriation of it), and more so under Willkie and Dewey, Republicans competed with Democrats on liberal, domestic and international fronts, inviting jeers of me-tooism. Robert Taft said flatly that the business of an opposition is to oppose, but Taft was jettisoned in favor of Ike, a war hero and popular president, but a political novice who proved unable to redeem his party. From an old-line conservative's angle of vision, the Republican record is one of bald opportunism which, to appropriate a line from one of Saroyan's characters, had "No foundations, all down the line."

More recently, Republicans have been guided by the Ev and Charlie formulas, which are essentially technical: Improve city organizations, find popular candidates, lift the party's face.[8] Still more recently, we have the Goldwater prescription—a dramatic, quasi-religious crusade with a broad-based ideological appeal highlighting ancient verities and immutable principles of the kind that are intended to send hearts soaring—in both parties.

An Arizona storekeeper, Barry Goldwater was first elected to the Senate in 1952, a Republican in a nominally Democratic state. He's a man of considerable substance and small learning. He flunked out of public high school in his freshman year, graduated from a military academy with distinction in military subjects only, and failed to complete his freshman year at the University of Arizona.[9] Evidently though, the Senator is not at all embarrassed in making *ex cathedra* pronouncements on the content and methods of contemporary education,

---

[8] *For a perceptive analysis of the conservative's political plight in today's party struggles, see Russell Baker, "Growing Dilemma of the G.O.P.," The New York Times Magazine, April 8, 1962, p. 30 ff.*

[9] *Shadegg, op. cit., pp. 89–92.*

publicly deploring as he does the domination of schools by the progressivism of John Dewey and his disciples.

Goldwater's early political capital consisted of a family name prominent in Arizona, a war record, and a wide acquaintance with Genus Arizonus gained through chatty talks while showing colored slides on Indians of the Southwest.[10] He came to national attention through televised hearings on labor racketeering, his bitter-ender speech on the Kennedy-Ervin Labor Bill, and his opposition to the Rockefeller-Nixon "New York Munich pact" at the time of the 1960 Republican Convention. The big reception accorded him by the Convention turned him into circuit rider in behalf of his brand of political fundamentalism and won for him the sobriquet of Mr. Conservative. Although he began to taper off shortly before the 1962 elections and expects to cut back drastically on his speaking in 1963, he has been averaging more than 35 speaking invitations per day at his peak.[11]

Regarded by the movie-minded as up to JFK's standards, Goldwater's matinee possibilities inspired Hubert Humphrey's quip: "Barry is under contract to 18th Century Fox." An authentic frontiersman—Arizona is our 48th state—Goldwater really sounds like just plain folks. His slightly twangy, dehydrated voice suggests that of cowboys on TV westerns. He is all reasonableness, even compassion as he urges private charity for the poor. Although the point is often made that he is no orator[12] (meaning no demagogue, I presume), as a speaker he succeeds in making an hour pass quickly, though the residue, in cool detachment of afterthought, seems skimpy and threadbare. With special attention to overtones and with benefit of analogues, let me suggest the affective components of his message that are calculated to stimulate and weld a community of conservative sentiment.

At bottom the Goldwater message is programmatic: A staged withdrawal of the federal government on the domestic front and an adventuresome foreign policy that he calls peace through victory. But however fundamental these hard elements of his credo, it is impossible to make a *crusade* today simply out of the materials of Social Darwinism, laissez-faire economics, and pre-nuclear military thinking. Surely then the *ultimate goal* must transcend mundane matters, and it does. In the Senator's words, "Conservatism holds the key to national salvation.

[10] Robert Sheehan, "Arizona Fundamentalist," Fortune, LXIII (May 1961), 137–140.

[11] For an interpretation of Goldwater's reduction in his speechmaking see Robert D. Novak, "Boost for Rocky Seen as Goldwater Curtails Nationwide Politicking," The Wall Street Journal, September 14, 1962, p. 1.

[12] Goldwater's most recent biographer is among those who downgrade his oratorical abilities. See Jack Bell, Mr. Conservative: Barry Goldwater (Garden City, N.Y., 1962).

. . ."[13] Now salvation is an eternal matter and nothing to trifle with. It is achieved by zealous pursuit of correct principles governing the nature of man, society, and the state. As the conservative sees things, the uniqueness of each individual refutes the liberal's passion for egalitarianism, since Nature and Nature's Author have made differentiation among the species a first principle. In the conservative philosophy, attention to economics is only a means to promote the individualism required for the development of the whole man; conversely, the liberal's ideal of a collectivized economy fosters gross materialism, wars with Nature, and ultimately destroys man's integrity and individuality. Says the conservative: The true role of the state is to extend freedom consonant with social order. The liberal, he contends, wittingly or not, propounds the ". . . first principle of totalitarianism; that the State is competent to do all things and is limited in what it actually does only by the will of those who control the State."[14]

If the polarities here seem distended and the conservative view somewhat rarefied, let me remind that the Senator is preaching salvation, and you don't equivocate about that. When pushed, in private interviews,[15] Goldwater can "er" and "ah" with the best of them, or back off with a "Well, damned if I know," but on the platform the choices before us emerge with the sharp clarity of copybook maxims: It's freedom or slavery; victory or appeasement. His impact, observers agree, derives basically from his reductionist views, his ability to make value judgments pass as facts, the simplicity and coherence of the whole presentation, and the religious cast of his rhetoric.

Goldwater offers sanctions. Conservatism, Emerson once remarked, is always plagued by a certain meanness. Goldwater offers a loftier version. The principles of conservatism, he asserts, piously echoing Burke and Kirk, ". . . are derived from the nature of man, and from the truths that God has revealed about His creation."[16] And to refute the charge that conservatism is an ill-concealed rationalization for acquisitiveness, the Senator insists that the ultimate object of individualism and competition is character-building. Which, of course, is the message of Andrew Carnegie, William Graham Sumner, Russell Conwell, and Horatio Alger —heroes all in the heyday of Social Darwinism.

As with all revealed Truths, those of conservatism are in contest with diabolism. Whereas McCarthy spoke darkly of traitors, Goldwater

[13] *Barry Goldwater,* The Conscience of a Conservative (*Shepherdsville, Kentucky, 1960), Foreword. This tract, which did so much to spread Goldwater's conservative philosophy, is largely derived from his speeches and broadcasts.*
[14] *Ibid., p. 16.*
[15] *For a brilliantly written account of his interview with Goldwater, see Gore Vidal, "A Liberal Meets Mr. Goldwater,"* Life, L (*June 9, 1961), 106–118.*
[16] *Goldwater, op. cit., Foreword.*

speaks of dupes, pacificists, socialists, or whatever you call them—trailing off, as he does, into vagueness. Goldwater gives greater stress to the pervasive presence of insidious ideas, inveighing against those that sap our integrity—ideas like progressive education and welfare statism—and these must be countered by the special sanity of conservatives.

And Goldwater offers redemption for all. You and I, he says in effect, must accept our portion of guilt for abandoning traditional ways of thought, then hurries on to embrace extreme Arminianism.[17] Redemption is possible for Democrats (who vote too) as well as for Republican backsliders, and it can be achieved by returning to old-time political and economic thought of the post-Appomattox period.

If there is a theological cast to the Senator's political fundamentalism, as there is, what happens to the religious purity of conservatism on the campaign trail? Goldwater, like every practical politician, has been forced to come to terms with an illogical party system, based not on ideology, but on blocs of interest. "Let us be done with all this talk about hyphenated Republicans," I heard him say in the 1962 congressional campaign. "I don't care if he's a Rockefeller Republican, a Nixon Republican, or a Goldwater Republican. I don't care what his color is, as long as he is Republican, can get himself elected, and has strength enough to stand up in the Congress to shout 'here'!" This is purity of principle? Apparently, Goldwater relies heavily on the human will to believe, and on the theory that once the image of Mr. Conservative is set through headlines and speeches, it will safely weather compromises and changes of campaigns. And he may be right. I do know though that some rightists already despair of him.

As indeed, he despairs of them—at least the Far Right. From the Ultras—the men of fevered brain, hot eye, and spittle-caked lips—Goldwater seems to recoil aesthetically. But except for extreme spoilers and outriders, the conclusion is inescapable that Goldwater and the Ultras end up at approximately the same point and with the same program. Goldwater's problem then is to retain their support while escaping the opprobrium that attaches to them. He is edgy when questioned, but he struggles to speak well of many Birchers, especially Arizona Birchers, while opposing Robert Welch. In short, Goldwater stands staunchly for a decapitated Birch Society.

In this age of the personality cult, the problem of bucking and eventually displacing the Establishment, headed by a popular President, is

---

[17] For an example of this pitch, see Goldwater's speech to the American National Cattlemen's Association, January 29, 1960, in A. G. Heinsohn, Jr., ed., Anthology of Conservative Writing in the United States, 1932–1960 (Chicago, 1962), pp. 205–210.

a tough one for any critic even when aligned with Zeus and the cosmic forces. Interestingly, the popularity of Kennedy and Goldwater, though not to be equated, is the product of an "image" each has assiduously projected. But here the President has the advantage of exposure that goes with his office. Hence, Goldwater, with some modifications, has shrewdly resorted to a tactic of early British parliamentarians, in an age when critics of the monarch were understandably circumspect. His or her majesty can do no wrong, courtiers were wont to say, but he or she can be misled by scheming ministers. Goldwater seems wary when stalking Kennedy but confident and abandoned when cracking the skulls of men who surround and mislead the popular young president—Arthur Schlesinger, Jr., Ted Sorenson, Walter Heller, Adlai Stevenson—that crowd. And he can always extract a good laugh plus a round of applause from wisecracks about Robert Kennedy's "splashmanship."

But the greatest obstacle of all to Goldwater's success is the ever-accelerating pace of our age, the adaptations it demands, and the pragmatic philosophy of Americans. The instinct for survival is strong, and only a dolt will fail to roll with the punch. Mind you, I do not minimize the essential role of enlightened conservatives in our political life even in, or particularly because of this age of incredible flux; but Goldwater's "was-ism," his crusade to recover a lost world to which he assigns an illusory coherence and relevance, does seem a quixotic adventure in the extreme, though not without consequences however difficult they are to assess. What has been the feedback to his campaigning that has kept him relentlessly at it? Is the Presidency the inducement? Since Arizona is not a good presidential launching pad and since he has no strong urban support, this seems to be an unreasonable ambition for Goldwater to entertain. But then again, who knows the power of this lure on the Senator? Is he seeking to enhance his influence in Congress? A notorious absentee, the Senator hasn't had much time to give to congressional business, and by all accounts his colleagues remain unimpressed by his efforts. Unlike Robert Taft, who was skilled in the art of legislative action, Goldwater has made negligible contributions. Does he hope to found a new party or accomplish a realignment of old parties along ideological lines? There is no chance of either result in the foreseeable future, and he knows this.

Though they are unmeasurable, traces of Goldwater's influence are best perceived or sensed in a public mood that he has worked hard to develop through his speaking campaign. Hard core conservatives whose car bumpers carry stickers such as "I am a Conservative" or "Goldwater in 1964," offer the clearest indication of his catalytic influence. Apparently he has also had some success in stimulating a revival of conservatism among college students. But the full measure of Goldwater's impact on the public mind lurks in the lower levels of consciousness where we cannot probe. In what ways and to what extent has he enlarged the anxieties and guilt of those who, though not enrolled in the camp of the selfconscious conservatives, fear we are plunging down history's highway marked catastrophe? Uncertain, fearful, and frustrated, the public is understandably vulnerable to a message fashioned by an attractive United States Senator, out of primitive economics, folk mythology, and religiosity. Goldwater's sharp dichotomies put things on the line, offering a clean-cut choice and inducement for the unsophisticated listener. Even professing liberals have been known to voice grudging admiration that betrays their own uneasiness: "You have to admit you know where Barry stands." Who can say, for example, to what extent the widespread approval of Kennedy's essentially unilateral power play in the Cuban crisis is attributable to Goldwater's conditioning of the public mind?

Admittedly, we are groping as we try to fathom the depth of the Senator's impact on our times. We can point with confidence to him, however, as the most conspicuous, peripatetic spokesman of conservatism today, and we may safely credit him with being its foremost moodmaker by intensifying popular nostalgia for the world of yesteryear.

3
THE EXPERIENTIAL
PERSPECTIVE

In the introductory essay to this book, we cited Thomas Kuhn's notions of paradigm and the breakdown of faith in paradigms as accounting for the historical pattern of science. We have adapted these notions to twentieth-century rhetorical criticism, and have described and illustrated a traditional perspective. Now we shall try to account for what appears to be a break-down of faith in the paradigm.

In the 1940s and 1950s a few voices were raised decrying the traditional approach to rhetoric and communication. The General Semanticists were the most vocal early group of protesters.[1] However, not until the 1960s could one say that a serious break from traditional rhetoric and criticism had developed. Edwin Black's *Rhetorical Criticism: A Study in Method* stands out as the book that announced the end of the neo-Aristotelian hegemony.[2]

Interesting evidence of the shift can be derived from studying Barnet Baskerville's bibliographical essay "Selected Writings on the Criticism of Public Address." To the essay, first published in 1957, Baskerville added an "Addendum, 1967."[3] A comparison of the two essays is informative.

In 1957 Baskerville testified to "an abundance of critical literature on speaking" without "a corresponding interest in discussing the act of criticism itself." Throughout the essay he clearly implied that the traditional neo-Aristotelian and historical modes dominated criticism. But a decade later he wrote, "It is probably not inaccurate to observe that we have more distinguished essays *on* criticism than essays *in* criticism" [emphasis in the original].[4] The shift in emphasis was not brought about by a decrease in the number of essays in criticism but by an outpouring of articles on the shortcomings of existing work and recommendations for new directions. The shift in emphasis from the application of an accepted theory to speculation about acceptable theory is consistent with Kuhn's description of a breakdown of faith in a paradigm.

---

[1] *See, for example, Irving Lee, "Four Ways of Looking at a Speech,"* The Quarterly Journal of Speech, *XXVIII, 2 (April 1942), 148–55.*

[2] Rhetorical Criticism: A Study in Method, *New York, Macmillan, 1965. This book was reprinted in 1978 by the University of Wisconsin Press, Madison, Wisconsin. To the book, Mr. Black added an "Author's Foreword."*

[3] *Baskerville's essay first appeared in* Western Speech *(Spring 1957) and is reprinted together with the "Addendum, 1967" in Thomas R. Nilsen, ed.,* Essays on Rhetorical Criticism, *New York, Random House, 1968.*

[4] Ibid., *pp. 174 and 184.*

Reasons for a loss of faith are always complex, but perhaps we can identify a few of the interrelated causes of the break from a well-established tradition.

First, providing a comprehensive rhetorical criticism as outlined by Wichelns is a challenge that few critics have met successfully. In practice, critics developed many shortcuts—providing only an historical analysis, focusing on a few Aristotelian topics, or being descriptive only—which reduced the adequacy of the method. Many critics who have decried traditional criticism have objected actually to its incomplete application.

A second, and deeper reason for the breakdown lies in a growing agreement that speakers (or writers or publicists) are as much a result of cultural forces as they are active participants in forming these forces. The critic, then, becomes interested in the cultural force itself, looking at discourse as something that permeates various sources yet is larger and more pervasive than any one or all of them. Thus, the traditional speaker orientation proves inadequate as the critic's interest in the speaker recedes, and the socio-politico-economic environment as a source of rhetorical potency increases.

Third, critics recognize that meaning in messages is not inherent—put there through the intentions of sources; rather, meaning is interpreted from every response to the message and its concomitants. Critics become aware of themselves as interpreters of events in which they are interested. Further, they are aware of the multitude of focuses possible. Any picture they present will be but one of several possibilities. Such a line of reasoning does not imply that any one interpretation is just as good as another; that question is not central to this tendency. Therefore critics must ask themselves what unique insights they can give into the phenomena that attract their concern. The result of their work must justify itself. In short, to borrow a phrase from the psycho-historian, Robert Jay Lifton, critics become aware of "an ever expanding use of the self as one's research instrument."[5]

The fourth reason is simply an amalgam of the second and third: The complex interaction of speaker, audience, and context over a period of time is what interests many critics today. Thus an extended political campaign or social movement may become a focus for their studies. Initially, critics attempted to adapt the traditional method to their expanded interest, but many soon began to look elsewhere for a more appropriate theory and a new perspective.

The break with faith in the traditional paradigm has been neither smooth nor complete. For several decades the field of rhetorical theory and criticism has seemed chaotic, with many specifying alternatives to the tradi-

[5] History and Human Survival, *New York, Random House, 1970, p. 5.*

tional methods while paying little attention to the general flow of other proposals. However, we believe that a few tendencies that might be called fresh perspectives have begun to emerge.

Roughly, we see the break with traditional criticism going in two directions. One direction, which we call experiential, will be described in this chapter; the other direction, which we call the way of the "New Rhetorics," is the subject of the next chapter.

Two remarks may be overly cautious, but we are wary enough to make them nonetheless. First, our groupings are rough. A finer-grained analysis might result in a somewhat different arrangement, but we believe that it is sensible to stress similarities and ignore differences at this juncture in the development of rhetorical criticism. Any tensions generated by such groupings may create a further evolution of critical thought and practice.

A second caution: We do not intend our ordering to suggest any priority of value between the two perspectives. In fact, arguments could be made that either could be handled first. As we pointed out at the beginning of this essay, one of the first strong challenges to the neo-Aristotelian hegemony was issued by the General Semanticists who offered a rather systematic alternative to which critics could repair with strong commitment. Again, the systematic and influential essay on the work of Kenneth Burke by Marie Hochmuth Nichols provided several generations of graduate students with an organizing vision and an attractive box of tools.[6] On the other hand, it is possible to argue that as critics began to reject the traditional perspective they shifted toward relying upon their judgmental use of historical and neo-Aristotelian methods before adopting a competing rhetorical theory as the basis for their criticism.[7] This view would describe experientialism as a temporary position prior to accepting a new rhetoric. This is not our position. Our preference for discussing the experiential perspective first is based on the observation that in the 1960s more critical essays followed this perspective, and it was not until the 1970s that the new rhetorics were employed with greater frequency.

Eclectic Approach

A fundamental urge that seems to mark what we are calling the experiential perspective is eclecticism, so we call one of the two strains within the

[6] "Kenneth Burke and the 'New Rhetoric,'" The Quarterly Journal of Speech, XXXVIII, 2 (April 1952), 133–44

[7] This shift away from traditional criticism is reflected in the third volume of A History and Criticism of American Public Address which was published twelve years after volumes one and two. Black's analysis of neo-Aristotelian criticism in Rhetorical Criticism, pp. 27–35, suggests in footnotes 27 through 31 that volumes one and two are more narrowly traditional than volume three. Further, Black uses Martin Maloney's criticism of Clarence Darrow from volume three as an example of a definite departure from the traditional perspective.

experiential perspective the "eclectic" approach. The other is a special sort of eclecticism which we call the "social reality" approach. As we label the two approaches we are aware that they are really only different in emphasis—they are not distinctly separate categories. Eclectic criticism generally assumes that reality is socially constructed, and social reality criticism is quite eclectic. Yet we find it useful to discuss two central tendencies in experiential criticism. The tendency to pick and choose from the parts of the culture that appeal to one is as ancient in Western thought as its records. Rudyard Kipling put the matter amusingly in these lines:

> When 'Omer smote 'is bloomin' lyre,
> He'd 'eard men sing by land an' sea;
> An' what he though 'e might require,
> 'E went an' took—the same as me!

Less graciously, many see the eclectic urge as akin to a lack of good sense rather than pilfering. The mind that is committed to the unity of thought as the highest mark of goodness is apt to object that one cannot dismember a system or a method, which, if worthwhile, is an organic whole, without obviating just that feature that makes it viable.

The conscientious eclectic is apt to be more interested in the immediacy of experience than the abstract integrity of a system or a method. Such a person will argue that all methods are but more or less complete sets of tools with instructions by which to build scaffoldings and framework. They will argue that when what is made is made, the tools are laid aside, the scaffolding torn down, and the framework absorbed. The eclectic approach stresses the critic's ability to assemble and absorb ways of working, subordinating these to the task at hand. The attitude of eclectic experientialism is well indicated by movie critic Pauline Kael:

> I believe we respond most and best to work in any art form [and to other experience as well] if we are pluralistic, flexible, relative in our judgments, if we are eclectic. But this does not mean a scrambling and confusion of systems. Eclecticism is the selection of the best standards and principles from various systems of ideas. It requires more orderliness to be a pluralist than to apply a single theory . . . criticism is exciting because you must use everything you are and everything you know that is relevant. . . .[8]

The ideal eclecticism may seldom be attained, but then ideals generally are striven for rather than reached.

In thinking about experientialism, the notion of *stance* seems especially vital. How does the critic stand vis à vis the critical task?

[8] I Lost It at the Movies, *Boston, Little, Brown, 1964, p. 309.*

Earlier we indicated that most critics developed shortcuts in the comprehensive traditional method outlined by Wichelns and that the complex, process nature of the rhetorical situation made critics realize that they could not achieve the objectivity assumed in traditional criticism. Some critics began to argue that they were starting with their perceptions of a rhetorical situation and were selecting from their rhetorical training and experience the analytic tools and standards appropriate for assessing any given rhetorical act. Black suggests this attitude toward criticism in the conclusion to *Rhetorical Criticism* when he says that rhetorical criticism is "the process by which, through the medium of language, a private attitude becomes a public faith." And when he closes the book, he states, "We simply do not know enough yet about rhetorical discourse to place our faith in systems [paradigms], and it is only through imaginative criticism that we are likely to learn more."[9]

In Black's context one could argue that "imaginative" is but another word for "stop-gap," arguing that when we know more we will be able to act differently. If that is a good gloss on the book published in 1965, then Black himself seems to retreat from that reasoning in the "Author's Foreword" to the 1978 reprinting of the book. In fact from that foreword one might glean a superb expression of the attitude that seems to us to drive the approach we are attempting to describe. Black says from his retrospective view, "Behind the composition of *Rhetorical Criticism: A Study of Method* was an idea that was too dimly understood by its author to possess the book as firmly as it would if the book were to be written now. That idea is that critical method is too personally expressive to be systematized."[10]

A number of critics have taken positions similar to the one Black later saw as his own. One of the first was Mark Klyn who wrote in his essay "Toward a Pluralistic Rhetorical Criticism" that "rhetorical criticism . . . only means 'intelligent writing about works of rhetoric'—or about works which are not 'rhetoric' in any formal sense but which can be illuminatingly treated from such a standpoint—in whatever way the critic can manage it. It does not imply a prescriptive mode of writing, any categorical structure of judgment, or even any judgmental necessity."[11]

It would be far from the spirit of either Klyn or Black to present them as saying, in effect, that one needs only to toss out all methods in order to see truth face-to-face. It seems possible that a critic could become objective by giving his allegiance to a method, and thus become a neutral manipulator of instruments (an ideal that is fast being taken as a myth in what we often call "the exact sciences"). This stance must be guarded against.

[9] *Black, p. 177.*
[10] *"Author's Foreword," p. x.*
[11] *Nilsen, p. 147.*

The result will not be subjectivism but intersubjectivism. Black cautions, "To say that criticism is a personal instrument is not to say that it is a private one. The critic does address a public and he thereby incurs public responsibilities."[12] A similar insight seems to us to motivate Wayne Brockriede in his often cited article "Rhetorical Criticism as Argument." He writes, "A person can function as critic either by passing judgment on the [concrete rhetorical] experience or by analyzing it for the sake of a better understanding of that experience or some more general concept or theory about such experience."[13] In any case, Brockriede holds, and we agree, that the eclectic critic should present an argument. The meaning of an argument, as Brockriede has made clear several times, is always open; the critic-as-arguer is an important concept if the experiential perspective is not to veer toward whim.

Given the triad of purposes that we posited in the essay that opened this book: description, interpretation, and evaluation, the experientialist critic will tend to absorb descriptive and evaluative tendencies toward the interpretive.[14] Another way to put the point is this: what the world is, is always problematic. Thus a critic examining rhetorical discourse will produce discourse, and if that discourse is argumentative, it will be rhetorical discourse. Thus there is a reflexiveness in the critical act; it seeks momentary closure in such a way as to remain open to further interpretation.

The point of view expressed in the last paragraph is essential to the experiential perspective. The key word, and the attitude that accompanies it, is probably essential to contemporary theorizing about rhetoric and to all the points of view toward criticism that we try to discuss and include throughout this book. The word, of course, is *act*. The significance for the term is well discussed in Malcolm Sillars's essay "Rhetoric as Act" in which he undertakes to elevate "rhetoric to the status of an act."[15] The separation of "facts" from "mere rhetoric" has plagued rhetorical thinking throughout

---

[12] *"Author's Foreword," p. xii.*

[13] *"Rhetorical Criticism as Argument,"* The Quarterly Journal of Speech, *LX, 2 (April 1974), 165.*

[14] *A pair of essays that will reward careful study are David L. Swanson's "A Reflective View of the Epistemology of Critical Inquiry,"* Communication Monographs, *XLIV, 3 (August 1977), 207–19; and "The Requirements of Critical Justification," XLIV, 4 (November 1977), 306–20. Swanson carefully labels his work "metacritical" rather than "critical," signaling that he is discussing the basis on which theorizing about criticism might proceed rather than setting forth critical theory. But in the first of these essays, he suggests that what we call "experiential criticism" bears a dim likeness to the outline that he tries to bring forward in bolder relief (p. 213). Throughout the second essay, it is clear that Swanson perfers criticism that interprets, but it is also clear that he believes that the act of interpretation as a critical act needs considerable explication in order to sort out the implications of various stances one may take toward it.*

[15] *"Rhetoric as Act," The Quarterly Journal of Speech, L, 3 (October 1964), 277–84.*

the history of Western culture. Taking the distinction at face value would seem to imply that the best criticism would be a sort of peeling away of the latter to reveal the former. Sillars's argument, widely accepted today among rhetorical theorists and critics, is that everything that the human can experience as meaningful is permeated with human participation, that is, what "means" does not stand apart from us but is embodied by us. To use the key word: acting in the world creates meaning.

Given this point of view, the experientialist stresses that the rhetorical critic is fundamentally a participant. The critic, then, must argue. Insofar as critical arguments constitute judgment (and, as we said, experientialists may subordinate that element of their critical statements), that judgment cannot be taken as objective measuring, but rather as an invitation to experience rhetorical phenomena as the critic has.

We suggest that experiential criticism may be seen as primarily eclectic. Yet within the flow of eclecticism, some critics give special attention to reality as socially constructed, and we label this tendency the social reality approach. But given the nature of this perspective, dividing the whole must be even more precarious than most acts of categorizing. If for no other reasons than momentary convenience and the conventions of book-making, some sort of divisions seem necessary.

We have chose two pairs of essays to illustrate eclecticism generally.

The first pair is by Lawrence W. Rosenfield. In his theoretical essay "The Anatomy of Critical Discourse," Rosenfield responds to the "ferment in rhetorical criticism" by challenging "critics to formulate more carefully their goals and methods." In his attempt at such a formulation, he creates a sort of matrix that may function as an open system for the critic as "expert-spectator" who has numerous methodological alternatives open to him. The guides he offers are of the sort that quicken the possibility of the scrupulous pluralism that Pauline Kael lauds.

In "A Case Study in Speech Criticism: The Nixon-Truman Analog," Rosenfield demonstrates one way in which the eclectic critic may work to maximize insights that hold promise of transfering from the case at hand to other cases. Although it seems to us that experiential criticism is not generally inclined toward "building theory," Rosenfield's work demonstrates that the possibility is not closed.

The second pair of essays illustrating eclecticism includes Wayne Brockriede's "Dimensions of the Concept of Rhetoric," and Wayne Brockriede and Robert L. Scott's "Khrushchev's 1959 American Tour." Brockriede's essay parallels Rosenfield's theoretical work in that it is concerned with a set of dimensions for the study of rhetorical communication. In the process of setting forth five assumptions implicit in establishing dimensions and their implications, he identifies major elements of a rhetorical act that an eclectic critic may treat, but he recognizes, at least implicitly, the uniqueness of each criticism and the importance of the critic's task in selecting a specific focus. The essay by Brockriede and Scott demonstrates one application of the pattern. Although tentativeness is common in the experiential perspective, perhaps even demanded by it, this essay is extraordinarily so; the authors seem to be at great pains to indicate alternatives and the possibility of different emphases in treating the skein of communications that make up Khrushchev's visit to the United States.

Social Reality Approach

Within the experiential perspective we notice a tendency that we label "social reality." In an earlier edition of this book we called this tendency the "sociocultural-psychological" approach. At that time we were responding to the tendency of critics to communicate an insight into a given rhetorical act through the use of a non-rhetorical concept or theory as the organizing feature of the criticism. Many rhetorical critics have used Freudian psychology or Hegelian dialectic as a basis for the organization and analysis of their criticism. We observed that critics developed an extended analogy, which they found heuristic in a given case. The two essays that we included to illustrate the theory and application of sociocultural-psychological criticism were Kenneth Burke's "Mind, Body, and the Unconscious"[16] and "The Rhetoric of Hitler's 'Battle.' "[17] We felt that they were excellent examples of Freudian theory and its application in rhetorical criticism. We still believe that these two essays will reward close study.

Criticism often seeks to explain some rhetorical act in terms of its economic, social, or psychological context. Some theorists and critics have extended their concern for context and process, which we identified earlier as a factor in the breakdown of the traditional perspective, to make it the starting point for what we label as the "social reality" approach to criticism. For these scholars, the seeming immediacy of economic, social, and psychological conditions, if probed, will reveal symbolic systems through which people interact to create these conditions.

We have already indicated that the experiential critic sees reality as intersubjective rather than objective. Social reality as a critical tendency focuses on and through this insight. Arthur Hastings, for example, identifies metaphor as central to one's view of reality: "We can say that every culture's view of reality is a metaphorical view which is structured into various frameworks of perception, values, beliefs, feelings and behaviors—all connected to language patterns."[18] Hastings goes further to argue that "a culture itself

[16] Lanaguage as Symbolic Action, *Berkeley, California, University of California Press, 1966.*
[17] The Philosophy of Literary Form, *Baton Rouge, Louisiana, Louisiana State University Press, 1941.*
[18] *"Metaphor in Rhetoric,"* Western Speech, *XXXIV, 3 (Summer 1970), 187.*

is a broad metaphor, and within a culture, subcultures have their own metaphors for relating to aspects of experience."[19]

In filling in the concept of the perspective, such essays as David Berg's "Rhetoric, Reality, and Mass Media" are useful in understanding rhetoric in the twentieth century as being indelibly imprinted by the mass media. As Berg writes, "The briefest reflection ought to verify sufficiently that, for most of us, the great issues of the day—Vietnam, Arab-Israeli confrontations, the national economy—are known only indirectly and usually via the mass media."[20] Berg concludes that "rhetorical criticism, consequently, if it is to remain a viable instrument for social analysis, must take cognizance of the media's influence on human communication behavior."[21]

Accepting this general view of rhetorical criticism, Ernest Bormann in "Fantasy and Rhetorical Vision: The Rhetorical Criticism of Social Reality" describes more specifically how a critic might proceed: "A critic can take the social reality contained in a rhetorical vision [an intersubjective world of common expectations and meanings created in speaker-audience transactions] which he has constructed from the concrete dramas developed in a body of discourse and examine the social relationships, the motives, the qualitative impact of the symbolic world as though it were the substance of social reality for those people who participated in the vision."[22]

Now our view of the "social reality" approach begins to take form. It is a rhetorical analysis of cultural artifacts, often associated with the mass media, in an effort to understand some aspect of the society-source-public relationship. This broadened approach to rhetorical criticism seems to us to be expressed tacitly in the report to the Wingspread Conference by its Committee on the Nature of Rhetorical Invention.[23]

The phrase and the tendency of "social reality" as basic to critical activity has been evident in a great deal of work appearing in professional journals in the 1970s. In "Reaffirmation and Subversion of the American Dream," Walter Fisher analyzed two interpretations of the American Dream [social reality] to explain the 1972 presidential election.[24] Moving from politics to film, Thomas Frentz and Thomas Farrell examined *The Exorcist* to discover a shift in society's approach to contemporary problems: "It [the film] at once crystalized America's disillusionment with Positivism and

[19] Ibid., *194*.

[20] *"Rhetoric, Reality, and Mass Media,"* The Quarterly Journal of Speech, *LVIII, 3 (October 1972)*, 255–56.

[21] Ibid., *263*.

[22] *"Fantasy and Rhetorical Vision: The Rhetorical Criticism of Social Reality,"* The Quarterly Journal of Speech, *LVIII, 4 (December 1972)*, 401.

[23] *Lloyd Bitzer and Edwin Black, eds.,* The Prospect of Rhetoric, *Englewood Cliffs, N.J., Prentice-Hall, 1971, pp. 228–33.*

[24] *"Reaffirmation and Subversion of the American Dream,"* The Quarterly Journal of Speech, *LIX, 2 (April 1973)*, 160–67.

at the same time reaffirmed transcendent Christian faith as the most viable means of coping with the problems of contemporary life."[25] More and more frequently, rhetorical critics are seeing television news not as a passive rendering but an active dramatizing. In "Television News: Reality and Research" Charles Bantz studied television as a creative source of symbols that participate in constructing what most of us are pleased to call "reality."[26] Richard Gregg's "The Rhetoric of Political Newscasting" interprets reality as fundamentally constructed by shared symbolic acts.[27]

Clearly the public speaking situation that dominated traditional rhetorical criticism no longer dominates experiential criticism, especially in its social reality mode. In that mode, the critic seeks whatever means seems appropriate for the purpose of examining the society-source-public relationship and often chooses data that have been generated through the electronic mass media.

"Social reality" criticism will be illustrated by two essays by Janice Hocker Rushing and Thomas Frentz. In their article "The Rhetoric of 'Rocky': A Social Value Model of Criticism," after establishing a reciprocal relationship between societal values and film, they present a five-phase social value model of rhetorical criticism designed to be "a heuristic vehicle for analyzing the political-rhetorical context. . . ." This "vehicle" seems to us to be well grounded in a mass of literature on rhetoric well absorbed by Rushing and Frentz; it is well pointed toward their task, although obviously they hope that it will be adaptable to other critics and other tasks. Their essay "The Rhetoric of 'Rocky': Part Two" applies the social value model to the film to gain insight into the pattern of social change reflected in that movie which became a cultural event by a startlingly strong acceptance by a broad public. The reciprocal relationship between the mass media and society allows the critic to gain significant insights into this relationship or into any of its elements by examining such rhetorical acts as films, television programs, or any other aspect of the popular culture.

Characteristics of the Experiential Perspective: A Summary

Rejecting, consciously or unconsciously, traditional rhetorical criticism, many critics have taken themselves and their own perceptions as a starting place. The critic takes the interactions of the socio-political-economic environment and the rhetorical forces as infinite and believes that the mind and experience must be drawn on creatively to form coherent views of the

[25] "Conversion of America's Consciousness: The Rhetoric of The Exorcist," The Quarterly Journal of Speech, LIX, 1 (February 1975), 40.
[26] "Television News: Reality and Research," Western Speech Communication, XXXIX, 2 (Spring 1975), 123–30.
[27] "The Rhetoric of Political Newscasting," Central States Speech Journal, XXVIII, 4 (Winter 1977), 221–37.

phenomena of discourse. Experientialism, of course, entails assumptions that are different from those of traditional rhetorical criticism.

First, from this perspective society is viewed as being in a continual state of process or change. Thus any statement critics make to describe or evaluate discourse must be quite tentative, since discourse is a part of the ever-shifting reality. Interested in relationships, experiential critics focus on what by definition are relative to point-of-view; the nature of social reality and a scrupulous appreciation of their own way of working tends to bring experientialists to assimilate descriptive and evaluative gestures to larger patterns of interpretation. To the traditional rhetorical critic, to judge justly was the preferred end of critical action (even though description was quite often the way-station achieved). To the experiential critic, to interpret openly in such a way as to encourage further individual interpretations seems preferable.

The tentativeness of experientialists goes well beyond normal scholarly reserve; they hold no theory as absolute and believe that all rules can be disregarded if the circumstances warrant. Experiential critics do not see process simply as a cycle, which would imply that the discarded principles can be reclaimed. Instead they are likely to see each day and its experiences as unique, requiring critical insight to understand the skein of passing phenomena and, especially, to act wisely in the face of changing circumstances.

Second, experiential critics, in contrast to traditional critics, tend to believe that an infinite number of concepts, strategies, and postures are available for the study of the rhetorical act; and they believe that a close interaction between the critic and the act itself is necessary for the selection of the correct concepts, strategies, and postures in given instances. As the world is a state of process that must be lived to be real, so is rhetorical theory. Thus fresh concepts and strategies, as well as different combinations of the old, must evolve if the critic is to work well.

A third assumption characteristic of the experiential critic follows from understanding both rhetoric and criticism as being interpretations of phenomena. This means that any critical vocabulary, in fact, any system of symbolizing, is arbitrarily established and does not reflect merely an external reality. Experiential critics are as likely as any others to be concerned about maintaining a close word-thought-thing relationship, because only through language can they communicate their interpretations. However, they are especially sensitive to the impact that the arbitrary process of selecting a symbol can have on the perceptive process. The word-thought-thing relationship is reciprocal. Not only does the referent influence the selection of the word but the word influences the understanding of what is referred to. Thus, the experiential critic is likely to stress the arbitrary nature of all interpretations of phenomena.

Clearly, the experiential stance obligates critics to be eclectic in their methods. That stance, however eclectic, does function within the compass of an orientation and a set of assumptions. That compass is a rough consensus. So let us summarize the experiential perspective in the three part manner that we are summarizing each of the perspectives that form the outline of this book:

1. Orientation. No single element or rhetorical principle can be assumed as the starting point for criticism. Thus, the critic, depending on his or her sensitivity and knowledge, must make the fundamental choice of emphasis.

2. Assumptions.

a. Society is in a continual state of process.

b. An infinite combination of concepts, strategies, and postures are available for the study of public discourse.

c. Any system of categorizing is arbitrary and does not accurately reflect an assumed external reality for extended periods of time.

3. Consensus. No special pattern exists for the study of public discourse. Therefore, discourse must continually be studied afresh.

We have argued that what we call experiential criticism represents a break from the traditional paradigm, and we believe that the essays that follow will help clarify the nature and potentialities of the experiential perspective. In chapter four we shall explain and illustrate with further essays another direction in the break of faith in the traditional paradigm.

THE ECLECTIC APPROACH

The Anatomy of Critical Discourse
by Lawrence W. Rosenfield

The recent ferment in rhetorical criticism generated by Professor Black's provocative *Rhetorical Criticism: A Study in Method* challenges critics to formulate more carefully their goals and methods. The attempt to raise critical procedures from an *ad hoc* status to something more systematic is not new,[1] but at least among rhetorical critics, it seems today to hold a place of special interest.

The discussion of some of the logical features of criticism contained in this essay responds to the call for a more formal understanding of the critical act. It is an effort to abstract the implicit assumptions of those whom we would clearly want to call critics, to consider the ways in which it would make sense for an ordinary but responsible user of the English language to talk about the behavior of critics and about their products (criticism).

It is the contention of this essay that criticism is most sensibly conceived of as a special form of reason-giving discourse. The nature of reason-giving in criticism becomes intelligible if we treat four particular questions concerning criticism: (1) What do we commonly mean when we call someone a "critic"? (2) What features of criticism distinguish it from other intellectual endeavors? (3) What kinds of questions does criticism seek to answer? (4) By what modalities (formulae) are reasons produced in criticism? Answers to these four questions, and hence support for the central assertion, constitute the bulk of this study.[2] Let us begin by raising the first question and asking of whom we are talking when we speak of "the critic."

Whenever the word "critic" comes up in conversation, a variety of images is liable to come to mind. Some think of the book reviewer or the drama critic for a newspaper. Others, who equate "critic" with "carper," are reminded of a sour, negative individual who cannot be pleased. Still others (particularly if they are conversant with too many

From *Speech Monographs*, XXV, 1 (March 1968), 50–69. Used by permission of the author and the Speech Communication Association. Dr. Rosenfield is professor of speech at Hunter College, New York.

[1] Cf. L. H. Levy, Psychological Interpretation *(New York, 1963), p. 30;* R. McKeon, "The Philosophic Bases of Art and Criticism," Critics and Criticism, Ancient and Modern, *ed. R. S. Crane (Chicago, 1952), pp. 147–175;* L. Thonssen and A. C. Baird, Speech Criticism *(New York, 1948).*

[2] *The reader should beware of confusing the remarks made in this essay about the nature of criticism with handbook directions on how to do criticism or with empirical descriptions of how criticism is* done. *The aim here is simply to offer a topology which suggests the characteristic formal relationships normally encountered by critics.*

Master's theses in public address) may imagine that "the speech critic" is a kind of reporter of public address in history.[3] Clearly, common usage has made the term so vague as to be practically meaningless. Is it possible to restrict the meaning of "critic" by adopting semantic boundaries which enable us to distinguish the legitimate critics from those for whom the label represents simply encomium (or invective)? To do so we would need to ascertain what actions we may ordinarily expect of one who is fulfilling the office of critic. If we investigate what I have chosen to call the "critical posture," or the stance habitually assumed by one who is fulfilling the logical requirements of critic, we can reach some consensus as to the behavior of the critic; we will then be in a better position to understand "criticism" itself. In order to clarify what is meant here, it may be helpful to draw a rough comparison between events discussed by critics and those events we commonly call "athletic." We shall discover that in the main the critical posture resembles the "spectator" half of an agent-spectator dichotomy.[4]

First of all, it is easy enough to understand that some sporting events are not only played but are observed as well—by individuals we call "spectators." And it is common that these spectators, if they are genuine fans, do more than simply purchase a ticket of admission so that they may sit in proximity to the athletic activity. They will also devote a certain time and effort to contemplating and discussing the events they observe. That is to say, the role of the spectator often entails reflection and communication about the athletic events. For instance, the baseball fan may attend winter Hot Stove meetings where particular plays will be recalled and mulled over; likewise, the Monday Morning Quarterbacks derive a certain satisfaction from assembling to debunk the maneuvers executed in recent football games.

This same quality of spectatorship seems to be common among those whom we might call fans of aesthetic events, whether their particular "sport" be painting or public communication.[5] One characteristic

[3] Cf. E. G. Bormann, Theory and Research in the Communicative Arts (New York, 1965), pp. 227–238, for a discussion of the confusion which often arises between the role of historian and that of critic.

[4] Cf. N. Smart, "Sense and Reference in Aesthetics," British Journal of Aesthetics, III (October 1963), 363–366; L. W. Beck, "Agent, Actor, Spectator and Critic," The Monist, XLIX (April 1965), 167–182; D. Van de Vate, Jr., "Disagreement as a Dramatic Event," The Monist, XLIX (April 1965), 248–261.

[5] Nothing esoteric is meant by "aesthetic." I intend only to convey the notion that the logical conditions mentioned here apply to the full range of interests open to the critic: dramatic productions, musical performances, traditional "fine art," as well as to orations and political dialogues. "Aesthetics" is derived from the Greek aisthetikos (of sense perception), and I use the term to suggest that the phenomena which provoke discussion by spectators are of the order which manifest themselves to the perceptions.

of the rhetorical critic, then, is his interest in observing and discussing instances of rhetorical discourse, be they speeches, essays, or advertisements, from the vantage of the spectator.

Another characteristic which critics share with at least some sports fans is that both show an appreciation for the execution of the event or object.[6] The involvement of some fans is limited to being loyal followers of a favorite team; they are mainly concerned to share in the exaltation of the home team's victories. For such "part-time" fans, the outcome of a contest is of paramount interest. True enthusiasts, however, seldom gather merely to report the results of games; they do not confine their comments to the immediate, utilitarian aspects of athletic events. Such fans derive satisfaction from watching a film replay of a game whose final score they already know, a satisfaction we may label as appreciation. This appreciation, whether in the fan or the critic, is not inherently related to enthusiasm or suspense over outcome.

A third similarity between the posture of the critic and that of the athletic fan is that heightened appreciation (and hence increased satisfaction or pleasure) accompanies increased knowledge of the events or objects observed. The football fan who knows more than the formal rules of the game (e.g., understands the tactics of blocking assignments and the relative merits of the T-formation and the single wing) derives a satisfaction from second-guessing the coach which the less informed "rooter for the home team" misses. In other words, consciousness of artistic principles contributes to appreciation.

A final commonality follows from the notion of heightened appreciation. Some spectators, because of especially fine training or acute sensitivity, attain the status of "experts." In the athletic sphere such persons are often hired to act as sportscasters and sports-writers, and in the aesthetic realm they may be called upon to act as "critics" in giving reviews of books, plays, and the like. However, their titles do not derive from the fact that they are appointed or paid to perform these tasks. Rather, it is because of their competence that they are asked to assume the critic's office. An expert can be an amateur and still be a fine sports analyst or critic. What matters is exceptional understanding. Accordingly, "critical posture" refers to *the capacity a person has to act as an expert commentator,* and the critic, if he is nothing else, must be one who is capable of fulfilling this role.

Simple *capacity* to render commentary is not yet criticism. The

---

[6] *The notion of execution should not be confused with the idea of intent. The football pass may have been an accident and still have been well executed. "Skill in execution" is not synonymous with "doing what the creator intended." Cf. M. Eshleman, "Aesthetic Experience, The Aesthetic Object and Criticism,"* The Monist, *L (April 1966), 281–291.*

expert-spectator who relishes the events he observes but does not relate his appreciation to others is not a critic, for "criticism" normally refers to the critic's verbal commentary on the event. Criticism is therefore the special variety of discourse which results when a person who has adopted a critical posture makes assertions, i.e., statements by an expert about "the way things are."[7] How then may we distinguish critical discourse from the general range of assertive discourse?

One procedure would be to examine several instances of discourse which we would definitely wish to call criticism and seek to discover its typical features. I refer the reader to two short essays dealing with a speech delivered by General Douglas MacArthur to a joint session of Congress (and through direct broadcast, to the nation) on April 19, 1951. The first essay is by journalist Richard Rovere, the second by Herbert Wichelns, a professor of speech.[8] Let them represent clear cases of discourse we would ordinarily consider rhetorical criticism. What characteristics make them intuitively admissible as criticism?

Richard H. Rovere

As a literary critic and political observer, I view the speech solely from the literary and political points of view. I am not qualified to criticize oratory or elocution.

As a piece of composition, the speech seemed to me a good deal but not a great deal better than the general run of public prose in the United States today. MacArthur has eloquence of a kind, but it strikes me as a rather coarse eloquence. He never shades his meanings, never introduces a note of humor, never gives the feeling that he is one man, only one, addressing himself to other men. His language is never flat and bloodless; neither is it flabby and loose-jointed, as so much writing of this sort is. But to me there is rather a fetid air about it. It does not leave me with the impression that a cool and candid mind has been at

---

[7] This places literary and rhetorical critics in the peculiar position of producing verbal objects as comment on other verbal objects (e.g., novels, plays, speeches, etc.), so that both types of critic are in fact engaged in producing discourse about discourse. Cf. A. Hillbruner, "Criticism as Persuasion," The Southern Speech Journal, XXXVIII (Summer 1963), 260–267; E. Black, "Moral Values and Rhetorical Criticism," lecture delivered at University of Wisconsin, July 12, 1965; Thonssen and Baird, pp. 13–14.

[8] Both essays are drawn from F. W. Haberman, "General MacArthur's Speech: A Symposium of Critical Comment," Quarterly Journal of Speech, XXXVII (October 1951), 321–331. They are reprinted in C. C. Arnold, D. Ehninger, and J. C. Gerber, The Speaker's Resource Book (Chicago, 1961), pp. 283–286. Cf. also P. Wylie, "Medievalism and the MacArthurian Legend," ibid., XXXVII (December 1951), 473–478; P. R. Beall, "Viper-Crusher Turns Dragon-Slayer," ibid., XXXVIII (February 1952), 51–56; K. R. Wallace, "On the Criticism of the MacArthur Speech," ibid., XXXIX (February 1953), 69–74; M. H. Nichols, Rhetoric and Criticism (Baton Rouge, La., 1963), pp. 68–69.

work on difficult matters of universal concern. Instead, it leaves me with the impression that a closed and in a sense a rather frantic mind has been at work to the end of making an appeal to history—not neglecting to use any of the rulebook hints on how to do it. I think not of history but of second-rate historian as I read the speech.

Form and content are, if not inseparable, very closely related. Politically, MacArthur's speech seemed extremely weak to me. This is not, I think, because I am opposed to his politics; I believe he could have made out a much stronger case for himself. But he never came to grips with the issues. For example, he wanted to have it that he was being persecuted for "entertaining" his particular views. This, of course, is rubbish. He got into trouble not for the political and military views he entertained (no doubt he was right in saying they were entertained by many of his colleagues) but for seeking to usurp the diplomatic function. He never sought to answer the objections to his position that rest on political and economic facts recognized by both sides; that if we followed him, we would be abandoned by several allies; that if Russia invaded Europe, which he has admitted might be an early consequence of his policy, the industrial balance would favor the Communist world; that, like it or not, American power does have its limitations. Mac-Arthur's policy may be sounder than Truman's. But the contention cannot be sustained without facing these stubborn facts about the world today. MacArthur, in his speech, never faced them.

Herbert A. Wichelns

Demosthenes had the problem too; how much to spell out, how formal and explicit to make his proposals. At times Demosthenes judged it best not to "make a motion" but merely to offer comment and advice at large. MacArthur made a similar choice. In the main he chose not to debate, in the sense of formulating proposals and defending them in full. Instead he indicated the heads for debate, leaving no doubt as to the direction of his policy. Definite proposals were few, and sharply limited to Formosa and Korea. Supporting reasons were very sparingly given, and sometimes confined to bare assertions (as on the extent of China's present military commitment and Russia's probable course). But the call for a harder and more aggressive policy is plain from the beginning ("no greater expression of defeatism"). The chief support for that policy is neither logical argument nor emotional appeal, but the self-portrait of the speaker as conveyed by the speech.

It is an arresting portrait. Certain colors are of course mandatory. The speaker respects Congress and the power of this nation for good in the world. He is free from partisanship or personal rancor. He sympathizes with the South Koreans and with his embattled troops. He prefers victory to appeasement. He seeks only his country's good. He hates war, has long hated it. If these strokes are conventional, they take little time, except for the last, on which the speaker feels he must defend himself.

More subtle characterizing strokes are found in the "brief insight into the surrounding area" which forms a good half of the speech. Here the General swiftly surveys the nature of the revolution in Asia, the island-frontier concept and Formosa's place in the island-chain, the imperialistic character of the Chinese communities, the regeneration of Japan under his auspices, the outlook for the Philippines, and the present government of Formosa. All this before reaching Korea. Most of these passages have no argumentative force. But all together they set up for us the image of a leader of global vision, comprehending in his gaze nations, races, continents. The tone is firmest on Japan ("I know of no nation more serene, orderly and industrious"), least sure on the Philippines, but always positive.

Rarely indeed have the American people heard a speech so strong in the tone of personal authority. "While I was not consulted . . . that decision . . . proved a sound one." "Their last words to me"—it is the Korean people with whom the General has been talking. "My soldiers." The conduct of "your fighting sons" receives a sentence. A paragraph follows on the General's labors and anxieties on their behalf. The pace at which the thought moves, too, is proconsular; this is no fireside chat. Illustration and amplification are sparingly used; the consciously simple vocabulary of the home-grown politician is rejected. The housewife who "understood every word" was mistaken; she missed on epicenter and recrudescence and some others. But having by the fanfare been jarred into full attention, she understood quite well both the main proposition of the speech—a harder policy—and the main support offered—the picture of a masterful man of unique experience and global outlook, wearing authority as to the manner born.

One feature these comments display, which is often noted as an essential of critical discourse, is that both contain verdicts (sometimes called judgments or evaluations). Not all assertive discourse contains appraisal as criticism does. Scientific reports, for instance, display an exploratory impulse rather than an evaluative one.[9] Nor is this to say that critical essays must reach a settled and final verdict, for clearly Wichelns is at pains to avoid assessing MacArthur's speech as good or bad. But criticism does eventuate in, or at least has as an ultimate objective, assessment. Professor Black has put it most succinctly:

[9] Bormann, pp. 227–229; E. Black, Rhetorical Criticism: A Study in Method (New York, 1965), p. 4.

*At the culmination of the critical process is the evaluation of the dis-
course or of its author; a comprehensive judgment which, in the best of
criticism, is the fruit of patient exegesis. . . . Even the purely technical
objective of understanding how a discourse works carries the assumption that it does work, and that assumption is an assessment. Similarly,
to understand why a thing has failed is at least to suspect that it has
failed, and that suspicion is an assessment. There is, then, no criticism
without appraisal; there is no "neutral" criticism. One critic's judgment
may be absolute and dogmatic, another's tentative and barely com-
mital; but however faint the judicial element in criticism may become,
it abides.*[10]

If Black is correct, we ought seldom to find a critic engaging in description of a rhetorical event for its own sake; and if we do, we ought
perhaps proceed most cautiously in determining whether to label the
product "criticism."[11]

Clearly our two samples of criticism meet the criterion of making assessments. Rovere is explicit:

*. . . the speech seemed . . . a good deal but not a great deal bet-
ter than the general run of public prose . . . there is a rather fetid air
about it. . . . Politically [the] speech seemed extremely weak. . . .*

Wichelns' appraisal is more complex. Avoiding any "good-bad" evaluation, he invites us to accept his verdict on how the speech was executed (i.e., what made it work as it did). In Wichelns' judgment the
speech called for a harder policy and this call was supported by the
speaker's self-portrait. Both Rovere and Wichelns present us with
settled, though not necessarily final or definitive, assertions as to the
character and/or worth of the speech; their critical comments betray
momentary terminations (benchmarks) in their thought processes, terminations which are expressed in the form of verdicts.

Once we grant that the assertive discourse of criticism strives for
appraisal, we should concurrently examine the "reasons" offered to

---

[10] Black, *"Moral Values. . . ."* Cf. Hillbruner, pp. 264–266; P. W. Taylor,
Normative Discourse (*Englewood Cliffs, N.J., 1961*), p. 52; W. Righter, Logic and
Criticism (*New York, 1963*), pp. vii–3; Bormann, p. 229; J. Holloway, "Symposium: Distinctive Features of Arguments Used in Criticism of the Arts," Proceedings of the Aristotelian Society (*supplement*), XXIII (1949), 173.

[11] A. Isenberg, "Critical Communication," Philosophical Review, LVIII (April
1949) 331. See also the following articles in The Monist, L (April 1966): M.
Scriven, "The Objectivity of Aesthetic Evaluation," 159–187; H. Osborne, "Reasons and Description in Criticism," 204–212; H. Morris-Jones, "The Logic of
Criticism," 213–221; P. Wilson, "The Need to Justify," 267–280.

justify the verdicts. The bulk of both critical essays consists of reasons justifying the judgments. Notice, for example, Wichelns' assertion that MacArthur's main form of proof was his own self-portrait. It is supported by three contentions: that it was an arresting portrait, employing both "mandatory colors" and "subtle . . . strokes"; that the speech otherwise is lacking in argument and abounding in assertion; and that the speech was couched in the language of personal authority. From these Wichelns is enabled to conclude that the speech offered "the picture of a masterful man of unique and global outlook" as support for MacArthur's claims.

Dealing as we are with evaluative discourse, it is only natural to speculate further about the relationship linking verdicts and reasons. Imagine for instance the following situation: a friend says, "I read the novel *Tom Jones* last week." You treat this statement as a factual report. But were your friend to co-append, "It struck me as a rather shallow book," there is an immediate change in conditions. You may then decide to treat the combined statements as criticism, with the second sentence serving as an appraisal and the first now transformed from a report into part of the justification for the judgment. Furthermore, it would be extremely odd if your friend were to utter the second statement and at the same time deny having ever read the novel, having had any contact with anyone who had read it, or having had access to any critical comments about it. Obviously, we expect a critical verdict to be in some way conditional upon the reasons offered in its support. We are not yet in a position to see why reasons are expected or to determine how they function as support, but that they do so function to make criticism a reason-giving activity is evident.[12]

A valuable first step in grasping the logical structure underlying this conditional relation of reasons-and-verdict is to realize that criticism is an exercise in forensic reasoning. The critic's commentary is analogous to that of the trial lawyer who bases claims as to the proper verdict in a case on his interpretation of the facts in the light of some legal code. What tactics are open to the legal advocate? He may in some circumstances accept a set of legal standards (canons or laws) and apply them rigorously to the facts in the case. He may on the other hand feel

---

[12] *Let us momentarily disregard a related problem, whether one's verdicts must follow inevitably from one's reasons, as in a valid syllogism, or whether there is some looser connection between the evaluations and the justificatory reasons, perhaps a relation of appropriateness instead of one of correctness. What matters here is that both components are inseparable parts of the critic's assertions, no matter what their bearing on each other. Cf. Righter, pp. 74–84; M. Weitz, "Reasons in Criticism," Journal of Aesthetics and Art Criticism, XX (Summer 1962), 427–437; B. C. Heyl, "The Critic's Reasons," ibid., XVI (Winter 1957), 169–179.*

that the laws as they are commonly interpreted hurt his case. In that event he could propose a new interpretation of the laws which does more justice to the position he is defending; or if his mind functions after the fashion of an Erskine, he could seek to "make law" by questioning the established norms and attempting either to amend them or to substitute a code of his own choosing as the standard of evaluation. Again, some circumstances may be such that the counsel will accept a verdict contrary to his position but then go on to try to mitigate the thrust of the verdict by showing how special factors in the case deserve attention. Or perhaps there is a conflict in the legal code such as a contradiction between two laws. In the case of such an overlap, the advocate may argue for the priority of one law over another. In each of these instances the essential forensic tactic is to measure facts or observations against a code or canon.

A similar juxtapositioning of observations and normative standards constitutes the essence of critical activity:

The code may be the law of the land, the theory of probabilities, the standards of historical research, the canons of artistic excellence [my italics], or their own standards for distinguishing truth from error. Whoever judges in these ways, then, needs two distinct kinds of knowledge: (1) knowledge about the facts or events he is to judge and (2) knowledge about the standards against which he is to measure the facts or events.[13]

We may thus expect that reasons offered in critical discourse will lay claim to being the product of a "measurement" (comparison of data observed and norm). This does not mean that the verdict need follow inevitably from the comparison, only that it will claim such a juxtapositioning as a warrant for its own worth.

If the notion of forensic reasoning as the foundation of critical strategy is plausible, we have further grounds for rejecting some evaluations which are offered as specimens of criticism. Though tradition recognizes as "movie reviews" the placement of stars next to film titles in newspapers (four stars equivalent to "excellent," one star meaning "terrible"), we need not accept such markings as criticism (or if we do, as more than decapitated criticism). Again, what should one make of an argument which runs, "I feel that MacArthur's speech was unsatisfactory because the General once insulted me"? Such a remark is ordinarily disturbing. In part this is because the comment does not

[13] J. F. Wilson and C. C. Arnold, Public Speaking as a Liberal Art (Boston, 1964), p. 97. Cf. Weitz; Isenberg, pp. 330–335; Taylor, pp. 9–14.

fulfill forensic requirements: the reason offered, although it explains why the commentator holds the position he does, is not admissible as a justification for the verdict. In this case the norm (such as it is) violates the critical posture, and there is in addition a failure to juxtapose the norm to facts about the speech.

Observe how Wichelns illustrates the forensic pattern. He opens his essay by distinguishing between speeches which offer advice and those which join a debate. He thereby establishes the norm. He then spends the remainder of his first paragraph drawing attention to those facts about the speech which place it in the category of speeches of advice. In his next paragraph Wichelns formulates the principle that some remarks are mandatory on this kind of occasion—and then observes the extent to which MacArthur met those demands. In his third paragraph the critic implies that some rhetorical tactics reveal a proconsular image and then presents facts which enable him to ascribe such an image to MacArthur. The forensic pattern is evident throughout Wichelns' essay.

But the notion of forensic reasoning highlights one curious feature of criticism: although both norms and observations are logically essential, they need not be expressed separately. This aspect of criticism is illustrated in the dialogue concerning *Tom Jones*. When your friend justifies his evaluation of the novel with "I read the novel last week," where is the standard of judgment? Clearly, if it exists at all it is only implicit. One might suspect that your friend really meant, "I read the novel, and it did not measure up to my taste in novels," but that would only be speculation. Or take Rovere as a case in point. True, he announces at the outset that his standards will be "literary" and "political" ones. But then he goes on to call MacArthur's eloquence "coarse" and to say that MacArthur's language is neither "flat and bloodless" nor "flabby and loose-jointed." Are these observations or verdicts? And what are Rovere's standards for eloquence? Apparently, Rovere demands that the reader accept the existence and the excellence of the norms on faith. The norms do not appear in the criticism, though they are presupposed by Rovere's comments.

This fusion of otherwise distinct components is not an accident of composition. When Rovere condemns MacArthur's prose for its unshaded meanings, its lack of humor, its fetid language, is he hypothesizing that "the occurrence of these three elements results in coarse eloquence" after the fashion of the experimental scientists? Or is he calling to attention these particular observable features which, in these particular rhetorical circumstances, lend an air of coarseness to this particular speech? Rovere is obviously affirming his possession of standards of eloquence; but the application of the standards to a particular aesthetic event is, as we shall discover when we treat the modalities of analysis, far more complex than the measurement of the length of a metal pipe. In aesthetic judgments the standards often defy expression as general propositions for any but the most gross (and hence, trivial) features. And the standards applied are bound to the particulars of the single event because the events are too diverse and complicated to be comprehended by universal precepts. Such is the case of Rovere seeking to illuminate the coarseness of MacArthur's prose. He would be unable to provide general rubrics for what makes prose coarse because too many factors enter in; but he is able to account for the "coarse eloquence" in this case, and he does so.[14]

To answer what features of criticism distinguish it from other types of reason-giving discourse, we have so far maintained that the term "criticism" is most sensibly reserved for that assertive discourse produced by expert-spectators whose judgments as to the execution of (in this case) rhetorical phenomena are supported by forensic arguments. We may now consider the two remaining questions posed at the beginning of this essay. Let us for present purposes exclude from attention questions concerning the goals of rhetorical criticism or the origin and validity of rhetorical canons, interesting as these questions may be. In this essay we shall take for granted that the rhetorical critic possesses certain a priori objectives; he engages in the critical act for the sake of some preestablished end(s) which need not be specified here. We shall also presume that if called upon to do so, the critic could vindicate by means extrinsic to the realm of criticism (e.g., by metaphysical justification of some sort) his adoption of whatever rhetorical concepts he employs in his criticism.[15] Our interest is not in why he acts and believes as he does, but in how he exploits the critical opportunities available to him.

We are consequently obliged to examine the array of methodological options open to the rhetorical critic. At least two method-related questions invariably confront the critic in the exercise of his office: 1) what shall be the major focus of his critical analysis (what data will he find primarily relevant)? 2) what sorts of measurements or readings shall he take on the rhetorical transactions under investigation (in what fashion shall he transpose and describe the data he chooses to fix upon)? How he elects to answer these questions will in part influence both the nature and function of the critical reasons produced. Let us first ad-

[14] Righter, p. 22.

[15] Cf. Taylor, pp. 128–138; McKeon, pp. 489–490; K. Burke, A Grammar of Motives (New York, 1945), p. 472; E. Olson, "The Poetic Method in Aristotle: Its Powers and Limitations," Aristotle's Poetics and English Literature, ed. E. Olson (Chicago, 1965), pp. 187–191.

dress ourselves to the alternative foci open to the critic of "public address."

If we schematize an instance of public communication encountered by the critic, we intuitively recognize four gross variables: the source(s) or creator(s) of the message, the message itself, the context or environment in which the message is received (including both the receivers and the social "landscape" which spawns the message), and the critic himself (who, especially in the study of public address of the past, is in a sense a unique receiver). For the sake of convenience, let us label the variables "S" (source), "M" (message), "E" (environment), and "C" (critic). Obviously, in a total interpretation of the communicative act all four variables are relevant. But equally obvious from past critical practice, such all-encompassing analysis will be rare if not impossible for the single critic. Perhaps the two most thoroughly examined messages in the English language are Shakespeare's *Hamlet* and Lincoln's *Gettysburg Address;* the very fact that criticism of these two is not yet exhausted attests to the impracticality of completely enveloping one verbal act with another. We are therefore forced to recognize that critics will have to concentrate on some permutation of the four variables as a means of making their critical tasks manageable.

For the rhetorical critic the one indispensable factor is M, the message. Exclusive concern for S, the source, is the biographer's business; study of E, the environment, is the historian's; studies relating speakers to audience apart from the substance of the message (as in explorations of the role of status or leadership in public affairs) are performed mainly by sociologists. The rhetorical critic sees the entire communicative transaction as somehow "suspended" from the language of the message under examination. For the rhetorical critic the verbal utterance constitutes a kind of linguistic architecture which supports and gives form to the total rhetorical act. In this belief the critic differs from the historian and sociologist, who may choose to treat the verbal factors as mere artifacts of the event. The rhetorical critic not only fastens his observation to M; he does so in the conviction that the message is fundamental to an appreciation of the entire event.[16]

The critic therefore occupies himself with some combination of variables which focus on the message: S-M, M-E, M-C, S-M-E, S-M-C, or M-E-C. These are combinations which constitute genuine critical options. It is not the critic's task to inspect these variables in isolation; neither is it sufficient for him to report that they all converged in a particular instance of public discourse.

Consider first the nature of the M-C focus, which represents an un-

[16] Cf. T. Clevenger, Jr., "Research Opportunities in Speech," Introduction to the Field of Speech, *ed. R. F. Reid (Chicago, 1965), pp. 222–224.*

ashamedly introspectionist stance. This focus seeks to gauge the critic's personal response to the aesthetic object.[17] The critic who directs his attention to the M-C relationship will conceive of himself as a kind of sensitive instrument, and his analysis will be comprised primarily of reports of his own reactions to the work apart from any impact the work may have had on any particular "public." In this vein, Anatole France remarked that the good critic:

> . . . is he who relates the adventures of his soul among masterpieces. . . . The truth is that one never gets out of oneself.[18]

Rovere's commentary suggests that he adopted a focus such as the one described by France.

The M-C orientation grounds its validation on the premise that communication is essentially a unique event, a private transaction between message and receiver which can never be known to a third party. The critic is simply one more receiver of the message, albeit more sensitive than the typical, untrained receiver. If one accepts the notion that critical interpretation is so uniquely personal, it then follows that no interpretation can expect to be more than a justification of the critic's own state of mind as he responds to the aesthetic object.

And if communication is inherently a private matter, then one's faith in the critic's explication and overall taste constitutes at least as important a means of support for the verdicts offered as do the critic's stated reasons for his evaluation. Hence, in the case of Rovere, we need to trust his sensitivity as much as we need to be persuaded by his analysis of the prose. It is even possible to imagine that the primary function served by reasons submitted by an observer with the M-C focus is to demonstrate to a reader the observer's competence as a critic, to "exhibit his credentials," to make authoritative judgments.[19]

---

[17] Cf. Heyl, p. 170; R. Wellek and A. Warren, The Theory of Literature (New York, 1949); W. Embler, "The Language of Criticism," Etc., XXII (September 1965), 261–277. This cryptic account is obviously not the entire story. The critic is not privileged simply to report his pleasure and/or pain on confronting the discourse. He is in some manner obligated to explain how and why the work justifies his particular response. It is also important to note that contemporary literary critics who claim to focus entirely on the work itself are in fact often employing the M-C paradigm; their failure to recognize the implications of their critical orientation results occasionally in rather odd exigeses.

[18] Anatole France, "The Literary Life," The Book of Modern Criticism, trans. and ed. L. Lewisohn (New York, 1919), pp. 1–3. Cf. I. A. Richards, Principles of Literary Criticism (New York, 1925), pp. 5–24.

[19] Embler, p. 265; M. Beardsley, Aesthetics: Problems in the Philosophy of Criticism (New York, 1958), pp. 129–134.

Such a conception of M-C analysis may account for the propensity of prominent critics to set forth lists of their favorite books, or of the best plays or speeches of all time. Having achieved eminence, they need no longer justify their selections, but are able to telescope or even abort their arguments in favor of short explications of why a particular book, play, or novel pleased them personally.

The next three foci are related to each other in their denial of an introspectionist critical stance and their advocacy of greater detachment. The S-M focus concentrates on understanding discourse as an expression of its creator. Most often the critic attempts to trace out the creative process by which the speaker externalized and structured the feelings, thoughts, and experiences contained within himself. The relation of source to message has prompted two general schools of criticism. One (which actually concentrates on the S$\rightarrow$M relationship) seeks to account for the rhetor's behavior as a function of the factors which influenced him: his education, the books he read, the persons who inspired him, and the like.[20] The other variation of the S-M focus, S$\leftarrow$M, is best typified by neo-Freudian critics who treat the aesthetic event as symptomatic of the artist's personal life and psychodynamics. The critic, in other words, acts as a kind of lay psychoanalyst, using the message as a key to understanding and evaluating the creator of the message.[21]

The M-E focus also incorporates two divergent streams of critical practice. In the one instance (M$\leftarrow$E), "environment" is interpreted broadly (as by historians and literary critics) to encompass the age and the civilization in which the message originated. The historian of ideas attempts to set the historical background in which particular works or clusters of works were produced, showing how the messages are themselves a reflection of their era. This emphasis finds its rationale in the assumption that to the extent that an aesthetic event can be considered typical of its age it will provide valuable insight into the intel-

[20] Cf. M. H. Abrams, The Mirror and the Lamp: Romantic Tradition (New York, 1953), pp. 21–25; J. Thorp, "The Aesthetics of Textual Critcism," PMLA, LXXX (December 1965), 465–482; L. D. Reid, "Gladstone's Training as a Speaker," The Quarterly Journal of Speech, XL (December 1954), 373–380; L. Crocker, "The Rhetorical Training of Henry Ward Beecher," The Quarterly Journal of Speech, XIX (February 1933), 18–24.

[21] Cf. H. D. Duncan, Communication and Social Order (New York, 1962), pp. 3–16; M. Maloney, "Clarence Darrow," in A History and Criticism of American Public Address, ed. M. K. Hochmuth, III (New York, 1955), 262–312; H. M. Ruitenbeek (ed.), Psychoanalysis and Literature (New York, 1964); N. Kiell (ed.), Psychological Studies of Famous Americans (New York, 1964); W. S. Scott, Five Approaches of Literary Criticism (New York, 1962), pp. 69–73; R. L. Bushman, "On the Uses of Psychology: Conflict and Conciliation in Benjamin Franklin," History and Theory, V (#3, 1966), 225–240.

lectual and social trends of that age.[22] Another direction which critics
with an M-E focus have chosen to follow, one which has gained its
widest acceptance among critics with a bent toward social science, interprets "environment" in a more prescribed sense, referring to the
specific audience which the message had. These critics consider the
"functional" relationship which existed between the discourse and its
receivers. They seek to determine how the receivers used the messages
presented to them as stimuli. The assumption underlying the functional
(M→ E) approach to the M-E relationship is that, whatever the speaker's intention, the auditor attends to a speech in a manner which fulfills
his own personal needs. An old man may attend a July 4th celebration,
not prepared to be persuaded or inspired to increased patriotism, but
simply because the ceremonial oratory reminds him of the speeches he
heard on similar occasions in his youth. Similarly, the daily newspaper
may function for some readers as a means by which they maintain an
intimate contact with their favorite celebrities. For such readers, news
of a Hollywood scandal is as welcome as a letter from home. In cases
such as these, the M-E critic might concern himself with determining
expectations of the audience as well as the extent to which those expectations were fulfilled by the discourse.[23]

Although it is possible for a rhetorical critic to employ any of the
three foci so far mentioned, the bulk of traditional speech criticisms has
not explored dyadic relationships but the triadic formulations of S-M-E.
Essentially, this "pragmatic" orientation treats the message as an effort at persuasion and ventures to assess the artistic skill of the speaker
in achieving his persuasive goals with his audience.[24] The extensive
use of the S-M-E framework can be justified if we accept the notion
that public address is, literally, discourse addressed to a public by a
speaker who is carrying on public business by his act of communication. Because the critic takes for granted the Janus-like quality of public

---

[22] For example, V. L. Parrington, Main Currents in American Thought (New
York, 1927), 3 vols.; R. T. Oliver, History of Public Address in America (Boston,
1965); M. Meyers, The Jacksonian Persuasion (New York, 1960); A. O. Lovejoy,
The Great Chain of Being (Cambridge, Mass., 1936); D. M. Chalmers, The
Social and Political Ideas of the Muckrakers (New York, 1964); G. Orwell,
"Boys' Weeklies," in A Collection of Essays by George Orwell (Garden City,
N.Y., 1954), pp. 284–313; Scott, pp. 123–126.

[23] Cf. Heyl, p. 169; D. Katz, "The Functional Approach to the Study of Atti-
tudes," Public Opinion Quarterly, XXIV (Summer 1960), 163–204; J. K. Galbraith,
Economics and the Art of Controversy (New York, 1955), pp. 3–31; L. W. Lichty,
"The Real McCoys and It's (sic) Audience: A Functional Analysis," Journal of
Broadcasting, IX (Spring 1965), 157–165; B. DeMott, "The Anatomy of Play-
boy," Commentary, XXIV (August 1962), 111–119.

[24] Abrams, pp. 16–21; W. N. Brigance, "What is a Successful Speech?" The
Quarterly Journal of Speech Education, XI (April, 1925), 272–277; Black,
Rhetorical Criticism, pp. 36–58; Thonssen and Baird, pp. 448–461.

address, revealing simultaneously the communicator and the social environment to which he seeks to adapt himself, the S-M-E critic emphasizes in his study the mediating nature of the message in moving (or failing to move) the audience toward the speaker's vision of how the demands of occasion ought to be met and resolved.[25]

The three foci—S-M, M-E and S-M-E—comprise a set because they share one quality which distinguishes them from the introspectionist reports of the M-C focus. This shared quality is a stress on objective, verifiable, critical statements. By placing the spectator outside the critical equation, each method attempts to make of criticism a dispassionate report of what actually "is," a judicious, unbiased account of properties which inhere in the communicative event itself. In so doing they imply that the critic should strive to produce an analysis of the essential nature of the phenomenon apart from any idiosyncrasies in his personal responses.[26]

None of the three "impersonal" approaches so far mentioned can serve the ends of the introspectionist, and hence, none of the three finds encourages critical reasons employed mainly to establish the critic's own credentials as a sensitive observer. Instead, the critic who strives for a dispassionate and reliable report of the rhetorical act will find that the reasons he gives in support of his verdicts function primarily to call to the attention of others those characteristics of the original communication which merit their further contemplation. The method is similar to that of the football announcer who uses an instant replay camera. A team scores a touchdown, and seconds later the television commentator says, "As we play back the scoring play, notice the excellent footwork of the man with the ball." The listener-viewer is thus primed to observe for himself a feature of the event which the expert-commentator feels merits attention. The same ostensive function applies to the selection of reasons by the impersonal, rhetorical critic; his reasons do not report, nor do they simply support a conclusion—they call on the reader to observe for himself.

The last two foci available to the critic, S-M-C and M-E-C, reject the cleavage between introspection and impersonal functions of critical discourse. Justification for these two foci stems from the recognition of contemporary science that the very act of observation alters the event observed and so distorts the information one is able to obtain about the event. The distortions can never be overcome by more precise ob-

---

[25] D. C. Bryant, "Rhetoric: Its Scope and Function," Quarterly Journal of Speech, XXXIX (December 1953), 401–424.

[26] B. Harrison, "Some Uses of 'Good' in Criticism," Mind, LXIX (April 1960), 206; A. H. Hanney, "Symposium: Distinctive Features of Arguments Used in Criticism of the Arts," p. 169.

servations or measurements, but can only be acknowledged by specifying a degree of uncertainty and looseness in one's formulations.

As applied to the critical act, such a position holds that criticism is
inevitably the product of the critic's encounter with the rhetorical event,
that the locus of criticism is neither critic nor ontic event but the
critic's intrusion upon the event. Such an intrusion may not directly influence the agents involved in the communication; we may wish to admit, for instance, that as he prepared his first inaugural address Thomas
Jefferson probably did not significantly alter his behavior in conscious
anticipation of twentieth-century rhetorical critics. But neither should we
misconstrue the dilemma faced by the critic who would do more than
resurrect the data of the past. His problem is less one of succumbing
to personal bias than it is of taking and formulating precise measurements on the event under investigation.[27] Our final two foci suit the
critic who has reconciled himself to the inevitable impossibility of making meticulously accurate statements about the events he observes,
who wishes instead the maximum fidelity possible within the limits imposed on his by the nature of perception and critical language. His
framework for observation indexes neither the event *in vacuo* nor his
own response to the event, but the relation which joins him to the
rhetorical act.

The critic who adopts the S-M-C focus assumes that a speech will
no more exist "out there" in some ontic world than does a symphony
reside "in" a musical score or a drama "in" a manuscript.[28] Instead, he
believes that we can discern an artistic intention in a work of art; and
the aesthetic experience, be it to speech or symphony, is the experiencing and articulation of that artistic intention. Artistic intention is understood as the peculiar way in which the elements of the message cohere
in the movement of confrontation with the observer-critic.

There are objective clues in the messages as to the meaning which
will be actualized by the interaction of observer and thing observed. It

[27] A. G. Van Melsen, The Philosophy of Nature (New York, 1953), p. 226; L.
Brillouin, Science and Information Theory (New York, 1962), p. 232; F. C. Frick,
"Some Perceptual Problems from the Point of View of Information Theory,"
Psychology: A Study of a Science, II (New York, 1959), 77; J. Rothstein, "In-
formation and Organization as the Language of the Operational Viewpoint,"
Philosophy of Science, XXIX (October 1962), 406–411; J. Ruesch, "The Ob-
server and the Observed: Human Communication Theory," Toward a Unified
Theory of Human Behavior, ed. R. R. Grinker (New York, 1956), pp. 36–54; M.
Bunge, Causality: The Place of the Causal Principles in Modern Science (New
York, 1963), pp. 348–349; P. Frank, Philosophy of Science (Englewood Cliffs,
N.J., 1957), pp. 207–231; A. Moles, Information Theory and Esthetic Perception
(London, 1958).
[28] Cf. A. G. Pleydell-Pearce, "On the Limits and Use of 'Aesthetic Criteria,' "
Philosophical Quarterly, IX (January 1959), 29–30.

becomes the critic's task to investigate that cooperation of elements and ratios in the message which gives rise to the artistic meaning-as-experienced. In other words, speaker, speech, and observer momentarily coalesce as the elements of the rhetorical event unite to move toward some terminal condition. The critic's objective is to explicate that condition and the communication factors which contribute to or retard the transaction. The critic seeks to determine the nature of the demands made by the rhetorical event upon the beholder of the event. He is of course obligated to be alert to his own predilections as an instrument of observation, but his attention is focused outward upon artistic intention rather than inward as with introspection.[29]

The source enters into this equation because it is posited that the artist's intention(s) in creating the message may provide a key to understanding the artistic intention embodied in the message. The critic assumes that the speaker, by virtue of his close connection with the message, is something of an authority on the event; that is, the speaker often possesses special knowledge about the speech which adds depth to the critic's own interpretation. Hence, a comparison of artist's intentions with artistic intentions may prove a valuable aid in centering interest on the decisive qualities of the work of art.

Consider, for example, John Kennedy's television address to the nation on the Cuban missile crisis in 1962: we might regard the policy enunciated on that occasion as rhetorically inappropriate. However, if we knew that Kennedy was privy to secret information indicating that the Russians would withdraw their missiles if we took a strong line, this knowledge would help clarify the forceful posture Kennedy chose to adopt and possibly alter our critical assessment of the artistic intention evidenced in the discourse. We might now see the message as primarily a warning to Russia rather than as a report to the nation.

Notice that the S-M-C focus does not obligate the critic to accept the artist's personal conception of his creation; the purpose of uncovering Kennedy's purpose in speaking is not to whitewash Kennedy but to understand the parameters within which his verbal behavior operated. We might still find that Kennedy chose an inappropriate rhetorical strategy. Or we might conclude that Kennedy was himself not fully aware of the real significance of the discourse he produced. Our search does not necessarily tell us anything about the ultimate character of the message for the artist's intentions are ancillary to our primary con-

---

[29] Cf. E. Berne, Transactional Analysis in Psychotherapy (New York, 1961); Ch. Perelman and L. Olbrechts-Tyteca, "Act and Person in Argument," Philosophy, Rhetoric and Argumentation, ed. M. Natanson and H. W. Johnstone, Jr. (University Park, Pa., 1965), pp. 102–125.

cern, which is artistic intention.[30] We seek to discover the speaker's point of view; the symptoms of artistic and intellectual choice thereby revealed may lend depth to our apprehension of the design of the message.

Like its S-M-C counterpart, M-E-C rests on a conception of the critical act as an encounter. And it also recognizes the importance of artistic intention, of the demands made by the work upon the recipient of the message. The primary distinction between the two frameworks is the emphasis that the M-E-C focus places on the rhetorical event as an act, a performance which is only fully consummated in that instant when message is apprehended by receiver. Just as a play is not theatre until it is being performed for an audience, so the rhetorical artifact (such as a speech manuscript) becomes discourse only when it is experienced in a public "arena" or forum.[31] The rhetorical critic therefore necessarily fastens his attention not on the moment of creation but upon the moment of reception, realizing all the while that by his intrusion he is mutilating the confrontation of message and audience.

One consequence of this shift in emphasis is that the M-E-C critic is less concerned with the speaker's influence on the message than is the S-M-C critic. As the French symbolist Paul Valéry has contended:

There is no true meaning to a text—no author's authority. Whatever he may have wanted to say, he has written what he has written. Once published, a text is like an apparatus that anyone may use as he will and according to his ability: it is not certain that the one who constructed it can use it better than another.[32]

Although there are important differences between symbolist literary criticism and the traits of M-E-C rhetorical analysis, they are in this respect similar.

Whereas the S-M-C focus concentrates on the aesthetic demands of

---

[30] Cf. R. Kuhns, "Criticism and the Problem of Intention," Journal of Philosophy, LVII (January 7, 1960), 5–23; S. Gendin, "The Artist's Intentions," Journal of Aesthetics and Art Criticism, XXIII (Winter 1964), 193–196; E. Roma III, "The Scope of the Intentional Fallacy," The Monist, L (April 1966), 250–266.

[31] M. O. Sillars, "Rhetoric as Act," The Quarterly Journal of Speech, L (October 1964), 277–284; H. Arendt, Between Past and Future (Cleveland, 1963), pp. 143–172; S. K. Langer, Problems of Art (New York, 1957), pp. 1–58; S. C. Petter, The Work of Art (Bloomington, Indiana, 1955); M. Natanson, "The Claims of Immediacy," in Philosophy, Rhetoric and Argumentation, ed. M. Natanson and H. W. Johnstone, Jr. (University Park, Pa., 1965), pp. 10–19; W. Sacksteder, "Elements of the Dramatic Model," Diogenes, LII (Winter 1965), 26–54; P. K. Tompkins, "Rhetorical Criticism: Wrong Medium?" Central States Speech Journal, XIII (Winter 1962), 90–95.

[32] Paul Valéry, The Art of Poetry (New York, 1958), p. 152.

the event upon *an* auditor (the potential interpretation which any sensitive recipient might make), M-E-C considers the aesthetic demands made by the event upon *the* auditors (the likely meaning of the message for a given public). To illustrate, the S-M-C critic would seek to assess the enduring worth of medieval morality plays, taking account of their original cast as inculcators of religious faith; the M-E-C critic, on the other hand, would distinguish between the meaning of a morality play for its original audience and its meaning (perhaps totally different) for a typical contemporary auditor. Constrained thus by context, the M-E-C critical focus is more particularized, with the critic acting as a kind of surrogate for the audience he projects into the communicative event.[33]

Nor is the M-E-C frame simply a variation of the more objective message-environment focus. M-E analysis offers a predominantly historical interpretation of "how it was" when the public confronted the speech. The M-E critic seeks to understand the nature of the transaction as it in fact originally occurred. He may even go so far as to evaluate the speech using the rhetorical norms of the period and society in which the speech was delivered. He has a tendency to work back from the context to the message as he engages in assessment.

In contrast, an historistic interpretation might be more appropriate to an M-E-C focus. The M-E-C critic would try to go beyond understanding the message *as* the original participants understood it and attempt also to understand it *better than* they did.[34] He would seek to determine "how it would have to be" if one were to derive the fullest significance implicit in the rhetorical event. It is likely that an observer with an M-E-C orientation would follow a course of action in which he first analyzed the message, then projected from his analysis a description of the public for whom the message would be most appealing, and finally compared the bulk of the actual audience with his composite ideal auditor.

It is suggestive for us to bear in mind that both frames originate in the physicist's efforts to accommodate his formulations to the inherent uncertainty of the cosmos. We might therefore expect S-M-C and

---

[33] *The problem of a possible shift in meaning for morality plays is raised in* F. J. Coleman, *"A Phenomenology of Aesthetic Reasoning,"* Journal of Aesthetics and Art Criticism, *XXV (Winter 1966), 197–203.*

[34] *The distinction has been alluded to by R. L. Scott in his review of E. Black's* Rhetorical Criticism (The Quarterly Journal of Speech, *LI [October 1965], p. 336). Scott suggests that one may go to extremes in appealing to the immediate audience as a decisive measure of rhetorical merit, that in such instances the critic may be more concerned with direct measures of audience response such as shift-of-opinion ballots than with the speech itself. An extremist M-E critic might indeed tend to fit such a description, but an M-E-C critic would be unlikely to find himself in such a posture.*

M-E-C critics to be somewhat more heedful of the limitations of their investigations and less inclined to construct a brief for a particular interpretation. They might be somewhat more prone to employ their reasons as part of a calculation of the validity of particular rhetorical concepts. Their primary objective would then be to modify rhetorical theory to accommodate their clinical observations rather than to establish their own credibility or assist readers to derive increased satisfaction from the rhetorical event under discussion. We would expect critics with this cast to be more tentative in their reason-giving, since their comments would operate less in an advocative capacity and more as a special kind of scientific discourse. Such a critic might very well take the view that if his reasons are sound those to whom he reports will *probably* attach greater value to his judgments. He would therefore seek to determine the strength of his reasons.[35]

Let us conclude consideration of alternative critical foci by reminding ourselves that the focus adopted by the critic determines what kind of questions he will find most interesting. Insofar as the critic chooses to relate the rhetorical event to its creator he will ask: How did the message come to be? Is it symptomatic of the speaker? What are the capacities of the rhetor as an artist? How does the man shape the message? The critic who regards the message as the initial stimulus in his formula will ask himself a complementary set of questions: How does the message reflect its context? What evidence is there that the message as created was appropriate to the climate in which it was employed? How did the message serve to influence its environment? How and why does my experience with this message differ from the likely experiences of other recipients? These are all legitimate questions for a critic to ask; but his decision as to which shall occupy his attention will be at least partially influenced by the focus he has chosen to adopt.

Although many more problems pertaining to the logic of rhetorical criticism remain, this essay will treat only one more topic, the procedures available to the critic for relating norm and observation. This topic is essential since reason-giving has been shown to be the fundamental aspect of the logic of critical discourse.

We can imagine judgments which do not entail even the possibility of supporting reasons, but we ordinarily treat such evaluations as capricious remarks when uttered by critics. The manner in which a critic relates fact and criterion is of some moment if we hope to under-

[35] *E. H. Hutten, "Uncertainty and Information," Scientia, IC (#9–10, 1964), 199–206; J. J. Kupperman, "Reasons in Support of Evaluations of Works of Art," The Monist, L (April 1966), 222–236; J. Rothstein, Communication, Organization, and Science (Indian Hills, Colo., 1958). The problem we face at this point in the discussion is that no clear instances of this critical stance are available as of this date.*

stand the character of his reason-giving. For our purposes, the term "modality" will refer to any characteristic manner (or formula) for joining observations and norms so as to produce justificatory reasons in criticism. The term's meaning is thus roughly comparable to the sense of "function" as used in calculus.[36] To explain this special use of "modality" it is necessary to begin with a clarification of the term "juxtapose."

Earlier in this essay the critic was compared to the lawyer pleading a case. It was then suggested that a critic's primary task is to formulate justificatory bases for his verdicts by "juxtaposing" descriptions and norms. The term "juxtapose" is purposely vague, and it must be understood in light of John Dewey's observation that criticism:

. . . is judgment engaged in discriminating among values. It is taking thought as to what is better and worse in any field at any time, with some consciousness of why the better is better and why the worse is worse.[37]

Now determination of better-and-worse may take several forms. One might "grade" a speech according to various criteria or rank it with respect to other speeches and along designated scales, or he might simply classify it by type as part of a general act of recognizing features (when one labels a speech "epideictic," what he in fact does is provide a shorthand notation of several qualities we expect to find in epideictic oratory).[38]

Whatever the informative pattern evident in criticism, we expect that two related features of the critical act will remain constant. The critic will first have alternative speeches in mind as he approaches the object of study. Better-and-worse implies better-or-worse-than something else. To say that Adlai Stevenson was a great speaker suggests that the critic can discriminate between the speeches of Stevenson and those of some not-so-great speakers. To find fault with Lyndon Johnson's style suggests that the critic has in mind alternative stylistic tactics which Johnson might employ to improve his style.

The second implication to be drawn from Dewey's comment is that the alternative(s) the critic has in mind will take the form of particular speeches or aspects of speeches. To illustrate: suppose we feel that "good" speeches generally require transitions between main points.

[36] Cf. R. P. Agnew, Analytical Geometry and Calculus with Vectors (New York, 1962), pp. 111–117.

[37] Cited in M. K. Hochmuth (ed.), History and Criticism of American Public Address, III (New York, 1955), 4.

[38] Hanney. p. 170; Righter, pp. 64–69; Kupperman, pp. 229–233; Levy, p. 11.

Should we find a speech lacking transitions is it perforce a "bad" speech? Obviously not. Some speeches do not need transitions. Hence, the rubric "good speeches have transitions" is merely a guiding principle which serves to canalize critical observations; it is a reminder to consider the possibilities of an alternative speech containing transitions. To judge a discourse deficient in its use of transitions we need to have in mind how the addition of transitions might improve the speech; we must have an alternative image of a speech which is better, in particular ways, than the one we are observing. The "juxtaposition" called for in criticism is not straightforward application of rules to events in the manner by which we measure the length of an object against a yardstick. There is instead an oblique, two-step process by which the critic either generates or selects an appropriate alternative discourse and then compares that specific alternative to the discourse under analysis. The two modalities we shall consider represent general procedures for so joining observations and rhetorical norms.

A model modality is employed when the critic starts by generating some sort of paradigm which he will use as a basis of comparison. Laymen commonly speak of models in reference to airplanes, toy houses, or sets of blueprints. They tend to associate the term with miniatures, objects and/or plans drawn to scale.[39] However, the more appropriate sense of "model" in criticism is one which roughly corresponds to "prototype" or to "exemplar of a kind." Drawing on his rhetorical theory, the critic generates a model representing his conception of what would have constituted the ideal speech for the situation. He then compares his archetype with the speech which was actually delivered in order to determine the degree and the nature of the disparity between paradigm and actual speech. The comparison precipitates a kind of diagnosis; if the model conforms to the critic's rhetorical theory (as we must assume it does if it is to be regarded as a paradigm), then disparity between the norm-discourse and the actual one should provide some insight into both the aesthetic excellence and the rhetorical weaknesses evident in the discourse being inspected.

This notion of the norm as a model presupposes that the critic can himself create a prototype which is neither a stock image ("the speech for all occasions") nor yet a capricious whim. His model must be one which in its essentials conforms to his rhetorical theory. As we noted earlier, no rhetorical theory is so detailed that it can account for every aspect of every speech except in general outline. The well-wrought model requires a sensitive creator who can use his theory as a point of departure in developing in his imagination the model uniquely suited

[39] M. Black, Models and Metaphors (Ithaca, N.Y., 1962), pp. 219–224.

to assess a particular message. The search for an explanation for the extent and character of deviation from the paradigm model will then constitute the invention of critical reasons .

Both Rovere and Wichelns illustrate the model modality of reason-giving. Rovere contrasts MacArthur's speech by means of a treatment of issues demanded by the controversy; on that basis he decides Mac-Arthur's effort is inappropriate to the occasion. Wichelns, too, seems to reason from an implicit prototype insofar as he comments on attributes present and lacking, mandatory and optional in MacArthur's prose. If Wichelns is unwilling to discuss the appropriateness of Mac-Arthur's tone of authority (and his silence on this score is revealing), he is at least willing to address himself to MacArthur's skill in executing the tactic; and such comments, responsibly made, entail a theoretical conception of how public image is conveyed in a speech.

The essential feature of the second tactic of comparison, the analog modality, is that the norm employed is some actual discourse and not a theoretically derived prototype. Imagine the behavior of a critic who wished to characterize the rhetoric of Fidel Castro on those occasions when Castro justifies his failure to hold popular elections. The critic might use his rhetorical theory to generate a model of what would be appropriate for Castro to say; he might, on the other hand, be reminded of the rhetoric of another revolutionary in similar circumstances, say Cromwell dissolving Parliament. In the latter case, the critic might choose to juxtapose Castro's discourse to Cromwell's. His norm would no longer be paradigmatic, for he would have no a priori grounds for judging either Castro or Cromwell the more worthy rhetorician.

In lieu of such assessments, the critic would use Cromwell's speeches for topological purposes, much as he would a road map. Cromwell's discourse would serve to focus and guide the critic in his interpretation of Castro. Critical judgments would thus assume the form of statements of more-and-less or better-and-worse respecting particular qualities evident in the discourses. Perhaps Cromwell is more likely to engage in personal invective while Castro is more discursive in justifying his policies.

An illustration of the analog modality is found in Professor Laura Crowell's criticism of the speaking of John Pym, the English Parliamentarian. Crowell is contending that a distinctive feature of Pym's address is his interpretation of new events within the context of already-accepted materials and attitudes:

To people whose world was changing from medievalism to modernism under their feet, the words of a man who consistently saw events in larger context and who had details ready at hand on Biblical, philosophical, legal, financial, and parliamentary matters were extremely comforting. A cocksure age is ready for persuasion to new proposals, easily abandoning the present, not fearing the leap. But a skeptical age, such as Pym's, asks a persuasion that keeps its hold upon the present even while raising questions; it needs to feel the security of the past even while rising to meet new problems.[40]

The contrast between the debate of Pym's time and contemporary debate over, say, social welfare enables the critic in this case to highlight a quality in Pym's discourse which might not be readily evident were one to attempt to conceive the ideal rhetorical strategy for Pym solely on the basis of a rhetorical theory.

The analog relation of two particulars without direct recourse to a set of precepts entails a special role for rhetorical theory in the interpretative act. In the model modality the critic's norm is generated and constrained by theoretical precepts. In the analog situation rhetorical theory constitutes a shorthand account of those rhetorical categories which are typically helpful to the act of comparison. In the latter instance the critic is less concerned with creating a prototype than he is with "characterizing" an actual discourse.[41]

The analogical modality opens realms of critical analysis which have been for the most part neglected by rhetorical critics. Let us imagine that a critic, having assessed Castro in the light of the rhetorically similar Cromwell, decides to compare him with some apparently unrelated speaker, such as William Faulkner accepting the Nobel Prize for literature. There is no logical reason why such a comparison would be fruitless, yet it is clear that such a juxtaposing would yield results quite different from the comparison of Castro and Cromwell. Theoretically, the possibilities of analysis are infinite. Why not compare messages across cultures (say inaugural addresses of Presidents and coronation speeches of Kings), or across genres (John Adams the speaker and John Adams the writer of diaries)? Why not juxtapose various rhetorical forms, such as Ingersoll's witty ripostes at the Lotus Club and the cryptic visions of a religious mystic? Or why not contrast totally different rhetorical objects (Burke to the electors of Bristol and Martin Luther King to a college audience)?

The model modality finds its optimal use in confirming or qualifying rhetorical theory, where the analog modality, because of its factorial character, provides a point of departure which enables the critic to derive new categories and precepts from his investigation. The model-

---

[40] L. Crowell, "The Speaking of John Pym, English Parliamentarian," SM, XXXIII (June 1966), 100.
[41] Levy, pp. 65–66.

based critic is asking whether the rhetorician met certain criteria which were established by a given rhetorical system; the analog critic compares and contrasts, searching out theoretical explanations to accommodate his discoveries. In both instances theory assists the critic in his task and is in turn refined by the act of criticism. But it is clear that slatternly reliance on rhetorical canons to perform critical tasks is futile in either modality. Even where the canons suggest no obvious fault in a particular discourse, it is always possible that the astute critic could imagine a better speech or pamphlet, it is always possible that a felicitous comparison might expose qualities beyond the scope of the rhetorical theory at hand.[42]

Conclusion

This essay began by asserting that criticism is distinguished as a form of discourse by its peculiar reason-giving qualities. The ensuing discussion of this assertion holds two implications for speech scholars. The first is the suggestion, implicit in our analysis of the terms "critic" and "criticism," that rhetorical criticism does not operate *in vacuo*. Speech criticism can be best understood within the broader context afforded by a general conception of criticism's logical features. It has been argued that among the formal aspects which unite speech criticism with other varieties of critical discourse is the expert-spectator posture assumed by all critics. Another feature common to all criticism and setting it apart from the bulk of public discourse is its reliance upon forensic reasons-in-support-of-verdicts as its primary method for advancing contentions.

The second implication derives from our consideration of critical foci and modalities: it is possible to discern a finite set of relatively clearcut methodological options open to the critic. There is, in other words, a system of alternatives inherent in critical endeavor; criticism is not the "blooming, buzzing confusion" it may at times seem. Thus, for example, conceiving of the critical act as encompassing the four gross components of the communicative event enables us to specify in at least loose terms the kind of questions to which a given critic has addressed himself. Indeed, the recognition that various critics will give primary emphasis to particular combinations of S, M, E and C helps us to understand (although not necessarily to resolve) controversies which pit

---

[42] *In at least one instance the model-analog distinction breaks down and the modalities seem to fuse. That is where the critic relies on a touchstone as a standard of comparison. The touchstone, or "classic of its kind," at once represents an ideal and is at the same time an actual discourse which could conceivably be replaced in its role of prototype by some other discourse yet to be discovered. That the touchstone fulfills this dual role may explain its attraction for many critics as well as the rarity of its appearance as an effective critical tool. Cf. Wilson, pp. 272–276.*

critics of one focus against those of another. We are at least aware that the issue in the debate is often not so much the validity of the critics' arguments or the acuity of their observations as it is the importance each school attaches to particular relationships among the four communicative variables.

We have also considered the two fundamental modalities open to the critic as he relates his artistic criteria to the rhetorical event. We have seen that the common conception of the critic as one directly applying his canons in the manner of a measure applied to an object is overly simplified. The relation of criteria to object is oblique, entailing the critic's own conception of what the rhetorical work might have been. And this need for a one-to-one comparison again reminds us that the critic's selection from among the methodological options available will influence the character of his discourse.

Criticism, in sum, reveals itself to be a peculiarly open-ended, frustrating, but not incomprehensible endeavor. If the general condition of the critical act is diversity of substantive and methodological options, there are still reasonable limits to the range of those options. In the final analysis it is perhaps this vast complexity of opportunity that makes understanding the formal facets of critical method tenuous and difficult, yet at the same time renders understanding virtually indispensable to the student of criticism.

A Case Study in Speech Criticism:
The Nixon-Truman Analog
by Lawrence W. Rosenfield

One of the most controversial public addresses of modern American history is also one on which rhetorical scholars have remained strangely mute. I refer to the radio-television broadcast by the then vice presidential candidate Richard Nixon on September 23, 1952, the famous "Checkers" speech in which Nixon explained to the American public his use of a special campaign fund.[1] There also exists a remarkably similar address, a broadcast by ex-President Harry S. Truman on November 16, 1953 in which Truman answered charges that while president he had allowed a Communist agent, Harry Dexter White, to hold high governmental office. The generic resemblance of the two speeches (both may be classified as mass-media apologia) invites what may be called analog criticism—comparing the speeches in such ways

From *Speech Monographs*, XXXV, 4 (November 1968), 435–450. Used by permission of the author and the Speech Communication Association. Dr. Rosenfield is professor of speech at Hunter College, New York.

[1] *The only formal scholarly reference to it is Professor Baskerville's sketch of the "Nixon affair" in F. W. Haberman (ed.), "The Election of 1952: A Symposium,"* Quarterly Journal of Speech, *XXXVIII (December 1952), 406–408.*

that each address serves as a reference standard for the other. The objective of such a method of comparison and contrast is two-fold: to specify the fundamental anatomical features which relate the two speeches (engage in a *factorial* analysis of the category of apologetic discourse exemplified by the messages) and to assess the relative artistic merit of each speech, compared to the other.[2]

Comparison of these particular speeches is fruitful on several counts. First, an element of objectivity (especially important when discussing contemporary partisans like Nixon and Truman) is introduced when the speeches are played off against each other in the critic's analysis. Second, the identification of similar qualities in the two messages suggests to the critic certain constants operating in an otherwise undefined form—use of instantaneous electronic media to answer accusations. In these two instances we have cases of relatively early efforts by public officials to cope with the rhetorical problems raised by the demands of apologiae nationally broadcast. Where we discover similarities in the messages, we have grounds for attributing those qualities to the situation or the genre rather than to the individual speaker. And should we at some future date find modified tactics in apologetic speeches, we would be in a position to determine whether an evolution occurred in the form itself. Finally, because the surface conditions of these two speeches are so similar, the critic will be alert to the distinctive qualities of each. And having recognized those differences, he will be justified in evaluating the configuration of unique features in each speech as evidence of the individual speaker's artistry in responding to the exigencies of the situation.

The remainder of this paper is divided into five sections. A brief sketch of the incidents surrounding the two speeches is followed by discussion of similarities in the rhetorical contexts which gave rise to the speeches, by specification of the common elements in the two addresses, by consideration of their divergent features, and by discussion of the critical and theoretical implications of the entire rhetorical analysis.

The Nixon fund affair occurred during the 1952 Eisenhower-Stevenson presidential race. On Thursday, September 18, the *New York Post* featured a story headlined "Secret Nixon Fund." It opened as follows:

The existence of a "millionaire's club" devoted exclusively to the financial comfort of Senator Nixon, GOP Vice Presidential candidate, was revealed today.[3]

---

[2] *For further discussion of the analog method as a tool for speech criticism see Rosenfield "The Logic of the Critical Act" in* Rhetorical Criticism, *ed. D. Burks and J. Cleary (in press).*

[3] *Richard M. Nixon,* Six Crises *(Garden City, 1962), pp. 80–81.*

Democratic National Chairman Mitchell, in a "great show of indignation over corruption," promptly demanded that all details of the fund, including contributors and expenditures, be made public, and he called on candidate Eisenhower to remove Nixon from the Republican ticket. The next morning the battle was joined when Nixon responded to the charges in a whistle-stop speech in Marysville, California, characterizing them as a smear by Communists and crooks.[4]

This puerile exchange might have been muffled in the campaign cacophony had not the Republicans been touchy on matters ethical. They had pinned their election hopes on a "crusade to clean up the corruption mess in Washington." Hence, they felt themselves being hoisted on their own petard as the charges against Nixon spread and as several prominent newspapers began to give editorial support to the proposal that Nixon be dropped from the ticket. Should they retain Nixon the "crusade" might take on the shabby appearance of a huckstering attempt to horn in on the proceeds of corruption. But dropping him would imply a plea of "no contest" on the corruption charge and would open them to scorn for having nominated a rook. In either event they would forfeit the corruption issue. The Republicans chose to skirt these painful alternatives and to throw the question of Nixon's future open to a national plebiscite—they purchased a half hour of national broadcast time and instructed Nixon to clear himself of the charges with the electorate.[5]

Thus it was that on September 23, a bare five days after the charges were leveled, Richard Nixon addressed in his own defense the largest television audience to that time, sixty million people. The speech had three sections: a denial of unethical conduct in maintaining a campaign fund, a revelation of Nixon's personal financial history, and a partisan counterattack on the ethical qualifications of the Democrats' nominees. The response to the speech was immediate and fantastic: the public was virtually unanimous in its support of Nixon. Within hours the Republican panic had turned to glee; the "crusade" issue was more vital than ever, and Democrat Stevenson was straining to account for his own personal campaign fund. With a single speech Richard Nixon had won a decisive initiative for his party.[6]

Ex-President Harry S. Truman's ordeal smacked somewhat less of Armageddon and more of a joust; and the outcome was for several reasons less distinct than in Nixon's case. On November 6, 1953, Republican Attorney General Brownell charged in a Chicago speech

---

[4] *Nixon, pp. 83–84;* New York Times, *September 20, 1952, p. 9.*

[5] *Nixon, pp. 95–112.*

[6] *Nixon, p. 118;* A. Hillbruner, Critical Dimensions: The Art of Public Address Criticism (*New York, 1966*), *p. 60.*

(some claimed it was a smokescreen to draw attention away from recent Republican congressional election losses) that one Harry Dexter White, an alleged Communist spy now dead, had been promoted to a sensitive position with the International Monetary Fund during the Truman administration despite knowledge of his spying activities by "those who appointed him."[7] Truman at first denied ever having seen such reports on White. In the verbal sparring of the next few days both parties hedged. As bits of evidence came to public attention, Truman acknowledged that an unfavorable report had been received concerning White but claimed that at the proper time he had "fired" White. Later Truman shifted again to claim that he had "forced White's resignation." For his part, Brownell watered his accusation to one of "laxity" by the Truman administration in meeting Communist infiltration.

The immediate stimulus for Truman's national broadcast was a subpoena served on November 10 by Representative H. H. Velde (Illinois Republican) directing Truman to testify before the House Un-American Activities Committee regarding the White controversy.[8] Truman rejected the subpoena as his "duty under the Constitution" and chose instead to make his broadcast to fifty million people on Monday, November 16.

Like Nixon, Truman divided his remarks into three parts. He explained his refusal to testify before the H.U.A.C., justified his handling of Harry Dexter White's promotion, and attacked Brownell for having raised the issue. There were no immediate political stakes in the Brownell-Truman clash, so reaction to the speech was undramatic. In the ensuing week F.B.I. Director J. Edgar Hoover's testimony before the Senate Internal Security Committee cast some doubt on the interpretations Truman had offered in his speech. But, by November 18, Eisenhower signalled an end to the confrontation when he expressed hope that the whole issue concerning Communist internal subversion would be history by 1954. Within a week public interest had waned as congressional investigators turned from the White case to other allegations of espionage. Editorials tended to scold both Brownell and Truman for intemperate statements; then most newspapers dropped the matter. In retrospect Truman's can be considered a qualified victory. Though not as conclusive in its effects as Nixon's, his speech served to clear him

---

[7] New York Times, *November 7, 1953, p. 1.*

[8] *Velde apparently acted in a fit of enthusiasm without consulting Republican congressional leaders. In any event the main effect of the subpoena, besides giving Truman an excuse to mount a national forum, was to embarrass the Eisenhower administration. During his November 11 press conference, President Eisenhower noted in typical fashion that he "personally wouldn't have issued a summons" to an ex-President. Cf.* New York Times, *November 12, p. 14.*

of the main accusations and ended public interest in the circumstances of White's advancement.

These sketches of the two controversies provide sufficient background to enable the reader to consider the rhetorical context from which the two speeches grew.

A prime resemblance between the two speaking situations can be found in the expectations of the two national broadcast audiences. The period 1952–1953 was not marked by any striking shifts in American public opinion on major political issues,[9] and virtually the same individuals comprised the bulk of the two audiences.

The reputations of the two speakers were also such that the public would probably expect much the same rhetorical posture of each. With careers punctuated by flamboyant partisan utterance, there was little hint in the political biographies of Nixon and Truman that either was disposed to seek bipartisan consensus of the sort made popular by Dwight Eisenhower or Lyndon Johnson. Each stood in the public mind as a partisan "slugger," a staunch, uncompromising combatant for his party. As often as not it had been Truman's and Nixon's public remarks that had caused each to perform in the limelight of controversy. Richard Nixon was blessed with a kind of notoriety for pugnacious campaign tactics and for his role in the Alger Hiss investigations. "Irascible" is perhaps the most apt description of Harry Truman's prior public address. It was not without reason that the rallying cry of his 1948 presidential campaign had been, "Give 'em Hell, Harry!" And a public which remembered Mr. Truman's threat to punch the nose of a music critic who had panned daughter Margaret's singing would presumably expect the ex-President to deliver some pungent remarks in any address of self-defense.

Subjected to a personal attack centering on charges of past misconduct in public office, each speaker was placed in a Demosthenic posture; he must go before the citizenry to clear himself of accusations leveled by political assailants. The appropriate argumentative strategy was clearly forensic. The listeners could expect arguments of accusation and defense relating primarily to the interpretation of past facts. To this extent one may say each speaker was propelled by the logic of his situation toward the same, overall rhetorical strategy.

Though it was common practice in ancient Greece for the accused to speak directly to his judges, the use of electronic media for such a purpose was unorthodox in mid-century America. By their decisions to by-pass the customary medium of contemporary public dialog, the

---

[9] Cf. N.O.R.C. public opinion surveys 312, 315, 329, 334, 339, 348 for the period 1951–1953 (The Roper Public Opinion Research Center, Williamstown, Mass.); A. O. Hero, Jr., "The American Public and the United Nations, 1954–1966," The Journal of Conflict Resolution, X (December 1966), 436–475.

press, and to go instead directly to the people, Nixon and Truman tell us something about the intense character of their situations. Their choice may have been in part simply a symptom of things to come; we appear to rely more and more on the air waves for our contact with current affairs. But one cannot escape the feeling that in these two instances the central figures found the struggle so intense (if not climactic) that they felt it necessary to avoid the inevitable distortion of messages which results from the intervention of the newsprint channel.[10] At any rate, they chose to risk the outcome of their battles on single national broadcasts.

In retrospect a fourth similarity of context becomes apparent: both conflicts were short, sharp, and quickly resolved. The Nixon debate lasted from September 18 to September 24, the day Eisenhower announced that Nixon was vindicated. The Harry Dexter White affair merited headlines from November 7 to November 19.[11]

Finally, the broadcasts were in each case watersheds in the controversies. Nixon's speech caused the collapse of sniping at his campaign funds; Truman's speech was the last public mention of the possibility that a congressional committee might subpoena an ex-President. In view of their importance in each conflict, it is especially remarkable how brief the speeches were. Truman spoke for twenty-three minutes and Nixon's speech ran just under a half hour. One is reminded by contrast of the protracted, even leisurely paced, nineteenth-century oratorical struggles. These modern clashes seem abrupt in any such comparison.

We cannot with assurance attribute the differences between contemporary and former controversies either to qualities inherent in current issues or to the development of electronic media. The cost of air time limits the length of speeches, but it does not prevent continuance of debate by other means. But we can say that the contextual factors here mentioned—a forensic issue, use of broadcast facilities to carry a case directly to the public, relatively limited exposure time, and the sharp, decisive quality of the encounter—seem not coincidentally present in the two cases we are examining. If we as yet have no basis for determining which of the factors were antecedent and which were consequent, which were essential and which accidental, we can at least

---

[10] C. E. Swanson, J. Jenkins, and R. L. Jones, "President Truman Speaks: A Study of Ideas vs. Media," Journalism Quarterly, XXVII (Summer 1950), 251–262; J. Ericson, "The Reporting by the Prestige Press of Selected Speeches of Senator Goldwater in the 1964 Presidential Campaign," unpubl. diss. (University of Wisconsin, 1966).

[11] Although reverberations were felt afterward in connection with other congressional investigations, it is fair to say that Truman's role in it was a scant two weeks.

hypothesize that other contemporary apologiae are likely to display the same combination of attributes. The two speeches under investigation asked national audiences of roughly the same backgrounds to decide the guilt or innocence of two colorful political spokesmen. In choosing to risk defense on a single short speech transmitted directly to the public, the two speakers revealed something of the urgency they must have attached to their acts. What then, may we expect when men of such stripe find it necessary to speak as advocates in their own behalves under circumstances such as these? For a tentative answer we may turn to the messages actually presented by Nixon and Truman.

Both speeches adhered to classic forensic strategies, and both displayed martial overtones. In his denial of the charges, Nixon resorted to arguments of motive and fact (*quale sit* and *an sit*). At the outset he asserted that the appropriate standard for judging his acceptance of campaign contributions must be purity of motive:

I say that it was morally wrong—if any of that $18,000 went to Senator Nixon, for my personal use. I say that it was morally wrong if it was secretly given and secretly handled.[12]

Having demonstrated that these moral precepts were not violated in his use of the funds, Nixon proceeded to a factual iteration of personal financial affairs. These considerations ranged from his need to work in the family grocery store as a boy through the current unpaid balance on his home mortgage. The point of the narrative was clear: there was no evidence of campaign funds diverted to personal use. Nixon denied the accusation with facts.

For Harry Truman, argument by fact was not an option. The public already had reason to believe that at the time he was promoted Harry Dexter White was at least suspected by authorities of subversive activities. Truman employed forensic arguments of motive and value (*quale sit* and *quid sit*) in his defense. He contended that White's promotion was engineered so as to minimize the security risk while at the same time keeping secret an ongoing F.B.I. investigation of subversion. Hence, the motives for Truman's past acts were honorable. He justified his refusal to appear before Representative Velde's committee by ap-

---

[12] *This and all following quotes from the Nixon speech are from an official speech transcript prepared by four National Broadcasting Company stenographers and printed in the* New York Times *of September 24, 1952, p. 22. The* Times *text was verified by comparison with a text appearing in* Vital Speeches of the Day, *XIX (October 15, 1952), 11–15. A variant text can be found in* U.S. News and World Report, *XXXIII (October 3, 1952), 66–70. For a discussion of the problem of textual authenticity see E. G. Bormann,* Theory and Research in the Communicative Arts *(New York, 1965), pp. 173–191.*

pealing to a higher value—such an appearance would represent a threat to the constitutional separation of the three branches of government because it would subject past executive decisions to Congressional review. Implicit in Truman's argument was the premise that constitutional prerogatives take precedence over investigations of national security breaches.

Forensic strategy normally entails accusation as well as defense. Whether from habit or because they perceived that their situations demanded such tactics, both Nixon and Truman chose invective as their mode of attack. It seems more than coincidental that their speeches abound in ad hominum innuendoes concerning the moral qualities of their accusers, that in each case roughly the last third of the speech is almost entirely devoted to this kind of forensic offensive.

According to Truman, the Eisenhower administration was guilty of "shameful demagoguery"; Mr. Brownell degraded his office by engaging in political trickery and skullduggery, by lying to the American people, by smearing a defenseless and patriotic American (Chief Justice Fred Vinson, now dead), and by displaying "mealy-mouthed" cowardice. Truman also drew a red herring across the issue when he slipped in a reference to Senator Joseph McCarthy:

It is now evident that the present administration has fully embraced, for political advantage, McCarthyism. I'm not referring to the senator from Wisconsin—he's only important in that his name has taken on a dictionary meaning in the world. And that meaning is the corruption of truth, the abandonment of our historical devotion to fair play. It is the abandonment of the "due process" of law. It is the use of the big lie and the unfounded accusation against any citizen in the name of Americanism and security. It is the rise to power of the demagogue. . . .[13]

---

[13] The Truman text is from the transcript in the November 17, 1953 New York Times, p. 26. Variant texts can be found in U.S. News and World Report, XXXV (November 27, 1953), 104–106 and the Kansas City Times, November 17, 1953, pp. 1–2. The New York Times version gives internal evidence of being the most accurate account of what Truman actually said except for its omission of the bracketed words in the following sentence (spoken in reference to the late Chief Justice Vinson): "But I deeply resent these cowardly in [sinuations against one who is] dead." Philip C. Brooks, Director of the Harry S Truman Library of Independence, Missouri, agrees that the selected text is the most accurate one available (there being no reading copy of the text); but in a personal letter he refers to the New York Times version as a "press release text," thus casting doubt on its accuracy. Since no tape recording seems to exist, close stylistic analysis which would demand the exact words uttered by Truman on the occasion has not been attempted. See J. Thorp, "The Aesthetics of Textual Criticism," PLMA, LXXX (December 1965), 465–482; R. W. Smith, "The 'Second' Inaugural Address of Lyndon Baines Johnson: A Definitive Text," SM, XXXIV (March 1967), 102–108.

The excerpt intrigues. Was Truman accusing the administration of merely aping McCarthy, or was he suggesting that McCarthy exerted a substantial influence in the government? His meaning was conveniently vague. What stands out in Truman's attack is that it is unanswerable, for it substitutes name-calling for an assessment of motive. Brownell, for instance, could only reply to the charge of being mealy-mouthed by hurling a more insulting label at Truman; it was here, as always, futile to treat such an accusation as a "charge" in the traditional, legal sense.

Although not as explicit, Richard Nixon proved more adept than Truman in his use of innuendo. The ex-President pinned the label "liar" on Brownell outright; candidate Nixon was content with a telling sideswipe at his opposition. Twice, as if in tossing it off in passing, Nixon reminded the public that his Democratic counterpart, vice-presidential candidate Sparkman, had his wife on the Senate payroll. Nixon in both instances hastened (almost too quickly, one might feel)[14] to add, "I don't condemn him for that," "that's his business." The critic detects the swish of a matador's cape here. Nixon's nobility ("I'm for fair play") is deftly juxtaposed to the crass conduct of Sparkman. Nixon doesn't plunge the sword—he is content to draw blood. Standing aside, as it were, Nixon left the audience to judge who was in fact honorable in the use of Senate funds, but by means of the sharp contrast the auditor was offered only one option.

This distinctive habit of juxtaposing black and white distinguished Nixon's acrid invective from Truman's forthright smears. Consider the following passages:

. . . I love my country. And I think my country is in danger. And I think that the only man that can save America at this time is the man that's running for President on my ticket, Dwight Eisenhower. You say, why do I think it's in danger? And I say, look at the record. Seven years of the Truman-Acheson Administration and what's happened? Six hundred million people lost to the Communists, and a war in Korea in which we have lost 117,000 American casualties.

*   *   *

You wouldn't trust a man who made the mess to clean it up. That's Truman. And . . . you can't trust the man who was picked by the man who made the mess to clean it up, and that's Stevenson.

And so I say, Eisenhower, who owes nothing to Truman, nothing to the big-city bosses—he is the man that can clean up the mess in Washington.

*   *   *

[14] Nixon documents his deliberate intent in his book. See Six Crises, p. 118.

I'm going to campaign up and down America until we drive the crooks and the Communists and those that defend them out of Washington, and remember, folks, Eisenhower is a great man. Believe me, he's a great man, and a vote for Eisenhower is a vote for what's good for America.

What is striking is Nixon's habit of joining off-handed insults of the opposition with knight-in-shining-armor depictions of him and his. By this uneasy combination of dropped lines and stereotypes a Nixon insult was made at once more provocative—and more suspect—than the ingenuous efforts of Mr. Truman. For listeners there was the satisfaction of discerning the *act* of attack often tinged, one may believe, with distaste at being told so bluntly and sweepingly that untarnished good imbued Republicans and unrelieved corruption permeated the Democratic Party.

In addition to common forensic strategies and *ad hominum* ploys, a third general similarity characterized the two speeches: the manner in which documentation was employed to support arguments. Had this been an oratorical contest between Nixon and Truman, one might be tempted to ask which speaker displayed the better looking set of facts. Nixon's speech is of course best remembered for the section which began:

And I'd like to tell you this evening that just about an hour ago we received an independent audit of this entire fund . . . and I have that audit here in my hand. . . .

The section ended with the famous anecdote which caused the speech to receive the popular title "the Checkers Speech": the story of how Nixon had accepted only one personal gift while in public office—the cocker spaniel, Checkers.[15] The section occupied the entire middle third of the address and contained all of the documentation used in the speech.

Is it only coincidental that all of Harry Truman's documentation, such as it was, was also located in the middle third of his speech? Truman did not have any records in his hands. Instead he announced his presentation of inartistic data in this way:

I have had my files examined and have consulted with some of my colleagues who worked with me on this matter during my term of office.

[15] *Nixon admits that he planted this anecdote as another barb at the Democrats. The inspiration for the ploy was F.D.R.'s "Fala" speech during the 1944 presidential campaign.* Six Crises, *p. 103.*

Truman then "reported" his findings as a narration interwoven with interpretation; his evidence tended to uphold the assertion that his decisions were the most expedient under the circumstances. He ended his narration with the death of White in 1948, after White's appearance before H.U.A.C.

Why both speakers should lump all documentation in the middle of their speeches, and why both should assign the same relative space to presentation of evidence I am not sure. The simple enumeration of quasi-documentary data found in both cases might be taken as proof of the contention that ours is an age which puts its faith in facts rather than reason, and that contemporary rhetorical strategies often reflect that trust.[16] It is in any case somewhat beside the point for the critic to test by the traditional logical criteria the soundness of conclusions drawn from such selective, factual data as Nixon and Truman presented.

It seems clear that in one sense it was less important that the materials these speakers presented should provide absolute corroboration of their assertions than that the core of each case should contain a disclosure of new data. These data constituted artifacts; their presence lent an air of scientific proof (note the actuarial tone of Nixon's revelations) which could serve an important rhetorical end in and of itself. Professor Baskerville has argued that Senator Joseph McCarthy relied on an illusion of scientific proof to gain belief.[17] I suggest that if we leave aside matters of inferential soundness we can detect both Nixon and Truman benefitting from public acceptance of confirmation-by-a-heap-of-new-information.[18] And this interpretation gains plausibility when one recalls that the "charges" being answered alleged the *existence* of a fund and the motive of an act.

One final resemblance between the two apologiae is related to the use of documentation. Aside from the "good looking" new data presented, there were, strictly speaking, no new arguments in either speech. All the key ideas, and even the insults, can be found scattered in public statements made by the two speakers in the weeks prior to their television addresses. As early as September 19, for exam-

---

[16] Cf. W. S. Howell, "The Declaration of Independence and Eighteenth-Century Logic," William and Mary Quarterly, XVIII (October 1961), 463–484; R. Weaver, The Ethics of Rhetoric (Chicago, 1953); Dwight Macdonald, "A Critique of the Warren Report," Esquire, LXIII (March 1965), 59ff.

[17] B. Baskerville, "The Illusion of Proof," Western Speech, XXV (Fall 1961), 236–242.

[18] This "faith in the fact" hearkens back in the American rhetorical tradition at least as early as the age of Muckraker journalism. Cf. D. M. Chalmers, The Social and Political Ideas of the Muckrakers (New York, 1964); G. Ashenbrenner, "The Rhetoric of the Muckrakers," unpubl. thesis (University of Wisconsin, 1967).

ple, Nixon was claiming that the charges against him were a "smear by Communists and crooks" intended to make him relent in his campaign. On that same day Nixon also made references to Mrs. Sparkman's drawing a Senate salary.[19]

The finding that major speeches grew out of series of minor speeches, that the act of rhetorical invention was in fact an act of *selection* from previously used ideas is not unusual in rhetorical criticism. Studies of the major speeches of Grady, Bryan, Martin Luther King, and many others reveal the same thing: the oratorical masterpiece delivered at a crucial juncture in history reveals the orator not so much rising to heights of inspiration as choosing judiciously from a repertory of past ideas an appropriate mix of materials.[20] If our small sample is at all typical, the speech in the moment of crisis is most likely to represent a climax, a summing up, of those rhetorical thrusts which seem to have been most effective with the public on previous dry runs.[21]

In the speeches under examination here, two possible implications seem to follow from the similar inventive processes. One is that under conditions of contemporary American public address little fresh adaptation of *content* is to be expected in a climactic message. Whether Nixon or Truman spoke to a whistle-stop crowd in Idaho, a group of reporters, or a national audience, the substance of the speaker's remarks remained the same. In either case adaptation was from the outset constantly directed to the American public as a whole rather than to the immediate audience.

The central place scholars have accorded speakers' adaptation of arguments to *specific* audiences may be somewhat less justified in explaining the characteristics of television apologiae than we might at first think. Indeed, the only original element in either of the speeches examined here was the inclusion of new facts. Disclosure of new information may be more significant as a rhetorical phenomenon in dis-

---

[19] New York Times, *September 20, 1952, p. 9.*

[20] *Cf. Baskerville, Q.J.S., p. 407; T. D. Harrison, "The 'New South' Revisited," paper presented at "debut" session of S.A.A. National Convention, December 1965; D. H. Smith, "Martin Luther King, Jr., Rhetorician of Revolt," unpubl. diss. (University of Wisconsin, 1964); R. T. Oliver,* History of Public Speaking in America *(Boston, 1965), pp. 484–485.*

[21] *The critic may, if he chooses, examine the process whereby Nixon and Truman "discovered" the materials they eventually used—but only if he reckons with the clusters of earlier minor statements made by both men. In limiting the scope of the critical study to the television addresses themselves, the rhetorical critic must perforce adjust his notion of invention to one which emphasizes the means each speaker employed in selecting materials already available rather than broadening the concept of invention to include research procedures the speaker may originally have used.*

course prepared for a mass audience than are specific tactics of adaptation to the immediate audience.

To the extent that this implication holds, it suggests another. What distinguished Nixon's television apologia from Nixon's remarks to the press during the week prior to his speech was not the substance but the form. The *manner* in which Nixon chose to array for a national audience the ploys he had by trial and error found successful on more limited platforms cannot alone account for the potentialities of his broadcast address. The elements of rhetorical artistry unique to apologiae will be better seen if we turn from consideration of overall strategies to individual differences Nixon and Truman manifested in their tactics of array and emphasis.

Close reading confirms that there were indeed fundamental differences in the fabrics of the two speeches. Three formal qualities become prominent when one undertakes to depict the artistic genius of each discourse: the inferential patterns, the foci of attack, and the relative emphases on public or personal affairs. These three elements seem to set Nixon apart from Truman as an apologist.

The first impression one draws on comparing the two speeches is that where Truman's message displays a kind of dynamic, structural progression, Nixon's is hortatory and reminds one of stone blocks cemented into an edifice. The instrument of Truman's kinetic coloration seems to be his tendency to fuse acceptable (from the point of view of the audience) universal principles and conditional propositions into short, direct, enthymematic inferences. In the following passage the first two sentences form the theoretical ground from which Truman, in the third sentence, drew the consequence. Let us assume that most auditors accepted the principle of maintaining the independence of the executive branch of government. By articulating that principle, Truman prepared them to accept the truth of his fourth and fifth sentences which extended the principle to cover his behavior as chief executive.

The separation and balance of powers between the three independent branches of government is fundamental in our constitutional form of government. A congressional committee may not compel the attendance of a President of the United States, while he is in office, to inquire into matters pertaining to the performance of his official duties. If the constitutional principle were otherwise, the office of the president would not be independent. It is just as important to the independence of the executive that the actions of the President should not be subjected to questioning by the Congress after he has completed his term of office as that they should not be questioned while he is serving as President. In either case, the office of President would be dominated by

Congress, and the Presidency might become a mere appendage of Congress.

There is a logical gap between premise and conclusion, but if we accept the notion of enthymematic inference it is not difficult to imagine that an auditor who fully granted the explicit major premise would be prepared to fill in for himself the implicit minor premise. Truman's "if" statement thus serves in this instance to intensify adherence to the basic principle and to prepare hearers to make the necessary logical leap.

A like inferential movement occurred in a section where Truman justified his disposal of the White case.

But following receipt of the F.B.I. report and the consultations with members of my cabinet, it was decided that he would be limited to membership on the board of directors of the International Monetary Fund. With his duties thus restricted, he would be subject to the supervision of the Secretary of the Treasury, and his position would be less important and much less sensitive—if it were sensitive at all—than the position then held by him as Assistant Secretary of the Treasury.

Tonight I want the American people to understand that the course we took protected the public interest and security and at the same time permitted the intensive F.B.I. investigation then in progress to go forward. No other course could have served both of these purposes.

Truman asked the audience to look to the consequences of his alternatives; he asked them to grant the worth of his dual objectives, and he devoted his verbal effort to convincing them (by mention of the F.B.I. report and cabinet consultations and by showing how the Secretary of the Treasury could better control White's activities) that the chosen policy was the most expedient.

It is no insult to Nixon to observe that his disposition suggests that of a catechism: he puts the question he wants the audience to consider and then he speaks to the question as if reading from a trial brief.

But then, some of you will say, and rightly, "Well, what did you use the fund for, Senator? Why did you have to have it?"

Let me tell you in just a word how a Senate office operates. . . .

* * *

But then the question arises, you say, "Well, how do you pay for these and how can you do it legally?"

And there are several ways that it can be done, incidentally, and it is done legally in the United States Senate and in the Congress. The first way is to be a rich man. I don't happen to be a rich man, so I couldn't use that.

And now I'm going to suggest some courses of conduct.

First of all, you have read in the papers about other funds, now. Mr. Stevenson apparently had a couple. . . .

These excerpts not only represent juncture points in Nixon's speech—they are also frames which shape the arguments. Given such over-powering lead-ins there is little room for an auditor's imagination to function. His mind remains riveted as the argument unfolds. Viewed as a performance-in-time, the inferences are pre-determined by the transitions, and the discourse stubbornly resists efforts by an auditor to participate independently in the communicative act. There are undoubted merits in such structure; but the organization does not permit enthymematic reasoning as did Truman's. It was perhaps this catechetical feature of Nixon's recital which lent that "harsh and boney" quality of pre-packaged argument, not fully digested by the speaker, which some respondents discerned in his address.

Opponents were for both men objects of scorn, but Nixon and Truman differed in the breadth with which they defined the enemy camp. For Truman the "enemy" was a single man—Herbert Brownell. At times, as in the opening words of the speech, he depicted Brownell as a tool of the administration, but for the most part his invective sought out Brownell alone.

There can't be any doubt that Mr. Brownell was talking about me. Now let me talk about Mr. Brownell and this phony charge he has made.

His charge is false, and Mr. Brownell must have known it was false at the very time he was making it.

Mr. Brownell has made a great show of detail. . . . As Mr. Brownell should have learned by this time. . . .

*   *   *

There is one aspect of this affair that should be clear to everyone. That is the obvious political motivations of this attack on me.

In the launching of this attack on me, the Republican attorney general worked hand in glove with the Republican National Committee. The manner and the timing of what has been done made it perfectly clear that the powers of the attorney general have been prostituted for hopes of political gain.

In all cases Truman's tactic was to *accuse* Brownell, thus using consistently an overall forensic strategy. The cumulative impact of Truman's strategy would leave one who took the ex-President's words at face value with the feeling that the confrontation was between Truman and Brownell alone. Both the partial and the neutral auditor were given grounds for believing that Brownell unjustly maligned Mr. Truman. The entire force of Truman's argument was thus channeled to turn the attack back upon his accuser.

The clear focus of Truman's invective can be seen from these figures: of 15 accusatory references in the speech, 7 concern Brownell's personal behavior (he lied, fooled the public, is the source of malicious charges); 3 accuse Brownell of cheapening his office; 4 charge that the administration used Brownell as its tool in this affair; 1 places Brownell in conspiracy with the Republican National Committee. Again, where Truman stated the charges against him, he invariably coupled those statements with counter-charges that Brownell lied in his accusation. Had he not been so consciously mounting an offensive against Brownell, Truman might have contented himself at those points with a simple denial of the charges, but roughly 45 percent of the Truman speech concentrated on the "sordid" role of Brownell. This is gross evidence of the sharp focus of Truman's invective.

The characteristics of Truman's attack are the more noteworthy because of the comparative diffusiveness of Nixon's invective. Where Truman carefully leveled his sights on a particular object of scorn, Nixon must appear to all but his most devoted listeners to be lashing out at a penumbral host of spectres. Consider the swath cut by the following excerpts.

My fellow Americans: I come before you tonight as a candidate . . . and as a man whose honesty and integrity has been questioned.

By whom? Nixon never makes clear who is accusing him.

I am sure that you have read the charge, and you've heard it. . . .

Again there is no recognition of a particular source for the charge.

And the record will show that [he had not exerted influence on behalf of fund contributors] the records which are in the hands of the Administration.

Is the source of the charges somehow in league with the Administration?

. . . and let me say that I recognize that some will continue to smear, regardless of what the truth may be. . . .

Here again, the sources of attack are everywhere; perhaps reasonably, Nixon seemed to see himself in a state of siege. Yet, however justified such a belief may have been, its expression could not contribute to a well-focused counterattack.

One other thing I probably should tell you, because if I don't they'll probably be saying this about me too. . . . [Nixon here employs the "Checkers" gambit.] And, you know, the kids love the dog, and I just want to say this, right now, that regardless of what they say about it, we're gonna keep it.

*   *   *

. . . I remember, in the dark days of the Hiss case, some of the same columnists, some of the same radio commentators who are attacking me now and misrepresenting my position, were violently opposing me at the time I was after Alger Hiss.

Is the squabble between Nixon and the press? Or is it the case that the unnamed columnists are joining forces with other sinister agents to destroy Nixon? No listener could tell *from the discourse,* for the last excerpt is as close as Nixon came to identifying his attackers.

Failure to name accusers would not be significant (it probably has certain redeeming features) were it not that a concomitant limitation must thereby be placed upon the impact of an apologia. Nixon could not thus control the vector of his counterattack as precisely as Truman. Hence the tone of Nixon's reply tended toward the petulant, as though the man were lashing out at unknown conspirators seeking to victimize him. A rough classification of approximately 20 attack-statements in Nixon's speech shows that one-third were references to unspecified opponents, another third were scattered digs at Mr. Sparkman, the State Department, Mr. Stevenson, etc., and the final third were epideictic magnifications of corruption in the Truman administration. There was, in short, no concerted effort on Nixon's part either to isolate the source of the accusations or to provide the audience an explanation for such attacks.

It may be objected that Nixon's two-fold goal of clearing himself and scoring election points would force him to employ this particular pattern in invective. But the pattern, it turns out, is a Nixon pattern, not one peculiar to the situation. As befits a campaigner, Nixon showed greater concern with the faults of his political opposition in 1952 than with the source and nature of accusations against him. But the consequences of this unfocused invective appear to have stretched beyond the political contest of 1952. Some years later Nixon was to refer to this apologia as the event which made possible his election as vice president and at the same time denied him the presidency in 1960.[22] It may be that the reputation for immaturity which attached itself to Nixon had its origins in the undisciplined, unfocused attacks found in this speech.

A third notable difference also distinguishes the two speeches. The tone of the public man doing public business pervades the Truman address, whereas Nixon offers a revelation of the personal morality of a private man. This difference in tone grew in part out of the exigencies of each speaker's self-defense; however, both men spoke as public officials, so the contrast may also be taken as in some degree an index to the habitual rhetorical postures of the men.

As Harry Truman dealt with it, Brownell's accusation concerned the conduct of a public official in the execution of his office; the official happened to be named Truman.

> When I became President, I took an oath to preserve, protect and defend the Constitution of the United States. I am still bound by that oath and will be as long as I live. While I was in office, I lived up to that oath. . . . Now that I have laid down the heavy burdens of that office, I do not propose to take any step which would violate that oath or which would in any way lead to encroachments on the independence of that great office.

Was Truman using the office to shield himself from public scrutiny? Let us grant that he was not, that he was sincere in perceiving the demand that he testify as a genuine threat to the independence of chief executives. Corroboration for this interpretation is provided by Truman's other references to himself. Virtually all of the new data he provided, for example, were designed to show the calculated wisdom of the policy he eventually chose to follow. His mentions of himself served chiefly to enliven and personalize the image of an official struggling to arrive at a rational course of action. In the two instances where he mentioned himself as a person, it was to diminish his personal significance and to place the issue in the larger perspective of public affairs.

> First, I would like to tell you, the people of America, why I declined to appear before that committee. On the surface, it might seem to be an easy thing to do, and smart politics, for Harry Truman, now a private citizen of Independence, Missouri, to use the committee as a forum to answer the scurrilous charges which have been made against me. Many people urged me to do that. It was an attractive suggestion and appealed to me.
>
> But if I had done it, I would have been a party with the committee to

22 Nixon, Six Crises, pp. 125–129.

an action which would have undermined the constitutional position of the office of President of the United States.

*   *   *

If this were a matter which merely involved the name and reputation of Harry S. Truman, private citizen of Independence, Missouri, I would not be as concerned as I am. I can take care of myself. I believe that the American people know me well enough from my service as captain of Battery D in World War I to my service as President of the United States to know that I have always acted with the best interests of my country at heart.

But Mr. Brownell knows that, in this matter, when the final decision was mine, I relied on my principal advisers. . . .

There is one aspect of this affair that should be clear to everyone. That is the obvious political motivations of this attack on me.

Clearly, Truman preferred the *persona* of the office, and he allowed it to slip for only the briefest, most stereotyped glimpses of the real man behind the mask.

Almost the reverse was the case with Richard Nixon. Let us grant to him, too, the sincerity of his utterance. It still remains that his self-references all highlight the human creature, Dick Nixon, not the United States Senator, a public figure seeking election to another office:

It was not a secret fund. As a matter of fact, when I was on "Meet the Press"—some of you may have seen it, last Sunday—Peter Edson came up to me, after the program, and he said, "Dick, what about this fund we hear about?" And I said. . . .

Nixon *could* have generalized his argument to a discussion of the dilemma faced by the public official who must avoid temptations to corruption even as he seeks campaign contributions. He began on this course when he briefly considered the difficulty of running a Senator's office on the meager funds allotted by Congress.[23] But in the main he chose to present an autobiographical recitation of The Life and Hard Times of Young Dick Nixon.

The baring of one's finances (Nixon called it baring his soul) is not lightly undertaken in our commercial society; it surely requires some self-sacrifice. Its spectacular quality leads one to wonder whether it was rhetorically essential to Nixon's apologia or whether it offers a special kind of reading on the speaker. A few, but only a few, public

[23] *Professor Baskerville argues in the Q.J.S. symposium that Nixon ought to have taken this tack. I would not go so far, but would simply point out the ultimate rhetorical consequences of the path Nixon chose to follow.*

figures publicly report the full details of their finances. My own inclination is to believe that the prominence of creature-Nixon in this discourse served dual ends. It would seem unlikely, for instance, that a struggling young couple renting an eighty-dollar-a-month apartment in Fairfax, Virginia could be benefitting from graft. The material presented is persuasive, even for the doubter; and it is touching. But at the same time the information offered is not entirely relevant, for it fails to address itself to the issue: "Was there a misuse of campaign funds?" Nixon had already treated that issue in his denial of dishonesty, in his description of the needs of a modern Senate office, and in his report of the audit. The impression remains that Nixon was more ready to display his personal self than is common among civic men.

This same impression is further confirmed when we notice that the homey tone pervaded Nixon's speech as thoroughly as the public tone colored Truman's address. In both cases there was, for example, the matter of justification for conduct. Nixon explained that he could have put his wife on his Senate payroll, as Sparkman had done:

> . . . but I have never done that for this reason: I have found that there are so many deserving stenographers and secretaries in Washington that need the work that I just didn't feel it was right to put my wife on the payroll.

Or consider Nixon's explanation of why he intended to continue to fight the smears:

> Because, you see, I love my country. And I think my country is in danger.

Nixon, it appears, persistently, as though habitually, accounted for his public behavior by reference to his personal sentiments. It seems reasonable to suggest that Harry Truman would probably have sought other, equally effective justifications and proofs had he been in Nixon's place. At any rate, his apologia was far less creature-centered than Nixon's.

It may be that this distinction between the image of a public figure and that of the private man accounts for the observer's subjective impression that Harry Truman's message all adds up to a public warning while Richard Nixon's message amounts to an extended claim: "They're out to get me." And this difference in the core of the messages may provide an additional clue as to why the "Checkers" speech, so effective with the immediate audience, could another day function as a barrier to Nixon's presidential ambitions.

The Nixon plea sacrificed the mystique of the public man. It displayed him as a living, breathing citizen—perhaps too suggestive of Dagwood Bumstead. News commentator, Eric Sevaried, may have expressed the long-range public judgment aptly when he tried to explain the defeat of homey though honest and capable candidates for office:

We say in a democracy that we like the ordinary man. But we don't like him that much.[24]

When Nixon spoke to 60,000,000 people of his desire to help one deserving steno rather than hire his wife, even his loyal followers must have wondered whether he expected to be believed totally and literally. With whatever sincerity, Nixon ensnared himself by his rhetorical choices: he portrayed himself as at least a touch too simple for a complex age and too insensitive to the demands of a national, public occasion. It seems even fair to say that not every listener's smirk was one of superiority, but some were smirks of embarrassment. Nixon's response to attack, though emotionally appealing, was not fully appropriate to the public man, at least in this century.

Let us now extrapolate from the foregoing analysis those characteristics which appear to shed light on the two speeches under investigation. Conceivably, these features may represent parameters which will define other apologiae presented via the mass media.

There are four similarities in the two discourses which I take, at this time, to represent constants in the apologetic equation. Recognizing that these similarities may be accidental, may reflect some underlying kinship of the two speakers, or may be genuine symptoms of the demands of the apologetic form, we may tentatively hypothesize that the broadcast apologia is likely to be a part of a short, intense, decisive clash of views. We may further predict that a speaker who chooses to argue in his own defense over the airwaves is unlikely to limit himself to defensive remarks. In all probability he will take the opportunity to engage in some form of invective. We may perhaps be more than ordinarily aware of the invective in these two addresses because of the speakers' reputations; therefore, future criticism ought to study the extent to which invective is a staple of the genre. A heaping of data without careful attention to their artistic use may or may not be unique to modern apologetics, but the lumping of facts in the middle third of both speeches seems more than coincidental. It may be that either the circumstances surrounding broadcasting or the forensic demands of apologiae exert particular influences in these connections. Finally, the apologists' tendency to reassemble previously used arguments for

---

[24] *Eric Sevareid, Columbia Broadcasting System election returns program, November 8, 1966.*

presentation from the national rostrum (as evidenced in the fact that these two speeches are simple composites of earlier remarks) may hold implications both for our conception of rhetorical invention and for the critic's selection of facets for interpretation.

Whether or not the similarities we have just reviewed represent constants in the apologetic equation, we may regard as variables the dimensions of individual difference which were observed. Here emerged three ways by which speakers may put their personal imprints on messages: the manner in which the inferential pattern controls the form of the address, the degree to which the speaker channels his attack and thereby directs his listeners' aggression, and the ratio of public-personal explanations which becomes prominent in messages employing otherwise intimate electronic media.[25] There may of course be other factors influencing the character of modern broadcast apologiae, and we cannot discount the probability that as men gain experience in the use of electronic media the forms and styles of apologiae will change. Be that as it may, the elements of form and style amplified here deserve further study in apologiae and other genres of rhetorical discourse.

Finally, we are in a position to draw some conclusions concerning specific qualities of the two speeches here analyzed. First, it seems patently unfair to hold either Mr. Nixon or Mr. Truman in contempt, as many have, because either "injected personalities" into his remarks. Even granting the mercurial nature of the two speakers, there is a possibility that resort to invective is virtually inevitable given the unique configuration of forces operating upon the apologist. Secondly, if we wish to judge the logical validity or weight of evidence in either speech, we shall need to distinguish formal standards (which are often drawn from the courtroom) from the relativistic norms inherent in apologetics or in the age. To accuse Mr. Nixon of inadequate support for his contentions is to overlook the impact of his evidence on his audience. If accusations are to be mounted in this connection they are better directed to a society which contents itself with piles of evidence in place of rigorous argument.[26]

Lastly, while recognizing the unfairness of many journalistic criticisms of Richard Nixon, it does seem reasonable to contend that the most curious short-coming of his "Checkers" speech, when compared with Truman's address, was its endurance in the public mind, its capacity to outlast the demands of the occasion. Whereas Harry Truman's discourse was totally relevant to specific rhetorical objectives, Nixon

[25] Cf. J. M. Ripley, "Television and Recreational Patterns," Television Quarterly, II (Spring 1963), 31–36; M. McLuhan, Understanding Media: The Extensions of Man (New York, 1965), pp. 297–337.

[26] On this matter of loose standards of assessment in a given society see Aristotle, Rhetoric, 1354a 15–24.

in a single stroke demolished both the opposition's case and injured his own standing as a public man. "Checkers" resulted in immediate victory for the campaigner; yet its traces admittedly continue to plague the political figure.[27]

Dimensions of the Concept of Rhetoric
by Wayne Brockriede

During recent years a state of cold war has existed in the field of speech. Humanists who seek to understand rhetoric primarily through the use of historical scholarship and behavioral scientists who seek to develop a communication theory primarily through empirical description and experimental research have tended to see one another as threatening enemies. Yet members of these factions have the common objective of studying similar phenomena. The student of communication who conceives his study as focusing on pragmatic interaction of people and ideas is concerned with the rhetorical impulse within communication events.[1]

The purpose of this essay is to sketch the beginning and to encourage the further development of a system of dimensions for the study of rhetorical communication. Five assumptions implicit in this attempt should be stated explicitly from the outset.

First, the conception of rhetoric broadly as the study of how interpersonal relationships and attitudes are influenced within a situational context assumes the presence of the rhetorical impulse in such diverse acts as a speaker addressing an audience face to face or through mass media, a group of people conferring or conversing, a writer creating a drama or a letter to an editor, or a government or some other institution projecting an image.

Second, the concept of rhetoric must grow empirically from an observation and analysis of contemporary, as well as past, events.[2] The dimensions should be selected, developed, structured, and continuously revised to help explain and evaluate particular rhetorical acts.

[27] Cf. E. Black, Rhetorical Criticism (New York, 1965), pp. 162–164.
From The Quarterly Journal of Speech, LIV, 1 (February 1968), 1–12. Used by permission of the author and the Speech Communication Association. Dr. Brockriede is professor of communication and drama at California State University, Fullerton. Colorado.
[1] Although my treatment differs from Dean C. Barnlund's excellent analysis in his "Toward a Meaning-Centered Philosophy of Communication," Journal of Communication, XII (December 1962), 197–211, the scope of my conception of rhetoric seems similar to the scope of his conception of communication. Gerald R. Miller in his Speech Communication: A Behavioral Approach (Indianapolis, Ind., 1966), makes explicit (p. 12) his synonymous usage of the terms rhetoric and speech communication.
[2] An argument which supports this claim is developed in my essay "Toward a Contemporary Aristotelian Theory of Rhetoric," QJS, LII (February 1966), 35–37.

Third, although the theorist, critic, or practitioner may focus his attention on a rhetorical act, such an act must be viewed as occurring within a matrix of interrelated contexts, campaigns, and processes.

Fourth, the rubrics of a rhetorical act are best viewed as dimensional, each reflecting a wide range of possible descriptions and not as expressing dichotomies.

Fifth, the dimensions of rhetoric are interrelational: each dimension bears a relationship to every other dimension.

This essay, therefore, represents an attempt to sketch a contemporary concept of interrelated interpersonal, attitudinal, and situational dimensions of a broadly conceived rhetorical act.

1

Traditional rhetoric places much less emphasis on interpersonal relationships than does the model presented in this paper. Even the concept of *ethos* frequently has been conceived as personal proof functioning rationalistically as a message variable.[3]

What are here developed as interpersonal dimensions may indeed function in an instrumental way, having some influence on a rhetorical act which aims primarily at attitudinal influence or situational appropriateness. But interpersonal dimensions themselves often represent the principal goals; and the establishment, change, or reinforcement of such interpersonal relationships as liking, power, and distance may exercise a controlling influence on the other dimensions.

Liking. This interpersonal dimension poses the question: how attracted to one another are the people who participate in a rhetorical act? Liking differs qualitatively and may refer to such continua as spiritual adoration—hate, sexual attraction—repulsion, friendship—enmity, and compatibility—incompatibility. In a dyadic act the feelings may or may not be mutual. When many people are involved—as in hearing a public address, participating in a discussion, or reading a best-seller, a single relationship may be characteristic—as when an audience becomes polarized, or relationships may vary—as when some discussants feel affection for a leader whereas others are repelled. Liking also differs in degree of intensity and in degree of susceptibility to change.

The change or reinforcement of the liking dimension may function as the primary purpose of a rhetorical act; courtship, for example, aims principally at affecting this relationship. Or increasing, maintaining, or decreasing the degree people like one another may be a by-product of

---

[3] *For example, in Lester Thonssen and A. Craig Baird's* Speech Criticism *(New York, 1948), the chapter on* ethos *(pp. 383–391) is subtitled "ethical proof in discourse."*

a situation which has other chief aims. Or the liking relationship, though it remains essentially unchanged during a rhetorical act, may have a profound influence on whether other dimensions vary, as well as on how they vary.[4]

Power. Power may be defined as the capacity to exert interpersonal influence. Power may be the ultimate purpose or function, as in a power struggle, or it may be a by-product of or an influence on the controlling dimensions. The power dimension includes two primary variables.

First, what are the kinds of power? One is the influence a person has because others like him. The word *charisma* denotes this kind of power when it reaches a great magnitude. But personal magnetism exists also in lesser degrees. The power of personal attractiveness represents a kind of intersection of liking and power. A second type of power stems from position or role in the social system. By having control over the assignment of sanctions, the allocation of rewards and punishments in a social system, a man merely by virtue of his office or role may be powerful. A third type is the control over the communication channels and other elements of the rhetorical situation. This situational power corresponds to what some people call the gatekeeper function. A fourth kind of power is an influence over the sources of information, the norms and attitudes, and the ideology. Such an influence seems to depend on the extent to which other people trust one's ideational competence generally and his special expertise on matters relevant to the rhetorical act, on their perceptions of his general willingness to express himself honestly and accurately and of his special candor on the particular relevant topics, and on their feelings of confidence in their abilities to predict accurately the meaning and significance attached to his statements and actions.[5] Finally, one exercises indirectly a degree of power by having access to and influence on other people who can exercise the other kinds of power more directly. So a first general variable of the power dimension is the degree with which people participating in a rhetorical act can manifest these kinds of power.

[4] *Hugh D. Duncan stresses this dimension in his* Communication and Social Order *(New York, 1962) when he says (p. 170) that "the study of how men court each other . . . will tell us much about the function of rhetoric in society." See also Kenneth Burke,* Rhetoric of Motives *in* A Grammar of Motives and a Rhetoric of Motives *(Cleveland, 1962), pp. 732–736. I make no attempt in this essay to catalogue the status of knowledge or to supply bibliographies concerning each of the dimensions discussed. I shall suggest, however, a source or two which will develop further each of the dimensions considered in this essay.*

[5] *Kenneth Andersen and Theodore Clevenger, Jr., provide an excellent synthesis of information on this kind of power in "A Summary of Experimental Research in Ethos,"* Speech Monographs, *XXX (June 1963), 59–78.*

A second variable is power structure. Knowing how much power of what kind each rhetorical participant has may be less immediately relevant than knowing the relationship among the power statuses of the people involved. That is, power is relative rather than absolute. The significance of the power of a writer, for example, regardless of the amount or kind he may possess, depends on how much power he has relative to that of his readers. Two questions especially are important in an analysis of the power structure. How disparate are the power positions of the various participants of an act, and does the act function to increase, maintain, or decrease the disparity? How rigid or flexible is the structure, and does the rhetorical act function to increase, maintain, or decrease the stability?[6]

Distance. The concept of distance is related to the other interpersonal dimensions. One generally feels "closer" to those persons he likes and "farther" from those he dislikes, but the greater the power disparity the greater the distance. Like all other dimensions, the establishment of an appropriate distance (whether decreasing, maintaining, or increasing it) may be a rhetorical act's primary function, an incidental outcome, or an influencing factor.

Two kinds of distance make up this dimension. One is an interpersonal distance between each two participants in a rhetorical act. The other is a social distance which exists within the structure of the group or groups within or related to the rhetorical act—such groups as audiences, committees, organizations, societies, and cultures. Although interpersonal and group distance are related closely and tend generally to covary, they are discrete variables in that two persons in a discussion group, for example, may move more closely together while the group structure is in the process of disintegrating.[7]

---

[6] *This dimension seems to have been ignored in the study of many rhetorical situations. It is only implied, partially, for example, in the public address doctrine of ethos. During recent years, however, under the headings of leadership and power structure, many small group specialists have emphasized it. See, for example, Dorwin Cartwright and Alvin Zander,* Group Dynamics: Research and Theory, *2nd ed. (Evanston, Ill., 1960), pp. 487–809. Among a number of useful works in the field of political sociology which are relevant to an understanding of the function of power in rhetorical acts, see* Class, Status, and Power, *ed. Reinhard Bendix and Seymour Martin Lipset, 2nd ed. (New York, 1966), pp. 201–352.*

[7] *One of the shortcomings of the concept of interpersonal distance is that the term is not readily operationalized into specifiable behaviors. Consciously or unconsciously, however, people seem to have a sense of closeness or distance from others; such a feeling can influence rhetorical interaction. The philosophical basis for Kenneth Burke's rhetoric is the view that men are fundamentally divided. His concepts of identification and consubstantiality suggest that one of rhetoric's functions is to reduce man's interpersonal*

Several questions about the role of interpersonal and group distance in rhetorical situations seem important. How much distance (of each type) is optimal in achieving certain kinds of interpersonal, attitudinal, and situational rhetorical functions? What conditions of the other dimensions are most likely to increase, maintain, or decrease the distance (of each type)?

2

Controversial ideas which involve a choice among competing judgments, attitudes, and actions form a necessary part of any rhetorical act. Very often, although not always, such a choice is the primary operation, and the various interpersonal and situational dimensions merely create the environment in which the choice is made and influence how the choice is made. Traditionally, rhetoric seems rather consistently to have made this sort of assumption. The principal function of some rhetorical acts is interpersonal interaction or situational appropriateness, however, and the influence on attitudes in the making of choices is secondary. Attitude may be defined as the predisposition for preferential response to a situation. Two kinds of attitudes have rhetorical significance: attitudes toward the central idea in a choice-making situation and the ideological structure of other related attitudes and beliefs.

Central Idea. Several features of attitudes toward the central idea of a rhetorical situation require study.

First, although attitudes customarily have been considered as a point on a scale, this view is inadequate. As Carolyn Sherif, Muzafer Sherif, and Roger E. Nebergall have pointed out, a person's attitude may be described more accurately by placing various alternative positions on a controversy within three latitudes—of acceptance, of rejection, and of non-commitment.[8] On the policy of the United States toward Vietnam, for example, a person may have one favored position but place other positions within his latitude of acceptance; such additional positions are tolerable. He may have one position that he rejects more strongly than any other but place other positions within his latitude of rejection. Finally, because he lacks information, interest, or decisiveness, he may place other positions within his latitude of non-commitment. To understand or predict the attitudinal interaction in a rhetorical situation one

---

distance from man. See, for example, Burke, pp. 543–51. Edward T. Hall treats distance literally as a variable in communication situations in his Silent Language (*Garden City, N. Y., 1959*), pp. 187–209. The concept of social distance is implied in such terms in small group research as group cohesiveness, primary groups, and reference groups.

[8] Attitude and Attitude Change: The Social Judgment-Ego Involvement Approach (*Philadelphia, 1965*), pp. 18–26.

must know whether its central idea falls within the participants' latitude of acceptance, rejection, or non-commitment.

Second, the degree of interest and the intensity of feeling with which the central idea confronted in a rhetorical act occupies a place in whatever latitude will influence potentially all other dimensions of that act.

Third, the way the various latitudes are structured is an influential variable. Sherif, Sherif, and Nebergall identify one such structure which they term ego-involvement. A person who is ego-involved in a given attitude tends to perceive relatively few discrete alternative positions, to have a narrow latitude of acceptance—sometimes accepting only one position, to have a broad latitude of rejection—lumping most positions as similarly intolerable, and to have little or no latitude of non-commitment.[9] The ego-involved hawk, for example, may accept only a strong determination to achieve a military victory, assimilating all positions close to that one; and he may reject all other stands, seeing little difference between unilateral withdrawal and attempts to negotiate that necessitate any genuine concessions to the adversary, and labeling anything less than total victory as appeasement.

Fourth, a person's persuasibility on the central idea of a rhetorical act is a relevant variable. How likely is a person to respond positively to attempts to change his attitude? This question suggests the superiority of the Sherif, Sherif, and Nebergall analysis. The question is not the simple one of how likely is a person to move from "yes" to "no" or from favoring a negotiated settlement in Vietnam which does not involve the possibility of a coalition government in South Vietnam to one which does. It is the far more complex question of whether positions which are now assigned to one latitude can be moved to another one. This concept recognizes, for example, that to move a person from a position of rejection to one of non-commitment is significant persuasion. A person's persuasibility is related, of course, to the nature, intensity, and structure of his attitude.[10] An ego-involved person who feels strongly about an idea is less likely to change his attitude than one who is less ego-involved or less intense.

What the preceding discussion suggests is that the nature, intensity, structure, or persuasibility of the attitude of any participant toward the central idea in a rhetorical transaction will influence the other dimensions and be influenced by them. In addition, the relationship of the attitudes of each participant to those of others in the situation will influ-

[9] Ibid., p. 233.

[10] In addition, an individual's personality may be one of the determinants of his persuasibility on controversial propositions. See Irving L. Janis, Carl I. Hovland, et al., Personality and Persuasibility (New Haven, Conn., 1959), and Milton Rokeach, The Open and Closed Mind (New York, 1960).

ence their interaction together. The issue here can be focused in a single question: how similar are the people in a rhetorical act with respect to the nature, intensity, structure, and changeability of their attitudes toward the idea under focus in the rhetorical act? Or, to put the question in a slightly different way: to what extent can people identify with the attitudes of one another?[11]

Ideology. An attitude does not exist in a vacuum. One idea does not occur by itself. Rather, attitudes have homes in ideologies. The ideologies evoked in a rhetorical act influence, and may sometimes dominate, the other dimensions.

Several ideological structures may be identified. Attitudes may relate to other attitudes, to systems of values and norms, to ethical codes, and to philosophic presuppositions about the nature of man, the nature of reality, the nature of language, and the nature of knowledge. About each of these contexts two questions may be raised: What is the nature of the ideological structures of each participant in the act? How similar or different are the ideologies of the various participants?

The central idea of any rhetorical transaction evokes not only attitudes toward that idea but attitudes toward related ideas. In recent years several theories and approaches have developed: balance theory, the theory of cognitive dissonance, the congruity hypothesis, and the social judgment approach.[12] Although these formulations differ and the differences are argued heatedly, one principle seems accepted by most attitude theorists: man has an urge to think himself consistent, to try to achieve homeostasis within his system of attitudes.

Although relatively few persons work out a careful formulation of an ideology which consciously monitors various attitudes, each person very likely has an implicit ideology which unconsciously affects the development of any attitude in the system. Anyone attempting to change one attitude of a person, therefore, will profit from the admittedly difficult task of identifying that person's other attitudes and of considering how they may facilitate or retard such an attempt and how the target-attitude will, if changed, affect other attitudes. In addition, to understand the rhetorical interaction on some central idea one must also consider how similar or different one person's attitudes toward related ideas are to those of other people in the rhetorical act.

---

[11] *Kenneth Burke's concept of identification seems to relate to the attitude dimension as well as to the dimension of interpersonal distance.*
[12] *See Fritz Heider, "Attitudes and Cognitive Organizations,"* Journal of Psychology, *XVL (April 1946), 107–114; Leon Festinger,* A Theory of Cognitive Dissonance (Evanston, Ill., 1958); *Charles E. Osgood, Percy Tannenbaum, and George Suci,* The Measurement of Meaning (Urbana, Ill., 1957); *and Sherif, Sherif, and Nebergall.*

A second ideological variable is the system of values and norms sub-
scribed to by the people in a rhetorical act. Just as a person's attitudes relate to his other attitudes, they relate also to more fundamental
principles which he values. Whereas the first relationship may be
viewed as a sort of part-to-part analogical inference, the second is a
part-to-whole (or whole-to-part) inference. General values both evolve
from many particular attitudes, and they also structure new experience
in the development of new attitudes toward new situations.[13]

One of the most important sources of each person's fundamental
values is his membership in small groups, organizations, societies, and
cultures. The argument can be made that all values can be traced generally to a social origin, but some values especially can be associated
closely with membership in a particular reference group—whether
small group, organization, society, or culture. Such shared values are
termed norms. When a rhetorical situation involves the actual or implied
presence of such groups, the norms of those groups predictably are
going to function as an ideology which will tend to set limits for attitudes of group members.[14]

A third kind of ideology is the ethical variable which raises two
questions: What personal morality or public ethic guides the interaction
of attitudes? Is the code of conduct acceptable to others who participate in the rhetorical act? A transaction of ideas viewed as unethical
by someone with whom a person tries to interact will have adverse
effects on many of the other dimensions.[15]

A fourth ideological variable consists of a person's philosophic presuppositions about the nature of man, the nature of reality, the nature
of language, and the nature of knowledge. This variable probably functions relatively rarely as the primary goal of a rhetorical act, perhaps
only when philosophers engage in dialogue, but it establishes a frame
of reference within which attitudes interact. Is a man an object to be
manipulated or a decision-maker in the process of making radical

---

[13] In their essay "The American Value System: Premises for Persuasion,"
Western Speech, XXVI (Spring 1962), 83–91, Edward D. Steele and W. Charles
Redding state, "Values, as they exist psychologically in the mind of the audience, have been generalized from the total experience of the culture and
'internalized' into the individual personalities of the listeners as guides to
the right way to believe or act" (p. 84). Karl R. Wallace argues that general
value premises function as the substance of rhetoric—as good reasons which
support propositions or value judgments. See "The Substance of Rhetoric:
Good Reasons," QJS, XLIX (October 1963), 239–249.

[14] See A. Paul Hare, Handbook for Small Group Research (New York, 1962),
pp. 23–61.

[15] Edward Rogge, in his "Evaluating the Ethics of a Speaker in a Democracy," QJS, XLV (December 1959), 419–425, suggests that the standards used
to evaluate a speaker's ethics be those established by the audience and the
society of which it is a part.

choices? To what extent does he behave rationally? To what extent is his rhetorical behavior determined for him and to what extent does he exercise free will? Does one take an Aristotelian, a Platonic, or a phenomenalistic stance on the question of the nature of reality? How does man acquire knowledge? To what extent does he come to know through *a priori* intellection, through revelation, through intuition, through memory, through empirical observation, through existential experience, or through scientific analysis?[16] How each person in a rhetorical act answers these questions, and the degree to which the various answers are similar, will influence how attitudes interact.

3

A rhetorical act occurs only within a situation, and the nature of that act is influenced profoundly by the nature of the encompassing situation. Furthermore, on certain ceremonial occasions situational dimensions dominate the act. A speaker's function in a funeral oration, for example, may be merely to meet the expectations of the occasion. Six situational dimensions form a part of the conceptual framework advanced in this essay: format, channels, people, functions, method, and contexts.

Format. The essential concern of this dimension is how procedures, norms, and conventions operate to determine who speaks and who listens.

Formats fall into two general types which anchor the ends of the dimension. At one extreme is a polarized situation in which one person functions as speaker or writer and others function as listeners or readers. At the other extreme is a type of conference situation in which the functions of the various participants rotate freely between speaking and listening.

Formats vary with respect to the degree of flexibility permitted rhetorical participants. In some situations, for example in written and electronic discourse, a rhetorician has little opportunity to revise his original plans within the act, although he may utilize feedback in designing subsequent acts in a campaign. In other situations a rhetorician has maximum opportunity to observe the reactions of others and to make appropriate decisions accordingly.[17]

---

[16] *The importance of the philosophic dimension of rhetoric is well argued by Otis M. Walter in "On Views of Rhetoric, Whether Conservative or Progressive," QJS, XLIX (December 1963), 367–382.*

[17] *See David K. Berlo,* The Process of Communication *(New York, 1960), pp. 111–116. Ironically, in public address, a format which offers considerable opportunity for communicative flexibility, the role of feedback has been analyzed very little.*

Channels. The role of channels in a rhetorical act is manifested in three variables. First, is the communication conveyed verbally, nonverbally, or through a mixture of the two modes? Radio speaking and written messages are instances of the verbal channel; a silent vigil and pictures employ the nonverbal channel; and face-to-face speaking, television, and books which feature graphic materials illustrate the mixed mode.[18]

Second, if language is employed, is it in oral or written form? Although the distinction between these two channels needs no clarification,[19] their modes of transmission require analysis. Traditional rhetoric has long studied delivery as one of the canons. Although students of written composition have paid far less attention to the study of transmitting messages, such features as the selection of paper, binding, cryptology, and the like may influence the interaction between writer and reader more than the persons playing either role recognize. Delivery, whether in oral or written channel, illustrates well the primary idea of this essay: that each dimension relates to every other dimension. Delivery will influence and be influenced by the interpersonal dimensions of liking, power, and distance; by the attitudes toward the central idea and toward those related to it; and by the other situational dimensions of format, people, functions, method, and contexts.

Third, is the rhetoric transmitted directly or indirectly? A direct channel is a system of communication in which one person relates to someone else without the interference or aid of a third person or a mechanical device. The oral interpretation act, the speaker who reaches the newspaper reader via a reporter, the tape recording, television, and the two-step flow of communication all illustrate the indirect channel.[20] But indirectness admits of degrees. Messages may be transmitted through only one intermediary person or agency, or they may follow a circuitous track, as in a typical rumor, between its originator and its ultimate, and perhaps indefinite, destination.[21]

---

[18] *Marshall McLuhan's* The Medium is the Massage *(New York, 1967) is a notable attempt to make the nonverbal code as important in a book as the verbal.*

[19] *Joseph A. DeVito's study of "Comprehension Factors in Oral and Written Discourse of Skilled Communicators,"* Speech Monographs, *XXXII (June 1965), 124–128, concluded that written discourse involved a more difficult vocabulary, simpler sentences, and a greater density of ideas than did oral discourse.*

[20] *The two-step flow of communication and the concept of opinion leadership has considerable applicability to rhetoric. See Elihu Katz and Paul F. Lazarsfeld,* Personal Influence *(Glencoe, Ill., 1955), and Elihu Katz, "The Two-Step Flow of Communication: An Up-to-Date Report on an Hypothesis,"* Public Opinion Quarterly, *XXI (Spring 1957), 61–78.*

[21] *The classic study of rumor is Gordon W. Allport and Leo Postman,* Psychology of Rumor *(New York, 1947).*

People. How rhetorical situations are populated forms six variables. One concerns the number of interacting people. Are they few or many?[22]

A second variable is the number of groups which function in the situation, whether as audiences or conferences. The range is from one to many. A speaker may address one particular audience or many audiences, either simultaneously or consecutively. A person may participate in a conference which operates virtually as a self-contained unit or in a conference involving multiple groups.

A third variable has to do with the degree to which the people are organized. The range is from a virtual absence of organization to the status of a highly structured and cohesive reference group.

A fourth variable, closely related to the third, involves the degree of homogeneity among the participating people. They may exhibit a high degree of homogeneity, they may be similar on some and different on other properties, or they may differ so much as to constitute essentially different groups even though they participate in the same situation.[23]

Fifth, participants in a rhetorical situation may vary widely in their degree of awareness of their roles and in their degree of involvement in the situation.

Sixth, those who people a rhetorical situation engage in a range of relationships to that situation. One, some, many, or all of the participants may regard themselves or be regarded by others as depersonalized stimulus objects; as members or agents of a culture, institution, or group; as performing a role; as projecting an image; as manifesting a set of properties or as selves with radical choices to make or commitments to uphold.

Functions. The functions of a rhetorical situation may be viewed from a general perspective or along interpersonal and attitudinal dimensions.

Some questions of situational function seem to apply both to the interpersonal and to the attitudinal aspects of a rhetorical act. To what extent are interpersonal relationships and/or attitudes to be reinforced or changed? What degrees of intensity of reinforcement or change does the situation call for? If change is to function, in what direction?

[22] *I am inclined to include the intrapersonal communication of self-address within the scope of rhetoric. An individual's roles may interact intrapersonally and attitudinally in a variety of situational contexts in ways closely analogous to the interpersonal and attitudinal interaction of two or more persons. For support of this position, see Barnlund, 199–201, and Burke, pp. 561–563.*

[23] *The effect of a group's homogeneity and receptivity on the integration and polarization of an audience is admirably discussed in Charles H. Woolbert's pioneer monograph "The Audience," Psychological Monographs, XXI, No. 92 (June 1916), 37–54.*

Other questions relate directly to the interpersonal dimension. Are people trying primarily to relate, identify, disengage, or in other ways to interact with others in the situation, or are they trying to express their "selves" conjointly? Are they trying to court, please, satisfy, tolerate, dissatisfy, or derogate one another? Are they trying to change or reinforce the power disparity or power structure of the situation? Are they trying to increase, maintain, or decrease social or interpersonal distance? Is group maintenance or group cohesiveness a relevant situational function?

Still other questions relate directly to three kinds of attitude influence. First, a person may present a message with a designative function—to present information, describe, define, amplify, clarify, make ambiguous, obfuscate, review, or synthesize ideas. Second, someone may present a message with an evaluative function—to praise, make commentary, hedge, criticize, or blame some person, object, situation, judgment, or policy. Third, someone may present a message with an advocative function—to solve a problem, create indecision, reinforce a present choice, foster delay, choose a change [*sic*] alternative, resolve a conflict, propose a compromise, or stimulate action.

The functions of rhetorical situations appear far more complex than implied by the traditional categories of inform, entertain, and persuade.

Method. Any situational function is manifested instrumentally through a number of message variables. These constitute the methodological dimension of the rhetorical act. Method is less often than other dimensions the ultimate function of the act; typically it plays the instrumental role of facilitating whatever dimension is primary.

Method includes the materials presented, the form in which they are structured, and the style in which materials and form are communicated.

Three questions about the material to be presented seem important. How much data should be presented? What kinds of data should be employed? From what sources should they be derived? These questions, of course, have no simple answers universally applicable.

The form variable may be analyzed in two ways. A distinction can be made between a sort of form-in-the-large which permeates the rhetorical method and a more microscopic set of structures which develops. The rhetorical act may be transacted through some conventional medium like an essay, a play, or a speech. A rhetorician may fulfill expectations by using identifiable forms in typical ways, or he may create new forms or employ old forms in new ways. Whether forms are appropriately new or old and whether their development is appropriately conventional or eccentric, of course, depends on the experience and expectations of the other people in the rhetorical act. The method may represent a straightforward management of materials to develop a central idea directly, or reflect an indirect ordering—for example, through the use of irony.[24] How prominent the form-in-the-large is to be is an important issue. Should the form become clearly evident in the discourse, or should it fulfill its function unobtrusively and not call any special attention to itself?

The form variable may also be viewed microscopically. This level of analysis includes a consideration of the logical connection between the material presented and the ideas advanced—which calls for the student of rhetoric to understand the logic of rhetorical interaction and the modes of reasoning appropriate to such interaction.[25] It includes a recognition of the structure which joins the ideas advanced into a pattern which amplifies or supports the central idea—which calls for an understanding of the patterns of expository and argumentative discourse, the analysis of a controversy into its issues, and the methods of problem-solving and negotiation.[26]

Specific formal structures may be recognizable immediately to others in the act and utilized in predictable ways, or they may be new and less obvious. Furthermore, the two levels of form in a discourse, the macroscopic and the microscopic, may function harmoniously toward the same end or constitute incongruity. Form, whether large or small, may be designed to facilitate information transfer or to disrupt it; to create a relatively narrow range of meanings and attitudinal responses or to maximize ambiguity; to present an optimal amount of material efficiently or to aim at redundancy; to achieve identification or alienation; to reinforce meanings and attitudes or to change them; and to increase or decrease the intensity of feelings toward the ideas.

Style, like form, may be viewed macroscopically or microscopically. Rhetorical style may be looked at from the point of view of broad symbolic strategy, a style-in-the-large. I take this concern to be behind

[24] For an excellent analysis of rhetorical irony, see Allan B. Karstetter, "Toward a Theory of Rhetorical Irony," Speech Monographs, XXXI (June 1964), 162–178.

[25] If one accepts the central idea of this essay that rhetoric is a system of interrelated dimensions, he must conclude that a rhetorical logic must accommodate the function of dimensions other than the one concerned with formal relationships among propositions. Irrelevant to rhetorical analysis is any logical system which assumes that man is only rational and that men do not vary, that ideas can be divorced from their affective content and from their ideological contexts, and that the only situation is that of the logician talking to the logician.

[26] Rhetoricians have tended to treat these various organizational patterns, like logic, as invariant structures, without due regard for the totality of the rhetorical situation—its people, its functions, and its contexts.

much of the writing of Kenneth Burke.[27] Or it may be analyzed by looking at smaller units of analysis—at the level of the phoneme, word, sentence, or paragraph. Perhaps the writing of modern linguists may provide better ways of analyzing style microscopically than rhetoricians have followed traditionally.[28]

Many of the questions raised about form appear to apply also to style. Whether looked at large or small, style, too, provokes such issues as efficiency of information transfer, clarity *vs.* ambiguity, conciseness *vs.* redundancy, confidence *vs.* uncertainty, and identification *vs.* alienation. The issues can be resolved only by studying the particular interaction of the other dimensions in each unique rhetorical act.

Contexts. The contexts of time and place may alter in various ways how other dimensions function in the act. In this regard context is typical of situational dimensions. The substance of a rhetorical act is rarely located in the situation: it more characteristically focuses on the interpersonal and attitudinal categories. Aspects of the situation, including context, although not fundamental or ultimate, however, can alter decisively the other categories and hence change the substance of the act.

In addition, time functions in another way. Each rhetorical act has some larger setting and fits into one or more ongoing processes.[29] For example, a novel may be a part of a movement or of several movements, a representation of an ideology or several ideologies, a moment in the career of the writer, a specimen of some formal or stylistic tendency, a phase in some long-term interpersonal relationship with a set of readers, *et cetera.* Several questions may suggest some of the ways a rhetorical act may relate to its contexts. Does an act occur relatively early or relatively late in one or more processes? To what extent is the act congruous with its larger framework? Does the act play one role in one context and a different, and perhaps conflicting, role in another?

[27] *Burke, for example, says (p. 567) that rhetoric "is rooted in an essential function of language itself, . . . the use of language as a symbolic means of inducing cooperation in beings that by nature respond to symbols." For Burke, rhetorical analysis is an attempt to unearth the essential linguistic strategies of the rhetorical agent.*

[28] *In "A Linguistic Analysis of Oral and Written Style," QJS, XLVIII (December 1962), 419–422, Jane Blankenship applied the system of analysis which Charles C. Fries described in his book* The Structure of English *(New York, 1952).*

[29] *Two recent books which display a contextual orientation to rhetoric are Wallace Fotheringham,* Perspectives on Persuasion *(Boston, 1966), and Huber W. Ellingsworth and Theodore Clevenger, Jr.,* Speech and Social Action *(Englewood Cliffs, N. J., 1967).*

4

Important to the student of rhetoric is the question of points of view. A rhetorical act will be perceived quite differently by each person who participates in it, and still differently by each person who observes and criticizes it from "the outside." Here, as elsewhere, "meanings are in people," not in discourses. Students of rhetoric must try to determine how the various participants and observers have perceived the dimensions of the act and to discover the extent to which such perceptions differ. The points of view of the relevant people become part of an important dimension of the act.

The consideration of point of view may have different implications for theorists, as compared with participants and critics. The theorist tends to be interested in generalizations at the highest level of abstraction he can achieve, whereas participants and critics tend to be interested in making decisions or judgments about one very particular and unique act.

Perhaps the most important single characteristic of rhetoric is that it is a matrix of complex and interrelated variables of the kind discussed in this paper. The theorist cannot meaningfully pluck from the system any single variable and hope to understand it apart from the others. How can one understand style, for example, without knowing how it interrelates with power structure, with distance, with attitudes and ideologies, with the demands of format and context—in short, with every other dimension of the act? Gross generalizations about stylistic characteristics which ignore the assumption that style functions very differently when placed in different combinations with the other variables simply will not do. Unfortunately for the prognosis of theoretical advances in rhetoric, the combinations and permutations of the alternatives afforded by the various dimensions are so many as to approach infinity. But methods will have to be developed to pursue the sort of interrelational kind of analysis which an adequate theory of rhetoric requires.[30]

The practitioner may use such an interrelational analysis before, during, and after a transaction as a guide to the decisions he must make to give himself the best chance of interacting with others as he wishes.

The critic may profitably identify the single most compelling dimen-

---

[30] *Warren Weaver has argued that science must "make a third great advance which must be even greater than the nineteenth-century conquest of problems of simplicity or the twentieth-century victory over problems of disorganized complexity. Science must, over the next fifty years, learn to deal with these problems of organized complexity." See "Science and Complexity," in* The Scientist Speaks, *ed. Warren Weaver (New York, 1945), p. 7. Implicit in my essay is the belief that rhetoric represents a problem of "organized complexity."*

sion of a rhetorical act under consideration and then investigate how that dimension interrelates with others which appear to be relevant. For example, a critic studying Nikita Khrushchev's interaction with the American public during his 1959 visit to this country might focus primary attention on Khrushchev's reduction of interpersonal distance between himself and his hosts in order to see how his distance-reducing rhetoric related to new American images of Khrushchev personally along liking and power dimensions; to his attempts to make attitudes and ideologies consubstantial; and to his use of various rhetorical situations for these functions. If a critic accepts the fundamental premise that each rhetorical act or process is unique, that dimensions interrelate in a way to create a unity never achieved in the past or in the future, then he commits himself to a search for a new way to select, structure, and weigh dimensions for each new act he criticizes.

My hope is that the dimensions described in this essay may provide a framework for theoretical development, practical decision-making, and critical analysis.

Reducing Rhetorical Distance:
Khrushchev's 1959 American Tour
by Wayne Brockriede and Robert L. Scott

The 1950s were tense years of policy disputes between the United States and the Soviet Union. For example, the Soviet Union pressed hard for a change in the status of Germany, especially Berlin, which Nikita Khrushchev described as "abnormal" and "a bone in my throat" but the United States was determined not to leave Berlin. From the point of view of policy, the status quo was frozen.

Beneath the surface of such a stalemate, however, existed a tacit agreement concerning how policy issues of the Cold War were to be disputed. Principal among these agreements was the recognition that neither side was willing to initiate a nuclear war. Since the Korean War both sides had cautiously refrained from taking action that would broaden the conflict to include an American-Soviet confrontation. The 1955 Geneva Conference made the understanding explicit. In spite of a rhetoric of liberation during the Dulles era, the United States did not intervene in the Hungarian revolt of 1956. The ultimatum Khrushchev had issued concerning Berlin was lifted in 1959. Although disputes were not immediately negotiable, any alteration of the status quo had to be attempted without risking nuclear war between the major powers.

No limitation existed on the rhetorical level. The leadership and the people on both sides had conditioned one another to engage in what Adlai Stevenson called "massive verbal retaliation." Charles O. Lerche claimed that "the Soviet Union has raised the art of vituperative propaganda to new heights of excess in language and vulgarity in presentation" (p. 47), but a Soviet observer could have evaluated United States verbal abuse toward the Soviet Union similarly. Urie Bronfenbrenner argues persuasively that both sides developed a "mirror image" of the other (see also Lerche and Osgood). Full scale verbal assaults were the order of the day.

On August 4, 1959, the two governments issued an announcement that Premier Khrushchev would make an official visit to the United States in September and that President Dwight D. Eisenhower would make a return visit to the Soviet Union later that autumn. Premier Khrushchev's visit, September 15–27, is a complex and rewarding phenomenon for rhetorical analysis. Although neither government seemed to expect any major policy settlements, the joint announcement of the visit expressed "the hope that the forthcoming visits will contribute to better understanding between the USA and USSR, and promote the cause of peace" (quoted in *Khrushchev in America,* p. 9). Although policies were to remain frozen, the agreement to keep the peace was to be reinforced, and the rhetorical distance between the two countries was to be reduced.

Before the Tour

What were the prevailing attitudes of Americans toward Premier Khrushchev and the Soviet Union, the hopes and fears of the American hosts, and the possible goals of the Soviet guest on the eve of the rhetorical transaction?

Some Americans had reacted negatively to the announcement of the exchange of visits. Boston's Cardinal Richard Cushing "denounced all Russians as spies, urged Catholics to recite the rosary and pray during Khrushchev's twelve-day visit" (*Time,* 8–31–59, p. 12). On August 13, 1959, Senator Thomas J. Dodd of Connecticut told the Senate:

I hope that during Khrushchev's visit we shall hear church bells in the land, tolling their remembrance for the murdered millions behind the Iron Curtain. . . . Let there be no cheers for the Red Dictator, no crowds assembled to greet him, no flattery or flowers. Let our people be civil but silent ("Khrushchev's Visit," p. 712).

Most people approved the visits, however. *Newsweek* reported that thirteen of Premier Khrushchev's recent American callers "were unanimous in the belief that President Eisenhower's invitation . . . [held] out more promise of improving international relations than risk of impairing them" ("How to Handle Khrushchev," p. 22). Surely the war-hero President would not become soft on communism and surely he could "take care of himself, and the cause of the free world" ("What Americans Think," p. 40).

Although Americans favored the visits, they viewed the Soviet Union and its Premier with suspicion and hostility. They saw the Soviet Union not merely as an opponent, but as the enemy with whom one must regard "the struggle as one of life or death" (Morris, pp. 160–161). "After 14 years of the Cold War," William V. Shannon observes, "any Russian ruler would be received with suspicion and reserve." Although Merle Fainsod in 1956 had recognized that Khrushchev was able to "project an image of personalized and humanized leadership" (p. 35), most Americans in 1959 viewed him as "an abstract concept," as "embodied evil" ("Without Horns or Tails," p. 43). The only personal characteristics of Premier Khrushchev that had come into reasonably clear focus were essentially negative—such pictures as "the monster of deceit and treachery, the drunken peasant, the mass killer" ("The Visit"), a "vodka-drinking, musical comedy clown" (Sheerin, "What We Learned," p. 80).

Yet many people looked forward hopefully to the visit. One cause for hope was the belief, as Howard K. Smith expressed it, that "something new must be tried to break the log-jam and ease tension" (*Images of Peace*, p. 51). Senator Everett M. Dirksen of Illinois explained that

if there can come some end to the tensions which now exist between nations, and some relief from the costly armament burden which sits so heavily on people in all parts of the world, I believe history will rank President Eisenhower as the boldest peacemaker in many generations ("The Range of Reaction in Congress," pp. 69–70).

A second cause for hope was the idea that the Premier's experience in the United States would give him a better understanding of this country and its purposes. Before the visit had been announced, Vice President Richard M. Nixon argued that Khrushchev has "some real misconceptions with regard to both our policies and our people. And I think that by going to the United States and seeing first hand our country and people, this will serve to reduce those misconceptions" (Caruthers, p. 1). On several occasions President Eisenhower stressed his hope that a visit would increase Premier Khrushchev's understanding of the United States.

Some people minimized this hope by declaring that Mr. Khrushchev

already knew a great deal about the United States and was not remarkably well motivated to learn more. After the tour, one observer
noted that "he seems to have come to America more in a spirit of
national self-assertion than of genuine inquiry; and in some respects
the tour may have confirmed his prejudices rather than removed them"
("The Glacier Moves"). Stevenson, who was an early and staunch advocate of the exchange of visits, nevertheless recognized and was impressed by Khrushchev's grasp of American affairs:

*I don't think Khrushchev is so abysmally ignorant of us as the Soviet
press, with its distorted image of America, would lead one to suppose.
For he is one of the privileged minority in Russia not dependent on
Pravda for the truth or Izvestia for the news. . . . I was struck by his
grasp of many details of the international situation and of our policy*
(p. 5).

Interestingly, few persons voiced the hope that the government or the
people of the United States might learn to know Premier Khrushchev or
his purposes better.

Those who feared or opposed the trip believed that the Soviet Premier had gained by the fact of the invitation a tremendous increase in
international prestige, especially among peoples in the Soviet satellites
and in the uncommitted nations. Daniel Schorr observed that in Poland,
for example, "there was a feeling that Khrushchev's visit . . . was a
public relations coup before it ever started" ("Khrushchev's 'Hard
Sell,' " p. 6; see also *The Crimes of Khrushchev,* p. 13). The one country for which the visit did not enhance Soviet prestige was China. Several observers argued that "Premier Khrushchev's decision to visit the
United States represented the point of no return in the deepening
schism between the Soviet Union and China" (Slusser, p. 200; see also
Morris, p. 151).

What were Premier Khrushchev's motives for seeking and accepting
an invitation to tour the United States? First, no doubt, he hoped that
the visit would provide a "propaganda opportunity to project a more
favorable impression of himself and of Soviet strength," by having a
"sounding board in a country with the world's most highly developed
system of mass communication" ("Questions of the Week," p. 39).

Second, he may well have hoped to enhance his power in the Soviet
government and his popularity among his own people. Contrary to a
widespread belief in 1959 that Khrushchev was an absolute dictator,
today many historians argue that Khrushchev's power was never unlimited and that some of his initiatives were designed to maintain and
increase his status as leader of an oligarchy. Richard Lowenthal ex-

presses this point of view: "Khrushchev disposes of all the levers of command, but he is not yet regarded as infallible within the inner circle. . . . Khrushchev's lack of historical achievements . . . [induces him to] hunt for spectacular prestige successes abroad" (p. 122).[1] Presumably, the Soviet Premier hoped that he could gain a "spectacular prestige success" in the United States.

Contrary to another widespread belief in 1959 that the opinion of the Soviet people was essentially irrelevant to policy determination, many Kremlinologists recognized that public opinion had a growing influence on Soviet policies. In a 1957 essay Harrison Salisbury, Soviet specialist of *The New York Times,* commented, "The Russian dictatorship, contrary to popular supposition, is not immune to the trends of public opinion. . . . Khrushchev himself . . . has tried to link his fortunes with all of the things which he thinks the Soviet people want" ("The Fatal Flaw in the Soviet System," p. 249).[2] Edward Crankshaw, London journalist, said in 1962 that the object of the visit was "to prove to the Soviet people . . . that he could bring them peace and an understanding in terms of equality with the greatest power in the world" (1962, p. 149).

Khrushchev's third motive undoubtedly was to speak frequently to the American people under conditions that would ensure maximum attention, to talk his way across the country and back. On a CBS newscast on September 15, 1959, Daniel Schorr conjectured that Khrushchev wanted to "put across the twin points of overwhelming Soviet power and overwhelming Soviet desire for peace. He's not sure he can sell our leaders; he does think he's enough of a salesman to make an effective pitch over their heads to the American people" (*Images of Peace,* p. 73; see also Frankland, p. 155).

Premier Khrushchev's tour is an unusually complex rhetorical transaction. Although ostensibly he spoke to a single audience, the American people, the people and governments of American allies, the Soviet Union, China, Soviet satellites, and uncommitted nations all responded to his message. The critic who looks at what Khrushchev said and did during the tour may focus on any of these audiences or on the way the responses of various audiences were interrelated. He may also wish to examine Khrushchev's rhetoric from the perspective of any of a number of rhetorical dimensions. Following are the dimensions we consider especially relevant:

1. Distance: How did Khrushchev try to decrease the interpersonal distance between himself and his hosts and the international distance between the Soviet Union and the United States?

---

[1] See also Crankshaw, "The Men Behind Khrushchev," p. 29; Linden, p. 7; and Rush, pp. 111–113.
[2] See also Petrov, p. 290; Pietromarchi, p. 87; and Schapiro, pp. 398–399.

2. Images: How did Khrushchev try to improve his own image and that of his country?
3. Power: How did Khrushchev try to improve his own power status and that of his country?
4. Maximizing agreement: How did Khrushchev employ the rhetorical strategy of de-emphasizing disagreement on specific controversies and emphasizing agreement that such disputes should not be allowed to result in a Soviet-American war?
5. Forcing a choice: How did Khrushchev employ the rhetorical strategy of the residues method of argument to force the United States to choose peaceful coexistence and nonmilitary competition as the only reasonable alternative to ideological conversion (dismissed as unrealistic) or to arms races and nuclear wars (dismissed as undesirable)?
6. Context: What is the function of the context in determining and evaluating the effect of a particular message on a specific occasion? What advantage has the critic in viewing the tour as a sequential campaign instead of as a disconnected series of speeches?
7. Channels: What were the roles of the interpreters and of the communication media in selecting (and sometimes in determining) what the public would see, hear, and read?

Each of these dimensions, as well as others that are not mentioned here, could function as a useful lens through which a critic can look at other dimensions in an attempt to frame a total picture of the rhetoric Premier Khrushchev employed from September 15 to September 27, 1959.

An Annotated Record of the Tour

At 12:24 P.M., September 15, the Soviet Premier and his party landed at Andrews Air Force Base in Maryland. After President Eisenhower led the way to a reception area and made a speech of welcome, Premier Khrushchev presented the first of twenty-four speeches he was to make in the United States.

The Speech At Andrews Field.[3] *Mr. President, ladies and gentlemen. Permit me at this moment, in first setting foot on American soil, to thank Mr. Eisenhower for the invitation to visit your country, and everyone present for the warm welcome accorded to us representatives of the Soviet Union.*[4]

---

[3] *The text is the interpreter's translation as transcribed and printed in* The New York Times, *September 16, 1959, p. 19.*
[4] *The opening paragraph serves the ceremonial function of satisfying audience expectations on such an occasion.*

Russians say every good job should be started in the morning. Our flight began in Moscow this morning and we now have the pleasure of first meeting you on American soil on the morning of the same day.[5]

As you see our countries are not so distant from each other.[6]

I accepted the invitation of the President of the United States to make an official visit to your country with great pleasure and gratitude and I will be glad to meet and talk with your statesmen, representatives of the business world, intellectuals, workers and farmers, and to learn about the life of the industrious and enterprising American people.

For our part we will be glad to receive Mr. Eisenhower, his family and those who will shortly accompany him to the Soviet Union. We will give the President a most cordial welcome and every opportunity to become familiar with the life of the Soviet people.[7]

We have always considered reciprocal visits and meetings of representatives of different countries as useful. Meetings and discussions between the statesmen of our two great countries, the Soviet Union and the United States of America, are especially important.

The people of all countries are profoundly interested in the maintenance and consolidation of peace and peaceful coexistence. War does not promise anyone any good, while peace is advantageous to all nations. This is the basic principle which we believe the statesmen of all countries should be guided by in order to realize the aspirations of the people.

We have come here with an open heart and good intentions. The Soviet people want to live in friendship with the American people. There are no obstacles to having relations between our countries develop as good neighborly relations.

The Soviet and the American people and the people of other countries fought well together in the Second World War against the common enemy and broke his backbone. In peaceful conditions we have even more reasons for friendship and cooperation between the people of our countries.[8]

---

[5] Early in Mr. Khrushchev's first speech he seems to want to establish an informal relationship. One can almost imagine two gregarious Americans discussing the topic on a transcontinental flight.

[6] Khrushchev is doing more than merely passing the time of day. He has been using an informal social amenity to reduce distance and to argue by analogy his dominant theme: peaceful coexistence. In effect, he is saying that as our physical distance decreases our interpersonal and international distance should decrease.

[7] The fourth and fifth paragraphs are more formal; they include what might be expected in a speech of this sort. The theme and some of the language echo the announcement of the visits.

[8] After his attempt to establish a conversational tone with his audience, Khrushchev begins his first substantive argument: his theme of peaceful coexistence. The "open heart" and "good intentions" were phrases widely quoted.

Shortly before this meeting with you, Mr. President, the Soviet scientists, engineers, technicians and workers filled our hearts with joy by launching a rocket to the moon.[9] A road has thus been blazed from the earth to the moon and the container of 390 kilograms with a pennant bearing the national emblem of the Soviet Union is now on the moon. Our earth has become somewhat lighter while the moon has gained several hundred pounds in weight.

I am sure that this historic achievement of peaceful science has brought joy not only to the Soviet people but to all who cherish peace and friendship among nations.

An atomic icebreaker has just been completed in the Soviet Union. This practical embodiment of the desire of all people to see nuclear energy put solely to peaceful uses is also a happy event.

We are aware, Mr. President, that the idea of the peaceful use of atomic energy is dear to you, and we note with gratification that your aims in this field coincide with ours.[10]

We have no doubt that the excellent scientists, engineers and workers of the United States of America who are engaged in the field of conquering the cosmos will also carry their pennant over to the moon. The Soviet pennant, as an old resident, will then welcome your pennant and they will live there together in peace and friendship, as we should live together on earth in peace and friendship and as all people should live who inhabit our common mother earth who is so generous to us with all her gifts.

In these first few minutes of our stay in the United States permit me to extend cordial greetings and best wishes to the American people on behalf of the Soviet Union, the Soviet Government and on my own behalf.[11]

Thank you.

In the Russian version of the speech the "live in friendship" slogan appears as "live in peace and friendship." The Soviet book in which these speeches are collected is entitled Live in Peace and Friendship.

[9] *Khrushchev's motivation for boasting of recent Soviet technological achievements could be twofold: (1) a feeling that such a statement would be expected of him by the Soviet people and government and (2) a desire to underscore Soviet technological might and hence to strike a note of urgency, even fear, which would favor accepting peaceful coexistence. Khrushchev's reference to lunar sputnik must have appeared to most Americans as an assertion of raw Soviet power. Furthermore, the condescension implied, later in the speech, by the image of the Soviet emblem patiently awaiting its delinquent American counterpart must have been abrasive to many Americans, who may have missed the speaker's attempt to relate the image to his theme of peaceful coexistence.*

[10] *The reference is to Eisenhower's "atoms for peace" proposal and represents the strategy of stressing agreement.*

[11] *The concluding paragraph, like the introductory one, is a rather perfunctory fulfillment of a ceremonial commitment. The relatively small amount of time Khrushchev characteristically spends on ritualistic rhetoric is striking.*

During Premier Khrushchev's first four days in this country, in Washington and in New York City, he made additional speeches at a White House dinner, at the National Press Club, at a meeting with congressional leaders and members of the Senate Foreign Relations Committee, at a dinner given for President Eisenhower at the Soviet Embassy, at a luncheon given by New York's Mayor Robert Wagner, at a dinner given by the Economics Club of New York, and at the U.N. at which, in a major address, he presented the Soviet proposal for "general and complete disarmament."

Premier Khrushchev's behavior during the first phase of the tour, covered extensively by the news media, was not especially dramatic. Large crowds lined up to see him in Washington and New York, but the people, though curious, were not demonstrative. A London reporter described the American response:

It is not easy to say what impact Mr. Khrushchev made on New York or it made on him. . . . The crowds lining the streets proved that the silence with which he was greeted in Washington was not simply a local phenomenon due to the restraining presence of President Eisenhower. The New Yorkers showed the same surprising, rather un-American reticence. Reporters, in their search for the right word to describe it, have run through a Roget's Thesaurus of adjectives: cool, chilly, restrained, reserved, aloof ("Communist's Progress," p. 1021; see also Shannon).

The rhetorical drama became more exciting on September 19, when Premier Khrushchev landed in Los Angeles. He was greeted so briefly by Mayor Norris Poulson that he discarded his prepared text and responded briefly in kind. Then at a luncheon at the studio of 20th-Century Fox, given by Eric Johnston, President of the Motion Pictures Association of America, and Sypros Skouras, President of 20th-Century Fox, Premier Khrushchev created the first major stir. After concluding his prepared text, he announced that, for security reasons, he would not be permitted to visit Disneyland:

But just now I was told that I could not go to Disneyland.[12] I asked, "Why not?" What is it, do you have rocket-launching pads there? I do not know. And just listen—just listen to what I was told—to what reason

[12] *The text was transcribed by a CBS affiliate, KNX-TV of Los Angeles, and appeared in* The New York Times, *September 20, 1959, p. 41. The reference to Disneyland is both ludicrous (a Soviet premier pouting over a denied pleasure) and appealing. Whatever else this passage may have done to modify American attitudes toward Khrushchev, it reduced distance by revealing something of the Premier's humanness.*

I was told. We, which means the American authorities, cannot guarantee your security if you go there.

What is it? Is there an epidemic of cholera there or something? Or have gangsters taken hold of the place that can destroy me? But your policemen are so tough they can lift a bull by the horns. And surely they can restore order if there are any gangsters around.

And I say, I would very much like to go and see Disneyland. But then, we cannot guarantee your security, they say. Then what must I do? Commit suicide?[13] *That's the situation I am in—your guest. For me, such a situation is inconceivable. I cannot find words to explain this to my people.*

The second explosion was more serious. It occurred that evening at a dinner sponsored by Los Angeles authorities and the Association of International Affairs. Mayor Poulson called attention to Mr. Khrushchev's celebrated "we will bury you" statement.[14] The Premier followed him to the podium. He waited until he had completed his prepared text before escalating tension to the peak of the tour.

The Threat.[15] *. . . Actually, that was the end of my prepared speech, but those—the speakers that preceded me raised a number of points which I cannot fail to answer.*[16] *I can put this text in my pocket now. I turn to you, Mr. Mayor, my dear host: in your speech you said that we wanted to bury you.*

You have shown us wonderful hospitality towards me and my comrades, and I thank you.

---

[13] *The Disneyland passage has a light and humorous touch likely to appeal to some Americans. Throughout his visit, Premier Khrushchev's attempts at humor probably had a good effect on his image.*

[14] *Khrushchev made the widely quoted statement on November 17, 1956, at a Kremlin reception. He had been irritated by an American refusal to respond reciprocally to a hint that Russia might withdraw from Hungary if the United States were to withdraw from some other part of Europe. The phrase "we will bury you" has been quoted out of context frequently. The entire passage is as follows: "If you don't like us, don't accept our invitations and don't invite us to come to see you! Whether you like it or not, history is on our side; we will bury you!!!" The time, the occasion, and the character of the speaker all suggest that these "flushed and impulsive words" are those "of a powerful but unsure man, shouting rather than whistling in the dark" (Lukacs, p. 151).*

[15] *The text of this extemporaneous explosion is taken from* The New York Times, *September 20, 1959, pp. 41–42.*

[16] *As in his earlier speech that day, Mr. Khrushchev drew a sharp line between the prepared text, which presumably represented carefully calculated rhetorical decisions, and his impromptu response to the occasion. One wonders if he welcomed the chance to take the hard line, to make explicit the alternative to peaceful co-existence. He may have felt that he should not complete the argument as a part of a prepared discourse.*

I want to say the truth. Can I do that here?[17] *I want to ask you why did you mention that fact? Already while I was here in the United States I have already had occasion to give clarification on that point. I trust that even mayors read the press. At least in our country the chairmen of the city councils read the press. If they don't, they risk not being elected next time.*[18]

Ladies and gentlemen, you want to get up on this favorite horse of yours and proceed in the same old direction. If you do get up on it and sit in the saddle, where can this horse lead you to? If you want a continuation of the arms race, you are doing right. You should then get up on this horse and go along in that old direction.

If you want to continue the arms race, if you want to have a war, then do get up on that horse. If you want to insist on this line, then there can be no talk of disarmament. There can only be talk of continuing the arms race.

If you are not ready for disarmament and you want to go on with the arms race, very well, we accept that challenge,[19] *for we now have the necessary strength and all the possibilities to create modern weapons, and as for the output of our rockets, those are on the assembly line.*[20]

I am talking seriously, because I have come here with serious intentions and you try to reduce the matter to simply a joke. It is a question of war or peace between our countries, a question of the life or death of the people.

[17] On several occasions Khrushchev precedes hard talk with a justification for speaking plainly, even bluntly. He seems to be trying to show an awareness of the normal expectations of guest-host relationships even though he feels moved to violate one of them.

[18] Khrushchev's decision to ridicule Mayor Poulson was risky. No doubt Khrushchev would lose favor with some of his audience for being openly contemptuous of the Mayor in his own city. He may have reasoned that some would oppose the Mayor and that others might see the validity of the accusation that Poulson had not read Khrushchev's Washington speeches and should have done so. Although Khrushchev treats the situation humorously, the humor is heavy, if not brutal.

[19] Perhaps the principal logic of Khrushchev's rhetoric throughout the tour is the attempt to stress that the Soviet Union and the United States had two choices: cold war or peace and friendship. Khrushchev's strategy is to put the burden of choosing on the United States rather than on Soviet Russia. The rest of this speech places considerable emphasis on the "war or peace" strategy.

[20] Not only does Khrushchev emphasize the choice of war or peace; here more than in any other speech he tries to underscore the urgency of that choice by referring to the strength of the Soviet Union and by suggesting the consequences of nuclear war. Perhaps a principal motive for the trip was Khrushchev's hope of demonstrating to his own people, to his allies, to neutralist nations, and to the United States and its allies that the Soviet Union had reached a position equal to that of the United States. The implication of the undesirability of an American choice of war rather than peace dominates the rest of the speech.

We are extending the hand of friendship, but if you don't want to—if you accept it, then you should manifest a reasonable approach to matters. One should not play upon words. We hold positions of too much responsibility and the consequences of a play upon words can be too sad for our peoples.

Ladies and gentlemen, I would like once again to clarify what I have already said once.[21] When I spoke of the burial, that should not be understood literally, word for word, as if somebody was going to take a spade and start burying somebody. What I meant was the development of history, the evolution of human society and that is what we believe in, according to our philosophy.

According to your philosophy, that is not so, but then let history be the judge of who is right. You live under capitalism and let us live under socialism. I have said that so many times that my tongue is tired of saying it. Let time show which social system is better. If the people see that your system is better, let that be proved.

If the people think that ours is better, let them take our system but let us not try to bury one another. If you prefer to live under your system, God be with you.

Ladies and gentlemen, your President Eisenhower invited me here as his guest, not just to have a cup of tea or perhaps a small glass of cognac. I have partners for that back home. I have not traveled thousands of miles for that. I am sure that your President also has enough partners at home without inviting me over.

The President offers me no hope of accepting our opinions, our philosophy regarding the development of human society, and I have no hope that the President will revert—will come over to the positions of communism. From that point of view, he is hopeless. And I have no such designs, just as I am sure that he has no designs of turning me into a capitalist.[22]

----

[21] Although Mr. Khrushchev shows impatience at having to explain his famous statement one more time, he does not set aside this question as "provocative" and unworthy of an answer—as he did in response to several questions earlier in the tour. He may have answered the question whenever someone raised it because he could use it as another springboard for stating the peaceful competition argument of his peaceful coexistence theme. Questions about Hungary or about his own relations with Stalin had no such value and were rejected.

[22] This statement represents the change in communist ideology announced in Khrushchev's 1956 speech to the 20th Party Congress: the doctrine that war to the finish with capitalism is not inevitable. What he sees as inevitable is history's verdict that communism will ultimately triumph. Furthermore, Khrushchev is able to tell his own people (as he did on several other occasions) that he was in no danger whatsoever of being persuaded by his American hosts. Khrushchev recognizes, however, that a capitalist leader will not be persuaded on a short-term basis to accept communism.

Then, why is it that—why is it that he invited me here? He showed, I think, state wisdom. He understood the duty to seek agreement with us, without feeling any esteem or respect for the teaching of communism. I assure you I am sure that you have no such esteem for that teaching, but we are neighbors, because the Pacific Ocean both divides us and unites us.

The question is one, ladies and gentlemen, of there being either peace or war between our two nations.

I am deeply concerned over these, I believe to be, conscious distortions of my thoughts which can lead to nothing but the aggravation of the "cold war." But choose for yourself the language you prefer to use.

I have not come here to appeal to you in any way. We are strong. We are no less strong than you are.

I have never in any of my addresses spoken or mentioned any rockets, but when I did so today, I had no other way out, because it would seem it could be made out from certain pronouncements that we have come here to beg something of you; that we have come here to beg you to eliminate the "cold war" because we are afraid of you.

If you think that the "cold war" is something which is profitable to you, then go ahead. Let us then compete in the "cold war."

The only thing is: that competition in the "cold war" means, with the modern means of—in the conditions of the existence of modern weapons.

The question as it stands now is one of whether this meeting of minds with President Eisenhower will lead to the elimination of the "cold war" or whether we will simply part.

After all, I am the first head of either Russia or the Soviet Union to have visited the United States in all your history, and yet we did live. If you do not accept these—all this, but I can go and I don't know when if ever another Russian Soviet Premier Minister will visit your country.

You may well say that without such a visit you too live in this world. That is true, certainly, but with equal certainty it is also true that it is much better to live in peace than to live in conditions—than to live with loaded pistols and guns trained at their objective.[23]

It is—[Applause].

It is better to have a friendly atmosphere—a friendly and a tranquil atmosphere so that people need not fear for their future, so they can

---

[23] *Khrushchev relieves a bit of the tension by shifting emphasis to the possibility and desirability of peace. The audience responded by applauding. The transcript that appeared in* The New York Times *indicates applause only at this point and after the next sentence, which underscores the advantage of peace.*

go to bed at night and be sure that war will not disturb their sleep neither today nor tomorrow nor the day after tomorrow; that they should be sure that peace will be eternal [Applause].

The though [sic] sometimes—the unpleasant thought sometimes creeps up on me here as to whether Khrushchev was not invited here to enable you to sort of rub him in your sauce and to show the might and the strength of the United States so as to make him—so as to make him shake at the knees. If that is so, then if it took me twelve hours to get here, I guess it will take no more than ten a [sic] half hours to fly back. . . .[24]

But I do believe that we will show more wisdom and find a common language and that we will all strive for this.

I am going to close. I have tired you out. I believe you suffered through my speech, but so was I made to suffer. I have such a nature that I do not want to remain in debt and I do not want to be misunderstood. . . .

The next day Premier Khrushchev traveled to San Francisco. Overnight, Khrushchev's mood and that of the Californians who went to see him had undergone a striking transformation. Security restrictions were relaxed; the Premier mingled more freely with people, and he received his first really warm welcome. A reporter from the London *Economist* described the change:

When the train stopped at Santa Barbara, . . . Mr. Khrushchev got off, breaking through the security that has thus far surrounded him, to shake hands and talk with the friendly throng waiting on the station platform to catch a glimpse of him.

These greetings, the first warm and spontaneous ones he had yet received in America, were followed by a hospitable welcome . . . from the Mayor of San Francisco and from a large cheering crowd that waited at the entrance to Mr. Khrushchev's hotel, high on Nob Hill ("Communist's Progress," pp. 1021–1022).

---

[24] Khrushchev's threat to return to Russia without completing the tour, without talking to Eisenhower at Camp David, created a major stir in the press. John Osborne described the moment: "When he made the coldest and bluntest statement of the tour, . . . his audience kept a deathly silence. When he threatened to break off his tour and fly home, the fright in the hall was a tangible and present thing. When he relaxed into a lighter vein, the relief among his hearers was almost as frightening as their fright." During the remainder of the tour, Khrushchev was given more freedom of movement, more opportunity to mingle with people, more immunity from hecklers, and more solicitous concern by his official host, Henry Cabot Lodge. These effects would seem to be precisely what Premier Khrushchev wanted.

Premier Khrushchev's interaction with San Franciscans was distinctly successful. Although his meeting with trade union leaders on September 20 was stormy, his speeches to the Longshoremen's Union and at the IBM Corporation Plant in San Jose were well received. Khrushchev's major address in the San Francisco area reflects his recognition that he is now getting the response he had been seeking. This speech was presented on September 21 at a joint dinner of the San Francisco Commonwealth Club and the World Affairs Council.

The San Francisco Address.[25] *Esteemed Mayor Christopher, esteemed Governor Brown, esteemed Chairman Rockwell, esteemed Chairman Johnson, ladies and gentlemen: I am very grateful to you for this invitation to address such a distinguished gathering.*

We came to San Francisco from Los Angeles. We traveled along a beautiful coast, enjoying the scenic beauties of California. We saw your wonderful land, and all along the route, the California sun shone as brightly as it did in the Crimea, where I rested before leaving for the United States.

But it is not sunlight alone that warms our hearts in this land so distant from our country. We have been cordially welcomed and received by the Californians, and I would like the friendship between our peoples to be as inextinguishable and bright as is your southern sun. . . . [26] *[He discusses the history and resources of California and deplores the decrease in Soviet-American trade.]*

I have already said on more than one occasion that we have come to the United States with an open heart and the best of intentions. We want but one thing and that is to live in peace and friendship with you and with other peoples.[27]

It is my opinion that the distinguished Californians here tonight share these sentiments and aspirations with us.

[25] *The text is taken from* The New York Times, *September 22, 1959, p. 23.*

[26] *If one analyzes this speech without considering the context of the tour and of the explosions in Los Angeles, Premier Khrushchev might seem merely to be playing the flattering itinerant politician. Yet the difference in tone between the speeches in Los Angeles and in San Francisco is startling; newsmen were quick to see it. The audience was different. They gave Khrushchev what Harrison Salisbury of* The New York Times *the next day called "something like an ovation" before he spoke (p. 1). Whether the warm response represented a pervasive difference between the attitudes of people in the two California cities or whether San Franciscans wanted to avoid any behavior that might justify Khrushchev's termination of the trip is uncertain. Khrushchev is also different. Along the California coast and in San Francisco he had just received the first genuine hospitality in America. At any rate, the interaction between speaker and audience is friendly.*

[27] *Having dispensed with his introductory friendly remarks, Premier Khrushchev turns once again to the principal substantive theme of the tour and repeats the phrases "open heart" and "peace and friendship."*

Americans who have visited the Soviet Union returned with different opinions about our country and its life, but they will all confirm that the words "peace" and "friendship" are to be heard everywhere in our country.

They are to be seen in the white stone of the slopes of railway tracks. They are to be seen written in flowers in our parks and gardens. They are to be seen traced on house walls. They are in the heart of every Soviet citizen, and this is because all Soviet people are seeking by their peaceful labor to safeguard themselves and the entire world against the horrors of war.

We know well what war means, and though we are strong, we do not want war with its consequences and its destruction ever again to be visited upon mankind.[28]

It goes without saying that the best way to prevent war is to nip it in the bud, and that is to destroy the means of conducting war. A few days ago the Soviet Government submitted to the United Nations a proposal for general and complete disarmament, with the establishment of unlimited control.[29] A little earlier, at the end of August, the Soviet Government decided not to resume nuclear tests in the Soviet Union unless such tests were resumed by the Western powers.[30]

The Soviet Union will continue to struggle for a complete cessation of nuclear tests regarding this as an important step toward the termination of the nuclear armed race and elimination of the threat to the life and health of millions of people.

It is well understood everywhere that these are not the only problems that are of cardinal importance if peace is to be preserved. The existence of remnants of World War II is likewise fraught with the danger of a new war, and therefore this problem, too, must be solved.

We do not seek any unilateral advantages or benefits in proposing the conclusion of a peace treaty with Germany and proceeding from the existence of two German states. Who can think of advantages when it is a matter of putting out the still glowing embers of an old fire. The Soviet Government has often stated that it wants to normalize the situation in Germany, which would also eliminate the abnormal situation in Berlin. . . .[31] [Khrushchev states the hope that his talks with the President will solve international problems.]

[28] Instead of using the open threat of assembly-line rockets, as in the Los Angeles speech, Khrushchev here says simply that Russia is strong.

[29] He is referring to his plan of "general and complete disarmament," which he had presented several days earlier in the U.N. He is careful to attribute the source of this proposal not to himself but to the Soviet government.

[30] This initiative taken by Khrushchev was probably timed to enhance his visit and message to the United States.

[31] The brevity of his reference to the principal trouble spot, Berlin, is consistent with Khrushchev's strategy of de-emphasizing disagreement.

We want better to understand you and your motives, but there must be reciprocity. You also should better understand us and our motives. The Soviet Union does not seek any advantages. We want only one thing, that war should never again menace people anywhere on earth.

Well, that actually brings me to the close of my prepared speech to this responsible gathering, but if you have no objections I would like to share with you some of the impressions that I gained after this text was prepared. . . .[32] [*He describes the trip to San Francisco, his meeting with the Longshoremen's Union, and his visit to the IBM plant. He expresses gratification at his welcome and praises the city of San Francisco.*]

The main thing is not to touch upon the questions that divide us. We're all, I believe, sick and tired of discussions—of fruitless discussion on such issues, but the main thing is to speak of those points that unite us, that bring us together, to seek out those points where we can find agreement without touching upon the cardinal issues between us.[33]

After all, it is of course inconceivable that you could persuade me that the capitalist system was better, just as it is inconceivable that I could convince you that the Communist system was better.

We will evidently all remain with our own convictions, but that should in no way hinder us from going ahead, from living together in peace and caring for the welfare of our respective people.

I want to assure you, ladies and gentlemen, that I am not trying to entice you over into the Communist kingdom when I say this, but you will perhaps one day remember my words, and I want to say that when you get to know better us Communists, when you better get to know the thoughts and aspirations that guide us[34]—*this will not happen today, I realize—but you will see how noble are these aspirations of Communists when we seek to build a Communist society.*[35]

This is not a thing of today. It is a thing of tomorrow, but we conceive

---

[32] *Again, Khrushchev demarcates the carefully prepared portion of his speech from the impromptu part. The following day Salisbury wrote in* The New York Times *that Khrushchev had presented "one of the longest and most rambling extemporaneous talks of his tour" (p. 1). Presumably Salisbury refers to the final two-thirds of the speech, which begins at this point.*

[33] *Khrushchev here makes explicit his dominant strategy: maximizing agreement.*

[34] *Perhaps the main reason for Khrushchev's eagerness to make the trip was strong belief that relations could improve if the Americans understood the Russians better. He acts as though his primary interpersonal task is to reduce distance between the two groups. This passage is just one instance among many during the tour.*

[35] *The "live and let live" topic is another frequent one; it is part of the agreement for arriving at peaceful coexistence by discarding the competing ideas of conversion and war.*

this aspiration of ours as most sacred, as something that is most sacred for us. . . . [He compares the teachings of communism to the precepts of Christianity. He praises Mayor George Christopher, his dinner, and a supermarket he visited.]

I consider it also my duty here in San Francisco to say a few words about your neighbor city, the city of Los Angeles. I trust you will manifest patience and hear me out. I want to say some good things about the people of Los Angeles.[36]

Now if I were to use a somewhat poetic word, you have virtually charmed us here. You really are charmers, magicians, you have managed to charm me, a representative of a Socialist state.

You have charmed my heart, but in my head I still think that our system is a good system. You evidently think that your system is a good one, well, God be with you! Live under it. . . . [Khrushchev attributes the denial of permission to visit Disneyland to a tomato thrown at a car in which the Los Angeles chief of police was riding; he calls the change in schedule "superstitious." The Soviet Premier calls the altercation with Mayor Poulson an "unhappy incident," declares the question "closed," and extends again an invitation he had first made before the Los Angeles Civic Dinner for the Mayor to visit Russia. Khrushchev concludes his speech by inviting all present to make such a visit and by expressing once more the hope that his visit might bring the United States and the Soviet Union closer together.]

From San Francisco, Premier Khrushchev journeyed to Des Moines, Iowa, where he made a speech on agriculture at a reception sponsored by the Des Moines Chamber of Commerce, and to Coon Rapids, Iowa, where he inspected the hybrid-corn farm of Roswell Garst. Then the tour led to Pittsburgh. Khrushchev spoke at a luncheon at the University of Pittsburgh and visited a factory. The friendliness generated along the California coast increased during Khrushchev's stays in Iowa and Pittsburgh. On September 25 *The New York Times* headline read "PITTSBURGH STOP WARMEST OF TOUR."

On the afternoon of September 24, Premier Khrushchev returned to Washington for a weekend of private discussions with President Eisenhower. The rhetoric that for more than a week had been conducted on a public level with the American people through the mass media would now be carried on in private by the two leaders. One can only speculate about the rhetorical transaction between Eisenhower and Khru-

[36] *The audience doubtless hoped that Khrushchev would relieve the tension he had generated in Los Angeles. If San Francisco diners were thinking about Khrushchev's previous impromptu conclusions, they may well have been anxious and attentive when he talked of Los Angeles.*

shchev; transcriptions are not available, and their joint communique leaves much unsaid.

The Joint Communique.[37] *The Chairman of the Council of Ministers of the USSR, N. S. Khrushchev, and President Eisenhower have had a frank exchange of opinions at Camp David. In some of these conversations United States Secretary of State Herter and Soviet Foreign Minister Gromyko, as well as other officials from both countries, participated.*

Chairman Khrushchev and the President have agreed that these discussions have been useful in clarifying each other's position on a number of subjects. The talks were not undertaken to negotiate issues. It is hoped, however, that their exchanges of views will contribute to a better understanding of the motives and positions of each and thus to the achievement of a just and lasting peace.

The Chairman of the Council of Ministers of the USSR and the President of the United States agreed that the question of general disarmament is the most important one facing the world today. Both governments will make every effort to achieve a constructive solution of this problem.[38]

In the course of the conversations an exchange of views took place on the question of Germany including the question of a peace treaty with Germany, in which the positions of both sides were expounded.

With respect to the specific Berlin question, an understanding was reached, subject to the approval of the other parties directly concerned, that negotiations would be reopened with a view to achieving a solution which would be in accordance with the interests of all concerned and in the interest of the maintenance of peace.[39]

In addition to these matters useful conversations were held on a number of questions affecting the relations between the Union of Soviet Socialist Republics and the United States. These subjects included the question of trade between the two countries.[40] *With respect to an in-*

[37] *The text is taken from* The Department of State Bulletin, 41 *(October 12, 1959), 499–500.*

[38] *This statement implies that the two governments were more interested in broadening agreement on the ground rules for their disputes so that war might be avoided than in settling substantive issues.*

[39] *On September 28 The New York Times reported that the talks at Camp David on Berlin did not "go well." Mr. Khrushchev is said to have concluded "that his way of settling the problem was the only way he knew of reaching a settlement" (Reston, p. 1).*

[40] *The question of increased trade was probably included in the document at Premier Khrushchev's urging. The lack of any statement of consequence beyond the "conversations" probably represents President Eisenhower's realization that in 1959 Americans were not ready for "normal trade relations."*

crease in exchanges of persons and ideas, substantial progress was made in discussions between officials and it is expected that certain agreements will be reached in the near future.[41]

The Chairman of the Council of Ministers of the USSR and the President of the United States argreed that all outstanding international questions should be settled not by the application of force but by peaceful means through negotiation.[42]

Finally it was agreed that an exact date for the return visit of the President to the Soviet Union next spring would be arranged through diplomatic channels.

The private rhetorical exchange between Khrushchev and Eisenhower may have mirrored the public exchange between the Soviet Premier and the American people. No policy changes or ideological shifts resulted from either transaction. On the private level, perhaps the tacit understanding between the two men that international disputes must not lead to a Soviet-American war was strengthened; on the public level, the American people may have become conditioned to accept such a stipulation now—especially if publicly endorsed by Eisenhower —even if earlier in the decade they had been conditioned differently by the rhetoric of brinksmanship. Just as Khrushchev and the American people may have experienced publicly a reduction of interpersonal distance, so Khrushchev and Eisenhower privately may have come to understand one another better. The public statements of the two men after their talks support this supposition. In his press conference the day after Khrushchev's departure, Eisenhower characterized his Soviet visitor as "a dynamic and arresting personality" ("In Their Own Words," p. 104). In speaking in Moscow immediately upon his return, Khrushchev said that he "got the impression from the talks and discussions of concrete questions with the United States President that he sincerely wishes to end the state of cold war, to create normal relations between our two countries, to promote the improvement of relations among all states" ("In Their Own Words," p. 105).

Interpreting the Tour

In analyzing a campaign as complex as Khrushchev's 1959 tour of the United States, a critic must make choices. First, he must select an audience on which to focus. Although Khrushchev appeared before

---

[41] *The statement on cultural exchange programs is much more hopeful than the one on trade.*

[42] *The policy of refraining from hot war between the two nations had been manifest by the behavior of both governments throughout the 1950s. This sentence extends manifest policy to rhetorical commitment.*

different groups of Americans, he seemed always to be addressing an image of American public opinion. Certainly he was concerned about the leaders of his host government, and surely he knew that the response of his colleagues in the Kremlin was vital. But for the latter audiences, and perhaps for others, his ability to appeal to Americans generally would have great instrumental value. We choose, therefore, to focus on the general American audience.

Second, a critic may select a single dimension on which to focus his judgment. Our evaluation is that the visit was an important rhetorical *transaction that may have reduced the rhetorical distance between the* United States and the Soviet Union in the Cold War. The other dimensions . . . will be treated as subsidiary.

Viewing Khrushchev's rhetoric as reducing distance with the American audience, and looking at the relationships of six other dimensions of that function, constitutes one interpretation of the transaction. It does not, of course, exhaust the possibilities of criticism. Stressing a different dimension and considering other dimensions as secondary would create a new focus; focusing differently is not merely legitimate, it is essential. The total picture of any significant rhetorical transaction changes as a critic gains new perspective through his own efforts and through sharing the results of the efforts of others.

Distance Reduction. Our judgment is that this dimension is the single most important route to an understanding of the rhetoric of the tour. All the dimensions we treat as subsidiary seem relevant to an analysis of how Khrushchev reduced his distance from American audiences. He reduced distance by developing a strong, concrete, and human image; by insisting on parity between himself and Eisenhower and between the Soviet Union and the United States; by finding common ground in a desire to keep the peace; by forcing the United States to choose peaceful coexistence after rejecting other alternatives; and by skillfully using a campaign strategy and communication channels.

Premier Khrushchev reduced distance between himself and the American public, in part, by his vivid physical presence. Mary McGrory explains this factor:

Everybody is still reeling from the shock of that potent personality and from the endless incongruities that dogged him every step of the way. . . . No one could have predicted the force of his presence. . . . Mr. Khrushchev in person had the unarguable presence of a rock or tree.

Then, too, Khrushchev turned out to be far more "American" than anyone had expected. He seemed to be

the sort of person towards whom Americans instinctively warm: tough-spoken but probably good-hearted, a stranger to diplomatic niceties, a decisive leader who obviously springs from the people he leads. He possesses many of the qualities which the American voters thought they detected in Mr. Eisenhower in 1952 ("Without Horns or Tails," p. 43).[43]

Although Americans probably could not help feeling somewhat closer to the Soviet Premier after they had been exposed to his physical presence for nearly two weeks and had been saturated with the events of the tour through the mass media, the Soviet leader reinforced this tendency by some of the rhetorical decisions he made. In particular, Khrushchev's California speeches appeared to reduce interpersonal distance between himself and America. The reduced interpersonal distance may have lessened the chasm between the Soviet Union and the United States.[44]

Image Improvement. How was Khrushchev perceived in the United States before and after the tour? Did perceptions change? Many observers say, "Yes. He registered." Mark Frankland believes that Khrushchev's greatest achievement during the tour was "to leave the American people with a lasting impression of his vivid and at times prickly personality" (p. 163). A London reporter claimed that Premier Khrushchev "came to the United States as an abstract concept; he leaves as flesh and blood" ("Without Horns or Tails," p. 43).[45]

What were the primary features of the new image? Two seem repeated most often. First, many noted Khrushchev's determined, dynamic ability. What had been an unmixed hostility toward his hardness carried a new note of admiration. Senator Wayne Morse of Oregon remarked that the senators with whom he (Morse) had talked recognized they "were dealing with an exceedingly able man, a determined man" ("The Khrushchev Campaign," p. 104). A London reporter commented: "After his visit, there are a number of not entirely flattering adjectives they would happily apply to him—'pugnacious,' 'self-assured,' 'ruthless,'—but the number of those who think he is malevolent or

[43] *See also "The Great Encounter,"* Newsweek, *9-21-59, pp. 38–39; Schorr, "Traveling Salesmen," p. 22; Osborne; and "Dictator at Close Range," p. 75.*
[44] *Sources useful in further study of this dimension include Lukacs; Schorr, "Traveling Salesmen"; "Without Horns or Tails"; "Communist's Progress"; McGrory; Morris; and Seabury.*
[45] *See also Frankland, p. 55, and Gibney, p. 8.*

hypocritical has been sharply reduced" ("Without Horns or Tails," p. 43).[46]

A second characteristic of Khrushchev's new image was the recognition that he was less menacing—that he was a political, yet humane person with whom Americans could interact. A report prepared for the Senate Judiciary Committee by the Foreign Policy Research Institute of the University of Pennsylvania summarized this view: "The notion probably gained headway that somehow or other Khrushchev may indeed be the apostle of a new and less menacing kind of communism. . . . He has undeniably succeeded in imparting to the conduct of Soviet affairs a style . . . seemingly more humane and more acceptable than 'Stalinism' " (p. 1). Many writers noted the politician in the man and speculated about how the Russian would have fared in American politics. An editorial writer for *The Nation* represents this view: "What we actually saw was a Communist politician, as opportunistic and long-winded as any of his capitalist counterparts, but wittier than most, and a horse trader from head to toe. . . . He emerged as an antagonist who could be dealt with at the conference table" ("The Visit").[47]

If one accepts the judgment that Khrushchev changed the image Americans had of him in the directions suggested above, he may ponder several questions. How did Khrushchev do it? What kinds of rhetorical methods accounted for such changes? What, for example, accounted for the radical shift in American response as the Premier went from Los Angeles to San Francisco? How did he· encourage a continuation of the San Francisco reaction in Coon Rapids and in Pittsburgh? Was he able to decrease the animosity toward the Soviet Union as he had decreased hostility toward himself? Did Americans feel closer to the new Khrushchev than to the old?[48]

Toward Power Parity. Many observers noted that Premier Khrushchev was able to get himself accepted as a powerful adversary after his visit to the United States. For example, Max Ascoli said:

Both fairness and the will to survive should compel us to pay tribute to a formidable enemy. During those 13 days he ran circles around the

[46] *See also Sheerin, "What We Learned From Khrushchev," p. 80; Dodd, "If Coexistence Fails," pp. 409–410; Salisbury, "Khrushchev's Visit"; and "The Great Encounter," Newsweek, 10-5-59, p. 19.*

[47] *See also Whitney, p. 2; Sheerin, "What We Learned From Khrushchev," p. 80; Dodd, "If Coexistence Fails," pp. 409–410; "The Great Encounter," Newsweek, 10-5-59, pp. 19–24; and Halle, pp. 311, 390–391.*

[48] *Sources useful in further study of this dimension include Crankshaw, Khrushchev; "Without Horns or Tails"; Ascoli; Black; Brontenbrenner; Dodd, "If Coexistence Fails"; Osborne; Sheerin, "Khrushchev Has Many Faces"; and "The Visit."*

American people and, it is to be feared, the high officials of the ad-ministration. . . . We had never been exposed to the sight of a high-powered live Communist. . . . We weren't immunized, and we were upset (p. 21).

Other observers commented on the Premier's attempt to communi-cate that he represented a powerful country. One writer put this idea succinctly in *U.S. News and World Report:* "He is after respectability, recognition as the legitimate ruler of Soviet Russia and its satellite states. He wants the world to know that Russia can talk to America as an equal" ("Questions of the Week," p. 39).[49] Khrushchev also wanted this sort of recognition from the United States. As Fred W. Neal has argued, the United States had "never really come psychologically to acceptance of the Soviet Union as a force with which we must deal on a basis of permanence and equality" (p. 53; see also *Current Digest of the Soviet Press,* 11-4-59, p. 5). Khrushchev undoubtedly wanted this distance in power reduced.

The critic who intends to pursue Khrushchev's drive for power parity confronts several questions: How did Khrushchev's attempt to manifest his personal authoritativeness complement his attempt to demonstrate the power of the Soviet Union? How did both attempts contribute to a reduction of distance? Is a person likely to identify with someone equal in power or with someone significantly stronger or weaker? Is one na-tion apt to have more in common with another nation equal in power or with one that is stronger or weaker? Can the speech at the Los Angeles Civic Dinner be interpreted as Khrushchev's simultaneous effort to stress his own power and that of the Soviet Union?[50]

Strategy of Maximizing Agreement. Throughout the tour Khrushchev played down policy disputes that were impossible to settle in 1959 and emphasized the need to handle the resulting conflict so that nuclear war could not erupt.

The most threatening issue in 1959 was German reunification, es-pecially the question of what to do about Berlin. The Premier refers to that controversy in only five of his twenty-four speeches in the United States; the references are usually brief, and he makes them without truculence. In none of his angry outbursts does he refer to Berlin. Nor does he raise the issue in his final press conference. When a reporter raises it, Khrushchev's reply is brief and restrained; it avoids controversy (*Khrushchev in America,* p. 193).

---

[49] See also "Report on Washington," and Morgenthau, p. 386.
[50] Sources useful in further study of this dimension include Lukacs; Con-quest; The Crimes of Khrushchev; Lowenthal; Morganthau; Neal; "Questions of the Week"; and "Report on Washington."

Aside from expressing his fury at questions concerning Hungary or his own activities during the Stalin era, Premier Khrushchev spent remarkably little time arguing about policy controversies. On the other hand, he stressed possible grounds of agreement. The principal common interest of the two countries, he argued, was the desire to avoid war. They had already arrived at a tacit understanding on this issue concerning policy. Lerche explains the agreement:

Lying beneath the surface indications of a total conceptual and operational confrontation is a substratum of agreement. . . . Probably the most fundamental manifestation of such agreement was . . . that the cold war could not be permitted to escalate into an armed conflict between the Soviet Union and the United States. . . . At the rhetorical level neither government pretends to take the other's word seriously, but operationally each counts upon at least this measure of restraint in estimating its opponent's intentions (p. 32).[51]

Premier Khrushchev seems to have adopted the strategy of extending the operational agreement to the rhetorical level. The need to avoid nuclear war is implicit in every speech, and arguments consonant with the need are made explicit in many. The final declaration by Eisenhower and Khrushchev in the joint communique amounts to a public commitment to avoid nuclear war and functions as a culmination of Khrushchev's strategy to maximize agreement.

Why did Khrushchev choose the strategy? How did he develop it? To what extent may his development of the strategy in speeches to the American people be viewed as a useful prelude to creating favorable conditions for the private discussions with Eisenhower? How did the emphasis on agreement reduce the distance between Khrushchev and his hosts?[52]

Strategy of Forcing a Choice. On several occasions Premier Khrushchev used a residues method of argument, presumably designed to induce Americans to accept the doctrine of peaceful coexistence because they had rejected the available alternatives. His fundamental argument is this: Because neither capitalism nor communism can convert the other side to its point of view, and because nuclear war is unthinkable, the only choice remaining is peaceful coexistence and nonmilitary competition.

When Khrushchev arrived in the United States, Schorr predicted on a CBS newscast, September 15, 1959, that the Premier wanted to "put

[51] *See also Seabury, p. 68, and "The Glacier Moves."*
[52] *Sources useful in further study of this dimension include Halle; Karol; Lerche; "The Glacier Moves"; and Seabury.*

across the twin points of overwhelming Soviet power and overwhelming Soviet desire for peace" (*Images of Peace,* p. 73). The "war or peace" strategy pervades all his speeches. At times Khrushchev recognizes that the ideological struggle between capitalism and communism cannot be settled instantly and declares the willingness of the Soviet Union to live and let live. At other times, as in Los Angeles, he stresses the military might of the Soviet Union and threatens either hot or cold war. But more frequently he is more optimistic and argues that peaceful coexistence is possible, indeed, that it is the only viable choice. A content analysis by the Foreign Policy Research Institute of the University of Pennsylvania reveals that the three most frequent themes of Khrushchev's speeches during the tour were improvement of Soviet-American relations; peaceful competition between the communist and the capitalist systems; and peaceful coexistence and the relaxation of international tensions (pp. 33–38).

If a critic wished to emphasize this dimension, he might investigate the forms in which Premier Khrushchev developed the argument. How does he argue that ideological conversion is unrealistic, that nuclear war is fearful, that peace is desirable? How does he vary his moods in creating and in relieving tensions as orchestration for the argument? How do the angry mood and warlike arguments of the speech at the Los Angeles Civic Dinner prepare the San Francisco audience for the friendly mood and conciliatory arguments? How does the "war or peace" strategy reduce distance?[53]

Context. Two contexts are especially important in a critical analysis of Khrushchev's tour. First, the tour took place within the context of the Cold War. A critic who is to understand the tour must understand the conflict itself. Second, each rhetorical action during the tour must be viewed within the context of the tour as a campaign.

The rhetoric of reducing distance did not develop as a result of a single remark or a single speech but as a result of the tour. The tour is a sequential campaign, not an independent series of speeches. Some of the themes and images recurred often enough to constitute a rhetorical strategy. A critic might investigate the timing of Khrushchev's various maneuvers (see Foreign Policy Research Institute, p. 9). For example, were the angry outbursts in Los Angeles well timed to create or promote a desirable campaign effect?[54]

---

[53] *Sources useful in further study of this dimension include Crankshaw,* Khrushchev's Russia; *Lerche; Schorr, "Khrushchev's 'Hard Sell' "; Kennan;* Khrushchev; "On Peaceful Coexistence"; *and Neal.*

[54] *Sources useful in further study of this dimension include the Foreign Policy Research Institute; Halle; Lerche; Lukacs; Whitney; and "Without Horns or Tails."*

Channels. Two channels are significant in this study: the interpreters and the mass media.

The two Soviet translators were Oleg Troyanovsky and Viktor Sukhodrev. Russian-speaking listeners claim that the American public did not receive the full force of Premier Khrushchev's language— that the translators, especially Troyanovsky, softened words in the speeches. Leon Volkov characterized Khrushchev's language as "colloquial, tough, and harsh. When angered, he threatens. One gets an almost frightening sense of ruthlessness on display. But Troyanovsky . . . dilutes the language so skillfully that the general purport comes through, but with most of the harshness extracted" (Volkov).[55] How did the interpreters influence the messages and images Premier Khrushchev tried to project? How did the interpreters vary in the decisions they made while translating the speeches?[56]

The various mass media—radio, television, newspapers, and news magazines—constitute a second influential channel. One effect was obvious: the intensive coverage of Khrushchev's behavior made them available to millions. Khrushchev capitalized on his opportunity in several ways. He was "accessible and responsive to newsmen," and played off "one reporter against another, handing out brief interviews, now to newspapermen, now to television reporters, 'mugging' for the nearest available cameraman, and hugely enjoying the entire process" (*Images of Peace,* p. 93).

The media may well have functions other than those of a passive channel through which messages and images flow. Did media specialists make rhetorical decisions of their own that may have either supplemented or contradicted those of Premier Khrushchev? To what extent did they create history as well as merely record it? Benjamin Bradlee argues persuasively that

the press did not cover the Khrushchev story. It smothered the Khrushchev story. In the process, it distorted almost beyond recognition the America Khrushchev saw, and by its very presence created other stories. . . . The truth is that in this Golden Age of Communications, whenever the press participates massively in history it changes history (p. 32).

One wonders to what extent reporters caused Premier Khrushchev to say and do things.

[55] *See also "Khrushchev's Outbursts" and the Foreign Policy Research Institute.*

[56] *Sources useful in further study of this dimension include* Images of Peace; *Foreign Policy Research Institute; Bradlee; "Khrushchev's Outbursts"; and* Volkov.

Each of these dimensions—and no doubt there are others—should be considered by the critic of rhetoric who analyzes Premier Khrushchev's 1959 visit to the United States. If a critic is imaginative and treats one dimension as primary and the others as subsidiary, he may be able to illuminate Khrushchev's exchange with the American public and with other audiences.

Our own conclusion is that Khrushchev's rhetorical decisions helped reduce distance between himself and the American public and, at least momentarily, between the Soviet Union and the United States. But that achievement was quickly undone by the U-2 incident.

Bibliography

Ascoli, Max. "Now That We've Seen Him," *The Reporter,* 21 (October 15, 1959), 18–22.

Black, Cyril E. "Soviet Political Life After Stalin," in Alex Inkeles and Kent Geiger (eds.), *Soviet Society.* Boston: Houghton Mifflin, 1961. Pp. 182–189.

Bradlee, Benjamin. "Saturation Coverage," *The Reporter,* 21 (October 29, 1959), 32–34.

Bronfenbrenner, Urie. "The Mirror Image in Soviet-American Relations: A Social Psychologist's Report," *Journal of Social Issues,* Vol. 17, No. 3 (1961), pp. 45–56.

Caruthers, Osgood. "Nixon Wants Khrushchev to See U.S. at First Hand," *The New York Times,* August 3, 1959, pp. 1, 8.

"Communist's Progress," *The Economist,* September 26, 1959, pp. 1021–1022.

Conquest, Robert. *Russia After Khrushchev.* New York: Praeger, 1965.

Crankshaw, Edward. *Khrushchev: A Career.* New York: Viking, 1966.

———. *Khrushchev's Russia.* Rev. ed. Baltimore: Penguin, 1962.

———. "The Men Behind Khrushchev," *Atlantic Monthly,* 204 (July 1959), 27–32.

The Crimes of Khrushchev. Prepared for the use of the House Committee on Un-American Activities. Washington, D.C.: U.S. Government Printing Office, 1959.

Current Digest of the Soviet Press, October 6, 1959–December 2, 1959.

"Dictator at Close Range—End of a Mystery," *U.S. News and World Report,* 47 (October 5, 1959), 74–76.

Dodd, Thomas J. "If Coexistence Fails: The Khrushchev Visit Evaluated," *Orbis,* 3 (Winter 1960), 393–423.

———. "Khrushchev's Visit," *Vital Speeches of the Day,* 25 (September 15, 1959), 706–712.

Fainsod, Merle. "The Communist Party Since Stalin," in "Russia Since Stalin," *Annals of the American Academy of Political and Social Sciences,* 303 (January 1956), 23–36.

Foreign Policy Research Institute, University of Pennsylvania. *Khru-shchev's Strategy and Its Meaning for America.* Washington, D.C.: U.S. Government Printing Office, 1960.

Frankland, Mark. *Khrushchev.* New York: Stein & Day, 1967.

Gibney, Frank. *The Khrushchev Pattern.* New York: Duell, Sloan & Pearce, 1960.

"The Glacier Moves," *The New Statesman,* 58 (October 3, 1959), 413.

"The Great Encounter," *Newsweek,* 54 (September 21, 1959), 37–47; (September 28, 1959), 33–38; (October 5, 1959), 19–24.

Halle, Louis J. *The Cold War as History.* New York: Harper & Row, 1967.

Hearst, William Randolph, Frank Coniff, and Bob Considine. *Ask Me Anything.* New York: McGraw-Hill, 1960. Pp. 232–252.

"How to Handle Khrushchev," *Newsweek,* 54 (August 17, 1959), 22–23.

Images of Peace. CBS booklet, 1960.

"In the Home Stretch," *U.S. News and World Report,* 47 (October 5, 1959), 43–48.

"In Their Own Words," *U.S. News and World Report,* 47 (October 12, 1959), 103–105.

Karol, K. S. "Khrushchev's View of the World," *The New Statesman,* 58 (October 24, 1959), 532–534.

Kennan, George F. "Peaceful Coexistence: A Western View," *Foreign Affairs,* 38 (January 1960), 171–190.

Khrushchev, Nikita S. "On Peaceful Coexistence," *Foreign Affairs,* 38 (October 1959), 1–18.

———. Speech at Andrews Field, Maryland, September 15, 1959. *The New York Times,* September 16, 1959, p. 19.

———. Speech at Dinner sponsored by the City of Los Angeles and the Association of International Affairs, Los Angeles, September 19, 1959. *The New York Times,* September 20, 1959, pp. 41–42.

———. Speech at Dinner sponsored by the San Francisco Common-wealth Club and the World Affairs Council, San Francisco, September 21, 1959. *The New York Times,* September 22, 1959, p. 23.

———. Speech at Luncheon at the 20th-Century Fox Studio, Los Angeles, September 19, 1959. *The New York Times,* September 20, 1959, p. 41.

———, and Dwight D. Eisenhower. "President Eisenhower and Chairman Khrushchev Issue Communique at Conclusion of Talks at Camp David." *The Department of State Bulletin,* 41 (October 12, 1959), 499–500.

"The Khrushchev Campaign in U.S.—What His Speeches Show," *U.S. News and World Report,* 47 (September 28, 1959), 96–109.

Khrushchev in America. New York: Crosscurrents Press, 1960.

"Khrushchev's Outbursts—and the Language Barrier," *U.S. News and World Report,* 47 (October 5, 1959), 71–72.

Lerche, Charles O. *The Cold War and After.* Englewood Cliffs, N.J.: Prentice-Hall, 1965.

Linden, Carl A. *Khrushchev and the Soviet Leadership.* Baltimore: Johns Hopkins Press, 1966.

Live in Peace and Friendship. New York: Crosscurrents Press, 1960.

Lowenthal, Richard. "The Nature of Khrushchev's Power," in Abraham Brumberg (ed.), *Russia Under Khrushchev.* New York: Praeger, 1962. Pp. 114–126.

Lukacs, John. *A New History of the Cold War.* 3rd ed. Garden City, N.Y.: Doubleday, 1966.

McGrory, Mary. "Gone But Not Forgotten," *America,* 102 (October 17, 1959), 63.

Morgenthau, Hans J. "Khrushchev's New Cold War Strategy: Prestige Diplomacy," *Commentary,* 28 (November 1959), 381–388.

Morris, Bernard. *International Communism and American Policy.* New York: Atherton Press, 1961.

Neal, Fred W. *U.S. Foreign Policy and the Soviet Union.* Santa Barbara, Calif.: Center for the Study of Democratic Institutions, 1961.

Osborne, John. "Final Image: A Man With Ironclad Views Who Left No Doubt About What He's After," *Life,* 47 (October 5, 1959), 42.

Osgood, Charles E. "An Analysis of the Cold War Mentality," *Journal of Social Issues,* Vol. 17, No. 3 (1961), pp. 12–19.

Petrov, Vladimir. "Whither Soviet Evolution," *Orbis,* 3 (Fall 1959), 282–296.

Pietromarchi, Luca. *The Soviet World.* Lovett F. Edwards (tr.). London: Allen & Unwin, 1965.

"Questions of the Week," *U.S. News and World Report,* 47 (September 21, 1959), 39–41.

"The Range of Reaction in Congress," *U.S. News and World Report,* (September 7, 1959), 69–72.

"Report on Washington," *Atlantic Monthly,* 204 (November 1959), 8, 11.

Reston, James. "Views Unchanged," *The New York Times,* September 28, 1959, pp. 1, 20.

Rush, Myron. *Political Succession in the USSR.* New York: Columbia University Press, 1965.

Salisbury, Harrison E. "Fatal Flaw in the Soviet System," in Samuel Hendel (ed.), *The Soviet Crucible: The Soviet Government in Theory and Practice.* Princeton, N.J.: D. Van Nostrand, 1959. Pp. 246–251.

———. "Khrushchev, in a Warm Speech, Renews Appeal for Friendship; President Again Asks Courtesy," *The New York Times,* September 22, 1959, pp. 1, 21.

————. "Khrushchev Visit: Impact in U.S.," *The New York Times,* September 20, 1959, p. E-5.

Schapiro, Leonard. "Has Russia Changed?" *Foreign Affairs,* 38 (April 1960), 391–401.

Schorr, Daniel. "Khrushchev's 'Hard Sell,' " *The New Leader,* 42 (October 19, 1959), 6–8.

————. "Traveling Salesmen for Two Ways of Life," *The New York Times Magazine,* March 13, 1960, pp. 22, 88–92.

Seabury, Paul. *The Rise and Decline of the Cold War.* New York: Basic Books, 1967.

Shannon, William V. "The Last Ten Days," *The New Statesman,* 58 (September 26, 1959), 379.

Sheerin, John B. "Khrushchev Has Many Faces," *The Catholic World,* 191 (August 1960), 264–268.

————. "What We Learned From Khrushchev," *The Catholic World,* 190 (November 1959), 79–80.

Slusser, Robert M. "America, China, and the Hydra-Headed Opposition: The Dynamics of Soviet Foreign Policy," in Peter H. Juviler and Henry W. Morton (eds.), *Soviet Policy-Making: Studies of Communism in Transition.* New York: Praeger, 1967. Pp. 183–269.

Stevenson, Adlai E. "Tour for Khrushchev—The Real America," *The New York Times Magazine,* July 5, 1959, pp. 5–7.

"The Visit," *The Nation,* 189 (October 3, 1959), 181.

Volkov, Leon. "The Tough and the Gentle," *Newsweek,* 54 (September 28, 1959), 37.

"What Americans Think," *Newsweek,* 54 (September 28, 1959), 39–40.

Whitney, Thomas P. "Introduction: The Tireless Voice of the Kremlin," in Thomas P. Whitney (ed.), *Khrushchev Speaks.* Ann Arbor: University of Michigan Press, 1963.

"Without Horns or Tails," *The Economist,* October 3, 1959, pp. 43–44.

THE SOCIAL REALITY APPROACH

The Rhetoric of "Rocky": A Social Value Model of Criticism
by Janice Hocker Rushing and Thomas S. Frentz

The film "Rocky" is a genuine enigma. It has all the sure-fire ingredients of cinematic failure. The theme of a local, mediocre club fighter's accidental shot at the World Heavyweight Boxing title is both implausible and potentially maudlin. The cast of characters—with the possible exception of Burgess Meredith—reads like a Who's-Not-Who in Hollywood. The screenplay was written by someone whose scripts had never been filmed and who withheld the film rights until he could play the leading role. When that was finally affirmed, the writer/actor all but converted the final product into a home movie by using virtually his entire family in some capacity (even the writer/actor's dog, Butkus Stallone, has a supporting role). If we were to document how to guarantee a film disaster, we could do worse than recommend the ingredients that went into the making of "Rocky."

But the film is not a failure. Incredibly, "Rocky" has charmed critic and public alike. Seldom has a low-budget, personally-produced, no-star film so captured the imagination of the American people.[1] Its universal appeal stems in large part from the unusual way in which "Rocky" deals with American values. Unlike other popular films which announce, predict, or reflect the deterioration of American morality (e.g., "The Exorcist," "One Flew Over The Cuckoo's Nest," "All the President's Men," and "Network," to name a few), "Rocky" both celebrates the American Dream and implies an innovative psycho-social process for identifying with its mythology. On the most basic level, it is idealistic optimism tempered by experiential reality that sets "Rocky" apart from other films making rhetorical statements about values.[2]

The importance of "Rocky," however, is that the film need not be experienced only on this basic level. When examined carefully, "Rocky" manifests a particular pattern of value change. Moreover, that pattern—while having specific symbolic import in the film itself—reflects a more general social value model of rhetorical criticism. To realize "Rocky's" import, we need to do more than simply evaluate a film, we must develop an appropriate model for its investigation. Thus in this initial essay, we will (1) discuss the relationship between societal values and film[3] and (2) outline a five-part social value model of rhetorical criticism. In the second essay (to

From the *Western Journal of Speech Communication*, XLII, 2 (Spring 1978), 63–72. Used by permission of Janice Hocker Rushing, Thomas S. Frentz, and the Western Speech Communication Association. Dr. Rushing and Dr. Frentz are professors of speech-communication at the University of Colorado at Boulder.

[1] *Chartoff-Winkler Productions report domestic box office receipts, as of November, 1977, at $100,000,000.*

[2] *For a similar view of "Rocky," see:* Newsweek, April 11, 1977, p. 71.

[3] *Lawrence W. Rosenfield describes the "model modality" of rhetorical criticism in "The Anatomy of Critical Discourse,"* Speech Monographs, 25 (1968), 50–69, *as one procedure for joining observations and rhetorical norms. The critic generates a paradigm which is used as a basis of comparison. For an excellent example of*

appear in the Fall issue of WJSC), we will employ the model to investigate the political context surrounding "Rocky," demonstrate the unusual pattern of value change presented in the film, and consider implications for future rhetorical criticism of such rhetorical statements.

Film and Society

Societal values and film are related in two fundamental ways. First, film and society reciprocally influence one another.[4] By projecting collective images of a culture, by serving as symptoms of cultural needs, and by symbolizing trends, dramatic media both reflect and create societal events. Second, socio-political processes, like film, are structured and perceived as essentially dramatic.[5] Film is clearly a potent vehicle for symbolizing socio-political change.

The reciprocity between film and society is manifested on three levels. First, film projects the collective images, fantasies, and values of the culture in which the film is created. Viewed historically, film reveals obvious correlations between ideals in fashion, male and female beauty, individual and nationalistic heroism, and family life. Martha Wolfenstein and Nathan Leites put this point well:

The common daydreams of a culture are in part the sources, in part the products of its popular myths, stories, plays and films. Where these productions gain the sympathetic response of a wide audience, it is likely that their producers have tapped within themselves the reservoir of common day-dreams.[6]

---

model rhetorical criticism in which the models used are described explicitly, see: James W. Chesebro and Caroline D. Hamsher, "Communication, Values, and Popular Television Series," in Television: The Critical View, *Horace Newcomb ed. (New York: Oxford University Press, 1976), pp. 6–25.*

[4] *See David M. Berg, "Rhetoric, Reality, and Mass Media," Quarterly Journal of Speech, 58 (1972), 256, who argues: "First, it is clear that media do more than merely reflect events; they also create them. 'Any medium,' as anthropologist Edmund Carpenter points out, 'abstracts from the given and codifies in terms of that medium's grammar. It converts "given reality" into 'experienced reality.' "*

[5] *See Ernest G. Bormann, "Fantasy and Rhetorical Vision: The Rhetorical Criticism of Social Reality," Quarterly Journal of Speech, 58 (1972), 396–407, who argues that the process by which fantasies generated in small groups become public enactments is also dramatic in nature.*

[6] *Martha Wolfenstein and Nathan Leites, Movies: A Psychological Study (Glencoe: Free Press), 1950, p. 13. See also Richard M. Merlman, "Power and Community in Television," in Newcomb, who argues that television's westerns, crime series, and situation comedies are "fertile sources of information about the collective projections of Americans. . . . Unconscious as well as conscious expectations of political behavior, individual morality and social norms are acted out in television entertainment series," p. 87. That films represent collective societal projections implies the "intentional fallacy"—that it is misleading to attribute meaning in any artistic creation only to what matches the source's intention. The artist can certainly lend insight to an interpretation of film, but often he or she is acting at least in part unconsciously as a representative of the culture and thus as a receptacle for its fantasies. See Rosenfield, p. 63.*

Second, film often dramatizes symptoms of particular societal needs of an era. By portraying external problems facing the entire country, conflicts among sub-cultural groups, or internal needs shared by a major segment of the public, films give tangible structure to social phenomena. Like dreams, films arouse an audience to recognize, with varying degrees of consciousness, the most critical societal problems and in a form that is appealing.[7] It is often easier to face social problems by identifying with attractive, humorous, or pathos-evoking characters engaged in some form of dramatic tension than by listening to politicians, ministers, or other public persuaders preaching about societal ills. As David M. Berg argues, mass media expands the awareness of issues facing humankind, and thus "increases the ratio of exigence to reality."[8]

This "symptomizing" relationship between film and society can be documented almost endlessly. Many 1940 war movies (e.g., "Guadalcanal Diary," "Iwo Jima") responded to a general public need to feel that the war was morally justified. Similarly, select 1950 science fiction films (e.g., "The Thing," "Invasion of the Body Snatchers") can be seen as thinly veiled reflections of the Communist Threat. The popular "youth films" of the 1960s (e.g., "The Graduate," "Easy Rider," "Five Easy Pieces") were symptomatic of a cluster of intracultural problems all relevant to the "generation gap." Nostalgia movies of the early 1970s (e.g., "Summer of '42," "American Graffitti") could be analyzed as symptomatic of a desire to return to more tranquil times following the turbulence of the Sixties.

Third, films often symbolize and reinforce societal trends.[9] Sometimes films have modeled for society complete re-orientations in value structure. For example, Thomas S. Frentz and Thomas B. Farrell argue that "The Exorcist" signaled an alteration from a positivistic to a more transcendent value orientation.[10] Other times, films, or film genres merely reflect a trend already in progress. Russell L. Merritt, for example, describes the "bashful

[7] Horace Newcomb makes a related point about the function of television in "Toward a Television Aesthetic," in Newcomb, pp. 273–89. Television dramatic programs, he says, often deal with contemporary historical concerns as subject matter, but place their characters within an older time frame. In this "mythical realm," where values and issues are more clearly defined and certain modes of behavior, such as violence, are more permissible, we recognize our own problems. "Our history is all too familiar and perplexing, so to deal with it we have created the myth of television," p. 286.

[8] Berg, p. 256.

[9] This assumption corresponds to Rosenfield's "M-E" or message-environment focus for criticism, in which focuses on the environment as the particular age and civilization in which the message was created. Rosenfield defined the focus as follows: "This emphasis finds its rationale in the assumption that to the extent that an aesthetic event can be considered typical of its age it will provide valuable insight into the intellectual and social trends of that age," p. 60.

[10] Thomas S. Frentz and Thomas B. Farrell, "Conversion of America's Consciousness: The Rhetoric of The Exorcist," Quarterly Journal of Speech, 61 (1975), 43.

hero"—typically played by Gary Cooper, James Stewart, Henry Fonda, and Will Rogers—as the rhetorical child of the Progressive era that emerged around the turn of the century, in which the prevailing philosophy was egalitarian, focusing upon the wisdom of the common man.[11]

Although film and overall social processes are inextricably related, it is with political processes that film is most symbiotically linked. For political acts, like film, are essentially dramatic and symbolic in form. Edelman captures this relationship well:

The parade of 'news' about political acts reported to us by the mass media and drunk up by the public as drama is the raw material of such symbolization. It has everything: remoteness, the omnipotent state, crises, and detentes. More than that, it has the blurring or absence of any realistic detail that might question or weaken the symbolic meanings we read into it. . . . If political acts are to promote social adjustment and are to mean what our inner problems require that they mean, then these acts have to be dramatic in outline and empty of realistic detail.[12]

If both political processes and film are experienced as dramatic events, then both are experienced as "spectator sports." Daniel J. Boorstin comments that Americans rarely confront political reality directly—that they instead witness "pseudo-events" that appear spontaneous and genuine, but are in fact designed to obscure the ambiguous situation behind the event.[13] And when this occurs, the experiencing of political change becomes analogous to the experiencing of, say, a football game or—more to the point here—a prize fight; the contact can be at once exhilarating while still somewhat detached.

Social Value Model

We have argued that an interdependent relationship exists between film and social phenomena in general, and political processes in particular.

---

[11] *Russell L. Merritt, "The Bashful Hero in American Film,"* Quarterly Journal of Speech, *61 (1975), 129.*

[12] *Murray Edelman,* The Symbolic Uses of Politics, *Urbana, University of Illinois Press, 1964, pp. 8–9. See also Murray Edelman,* Politics as Symbolic Action *(Chicago: Markham, 1971).*

[13] *Daniel J. Boorstin,* The Image *(New York: Atheneum, 1962), pp. 9–12. Dan Nimmo,* The Political Persuaders: The Techniques of Modern Election Campaigns *(Englewood Cliffs: New Jersey, Prentice-Hall, 1970), cites three recent trends in publicizing political candidates on television; the quest of the news media for entertaining events to report, the ritualistic television coverage of such public events as party conventions and inaugurations, and the attempt of TV stations to perform a "public service" by staging debates between candidates, p. 155. For a rhetorical perspective on the relationship between mass media "spectacles" and social knowledge, see Thomas B. Farrell, "The Forms of Social Knowledge: Praxis and Spectacle," paper presented at the Speech Communication Association's Convention, San Francisco, California, December, 1976.*

Societal change, however, does not unfold capriciously; it has an underlying structure. This pattern has seldom been explored by social and rhetorical critics. If knowledge of the form of social change—particularly in regard to values—is necessary to understand fully such change, then we must generate a model that explicates that form. To the extent that the model is explicitly formulated and functionally clear, it should operate heuristically to reveal the nature of the political context that impinges on a film, such as "Rocky," and the specific exigence to which it is a response. We propose a five-part model to serve this function, we call it a social value model. The remainder of this essay will be devoted to detailing its structure.

Dialectical Opposition

The "collective consciousness" of a society is composed primarily of broad clusters of values that take the form of images, dreams, and myths that are self-reflexive.[14] The values basic to a culture's thought and rituals exist frequently in a fragile pattern of dialectical opposition—a state of tension, real or potential conflict or change.

Several critics note the existence of such dichotomous value schemes. For example, Alvin W. Gouldner argues that any culture's outlook on its own future is manifested in opposing values—those comprising a "tragic" vision and those comprising a "utopian" vision. The tragic viewpoint incorporates the belief that positive societal growth is not possible and that the continuing endurance of suffering is the most realistic stance. By contrast, the utopian framework is based on the assumption that the discrepancies between the real and the ideal are surmountable; utopianism strives for perfection.[15] Each vision co-exists in "profound tension" with the other.[16] Since utopianism does not focus on what already has been accomplished, Gouldner says, "It is continuously poised on the brink of a new despair and pessimism, to which it is vulnerable, so that one unintended outcome of the striving to enact the utopian vision is to regenerate the tragic vision. The pursuit of utopia prepares for a regression to the tragic view."[17]

---

[14] *Marshall McLuhan argues that the existence of widely shared mass media images creates a situation in which the "globe is no more than a village," and everyone is necessarily involved in the lives of everyone else. See* Understanding Media: The Extensions of Man *(New York: McGraw-Hill, 1964), p. 5. By "myth," we refer to a society's collectivity of persistent values, handed down from generation to generation, that help to make the world understandable, support the social order, and educate the society's young. Myths change slowly, and are widely taught and believed. They are expressed in the dominant symbols and rituals of the culture.*

[15] *Alvin W. Gouldner,* The Dialectic of Ideology and Technology: The Origins, Grammar, and Future of Ideology *(New York: Seabury, 1976), pp. 69–88. A variant of the utopian view is the "ideological," which accepts universal imperfection and merely strives for better conditions in life.*

[16] *Gouldner, p. 88.*

[17] *Gouldner, p. 89.*

A similar dialectical opposition among social values may be observed—in slightly different form—in American history. For example, Frentz and Farrell argue:

Throughout the history of American thought, two countervailing impulses have alternatively dominated the nation's consciousness. There is . . . a positivist inclination [that] . . . regards any statement to be meaningful only in terms of its verifiable and observable referents, . . . distrusts the abstract, is contemptuous of disorder, and compensates for its skepticism with a firm confidence that reductionism, prediction, and control are valued intellectual pastimes.[18]

By contrast,

The counterpart of Positivism in American thought, Transcendence, . . . yearn(s) for that which is general and ideal, . . . finds meaning in that which is good; . . . harkens after the ahistorical; . . . compensates for naive insecurity by piously anticipating a reemergence of utopian innocence.[19]

The generic names as well as the values underlying these dialectical oppositions vary; in this paper, however, we are most concerned with the specific form value opposition took in the socio-political context surrounding "Rocky." Walter R. Fisher aptly defines the dichotomy in the distinction between materialism and moralism. The materialistic myth

is grounded on the puritan work ethic and relates to the values of effort, persistence, 'playing the game,' initiative, self-reliance, achievement, and success. It undergirds competition as the way of determining personal worth, the free enterprise system, and the notion of freedom, defined as the freedom from controls, regulations, or constraints that hinder the individual's striving for ascendency in the social-economic hierarchy of society.[20]

In tension with the materialistic myth, the moralistic myth

. . . is well expressed in basic tenets of the Declaration of Independence: that 'all men are created equal,' men 'are endowed by their Creator with certain inalienable rights,' 'among these are life, liberty, and the pursuit of Happiness,' . . . These tenets naturally involve the values of tolerance,

[18] *Frentz and Farrell, pp. 40–41.*
[19] *Frentz and Farrell, p. 41.*
[20] *Walter R. Fisher, "Reaffirmation and Subversion of the American Dream,"* Quarterly Journal of Speech, 59 (1973), 161.

charity, compassion, and true regard for the dignity and worth of each and every individual.[21]

As we shall demonstrate, the tension between moralism and materialism is particularly relevant to understanding "Rocky."

Symbolic Conflict

If the values of a society live in delicate tension, we may ask what the conditions for change are and if such change has an identifiable communicative form. Some sort of value change is inevitable whenever the dominant form of the prevailing myth or value cluster is incapable of solving social problems.[22] Although societal members may begin to question the values of a myth individually, the *collective* premonition of inadequacy must be acknowledged before actual changes can occur. Several forces operate simultaneously in the emergence, consensual validation, and communication of value change to a public. Social and artistic critics, for instance, usually alert the public that its general mood is due for a change by decrying the decline of values.[23]

Because values exist in a state of dialectical opposition, however, communicative *conflict* is the most common and powerful form for enacting change. This conflictual form of value change is clearly reflected in political acts as well as in film. In political change, Gouldner observes, "A good part of the sense of men's potency rests on *conflictual* validation, the conduct of *successful* conflict, struggle, contest, and also war."[24] Certainly, "collective non-movements,"[25] loosely structured groups of people conspicuously demonstrating alternative ways of life, and rhetorical movements, groups attempting to pressure the society at large for change, are political, conflictual ways of bringing about value change.[26]

---

[21] *Fisher, p. 161.*

[22] *Frentz and Farrell claim: "The end of an era is usually marked by the increased incapacity of one dimension of consciousness to solve contemporary social problems," p. 42.*

[23] *Frentz and Farrell note that the demise of Positivism in America was accompanied by an intensified concern with the American psyche on the part of social critics, p. 43.*

[24] *Gouldner, p. 69.*

[25] *According to Ron E. Roberts and Robert Marsh Kloss, Social Movements: Between the Balcony and the Barricade, St. Louis, C. V. Mosby, 1974, p. 41, a "collective non-movement refers to a solution to a problem which does not attempt to influence the labor or property relations of a given society." That is, collective non-movements, as opposed to movements, depend on psychological reorganization rather than social change to solve problems. Joseph Gunsfield makes a similar distinction in Symbolic Crusade: Status Politics and the American Temperance Movement (Urbana: University of Illinois Press, 1966). He identifies psychologically oriented movements with status politics and economically oriented movements with class politics.*

[26] *Roberts and Kloss consider collective non-movements and movements to be evidence of a "dialectical process"; that is, a social trend produces its own opposition by fostering within a group of people the psychological need for negation of the trend, p. 19.*

Film, with its dramatic affinity to political events, is also adept at depicting value changes through symbolic conflicts. As Marsha Kinder and Beverle Houston note, film is particularly suited to representing myth for an audience:

Since their beginnings movies have had the special qualities of a mythic medium. Like the ballad, the circus, and other popular art forms, they have drawn a mass audience. In images larger than life, they both reflect and shape popular myths. One of their strongest powers lies in their ability to project dreams and fantasies under quiet, darkened conditions, which enhance their effectiveness.[27]

In both politics and film, the conflict is often expressed as a verbal or physical battle between two opposing individuals or groups of individuals. Thus, Fisher argues that the 1972 Presidential campaign was a symbolic struggle between Nixon as the flag carrier of the materialistic myth and McGovern as the symbol of the moralistic myth. Frentz and Farrell maintain that the struggle between Father Karras and the Demon in "The Exorcist" symbolizes a similar conflict, a battle between transcendent Good and positivistic Evil. And, as we shall demonstrate, a comparable conflict is central to the meaning of "Rocky."

Patterns of Change

Symbolic conflict, then, is the necessary condition of value re-orientation—both in politics and in film. There are, however, two different patterns that such symbolic conflict can take, each pattern having its own peculiarities and necessary pre-conditions to enactment: *dialectical transformation* and *dialectical synthesis*. One pattern entails an inversion from one prevailing set of values to the other—a *dialectical transformation.*[28] In terms of the concepts discussed previously, this pattern would be exemplified in a transformation from tragedy to utopia, from positivism to transcendence, or from moralism to materialism (or, of course, vice-versa). Of the two patterns, dialectical transformation is the simplest because it does not necessitate the creation of a new value structure, but only the shift from one dominant set of values to another—where both value sets are previously known and experienced. In addition, dialectical transformation

[27] *Marsha Kinder and Beverle Houston,* Close-Up: A Critical Perspective on Film *(New York: Harcourt, Brace Jovanovich, 1972), p. 282.*

[28] *There is some evidence of this pattern. Of Positivism and Transcendence, Frentz and Farrell argue that "Because of their antithetical nature, these two dimensions of American consciousness have ebbed and flowed in an irregular but recurrent cycle," p. 41. Gouldner claims that the modern consciousness "is precariously divided internally so that one decade may be passive and profoundly gloomy while the very next is activistic and optimistic," p. 75.*

is a non-zero-sum game; as one set of values replaces the other as the underlying myth of social life, the value set that is replaced "loses" in a symbolic sense. This pattern is marked by competition.

The competitiveness of a dialectical transformation has not gone unnoticed among political and film critics. Frentz and Farrell express concern over the possible "debilitating effect of a total reliance on one dimension of consciousness to the exclusion of the other."[29] Fisher, commenting on the consequences of the 1972 Presidential campaign, warns:

The gravest danger that the election may have fostered is an increased loss of faith in the American Dream, the whole dream. . . . American needs heroes and rituals, presidents and elections, to signify her whole meaning—moralistic and materialistic; she requires symbols that her citizens can identify with and can gain sanction from for what they are as individuals and what they represent as a nation.[30]

The second pattern of value change is more complex conceptually and more difficult to enact symbolically. In a dialectical synthesis the old is not merely replaced with the new, but rather an integration of the old with the new is formed in such a way that the relationship among the participants is reaffirmed. In other words, this pattern of change renews a sense of independence and community among those involved. Moreover, there are no "losers" in a dialectical synthesis process, because all parts are preserved, the symbolic conflict is characterized by intense effort that is more cooperative than competitive.

Psychological Prerequisites

Change agents—be they politicians or characters in a film—are not totally free to choose either pattern of value change; any change agent must manifest internally a value ensemble consistent with the pattern to be followed. This principle is based upon the assumption that agents of social change can only be effective to the extent that they have experienced psychologically the new values. For change agents to implement the dialectical transformation pattern of symbolic conflict would require that they have psychological knowledge of one of the two competing sets of values. For individuals or groups dialectically to synthesize opposing values, however, they would have to have already synthesized the values in question internally, to have "psychologically previewed" the synthesis process to be enacted in the socio-political arena. It may well be that the rarity with which the synthesis pattern is enacted stems from the difficulty of achieving the psychological prerequisites.

[29] *Frentz and Farrell, p. 41.*
[30] *Fisher, p. 167.*

Audience Role

The final component of our critical model involves the role of the audience, the spectators for which symbolic conflict is enacted. The audience's role in either dialectical pattern varies from intensified awareness to active participation. This general intensified awareness is traceable to dissatisfaction with a given value orientation that is no longer meeting societal needs—to a yearning for something different. The audience seems to be most actively involved, however, when the pattern of change is synthetic; for dialectical synthesis is an emergent pattern—a pattern in which the change agents creatively force a new phenomenon. Thus, when individuals witness such change, they identify with an inventional process. Ideally, they are contributors to the generative process; they both learn and vicariously help create that which did not exist before the pattern was enacted.

The five-phase social value model of rhetorical criticism we have outlined is schematized in Figure 1.

In this essay, we have argued that film and social change are inextricably related and, as such, to understand either demands understanding that interrelationship. We then created a five-part social value model of rhetorical criticism. In the second essay, we shall use the social value model as a heuristic vehicle for analyzing the political-rhetorical context in which "Rocky" occurred and for evaluating the film as an expression of value change in American society.

Figure 1
Social Value Model

1. Values exist in dialectical opposition.

2. Symbolic conflict is the necessary condition for value re-orientation.

3. There are two patterns of symbolic conflict:
   —dialectical transformation;
   —dialectical synthesis.

4. Psychological prerequisites:
   —dialectical transformation necessitates non-integrated change agent;
   —dialectical synthesis requires integrated change agent.

5. Audience role:
   —participation in a generative process heightens experiential involvement in dialectical synthesis.

The Rhetoric of "Rocky": Part Two
by Thomas S. Frentz and Janice Hocker Rushing

In part one of this essay, we observed that the film "Rocky" was an oddity. It combined elements that should have led to cinematic disaster, but in fact, it captured the imagination and pocketbooks of the American public.[1] To explain the rhetorical appeal of "Rocky," we undertook three tasks. First, we argued that film and social processes are interdependent. Second, we noted that a crucial dimension of that interdependence was that film and social processes manifest similar patterns of value change. Third, we created a model of value change that can account for the rhetorical force underlying both film and more general social processes.

The social value model has five dimensions. First, societal values exist in dialectical opposition. Second, symbolic conflict is the dominant form for value change. Third, this symbolic conflict may assume the pattern of either *dialectical transformation,* involving an inversion of power between dominant value systems, or *dialectical synthesis,* demanding a conceptual integration between existing value systems. Fourth, each pattern requires specific psychological conditions within the change agents; dialectical transformation requires only knowledge of the value systems in question, while dialectical synthesis necessitates both knowledge of the existing value systems and an internal capacity to integrate them into a unified whole. Finally, since there is greater identification by an audience in a change process that is cooperative and integrative, a more intensified sense of involvement is found in the pattern of dialectical synthesis than in dialectical transformation.

We will use this model as the basis of our criticism of "Rocky." We begin by considering the pattern of value change in the rhetorical context of the film—namely, the state of mind reflected by the 1976 Presidential campaign. We then examine how the pattern of value change in "Rocky" extends the pattern begun in that campaign. Finally, we offer implications for future studies of value change in rhetorical events.

The Rhetorical Context of "Rocky"

Because of its relevance to the contemporary American political scene, we shall use Fisher's distinction between the moralistic and materialistic

From the *Western Journal of Speech Communication,* XLII, 3 (Fall 1978), 209–221. Used by permission of Thomas S. Frentz, Janice Hocker Rushing, and the Western Speech Communication Association. Dr. Frentz and Dr. Rushing are professors of speech-communication at the University of Colorado at Boulder.

[1] Janice H. Rushing and Thomas S. Frentz, "The Rhetoric of 'Rocky': A Social Value Model," Western Journal of Speech Communication, *42 (1978),* 63–72.

myths as our dominant value terms.[2] At the outset of 1972, it was obvious that the American value system was badly fractionated and that massive public disillusionment had formed concerning materialism as the dominant purveyor of social action. For example, if Nixon embodied the values underlying materialism, then Watergate and the first Presidential resignation in history dealt perhaps the severest blow yet experienced to those values for most Americans. A poll conducted by the University of Michigan showed that the number of people who trusted government had slipped to 36 percent in 1974; in 1958, it was 71 percent. Although 1958 was a recession year, 74 percent of the public believed that government benefited all the people; in 1974, the figure had fallen to 25 percent.[3]

Similarly, if McGovern symbolized moralistic values for the American people, his loss in the 1972 election signalled the decline of that myth as well. McGovern was perhaps the last heir to the Democratic politicians of the 1960s—politicians capable of generating optimism, activism, and an entire youthful generation bent on egalitarian reforms. The enormity of his defeat, the continuation of social and racial suppression, the inequality of life-standards, and seemingly incomprehensible environmental problems all took their toll on the de-radicalization of American politics. By mid-1976, ironically the Bicentennial year, both dimensions of American values were badly in need of repair.

Onto this scene came Jimmy Carter—in many ways a political enigma. The born-again Baptist Sunday school teacher from Plains, Georgia, was a curious blend of both myths. He was fervently moralistic, stressing that the people believed the country had lost its moral and spiritual underpinnings, and he was fond of promising a government "as decent . . . as compassionate . . . as filled with love as our people are."[4] This moralistic bent was certainly not lost on the press. Newsweek, for instance, declared that "He may be the most unabashed public moralist to seek the Presidency since William Jennings Bryan. . . ."[5]

[2] Walter R. Fisher, "Reaffirmation and Subversion of the American Dream," Quarterly Journal of Speech, 59 (1973), 160–67.

[3] Surveys conducted by the Survey Research Center and the Center for Political Studies, University of Michigan, as quoted in Thomas B. Farrell, "Campaign '76 as Comedy or Why Aren't These Men Laughing?" a paper presented at the Speech Communication Association Convention, San Francisco, California, December, 1976, p. 4.

[4] Jan Schuetz and Wayne A. Beach point out that Carter created a positive moral impression of his potential supporters and then interjected his own image into their personal views. See "Rhetorical Sensitivity and the Campaign of Jimmy Carter," a paper presented at the Western Speech Communication Association Convention, San Francisco, California, November, 1976.

[5] Newsweek, September 13, 1976, p. 23. Newspaper headlines repeatedly emphasized the moral aspects of the entire Democratic campaign. For instance, on July 13, 1976, the Los Angeles Times headlined a story on the Democratic Convention, "Democrats Hear Call for Morality."

But Jimmy Carter was more than a moralist. Carter was a wealthy agribusinessman, having turned a financially precarious family business into a five million dollar family fortune.[6] He controlled a political machine that rivaled that of the late John F. Kennedy for sophistication and precision. Carter revelled in hard work and was continuously shown in television ads in a plaid shirt and comfortable old hiking boots walking through the fields of his peanut plantation. Here was a man proud of his image, composed as much from rags-to-riches ingredients as from spiritual constituents.

Thus, Jimmy Carter was a person in which materialism and moralism had been integrated, and as such, he possessed the psychological pre-requisites to turn the 1976 Presidential election into a ritual of dialectical synthesis. For example, Carter's platform encompassed not only the con-cerns of his Democratic party, but also many of the important proposals of the Republican platform as well. Because of this amalgam of positions, many charged that Carter was vague on issues. Moreover, Carter did not attempt to depict Ford as the reincarnation of the Demon from San Cle-mente. In fact, Ford's own credibility grew during the campaign and pri-marily the nagging reminder of the pardon prevented an even greater spirit of respect between the candidates.[7] Ford lost the election—just as Rocky lost the fight—but both Ford and Rocky gained a great deal; for many, Ford's courage and effort against insurmountable odds elevated his stature as a person. Finally, because the 1976 election campaign mani-fested the pattern of dialectical synthesis, it became a powerful vehicle of social change. For, as Edelman puts it, "They [election campaigns] give people a chance to express discontents and enthusiasms, to enjoy a sense of involvement."[8]

While the 1976 campaign reflected the pattern of dialectical synthesis, the election itself did not, in that a winner was declared. As we have pointed out, the campaign was a conflict between competing value sys-tems—moralism and materialism. Such conflict is an essential constituent of this pattern of change. The exigence of the campaign, recognized keenly by Carter, was the need to restore the health of the American Dream. As he said: "It is a time for healing."[9] Just as Carter sought to provide a remedy for the nation's illness, so does "Rocky," but in a way that only film can realize.

[6] Newsweek, September 13, 1976, p. 33.

[7] Following the Republican Convention, Ford started the campaign farther behind than any President in scientific polling history; a Gallup survey showed Carter ahead 50–33, and Harris gave Carter a 61–32 margin, according to Newsweek, August 30, 1976, p. 16. By late October, Gallup gave Carter only a 47–41 lead; Harris gave him a 45–42 lead; Associated Press showed Ford ahead for the first time, 49–45, Newsweek, November 1, 1976, p. 18.

[8] Murray Edelman, The Symbolic Uses of Politics (Urbana: University of Illinois Press), 1964, p. 3.

[9] CBS Convention Coverage, July 15, 1976.

"Rocky" As Dialectical Synthesis

Five interrelated dimensions of "Rocky" become apparent when viewed from the perspective of our model of social value.

Value Opposition

First, the film dramatizes value opposition. In the opening scene, a closeup view of a particularly brutal, physical battle between Rocky and some unknown opponent is shown. Subtly present in the background is a painting of a madonna hanging as a reminder of another set of values. At the very outset, then, we experience the materialistic value of competition and winning against the moralistic backdrop of religious love and compassion. This opposition recurs scenically throughout the film.

Symbolic Conflict

The conflict between moralism and materialism in "Rocky" is triggered by the protagonist's anger. Rocky is angry at his own initial inability to make any form of significant human contact, at his inability to succeed in the fight profession, at having to work for a loan shark in order to survive, and, most directly, at those forces of materialism and wealth that keep Rocky and the millions like him in the slums of south Philadelphia. In short, Rocky is angry at himself and his situation.

Anger often underlies human conflict—whether that conflict be physical and destructive, as in the case of the Watts riots, or more detached and controlled, as in the case with political elections. Throughout the film, we see resentment and hostility building both in Rocky and in his associates. When Rocky is offered the chance to fight Creed, his anger takes specific focus and becomes goal-directed.

Psychological Prerequisites

Neither the awareness of value opposition nor the presence of the conflict is responsible for the audience's reaction to "Rocky." An essential attribute of the film is its evocation of sympathy and support for Rocky as he grows in character. As one critic put it, "Rocky" is a study in self-actualization.[10] The *progressive* nature of that self-actualization process is what is important. After all, Rocky is not a dualing dialectician—the Eric Hoffer of the ring. He is at the outset of the film—most charitably put— a rather ordinary person with a remarkable potential for growth and change.

As the film progresses, we witness a gradual, but certain process of value synthesis within Rocky. Rocky's arduous training program reflects

---

[10] Nancy L. Street, " 'Rocky': The Moral Imperative" a paper presented at the Western Speech Communication Association Convention, Phoenix, November, 1977.

clearly his endorsement of the puritan work ethic, his increasing need to "win" a place for himself, and his unequivocal acceptance of direct, physical competition as the determiner of a person's worth. Rocky exhibits extreme compassion: for Mickey, the fight manager of questionable motives; for Adrian, the painfully shy lover-to-be; for an unidentified man, who cannot pay a debt owed to the loan shark for whom Rocky works; and even for Adrian's brother, whose most redeeming feature seems to be his inability to exploit Rocky. Moreover, Rocky searches with increasing clarity for his own dignity and self-worth—two deep-rooted facets of moralism. The very night before his fight with the champion, Rocky tells Adrian, "If I can go the distance, I'll know for the first time in my life I'm not just another bum from the neighborhood." Rocky's self-actualization is dramatic evidence of his internalization of materialistic and moralistic values.

To be aware of the importance of opposing value systems is one thing; to integrate those systems within oneself is quite another. But that is precisely what occurs within Rocky as the film progresses. For example, in his pre-fight training program, Rocky seems to understand tacitly both the materialistic and the moralistic senses of "purification." Rocky endures the hard work of training and at the same time he experiences the pain of self-sacrifice. (Not only does he rise before dawn and gulp down five raw eggs prior to his daily jogging ritual, but he also tells Adrian that "fooling around" will sap his energy.) The effort of training is clearly materialistic, linked again to the puritan work ethic. But the experiencing of pain through self-sacrifice is moralistic, an experience commonly advocated by spiritual leaders.[11] In the act of training, then, Rocky exhibits materialistic and moralistic values.

Further evidence of Rocky's internal synthesis of values can be found in his ability to avoid most of the weaknesses inherent in each myth as it stands alone.[12] Rocky is *self-interested* but not *self-centered*. The self-absorption of materialism is avoided most clearly in the scene in which Rocky has finally coaxed the timid Adrian into his apartment. As Rocky approaches the woman, the camera emphasizes the difference in their

---

[11] *Martin Luther King, Jr., for instance, believed in the necessity of 'self-purification" of those engaging in nonviolent direct action against their oppressors; this involved spiritual preparation for resistance through training sessions, discussions, and role-playing. Suffering and self-denial were considered to be dignified and redemptive. See* Letter From Birmingham City Jail *(Philadelphia: American Friends Service Committee, 1963).*

[12] *Fisher notes that each myth has weaknesses, and thus is susceptible to rhetorical subversion. The weaknesses of the materialistic myth relevant to this study are that it is suspect for those who are troubled by its real-life manifestations of avarice, resentment, envy, and vindictiveness; it is compassionless and self-centered; it encourages manipulation and leads to exploitation. Relevant weaknesses of the moralistic myth are that its advocates often appear self-righteous, "holier-than-thou," scolding, and unrealistic, pp. 161–62.*

sizes. We are led to expect an ugly scene—perhaps even a rape attempt. But instead of removing Adrian's clothes, Rocky removes her glasses, saying, "I always knew you were pretty." Similarly, although Rocky doggedly goes after the black champion, Apollo Creed, he refuses to hate or even envy his opponent—another proclivity of the materialistic orientation. Though he pursues what he wants persistently, Rocky avoids the pitfalls of manipulation, exploitation, and lack of compassion so often associated with materialistic values.

Neither does Rocky resemble anything like a self-righteous, holier-than-thou scold; the film is not a melodramatic morality play with Rocky as Virtue and Apollo as Vice. Rather, Rocky is portrayed with all his faults—he does legwork for a loan shark, he does get angry at Adrian's brother Pauli, he undermines Mickey's self-respect before he restores it. He learns through a series of painful failures how to be a man of dignity; that is, his character is transformed in the film. "Rocky" is more like a parable than a sermon; as the audience progressively identifies with a quite human hero, it experiences vicariously a crucial blending of freedoms which are usually antithetical in both conception and practice: the freedom to do and the freedom to be.[13] As before, we are not claiming that Rocky was consciously aware of the integration process that was occurring. We are claiming, however, that such a process did occur and that there is ample evidence in the film to substantiate the claim.

Resolution Through Dialectical Synthesis

Because Rocky had integrated an antithetical set of values, he had the potential to define the impending fight as dialectical synthesis. But to understand fully the rhetorical impact of the fight sequence, we need to examine the pre-fight orientations of the champion, Apollo Creed, as well as Rocky.

We have already hinted at Rocky's pre-fight choices. For Rocky, the fight would be—if he had his way—an enactment of integration. As such, it would not be a pre-arranged "circus" in which the outcome was already determined, but an event in which he and champion Creed would "competitively cooperate" to forge a synthesis of values. For many in the audience, the experiential impact of the fight stemmed from the creative energy entailed in enacting dialectical synthesis.

But the choice of form for the fight is not Rocky's to make—at least not without a struggle. An adversary (the antithesis to a thesis) always has a say in the choice of patterns, and Creed is no exception. Blatantly mod-

---

[13] Fisher notes: "Where the materialistic myth involves a concept of freedom that emphasizes the freedom to do as one pleases [freedom from controls], the moralistic myth tends toward the idea of freedom that stresses the freedom to be as one conceives himself," p. 162.

eled after Mohammed Ali, Apollo Creed manifests, in caricature, the myth of materialism. When Creed (rhymes with greed) hits upon the idea of getting an unknown Italian to fight him on the Bicentennial ("Who discovered America—an Italian—right"), he exchanges these words with his promoter:

> *Promoter: "Apollo, I like it—it's very American."*
> *Creed: "It's very smart."*

As a symbol of materialism, Apollo Creed merely reflects the predominance of that myth. Because he desires no change at all, but rather a "show" of power and superiority, he approaches the fight with a set of predetermined rules—rules he naively thinks that Rocky shares. Of course, there is always the possibility that an inversion could occur—that Creed, the materialistic champion, would lose to his challenger. But that probability is very unlikely, particularly if Creed can choose his opponent.

Hence we can see in the pre-fight drama a difference between Rocky and Creed in regard to the patterns they each would enact in the impending conflict. A clear example of the pre-fight contrast occurs when Apollo's manager happens to watch Rocky on television pounding a side of beef in a meat locker:

> *Manager: "Hey, take a look at this guy you're gonna fight. He means business!"*
> *Creed: "Yeah, I mean business, too."*

The play on the word *business* is important. For the manager (who, by his growing realization of what is happening, reflects Rocky's consciousness), *business* means seriousness, effort, uncertainty of outcome. For Apollo, *business* is money from a show. For Creed, the fight would serve to increase his celebrity status and his pocketbook. For Rocky, the fight would be a chance not only to prove himself "not just another bum from the neighborhood," but also would serve as an arena in which an integrated set of values would be created through their combat.

The synthesis is most dramatically determined, however, in the fight itself. Rocky wins the choice of pattern near the end of the first round with a left field punch that almost decapitates the champion. Apollo's manager, who seemed to sense all along that this fight would be different, will not let Creed miss the choice that has just been made for him. After the first round, the manager whispers urgently into the dazed champion's ear: "He doesn't know it's a damn show! He thinks it's a damn fight! Finish this bum and let's go home!"

Begrudgingly, Creed accepts—as he must—the form of the fight that has been imposed upon him. Rounds 2 through 15 exemplify well conflict through dialectical synthesis. The concept neatly explains that rare bond of respect that grows between the fighters as the rounds pass. Though each man systematically reduces the other to a bloody pulp (after all, who ever said that dialectical synthesis would be easy?), there is a poignant realization of their joint effort in their closing exchange at the final bell:

Creed: *"Ain't gonna be no rematch! Ain't gonna be no rematch!"*
Rocky: *"Don't want none!"*

Just as ancient dialecticians acknowledged the products of their loving intellectual combat, so too do these combatants salute each other in mutual respect and acknowledgment of what they have created.

As we might expect from a conflict of dialectical synthesis, no one loses. Both win. Creed maintains his title—if by the narrowest of margins—and by so doing, the integrity of the materialistic myth is preserved. But Rocky wins, too, and for some, his victory is much more significant. He wins his self-respect, his worth, and his freedom. Most significantly, though, Rocky wins for us—albeit in ill-defined form—a broadened perspective on social values. For many Americans, Rocky, along with Carter, provided a renewal of hope.

Audience Role

As already noted, experiencing value change through dialectical synthesis creates strong identification between the audience and the change agents. Such was the case with "Rocky." Few who saw the film did not become engrossed in the fight sequence between Creed and Rocky. Reactions varied from states of anxiety and tension to acts of standing, screaming, and pantomiming what Rocky should do in order to knock Creed out. Curiously enough, the visceral reaction to the fight was, for many persons, a reality independent of whether they "liked" the film or not.

What could be the cause of this degree of involvement by the film audience? Several reasons seem insufficient. For one, the fact that the sequence was a physical prizefight seems inadequate to explain the intensity of its effect. There have been numerous such scenes in, for example, films like "Requiem for a Heavyweight," "Somebody Up There Likes Me," "The Joe Louis Story," and so on. Many of the fight sequences in these films contain as much drama, uncertainty, and physical brutality as the sequence in "Rocky." Neither could the technically superb choreography account fully for the effect of the sequence. For if it could, then the same persons who stood and cheered in "Rocky" would stand and cheer for film documentaries of fights—where the techniques do not have to be staged.

We argue that American audiences know—tacitly, of course—that more was at stake in that fight sequence than the identity of the next Heavyweight Boxing Champion. Audiences experienced in "Rocky" the creation of an integrated set of values that merged materialism and moralism, which reaffirmed the central worth of both value orientations. And for many, it could well have been their participation in the generative process of dialectical synthesis that gave the fight its magentic appeal.

Implications

Like any heuristic concept, the model of social change presented here is not a cookie cutter; it cannot replace the creative insights of the intelligent critic. We hope that future study in rhetorical criticism would explore at least two avenues suggested by the model. First, the model needs to be conceptually and methodologically refined. Second, since values—their formation, affirmation, and subversion—have always occupied a dominant place in rhetorical messages, perhaps the model could be extended to other rhetorical arenas than political acts and films. Insofar as the model alerts critics to how values function rhetorically, we may gain insight into the overall process of social change.

Our analysis of "Rocky" also implies that "undergods" must come to understand the total value structure of the society from which they are alienated if they are to achieve dignity within it. (For how can one change what one does not know?) Ideally, subordinates proceed through unfocused alienation to increased psychological awareness (i.e., through either dialectical transformation or synthesis) of the dominant value structures that exist in tension. And if the "common people" seek *cultural* as well as personal change, they must educate representatives of the power elite to the necessity of change through some sort of symbolic confrontation. That is, because the persons endorsing the dominant value system in a society very rarely redistribute power or re-orient their values voluntarily, the subordinates have an obligation to make them aware of the maladies within the existing system.[14] As we have shown in "Rocky," often this educational process can make the power elite aware of the situation and, occasionally, can dictate the options of individual and social action. Rocky, it will be recalled, defined for Apollo Creed quite clearly and dramatically the pattern that their conflict was to take.

Nor should the humanistic potential of the dialectical synthesis pattern be underestimated. For when this pattern can be enacted, when at least one of the combatants has experienced this pattern internally, then symbolic conflict does not have to be competitive, such that when one wins,

[14] *Martin Luther King, Jr., for instance, stressed that it is the job of the nonviolent resister to educate the majority not only to the societal problem, but also to the intentions of the mass movement to exercise "power under discipline," in* Stride Toward Freedom *(New York: Harper and Row, 1958), pp. 211–219. J. Robert Cox notes that many liberals believed that it was their duty to educate the majority as to the evils of the Vietnam War, in "Perspectives on Rhetorical Criticism of Movements: Antiwar Dissent, 1964–1970,"* Western Speech, 38 (1974), 254–68.

the other must lose. It is equally true, as we have noted throughout, that dialectical synthesis is the exception and not the rule. The rule is dialectical transformation, a situation in which there must be a winner and loser (the loser usually being the underdog). The implication of the film, of course, is that a viable, though difficult, alternative does exist.

Herbert W. Simons notes the prominence of the "system-as-organism" metaphor—the idea that protestors are "pathological," "unhealthy," a "disease." These aspects of the metaphor surely stress the dialectical transformation pattern where subordinates are conceived as losers—losers that are dangerous to the system. But he counters that even the organic metaphor does not demand that the sole function of the system (enforced by those in power) should be to maintain homeostasis:

Besides maintaining basic life functions, the 'healthy' system or organism changes, grows, adapts to problems. Single-minded preoccupation with preserving life functions is indeed a sign of an aged and withered organism, one not contributing very much and not likely to survive for very long.[15]

Indeed, those in control may *adjust* to the challenger's demands rather than totally *capitulate*.[16] Dialectical synthesis at once preserves the social order (after all, Creed *did* retain his championship), while at the same time allows the challengers to achieve their own measure of victory and success. "Rocky" promotes the possibility of a social order one step beyond peaceful coexistence—that of mutual transcendence through cooperative action.[17]

Finally, there is a haunting worrisomeness about "Rocky." It could be rooted in a gnawing discomfort that some astute political observers find in Jimmy Carter as well. For how permanent *are* the consequences of the dialectical synthesis process or, for that matter, *any* primarily symbolic ritual of conflict? What becomes of the American voter two years after Carter takes office? What becomes of Rocky and Adrian two years after their "moment"? One can rather easily imagine Rocky, still in the Philadelphia slums, stumbling up to someone in a bar and slurring, "You shoulda seen me in there with Creed—I was really somethin'!"

[15] *Herbert W. Simons, "Persuasion in Social Conflicts: A Critique of Prevailing Conceptions and a Framework for Future Research," Speech Monographs, 29 (1972), 238.*

[16] *For a description of various strategies that control may employ, including adjustment and capitulation, see John Waite Bowers and Donovan J. Ochs, The Rhetoric of Agitation and Control, Reading, Massachusetts, Addison-Wesley, 1971, pp. 39–56.*

[17] *Although we have focused on dialectical synthesis as a method of value integration, the method need not be restricted to conflicts in value. For example, one of the more imaginative applications of the method occurs in "Close Encounters of the Third Kind," where music is the medium, dialectical synthesis is the method, and initial communicative contact between ontologically different beings is the goal.*

4
THE "NEW RHETORICS" PERSPECTIVE

In the late 1950s and into the 1960s the academic fields of speech-communication and English, and even sociology, political science, and history, were astir with talk of a "New Rhetoric." L. H. Mouat, responding to the "confusion and disagreement among rhetorical critics" and attempting to reduce such confusion for future critics, called for "A *single* [emphasis in original] set of principles" to evaluate the new rhetoric.[1] Then in writing about the increasing tempo of activity, Martin Steinmann, Jr., remarked, "I say 'new rhetorics' rather than 'a new rhetoric' because modern concepts of rhetoric are so diverse that a family of new disciplines rather than a single one seems to be evolving."[2] We would join Steinmann and others in stressing the plural. But we believe that within the diversity there is a family resemblance—especially when the new rhetorics are applied to criticism—that helps us discern a second direction in the breakdown of faith in the traditional perspective which is different from the experiential perspective.

Both of these fresh directions share a rejection of the speaker orientation of the traditional perspective, but the perspective of the "New Rhetorics" also rejects the experiential centering on the critic. The "new" rhetoricians, like the traditional, follow Mouat's call for "a *single* set of principles" and look toward a unified theory to inform their criticism, but their faith tends to be in a non-Aristotelian system. Some of these critics seem to harbor the hope that their particular embryonic theory will grow to be a new paradigm for criticism, but at this point there is little evidence to suggest that any single theory will gain a position equal to that of Aristotelianism in traditional rhetorical criticism.

As we have indicated, prior to the rather clear breakdown of the paradigm in the 1960s, some spokesmen not only registered their dissatisfaction with traditional theory and criticism but attempted to establish new systems that would be more compatible with contemporary views of man and reality. Alfred Korzybski, author of *Science and Sanity,* provided one source of impetus.[3] A few critics drew from Korzybski for their critical method; they were also influenced by his disciples in the general semantics movement—such persons as Irving Lee, Wendell Johnson, S. I. Hayakawa, Anatole Rapoport, and Stuart Chase. The General Semanticists

---

[1] *"An Approach to Rhetorical Criticism," in* The Rhetorical Idiom, *Donald C. Bryant (ed.), New York, Russell & Russell, 1966, p. 165.*
[2] New Rhetorics, *New York, Scribner's, 1967, p. iii.*
[3] Science and Sanity, *Lakewood, Conn., Institute of General Semantics, 1933.*

shared the belief that traditional rhetoric was prescientific and elementistic and, as a result, was the source of many problems, including mental ills.

Another writer who rejected the traditional perspective prior to the 1960s was Kenneth Burke. Burke's rhetorical philosophy evolved through literary criticism into social criticism, with the result that his dramatistic approach has a markedly sociopsychological tone. His rejection of the Aristotelian rhetoric differs from the General Semanticists' in that he builds on the Aristotelian philosophy and extends its range. Burke's rhetoric was introduced into the field of speech-communication in 1952 by an essay in *The Quarterly Journal of Speech* written by Marie Hochmuth Nichols.[4] Her essay was immediately followed in the same journal by two articles by Burke himself: "A Dramatistic View of the Origins of Language" and "Postscripts on the Negative."[5] With these examples before them, critics in the field of speech-communication began to use a Burkeian vocabulary, although in a manner reminiscent of neo-Aristotelianism, that is, mechanically, aiming at description by affixing a series of labels. In fact, Virginia Holland and Dennis Day analyzed Burke's dramatism as an extension of, rather than a departure from, traditional rhetorical theory.[6] Day even concluded, "Burke's theory of rhetoric in terms of identification is not a 'new' *rhetoric;* it is, rather, a 'new' *perspective* from which to view the 'old' rhetoric.[7] To us, this effort to interpret Burke's theory simply as a new perspective on the Aristotelian tradition was a strategy to repair and maintain the traditional paradigm. Kuhn points out that whenever a paradigm is in danger of being rejected its proponents will adapt the theory of the opponents in an effort to save the tradition. If we are correct in our judgment the situation was ironic, for much of Burke's writing in the later 1930s and 1940s was motivated by what he considered to be the mechanical and inadequate explanations of human behavior that were then current in the social sciences.

Another sign of the break from traditional rhetoric was the publication in 1959 of Daniel Fogarty's *Roots for a New Rhetoric.*[8] He saw an amalgam

[4] *"Kenneth Burke and the 'New Rhetoric,'"* The Quarterly Journal of Speech, XXXVIII, 2 (April 1952), 133–44.

[5] *"A Dramatistic View of the Origins of Language,"* The Quarterly Journal of Speech; "Part One," XXXVIII, 3 (October 1952), 251–64; "Part Two," XXXVIII, 4 (December 1952), 446–60; "Part Three," XXXIX, 1 (February 1953), 79–92; and "Postscripts on the Negative," The Quarterly Journal of Speech, XXXIX, 2 (April 1953), 209–16.

[6] Holland, "Rhetorical Criticism: A Burkeian Method," The Quarterly Journal of Speech, XXXIX, 4 (December 1953), 444–50; Holland, "Kenneth Burke's Dramatistic Approach in Speech Criticism," The Quarterly Journal of Speech, XLI, 4 (December 1955), 352–58; and Day, "Persuasion and the Concepts of Identification," The Quarterly Journal of Speech, XLVI, 3 (October 1960), 270–73.

[7] Day, p. 273.

[8] Roots for a New Rhetoric, New York, Columbia University Teachers College Press, 1959.

of three theories—those of I. A. Richards, Kenneth Burke, and the General Semanticists—as providing the basis for a unified system. Fogarty seemed hopeful that the new rhetoric would be paradigmatic, but even though rhetorical critics have drawn heavily upon these theories, the decades of the 1960s and 1970s have scarcely fulfilled his hope.

After studying the current theory and application, we have concluded that it may be useful to differentiate two basic approaches within the general perspective of the new rhetorics. One of these we call the "language-action"[9] approach and the other, the "dramatistic" approach.

Language-action Approach

Within the language-action approach we not only bring together such theorists as I. A. Richards and the General Semanticists but also classify much of the work being done by our colleagues in English departments on style and stylistics. Representative of such an approach is the work of Richard Ohmann, Martin Steinmann, Jr., and W. Ross Winterowd.

Furthermore, a marked interest has arisen lately in the "speech act theory" of the philosophers J. L. Austin and John Searle. Rhetoricians have discussed that theory and its implications in a number of convention programs and journal essays, but it has yet to take shape in critical theory and application.[10] We expect increasing activity stemming from this particular interest.

In 1933, Alfred Korzybski launched the movement of General Semantics, and throughout the 1930s and 1940s his followers became a vocal group within speech communication. An early statement by Irving J. Lee, "Four Ways of Looking at a Speech," attempted to establish General Semantics (along with rhetoric, logic, and semantics) as a viable method of speech criticism.[11] In a further effort to make General Semantics readily available as an instrument of speech criticism, Lee reviewed the academic

---

[9] *The term "language-action" has been taken from the article "Language-Action: A Paradigm for Communication" by Thomas S. Frentz and Thomas B. Farrell,* The Quarterly Journal of Speech, *LXII, 4 (December 1976), 333–49, because it represents a label for and embodies the philosophy of much of the work that uses language as the starting point for its analysis.*

[10] *See J.L. Austin,* How to Do Things with Words, *Oxford: Oxford University Press, 1962; and John R. Searle,* Speech Acts: An Essay in the Philosophy of Language, *Cambridge: Cambridge University Press, 1976. Among rhetoricians who have discussed speech acts and the uses of theories stemming from such analyses are: Karl R. Wallace,* Understanding Discourse: The Speech Act and Rhetorical Action, *Baton Rouge, Louisiana: Louisiana State University Press, 1970; Robert E. Sanders, "Utterances, Actions, and Rhetorical Inquiry,"* Philosophy and Rhetoric, *XI, 2 (Spring 1978), 114–133; and Paul Newell Campbell, "A Rhetorical View of Locutionary, Illocutionary, and Perlocutionary Acts,"* The Quarterly Journal of Speech, *LIX, 3 (October 1973), 284–96.*

[11] *"Four Ways of Looking at a Speech,"* The Quarterly Journal of Speech, *XXVIII, 2 (April 1942), 148–55.*

progress of the movement a decade later in his "General Semantics[1952]."[12] The concepts and tools developed by the General Semanticists were presented in a highly popular form by S. I. Hayakawa in his book *Language in Thought and Action.*[13]

The relationship between words and things, or probably better put, among three elements—what we say, what we think, and what we perceive in our environments, is a problem that has long been both troublesome and fascinating. Immediately pre-dating the General Semanticists, C. K. Ogden and I. A. Richards in *The Meaning of Meaning* struggled to clarify what they believed it means to "refer" to something.[14] Their formalization of the problem has been stimulating on a broad front and seems to us to underlie much that is now being worked out as "language-action" even though most writers who exemplify this approach would reject the passivity in any theory of language that depends heavily on the notion of reference to fix meaning. I. A. Richards, himself, worked toward a much more active, that is, interpretive, sense of language in his *The Philosophy of Rhetoric* where he emphasizes the essential role of metaphor in creating meaning.[15]

In contrast with the General Semanticists' positivist belief that language should conform as closely as possible to an external reality, Richard Weaver took the idealist stance that "true rhetoric involves choices among values and courses of action; it aims at showing men 'better versions of themselves' and better visions of an ultimate Good."[16] Weaver presented much of his philosophy in *Ideas Have Consequences* and extended his thinking explicitly to rhetoric and to criticism in *The Ethics of Rhetoric* and in his often cited essay, "Language Is Sermonic."[17]

In the 1970s research and criticism in the field of speech-communication that has approached language as the starting point has been quite diverse. John R. Stewart in "Concepts of Language and Meaning: A Comparative Study" reviewed studies of language in speech-communication and encouraged scholars to use ordinary language methods.[18] Arguing

[12] *"General Semantics[1952],"* The Quarterly Journal of Speech, *XXXVIII, 1 (February 1952, 1–12.*

[13] Language in Thought and Action, *New York, Harcourt, Brace & World, Inc., 1964.*

[14] The Meaning of Meaning, *London, Routledge and Kegan Paul, Ltd., 1923.*

[15] The Philosophy of Rhetoric, *New York, Oxford University Press, 1936.*

[16] *Richard L. Johannesen, Rennard Strickland, and Ralph T. Eubanks, eds.,* Language is Sermonic: Richard M. Weaver on the Nature of Rhetoric, *Baton Rouge, Louisiana State University Press, 1970, p. 30.*

[17] Ideas Have Consequences, *Chicago, University of Chicago Press, 1948;* The Ethics of Rhetoric, *Chicago, Henry Regnery Co., 1965; and "Language is Sermonic," in* Dimensions of Rhetorical Scholarship, *Roger E. Nebergall (ed.), Norman, University of Oklahoma Department of Speech, 1963.*

[18] *"Concepts of Language and Meaning: A Comparative Study,"* The Quarterly Journal of Speech, *LVIII, 2 (April 1972), 123–33.*

that "language has the nature of an open-ended social institution," Stanley Deetz recommended approaching language as more constitutive than simply referential, that is, proceeding "from the lived experience prior to conceptualization" the perceiver actively forms meaning in a social milieu. Deetz's title indicates the break this sort of thinking makes with older word-thought-thing representations: "Words without Things: Toward a Social Phenomenology of Language."[19]

An active interest in metaphor has long marked rhetorical criticism. The shift in what we are calling the language-action approach resides in moving from metaphor as decoration or elaboration to metaphor as indigenous to meaning. The work of Michael Osborn, beginning with his fine essay with Douglas Ehninger in 1962, "The Metaphor in Public Address," and continuing through his case studies of what he calls "archetypal metaphor" is especially vital.[20] Thomas S. Frentz conducted behavioral tests on three psychological models of metaphor and discovered support for the generative semantics approach to linguistics as contrasted to the classical theory.[21] Paul Newell Campbell, in "Metaphor in Linguistic Theory," argued that "dictionaries have little hope of compassing the varying meanings of words when metaphor can, at the same time, so forcibly question the distinction between the two."[22]

The language-action approach is based on the assumption that the rhetorical critic should begin analysis with the speaker's or writer's use of language. As Thomas S. Frentz and Thomas B. Farrell strive to demonstrate, "a language-action paradigm for human communication" that "reaffirms the centrality of language (i.e., both verbal and nonverbal code systems) to communication [and rhetorical] theory" is vital to a full understanding of discourse.[23] Typically language-action critics make either qualitative or quantitative textual analyses in an effort to establish language patterns that will increase the understanding of the rhetorical act. For example, Richard Ohmann in *Shaw, the Style and the Man* uses Roman Jakobson's theory of arrangement to analyze Shaw's "modes of expression," "habitual patterns of thought," and "lines of connection be-

---

[19] *"Words without Things: Toward a Social Phenomenology of Language,"* The Quarterly Journal of Speech, VIX, 1 (February 1973), 50.

[20] *"The Metaphor in Public Address,"* Speech Monographs, XXIX, 3 (August 1962), 223–34; and *"Archetypal Metaphor in Rhetoric: The Light-Dark Family,"* The Quarterly Journal of Speech, LIII, 2 (April 1967), 115–26.

[21] *"Toward a Resolution of the Generative Semantics/Classical Theory Controversy: A Psycholinguistic Analysis of Metaphor,"* The Quarterly Journal of Speech, LX, 2 (April 1974), 125–33.

[22] *"Metaphor in Linguistic Theory,"* The Quarterly Journal of Speech, LXI, 1 (February 1975), 12.

[23] *Frentz and Farrell, p. 347. The authors do not use the term "paradigm" in the Kuhnian sense.*

tween rhetoric and conceptual schemes."[24] Quite different from Ohmann's adaptation of a linguistic frame of analysis,[25] John Sommerville's "Language and the Cold War" adapts a General Semantics approach to argue for a cross-cultural semantic analysis to end the cold war.[26] We classify both works as falling in the broad range of the language-action approach.

As our examples indicate, many competing theories under different labels are current. We would classify any critical application as language-action if (1) the stress falls on the language itself as the starting point of analysis and (2) the critic sees language as embodying action not simply reflecting, or presenting, or pointing toward it.

We have chosen Richard Weaver's essay, "Some Rhetorical Aspects of Grammatical Categories," to illustrate how a critic can construct theory within the language-action frame. In his *The Ethics of Rhetoric,* Weaver covers a number of rhetorical topics in broad strokes: he discusses the relationship between ideology and strategy in the essays "Edmund Burke and the Argument from Circumstances" and "Abraham Lincoln and the Argument from Definition"; he considers the substantive value of rhetoric in "The Rhetoric of the Social Sciences"; and he contrasts the conflict of assumptions in "Dialectic and Rhetoric at Dayton, Tennessee." Initially these essays seem quite diverse, but they all have a common methodological characteristic: the conclusions are based upon a careful analysis of the language. In "Some Rhetorical Aspects of Grammatical Categories" Weaver makes explicit some aspects of grammatical analysis. Introducing his point of view, Weaver puts well the characteristic thrust of language-action analysis: "All this amounts to saying what every sensitive user of language has sometimes felt; namely, that language is not a purely passive instrument, but that, owing to this public acceptance, while you are doing something with it, it is doing something with you, or with your intention."[27]

To illustrate the application of the language-action approach we have chosen Hermann Stelzner's analysis of Franklin Roosevelt's "War Message" speech. Stelzner makes a close textual analysis by focusing on Roosevelt's stylistic choices as strategies designed to make the acceptance of his proposed action a foregone conclusion. The essay represents a qualitative rather than a quantitative language-action approach to rhetorical criticism.

---

[24] Shaw, The Style and the Man, *Middlebury, Conn., Wesleyan University Press, 1962.*

[25] *We considered using the term "linguistic" for this approach rather than "language-action," but decided that, since contemporary linguists often limit their analysis to the syntactic relationships, the former label might be misleading and the admittedly clumsy but broader label was perhaps more apt.*

[26] *"Language and the Cold War,"* A Review of General Semantics, XXIII, 4 *(December 1966), 425–34.*

[27] Ethics of Rhetoric, *p. 116.*

For a second application of the language-action approach we have chosen Jane Blankenship's "The Search for the 1972 Democratic Nomination: A Metaphorical Perspective." Blankenship analyzes print media coverage of the democratic presidential nomination and discovers twelve metaphors used by reporters and the candidates themselves in discussing the political process. She explains how metaphor plays a significant role in the "reality" constructed by the press.

Dramatistic Approach

To label another approach within the perspective of the "New Rhetorics," we have chosen one of Kenneth Burke's key terms, "dramatistic." In transcending the traditional speaker orientation, Burke shifts the focus of rhetoric from persuasion (the speaker's purpose) to identification (the result of all the components in the rhetorical act). He highlights the psychological constituent of rhetoric by concentrating on the analysis of motive. Among Burke's many books those that pertain most directly to rhetoric are *A Rhetoric of Motives, The Rhetoric of Religion,* and *Language as Symbolic Action.*[28] So successful is Burke in weaving all his concepts into a pattern and creating a feeling of Gestalt, that one cannot fully understand the dramatistic without familiarity with all his work.

Because of the enormous effort necessary to grasp his system, Burke has gained a number of interpreters and translators. An early attempt at describing Burke's rhetoric and evaluating his influence was made by Stanley E. Hyman in his essay, "Kenneth Burke and the Criticism of Symbolic Action."[29] This essay was followed by that of Marie Hochmuth Nichols, mentioned before, and by such books as George Knox's *Critical Moments: Kenneth Burke's Categories and Critiques,* and L. Virginia Holland's *Counterpoint: Kenneth Burke and Aristotle's Theories of Rhetoric.* But probably the most understandable and useful interpretation is supplied by William Rueckert in his book *Kenneth Burke and the Drama of Human Relations.* Rueckert also edited *Critical Responses to Kenneth Burke,* a book that demonstrates Burke's tremendous influence in such fields as sociology, communication, theater, education, and literary criticism.[30]

---

[28] A Rhetoric of Motives, *Berkeley, University of California Press, 1969;* The Rhetoric of Religion, *Boston, Beacon Press, 1961; and* Language as Symbolic Action: Essays on Life, Literature, and Method, *Berkeley, University of California Press, 1966.*

[29] The Armed Vision: A Study in the Methods of Modern Literary Criticism, *New York, Knopf, 1948, pp. 347–94.*

[30] *Knox,* Critical Moments: Kenneth Burke's Categories and Critiques, *Seattle, University of Washington Press, 1957; Holland,* Counterpoint: Kenneth Burke and Aristotle's Theories of Rhetoric, *New York, Philosophical Library, 1959; Rueckert,* Kenneth Burke and the Drama of Human Relations, *Minneapolis, University of Minnesota Press, 1963; and Rueckert (ed.),* Critical Responses to Kenneth Burke, *Minneapolis, University of Minnesota Press, 1969.*

In recent years Burke's dramatistic approach has been more widely accepted as a critical method; speech-communication journals reflect the numerous ways Burkeian concepts have been applied. John W. Kirk explained and illustrated how Burkeian dramatism could be applied to theatre. S. John Macksoud analyzed George Bernard Shaw's play *Saint Joan* from a Burkeian rhetorical perspective. Jeanne Y. Fisher applied Burke's dramatism to a multiple murder and suicide. Then, in what could also be called a generic criticism, Robert L. Ivie constructed a method for Burke's dramatism and applied it to selected presidential war messages. And Carol Berthold followed Burke's method of agon and cluster analysis in criticizing speeches of President John F. Kennedy.[31] These articles, and others, certainly suggest that Burke's dramatism can be applied to rhetorical acts in a variety of fashions.

However, it is important to note that the dramatistic approach is not limited to the work of Kenneth Burke, though most scholars of dramatism acknowledge him as a philosophical and inspirational source. A good example is the book *Drama in Life: The Uses of Communication in Society*, edited by James E. Combs and Michael W. Mansfield. This book brings together in one volume such scholars as Hugh Duncan, Peter Berger, and Erving Goffman from sociology; Eric Berne and Ernest Becker from psychology; Walter Lippmann from journalism; Daniel Boorstin from history; Joseph Gusfield, Dan Nimmo, Murray Edelman, and Orrin Klapp from political science; and movie critic Pauline Kael.[32] The editors indicate in the preface, "Many contemporary social scientists have abandoned physical metaphors as inadequate, and find that the dramaturgical perspective developed by Burke has a depth and explanatory power denied to other paradigms."[33]

Still another form of dramatism in communication has been initiated by Ernest Bormann. Drawing on the fantasizing of small groups, Bormann explains how dramatizations in public messages spread out across larger publics.[34] Bormann's fantasy theme analysis has become another popular method of dramatistic criticism.[35]

---

[31] Kirk, *"Kenneth Burke's Dramatistic Criticism Applied to the Theatre,"* The Southern Speech Communication Journal, XXXIII, 3 (Spring 1968), 161–77; Macksoud, *"Voices in Opposition: A Burkeian Rhetoric of Saint Joan,"* The Quarterly Journal of Speech, LVII, 2 (April 1971), 140–46; Fisher, *"A Burkean Analysis of the Rhetorical Dimensions of a Multiple Murder and Suicide,"* The Quarterly Journal of Speech, LX, 2 (April 1974), 175–89; Ivie, *"Presidential Motives for War,"* The Quarterly Journal of Speech, LX, 3 (October 1974), 337–45; and Berthold, *"Kenneth Burke's Cluster-Agon Method: Its Development and an Application,"* The Central States Speech Journal, XXVII, 4 (Winter 1976), 302–9.

[32] Drama in Life: The Uses of Communication in Society, New York, Hastings House, 1976.

[33] Ibid., p. xix.

[34] *"Fantasy and Rhetorical Vision: The Rhetorical Criticism of Social Reality,"* The Quarterly Journal of Speech, LVIII, 4 (December 1972), 396–407.

[35] We would like to cite a number of qualitative and quantitative applications of

To illustrate dramatistic theory, we have included an essay written specifically for this book by Bernard L. Brock, "Rhetorical Criticism: A Burkeian Approach." Brock has found Burke's concepts especially useful in
the rhetorical criticism of contemporary political persuasion, as can be
seen in his essay, "Political Speaking: A Burkeian Approach."[36]

Illustrating the application of dramatistic criticism, we have chosen
David Ling's article, "A Pentadic Analysis of Senator Edward Kennedy's
Address to the People of Massachusetts." In addition to utilizing effectively
Burke's pentad, Ling shows how the critic can discover and communicate
an insight that would likely remain hidden except for the application of the
dramatistic method.

For a dramatistic application that is not directly Burkeian, we have
chosen Ernest Bormann's "The Eagleton Affair: A Fantasy Theme Analysis." Utilizing fantasy theme analysis Bormann discovered how George
McGovern's handling of the Eagleton vice-presidential nomination created
a negative image that was inconsistent with McGovern's earlier one.

Characteristics of the "New Rhetorics"

Even though we do not see a *single* new rhetoric emerging from the
break from tradition, we do believe that a rough consensus can be discerned, and several assumptions differentiate the perspective of the "New
Rhetorics" from the traditional and the experiential.

First, like the experiential, the perspective of the "New Rhetorics"
stresses society as being in a continual state of process. Thus, critics
working from this perspective will stress interaction and change. However,
unlike the experiential, the "New Rhetorics" seem to assume that stable
relationships can be discovered within the complex interactions of man
and his social and physical context. From these stable relationships, they
believe that it should be possible to construct a unified rhetorical theory.

Second, the belief in stable relationships is an assumption much like
that of the traditional perspective. At the moment, a number of competing

---

Bromann's fantasy theme analysis. Ernest G. Bormann, "Fetching Good Out of Evil:
A Rhetorical Use of Calamity," The Quarterly Journal of Speech, *LXIII, 2 (April
1977), 130–39; Laurinda W. Porter, "The White House Transcripts: Group Fantasy
Events,"* The Central States Speech Journal, *XXVII, 4 (Winter 1976), 272–79; Rich-
ard J. Ilkka, "Rhetorical Dramatization in the Development of American Commun-
ism,"* The Quarterly Journal of Speech, *LXIII, 4 (December 1977), 413–27; Ernest
G. Bormann, Jolene Koester, and Janet Bennett, "Political Cartoons and Salient
Rhetorical Fantasies: An Empirical Analysis of the '76 Presidential Campaign,"*
Communication Monographs, *XLV, 4 (November 1978), 317–29; David L. Rarick,
"The Carter Persona: An Empirical Analysis of the Rhetorical Visions of Campaign
'76" and John F. Cragan and Donald C. Shields, "Foreign Policy Communication
Dramas: How Mediated Rhetoric Played in Peoria in Campaign '76,"* The Quarterly
Journal of Speech, *LXIII, 3 (October 1977), 258–89.*
[36] *Rueckert,* Critical Responses, *pp. 444–55.*

systems, or at least moves toward competing systems, mark the new rhetorical criticism. If the assumption concerning the degree of social stability is correct, continued work ought to lead toward a critical consensus on a method flexible enough to enable the critic to analyze rhetorical patterns typical of the social process.

A third assumption flows from the word-thought-thing relationship. Again, this perspective is like that of the experiential critics. The word-thought-thing relationship is reciprocal, that is, not only does the nature of the object (of relationship) affect the selection of words but the use of a symbol system affects a person's perception of reality. However, the "New Rhetorics" critic would generally go further than the experientialist in stressing the dominance of the word in the presumed interactions of language and reality as a focal point for criticism.

"New Rhetorics" critics look to a unified rhetorical theory to inform their criticism as they apply their theory in a flexible manner. Again, even though a single theory has not emerged there is a rough consensus for an orientation and a set of assumptions. So we will summarize the "New Rhetorics" in the same manner we have summmarized the two previous perspectives.

1. Orientation. The critic must find stable relationships in understanding the interaction of people and their social environment.

2. Assumptions.

a. Society is in process, but fairly stable relationships can be found that govern human interactions with the environment.

b. A flexible framework may be constructed for the study of public discourse.

c. A specific symbol system influences one's perception of reality.

3. Consensus. A unified rhetorical framework is necessary for the productive study of rhetoric and criticism.

As one considers the works that demonstrate a concern with the "New Rhetorics," one is inevitably struck by the rich variety of theorizing and the comparatively recent concern for critical application. Again, we must say that this situation is consistent with Thomas Kuhn's contention that the normal business of science—and we would extend the generalization to criticism—is to apply theory to as many different circumstances as possible once a paradigm is agreed upon. In looking at both the experiential and the "New Rhetorics" perspectives, we would still conclude that rhetoric and rhetorical criticism are pre-paradigmatic.

THE LANGUAGE-ACTION
APPROACH

Some Rhetorical Aspects of Grammatical Categories
by Richard M. Weaver

In an earlier part of this work we defined rhetoric as something which creates an informed appetition for the good. Such definition must recognize the rhetorical force of things existing outside the realm of speech; but since our concern is primarily with spoken rhetoric, which cannot be disengaged from certain patterns or regularities of language, we now turn our attention to the pressure of these formal patterns.

All students of language concede to it a certain public character. Insofar as it serves in communication, it is a publicly-agreed-upon thing; and when one passes the outer limits of the agreement, one abandons comprehensibility. Now rhetoric affects us primarily by setting forth images which inform and attract. Yet because this setting forth is accomplished through a public instrumentality, it is not free; it is tied more or less closely to the formalizations of usage. The more general and rigid of these formalizations we recognize as grammar, and we shall here speak of grammar as a system of forms of public speech. In the larger aspect, discourse is at once bound and free, and we are here interested to discover how the bound character affects our ability to teach and to persuade.

We soon realize that different ways of saying a thing denote different interests in saying it, or to take this in reverse as we do when we become conscious users of language, different interests in a matter will dictate different patterns of expression. Rhetoric in its practice is a matter of selection and arrangement, but conventional grammar imposes restraints upon both of these. All this amounts to saying what every sensitive user of language has sometimes felt; namely, that language is not a purely passive instrument, but that, owing to this public acceptance, while you are doing something with it, it is doing something with you, or with your intention.[1] It does not exactly fight back; rather it has a set of postures and balances which somehow modify your thrusts and holds. The sentence form is certainly one of these. You pour into it your meaning, and it deflects, and molds into certain shapes. The user of language must know how this counterpressure can

[1] *To mention a simple example, the sarcasm uttered as a pleasantry sometimes leaves a wound because its formal signification is not entirely removed by the intonation of the user or by the speech situation.*

be turned to the advantage of his general purpose. The failure of those who are careless, or insensitive, to the rhetoric of grammar is that they allow the counter force to impede their design, whereas a perspicacious use of it will forward the design. One cannot, for example, employ just any modifier to stand for a substantive or just any substantive to express a quality, or change a stabilized pattern of arrangement without a change in net effect, although some of these changes register but faintly. But style shows through an accumulation of small particulars, and the artist in language may ponder a long while, as Conrad is said to have done, over whether to describe a character as "penniless" or "without a penny."

In this approach, then, we are regarding language as a standard objective reality, analyzable into categories which have inherent potentialities. A knowledge of these objective potentialities can prevent a loss of force through friction. The friction we refer to occurs whenever a given unit of the system of grammar is tending to say one thing while the semantic meaning and the general organization are tending to say another. A language has certain abilities or even inclinations which the wise user can draw into the service of his own rhetorical effort. Using a language may be compared to riding a horse; much of one's success depends upon an understanding of what it *can* and *will* do. Or to employ a different figure in illustration, there is a kind of use of language which goes against the grain as that grain is constituted by the categories, and there is a kind which facilitates the speaker's projection by going with it. Our task is an exploration of the congruence between well understood rhetorical objectives and the inherent character of major elements in modern English.

The problem of which category to begin with raises some questions. It is arguable that the rhetoric of any piece is dependent upon its total intention, and that consequently no single sentence can be appraised apart from the tendency of the whole discourse. Our position does not deny that, since we are assuming merely that within the greater effect there are lesser effects, cooperating well or ill. Having accepted that limitation, it seems permissible for us to begin with the largest unit of grammar, which is the sentence. We shall take up first the sentence as such and then discriminate between formal types of sentences.

Because a sentence form exists in most if not all languages, there is some ground to suppose that it reflects a necessary operation of the mind, and this means not simply of the mind as psychologically constituted but also as logically constrained.

It is evident that when the mind frames a sentence, it performs the basic intellectual operation of analysis and re-synthesis. In this complete operation the mind is taking two or more classes and uniting them at least to the extent at which they share in a formal unity. The unity

itself, built up through many such associations, comes to have an existence all its own, as we shall see. It is the repeated congruence in
experience or in the imagination of such classes as "sun-heat," "snow-
cold," which establishes the pattern, but our point is that the pattern
once established can become disciplinary in itself and compel us to
look for meaning within the formal unity it imposes. So it is natural for
us to perceive through a primitive analysis the compresence of sun
and hot weather, and to combine these into the unity "the sun is hot";
but the articulation represented by this joining now becomes a thing
in itself, which can be grasped before the meaning of its component
parts is evident. Accordingly, although sentences are supposed to
grow out of meanings, we can have sentences before meanings are
apparent, and this is indeed the central point of our rhetoric of grammar. When we thus grasp the scope of the pattern before we interpret
the meaning of the components, we are being affected by grammatical
system.

I should like to put this principle to a supreme sort of test by using a
few lines of highly modern verse. In Allen Tate's poem "The Subway"
we find the following:

> I am become geometries, and glut
> Expansions like a blind astronomer
> Dazed, while the wordless heavens bulge and reel
> In the cold reverie of an idiot.

I do not propose to interpret this further than to say that the features
present of word classification and word position cause us to look for
meaning along certain lines. It seems highly probable that we shall have
to exercise much imagination to fit our classes together with meaning
as they are fitted by formal classification and sentence order ("I am
become geometries"); yet it remains true that we take in the first line
as a formal predication; and I do not think that this formal character
could ever be separated entirely from the substance in an interpretation. Once we gain admission of that point with regard to a sentence,
some rhetorical status for grammar has been definitely secured.

In total rhetorical effect the sentence seems to be peculiarly "the
thing said," whereas all other elements are "the things named." And
accordingly the right to utter a sentence is one of the very greatest
liberties; and we are entitled to little wonder that freedom of utterance
should be, in every society, one of the most contentious and ill-defined
rights. The liberty to impose this formal unity is a liberty to handle the
world, to remake it, if only a little, and to hand it to others in a shape
which may influence their actions. It is interesting to speculate whether
the Greeks did not, for this very reason, describe the man clever at

speech as δεινός, an epithet meaning, in addition to "clever," "fearful" and "terrible." The sentence through its office of assertion is a force adding itself to the forces of the world, and therefore the man clever with his sentences—which is to say with his combinations—was regarded with that uneasiness which we feel in the presence of power. The changes wrought by sentences are changes in the world rather than in the physical earth, but it is to be remembered that changes in the world bring about changes in the earth. Thus this practice of yoking together classes of the world, of saying "Charles is King" or "My country is God's country" is a unique rhetorical fact which we have to take into account, although it stands somewhat prior to our main discussion.

As we turn now to the different formal types of sentences, we shall follow the traditional grammatical classification and discuss the rhetorical inclination of each in turn.

Through its form, the simple sentence tends to emphasize the discreteness of phenomena within the structural unity. To be more specific, its pattern of subject-verb-object or complement, without major competing elements, leaves our attention fixed upon the classes involved: "Charles is King." The effect remains when the simple sentence compounds its subject and predicate: "Peaches and cantaloupes grew in abundance"; "Men and boys hunted and fished." The single subject-predicate frame has the broad sense of listing or itemizing, and the list becomes what the sentence is about semantically.

Sentences of this kind are often the unconscious style of one who sees the world as a conglomerate of things, like the child; sometimes they are the conscious style of one who seeks to present certain things as eminent against a background of matter uniform or flat. One can imagine, for example, the simple sentence "He never worked" coming after a long and tedious recital which it is supposed to highlight. Or one can imagine the sentence "The world is round" leaping out of a context with which it contrasts in meaning, in brevity, or in sententiousness.

There is some descriptive value in saying that the simple sentence is the most "logical" type of sentence because, like the simple categorical proposition, it has this function of relating two classes. This fact, combined with its usual brevity and its structural simplicity, makes it a useful sentence for beginnings and endings (of important meaning-groups, not so much of formal introductions and conclusions). It is a sentence of unclouded perspective, so to speak. Nothing could be more beautifully anticipatory than Burke's "The proposition is peace."

At the very minimum, we can affirm that the simple sentence tends to throw subject and predicate classes into relief by the structure it presents them in; that the two-part categorical form of its copulation indicates a positive mood on the part of the user, and that its brevity often induces a generality of approach, which is an aid to perspicuous style. These opportunities are found out by the speaker or writer who senses the need for some synoptic or dramatic spot in his discourse. Thus when he selects the simple sentence, he is going "with the grain"; he is putting the objective form to work for him.

The complex sentence has a different potentiality. Whereas the simple sentence emphasizes through its form the co-existence of classes (and it must be already apparent that we regard "things existing or occurring" as a class where the predicate consists only of a verb), the complex sentence emphasizes a more complex relationship; that is to say, it reflects another kind of discriminating activity, which does not stop with seeing discrete classes as co-existing, but distinguishes them according to rank or value, or places them in an order of cause and effect. "Rome fell because valor declined" is the utterance of a reflective mind because the conjunction of parts depends on something ascertainable by the intellect but not by simple perception. This is evidence that the complex sentence does not appear until experience has undergone some refinement by the mind. Then, because it goes beyond simple observation and begins to perceive things like causal principle, or begins to grade things according to a standard of interest, it brings in the notion of dependence to supplement that of simple togetherness. And consequently the complex sentence will be found nearly always to express some sort of hierarchy, whether spatial, moral, or causal, with its subordinate members describing the lower orders. In simple-sentence style we would write: "Tragedy began in Greece. It is the highest form of literary art." There is no disputing that these sentences, in this sequence, could have a place in mature expression. But they do not have the same effect as "Tragedy, which is the highest form of literary art, began in Greece" or "Tragedy, which began in Greece, is the highest form of literary art." What has occurred is the critical process of subordination. The two ideas have been transferred from a conglomerate to an articulated unity, and the very fact of subordination makes inevitable the emergence of a focus of interest. Is our passage about the highest form of literary art or about the cultural history of Greece? The form of the complex sentence makes it unnecessary to waste any words in explicit assertion of that. Here it is plain that grammatical form is capital upon which we can draw, provided that other necessities have been taken care of.

To see how a writer of consummate sensibility toward expression-forms proceeded, let us take a fairly typical sentence from Henry James:

Merton Densher, who passed the best hours of each night at the office of his newspaper, had at times, during the day, a sense, or at least an appearance, of leisure, in accordance with which he was not infrequently to be met, in different parts of the town, at moments when men of business were hidden from the public eye.[2]

Leaving aside the phrases, which are employed by James in extension and refinement of the same effect, we see here three dependent clauses used to explain the contingencies of "Merton Densher had an appearance of leisure." These clauses have the function of surrounding the central statement in such a fashion that we have an intricate design of thought characterized by involution, or the emergence of one detail out of another. James' famous practice of using the dependent clause not only for qualification, but for the qualification of qualification, and in some cases for the qualification of qualification of qualification, indicates a persistent sorting out of experience expressive of the highly civilized mind. Perhaps the leading quality of the civilized mind is that it is sophisticated as to causes and effects (also as to other contiguities); and the complex sentence, required to give these a scrupulous ordering, is its natural vehicle.

At the same time the spatial form of ordering to which the complex sentence lends itself makes it a useful tool in scientific analysis, and one can find brilliant examples of it in the work of scientists who have been skillful in communication. When T. H. Huxley, for instance, explains a piece of anatomy, the complex sentence is the frame of explanation. In almost every sentence it will be observed that he is focussing interest upon one part while keeping its relationship—spatial or causal—clear with reference to surrounding parts. In Huxley's expository prose, therefore, one finds the dominant sentence type to consist of a main clause at the beginning followed by a series of dependent clauses which fill in these facts of relationship. We may follow the pattern of the sentences in his account of the protoplasm of the common nettle:

Each stinging-needle tapers from a broad base to a slender summit, which, though rounded at the end, is of such microscopic fineness that it readily penetrates, and breaks off in, the skin. The whole hair consists of a very delicate outer case of wood, closely applied to the inner surface of which is a layer of semi-fluid matter full of innumerable granules of extreme minuteness. This semi-fluid lining is protoplasm, which thus constitutes a kind of bag, full of limpid liquid, and roughly corresponding in form with the interior of the hair which it fills.[3]

---

[2] The Wings of the Dove (*Modern Library ed., New York, 1937*), p. 53.
[3] "*On the Physical Basis of Life,*" Lay Sermons, Addresses and Reviews (*New York, 1883*), pp. 123–24.

This is, of course, the "loose" sentence of traditional rhetorical analysis, and it has no dramatic force; yet it is for this very reason adapted to the scientist's purpose.[4] The rhetorical adaptation shows in the accommodation of a little hierarchy of details.

This appears to be the sentence of a developed mentality also, because it is created through a patient, disciplined observation, and not through impression, as the simple sentence can be. To the infant's mind, as William James observed in a now famous passage, the world is a "buzzing, blooming confusion," and to the immature mind much older it often appears something done in broad, uniform strokes. But to the mind of a trained scientist it has to appear a cosmos—else, no science. So in Huxley the objective world is presented as a series of details, each of which has its own cluster of satellites in the form of minor clauses. This is the way the world has to be reported when our objective is maximum perception and minimum desire to obtrude or influence.

Henry James was explaining with a somewhat comparable interest a different kind of world, in which all sorts of human and non-material forces are at work, and he tried with extreme conscientiousness to measure them. In that process of quantification and qualification the complex sentence was often brought by him to an extraordinary height of ramification.

In summation, then, the complex sentence is the branching sentence, or the sentence with parts growing off other parts. Those who have used it most properly have performed a second act of analysis, in which the objects of perception, after being seen discretely, are put into a ranked structure. This type of sentence imposes the greatest demand upon the reader because it carries him farthest into the reality existing outside self. This point will take on importance as we turn to the compound sentence.

The structure of the compound sentence often reflects a simple artlessness—the uncritical pouring together of simple sentences, as in the speech of Huckleberry Finn. The child who is relating an adventure is likely to make it a flat recital of conjoined simple predications, because to him the important fact is that the things were, not that they can be read to signify this or that. His even juxtapositions are therefore sometimes amusing, for now and then he will produce a coordination that unintentionally illuminates. This would, of course, be a result of lack of control over the rhetoric of grammar.

On the other hand, the compound sentence can be a very "mature"

---

[4] On this point it is pertinent to cite Huxley's remark in another lay sermon, "On the Study of Zoology" (ibid., p. 110): "I have a strong impression that the better a discourse is, as an oration, the worse it is as a lecture."

sentence when its structure conforms with a settled view of the world. The latter possibility will be seen as we think of the balance it presents. When a sentence consists of two main clauses we have two predications of similar structure bidding for our attention. Our first supposal is that this produces a sentence of unusual tension, with two equal parts (and of course sometimes more than two equal parts) in a sort of competition. Yet it appears on fuller acquaintance that this tension is a tension of stasis, and that the compound sentence has, in practice, been markedly favored by periods of repose like that of the eighteenth century. There is congeniality between its internal balance and a concept of the world as an equilibrium of forces. As a general rule, it appears that whereas the complex sentence favors the presentation of the world as a system of facts or as a dynamism, the compound sentence favors the presentation of it in a more or less philosophical picture. This world as a philosophical cosmos will have to be a sort of compensatory system. We know from other evidences that the eighteenth century loved to see things in balance; in fact, it required the idea of balance as a foundation for its institutions. Quite naturally then, since motives of this kind reach into expression-forms, this was the age of masters of the balanced sentence—Dryden, Johnson, Gibbon, and others, the *genre* of whose style derives largely from this practice of compounding. Often the balance which they achieved was more intricate than simple conjunction of main clauses because they balanced lesser elements too, but the informing impulse was the same. That impulse was the desire for counterpoise, which was one of the powerful motives of their culture.

In this pattern of balance, various elements are used in the off-settings. Thus when one attends closely to the meanings of the balanced parts, one finds these compounds recurring: an abstract statement is balanced (in a second independent clause) by a more concrete expression of the same thing; a fact is balanced by its causal explanation; a statement of positive mode is balanced by one of negative mode; a clause of praise is balanced by a clause of qualified censure; a description of one part is balanced by a description of a contrasting part, and so on through a good many conventional pairings. Now in these collocations cause and effect and other relationships are presented, yet the attempt seems not so much to explore reality as to clothe it in decent form. Culture is a delicate reconciliation of opposites, and consequently a man who sees the world through the eyes of a culture makes effort in this direction. We know that the world of eighteenth century culture was a rationalist world, and in a rationalist world everything must be "accounted for." The virtue of the compound sentence is that its second part gives "the other half," so to speak. As the pattern works out, every fact has its cause; every virtue is compensated for by a vice;

every excursion into generality must be made up for by attention to concrete circumstances and vice versa. The perfection of this art form is found in Johnson and Gibbon, where such pairings occur with a frequency which has given rise to the phrase "the balanced style." When Gibbon, for example, writes of religion in the Age of Antonines: "The superstition of the people was not embittered by any mixture of theological rancour; nor was it confined by the chains of any speculative system,"[5] we have almost the feeling that the case of religion has been settled by this neat artifice of expression. This is a "just" view of affairs, which sees both sides and leaves a kind of balanced account. It looks somewhat subjective, or at least humanized; it gives us the gross world a little tidied up by thought. Often, moreover, this balance of structure together with the act of saying a thing equivocally—in the narrower etymological sense of that word—suggests the finality of art. This will be found true of many of the poetical passages of the King James Bible, although these come from an earlier date. "The heavens declare the glory of God; and the firmament sheweth his handiwork"; "Man cometh forth as a flower and is cut down; he fleeth also as a shadow and continueth not." By thus stating the matter in two ways, through balanced clauses, the sentence achieves a degree of formal completeness missing in sentences where the interest is in mere assertion. Generally speaking the balanced compound sentence, by the very contrivedness of its structure, suggests something formed above the welter of experience, and this form, as we have by now substantially said, transfers something of itself to the meaning. In declaring that the compound sentence may seem subjective, we are not saying that it is arbitrary, its correspondence being with the philosophical interpretation rather than with the factual reality. Thus if the complex sentence is about the world, the compound sentence is about our idea about the world, into which some notion of compensation forces itself. One notices that even Huxley, when he draws away from his simple expositions of fact and seeks play for his great powers of persuasion, begins to compound his sentences. On the whole, the compound sentence conveys that completeness and symmetry which the world *ought* to have, and which we manage to get, in some measure, into our most satisfactory explanations of it. It is most agreeable to those ages and those individuals who feel that they have come to terms with the world, and are masters in a domain. But understandably enough, in a world which has come to be centrifugal and infinite, as ours has become since the great revolutions, it tends to seem artificial and mechanical in its containment.

Since the difference between sentence and clause is negligible as

[5] Decline and Fall of the Roman Empire (*Bury's ed., London, 1900*), *I, 28.*

far as the issues of this subject are concerned, we shall next look at the word, and conclude with a few remarks on some lesser combinations. This brings up at once the convention of parts of speech. Here again I shall follow the traditional classification, on the supposition that categories to which usage is referred for correction have accumulated some rhetorical force, whatever may be said for the merits of some other and more scientific classification.

The Noun

It is difficult not to feel that both usage and speculation agree on the rhetorical quality of nouns. The noun derives its special dignity from being a *name* word, and names persist, in spite of all the cautions of modern semanticists, in being thought of as words for substances. We apprehend the significance of that when we realize that in the ancient philosophical regimen to which the West is heir, and which influences our thought far more than we are aware at any one moment, substances are assigned a higher degree of being than actions or qualities. Substance is that which primordially *is,* and one may doubt whether recent attempts to revolutionize both ontology and grammar have made any impression at all against this feeling. For that reason a substantive comes to us as something that is peculiarly fulfilled;[6] or it is like a piece in a game which has superior powers of movement and capture. The fact that a substantive is the word in a sentence which the other words are "about" in various relationships gives it a superior status.[7]

Nouns then express things whose being is completed, not whose being is in process, or whose being depends upon some other being. And that no doubt accounts for the feeling that when one is using nouns, one is manipulating the symbols of a self-subsistent reality.[8] There seems little doubt that an ancient metaphysical system, grown to be an *habitus* of the mind through long acceptance, gives the substantive word a prime status, and this fact has importance when we come to compare the noun with the adjective in power to convince by

---

[6] Cf. *Kenneth Burke,* Attitudes Toward History *(New York, 1937), I, 82–83:* "Looking over the titles of books written by Huysmans, who went from naturalism, through Satanism, to Catholicism, we find that his titles of the naturalistic period are with one exception nouns, all those of the transitional period are prepositions actually or in quality ("A-Vau-l'Eau," "En Rade," "A Rebours," "La Bas," "En Route") and all in his period of Catholic realism are nouns."

[7] *In German all nouns are regularly capitalized, and the German word for noun substantive is* Hauptwort *or "head word." In this grammatical vision the noun becomes a sort of "captain" in the sentence.*

[8] *Cf. Aristotle,* Rhetoric, *1410 b: "And let this be our fundamental principle: for the receiving of information with ease, is naturally pleasing to all; and nouns are significant of something; so that all those nouns whatsoever which produce knowledge in the mind, are most pleasing."*

making real. Suffice it to say here that the noun, whether it be a pointer to things that one can touch and see, as *apple, bird, sky,* or to the more or less hypothetical substances such as *fairness, spook, nothing-ness,* by rule stands at the head of things and is ministered to by the other parts of speech and by combinations.

The Adjective

The adjective is, by the principle of determination just reviewed, a word of secondary status and force. Its burden is an attribute, or some-thing added. In the order of being to which reference has been made, the noun can exist without the adjective, but not the adjective without the noun. Thus we can have "men" without having "excellent men"; but we cannot have "excellent" without having something (if only something understood) to receive the attribution. There are very prac-tical rhetorical lessons to be drawn from this truth. Since adjectives ex-press attributes which are conceptually dispensable to the substances wherein they are present, the adjective tends to be a supernumerary. Long before we are aware of this fact through analysis, we sense it through our resentment of any attempt to gain maximum effect through the adjective. Our intuition of speech seems to tell us that the adjective is question-begging; that is to say, if the thing to be expressed is real, it will be expressed through a substantive; if it is expressed mainly through adjectives, there is something defective in its reality, since it has gone for secondary support.[9] If someone should say to us, "Have some white milk," we must suppose either that the situation is curious, other kinds of milk being available, or that the speaker is trying to im-pose upon us by a piece of persiflage. Again, a mountain is a mountain without being called "huge"; if we have to call it huge, there is some defect in the original image which is being made up. Of course there are speech situations in which such modifiers do make a useful contri-bution, but as a general rule, to be applied with discretion, a style is stronger when it depends mainly upon substantives sharp enough to convey their own attributes.

Furthermore, because the class of the adjective contains so many terms of dialectical import, such as *good, evil, noble, base, useful, use-less,* there is bound to exist an initial suspicion of all adjectives. (Even when they are the positive kind, as is true with most limiting adjectives, there lurk the questions "Who made up the statistics?" and "How were they gathered?") The dialectical adjective is too often a "fighting word" to be used casually. Because in its very origin it is the product of dis-

[9] *Compare the following passage by Carl Sandburg in "Trying to Write,"* Atlantic Monthly, *Vol. 186, No. 3 (September, 1950), p. 33: "I am still studying verbs and the mystery of how they connect nouns. I am more suspicious of ad-jectives than at any other time in all my born days."*

putation, one is far from being certain in advance of assent to it. How would you wish to characterize the world? If you wish to characterize it as "round," you will win a very general assent, although not a universal one. But if you wish, with the poet, to characterize it as "sorry," you take a position in respect to which there are all sorts of contrary positions. In strictest thought one might say that every noun contains its own analysis, but an adjective applied to a noun is apparatus brought in from the outside; and the result is the object slightly "fictionized." Since adjectives thus initiate changes in the more widely received substantive words, one has to have permission of his audience to talk in adjectives. Karl Shapiro seems to have had something like this in mind in the following passage from his *Essay on Rime:*

> for the tyrannical epithet
> Relies upon the adjective to produce
> The image; and no serious construction
> In rime can build upon the modifier.[10]

One of the common mistakes of the inexperienced writer, in prose as well as poetry, is to suppose that the adjective can set the key of a discourse. Later he learns what Shapiro indicates, that nearly always the adjective has to have the way prepared for it. Otherwise, the adjective introduced before its noun collapses for want of support. There is a perceptible difference between "the irresponsible conduct of the opposition with regard to the Smith bill" and "the conduct of the opposition with regard to the Smith bill has been irresponsible," which is accounted for in part by the fact that the adjective comes after the substantive has made its firm impression. In like manner we are prepared to receive Henley's

> Out of the night that covers me,
> Black as the Pit from pole to pole

because "night" has preceded "black." I submit that if the poem had begun "Black as . . ." it would have lost a great deal of its rhetorical force because of the inherent character of the opening word. The adjective would have been felt presumptuous, as it were, and probably no amount of supplementation could have overcome this unfortunate effect.

I shall offer one more example to show that costly mistakes in emphasis may result from supposing that the adjective can compete with the noun. This one came under my observation, and has remained with

[10] Essay on Rime (*New York, 1945*), p. 43, ll. 1224–1227.

me as a classical instance of rhetorical ineptitude. On a certain university campus "Peace Week" was being observed, and a prominent part of the program was a series of talks. The object of these talks was to draw attention to those forces which seemed to be leading mankind toward a third world war. One of the speakers undertook to point out the extent to which the Western nations, and especially the United States, were at fault. He declared that a chief source of the bellicose tendency of the United States was its "proud rectitude," and it is this expression which I wish to examine critically. The fault of the phrase is that it makes "rectitude" the villain of the peace, whereas sense calls for making "pride." If we are correct in assigning the substantive a greater intrinsic weight, then it follows that "rectitude" exerts the greater force here. But rectitude is not an inciter of wars; it is rather that rectitude which is made rigid or unreasonable by pride which may be a factor in the starting of wars, and pride is really the provoking agent. For the most fortunate effect, then, the grammatical relationship should be reversed, and we should have "rectitude" modifying "pride." But since the accident of linguistic development has not provided it with an adjective form of equivalent meaning, let us try "pride of rectitude." This is not the best expression imaginable, but it is somewhat better since it turns "proud" into a substantive and demotes "rectitude" to a place in a prepositional phrase. The weightings are now more in accordance with meaning: what grammar had anomalously made the chief word is now properly tributary, and we have a closer delineation of reality. As it was, the audience went away confused and uninspired, and I have thought of this ever since as a situation in which a little awareness of the rhetoric of grammar—there were other instances of imperceptive usage—could have turned a merely well-intentioned speech into an effective one.

Having laid down this relationship between adjective and substantive as a principle, we must not ignore the real or seeming exceptions. For the alert reader will likely ask, what about such combinations as "new potatoes," "drunk men," "a warlike nation"? Are we prepared to say that in each of these the substantive gets the major attention, that we are more interested in "potatoes" than in their being "new," in "men" than their being "drunk," and so forth? Is that not too complacent a rule about the priority of the substantive over the adjective?

We have to admit that there are certain examples in which the adjective may eclipse the substantive. This may occur (1) when one's intonation (or italics) directs attention to the modifier: "*white* horses"; "*five* dollars, not four." (2) when there is a striking clash of meaning between the adjective and the substantive, such that one gives a second thought to the modifier: "a murderous smile"; "a gentleman gambler." (3) when the adjective is naturally of such exciting associations that it has become a sort of traditional introduction to matter of moment: "a warlike nation"; "a desperate deed"; etc. Having admitted these possibilities of departure from the rule, we still feel right in saying that the rule has some force. It will be found useful in cases which are doubtful, which are the cases where no strong semantic or phonetic considerations override the grammatical pattern. In brief, when the immediate act of our mind does not tell us whether an expression should be in this form or the other, the principle of the relationship of adjective and substantive may settle the matter with an insight which the particular instance has not called forth.

The Adverb

The adverb is distinguished from the other parts of speech by its superior mobility; roughly speaking, it can locate itself anywhere in the sentence, and this affords a clue to its character. "Certainly the day is warm"; "The day certainly is warm"; "The day is certainly warm"; "The day is warm certainly" are all "normal" utterances. This superior mobility, amounting to a kind of detachment, makes the adverb peculiarly a word of judgment. Here the distinction between the adverb and the adjective seems to be that the latter depends more upon public agreement and less upon private intention in its applications. It is a matter of common observation that the adverb is used frequently to express an attitude which is the speaker's projection of himself. "Surely the war will end soon" is not, for example, a piece of objective reporting but an expression of subjective feeling. We of course recognize degrees of difference in the personal or subjective element. Thomas Carlyle is much given to the use of the adverb, and when we study his adverbs in context, we discover that they are often little more than explosions of feeling. They are employed to make more positive, abrupt, sensational, or intense whatever his sentence is otherwise saying. Indeed, take from Carlyle his adverbs and one robs him of that great hortatory sweep which makes him one of the great preachers in English literature. On the other hand Henry James, although given to this use to comparable extent, gets a different effect from his adverbs. With him they are the exponents of scrupulous or meticulous feeling; they are often in fact words of definite measure. When James says "fully" or "quickly" or "bravely" he is usually expressing a definite perception, and sometimes the adverb will have its own phrasal modifier to give it the proper direction or limitation of sense. Therefore James' adverbs, instead of having a merely expletive force, as do many of Carlyle's, tend to integrate themselves with his more objective description. All this amounts to saying that adverbial "judgments" can be differently based; and the use of the adverb will affect a style accordingly.

The caution against presumptuous use of the adjective can be repeated with somewhat greater force for the adverb. It is the most tempting of all the parts of speech to question-beg with. It costs little, for instance, to say "certainly," "surely," or even "terribly," "awfully," "undoubtedly"; but it often costs a great deal to create the picture upon which these words are a justifiable verdict. Asking the reader to accept them upon the strength of simple assertion is obviously a form of taking without earning. We realize that a significant part of every speech situation is the character of the speaker; and there are characters who can risk an unproved "certainly" or "undoubtedly." They bring to the speech situation a kind of ethical proof which accentuates their language. Carlyle's reflective life was so intense, as we know from *Sartor Resartus* and other sources, that it wins for him a certain right to this asseverative style. As a general rule, though, it will be found that those who are most entitled to this credit use it least, which is to say, they prefer to make their demonstrations. We point out in summary that the adverb is frequently dependent upon the character of its user, and that, since it is often the qualifier of a qualifier, it may stand at one more remove from what we have defined as the primary symbol. This is why beginners should use it least—should use it only after they have demonstrated that they can get their results by other means.

The Verb

The verb is regularly ranked with the noun in force, and it seems that these two parts of speech express the two aspects under which we habitually see phenomena, that of determinate things and that of actions or states of being. Between them the two divide up the world at a pretty fundamental depth; and it is a commonplace of rhetorical instruction that a style made up predominantly of nouns and verbs will be a vigorous style. These are the symbols of the prime entities, words of stasis and words of movement (even when the verb is said to express a "state of being," we accept that as a kind of modal action, a process of going on, or having existential quality), which set forth the broad circumstances of any subject of discussion. This truth is supported by the facts that the substantive is the heart of a grammatical subject and the verb of a grammatical predicate.

When we pass beyond the matter of broad categorization to look at the verb's possibilities, we find the greatest need of instruction to lie in the verb epithet. It may be needless to impress any literate person with the verb's relative importance, but it is necessary to point out, even to some practiced writers, that the verb itself can modify the action it asserts, or, so to put it, can carry its own epithet. Looking at the copious supply of verbs in English, we often find it possible to choose one so selective in meaning that no adverb is needed to accompany it. If we wish to assert that "the man moves *quickly*," we can say, depending on the tone of our passage and the general signification, that he *hastens, rushes, flies, scrambles, speeds, tears, races, bolts,* to name only a few. If we wish to assert that a man is not telling the truth, we have the choice of *lies, prevaricates, falsifies, distorts, exaggerates,* and some others. As this may seem to treat the matter at too didactic a level, let us generalize by saying that there is such a thing as the characterizing verb, and that there is no telling how many words could have been saved, how many passages could have dispensed with a lumbering and perhaps inaccurate adverb, if this simple truth about the verb were better appreciated. The best writers of description and narration know it. Mark Twain's most vivid passages are created largely through a frequent and perceptive use of the verb epithet. Turn to almost any page of *Life on the Mississippi:*

Ship channels are buoyed and lighted, and therefore it is a comparatively easy undertaking to learn to run them; clear-water rivers, with gravel bottoms, change their channels very gradually, and therefore one needs to learn them but once; but piloting becomes another matter when you apply it to vast streams like the Mississippi and the Missouri, whose alluvial banks cave and change constantly, whose snags are always hunting up new quarters, whose sand-bars are never at rest, whose channels are forever dodging and shirking, and whose obstructions must be confronted in all nights and all weathers without the aid of a single lighthouse or a single buoy, for there is neither light nor buoy to be found anywhere in all this three or four thousand miles of villainous river.[11]

Here there occurs not just action, but expressive action, to which something is contributed by Twain's subtle appreciation of modal variations in the verb.

There is a rough parallelism between the use of the complex sentence, with its detail put away in subordinate constructions, and the use of the verb epithet. In both instances the user has learned to dispense with a second member of equal or nearly equal weight in order to get an effect. As the adverbial qualification is fused with the verb, so in lesser degree, of course, is the detail of the complex sentence fused with its principal assertion. These devices of economy and compression, although they may be carried to a point at which the style seems forced and unnatural, are among the most important means of rhetoric.

The Conjunction

The conjunction, in its simple role as joiner, seems not to have much character, yet its use expresses of relatedness of things, which is

[11] Life on the Mississippi (*New York, 1903*), *p. 73.*

bound to have signification. As either coordinator or subordinator of entities, it puts the world into a condition of mutual relationship through which a large variety of ideas may be suggested. From the different ways in which this relationship is expressed, the reader will consciously and even unconsciously infer different things. Sometimes the simple "and . . . and" coordination is the expression of childlike mentality, as we saw in our discussion of the compound sentence. On the other hand, in a different speech situation it can produce a quite different effect: readers of the King James version of the Bible are aware of how the "and" which joins long sequences of verses sets up a kind of expectancy which is peculiarly in keeping with sacred text. One gets the feeling from the reiteration of "and" that the story is confirmed and inevitable; there are no contingencies, and everything happens with the double assurance of something foretold. When this pattern is dropped, as it is in a recent "American" version of the Bible, the text collapses into a kind of news story.

The frequent use of "but" to join the parts of a compound sentence seems to indicate a habit of mind. It is found congenial by those who take a "balanced view," or who are uneasy over an assertion until it has been qualified or until some recognition has been made of its negative. Its influence is in the direction of the cautious or pedantic style because it makes this sort of disjunction, whereas "and" generously joins everything up.

Since conjunctions are usually interpreted as giving the plot of one's thought, it is essential to realize that they have implicit meanings. They usually come at points where a pause is natural, and there is a temptation, if one may judge by indulgence in the habit, to lean upon the first one that comes to mind without reflecting critically upon its significance, so that although the conjunction may formally connect at this point, its semantic meaning does not aid in making the connection precise. A common instance of this fault is the casual interchange of "therefore" and "thus." "Therefore" means "in consequence of," but "thus" means "in this manner" and so indicates that some manner has already been described. "Hence" may take the place of "therefore" but "thus" may not. "Also" is a connective used with unimaginative regularity by poor speakers and writers, for whom it seems to signalize the next thought coming. Yet in precise meaning "also" signifies only a mechanical sort of addition such as we have in listing one item after another. To signalize the extension of an idea, "moreover" is usually more appropriate than "also." Although "while" is often used in place of "whereas" to mean "on the other hand," it has its other duty of signifying "at the same time." "Whereas," despite its pedantic or legalistic overtone, will be preferred in passages where precise relationship is the governing consideration. On the whole it would seem that the average writer suffers, in the department, from nothing more than poverty of vocabulary. What he does (what every writer does to some extent) is to keep on hand a small set of conjunctions and to use them in a sort of rotation without giving attention to how their distinctive meanings could further his purpose.

The Preposition

The preposition too is a word expressing relationships, but this definition gives only a faint idea of its great resources. When the false rules about the preposition have been set aside, it is seen that this is a tremendously inventive word. Like the adverb, it is a free rover, standing almost anywhere; it is constantly entering into combinations with verbs and nouns, in which it may direct, qualify, intensify, or even add something quite new to the meaning; at other times it combines with some other preposition to produce an indispensable idiom. It has given us "get out," "put over," "come across," "eat up," "butt in," "off of," "in between," and many other expressions without which English, especially on the vital colloquial level, would be poorer indeed. Thornton Wilder maintains that it is in this extremely free use of the preposition that modern American English shows its superiority over British English. Such bold use of prepositional combinations gives to American English a certain flavor of the grand style, which British English has not had since the seventeenth century. Melville, an author working peculiarly on his own, is characterized in style by this imaginative use of the preposition.

Considered with reference to principle, the preposition seems to do what the adverb does, but to do it with a kind of substantive force. "Groundward," for example, seems weak beside "toward the ground," "lengthwise" beside "along the length of," or "centrally" beside "in the center of." The explanation may well lie in the preposition's characteristic position; as a regular orderer of nouns and of verbs, it takes upon itself something of their solidity of meaning. "What is that for?" and "Where did you send it to?" lose none of their force through being terminated by these brief words of relationship.

The Phrase

It will not be necessary to say much about the phrase because its possibilities have been fairly well covered by our discussion of the noun and adjective. One qualifying remark about the force of the prepositional phrase, however, deserves making. The strength normally found in the preposition can be greatly diminished by connection with an abstract noun. That is to say, when the terminus of the preposition is lacking in vigor or concreteness, the whole expression may succumb to vagueness, in which cases the single adjective or adverb will be stronger by comparison. Thus the idea conveyed by "lazy" is largely frustrated by "of a lazy disposition"; that of "mercenary" by "of a mercenary character"; that of "deep" by "of depth," and so on.

After the prepositional phrase, the most important phrasal combination to examine, from the standpoint of rhetorical usages, is the participial phrase. We could infer this truth from the fact alone that the Greeks made a very extensive use of the participle, as every student of that marvellous language knows. Greek will frequently use a participle where English employs a dependent clause or even a full sentence, so that the English expression "the man who is carrying a spear" would be in Greek "the spear carrying man"; "the one who spoke" would be "the one having spoken" and further accordingly, with even more economy of language than these examples indicate. I am disposed to think that the Greeks developed this habit because they were very quick to see opportunities of subordination. The clarity and subtlety of the Greek language derives in no small part from this highly "organized" character, in which auxiliary thoughts are compactly placed in auxiliary structures, where they permit the central thought to emerge more readily. In English the auxiliary status of the participle (recognized formally through its classification as an adjective) is not always used to like advantage.

One consequence of this is that although English intonation and normal word order tend to make the last part of a sentence the most emphatic, unskillful writers sometimes lose this emphasis by concluding a sentence with a participial phrase. We may take as examples "He returned home in September, having been gone for a year"; and "Having been gone for a year, he returned home in September." The second of these puts the weightier construction in the emphatic position. Of course the matter of their relative merit cannot be separated from their purpose; there are sentences whose total meanings are best served by a *retardo* or *diminuendo* effect at the end, and for such closes the participial phrase is well suited for reasons already given. But in the majority of utterances it contributes best by modifying at some internal position, or by expressing some detail or some condition at the beginning of the sentence. The latter use may be quite effective in climactic orderings, and it will be found that journalists have virtually stereotyped this opening for their "lead" sentences: "Threatened with an exhausted food supply by the strike, hospitals today made special arrangements for the delivery of essentials"; "Reaching a new high for seven weeks, the stock market yesterday pushed into new territory." This form is a successful if often crude result of effort toward compact and dramatic presentation.

But to summarize our observations on the participial phrase in English: It is formally a weak member of the grammatical family; but it is useful for economy, for shaded effects, and sometimes the phrase will contain words whose semantic force makes us forget that they are in a secondary construction. Perhaps it is enough to say that the mature writer has learned more things that can be done with the participle, but has also learned to respect its limitations.

In Conclusion

I can imagine being told that this chapter is nothing more than an exposition of prejudices, and that every principle discussed here can be defied. I would not be surprised if that were proved through single examples, or small sets of examples. But I would still hazard that if these show certain tendencies, my examples show stronger ones, and we have to remember that there is such a thing as a vector of forces in language too. Even though an effect may sometimes be obtained by crowding or even breaking a rule, the lines of force are still there, to be used by the skillful writer scientifically, and grammar is a kind of scientific nomenclature. Beyond this, of course, he will use them according to art, where he will be guided by his artistic intuition, and by the residual cautions of his experience.

In the long view a due respect for the canons of grammar seems a part of one's citizenship. One does not remain uncritical; but one does "go along." It has proved impossible to show that grammar is determined by the "best people," or by the pedants, or by any other presumptive authority, and this is more reason for saying that it incorporates the people as a whole. Therefore the attitude of unthinking adoption and the attitude of personal defiance are both dubious, because they look away from the point where issues, whenever they appear, will be decided. That point seems to be some communal sense about the fitness of a word or a construction for what has communal importance, and this indicates at least some suprapersonal basis. Much evidence could be offered to show that language is something which is born psychological but is ever striving to become logical. At this task of making it more logical everybody works more or less. Like the political citizenship defined by Aristotle, language citizenship makes one a potential magistrate, or one empowered to decide. The work is best carried on, however, by those who are aware that language must have some connection with the intelligential world, and that is why one must think about the rhetorical nature even of grammatical categories.

"War Message," December 8, 1941:
An Approach to Language
by Hermann G. Stelzner

I

Two recent books[1] are responses to an uneasiness with much rhetorical criticism which has appeared in print. In raising questions the
authors hope to stimulate more meaningful and insightful analyses of
rhetorical activities and processes. They goad critics to experiment, to
describe and to evaluate in ways heretofore little practiced. Both authors ask that "beginnings" be made.

Reviewers have pointed to difficulties. Arnold's review of Nichols'
work asks for a sample of the criticism "I am exhorted to produce.
. . . " He feels that Nichols "does not illustrate in pointed ways how
criticism may, in practice, resolve the . . . issues raised. . . ."[2] Responding to Black's work, Ehninger agrees with Black's assessment of
much criticism but believes Black's alternatives "are not worked out in
enough detail to be viable." The "ingredients . . . are not developed
into anything approaching a critical method" nor are "characteristics
and possibilities . . . systematized into a program of attack and procedure which the critic . . . may apply."[3] Yet neither Black nor Nichols sets out to develop systems. Black observes:

We have not evolved any system of rhetorical criticism, but only, at
best, an orientation to it. An orientation, together with taste and intelligence, is all that a critic needs. If his criticism is fruitful, he may end
with a system, but he should not, in our present state of knowledge,
begin with one. We simply do not know enough yet about rhetorical discourse to place our faith in systems, and it is only through imaginative
criticism that we are likely to learn more.[4]

Concluding her remarks on I. A. Richards, Nichols states:

One of the most useful things about I. A. Richards . . . is his demonstration of the possibility of finding an orderly methodology. . . . I do

From Speech Monographs, XXXIII, 4 (November 1966), 419–437. Used by permission of the author and the Speech Communication Association. Dr. Stelzner is
professor of speech at the University of Massachusetts.

[1] Marie Hochmuth Nichols, Rhetoric and Criticism (Baton Rouge, La., 1963);
Edwin Black, Rhetorical Criticism (New York, 1965).

[2] Carroll C. Arnold, review of Rhetoric and Criticism in Southern Speech
Journal, XXX (Fall 1964), 62.

[3] Douglas Ehninger, "Rhetoric and the Critic," Western Speech, XXIX (Fall
1965), 231.

[4] Black, p. 177.

*not mean that Richards' method should be adopted. . . . What I do
mean is that we also should be looking for an orderly methodology.*[5]

The thrust of Nichols' and Black's analyses is macrocosmic. Most
criticism, Black states, is limited to "an estimate of the historically factual effects of the discourse on its relatively immediate audience."[6] He
argues for enlargement, for an "interpretation of the discourse that
realizes all that is in it and that aims 'to see the object as it really
is.' . . ."[7]

A rhetorical act is both rich and complex. To probe it fully requires
all the critical postures, approaches, and talents described by Stanley
Hyman in his portrait of an "ideal" critic.[8] Full disclosure is the ideal.

The posture of this study is microcosmic. We center on the language
of Franklin D. Roosevelt's "War Message" to Congress, December 8,
1941. The analysis is motivated by the treatment of language found in
much traditional criticism. Often critics fragment discourse, investigate
chosen samples of language as independent variables and draw conclusions. One analyst, after studying Stevenson's 1952 campaign addresses, reported that Stevenson had a "middle" style, "neither plain
nor grand."[9] To the traditional procedures, Nichols has responded:
"Hoary with age. . . ."[10] She believes that the usual approaches have
failed to treat language adequately: "Year after year, language, if it
is handled at all, gets a few words about rhetorical questions, antithesis,
and metaphors. . . ."[11] Ehninger's description of existing criticism
includes like comments:

*Instead of describing what is going on in a discourse as it works to
achieve its ends, they [critics] focus on how the discourse came into
being, on the circumstances under which it was delivered, and on the
reactions or results it produced. Analysis of the speech itself not only
is slanted, but to the extent that it is present it tends to consist of a
classification of certain grosser properties, cast under the heads of the
traditional modes and canons—to be a mechanical accounting or summing up of how well the speech fits an a priori mold.*[12]

The present approach to Franklin D. Roosevelt's "War Message" is
"topographical." The speech is the "particular place" and, to assess

[5] *Nichols, pp. 106–107.*
[6] *Black, p. 48.*
[7] Ibid.
[8] *Stanley Edgar Hyman,* The Armed Vision (*New York, 1955*), *pp. 386–391.*
[9] *Nichols, p. 107.*
[10] Ibid.
[11] Ibid.
[12] *Ehninger, p. 230.*

the configurations of its language, its "roads," "rivers," "cities," "lakes," and "relief" are examined. To shift the figure, fragments of language are not selected from the speech and regarded as the dominant lights, independent and autonomous. The concern is with the constellation, not the major stars alone. Interest centers on the order, movement, meanings, and interrelations of the language; the object is to discover not only what goes on, but how it goes on. The aim is full disclosure.

We explicate. We try, inductively, a kind of "statistical inspection"[13] to find out what goes on and how the "on-going" is generated. We note development *"from what through what to what,"*[14] shifting from grammar to syntax to diction to logic to rhythm to figure or whatever, when the speech itself demands a shift to account for the totality of tensions in the language. Speeches, including those of the expository genre, are more than collections of statements. Explicating is more than paraphrasing. It is "the ex*plicit*ation of the implicit."[15] We explore the lexical possibilities of words and word combinations. As a way of demonstrating what is going on in a speech, explication is analogous to Hyman's description of Burke's mode: "Use All There Is to Use," which means "the rather disorganized organizing principle of investigating every possible line of significance."[16]

The speech provides the clues. The available drafts of Roosevelt's address have been examined and, when variations in the drafts bear on the analysis, we cite them.[17] However, the primary purpose is not to trace the *development* of the "War Message" of December 8, 1941. How the speech *is,* not how it came to be, is the concern.

We do not suggest that Roosevelt himself consciously structured the relationships we explore and evaluate. It "cannot be said too often that a poet does not fully know what is the poem he is writing until he has written it"[18] applies to all composition. Burke argues it is not until *"after the completion* of the work"[19] that interrelationships in it can be

---

[13] *Kenneth Burke,* The Philosophy of Literary Form *(New York, 1957), p. 59; on p. 75 Burke refers to the examination as an "inductive inspection."*

[14] *Ibid., p. 60; italics his.*

[15] *W. K. Wimsatt, Jr.,* The Verbal Icon *(Lexington, Ky., 1954), p. 249; italics his.*

[16] *Hyman, p. 390.*

[17] *The Franklin D. Roosevelt Library, Hyde Park, New York, has four drafts of this message. They were examined and are referred to by number. Changes from draft to draft are not extensive. Grace Tully, Roosevelt's secretary, indicates that the address was delivered in almost the identical form in which it was originally dictated to her by the President. See Grace Tully,* F. D. R., My Boss *(New York, 1949), p. 256.*

[18] *C. Day Lewis,* The Poetic Image *(London, 1947), p. 71.*

[19] *Burke, p. 18; italics his.*

analyzed; analysis of these involves both "quantitative and qualitative considerations":[20]

Now, the work of every writer contains a set of implicit equations. . . . And though he be perfectly conscious of the act of writing, . . . he cannot possibly be conscious of the interrelationships among all these equations. . . . The motivation out of which he writes is synonymous with the structural way in which he puts events and values together when he writes; and however consciously he may go about such work, there is a kind of generalization about these interrelations that he could not have been conscious of, since the generalization could be made by the kind of inspection that is possible only after the completion of the work.[21]

Because this analysis is limited to the language of a single speech, we cannot generalize from it to "style." The inability to generalize from a single example presents the reverse of a difficulty which reviewers saw in Nichols' and Black's macrocosmic postures: the difficulty of implementation. And microscopic analysis, no matter how successful, does not shed much light on discourse in general. Yet William E. Leuchtenburg's insightful essay, "The New Deal and the Analogue of War,"[22] offers possibilities for extending the analysis undertaken in these pages. He points out that much New Deal policy was accomplished through the figure of war. Roosevelt himself often applied the topic, "war," to social and economic problems. In a sense his December 8, 1941 "War Message" was but another treatment of that topic. Scrutiny of a number of his addresses might provide insights into his use of language, his "style," on the topic "war"; generalization would then be possible. Speaking to the point of generalization, Burke states that it is first necessary to trace down the "interrelationships as revealed by the objective structure of the book itself":

The first step . . . requires us to get our equations inductively, by tracing down the interrelationships as revealed by the objective structure of the book itself. [Eventually one may] . . . offer 'generalizations atop generalizations' whereby different modes of concrete imagery may be classed together. That is, one book may give us 'into the night' imagery; another 'to the bottom of the sea' imagery; another the 'apo-

---

20 Ibid., *p. 59.*
21 Ibid., *p. 18; italics his.*
22 *William E. Leuchtenburg, "The New Deal and the Analogue of War," in* Change and Continuity in Twentieth-Century America, *ed. John Braeman (Columbus, Ohio, 1964), pp. 81–143.*

*plectic' imagery . . . and we may propose some over-all category
. . . that would justify us in classing all these works together on the
basis of a common strategy despite differences in concrete imagery.*[23]

The objective structure of a speech, as well as of a book, is a composite of subtly balanced meanings; all language is weighted toward something, hence away from something; for something, hence opposed to something. A "statistical inspection" of a speech reveals what the speaker talked about, and from that knowledge the balance of his meanings can be established. For example, in the "War Message" of December 8, 1941 "time" is central to Roosevelt's discussion. He uses the future and the past, even as he speaks in, about, and to the present. Future is balanced against Past; these are poles of a continuum along which "goods" and their opposites balance antithetically. The past is given negative valence in Roosevelt's address; and in like manner other concepts, entities, and conditions are antithetically balanced. The balanced meanings are listed below. Those on the left have "positive" quality; those on the right are "negative." *Successive* balances emerge as the speech advances and they, hence, constitute a structural pattern according to which analysis of the address may proceed.

An arrangement of the balanced meanings of an address, such as the arrangement just set forth, describes the relationships of the topics discussed by the speaker; the arrangement does not, however, explicate these relationships. There remains the task of revealing not only the weight of each pole in a particular balance of meaning but how the weighting, hence relationship, was rhetorically achieved.

Future time	*Past time*
God	*"Devil"*
United States	*Japan*
government	*government*
military	*military*
people	*people*
Absence of Danger (presence	*Presence of Danger (absence*
of peace)	*of peace)*
International involvement	*Isolationistic non-involvement*
"I" of address	*Non-"I"*[24]

---

[23] *Burke, p. 59.*

[24] *In a speech situation, the speaker, the "I," is never wholly absent. Listeners may respond to his voice and/or his physical presence even when he handles materials largely denotative and expository in character. The continuum of "presence-absence" is one of convenience, establishing poles and making possible relative weighting.*

We may turn now to the text of Roosevelt's address:

War Message[25]

II

The man who writes or speaks of an "anticipated war . . . must select his material out of the past and the present."[26] He is committed to speak in some fashion about history. On December 7, 1941, history was made suddenly and directly. The equally direct, initial, verbal response (1–3) parallels the historical facts which made statement necessary. Moreover, the mass media had described fully the international activities of December 7, 1941, and listeners could easily fit the speaker's initial statement into a larger and ordered background.

"Yesterday" quickly anchors the address to the immediate historical

[25] *This text is the transcript of the message as delivered. Text from Franklin D. Roosevelt Library, Hyde Park, New York.*

1   *Yesterday, December 7, 1941—a date which will live in infamy—the United*
2   *States of America was suddenly and deliberately attacked by naval and air forces of*
3   *the Empire of Japan.*
4   *The United States was at peace with that nation and, at the solicitation of*
5   *Japan, was still in conversation with its Government and its Emperor looking toward*
6   *the maintenance of peace in the Pacific.*
7   *Indeed, one hour after Japanese air squadrons had commenced bombing in the*
8   *American island of Oahu, the Japanese Ambassador to the United States and his colleague*
9   *delivered to our Secretary of State a formal reply to a recent American message. And*
10   *while this reply stated that it seemed useless to continue the existing diplomatic*
11   *negotiations, it contained no threat or hint of war or of armed attack.*
12   *It will be recorded that the distance of Hawaii from Japan makes it obvious that*
13   *the attack was deliberately planned many days or even weeks ago. During the inter-*
14   *vening time the Japanese Government has deliberately sought to deceive the United*
15   *States by false statements and expressions of hope for continued peace.*
16   *The attack yesterday on the Hawaiian Islands has caused severe damage to American*
17   *naval and military forces. I regret to tell you that very many American lives have*
18   *been lost. In addition American ships have been reported torpedoed on the high seas*
19   *between San Francisco and Honolulu.*
20   *Yesterday the Japanese Government also launched an attack against Malaya.*
21   *Last night Japanese forces attacked Hong Kong.*
22   *Last night Japanese forces attacked Guam.*
23   *Last night Japanese forces attacked the Philippine Islands.*
24   *Last night the Japanese attacked Wake Island.*
25   *And this morning the Japanese attacked Midway Island.*
26   *Japan has, therefore, undertaken a surprise offensive extending throughout the*
27   *Pacific area. The facts of yesterday and today speak for themselves. The people of*
28   *the United States have already formed their opinions and well understand the impli-*
29   *cations to the very life and safety of our nation.*
30   *As Commander-in-Chief of the Army and Navy I have directed that all measures*
31   *be taken for our defense. But always will our whole nation remember the character*
32   *of the onslaught against us.*
33   *No matter how long it may take us to overcome this premeditated invasion, the*
34   *American people in their righteous might will win through to absolute victory.*
35   *I believe that I interpret the will of the Congress and of the people when I*
36   *assert that we will not only defend ourselves to the uttermost but will make it*
37   *very certain that this form of treachery shall never again endanger us.*
38   *Hostilities exist. There is no blinking at the fact that our people, our*
39   *territory and our interests are in grave danger.*
40   *With confidence in our armed forces, with the unbounding determination of our*
41   *people, we will gain the inevitable triumph—so help us God.*
42   *I ask that the Congress declare that since the unprovoked and dastardly*
43   *attack by Japan on Sunday, December 7, 1941, a state of war has existed between the*
44   *United States and the Japanese Empire.*
[26] *Burke, p. 203.*

past, to the events of December seventh. It suggests that the speaker does not intend to go deeply into the past or to discuss it as part of the recommendations he will ultimately make.[27] The meaning of the immediate past was clearly less important than the present and the future. This placement of yesterday contributes to the overall past-present-future structure of the address and to the connotative values of "time" in it. The direct announcement (1–3) ruptures "yesterday," a time of reasonable stability and peace. That mind which wished to wander even fleetingly back over time, is restrained and controlled by the appositive, December 7, 1941. The speaker acknowledges that his listeners understood (27–29) the "leisure," the peaceful "timelessness" of yesterday had gone; but he impresses the point upon them.

The appositive, December 7, 1941, not only defines the specific yesterday among the potentially many. It establishes the date, which for historical purposes is more important than the day, Sunday, here omitted. The personal value judgment—"a date which will live in infamy"—colors the appositive and introduces the future into the discussion. Introduced as an "aside," the future already acts, offering judgments about the present. The matter is carefully handled. The speaker did not say: the date will live in infamy. A shift from the indefinite to the definite article and the excision of the relative pronoun *which* makes the speaker's personal judgment categorical, forcing on the historical future a value judgment which only the historical future can rightfully make.

That a sense of and a sensitivity to history operates[28] can be seen by testing alternatives: *Yesterday, a day which will live in infamy. . . .* Here the appositive is omitted, a possibility because it was unlikely that any member of the immediate audience would have been unaware of the date. History, however, catalogues dates, not yesterdays or days; the date is supplied. Omitting the appositive also makes necessary the revision of "a date which" to "a day which"; the former is somewhat more precise and sustains better the historical overtones of the initial announcement (1–3). Thus, the first twelve words of Roosevelt's ad-

---

[27] Tully, p. 256, reports that when the message was being prepared Roosevelt called Secretary of State Cordell Hull to the White House to examine a draft. "The Secretary brought with him an alternative message drafted by Sumner Welles, longer and more comprehensive in its review of the circumstances leading to the state of war. It was rejected by the Boss. . . ."

[28] Roosevelt "regarded history as an imposing drama and himself as a conspicuous actor. Again and again he carefully staged a historic scene: as when, going before Congress on December 8, 1941 to call for a recognition of war with Japan, he took pains to see that Mrs. Woodrow Wilson accompanied Mrs. Roosevelt to the Capitol, thus linking the First and Second World Wars." Allan Nevins, "The Place of Franklin D. Roosevelt in History," American Heritage, XVII (June 1966), 12.

dress join past and future; the present is represented by speaker and audience. And the immediate present—unsettled, disrupted, and anxiety-provoking—is somewhat stabilized by the past-future continuum which provides a sense of continuity. In the speaker's judgmental aside, the future renders a verdict on present activities which favors us; implicatively the future is on "our side."

The passive voice of the initial announcement makes possible some specific relationships between time, the actors in time, and the judgmental aside about the time. Though the statement's subject is the naval and air forces of the Empire of Japan, in the passive voice the subject becomes a marginal, omissible part of the sentence and its sense. The speaker could have said: . . . *the United States of America was suddenly and deliberately attacked.* But as delivered, the first statement treats the Japanese Empire as "marginal," subordinate. The passive emphasizes the United States as receiver of the action on a specific date, a day of peace until the attack which was infamous in character. The interrelationship of the three allows the immediate audience and history to record these facts. The initial statement might have been active: *Yesterday, December 7, 1941, a date which will live in infamy, naval and air forces of the Empire of Japan suddenly and deliberately attacked the United States.* Not only would the Japanese Empire have become central and active, but the United States would have been removed from its relationship to time. Yet time is essential to the well-being of the country. Past time treated her badly; future time (33–34, 40–41) will heal her wounds.

Even as yesterday was ruptured, the formal, settled, and trusted diplomatic conventions (4–6) were in process. These, too, will be broken (9–15) as the speaker particularizes some of the specific details in the deliberations. The formal and elevated diplomatic language describes. "Nation" (4) is more formal and concrete than a possible alternative, *country.* "Solicitation" (4) is more formal than *request,* and "conversation" (5) is more formal than *discussion* or *conference.* Consistent with the formality of the language is its loose, alliterative quality, more pronounced here than in any section of the address. "Peace" (4, 6) opens and closes the section, its sound sense somewhat reinforced by a weak alliterative echo: "Pacific." Between these points, "nation," "solicitation," "conversation" occur in rapid order; "maintenance," modifies the pattern by introducing a different, though not wholly dissimilar, sound tension.

Time remains central to the development. "The United States was at peace"[29]—past, "still in conversation"—present, "looking toward the

---

[29] *In drafts I, II, and III the line reads: "The United States was at the moment at peace. . . ." The "at the moment" phrase emphasizes time unnecessarily;*

maintenance"—future. The actors in the drama are polarized. Responding to a Japanese "solicitation," we were still concerned with tomorrow, even as they were not. The formal, diplomatic language (4–6) symbolizes a mask behind which duplicity is hidden. The duplicity, one dimension of a key term, "infamous" (1), is woven into the texture of the address. For example, the close relationship of "yesterday" (1, 16, 20) to the repeated "deliberately" (2, 13, 14) intensifies and supports the duplicity or infamy. The formal language (4–6) foreshadows the recital of specific events (7–11).

"Indeed," injecting emphasis and force, begins the recitation and colors the neutrality of formal, diplomatic language. Not *yet, still, but,* nor *however* would have functioned as well to introduce the formal, but false, overtures of the Japanese. "Indeed" imprints a reaction of the individual "I" on the yet-to-be-stated particulars. Moreover, "indeed" gains force and support from the earlier "yesterday," "infamy," "deliberately," "at peace," "still in conversation," and "maintenance of peace." Following the expletive, the speaker says "one hour after" (7), not merely *after.* "One hour after" makes time concrete, supports the emotional dimensions of "indeed," and forecasts the brazen, formal action of the Japanese Ambassador and the duplicity behind his formality. Also supporting duplicity is a subdued temporal pattern (7–11): after Japanese air squadrons attacked—past, the Ambassador delivers his reply—present, concerning *future* relationships.

"Japanese air squadrons" (7) were the instruments of attack. The phrase might have been rendered: *after the Japanese air force* or *after Japanese air forces.* These alternatives parallel better the first reference to the Japanese military (1); but therein lies a weakness. The modified repetition provides some variety. More important is the matter of image. *Air force* and *air forces* denote and connote mass, a large quantity which blankets a sky. Such a mass moves, but in droning and lumbering fashion. "Air squadrons" is a sharper, definable form of the force, as an image in the mind's eye. The image is of small groups, of well-defined patterns in the total mass, of tightly knit units sweeping in and out over the target.

"Air squadrons" is quantitative, definitive, and repetitive. To the extent that squadrons are patterns, the image presents formal patterns inflicting damage. Formal patterns are the enemy: of the past—"one hour

---

it contributes little to clarity or sense, and its excision is merited. Further, its excision diminishes the possibility of the immediate listeners' setting up the balance: was at the moment—is at this moment. "At this moment" (i.e., the moment of the address) the United States was in practical terms at war. Yet the President was speaking formally to the Congress to whom the legal right formally to declare war belonged. "At this moment" we were "legally" still at peace. Excision of "at the moment" diminished the possibility of a mistaken response by either the Congressional or the general audience.

after" (7), as well as the near present—"the Japanese Ambassador
. . . delivered" (8–9). The formality of pattern connoted by "Japanese
air squadrons" is also explicitly denoted of the Ambassador's act; he
delivers a "formal reply" (9), which is contrasted to a slightly less formal "American message" (9). Had the description been of an *American
note,* it would have been overly informal. Slightly more formal and rigid
than "our Secretary of State" (9) is "the Japanese Ambassador" (8). If
there is in these lines a heightened sense of the "formal" and if formality marks the enemy, all formality becomes symbolic—a mask—for
duplicity and infamy. The closed, distant, difficult-to-read "formal" opposes the somewhat easier-to-read, open "informality." Such suggestion is consistent with the Western, especially American, stereotype of
the Orient and Oriental, *circa* 1941. Duplicity masked by formality is
thus further intensified. On first glance the construction of line 11[30]
appears anticlimactic. "War" (11) is more encompassing and potentially more dangerous than "armed attack." However, "war" connotes a
formal, open declaration of conflict. The Japanese dispensed with that
formality, favoring "armed attack," an action outside the conventions
of diplomacy.

Thus far no objective evidence has been offered to support the
charge of duplicity. The speaker has been reporting diplomatic relationships (4–6) which the listeners themselves cannot verify; they are
dependent upon him. But the shift is now to a geographical relationship (12) which supports the charge. "It will be recorded. . . ." By
whom? The immediate audience certainly, but the historical audience
as well. The verb "record" alters the speaker's stance and the passive
"will be recorded" his perspective. The speaker's verb refers to, points
to, the intellectual activity of man. Together, in concert, the speaker
and the listeners function as detached observers—they measure mileage—and as commentators. "Makes it obvious" (12) is a phrase which
befits such activity—of seeing, of reasoning, of understanding. The passive allows the evidence to be offered in dependent clauses, which
contain the signs upon which the conclusion depends; it provides the
"distance" necessary to detached, intellectual analysis. All the signs,
and especially the final, objective, mileage sign, which is positioned
nearest the conclusion which all signs support, contribute to one judgment: infamous duplicity. Finally, "the distance of Hawaii from Japan"

[30] *In draft II lines 10–11 read: "This reply contained a statement that it
seemed useless to continue the diplomatic negotiations, but it contained no
threat nor hint of war or of armed attack." Drafts III and IV are consistent with
the final text (pp. 422–423). The draft II version is a compound sentence and
fails to stress the "no threat nor hint of war. . . ." The revision, a dependent-
independent arrangement, emphasizes the "no threat nor hint of war. . . ." It
emphasizes duplicity.*

(12), a particular sign, is embedded in a sentence which itself spans syntactical distance.

The passive construction makes possible analysis of events which are outside the direct experience of the speaker. Events of the more immediate past (14–15) are handled differently; they are not in dependent clauses and the subject of detached, intellectual analysis. Of these events, the speaker has direct knowledge, and he shifts to the active voice. Japan acts. The language which responds is categorical and conclusive: "deliberately sought to deceive the United States by false statements and expressions of hope . . ." (14–15). Was the deception successful? The ambiguous "sought" leaves the question open, even as the speaker's emphasis on Japan's deliberateness and falsity tend to forestall the asking of it.

As further details are enumerated, time shifts slightly in importance. In "the attack yesterday" (16), the act is more important than the time. The emphasis on time could have been maintained: *yesterday's attack.* The new arrangement is less emphatic. The shift in emphasis does not however alter the basic time-act or act-time relationship. A legitimate alternative would have considerably weakened, if not broken, it: *the attack on the Hawaiian Islands yesterday.* . . .

From the description the personal "I" (17) emerges to link the speaker with the "blackest" event yet—the specific human tragedy. Both the "I" and the tragedy gain stature from the relationship. Had the "I" chosen a compound sentence, he could have avoided announcing the loss of life: the attack . . . *caused* . . . *damage to* . . . *forces and very many American lives have been lost.* Or he might have said simply: *Very many American lives have been lost.* These choices diminish both the ethical posture of the "I" and the dignity of the men who lost their lives. The "I" reveals (17–18), explicitly and implicitly, something of his regard for life—he separates it from the materials of war—and of his concept of duty, as a human being and as President and Commander-in-Chief. He demonstrates his understanding of and his respect for the conventions of tragic announcement. Moreover, he emerges "to tell" (17) his listeners. The direct, common verb suggests closeness—he to them and they to him. A close relationship must exist between the bearer and the receivers of tragic tidings for the verb "tell" to operate. When there is distance the tendency is toward formality, neutrality, and elevation: to *inform,* to *report,* or to *announce.*

"In addition" (18) adds still another detail. Is it of equal, more, or less importance than others? That depends upon the reaction of the listener to the total configuration. But the speaker by his placement of it reveals his assessment of its importance. Japanese submarines have approached the United States; they act not at far-off Hawaii, but nearer home. For an already upset nation the news is serious and distressing. The distress is minimized somewhat by placing it following the announcement of the loss of life, which absorbed most, if not all, emotional energies. The statement which follows the news helps to minimize the danger from the submarines. Attention and concern are diverted by the quick, crisp movement to Malaya (20)—about as far as danger could be removed.

Additional forces further diminish the submarine threat; distance is achieved by having the ships torpedoed on the high seas between San Francisco and Honolulu. The language moves danger "away from" the shores of the United States. The proper nouns, San Francisco and Honolulu (19), are necessary to the overall effect. Let the speaker say: *In addition, American ships have been reported torpedoed on the high seas.* Responses become: Where? Everywhere? Close to the United States? How close? Distant? How distant? The proper nouns meet some of the questions. Where? On a direct path between San Francisco and Honolulu. One can almost see it on the wall map of the mind—the narrow, well-defined shipping route. Close? How close? Ambiguously the image suggests movement *away from.* One may speculate on the range of possible responses had the speaker said, *on the high seas between Honolulu and San Francisco,* or merely *on the high seas.*

The choice and arrangement of the proper nouns diminish danger; a vague term in the same sentence (18–19) functions similarly. "Have been reported torpedoed . . . ," said the speaker. "Reported" has truth-value, but relative to source and circumstance. Reports of that time were somewhat chaotic and unreliable. The speaker hints at doubt and uncertainty. The weight of the office of President and Commander-in-Chief does not support the reports. An alternative could diminish doubt: *American ships have been torpedoed.* The specific and the concrete joined in the same sentence to the vague and ambiguous moderate danger.

The announcement of the attack against Malaya (20), which partially relieved concern for the movement of Japanese submarines, has another function. It quietly extends the conflict, joining the United States as partner and ally of the British. The United States' involvement is not to be limited; it will become global. "Also" (20) signals this extension, though "Malaya" and "Hong Kong" must be heard to make the idea meaningful. The concluding generalization, "a surprise offensive extending throughout the Pacific area" (26–27), also quietly involves the country with allies and quietly prepares it for total involvement without the speaker's need to expend ethos to stress the necessity of an international commitment.[31]

[31] *James Reston,* New York Times, *December 9, 1941, p. 5, wrote: "Two facts seemed to impress this gathering [Congress] more perhaps than the*

The announcement of the attack against Malaya (20) also introduces a shift in the movement and tone of the address. The former will be quickened, the latter be made emphatic. The statement of the attack against Malaya parallels in substance lines 1–3; it begins "yesterday"; its subject is Japanese activity. However, its voice is active; it has neither qualifiers nor dependent clauses; its verb is simple, past tense. No other statement in the address thus far is as compressed or moves as quickly.

The "yesterday" which introduces the attack against Malaya concludes a compression among the yesterdays; note only the distance between them (1, 16, 20). This compression occurring over time and distance foreshadows, even as it is counterbalanced by, the tightly compressed "last night" series (21–24), including as well the modified restatement of time: "this morning" (25). These compressions of time herald the end of discussion about events in the immediate past. Attention will soon be directed (27–29) to what must be done today and tomorrow.

The tonalities of the "last night" series (21–25) are controlled by line 20 which begins formally: "the Japanese Government." The verb, "launched," quickly tarnishes the formal recognition. Rather than "launched," why not *began, commenced,* or the still simpler *attacked?* None of these verbs reinforces or sustains as well the connotations of "suddenly and deliberately attacked" (2) and "deliberately planned" (13), which emphasize that Japanese activities were outside the conventions of diplomacy. Had they been within those conventions, "launch" might have been an inappropriate description. A verb of strong thrust and impulse, "launch" has sufficient energy to encompass all remaining action (21–25).

Formal agents and agencies, "Japanese forces" (21–23), advance the action. Soon the less formal and somewhat ambiguous "the Japanese" (24–25) forward it. Is the referent only the Japanese Government and/or its agents? Or has there been a subtle expansion to include the citizens of Japan, as well? The choice of "Japan" (26) suggests the latter explanation. "Japan"—not the Empire of Japan, nor the Emperor, nor the Ambassador, nor the Government—merely Japan; the common term describes the nation. The Government and its agents are the explicit enemy; by implication the people are also numbered among the enemy. Nowhere before has the term, Japan, been used in this naked fashion. The "Japan" of line 5 occurs within the context of elevated, diplomatic language; in line 12 the reference is a straightforward, geographical one. The common term is later repeated (43) and tarnished completely

---

simple words of the speech. By not the slightest inflection did he suggest that the facts of the world situation had finally justified his policy, as even his opponents were admitting today he might very well have done."

by "unprovoked and dastardly" (42). The national name is finally too good to serve to describe the country. Reduction of Japan is effected by carefully controlled and disciplined language. Men in the street could and did say "Japs." The speaker could not. To have done so would have diminished not only the stature of the office of President but also the occasion and the place, the formal chambers in which affairs of state were conducted. Equally important, to have said "Japs" would have reduced the leader to the level of the led; distance, however defined, is necessary to effective leadership.

The "last night" series (21–24) supports the pace and quality of the attacks. Logically, last night, a part of yesterday, is illogical. The compressed "last nights," figuratively ticking off the clock, bring yesterday to a climactic end. The three "yesterdays" (1, 16, 20) spanned time and space; the night and the events in the night move faster. Simple declarative sentences present facts—actor, action, acted upon. The lengthy iteration is necessary to establish the magnitude of the Japanese thrust. However, had it been extended by the addition of only a few details, it would have been compromised, having its force, pace, and energy enervated. Finally, the verb "launched" more than attacks; it launched a series of sentences which structurally (i.e., in form) harmonize with the acts embedded in them. The actions (i.e., their substance) and the manner of describing them (form) are one. The syntax is itself symbolic of the fast moving military operations.

The connotations from the cluster of "last nights" do more than support the emotional responses rising from "in the quiet of the night when all were abed and defenseless." The cluster is the turning point in a chain of emotive phrases. Prior to the "last night" series, descriptions are relatively mild and basically denotative: "suddenly and deliberately" (2), "deliberately planned" (13), "deliberately sought to deceive" (14), and "false statements" (15). Following the cluster and supported by it is a chain of increasingly stronger phrases: a mild "surprise offensive" (26), a slightly stronger "premeditated invasion" (33), the strong "this form of treachery" (37), and the vehement "unprovoked and dastardly" (42). As the descriptions of the Japanese actions become stronger, so also does the language which responds. Later shifts in verb and voice which describe the response of the United States will be noted.

Finally, the stress which the language contributes, sustains and intensifies the general emphasis of the "last night" passage (20–25). "Yesterday" has three syllables, the first being accented. The phrase "last night" has two accented syllables, relatively equal in stress. Each "last night" is encircled by "attack" or "attacked." The stress pattern of the language is a bombardment. The final line (25) begins with a conjunction which readies the listener for the final "to top it all off." Thus "and," too, is a term of some stress and strength. "And this morning," a phrase of four syllables, the first three accented, concludes the bombardment.

How well this discourse is managed is seen best by examining some alternatives. Compare "Last night Japanese forces attacked Hong Kong" (21) with: (a) *Japanese forces attacked Hong Kong last night,* or (b) *last night Hong Kong was attacked by Japanese forces.* Alternative (a) maintains the active voice, emphasizing Japanese forces. But the immediacy of "last night" is lost when the phrase concludes the thought. The arrangement also negates the effect produced by accent and stress. "Japanese" contains three syllables, relative stress being unaccented, unaccented, accented. Bombardment by stress is weaker. Further, alternative (a) significantly changes the range of the connotative values of "last night," which now modifies Hong Kong and which divides the emotional response. Sympathy goes out to the people of Hong Kong who experienced catastrophy during the night, yet this relieves somewhat the intensity of the negative emotional response centered on the Japanese, the central actors in the night. Alternative (b) is also unable to capitalize fully on the connotative values of "last night." The passive construction of (b) slows the pace; it also makes the subject, "Japanese forces," a marginal part of the sense. Yet the "last night" series (20–25) is the speaker's final statement about yesterday's activities. He soon directs his listeners (27–29) to respond positively. Their active responses are directed to and focused on something central, not marginal.

Finally, the passive construction of alternative (b) puts the places attacked prior to the act of attack and the attacking forces. Place names, Malaya, Hong Kong, Guam, are presented to the listener first, and though the places are scattered over geography, mentioning them first tends to fix them within a general geographical framework. Anchoring the place names makes the image somewhat static. In the active construction (20–25), the image has more movement. The attacks push on places which are in turn pushed over geographical distance enlarging the area of the conflict. The image thus better foreshadows the concluding, explicit reference to a surprise offensive "extending throughout the Pacific area" (26–27).

Roosevelt's conclusion is introduced by the formal, logical sign, "therefore" (26). His demonstration concluded, the speaker again shifts posture, removing himself altogether from the discussion. He chooses to let a transcendental power suggest action. He personifies: "The facts . . . speak for themselves" (27). The information could have been conveyed in other ways: *the facts . . . are clear; the facts . . . are obvious; the facts . . . are self-evident; the facts . . . are self-explanatory.* But, "facts . . . speak. . . ." To whom? Directly, which none of the alternatives above manages quite as well, to "the people of the United States," the subject of the following sentence. How do the people respond? What do they do? Verbs (28) indicate that they use their intellects and power to reason. They have "formed their opinions and well understand." So powerful were the facts that they spoke; so reasoned were the people that they needed no guidance to arrive at a conclusion. No intermediary stands between the facts and the people of intellect. What conclusion had the people "already" (28) reached? To support the action which the speaker announces he has "already" taken (30–32).

The people of the United States are presented as acting on the danger before their Government. Though the danger is not well defined, they understand the "implications" and react positively. When the speaker first mentions the danger he embeds it in his statement about the people (27–29). Their positive response envelops danger, thereby minimizing it.

The speaker's treatment of the situation and the course of action asserts a commonplace of democratic decision making: the people (27–29), the president (30), the troops (30–31) act jointly. Though they act jointly, the people are presented as having the power to effect decisions.[32] The point is demonstrated by rearranging the speaker's language so that it violates the commonplace:

The facts of yesterday and today speak for themselves. As Commander-in-Chief of the Army and Navy, I have directed that all measures be taken for our defense. The people of the United States, understanding well the implications to the very life and safety of our nation, have already formed their opinions as to the necessity of this action.

[32] *The power structure upon which the democracy rests compares favorably with that of the enemy: the Emperor, the troops, the people, the latter recognized by their omission. Two reasons partially explain the absence of any formal recognition of the Japanese people, thereby implicatively numbering them among the enemy. First, the conflict does not become one between people; the enemy scapegoat is clearly displayed and well-defined to allow reactions to center on it. Second, the people have to be handled as a totality, as an entity. Even were it possible to define some as "enemy" and others as "friend" the difficulties would have been great. Fine distinctions would have necessitated logical and legalistic development which would have slowed and weakened the movement of the address. The problem would have been only slightly less difficult had the speaker said categorically: The United States has no quarrel with the Japanese people. (Substitute the word German for Japanese in this sentence and it becomes Woodrow Wilson's position in his "War Message" on April 2, 1917. Roosevelt's treatment of the Japanese people is quite different from Wilson's treatment of the German people.) Quite apart from the fact that the Japanese had made American citizens part of the conflict, the speaker, perhaps ahead of the mass of men, realized that such a statement, with its overtone of righteousness, had no place in the mid-twentieth century. War was total. To have said publicly that the people of Japan were not a part of the conflict would have involved the speaker in an untruth, at worst, or in "mere rhetoric," at best. These charges he had earlier levied against Japan.*

To take the action which the logic of the people demanded, man must act. The speaker shifts stance to act in their behalf: "directed" (30) and "taken" (31) indicate reinvolvement with immediate circumstances. He has been reporting. Now he leads: "I direct" (31), "I believe" (35), "I interpret" (35), "I assert" (36), "I ask" (42). Henceforth energies are marshalled and thrust upon the circumstances which face the country. In the prepositional phrase of interrelation and interaction, "between the United States and the Japanese Empire" (43–44), the United States is mentioned first, giving an additional sense of thrust to our energies. After the speaker announces that the "facts of yesterday . . . speak for themselves," the United States becomes active and positive in its response to those facts. The shift in movement is marked when compared to earlier activity, lines 1–3 being but one example.

The turning point in this address having been reached, the events of yesterday now sustain and support the energy of the country. "That always will our whole nation remember the character of the onslaught against us" (31–32)[33] is in a syntactically dependent position. Though the clause is somewhat awkward and forced, it does foreshadow the first comment about the ultimate outcome (33–34): "no matter how long it may take" (33) which tempers hopes of a quick conclusion. The introductory qualification needs its present emphasis so that listeners' hopes may not be falsely supported. Had the speaker said: *the American people . . . will win through to absolute victory, no matter how long it may take,* listeners might have missed the qualification. Patience, determination, and fortitude are connoted to counterbalance the zeal with which the people, who had "already" (28) reached a judgment, meet the challenge. The zeal is not destroyed, but protected: zeal often becomes impatient when detours or setbacks delay progress. The "righteous might" (34) not only provides alliteration and balance for "premeditated invasion" (33), but also triggers a new chain of images: from "righteous might" (34) to "God" (41) to "Sunday" (43). "God" in medial position reflects backward and forward.

Though the specific "I" has emerged to act, his actions vary. What he is and what he does are partially revealed by the choice of verbs. Three verbs (35–37) point to intellectual activity: "I believe," "I interpret," "I assert." Having earlier "directed" and "taken" (30–31), he now becomes an observer of evidence and a commentator thereon. A

---

[33] *In drafts I, II, and III this line reads: "Long will we remember the character of the onslaught against us." In draft III "long" is struck and "always" substituted. "Always," positive and categorical, is stronger than "long," a relative term. "Always" also better suits the historical overtones in the address and the emphasis on future time. "Long" appears again in line 33, but the repetition serves no rhetorical purpose.*

slow reading of lines 35–37 reveals the tentative, cautious, distant quality of the prose. These lines contain three dependent clauses; no other lines in the address contain as many. Moving through the clauses, the speaker searches for and examines present signs as a basis for his "assertion" (36): "that this form of treachery shall never again endanger us."[34]

Following this intellectual-activity statement, long in the sense of distance and tone and by word count the longest in the address, Roosevelt shifts posture again, jolting listeners to a blunt recognition of present difficulty. "Hostilities exist" (38) is his shortest and most direct statement. Yet so mild, so objective, and so matter-of-fact is it that it functions as understatement. Responses spill out and over it; reactions are some variant of "that puts it mildly." Emotional responses to the events are stronger than this statement about the events. Thus, some response spills into lines 38–39 finding resolution in, and providing support for, the judgment, "grave danger" (39).

"Hostilities exist" has another function. Though the future is of concern, listeners could not long tolerate intellectual analysis of the present and future. They might allow the speaker to speculate, but their impulses were for direct action, having "already" (28) reached a judgment. Yet the distant quality of understated assessment dulls somewhat the listener's emotional edge, taking his mind momentarily off the present; it rests the mind before that mind has to accept the judgment of "grave danger" (39). When the speaker turns from intellectual analysis to the present, he indicates that he has not forgotten immediate concerns. He meets the present head-on.

Earlier the facts spoke to the people. They must now look directly at the facts: "There is no blinking at the fact that our people, our territory and our interests are in grave danger" (38–39). In the first three drafts, this line read: "There is no mincing the fact. . . ." The revision is clearer and stronger. To give "no mincing" meaning, an auditor might have to find a context which helped explain it; for example, I'll not mince words. "Blinking at" is clearer; its meaning is rooted in a com-

---

34 In drafts I, II, and III line 35 begins: "I speak the will of the Congress and of the people. . . ." This construction is much more emphatic and direct than what the speaker actually said, and he would not have been inaccurate had he said it. Yet his actual statement better suits the commonplace of democracy which holds that the President speaks as a result of what the people and their representatives will. He does not say: I speak your will; but rather, "as a result of your will, I speak." And he gives the appearance of "sounding out" the will and responding to it, even as he knows what that will is. Also in drafts I, II, and III lines 36–37, "but will make it very certain" read "but will see to it." The latter expresses the tone of determination but not the finality of the result. The actual statement is categorical in a way which "see to it" is not; moreover "see to it" is somewhat more colloquial than "make it very certain."

mon physiological process and in common usage. Moreover, a sound-sense equivalent to "blinking at" is "winking at"; and if sense were a problem the latter would easily furnish it. A sound-sense equivalent to "mincing" is "wincing"; the listener who sought meaning analogically would be misled.

The degree of danger is finally stated explicitly. Though "grave" (39) is judgmental, it stands as "fact" (38). Heretofore "grave danger" has been suggested in various ways: "character of the onslaught against us," "premeditated invasion." The statement, "There is no blinking at the fact that our people, our territory and our interests are in grave danger," is a modified repetition and an extension of "The people of the United States have already formed their opinions and well understand the implications to the very life and safety of our nation." New meaning is given to "implications." They are "grave."

However, the gravity (38–39) is tempered by its position in the general pattern. It is preceded by the statement which indicates that we shall respond so that this "form of treachery shall never again endanger us" (35–37) and followed by a statement prophesying "inevitable triumph" (40–41). The tensions created by gravity are counterbalanced by terms of positive outlook and mounting force: "confidence," "unbounding determination," "inevitable triumph," "God." The danger, though grave, is relative and does not connote absolute destruction; "unbounding," "inevitable," and "God" are positive, categorical, and absolute. The swing of the pendulum of construction is longer, stronger, and more forceful than the swing of destruction. Contributing to the strength of the categorical language of lines 40–41 is the loose, but recognizable and felt, iambic meter, which moves firmly to the inevitable triumph, "so help us God."

"With confidence in our armed forces, with the unbounding determination of our people, we will gain the inevitable triumph, so help us God" is the leader-speaker's oath, publicly taken.[35] So commonplace is its structure, diction, and rhythm that once underway the line cannot be turned nor resisted. Its sweep catches all. The well-being of the country is set in the timeless future. Rearranging the structure, diction,

---

[35] Lines 40–41 do not appear in drafts I, II, and III. Harry Hopkins suggested the addition, though his second phrase read: "with faith in our people," Roosevelt altered this to "with the unbounding determination of our people." Since Roosevelt's entire statement (40–41) is a confession of faith, the excision of "faith" in Hopkins' second phrase is appropriate. Too, "faith" has but one syllable, making Hopkins' second phrase shorter than his first and third and restricting somewhat the "swelling" movement of the entire confession. Roosevelt's "the unbounding determination of" is not only phonetically more expansive, but the additional syllables support better the rhythmical movement to the climactic "so help us God."

and rhythm upsets the sweep of the statement and weakens it as an article of faith: *We have confidence in our armed forces; our people have unbounding determination; we will gain the inevitable triumph, so help us God.*

The oath taken, no further thematic development is necessary. Only the formal declaration of war (42–44) remains.[36] However, additional modified repetitions woven into the formal declaration enlarge and emphasize thoughts, values, and feelings in the address. "Unprovoked and dastardly" (42) not only balances but also intensifies and enlarges "suddenly and deliberately" (1). The common "Japan" (43) is elevated to the "Japanese Empire" (44) which parallels the formality of "Empire of Japan" (3). The final elevation is one of form only; "dastardly Japan" is the subject. The day, as well as the date, has value. "Sunday" (43) extends and reinforces the connotations of "last night"; its proximity to "dastardly" (43) intensifies the connotations of that term, even as "Sunday" itself gains value and support from its relationship to "God" (41).

The generic negation, the Devil term, is "dastardly" (42).[37] Its appearance is surprising; its choice, apt. Though not a term of the vernacular, it is clear, conveying a dimension of the speaker's moral indignation. As the Devil term, it stands in antithesis to "righteous might" (34), "Sunday" (43), and "God" (41). It has another function. It is as close as the President, speaking to the country in a public chamber, could come to profanity. The movement from "dastardly" to "bastardly" is slight and swift; the latter epitomizes one dimension of the public mood on December 8, 1941. Infamous duplicity has become bastardly duplicity. The leader-speaker controls his emotions before his public and again maintains his distance from his public. Yet the adroit and adept rhetorical choice effects a public catharsis.

The dependent clauses in the final statement (42–44) allow the speaker his judgment of "unprovoked and dastardly" and permit a return to the past: "a state of war has existed." Though the safe and settled formal language of diplomacy and the settled and safe historical past are upset and sundered by the declaration, its formality suggests that the United States respects the conventions of diplomacy even when confronted by dastardly actions outside the accepted conven-

---

[36] *In drafts I, II, and III line 42 begins: "I, therefore, ask that . . ." The formal, logical sign is unnecessary; Roosevelt's logical and rhetorical conclusion was lines 40–41; lines 42–44 are a formal, ceremonial statement dictated by the nature of the occasion and the place.*

[37] *For an interesting observation on the word "dastardly," which bears on the discussion here, see Barbara W. Tuchman, "History by the Ounce," Harper's, CCXXXI (July 1965), 74.*

tions. Formality marks the conclusion as well as the beginning. The address has come full circle.

III

Elements of the "War Message," which sets forth Roosevelt's doctrine of demonology, need to be placed in the larger context of culture. We do not suggest that a direct, causal relationship exists between the speech and events in the culture. Cultural conditions have multiple causes; only rarely have they single causes. We do maintain that an address helps to create and sustain a "climate" which justifies activities, even though the speech itself is not *the* cause of any activity. The language of an address by the President of the United States in a time of crisis helps to create and sustain a "climate." It also begins to pattern the perceptions and the behaviors of those who hear it. Optimum language bears on perceptions and behaviors in a cohesive way.

The emphasis which Roosevelt gave to topics in his address provided his listeners an orientation to the Japanese and to the nature of the conflict; these had immediate and long-range consequences. He emphasized the infamous duplicity behind the Japanese attacks; they carefully and deliberately prepared their military onslaught, masking their preparations behind neutral and formal diplomatic negotiations. American political folklore and the folklore of the people generally hold such behavior in low esteem; the regard is revealed by popular maxims: the man who wears two hats; the man who works both sides of the street; the man who talks out of both sides of his mouth. Roosevelt's portrayal of the Japanese and their activities fits the sense of such widely known and well-understood commonplaces.

Too, the people of the United States generally knew little about the Orient, and stereotypes were associated with it and the Oriental long before December 7, 1941. Even in California, Washington, Oregon, and Arizona, where most of the Japanese in the United States lived, they were little known. The "War Message" enlarged and intensified the stereotypes. These long-standing cultural raw data were supported. On December 7–8, 1941, additional raw data came to the country from the news reports of the conflict. The latter data especially were confusing and anxiety-provoking. To them, Roosevelt gave meaning as he structured a climate of opinion and orientation.

The President's description of the Japanese Government as marginal, fraudulent, dangerous, and capable of dastardly-bastardly behavior has its parallels in the treatment of the Japanese people in the United States. For example, the Commanding General of the Western Defense Command, John L. DeWitt, agreed, as did others, that the Japanese on the West Coast had not engaged in any sabotage after Pearl Harbor. Yet on February 14, 1942, General DeWitt publicly cited the absence of sabotage as "a disturbing and confirming indication that such action will be taken."[38]

On February 6, 1942 in Los Angeles, Mayor Fletcher Brown, "an able and honest public official,"[39] said in a radio broadcast: "If there is intrigue going on, and it is reasonably certain that there is, right here is the hot bed, the nerve center of the spy system, of planning for sabotage." The Mayor recommended "removal of the entire Japanese population—alien and native born—inland for several hundred miles."[40] Ultimately Japanese were removed to relocation centers, but those details lie outside the present concern.

United States military policy toward Nisei, American citizens of Japanese-American ancestry, reflected Roosevelt's portrayal of the Japanese in his "War Message." Nisei inducted into military service before Pearl Harbor were, shortly after December 7, 1941, given honorable discharges, with no specification of cause of dismissal. In March, 1942, potential Nisei inductees were arbitrarily assigned IV-F, ineligible for service because of physical defects; on September 1, 1942, this classification was changed to IV-C, the category ordinarily used for enemy aliens.[41]

Not until January 28, 1943 were Japanese-American citizens eligible for military service on the same basis as other citizens. President Roosevelt publicly approved, saying "no . . . citizen of the United States should be denied the democratic right to exercise the responsibilities of his citizenship, regardless of his ancestry."[42]

Of course the general anxiety of the civilian population immediately after December 7, 1941 contributed to development of hostility toward Japanese-Americans. It also made the civilian population susceptible to the rantings of professional patriots, witch hunters, alien haters, and others with private aims, who used the cover of wartime patriotism to achieve what they wanted to do in peace time—rid the West Coast of the Japanese.

Numerous private citizens and officials of Government sought to redress such attacks upon the Japanese-Americans. For example, the San Francisco *Chronicle*, December 9, 1941, said editorially: "The roundup of Japanese citizens in various parts of the country . . . is not

[38] *Carey McWilliams*, Prejudice: Japanese-Americans, Symbol of Racial Intolerance (*Boston, 1945*), *p. 110; Dorothy S. Thomas and Richard S. Nishimoto*, The Spoilage (*Berkeley, Calif., 1946*), *p. 6.*
[39] *McWilliams, p. 252.*
[40] *Alexander H. Leighton*, The Governing of Men (*New York, 1964*), *p. 20.*
[41] *Thomas and Nishimoto, p. 56.*
[42] Ibid.

a call for volunteer spy hunters to go into action. Neither is it a reason to lift an eyebrow at a Japanese, whether American-born or not. . . ."[43] On balance, the voices of tolerance and fair play were the weaker.

President Roosevelt's "War Message" prepared the United States for a long military operation against the Japanese Empire. The nature of the political and military enemy abroad was clear. Indirectly, he supported a civilian army, equally anxious to do its duty, in its march against the civilian "enemy" at home. The "War Message" offered no protection to Japanese-Americans. In the terms of the analysis here presented these people were given "no weight." Two phrases, "the people of the United States" (27–28) and "the American people" (33–34), only implicitly recognize this group, and as a group they were a minority and a marginal part of the culture. Moreover, the two phrases do not contain positive terms; they contain dialectical terms, which reflect value judgments.[44] In this connection, note that Roosevelt's public statement in support of the induction of Nisei into the military service (p. 435) did contain the positive term, "citizen," which transcends even as it anchors such dialectical phrases as "the American people."

We do not suggest that had the "War Message" contained and emphasized the term, citizen, the address itself would have diminished attacks upon Japanese-Americans in the United States. We note only the absence of any protection, a matter of weighting, and thus conclude that the address contributed to the development of a climate for the attacks by strengthening the attitudes of those who, for whatever reasons, wished to attack. Equally important, those wishing to counter such attacks could find in the "War Message" of the President little to support them and the Japanese-Americans.

Though the primary concern of this analysis has been the language of the "War Message," we have in the paragraphs above extended the analysis and speculated upon possible cultural effects. We have done so because the major elements of any speech work on listeners' perceptions and when other factors, rhetorical and non-rhetorical, are present, perceptions become translated into behavior.

IV

We have centered on the language of an address because in much published criticism language has been neglected in favor of analysis of other factors in the rhetorical environment. What goes on in a speech? has been the question. To say that the "last night" series (20–25) is parallel and repetitive, thus contributing force and energy, is

---

[43] Ibid., pp. 17–18. Also see, McWilliams, pp. 271–273.
[44] Richard M. Weaver, The Ethics of Rhetoric (Chicago, 1953), pp. 16; 187–188.

to say too little. We have tried to link the section with preceding and following configurations of language and to analyze closely the section itself. The "last night" series is not in the active voice merely because the active voice is clear, direct, and emphatic, among other things. Had the series been structured differently (see p. 310) the image would have become static and less able to sustain the speaker's conclusion about the magnitude of Japanese activity: "a surprise offensive extending throughout the Pacific area" (26–27). The "last night" series is the turning point in the address; following it the United States becomes active, reacting to the events of yesterday. Had the series been structured differently, the Japanese actors would have become less central and the reaction of the United States more difficult to direct and focus. Though it makes sense for the speaker to choose to handle the Japanese Empire as "marginal" in his first recognition of the enemy (1–3), it makes equal sense for him to place the Japanese in a central position in the "last night" series. To expose linguistic strategies of rhetoric one needs thus to see language as "moving," and "linking," and as "ordering a hierarchy."

The critical posture here has been microcosmic; the analysis, microscopic. Such analysis does not reveal much about discourse in general. Yet it may be helpful to those who search for orderly methodologies for dealing with all rhetorical activities and processes. The interplay of the microcosmic and the macrocosmic may yield insights which will lead to more fruitful and productive rhetorical criticism.

The Search for the 1972 Democratic Nomination:
A Metaphorical Perspective
by Jane Blankenship

"Naming," Kenneth Burke argues, is an "interpretive act" and thus a guide to act in one way or another toward the thing named.[1] This is so in part because of the "magical decree" which is "implicit in all language."[2] "If you size up a situation in the name of regimentation," as Burke points out, "you *decree* it an essence other than if you size it up in the name of

From *Rhetoric and Communication*, ed. by Jane Blankenship and Hermann Stelzner, University of Illinois Press, Urbana, 1976, pp. 236–260. Used by permission of the author. Dr. Blankenship is professor of speech-communication at the University of Massachusetts, Amherst.

[1] *For the basis of Kenneth Burke's argument see, for example,* Permanence and Change: An Anatomy of Purpose *(Indianapolis, Ind.: Bobbs-Merrill, 1965), pp. 176–91, and* Philosophy of Literary Form, *rev. ed. (New York: Vintage Books, 1941), 5–7, 121–29.* Permanence and Change *was first copyrighted in 1935;* Philosophy of Form *in 1941.*

[2] *Burke,* Philosophy of Literary Form, *p. 5.*

planned economy."[3] Thus the "command" that one act one way rather than another is "*implicit* in the name."[4]

For Burke, words are "acts upon a scene" which in part *arise from* that scene and which in turn *shape* that scene.[5] In many respects the presidential election scene in 1972 was no different from any other. There were sleeper issues and gut issues, some of which were defused while others never caught fire, some of which were scrapped and on which some candidates waffled, white-washed, and soft-pedaled.

Candidates were still drumming up support, beating the daylights out of opponents, swallowing bitter pills, making pilgrimages, putting up straws in the wind, leaving doors open, creating sparks, sending up trial balloons, swinging into high gear, wooing the voters, tossing hats into the ring, and jumping on bandwagons.

The press continued to fuel speculation, bombard the candidates with questions, and claim to be made whipping boys.

Audiences still flocked to hear candidates, voted in beauty contests, gave candidates enough money to be called fat cats, or only enough to be called skinny cats. They observed meteoric declines, long shots, lame ducks, and changes of heart.

Others have provided a fuller political lexicon of past elections, much of which is clearly in use today.[6] This essay examines the metaphors used about and by the candidates in the print media for the democratic presidential nomination from January 1, 1971, to August 5, 1972. The analysis is based primarily on eight daily newspapers and four weeklies.[7] The metaphors, grouped in twelve categories, were selected because they were, in a loose quantitative sense, the most pervasive. Category one reflects the kinds of metaphors used the most times; category twelve, the least.[8]

[3] Ibid., *p. 7.*

[4] *Kenneth Burke,* Attitudes Toward History *(Boston: Beacon Press, 1959), p. 339. First copyright, 1937.*

[5] *Burke,* Philosophy of Literary Form, *p. vi. For a fuller discussion see Burke's later works:* A Grammar of Motives, *(New York: Prentice-Hall, 1945);* A Rhetoric of Motives *(New York: Prentice-Hall, 1950); and* Language as Symbolic Action *(Berkeley: University of California Press, 1966).*

[6] *A recent example is William Safire,* The New Language of Politics *(New York: Random House, 1968). See also Hans Sperber and Travis Trittschuh,* American Political Terms *(Detroit, Michigan: Wayne State University Press, 1962); Jack Plano and Milton Greenbert,* The American Political Dictionary *(New York: Holt, Rinehart and Winston, 1965); and Wilbur W. White,* White's Political Dictionary *(New York: World Publishing, 1947).*

[7] *The dailies were:* New York Times, Los Angeles Times, Washington Post, Christian Science Monitor, Boston Globe, Springfield (Massachusetts) Union, Akron (Ohio) Beacon Journal, Huntington (West Virginia) Herald Dispatch. *The Weeklies were* National Observer, New Republic, Newsweek, *and* Time.

[8] *Percentage totals for the first eight categories were: general violence (16 percent); warfare (15 percent); sports and games (15 percent); natural phenomena (14 percent); animals (9 percent); vehicles (6 percent); other types of persons (5.5 percent); and show biz (5.5 percent).*

These twelve categories of metaphors provide a set of "common topics" used by reporters to describe the 1972 nomination process. The examples noted under each category illustrate the "special topics" which varied with the candidate, reporter, situation, or some other element in the search for the nomination.

By examining the way the press talked about a significant part of the political process, the selection of a presidential nominee, we may be reminded that while we are using language, it is using us. Thus the way we talk *about* a political campaign may, in the end, be not merely descriptive but "prescriptive" as well.[9]

General Violence

Politics "is a brass-knuckles business," James Reston pointedly reminded us in 1972. By far the largest number of verbal and nominal metaphors could be placed under the category of general violence, even when those specifically referring to war and contact sports are excluded.[10]

The violence took many forms. Candidates "assaulted" and were assaulted, "attacked" and were attacked, "tussled," "flayed," "slapped," "jostled" each other. They "needled" and tried to "nail" each other.

By early 1971, McGovern had "already taken a few swipes at front runner Muskie...." He "hit" hard at the POW issue, "jabbed" at Humphrey and Muskie on their vote to cut N.A.T.O., and offered an economic policy that would "wallop the wealthy." One "top union official" complained of McGovern campaigners: "They preach nonviolence... but the first chance they get they poke you in the snoot."

The candidates hammered away at each other or at the issues. Wallace "in his neo-populist style hammered away at busing." Muskie's rivals "hammered away" at his absence from a meeting of the Manchester, New Hampshire, Democratic committee. In nationally televised debates with McGovern, reviewers say "Humphrey hammering away at... the issues of jobs and national security...."

Everyone "blasted" everyone else. Muskie "blasted" Wallace for "practicing 'the politics of exclusion.'" A Humphrey aide forecast that Nixon

---

[9] Even if language and conceptualization were not so intimately related, Richard Weaver's comment would approach this position in yet another way, "Language which is ... predicative, is for the same cause sermonic. We are all of us preachers in private or public capacities. We have no sooner uttered words, than we have given impulse to other people to look at the world, or some small part of it, in our way." "Language is Sermonic," in Roger E. Nebergall (ed.), Dimensions of Rhetorical Scholarship (Norman: University of Oklahoma, Department of Speech, 1963), p. 62.

[10] The number of metaphors cited in this paper generates 400 plus items. Even with severely abbreviated footnote form, the end result appeared so unwieldy that the decision was made simply to list the dailies which formed the basis for the classification scheme and for the statistical data. Specific citations may be obtained from the author.

would, "blow" McGovern "right out of the water." And, David Broder pointed out "The Democrats . . . could not bear to wait for Miami Beach to blow their convention and their party sky-high."

The candidates cut and got cut. McCarthy "knifed into the Democratic leadership that fought him in 1968. . . ." The AFL-CIO treasurer-secretary, "privately warned that labor would 'cut Muskie to ribbons.' . . ." Humphrey accused McGovern of "cutting into the very fiber and muscle of our defense establishment. . . ."

The *effects* of such violence were clear. The 1972 campaign was a "bloody" and "suicidal" campaign. By mid-1971 many old guard Democrats "made clear they [preferred] Muskie. But after being bloodied by the party's left so often, they doubt[ed] their ability to influence [the] wild-and-wooly [New York] Democratic primary." So they worked to "prevent another bloodbath. . . ."

Just before the primaries started we were down "to the candidates whose strategy [was] either to prove themselves in the early primaries or to stand aside while the others bleed themselves in state after state. . . ." "The sudden collapse of the Muskie bandwagon," according to Evans and Novak, threatened "uncontrolled bloodletting. . . ."

Some Democrats became increasingly concerned over the possibility of "Convention Floor Blood." The Democrats, William S. White observed, "don't at all mind coming over the tube as hand-to-hand combatants, in living color." He predicted that the G.O.P. conventions would be "pretty weak tea as against the gladiatorial entertainments offered by the Democrats."

With the California credentials decision the "explosion" some "feared and predicted, was triggered prematurely . . . at the Sheraton-Park Hotel, and they were . . . clearing up the blood and debris from Capitol Hill to California. . . ." After the convention there was some relief that it had taken place "without the predicted spilling of rivers of blood across millions of color TV screens. There was blood enough, but well short of the massive public carnage many had foreseen."

Two candidates used particularly violent language. George Wallace promised: "I'm Gonna Shake Their Eyeteeth Out." He talked about "sending a few shock waves" by winning some primaries. To the question "How do you think you'll be treated in Miami?," he replied: "I might get to Miami Beach and they throw me through the rooftop."

John Lindsay's language was also especially violent. When Governor Rockefeller "expressed approval of the sanitation men's terms," Lindsay "accused him of giving in to 'extortionist demands.' " He bitterly complained that his "community of New York and every community is ravaged by inflation. . . ." He said his "city was 'raped' by the state legislature in the annual budget battle. . . ."

Lindsay also was *perceived* in violent terms. Some predicted that he would "run like gangbusters" in the urban and big delegate states and that his appearance on the primary scene would send "tremors through the camp of every presidential hopeful." His encounters were described violently. Lindsay and Rockefeller were seen "stabbing at each other . . . with the vindictiveness of back-alley brawlers." At a Queens, New York, $50-a-plate dinner, Kennedy reportedly "wielded his political mace and ordered Lindsay disinvited."

Muskie, on the other hand, was often described as one who "conspicuously lacks the power to hurt, the muscle to assert against competitors." "Some politicians have an instinct for the jugular," explained one delegate, "but Muskie has an instinct for the capillaries."

Almost everybody wanted to "get back" at somebody or something. Shirley Chisholm wanted to "punch history in the face." An Ohio machinist supported McGovern because "he wants to kick them in the tail, too." A Philadelphia precinct worker explained: "People really don't like Wallace, but they want to give the Establishment a kick in the pants."

To avoid "civil war" and *fratricidal* violence, a variety of tactics were dreamed up but by April, 1972, "the Democratic fratricide [increased] in intensity and the bodies of the slain [piled] higher."

Much was made of the Democrats' "deathwish." By May, James Reston saw the Democrats "in a suicidal mood: broke, divided and . . . getting a little nasty. . . ." Wallace's campaign manager saw the platform adopted in Miami Beach as a "suicide note for November." Despite these dire predictions, Arthur Krock pointed to a "lesson" of history: "The Democratic Party is teetering again on that high, well-known window ledge, threatening to commit suicide. This posture is a cherished tradition of the oldest national political organization in the United States, and sometimes it has jumped as advertised. . . . The lesson of political history . . . is that it can quadriennially jump to apparent death in the summer and emerge miraculously resurrected in the Fall."

In 1972, the candidates did violence to each other and to the issues. The *kinds* of violence were varied and the violence was pervasive. The violent were perceived affirmatively, those candidates who "lacked the power to hurt," negatively. The general public and convention delegates alike identified mainly with those who wanted to kick some generalized "them" in the tail.

Warfare

The primaries were fought on a variety of "battlegrounds." Some claimed that the "real" battleground was the suburbs, but several famous battlefields were recalled as well. James Perry of the *Observer* wrote in June, 1971: "I do suspect that the Wallace movement crested in 1968, much as the Confederacy crested at Cemetery Ridge. It is worth remembering, though, that there was a lot of bloody business after Gettysburg." As TV zoomed in for a "beachhead" at Miami, Walter Cronkite likened working the convention to a famous World War II battle: " 'We're not going to be able to get the guns on shore,' the general said before landing in North Africa. . . . 'We're going to have to take the Casbah with cold steel.' "

Not all the warriors used the same tactics. Harold Hughes, for a brief time a contender himself, said that Muskie was "more a conciliator and compromiser than a charge-of-the-light-brigade type. . . ." John Lindsay joined the Democratic party because he was unwilling to undertake "a 'kamikaze mission' . . ." in the increasingly conservative Republican party. Gary Hart, McGovern's campaign manager, believed Mayor Richard Daley would help against Nixon because "Daley's not a bomber. . . ."

All the generals had their troops. Reminded that as a declared candidate she would automatically be placed on the ballot in some states, Chisholm said, "I might shoot my foot soldiers into some of these states. . . ." Among McGovern's assets were "the kids" who were "his shock troops, his envelope-stuffers. . . ."

The press talked of battalions, phalanxes, and juggernauts. Describing a "grassroots fair" for McGovern, the *Post* included in supporters "about two battalions of tiny tots. . . ." Humphrey had a "phalanx" of labor leaders "ready to do battle. . . ." However, there was talk that Humphrey would be an early casualty of "the Muskie 'juggernaut.' "

Blitzes and bombardments proved to be handy tools of war. In Ohio, McGovern waged a "massive, last-minute, radio-television blitz. . . ." McGovern's "call to share the wealth" proved to be a "soft bombshell." One shot in the "barrage" of Humphrey accusations plainly "hit" McGovern. For, according to Joseph Kraft: "The McGovern program is way out and not only on welfare."

Many of the candidates foresaw a long battle, "from the late spring primaries to a battle on the floor" of the Democratic National Convention. In *chronology* the war drama went like this: As early as July, 1971, Mayor Sam Yorty directed "the heavy artillery in his rhetoric" at Muskie and, at the same time, conducted "guerrilla warfare on Senator Henry Jackson. . . ." A "top aide" in the Muskie camp voiced public concern "that individual candidates from either wing might 'one-shot us' fatally in the early primaries. . . ." In Arizona, Evans and Novak predicted that Muskie's strength would be thinly spread while his opponents would concentrate in small areas and " 'bullet-vote' for the delegate-candidates pledged to them." Robert Haldeman's charge "that President Nixon's Vietnam critics are 'consciously' aiding the enemy set off a fusillade of counterfire from high ranking Democrats. . . ." By April, 1972, Jackson aimed "his guns directly at McGovern" in a "frontal assault on a prime plank in McGovern's candidacy."

In Virginia, McGovern backers "captured" a big bloc of delegates from Fairfax County. They set up a Texas "ambush" and went on a "foray" to the governor's conference in Houston.

Before and at Miami Beach the usual "male dominated convention [came] under fire. . . ." Most of those attending were at their first political convention and stayed, like good troops, pretty much under control. But by Thursday of the convention they finally "broke loose" like a "boot-camp Marine on 'his first weekend pass.' " There were, of course, after-the-convention letdowns, aptly described by one reporter as "the Glums of August."

The "beaten generals" who had tried to stop McGovern appeared, briefly at least, to be "politically shell-shocked." Tom Braden accurately predicted that many who lost would "turn out . . . to be good soldiers." There was even a kind of "sentimental balm" for some of the losers. As Holmes Alexander pointed out: "Two fallen warriors, George Wallace and Hubert Humphrey, are more dear to the hearts of their countrymen than when they were riding high."

Much of the violence in 1972 was patently warlike. The candidate-generals marshaled their troops in concerted attacks not only on each other but on their onlooker-constituents as well. Few, for example, were spared the propaganda barrages of the electronic media or direct mail.

Sports/Games

Picking presidential nominees, observed Jack Waugh, "is one of the great American spectator sports." The Democrats, for example, engaged in a wide variety of games: "tinker toys," "a painful game of musical chairs," "a jigsaw puzzle," "marbles," and "darts." But mostly they went to the horse races, played football, boxed, played baseball and cards, and participated in track events. They also "gambled" a lot: at dice, roulette, high stakes poker, and craps.

In June, 1971, a *Monitor* survey suggested "the real possibility of a Democratic 'horse race' before the final selection is made. . . ." A variety of name politicians endorsed Edmund Muskie's candidacy early, saying: "Fortunately for us, Muskie happens to be the best horse to ride in most states." After the Wisconsin primary, however, "Muskie's fourth-place showing . . . raised new doubts that the tiring Maine entry can go the distance."

When John Lindsay entered the race, the *Akron Beacon Journal* commented: "With the track already crowded with candidates, the reaction was 'who needs Lindsay?' " Some called him the "fairest dark horse of them all" but others were more skeptical. One journalist punned prophetically: "John V. Lindsay has finally decided to change hearses in mid-stream."

The "stalking-horse" notion started early and hung on. Nichols von Hoffman poked fun at its overuse: "McGovern is a stalking-horse for Kennedy and Fred Harris is a stalking-horse for McGovern, and Muskie is a stalking-horse for Humphrey, who is probably a stalking-horse for Bayh. . . ." With the "starters . . . at the Gate," journalists took a look at "how the Winter book might rate candidates. . . ."

Second only to horse racing was football. Godfrey Sperling, for example, foresaw the campaign for the Democratic nomination through the eyes of President Nixon: "Muskie has the ball and is already approaching the goal line. The Muskie forces have been moving forward steadily and, clearly, have the momentum. Now comes the big test for the other team (McGovern, Lindsay, Humphrey, Jackson, et al.). As Muskie gets closer to the goal will they be able to hold—as did Stanford against Michigan and Miami against Baltimore in key defensive stands that turned those recent ballgames around?" The "Game plan" proved to be easier to implement on paper than in action and Ohio's Governor Gilligan grew upset with Muskie's campaign; he complained: "He's in the position of a quarterback in football. If you can't get a running game established, then, it's harder to pass, and the whole thing comes apart."

Vice-President Agnew, himself fond of sports imagery, depicted Larry O'Brien as testing candidates for "the quarter-back slot in a triple option offense." Agnew continued: "George McGovern wanted to pitch out to a trailing back—but couldn't find anyone trailing him. . . . George Wallace found he had reported to the wrong team. Coach Larry O'Brien won't even talk to him or show him the play book. Vance Hartke thought about using a quarterback sneak. But unfortunately, Jack Anderson was out of town." On another occasion, Agnew compared Hubert Humphrey to a quarterback who "operates out of a 'moving pocket' in his policy statements on major issues."

If the game went badly enough Tom Braden speculated that Edward Kennedy might be called off the bench:

. . . the Democratic Party is not moving the ball. Quarterback Edmund Muskie is losing ground. McGovern, Lindsay, Jackson have not done as well as he. The crowd is yelling for Kennedy, who has been on the bench for two years with an injury once considered serious. The question is whether or not he is fit to play. . . . Perhaps that is the way it will end—with Kennedy brightly pointing out weaknesses from the sidelines, while somebody else tries to move the ball.

But the political history of the last few weeks suggests that the time may come when the pressure is irresistible, when a party about to lose an election looks down its bench, and says, so to speak, "Injured or not, let's put in the first team."

The "first team" appeared to be necessary, because the Democrats "seemed baffled by the broken-field running of the last three years [by the Nixon administration and were] reduced to sputtering about used cars. . . ." The Democrats, however, continued to ask: "Would you buy a used car from this man?"

Boxing also occupied the attention of many reporters. As early as New Hampshire, the contenders were described in "fighting" terms. For example, the candidates "like fighters aiming for points before the final bell in the last round [swung] at all kinds of targets. . . ." In Florida, a "third-spot finish for Muskie behind Wallace and Humphrey . . . wouldn't come close to a knockout blow against Muskie." But it would raise this question "If Ed Muskie can't deliver a knockout blow against Humphrey in Florida, can he take President Nixon in November?" Wisconsin was "round four" for George McGovern. His near tie in Ohio "was a body blow to Humphrey's claim of industrial support." In California, many journalists conceded that: "The 1972 presidential primaries are ending like the final round of an evenly matched prize-fight—two men, toe to toe, slugging it out." After California, McGovern climbed "away from the last of the prelims toward the title."

There was also time for baseball. The Wisconsin primary was like "the Fourth of July is to major league baseball—the first chance to reckon how the pennant race is shaping up." Later, at the convention, the Old Guard turned to baseball to describe their feelings. One commented, for example: "I feel like Warren Spahn must feel in Cleveland. Spahn must feel he can still pitch, and I do too, but nobody is calling me to do anything."

Wallace's first two major Michigan appearances were termed " 'double-header' triumphs. . . ." McCarthy sat "out in left field, threatening to enter the ballgame." And Ohioan Howard Metzenbaum apologized for endorsing McGovern at a Humphrey speaking engagement by saying: "I was off base and I'm prepared to admit it."

On the track, McGovern and Humphrey looked "like milers who are running close together at the midpoint of their race, with neither giving an indication of who will spurt to victory and who will falter in the stretch." All in all, the Democratic presidential primaries and caucuses seemed a puzzling decathlon: "Like the decathlon where one fellow may be better at the broad jump and another at discus-throwing, the variousness of the states gives every primary candidate at least a chance to display his talents best. But who would have thought that an all-rounder like Ed Muskie would have such trouble clearing so many hurdles?

In explaining "Why I'm for Muskie," Harold Hughes observed: "The contest for the nomination and for the presidency is a distance run, not a 50-yard dash. . . . I am convinced that he has the staying power to maintain the pace." But by mid-April even "Boston marathoners" got weary:

"Ed Muskie at this stage of the race is like one of those marathoners who torture-toed through Coolidge Corner yesterday. The grimace of pain and shortness of breath seemed just moments away from the dry heaves at Kenmore Square and whoever said running was fun?"

In addition to sports, some of the candidates also found time for cards. Edmund Muskie's "image of Yankee integrity" was his "strong suit." "All I have is my intellect," Shirley Chisholm commented, "but that gives me some trump cards. . . ." George Wallace, the "wild card" in the primaries, found school busing to be *his* "trump card." George McGovern's "ace in the hole" was "the youth vote."

The Democrats also seemed preoccupied with gambling. Even in December, 1971, some were guessing that Muskie's toughest foe in California would probably be Hubert Humphrey, "still the favorite of the state's high-rolling contributors." Wallace was promised a "fair shake of the dice" at the convention. Humphrey likened Nixon's policy on spending money overseas to an "international crap game."

In March, Muskie said, as he autographed a sample ballot in New Hampshire, "Now that's a big lottery ticket." All along, journalists were claiming that: "One of the handicaps of the favorite . . . is that a lot of people put bets on him." In California the "stakes" were high and the game was "winner-take-all." At Democratic headquarters the "old hands . . . [hedged] their bets" on whether 50 percent of the delegates would, as the rule dictated, be women.

In 1972 the candidates engaged in a wide variety of sports and games, most of which were gladiatorial in nature. Spectators clearly outnumbered participants in the arena. Those who sat on the sidelines could view the gladiatorial fray with the full enjoyment of one who is both vicariously "bloodied" and yet left basically unscarred by the whole business. They both knew the "plays" and egged the candidates on; yet they were somewhat superior creatures who knew better than to *actually* play the game.

Natural Phenomena

"Voting tides," William Stringer suggested, "can be as unpredictable as was tropical storm Agnes." Muskie was perhaps most aware of the truth of Stringer's observation about the "ebb and flow of candidates." A Los Angeles reporter crisply put it: "I don't think Muskie can win anymore. . . . The tide is turned." When this became abundantly clear, the *Monitor* editorialized: "The tides of political fortune, always fickle, often work their meanest truth against those who deserve them least."

Announcements for a presidential try were described in terms of water. By October, 1971, Chisholm spoke of "testing the water." Some pled "openly with the Mayor [Lindsay] to jump feet first into the . . . Presidential pool." There were "oceans of speculation" about a Lindsay candidacy and some Muskie supporters also wanted an earlier announcement but Muskie still stopped "at the water's edge."

Floods, drownings, and sinkings were often predicted and often materialized. The *Observer* predicted that the media would "cover John Lindsay like he was the Johnstown Flood." Charles Snider, Wallace's campaign manager, believed that the Democratic platform "weighted the Party down with 100 tons of cement in ocean-deep water." But perhaps the most picturesque of such images involved, not the ocean, but a bay: "The nation's press does have an eastward tilt, and all of us are going to tumble into Jamaica Bay, like it or not. I advise everyone: Grab hold of anything that's nailed down, pull on your life preserver, and together we'll sing *Nearer My God to Thee.*"

In the year 1972 fires were "rekindled," "fueled," and "heated up." At least one candidate was accused of "shouting fire" in a crowded political theater, the constituents of another were seen as willing to "commit arson" for their candidate, and one called his previous presidential bid a "refining fire."

Some candidates were able to ignite "sparks"; others were luckless in that ability. None of the four candidates appearing in Wisconsin by mid-May, 1971, Bayh, Hughes, Muskie, and McGovern, "set Wisconsin Democrats on fire with enthusiasm." The Lindsay candidacy was seen by some as having potential sparkle: "What he says isn't much different from what Senator George McGovern or Senator Birch Bayh or Senator Fred Harris, or even Ed Muskie, are saying. But somehow [Lindsay] can create sparks in crowds which they leave nodding." There *was* "an opportunity for someone to catch fire in Florida and really ignite the voters. . . ." Lindsay, however, proved "fireless in Florida and Max Lerner observed: "Even before his candidacy had taken fire, it struck many as a burned-out case."

Some saw McGovern as a man who "throws off no sparks." He was "a virtuous man but . . . no lighter of prairie fires. . . ." He delivered "the populist message with less fire but probably a great deal more substance [than Wallace]." Kennedy, however, said of McGovern's campaign that it "has 'caught its old fire and is on a definite upward course. A spark has been ignited, the flame is spreading and it's going to sweep across the country.' "

The candidates, fireless or not, operated on a scene in which the "fires of inflation threaten[ed] to rage out of control." And conservatives in both parties wondered, as did Henry Jackson, whether President Nixon was "using the 'smoke screen of summitry to cover up' de facto acceptance" of growing Soviet influence in the Middle East and elsewhere.

Storms, real or predicted, constantly loomed on the horizon. When Wallace "casually" let the *New York Times* know he would run in Florida, he "stole some thunder" from Muskie's formal declaration of candidacy on the same day. Wallace's decision to enter the Florida primary, in particular, threw "a cloud over the campaign of Senator Jackson. . . ." Nor were Jackson and Muskie to be the only storm watchers: "The storm signals [Wallace's strength in Florida] have not been lost on the other Democratic candidates." But long before Miami, it was clear that three "great political imponderables"—the eighteen-year-old vote, the independent vote, and taxes—plus the China-Russia diplomacy would "cloud the vision of all forecasters. . . ."

In addition to weather forecasts there were also alerts for "erosions," "avalanches," "earthquakes," and "icebergs." But despite this array of natural disasters, some "greening" did occur. Early in 1971, George McGovern took care to dig the "grass roots" and to prune the "money-tree." There was, as Tom Braden pointed out, "a dispute among money-tree experts about whether the tree shakes as vigorously for one man as it does for another. The hardhats among them think it all depends upon careful selection of the seedlings and constant pruning thereafter." The April, 1972, "flowering" of George McGovern was credited by James Kilpatrick, "in significant part to old-fashioned organization, to a methodical tilling of the soil."

The 1972 search for the nomination appeared, thus, to the media, a "natural" thing. However, that aspect of nature most seen was the violent side. Floods, drownings, brush fires, and avalanches seemed to be the lot of candidates, issues, and constituencies alike. The two candidates most often perceived as natural phenomena were George Wallace and George McGovern, both proclaimed "populist candidates." Both were perceived as disruptive natural forces, but McGovern was *also* perceived as one who "blossoms" and "flowers." The press sometimes seemed to have co-opted the McGovern campaign button metaphor, "I am a Grassroot."

Animals

By far the animal used most to describe the Democratic candidates was the ever present horse: Hubert Humphrey, the old warhorse; John Lindsay, the pale dark horse, and the like. Because most of the horse metaphors refer to horse racing, they were discussed under sports/games.

The verbal metaphors were for the most part prosaic. Muskie "crawled home" in the Florida primary. Lindsay "flushed out" other candidates and "unleashed" his Deputy Mayor Richard Aurelio on the campaign trail. Wallace "twisted tails." And, Humphrey, like the others, "corraled" votes and was "shepherded" from place to place. In 1972 the Democrats "weaseled around," "stalked," alternately "snarled" or "purred," and "flocked" or "stampeded" toward various of the candidates. If the verbal metaphors were commonplace, not so some of the nominal metaphors. Reminding us that most of the contenders were from the Senate and that only a few such as Wilbur Mills came forth from the House, one political commentator offered an explanation: "In contrast to the proud and glamorous stags that stalk the aisles of the Senate, the House of Representatives is populated mostly by prosaic and homespun men." And Mills himself provided one of the few references to the animals of antiquity when the secretary of the treasury discussed administration economic policy before the House Ways and Means Committee. He accused John Connally of "bringing into the committee room a Trojan Horse."

The description of George Wallace and Wallace's description of the political scene provided some interesting examples; for example, Wallace of his chief opponents, Humphrey and McGovern: "Everytime I trot out a li'l old bone of an issue, these big boys grab it and run off." Florida proved rich Wallace country, metaphorically, as well as in vote tally; for example, the headline proclaiming, "In Florida, Wallace Is the Big Gator." We were reminded also that "Florida loves strong men and beautiful women. If it weren't for the offshore shark (who has a beautiful lady of his own), the Jackson entry would look unbeatable here."

Of the candidates, Henry Jackson was the most persistent user of bird imagery; for example, when speaking of defense expenditures, he observed: "The ostriches say, 'Let's bury our heads in the sand and leave our rear ends exposed.' . . . I say we must stand for a prudent defense posture to protect our liberty." In a variation on the theme, he compared the blind ostrich to the keen-sighted owl." " 'Ostriches and owls,' hoots Scoop. 'We are entering an age of ostriches and owls. The ostriches bury their heads in the sand and refuse to recognize the implications of what they're saying. The owls keep their eyes open, always remembering what they do today will have repercussions tomorrow.' " To this metaphorical aviary, he added yet another bird: "If you leave the offensive weapons out [of disarmament agreements], you've let the fox in the chicken coop. . . ."

Not only candidates but constituents were also perceived by the press in birdlike metaphors. Birch Bayh's supporters existed in "little nests . . . in key states" and "assorted gaggles of curious tourists" hovered around the Kennedy compound. As convention time neared, one reporter suggested that readers not forget "a whole covey of Democrats out there in the hustings . . . who [will] flock to the convention clutching a half or quarter or less of a single vote."

Senator Edward Kennedy talked of and was talked about in terms of "lemminglike" behavior. In describing the record of the Nixon administration, Kennedy observed: "It isn't just the bad results. It's the way they've gone about them—the lemminglike pursuit of clearly failing policies, the rosy picture painted of every bad development. . . ." While the senator saw a lemminglike tendency in the Nixon administration, one political observer accused Kennedy supporters of the same tendency: "Lemmings have their pellmell stampede to the sea, penguins their wobbling and single-minded return to the rookery, salmon their upstream odyssey home to spawn. With political animals, the cycle is a more sober and calculated affair: a quadrennial flocking to presidential politics. And nowhere is the urge to be involved more sharply etched than in Camelot—the camp of Senator Edward M. Kennedy."

Domestic animals were also to have their day in the press. Deferring the full revision of the party charter was "a bone being tossed to George Meany. . . ." Muskie was declared as "clean as a houndstooth," Humphrey vowed to be no "hangdogger," and, a victim of credentials fight challenges, Mayor Richard Daley, was left, "according to one associate, 'like a puppy curled up in a corner after a licking.' "

James Hoffa was, perhaps, the bluntest about Democratic chances in November, declaring that only Kennedy could defeat Nixon: "I don't think these other mutts have a chance." Not all were that optimistic about Kennedy's chances: "Though Americans admire underdogs, perhaps they distinguish between breeds. It may be that politicians who stubbornly fight even foolish wars against the country's alleged enemies win elections. Those who become underdogs because of their indiscretions do not win elections. It makes a kind of sense, even if you don't like it."

Bovines were not to be outdone. Edmund Muskie folksily reminded his potential contributors: "The way to keep a cow fresh is to milk her early and often." The backers, we are told, "laughed as if it didn't hurt." At the Democratic convention, we were reminded that "old bulls never quit until the young bulls run them out. The old bulls are dead, but don't forget that the young bulls eventually become old bulls too."

Not only were candidates and constituents described in animal-like metaphors, but issues as well. George Wallace insisted that issues ought to be presented simply, vowing that he would "put the hay down where the goats can get it." McGovern's socioeconomic policies were his "albatross." And, for all the "presidential politicians, the Vietnam war issue is something like chasing a greased boar at the country fair. It's hard to get hold of and no sensible man should want to get within miles of it, but once he gets in the arena he doesn't have much choice but to go after it."

In 1972, then, the Democrats displayed a veritable "zoo of creatures" to the country. Animal metaphors so proliferated that not only were "animals" being viewed, but they were being viewed by other animals who "flocked" or "stampeded" to see them. Small wonder then that the "food for thought" both viewer and viewed tossed back and forth was "bones." Perhaps on such an animal farm it was not to be unexpected that the near *mythical* creature, "the" tortoise, would emerge with the nomination.

Vehicles

Ships of several varieties sailed the 1972 Democratic seas. At a mid-summer meeting, the AFL-CIO executive council expressed distrust of Lindsay as "a showboat." Kennedy described the visit of the American ping pong team to China as an "icebreaker plowing through a frozen sea" opening up "a new passage to improved relations. . . ."

Sailcraft, however, were most visible. In May, 1971, Humphrey declared, "I've got the sails up and I'm testing the water." He did, indeed, "set sail." In Little Rock, Arkansas, McGovern refused "to trim his sails on school busing or defense cuts. . . ." And Dan Walker offered this more *general* advice: "Anyone who thinks . . . McGovern plans to trim his sails . . . is in for a disappointment."

The political seas were strewn with sinking and abandoned ships. When the Michigan Democratic party left him off the guest list for a dinner, George Wallace held another, better attended dinner at the same time. "The snub," as one columnist put it, "proved somewhat like renting a deck chair on the *Titanic*." Early in the campaign "hapless survivors of ill-starred candidacies, already sunk or sinking, were being gladly welcomed aboard other campaigns." There was "only a momentary pause" for "the quietly disappearing hulks of the doomed candidacies—the Harold Hughes, Fred Harrises and Birch Bayhs. . . ." After the Massachusetts primary, "Establishment Massachusetts's politicians, for a time fighting among themselves to board the Muskie bandwagon . . . all but abandoned ship. . . ." By June, Humphrey "had to lay off some of his staff . . . and scavenge for $200,000 to stay afloat till the convention."

With the party in disarray, some thought of Kennedy as the "only port in the political hurricane now besetting the Democratic Party." Another reporter found Kennedy "restless in safe harbor" and thought he might declare his candidacy. And, when the nomination went to George McGovern, a *Monitor* editorial asked: "Was it shrewd or foolish politics for Mr. McGovern to so downgrade the once mighty bulwarks of his party?" The internecine feud that followed left McGovern and "his people . . . trying to stabilize the purists who still want to rock the boat."

Bandwagons were sometimes in fashion. From December, 1971, until the "launching" of a McGovern bandwagon in April, 1972, much of the talk focused on one particular wagon, that of Edmund Muskie. James Perry of the *Observer* denied there ever *was* a Muskie bandwagon, saying it was "more a solid old-fashioned beer wagon" delivering "on schedule."

Diesels gave way to steam engines. Contributors were "slow to board Muskie's campaign train." There was, however, an occasional "spurt of steam" for Muskie. Even at its slowest speeds, there was a "sputter in the engine" now and then and that "rumble" continued to produce "disquiet in the camps of Muskie rivals." There was some concern about George

Wallace in July because he "seemed to pick up steam the nearer he got to Miami." But it was McGovern's "little engine, which kept puffing, 'I think I can; I think I can'. . . ." that made it to the station.

An occasional plane or rocket flashed through the air. *Atlantic* sighed in March that the Democratic quest for the presidency began long ago, "lost in the criss-cross of hopefuls' planes increasing the mid-air collision rush. . . ." When Muskie announced his intention of withdrawing from the primaries, a "Muskie man in the Senate" advised a reporter, "we're in a holding pattern."

In 1972, the candidates rode out to do battle in a variety of crafts most of which were in a state of disrepair or in imminent danger of collision or sinking. Thus, there was little certainty that any candidate had constructed a craft capable of riding out the buffeting of the campaign. It seemed difficult for candidates and their supporters to distinguish between reality and appearances. What seemed to be a sleek, durable vessel turned out to be a *Titanic* or, worse still, no craft at all. What some thought were "bandwagons" were not and what most did *not* see as a bandwagon *was* one. It was, however, a near mythical craft from a children's story that emerged the most durable craft of all, a little engine that could.

Other Persons or Types of Persons

Almost all the candidates were compared with someone else and not always admiringly so; for example, Wills suggested that Eugene McCarthy had "become another Stassen." Von Hoffman saw Birch Bayh "as a kind of WASP Sammy Glick. . . ." When Hubert Humphrey offered "What this country needs is a nice man as President of the United States," Jenkins in the *New York Times Magazine* observed: "Like Willie Loman he sets great store by being well-liked."

David Broder suggested that with "his pompadour carefully fluffed to give him every possible quarter-inch of extra height," Wallace "looked just a bit like an aging musical comedy star brought back from retirement for a revival of 'Dames at Sea.' "

"Running for office—particularly the heady excitement of the big time, the Presidency" the *Observer* recorded, "is probably what [Wallace] enjoys doing most in life; he could no more pass it up than Sky Masterson could resist a bet on Don Juan as a pretty face." In Maryland, Wallace appeared to be the "sole vendor of vanilla ice cream, when everyone else is offering chocolate. With the chocolate fanciers thus divided, it is obvious that the unique vanilla vendor can hope to sell more ice cream cones than anyone else, even if he gets under 20 percent of the total market." One headline opined, "Wallace: Pied Piper of the Dissatisfied."

John Lindsay may have suffered most from comparisons. Reston called him "the Lochinvar of the late night shows. . . ." Some Democrats viewed him as a "carpetbagger." *Newsweek* reminded their readers: "Lindsay . . . came to City Hall a term and a half ago rather like Henry V to Agincourt, pledging at his inaugural not just to work the usual civic and fiscal wonders but to strike up 'new light in tired eyes and the sound of laughter in homes.' . . . Lindsay today is far less a hero at home than to the national audience he has cultivated and won as knight-errant for all urban America. His reign has been beset by crises from its very first day. . . ." Lindsay's challenge of Wallace to a TV debate in Florida prompted one reporter to suggest that was rather "like Tiny Tim asking Joe Frazier to step outside 'so we can settle this thing.' "

McGovern's "weakness" was likened to "that of Aristides: People are numbed by his liberal virtures, and are tired of hearing him called the Just." "To a round table jammed with seventy knights, clad in battered armour, he brings the Galahad Touch," declared James Kilpatrick. At least one reporter recalled McGovern's six-week campaign for the 1968 presidential nomination, saying it "seemed to confirm an image of a wildly unrealistic tilter at windmills."

When the Dixie governors "looked askance" at McGovern, the Hatfields seemed closer to "the McCoys than Senator George McGovern . . . [to] the U.S. South." By May he suddenly became "Prince Valiant" in the media. Princely or not, it was Kennedy who remained the romantic and perhaps tragic figure to some; for example, the *Globe* was reminded of Billy Budd:

They [McGovern sympathizers] don't just plan to draft Kennedy, since he can always object to that. They plan something more severe, more like an "impressment" of the Massachusetts senator, similar to the recruiting techniques used by the British Navy before the War of 1812. . . . As Kennedy sails the seas off Cape Cod, the flotilla of the Committee for an Open Convention is hard astern, seeking his services for the journey to November. Like Billy Budd, Melville's innocent foretopman, he may be taken from his peaceful merchant vessel and placed on the deck of a man 'o war. He may go quietly or he may protest. Either way, he's bound to be impressed.

Don Oberdorfer reminded *Post* readers that a number of people had scoffed when McGovern "sat down to play, a seemingly hapless and hopeless one note Johnny from South Dakota applying for the biggest job in the nation. . . ." Also playing on the keyboard metaphor Perry recalled: "Everybody laughed when poor old clodhopping George McGovern sat down to play the piano. Nobody's laughing now: he plays with the skill of a Van Cliburn."

Newsweek recalled how "Democratic regulars" had watched McGovern's "accelerating march toward the nomination as dismally, and as helplessly, as Rome watching the advance of Attila the Hun across Europe." Even then it was Kennedy, not McGovern, who was likened to the Greek heroes: "The day Senator Edward Kennedy of Massachusetts got into the Democratic campaign was like one of those moments in the Trojan War when things had been going badly for the Greeks and then one or another of their heroes, an Achilles or an Ajax, buckled on his armour and entered the fray."

In 1972, the candidates were often not perceived as senators and congressmen running for the presidential nomination but other types of persons engaged in other trades—they were Don Juans or ice cream vendors. More often than not they were larger or smaller than life, but rarely lifelike. Thus, the campaign appeared to be populated chiefly by royalty of various courtly ranks or by characters more to be disdained or pitied than admired. Constituents (when they were not masquerading as animals of several species, domestic and wild) were not citizens listening to campaigners' talks about issues, but, rather, buyers of ice cream easily seduced by the enticing tune of a Pied Piper marching throughout the land.

Show Biz

Vice-President Agnew agreed that the Democratic campaign was "an open book." He quipped: "I understand the author is Clifford Irving." While the press may have not agreed on the authorship of the piece, that there was a scenario they were sure. By May, 1971, it seemed clear "that the irrepressible Humphrey would like to write the comeback scenario of the 1970s." In mid-1971, Edmund Muskie tried out his "scenario for a front-runner" to see if it would move. An April New Republic cover story previewed at length, "A Scenario for Kennedy." If McGovern turned out to be a strong candidate, speculated one reporter, that "of course, would tear Mr. Kennedy's 'I am not a candidate' scenario to pieces."

Some of the candidates performed with more verve than others; for example, "John Barrymore Lindsay" gave a "bravura performance: when he announced his switch to the Democratic party. Others saw Edward Kennedy as the "number one sweater boy of politics" who at an occasion in Arkansas honoring Wilbur Mills "scattered magnolia blossoms with Rhett Butler abandon. . . ."

As late as July some Democrats held on to "a last hope—the feverish vision of a Last Hurrah, the sweet scenario of Ted's conscription as candidate Kennedy III, followed by his conquest of the usurper in November and his coronation in January as Sovereign of the Restoration."

There were those, however, who saw the election as less heady stuff. In 1971, one reporter thought Birch Bayh would be "cast as the juvenile lead in the Democratic follies. . . ." Bayh dropped out of the race even before the play "tried out" in the primary states but the show did, in fact, go on. "The Follies Begin," Perry of the *Observer* declared in January. The Florida primary turned "out to be the most fantastic local show since Walt Disney opened in Orlando. . . ." A later version of the "show" in Wisconsin starred the "odd couple," McGovern and Wallace. By mid-June some complained that the "real McGovern" still remained "under the greasepaint."

Many viewers agreed that there was "nothing quite like" a Wallace rally calling it "a country carnival, a phenomenon. . . ." The coming of George Wallace seemed to be "an event—rather like the coming of the circus in the spring." William Raspberry saw the Wallace rally as a "minstrel show" and Godfrey Sperling likened it to the "finish to a Billy Graham revival."

Shades of the old West sometimes walked the streets. "Showdowns" occurred from New York to California. Voters were tracked "along the Chisholm Trail." The *Monitor* speculated: "Lindsay may cut off Muskie at the Gap." But it took the California primary to recall two classic Western movies. A McGovern primary aide suggested: "California is the gunfight at the O. K. Corral." The *Monitor* went further back in film history: "California may have lost the crowd scene of the Republican convention, but it is almost sure to provide a 'High Noon' backdrop for a Democratic primary climax. The big scene now is the Hubert Humphrey-George McGovern 'shootout.' . . ."

Westerns were not the only genre for which the press had a fondness. There was, of course, one conspicuous event, that was, at first, treated like a spy-spoof, the Watergate break-in and subsequent coverup. "Mission Incredible," first described as a "caper," a "cloak-and-dagger" affair, remained for some a "political soap opera" but became for others a "national tragedy."

The "Barnum and Bailey world of politics '72" tilted "on its axis toward the party conventions. . . ." Until the last minute, "Humphrey scorekeepers challenged McGovern's arithmetic and guessed that his Great American Dream Machine would die around the second ballot." As the convention began, the "drama" of the three Georges (McGovern, Meany, Wallace) held the Miami "stage." Some claimed that the convention "in that stalest of all tags looked like the cast of 'Hair.' " And, as the convention ended and all the rivals stood with arms around each other on the podium, the "Democrats staged a smash rock-opera version of the old party show, 'United We Stand, Divided We Fall.' . . ." McGovern, the star of that show, caused some labor leaders concern: "We're [labor] going to have a real fight. . . . The Archie Bunkers think McGovern is too radical to vote for." The question asked much earlier, after Florida: "Was it *all* Archie Bunkers?," returned to haunt the Democrats again.

The search for the 1972 Democratic nomination turned primary season into the "great American road show." First one candidate and then another "leapt center stage" in several versions of the scenario for winning. This year the writers selected not only the older more conventional forms in which to write, but also dipped into the newer forms such as the rock opera. The play had an unusually large cast calling for a variety of actor-types—glamour boys, juvenile leads, stalwart protectors of the peace, and fumbling villains. Even with so large and varied a cast, show biz remained largely a spectator phenomenon, more to be watched than participated in. The spectators could enjoy the vicarious excitement of a shoot-out in Dodge City or the super cool antics of master spies. They could laugh at the clowns and the slightly aging musical comedy stars. But *they* did not actually put on the greasepaint and thus did not feel responsible when the play proved to be a flop.

Other Categories

The first eight categories accounted for 86 percent of the metaphors cataloged in this study. But four other categories need to be mentioned: courtship; food/cookery; religion; and health/illness.[11]

The 1972 presidential swains wooed and were wooed, courted and were courted. Only reporter predilection seems to have determined who "wooed" (and was wooed) and who "courted" (and was courted). Courted or wooed, the South, in the end, felt like a "bride who got left at the altar."

At least one suitor, Humphrey, was affectionately chastised by David Broder for his superabundance of ardor: "Humphrey can be faulted for his excesses, but they are the excesses of a generous spirit, not an angry or embittered heart. His exaggerations are like a lover's lies—and at 61, Humphrey is still engaged in reckless love affairs with his country, and, indeed, with all of life." All in all, however, the press appears to have seen little that was glamorous or courtly about the quest for the 1972 nomination. As one columnist put it: "The question is whether in the process of the courtship the lovely and elusive prize get so ravished and mutilated that the swains will wonder if the quest was worth it."[12]

Some judged the election to be "mostly about who gets what share of the money pie." The press saw celestial pie as largely bipartisan: "Pie-in-the-sky is a bi-partisan confession. It's a dish that Democrats and Republican candidates serve up with a flourish each presidential election year

[11] Percentage totals for categories 9 to 12 were: food/cookery (4 percent); courtship (3 percent); religion (3 percent); and health/sickness (3 percent).
[12] For a treatment of the political courtship of Hubert Humphrey and John F. Kennedy with West Virginia in 1960, see Hermann G. Stelzner, "Humphrey and Kennedy Court West Virginia, May 3, 1960," Southern Speech Journal, 37 (Fall, 1971), 21–33. A more general treatment of the persuader as wooer may be found in Wayne Brockriede, "Arguers as Lovers," Philosophy and Rhetoric, 5 (Winter, 1972), 1–11.

and a race between George McGovern and Richard Nixon could become a Chef's Derby."

The other Democratic dishes ranged in elegance from stew to hors d'oeuvres. When George Wallace tossed the Alabama state legislature "an impressive stew of populist legislation" it swallowed "only a spoonful." The candidates did not always manage to choose the appropriate fare for their audiences. For example, one local politician "fumed" about Lindsay's appearances in Indiana: "They wanted red meat and he's dishing up fancy hors d'oeuvres."

Consumers were warned by a variety of people; for example, Vice-President Agnew felt the contenders for the Democratic presidential nomination were only rewarding voters with " 'Leap Year lollipops' by using 'the old soak-the-rich, share-the-wealth ploy' as a campaign issue." Elizabeth Janeway's consumer advocacy took on a more bipartisan air: "It would appear that what politicans offer us is also a product to consume; plans, programs and policies cooked up in huge stainless steel vats somewhere behind the scene and marketed in convenient cans bearing a label that declares the contents are just what grandma used to make. . . . To the sellers of politics, we, the voters, are simply consumers and the chief question becomes how best to tickle our taste buds." In 1972, the "wares" of the Democratic party clearly did not "whet" the appetites of the American public.

The "Christian witness" of George McGovern and the political "conversion" of John Lindsay dominated the religious metaphors. Henry Jackson's much reprinted comment about Lindsay's switch to the Democratic party is indicative of the tone of many: "We believe in the right of redemption. But if you join the church on one Sunday you can't expect to be chairman of the board of deacons the following Sunday." Jackson proved to be more prophetic than the columnist who observed: "The ticket could be enlivened with the very newest Democrat around, one still fresh and dripping from the political baptism font, rechristened party man John Lindsay."

Lindsay, as he campaigned for the nomination, reminded one of "an attractive young Episcopal bishop from perhaps Old Greenwich, who says most of the right things and looks princely in the robes and trappings of his ecclesiastical office." If John Lindsay was likened to an Episcopal bishop, George McGovern was described in more fundamentalist terms. His "style" seemed "more like that of a Christian witness than that of [a] charismatic leader." As some McGovern Democrats sought to persuade Humphrey Democrats to join them, William Buckley provided this reminder for onlookers: "[It] isn't as simple as that Humphrey's emphases are different from McGovern's. What it is, is sacrilege. McGovernism is something of a religion. . . . It is off-putting to be asked to vote for McGovern as a religious exercise. It is one thing to seduce the Humphrey Democrat by appealing to his party loyalty or by his disapproval of Richard Nixon. It is something else to try to co-opt him into a new religious order."

Only Kennedy was persistently sanctified. One political observer noted: "Watching the summer tourists approaching Ted Kennedy in the halls of Congress is a little like watching pilgrims coming to a shrine. . . . The supplicants stand in line for pictures, autographs, or a handshake." One writer went so far as to metaphorically *deify* him: "He is a man of destiny, like it or not. And he does not want it. Deep down he is trapped in his own Gethsemane. He would like the chalice to pass. . . ."

Some came to view both the Wallace and the McGovern campaigns as "crusades." California was at once McGovern's "finest hour and the epiphany of all his larger political problems." As with most candidates, "Where his cup runneth over, where he is rich beyond measure, is in a superabundance of unsolicited advice." By September, 1972, it was clear of the old pols that "they really weren't terribly eager to recruit the 1972 'sacrificial lamb' from their own kind." Thus, it was "St. George" who went out to fight "the Dragon, Richard Nixon."

The year 1972 "brought boils to the surface to be lanced." "Front runner's miseries" dominated much of the early press coverage but the "sick list" extended to most of the candidates. It is perhaps not unexpected that the author of *In Critical Condition: The Crisis in America's Health Care* would, in these press accounts, make the most metaphorical use of health/sickness. For example, Senator Kennedy saw the I.T.T. affair as "symptomatic of a disease that infects all levels of government and all parties." He assured the South that they were "no longer swallowing . . . patent Yankee medicines." And he commented on the financial community's response to McGovern's defense of his socioeconomic policies in the California debates: "If Wall Street sneezed over George McGovern in California in 1972, it is positively caught pneumonia over President Nixon's invasion of Cambodia. . . ."

Kennedy himself was seen by the press in terms of health aid to an ailing McGovern; for example, he was called a "crutch" for McGovern and was certified a "tonic" for the South Dakota senator. "Advised that he trailed in every state except two, George McGovern took a powerful tonic—with built-in side effects. The tonic is called Edward Kennedy. And McGovern now has symptoms of charisma shock."

"Fractures" accounted for many 1972 miseries. The health/illness category is inextricably associated with the violence category, for surely candidates and constituencies alike would require time and treatment to recover from so much "flaying," "rattling of eyeteeth," "sandbagging," and the like.

The actors in the 1972 election, on occasion, indulged themselves in certain religious practices. But, there was, in 1972 at least, no biz like show biz, unless it was courting, cooking or diagnosing illnesses. It was, for the metaphor-makers at least, "a very good year."

Conclusion

In 1971 to 1972, twelve "common topics" appeared to dominate the way the press described the search for the Democratic nomination. For each of these "common topics" or essential metaphors, a variety of examples illustrate the range of "special topics" within them.

The readership of the print media sampled in this study numbered many millions of people. They were exposed to these particular common topics for at least eighteen months. One can only speculate to what extent the language describing the 1972 (or any) nomination process is "prescriptive" as well as descriptive. If Burke and others are correct in their suggestion that a "name" directs the way one acts toward the thing named, then language is prescriptive as well as descriptive. As he suggests, "The mere act of naming an object or situation decrees that it is to be singled out as such-and-such rather than something-other."[13] Thus, in "its essence" language is "not neutral." For as Burke argues: "Far from aiming at suspended judgment [the speech of people] is loaded with judgments. . . . Its names for objects . . . give us . . . cues as to how we should act toward these objects.[14]

There has been a serious cautionary note in this essay for, as Hermann G. Stelzner observed, metaphors "may become current coin before there is explicit recognition [Burke would suggest even 'implicit' recognition] that an *analogy* and not an identity is involved."[15] An identity may be presumed for so long that the analogy, *if* it is seen *as* an analogy, may be perceived as more exact than originally, in fact, it was. Moreover, as Marie Nichols reminds us: "Language is not an objective tool; its symbols are not empty but freighted with the experiences of men who are its makers, and interpreted by men who bring to it the feelings and experiences of their existential selves."[16]

If "to understand ourselves, we must study our symbolic behavior,"[17] this examination may prod us to ask: What does the way the press (and the candidates as reported in the press) talked *about* the 1972 Democratic presidential nomination tell us about the way press and candidates

[13] *Burke*, Philosophy of Literary Form, *p. 5.*
[14] *Burke*, Permanence and Change, *pp. 176–77.*
[15] *Hermann G. Stelzner, "Analysis by Metaphor,"* Quarterly Journal of Speech, *51 (February 1965), 60.*
[16] *Marie Hochmuth Nichols, "Rhetoric and Style," in* Patterns of Literary Style, *ed. Joseph Strelka (University Park: The Pennsylvania State University Press, 1971), p. 136.*
[17] *Karl R. Wallace,* Understanding Discourse *(Baton Rouge: Louisiana University Press, 1970), p. 5.*

have come to view that part of our political process? As consumers of these metaphors, we may want to go beyond that question to another question, "What do our interpretations of them tell us about *our* existential selves?" Again, Burke provides us with useful clues by reminding us that a symbol provides us with "a terminology of thoughts, actions, emotions, attitudes, for codifying a pattern of experience."[18] He points to the close relation between symbol and situation or scene. The symbol provides either an "*orienting* of a situation, or an *adjustment* to a situation," or in good Burkeian fashion, *both*.[19] Thus, symbols are linguistic encompassings of situations.

Existentially then, for the printed press, the nomination process is one in which violence is the norm rather than the exception. "Flaying" is the essential activity, whether the candidates direct it at each other or at the issues. The encounters of the candidates with one another and their tactics are, then, generally violent if not specifically warlike. Moreover the violence is multidirectional; it is directed not only at fellow candidates but at constituencies as well; for example, audiences are treated much like a people under siege. Small wonder that after more than a year of bruising battle, not only are the candidates bloodied and impotent but their constituencies as well. Thus there is little place for the careful, reflective consideration of issues during the nominating process and little will or capacity for it immediately after a campaign.

There is a gamelike nature to all of this. The "carnage" is both real and unreal. The favorite "games" (horse racing, football, and boxing) in the nomination process are "gladiatorial" in nature. They are, first of all, largely spectator sports. Few players actually get bloodied (in the one, horse racing, it is not even humans who feel the prod of the stick) and many can watch at a safe distance. Fans not only participate vicariously in the "fray" but by gambling on the outcome they add dimensions of excitement that applause and lip service alone do not generate. They are one step closer to the fray but still largely unbloodied.

Politics also often appears to be a genre of "show biz," again more to be watched than participated in. The cast, in 1971 to 1972, is still predominantly male. Some aspirants try out for their roles and occasionally one has the potential at least of stepping into the starring role without "trying out" for it.

The playbill consists more of musicals ("follies" and the like) and situa-

---

[18] *Kenneth Burke,* Counterstatement *(Berkeley: University of California Press, 1968), p. 154. Original copyright, 1931.*
[19] *Ibid., p. 156. Italics added.*

tion comedies (for example, the "Odd Couple") than of serious fare. But, Westerns and cloak-and-dagger "capers" occasionally are available for divertissements. When the viewer realizes that the "caper" is less the stuff of which James Bonds are made of and more the stuff of serious drama, some decide the play has run too long and move on to something else.

Scenarios prepared by campaign staffs are rewritten or discarded as the drama is played out before audiences. And, in politics as in show biz, "comebacks" are often more easily dreamed of than enacted.

The near obsession for "likenesses" is clear. Since the "roles" in the political process are either ill-defined, unconsidered, or disliked, candidates are seen "in terms of" something else. They are seen as other people—as Sammy Glicks, Willie Lomans, or as Billy Budds and Prince Valiants. The *range* is wide indeed, but people largely stand at either end of the continuum. Even the "piano" is only played by a "Johnny-one-note" or a Van Cliburn. Thus, our political figures seem either smaller than life or larger than life.

Often, indeed, the political scene is inhabited not by candidates but by animals of all varieties, more domestic than wild. Moreover, it is "peopled" not by a constituency carefully considering the issues but by "coveys" and "flocks" who are "corraled" or "herded" into their decisions. Thus, if one does not want to go to gladiatorial games or to the theater, one might well go to the zoo—there, again, mostly to look.

All of these proceedings are viewed, not as exceptional, but as natural. Candidacies "blossom" as readily as plants. If we are to agree with the metaphor-makers, the McGovern and Wallace candidacies seem the most "natural" for 1972.[20] Even in this category, "violent" imagery persists; for example, "drought," "washouts," or "earthquakes" are the fate of many. Still, amid all of the "avalanches" and "floods," some "greening" persists.

If this *is* the nature of the "reality" the press has constructed under the label "political process," one may pause to ask whether the political process would be greatly enriched were we to respond to it in other ways and to look for other symbols with which to "encompass" it. Such new vocabulary might reveal that we require our *candidates* to act like something more than rival quarterbacks who see their task as devising game plans and calling audibles. And we might require of *ourselves* a more thoughtful and active role in the political process.

[20] *Natural phenomena was the largest single category of metaphors used by and about George McGovern in this particular press sample; of those used by and about George Wallace in the sample, natural phenomena was the second largest category. (For Wallace, general violence was the largest category; for McGovern, it was the second largest category.)*

THE DRAMATISTIC APPROACH

Rhetorical Criticism: A Burkeian Approach
by Bernard L. Brock

Rhetorical criticism requires that a critic make a descriptive, interpretative judgment regarding the effectiveness of rhetoric. In this process the critic not only needs a language to describe man as he responds to his world but also a theoretical framework for understanding man's basic rhetorical tendencies. Kenneth Burke's dramatistic approach to rhetoric provides the critic with such a language and theoretical structure; thus many critics have turned from Aristotle to Kenneth Burke for a rhetorical theory to guide them in making critical judgments.

Kenneth Burke's rhetorical philosophy evolves from the view that language is a strategic response to a situation.[1] This view underlies all his major works: *Counter-Statement*, 1931; *Permanence and Change*, 1935; *Attitudes Toward History*, 1937; *The Philosophy of Literary Form*, 1941; *A Grammar of Motive*, 1945; *A Rhetoric of Motives*, 1950; *Rhetoric of Religion*, 1961; and *Language as Symbolic Action*, 1966. His writing, though unified, is quite complex, and thus has been difficult to apply as a system of rhetorical criticism.

Structuring Burke's rhetorical theories into a system of rhetorical criticism necessitates (1) identifying his philosophy of rhetoric, (2) framing a structure that reflects his philosophy, and (3) showing how the dramatistic approach unites substance and rhetorical devices. Then, one can suggest specifically how the rhetorical critic might use Kenneth Burke's dramatistic approach.

Burke's Philosophy of Rhetoric

The foundation of Burke's rhetorical philosophy can be found in *Attitudes Toward History*. He indicates that one assesses the "human situation" and shapes appropriate attitudes by constructing his conception of the world around him. In the process he perceives "certain functions or relationships as either friendly or unfriendly," and then, weighing his own potential against probable opposition, he selects his strategies for coping with the "human situation."[2] These strategies or stylized answers are symbols that reflect attitudes.[3]

By starting with man as he reacts symbolically to his environment, Kenneth Burke arrives at the function of rhetoric—"the use of words

[1]*Kenneth Burke*, The Philosophy of Literary Form, *New York, Random House, 1957, p. 3.*

[2]*Kenneth Burke*, Attitudes Toward History, *Boston, Beacon Press, 1961, pp. 3 and 4.*

[3]*Burke*, The Philosophy of Literary Form, op. cit., *p. 3.*

by human agents to form attitudes or to induce actions in other human agents."[4] Rhetoric originates not from "any past condition of human society," but from "an essential function of language itself." The act of using language to induce cooperation among people automatically focuses one's attention upon the language or the symbols employed.[5] From roots within its function two major concepts of Burke's philosophy of rhetoric evolve: Verbal symbols are meaningful acts in response to situations from which motives can be derived and society is dramatistic in nature.

Burke clearly demonstrates his view that verbal symbols are meaningful acts from which motives can be derived when he discusses the relationship betwen symbols and action. He points out that in acting wisely "we must name the friendly or unfriendly functions and relationships in such a way that we are able to do something about them."[6] The words that one assigns to these functions and relationships not only reveal the process of sorting out the world but also communicate an attitude that is a cue for the behavior of others. Burke clearly indicates that the act of selecting one symbol over another locks the speaker's attitude into the language. For this reason verbal symbols are meaningful acts from which human motives can be derived. These motives constitute the foundation or the substance of the speech, and through the ability to identify them by the cues in verbal symbols, Burke constructs a philosophy of rhetoric.

In considering the nature of society as fundamental to Burke's philosophy of rhetoric, one can turn to *Permanence and Change*. Burke explains that "action and end" as opposed to "motion and position" and "dramatistic terms" rather than "theories of knowledge" are appropriate in discussing human conduct.[7] The human tendency toward action makes a dramatistic vocabulary appropriate to the study of man. Burke describes man's society as a dramatistic process, which includes the elements of hierarchy, acceptance and rejection, and guilt, purification, and redemption.

Hierarchy generates the structure of our dramatistic society. In society the social, economic, and political powers are unevenly divided. Power endows individuals with authority. Authority, in turn, establishes definite relationships among people, reflecting the degree to which they possess power. These relationships can be viewed as a ladder of authority or the hierarchy of society.[8] As people accept their positions

[4] *Kenneth Burke,* A Rhetoric of Motives, *New York, Prentice-Hall, 1950, p. 41.*
[5] *Ibid., p. 43.*
[6] *Burke,* Attitudes Toward History, op. cit., *p. 4.*
[7] *Kenneth Burke,* Permanence and Change, *Los Altos, Calif. Hermes, 1954, p. 274.*
[8] *Ibid., p. 276.*

and work within a hierarchical structure, the structure is "bureaucratized" or given a definite organization. With the bureaucratization of the hierarchy comes order in society. This process makes hierarchy the structural principle of a dramatistic society.[9]

Another element of the dramatistic society is the concept of acceptance and rejection. Burke's philosophy of rhetoric is based upon man's propensity to accept or reject the "human situation" and his attempts to symbolize his reaction. The concept of acceptance follows from a positive reaction to the human situation and rejection from a negative reaction. Burke explains, however, that language allows the negative or rejection: "The essential distinction between the verbal and the non-verbal is in the fact that language adds the peculiar possibility of the Negative."[10] In nature everything is positive: What exists, simply exists. The negative or nonexistence results from language or the separation of a symbol from the thing that it represents. Burke further points out that historically, since there is no negative in nature, the negative in language has probably developed through the negative command, "Do not do that."[11] Language enables man to accept or reject his hierarchical position or even the hierarchy itself. Acceptance results in satisfaction and order, whereas rejection results in alienation and disorder.

To complete the dramatistic process, guilt, purification, and redemption must be understood. These terms represent the effects of acceptance and rejection of the hierarchy. Whenever man rejects the traditional hierarchy, he "falls," and thereby acquires a feeling of guilt. Burke feels that guilt is inherent in society because man cannot accept all the impositions of his traditional hierarchy. Conditions change, resulting in the rejection of some of the traditional modes. Also, each social institution—the family, school, church, clubs, and other "bureaucracies"—has its own hierarchy, and when any one of these hierarchies is in conflict with another, rejection of one will inevitably occur.[12] Since man cannot satisfy all the requirements of his traditional hierarchies, he is saddled with eternal guilt.[13]

The nature of hierarchy itself is another source of eternal guilt. Hierarchy, representing differences in authority between superiors and inferiors in society, always creates mystery. Moreover, inferiors always want to move up within the hierarchy or to change its nature. The

---

[9] Ibid., pp. 282 and 283.
[10] Kenneth Burke, "A Dramatistic View of the Origins of Language: Part One," The Quarterly Journal of Speech, XXXVIII (October 1952), p. 252.
[11] Ibid., p. 253.
[12] Burke, Permanence and Change, op. cit., p. 283.
[13] Ibid., p. 284.

sense of mystery that one class holds for another class and the upward tendencies of the lower classes create a guilt that is inherent in the hierarchy itself.[14]

Burke compares the eternal secular guilt with original sin. However, neither secular guilt nor original sin result from man's "personal transgression, but by reason of a tribal or dynastic inheritance."[15] In spite of this fact, guilt still sets off a psychological reaction in man. Guilt reduces social cohesion and gives man the feeling of being less than whole, so that he strives to have his guilt canceled or to receive redemption. The act of purification may be either mortification or victimage. Mortification is an act of self-sacrifice that relieves man of his guilt, whereas victimage is the purging of guilt through a scapegoat that symbolizes society's guilt. To be effective, the process of purification and redemption must be balanced: The act of purification must be equivalent to the degree of guilt if one is to receive redemption. Psychological guilt, purification, and redemption result from the rejection of hierarchy.

Burke believes that the dramatistic nature of society may be explained by considering the interrelationships among the (1) concepts of the hierarchy, (2) acceptance and rejection, and (3) guilt, purification, and redemption. This assumption together with the belief that verbal symbols are meaningful acts in response to situations from which motives can be derived, is the philosophic foundation of Kenneth Burke's system of rhetoric.

Structure in Burke's Rhetoric

Burke's dramatistic approach to rhetoric supplies a language that describes man as he responds to his world, but to be useful to the critic, this language must be transformed into a more definite structure. Two concepts are basic to such a structure: identification and the pentad. These concepts can be used as rhetorical tools to discover the attitudes expressed within a speech and to describe its dramatistic process. Identification is the major tool used to discover the attitudes and the dramatistic process: The pentad provides a model for their description.

In Burke's philosophy of rhetoric the verbal symbol carries within it the attitude of the speaker. Burke states that the basic function of rhetoric is "the use of words by human agents to form attitudes or to induce actions in other human agents."[16] In connection with this function Burke introduces identification, which is defined in A Rhetoric of

[14] Ibid., p. 287.
[15] Ibid.
[16] Burke, A Rhetoric of Motives, op. cit., p. 41.

Motives: "A is not identical with his colleague, B. But insofar as their interests are joined, A is *identified* with B. Or he may *identify himself* with B even when their interests are not joined, if he assumes that they are, or is persuaded to believe so."[17]

Burke sees identification as an "acting together" that grows out of the ambiguities of substance. Both division and unity exist simultaneously, division because each person remains unique and unity or "consubstantiality" to the extent that the actors share a locus of motives.[18] The speaker, whose attitudes are reflected in his language, will accept some ideas, people, and institutions, and reject others; his audience will to some extent both agree and disagree with him. To the extent that the audience accepts and rejects the same ideas, people, and institutions that the speaker does, identification occurs. The speaker's language will reveal the substance out of which he expects to identify with his listeners. Consciously or unconsciously his words will reveal his attitudes or stylized answers to the obvious divisions. The concept of identification will help the critic structure his insight into a speaker's sense of unity by grouping strategies into "clusters" until relationships indicate the speaker's concept of hierarchy and reflect the process of guilt, purification, and redemption. Identification, the tool that is applied directly to verbal symbols for the purpose of uncovering relationships among these symbols, is the critic's key to the speaker's attitudes and the dramatistic process.

Kenneth Burke labels one of his procedures as "statistical." He advises gathering lists of recurrent terms until the critic begins to sense those that are essential—which terms cluster and where. Beginnings and endings, he argues, are particularly likely to reveal key terms. The critic may verify the hypotheses he constructs by making a reasoned case for the consistencies of the parts and the whole, that is, for the manner in which the terms fit the apparent situation. In his work there is no substitute for intelligence and effort, both made sensitive by wide experience. But Kenneth Burke does suggest one more aid to finding and proving rhetorical structure.

Kenneth Burke's well-known pentad is this aid. He uses the device as a model to describe the dramatistic nature of society. In *A Grammar of Motives* Burke attempts to answer the question, What is involved when we say what people are doing and why they are doing it? As an explanation he introduces and defines the pentad:

We shall use five terms as generating principle of our investigation. They are: Act, Scene, Agent, Agency, and Purpose. In a rounded state-

---

[17] Ibid., *p. 20. Emphasis Burke's.*
[18] Ibid., *p. 21.*

ment about motives, you must have some word that names the act
(*names what took place, in thought or deed*), *and another that names
the* scene (*the background of the act, the situation in which it occurred*); *also, you must indicate what person or kind of person* (agent)
performed the act, what means or instruments he used (agency), *and
the* purpose.[19]

Men will disagree about the nature of these terms or what they represent, but they necessarily must provide some answer to these five questions: "what was done (act), when or where it was done (scene), who
did it (agent), how he did it (agency), and why (purpose)."[20] Thus, these
terms are the key to human motives, because statements assigning
motives "arise out of them and terminate in them."

Any man, Kenneth Burke argues, will tend to feature in his thought
one of these terms—although, of course, each may have his own vocabulary that reveals the set that dominates his thinking and speaking.
Some men, for example, will ask "What?" and then "Who?" Others
"Who?" and then "What?" In Burke's language an "act-agent" ratio
properly labels the first sequence of questions, and an "agent-act" the
second. Given his starting place (and starting places tend to be ending
places), we can trace a constellation of ratios in a coherent, well-
formed piece of rhetorical discourse. Domination by agent may reveal
agent-act concern, then agent-purpose, then agent-scene. Given a
man's dominant set or his term, a critic may trace the complete pentad
in a discourse; but probably a few ratios, and especially one term, will
typify that discourse.

The pentad, together with a knowledge of identification and the in-
nately dramatistic nature of human society, provides the critic with a
vocabulary and way of proceeding. To understand the process, however, the critic must understand each term of the pentad with its corresponding philosophy and terminology.

Following from the belief that society is dramatistic in nature, the
act for Burke is the central term in the pentad. The act answers the
question, What is done? Burke explains that when the act is *featured* in
discourse, the philosophy that dominates within the speech is realism.[21]
In defining realism Burke cites Aristotle: "Things are more or less real
according as they are more or less *energeia* (*actu*, from which our
'actuality' is derived)."[22] The act or realism is not just existence, it is
"taking form." The realist grammar begins with a tribal concept and

[19] *Kenneth Burke,* A Grammar of Motives, *Englewood Cliffs, N.J., Prentice-
Hall, 1945, p. x. Italics Burke's.*
[20] Ibid. *parentheses Burke's.*
[21] Ibid., *p. 128.*
[22] Ibid., *p. 227.*

treats the individual as a participant in substance. The terminology that is associated with the act would suggest an emphasis upon verbs.[23]

The term scene corresponds with a philosophy of materialism. Burke cites Baldwin's *Dictionary of Philosophy and Psychology* to define materialism, "that metaphysical theory which regards all the facts of the universe as sufficiently explained by the assumption of body and matter, conceived as extended, impenetrable, eternally existent, and susceptible of movement or change of relative position."[24] Darwin's *The Origin of the Species* illustrates some of the terminology that accompanies the domination of the scene: "accidental variation," "conditions of existence," "adjustment," "natural selection," and "survival of the fittest."[25]

The scene, which is the background or setting for the drama, is generally revealed in secular or material terms. Since it is the background, the emphasis can easily shift from the scene to the act, agent, agency, or purpose. But these shifts, which will be slight if the rhetoric is consistent, will continue to reveal the determinism of the material situation characteristic with the domination of a mind by the scene.

The philosophy corresponding to *agent* is idealism. Burke again turns to Baldwin's dictionary in defining idealism: "In metaphysics, any theory which maintains the universe to be throughout the work of reason and mind."[26] Burke points to terms such as "ego," "self," "superego," "mind," "spirit," and "oversoul" as a sign of a stress on agent. He also suggests that treating ideas—church, race, nation, historical periods, cultural movements—as "personalities" usually indicates idealism. Furthermore, the dominance of agent grows out of the spiritualization of the family. Whenever important human economic relations have become idealized or spiritualized, the agent is featured.

We have considered three terms from the pentad—act, scene, and agent. For convenience of explanation, we may draw together agency and purpose in a means-ends relationship. Burke points out that "means are considered in terms of ends." But as "you play down the concept of final cause (as modern science does), . . . there is a reversal of causal ancestry—and whereas means were treated in terms of ends, ends become treated in terms of means."[27] To illustrate this shift between means and ends Burke shows that money, which is the means (agency) of obtaining goods and services, simultaneously is the end (purpose) of work.[28]

[23] Ibid., *p. 228.*
[24] Ibid., *p. 131.*
[25] Ibid., *p. 153.*
[26] Ibid., *p. 171.*
[27] Ibid., *p. 276.*
[28] Ibid., *pp. 108 and 276.*

In featuring the means, or agency, the pragmatic philosophy is dominant. Pragmatism is defined by Kant as "the means necessary to the attainment of happiness."[29] John Dewey refers to his pragmatist doctrine as Instrumentalism. In modern science, method or agency dominates all other terms of the human drama. Along with modern science and pragmatism, the technologically oriented line of action has appeared and is identified with terms such as "useful," "practical," and "serviceable."[30] William James not only asserts that Pragmatism is "a method only," but he goes on to indicate that "consequence," "function," "what it is 'good for,'" and "the difference it will make to you and me" are pragmatic evaluations. However, pure pragmatism goes beyond James to transcend purpose, as in the applied sciences, when the method is built into the instrument itself. At this point agency becomes the focus of the entire means-ends relationship.

The process may be reversed, featuring *purpose* rather than agency. The philosophy corresponding to purpose is mysticism.

The Baldwin dictionary describes the philosophy of mysticism:

> . . . *those forms of speculative and religious thought which profess to attain an immediate apprehension of the divine essence or essence or the ultimate ground of existence. . . . Penetrated by the thought of the ultimate of all experience, and impatient of even a seeming separation from the creative source of things, mysticism succumbs to a species of meta-physical fascination.*[31]

Mysticism equals purpose because of such references as "the divine essence" and "the creative source." In mysticism the element of unity is emphasized to the point that individuality disappears. Identification often becomes so strong as to indicate the "unity of the individual with some cosmic or universal purpose."[32] The universal purpose becomes a compulsive force against which everything else is judged.

Aristotle and Plato reflect elements of mysticism. Aristotle's mystic absolutism can be seen in his purpose for society—happiness. Plato's mysticism goes well beyond that of Aristotle and completely equates "good" and "purpose." His concept of reality is drawn from his idea of the "good," and the rest of the world is arranged in accordance with this ideal.[33]

---

[29] Ibid., *p. 275.*
[30] C. *Wright Mills,* Power, Politics and People, *New York, Ballantine, 1963, p. 441.*
[31] *Burke,* A Grammar of Motives, op. cit., *p. 287.*
[32] Ibid., *p. 288.*
[33] Ibid., *pp. 292–294.*

In any discussion of human motivation all five terms of the pentad are necessary. To the extent that these terms are represented as separate elements there is division; however, to the extent that one term is featured and the other terms seem to grow out of this term, there is unity. As a model, the pentad can express both possibilities, unity and division.

To illustrate the operation of the pentad Kenneth Burke compares it to the human hand. He likens the five terms to the fingers, which are distinct from each other and possess their own individuality; yet, at the same time, they merge into a unity at the palm of the hand. With this simultaneous division and unity (identification) one can leap from one term to another or one can move slowly from one to another through the palm.[34] The analogy illustrates both aspects of the operation of the pentad—flexibility of movement and unity and division. The analogy also brings out another aspect of Burke's rhetorical philosophy and structure (which will be discussed later), whereby the palm represents the unity of the terms or substance of the speech that is discovered by determining which of the terms is featured in the discourse.

At this point identification and the pentad merge as tools in Burke's rhetorical structure. The speaker may use the strategy of featuring the agent, then, in proving a point, proceed to an agent-scene or agent-act ratio. Then he may move to purpose and finally to agency. Each step represents an act that symbolizes an attitude, and the total series represents the dramatistic process in action as the speaker sees it. Using identification one can discover each step that reflects the speaker's stylized answers to situation or strategies, and with the pentad as a model the steps can be plotted so as to describe the dramatistic process operating in the speech.

Unity of Substance and Rhetorical Devices

The structural tools of identification and the pentad bring about a unity of strategies or rhetorical devices and substance. This unity aids the critic in understanding and explaining man's basic rhetorical tendencies.

Substance, according to Burke, is the philosophical foundation of the message in the speech. In the analogy with the hand, substance represents the palm—the place where all other elements are unified. To define substance Burke starts with Webster's dictionary, "the most important element in any existence; the characteristic and essential import, purpose."[35] He concludes, literally, that substance is that which stands beneath something. The principle of substance is important in

---

[34] Ibid., p. xxiv.
[35] Ibid., p. 21.

Burke's rhetorical criticism because all speeches must establish a substance that is the context for the speech or the key to the speaker's attitudes. Burke defines four types of substance: familial, directional, geometric, and dialectic. Each type of substance is established when a given term from the pentad is featured to the point that it dominates the speech.

Geometric substance places an object in its setting as "existing both in itself and as part of its background."[36] This featuring leads to a materialistic notion of determinism, which is most consistent with the term scene from the pentad.

When agent is featured, a familial substance evolves. "It stresses common ancestry in the strictly biological sense, as literal descent from material or paternal sources."[37] However, the concept of family is often spiritualized so as to include social and national groups and beliefs.

Directional substance is also biologically derived; however, it comes "from a sense of free motion."[38] The feeling of movement provides a sense of motivation from within. All generalizations such as "the reasonable man" or "the economic man" fall in this category. Also, "terminologies that situate the driving force of human action in human passion"[39] and treat emotion as motive are classified as directional substance. Finally, "doctrines that reduce mental states to materialistic terms treat motion as motive," and encourage "sociological speculation in terms of 'tendencies' or 'trends.'"[40] The term agency follows from this context.

The last type of substance, dialectic, reflects "the ambiguities of substance, since symbolic communication is not a merely external instrument, but also intrinsic to men as agents. The motivational properties of dialectic substance characterize both the 'human situation' and what men are 'in themselves.'" The ambiguity of external and internal motivation creates dialectic substance. "The most thoroughgoing dialectic opposition, however, centers in that key pair: Being and Not-Being."[41] For example, Burke shows how dialectic substance can transcend to the "ultimate abstract Oneness." "The human person, for instance, may be derived from God as a 'super-person.' Or human purpose may be derived from an All-Purpose, or Cosmic Purpose, or Universal Purpose, or Absolute Purpose, or Pure Purpose, or Inner Purpose, etc."[42] The term central to dialectic substance is *purpose*.

---

[36] Ibid., *p. 29.*
[37] Ibid.
[38] Ibid., *p. 31.*
[39] Ibid., *p. 32.*
[40] Ibid.
[41] Ibid., *p. 34.*
[42] Ibid., *p. 35.*

Substance as the context of the speech is the source of the subject matter for the speech, of the motives and attitudes of the speaker, and of the strategies or rhetorical devices used by the speaker. The structural tools—identification and pentad—are useful in determining and describing both the substance of the speech and the speaker's rhetorical strategies. The critic is able to uncover the substance of the speech and the rhetorical strategies used by the speaker for three reasons: (1) because verbal symbols are meaningful acts that are strategies reflecting the attitudes of the speaker, (2) because these attitudes represent the speaker's acceptance and rejection of the present hierarchy of society, and (3) because acceptance and rejection results in the eternal process of guilt, purification, and redemption for society. The total interrelationship of terms and processes represents Kenneth Burke's dramatistic approach to rhetoric.

In addition to the basic dramatistic structure of his rhetorical system, Burke discusses various special rhetorical elements. The two most significant ones for rhetorical criticism are the forms of style and the levels of symbolic action. These special devices aid in describing the dramatistic process but are subordinate to the process. In *Counter-Statement* Burke indicates that form "is an arousing and fulfillment of desires."[43] Form provides sequence—one portion of the speech prepares the audience for another part. The kinds of form that Burke discusses are syllogistic and qualitative progression, repetitive form, conventional form, and minor or incidental form.[44] Because each speaker will structure his speech differently, various kinds of form aid the critic in establishing patterns for the development of the dramatistic process that takes place. Syllogistic progression is a step-by-step method of presenting an argument: "To go from A to E through stages B, C, and D is to obtain such form."[45] Qualitative progression is more subtle in its development. The speaker's ideas progress through the construction of a mood or a quality rather than in a step-by-step manner. Repetitive form is the process of restating a principle in a slightly different manner. The speaker may vary the details of the support with each restatement but the principle is consistent. Conventional form is the persuasive appeal resulting from "form as form." A syllogism or analogy has appeal simply as form, independent of the argument constructed. Any work also has minor or incidental forms "such as metaphor, paradox, disclosure, reversal, contraction, expansion, bathos, apostrophe, series, chiasmus—which can be discussed as formal events in themselves."[46]

---

[43] *Kenneth Burke,* Counter-Statement, *Chicago, University of Chicago Press, 1957, p. 124.*
[44] Ibid., *pp. 124–126.*
[45] Ibid., *p. 124.*
[46] Ibid., *p. 127.*

After describing the types of form, Burke indicates that there is both interrelation and conflict of forms. "Progressive, repetitive, and conventional and minor forms necessarily overlap."[47] However, the important thing is not that they overlap but that their use should be identified. The critic should discover the circumstances under which various forms are used. Not only do formal principles intermingle, they also conflict. Burke suggests that a writer may create a character who, according to the plot or the logic of fiction, "should be destroyed." But if this character is completely accepted by the audience, it may desire "the character's salvation." "Here would be a conflict between syllogistic and qualitative progression."[48] Burke also indicates that syllogistic and repetitive forms, as well as repetitive and conventional forms, may conflict. The form that the dramatistic process takes is another tool available to the rhetorical critic.

In describing the dramatistic process, the levels of symbolic action can also be of value to the critic. The speaker strategically selects verbal symbols that represent his attitudes and which he feels will be effective in inducing "identification" with his audience. One method of describing these symbols is to categorize them according to their level of symbolic action or level of abstraction. In *The Philosophy of Literary Form* Burke considers three levels of symbolic action: the bodily or biological level, the personal or familistic level, and the abstract level.[49] In *Rhetoric of Religion* he discusses "four realms to which words may refer. . . . First, there are words for the natural. . . . Second, there are words for the socio-political realm. . . . Third, there are words about words,"[50] and fourth, there are "words for the 'supernatural.' "[51] Again, these levels of symbolic action and realms for words will overlap in discourse, but the critic should identify their occurrence along with the circumstances in which they occur.

Burke's special devices of form, levels of symbolic action, and realms to which words may refer represent tools for rhetorical criticism that can be used in conjunction with his basic dramatistic structure of rhetoric. These techniques, taken together, constitute a definite system in which the substance of the speech and the rhetorical tools used by the speaker interlock.

Suggestions for the Rhetorical Critic

In executing rhetorical criticism the critic not only describes man's rhetorical efforts but also makes interpretative judgments based upon

[47] Ibid., *p. 128.*
[48] Ibid., *p. 129.*
[49] *Burke,* The Philosophy of Literary Form, op. cit., *pp. 31–33.*
[50] *Kenneth Burke,* The Rhetoric of Religion, *Boston, Beacon Press, 1961, p. 14.*
[51] Ibid., *p. 15.*

rhetorical norms or principles. Burke's dramatism gives the critic a method of analysis capable of establishing, at least tentatively, rhetorical norms through repeated application. Only through such application, sufficiently wide and varied to give a thorough test to the principles that arise, can critics be certain that they have a firm basis for judgment. But the long-range task necessitates consistent use of a critical vocabulary. The point of this essay has been to outline such a vocabulary and to suggest how the terms that compose it work together and aid the critic in making rhetorical judgments.

The following are some specific ways that a critic can use Burke's dramatistic rhetoric in establishing norms or principles for judgment:

1. Each of the Burkeian rhetorical concepts can be used to discover stylistic characteristics of a given speech or speaker.
2. The critic can observe the conditions under which various strategies are employed, thereby inductively constructing a theory about their use.
3. He can identify correlations in the use of various strategies to learn more about man's basic rhetorical tendencies and patterns. The relationship between substance and other strategies could be especially interesting.
4. The critic should study the stages in the dramatistic process—acceptance and rejection, and guilt, purification, and redemption—and determine how each stage is developed and stressed.
5. He should also discover the circumstances in which incompatible strategies are used—for example, when two terms from the pentad receive equal stress so that no discernible substance evolves.

Kenneth Burke's dramatistic approach to rhetoric provides the critic with a language and theoretical structure that allows him to describe man as he responds to his world and to understand man's basic rhetorical tendencies. With such a system the critic is able to make descriptive, interpretative judgments regarding the effectiveness of rhetoric.

A Pentadic Analysis of Senator Edward Kennedy's Address to the People of Massachusetts, July 25, 1969
by David A. Ling

On July 25, 1969 Senator Edward Kennedy addressed the people of the state of Massachusetts for the purpose of describing the events surrounding the death of Miss Mary Jo Kopechne. The broadcasting net-

From the *Central States Speech Journal*, XXI, 2 (Summer 1970), 81–86. Used by permission of the author. Dr. Ling is professor of speech at Central Michigan University.

works provided prime time coverage of Senator Kennedy's address, and a national audience listened as Kennedy recounted the events of the previous week. The impact of that incident and Kennedy's subsequent explanation have been a subject of continuing comment ever since.

This paper will examine some of the rhetorical choices Kennedy made either consciously or unconsciously in his address of July 25th. It will then speculate on the possible impact that those choices may have on audience response to the speech. The principle tool used for this investigation will be the "Dramatistic Pentad" found in the writings of Kenneth Burke.

The Pentad and Human Motivation

The pentad evolved out of Burke's attempts to understand the bases of human conduct and motivation. Burke argues that "human conduct being in the realm of action and end . . . is most directly discussible in dramatistic terms."[1] He maintains that, in a broad sense, history can be viewed as a play, and, just as there are a limited number of basic plots available to the author, so also there are a limited number of situations that occur to man. It, therefore, seems appropriate to talk about situations that occur to man in the language of the stage. As man sees these similar situations (or dramas) occurring, he develops strategies to explain what is happening. When man uses language, according to Burke, he indicates his strategies for dealing with these situations. That is, as man speaks he indicates how he perceives the world around him.

Burke argues that whenever a man describes a situation he provides answers to five questions: "What was done (act), when or where it was done (scene), who did it (agent), how he did it (agency), and why (purpose)."[2] Act, scene, agent, agency, and purpose are the five terms that constitute the "Dramatistic Pentad." As man describes the situation around him, he orders these five elements to reflect his view of that situation.

Perhaps the clearest way to explain how the pentad functions is to examine Burke's own use of the concept in *The Grammar of Motives*.[3] In that work, Burke argues that various philosophical schools feature different elements of the human situation. For example, the materialist school adopts a vocabulary that focuses on the scene as the central element in any situation. The agent, act, agency and purpose are

---

[1] *Kenneth Burke*, Permanence and Change (*Los Altos, California: Hermes Publications, 1954*), *p. 274.*
[2] *Kenneth Burke*, A Grammar of Motives and a Rhetoric of Motives (*Cleveland: The World Publishing Company, 1962*), *p. xvii.*
[3] Ibid., *pp. 127–320.*

viewed as functions of the scene. On the other hand, the idealist school views the agent (or individual) as central and subordinates the other elements to the agent. Thus, both the materialist and the idealist, looking at the same situation, would describe the same five elements as existing in that situation. However, each views a different element as central and controlling. In Burke's own analysis he further suggests philosophical schools that relate to the other three elements of the pentad: the act, agency and purpose. What is important in this analysis is not which philosophical schools are related to the featuring of each element. What is important is that as one describes a situation his ordering of the five elements will suggest which of the several different views of that situation he has, depending on which element he describes as controlling.

This use of the pentad suggests two conclusions. First, the pentad functions as a tool for content analysis. The five terms provide a method of determining how a speaker views the world. Indeed, this is what Burke means when he says that the pentad provides "a synoptic way to talk about their [man's] talk-about [his world]."[4]

A second conclusion that results from this analysis is that man's description of a situation reveals what he regards as the appropriate response to various human situations. For example, the speaker who views the agent as the cause of a problem, will reflect by his language not only what Burke would call an idealist philosophy, but he will be limited to proposing solutions that attempt to limit the actions of the agent or to remove the agent completely. The speaker who finds the agent to be the victim of the scene not only reflects a materialist philosophy but will propose solutions that attempt to limit the actions of the agent or to remove the agent completely. The speaker who finds the agent to be the victim of the scene not only reflects a materialistic philosophy but will propose solutions that would change the scene. Thus, an individual who describes the problem of slums as largely a matter of man's unwillingness to change his environment will propose self-help as the answer to the problem. The person who, looking at the same situation, describes man as a victim of his environment will propose that the slums be razed and its inhabitants be relocated into a more conducive environment. The way in which a speaker describes a situation reflects his perception of reality and indicates what choices of action are available to him.

The Pentad and Rhetorical Criticism

But what has all this to do with rhetoric? If persuasion is viewed as the attempt of one man to get another to accept his view of reality as

[4] Ibid., p. 56.

the correct one, then the pentad can be used as a means of examining how the persuader has attempted to achieve the restructuring of the audience's view of reality. Burke suggests how such an analysis might take place when he says in *The Grammar:* "Indeed, though our concern here is with the Grammar of Motives, we may note a related resource of Rhetoric: one may deflect attention from scenic matters by situating the motives of an act in the agent (as were one to account for wars purely on the basis of a 'warlike instinct' in people): or conversely, one may deflect attention from criticism of personal motives by deriving an act or attitude not from traits of the agent but from the nature of the situation."[5]

Thus, beginning with the language of the stage, the Pentad, it is possible to examine a speaker's discourse to determine what view of the world he would have an audience accept. One may then make a judgment as to both the appropriateness and adequacy of the description the speaker has presented.

Edward Kennedy's July 25th Address

Having suggested the methodology we now turn to a consideration of Senator Edward Kennedy's address of July 25th to the people of Massachusetts. The analysis will attempt to establish two conclusions. First, the speech functioned to minimize Kennedy's responsibility for his actions after the death of Miss Kopechne. Second, the speech was also intended to place responsibility for Kennedy's future on the shoulders of the people of Massachusetts. These conclusions are the direct antithesis of statements made by Kennedy during the speech. Halfway through the presentation, Kennedy commented: "I do not seek to escape responsibility for my actions by placing blame either on the physical, emotional trauma brought on by the accident or on anyone else. I regard as indefensible the fact that I did not report the accident to the police immediately."[6] Late in the speech, in discussing the decision on whether or not to remain in the Senate, Kennedy stated that, "this is a decision that I will have finally to make on my own." These statements indicated that Kennedy accepted both the blame for the events of that evening and the responsibility for the decision regarding his future. However, the description of reality presented by Kennedy in this speech forced the audience to reject these two conclusions.

Edward Kennedy—Victim of the Scene. The speech can best be examined in two parts. The first is the narrative in which Kennedy explained

---

[5] Ibid., *p. 17.*
[6] *This and all subsequent references to the text of Senator Edward Kennedy's speech of July 25, 1969 are taken from* The New York Times, *CXVII (July 26, 1969), p. 10.*

what occurred on the evening of July 18th. The second part of the speech involved Kennedy's concern over remaining in the U.S. Senate.

In Kennedy's statement concerning the events of July 18th we can identify these elements:

The scene (the events surrounding the death of Miss Kopechne)
The agent (Kennedy)
The act (Kennedy's failure to report immediately the accident)
The agency (whatever methods were available to make such a report)
The purpose (to fulfill his legal and moral responsibilities)

In describing this situation Kennedy ordered the elements of the situation in such a way that the scene became controlling. In Kennedy's description of the events of that evening, he began with statements that were, in essence, simple denials of any illicit relationship between Miss Kopechne and himself. "There is no truth, no truth whatever to the widely circulated suspicions of immoral conduct that have been leveled at my behavior and hers regarding that night. There has never been a private relationship between us of any kind." Kennedy further denied that he was "driving under the influence of liquor." These statements function rhetorically to minimize his role as agent in this situation. That is, the statements suggest an agent whose actions were both moral and rational prior to the accident. Kennedy then turned to a description of the accident itself: "Little over a mile away the car that I was driving on an *unlit* road went off a *narrow bridge* which had *no guard rails* and was built on a *left angle* to the road. The car overturned into a *deep pond* and immediately filled with water" (emphasis mine). Such a statement placed Kennedy in the position of an agent caught in a situation not of his own making. It suggests the scene as the controlling element.

Even in Kennedy's description of his escape from the car, there is the implicit assumption that his survival was more a result of chance or fate than of his own actions. He commented: "I remember thinking as the cold water rushed in around my head that I was for certain drowning. Then water entered my lungs and I actually felt the sensation of drowning. But somehow I struggled to the surface alive." The suggestion in Kennedy's statement was that he was in fact at the mercy of the situation, and that his survival was not the result of his own calculated actions. As an agent he was not in control of the scene, but rather its helpless victim.

After reaching the surface of the pond, Kennedy said that he "made repeated efforts to save Mary Jo." However, the "strong" and "murky" tide not only prevented him from accomplishing the rescue, but only succeeded in "increasing [his] state of utter exhaustion and alarm."

The situation described is, then, one of an agent totally at the mercy of a scene that he cannot control. Added to this was Kennedy's statement that his physicians verified a cerebral concussion. If the audience accepted this entire description, it cannot conclude that Kennedy's actions during the next few hours were "indefensible." The audience rather must conclude that Kennedy was the victim of a tragic set of circumstances.

At this point in the speech Senator Kennedy commented on the confused and irrational nature of his thoughts, thoughts which he "would not have seriously entertained under normal circumstances." But, as Kennedy described them, these were not normal circumstances, and this was *not* a situation over which he had control.

Kennedy provided an even broader context for viewing him as the victim when he expressed the concern that "some awful curse did actually hang over the Kennedys." What greater justification could be provided for concluding that an agent is not responsible for his acts than to suggest that the agent is, in fact, the victim of some tragic fate.

Thus, in spite of his conclusion that his actions were "indefensible," the description of reality presented by Kennedy suggested that he, as agent, was the victim of a situation (the scene) over which he had no control.

Kennedy's Senate Seat: In the Hands of the People. In the second part and much shorter development of the speech, the situation changes. Here we can identify the following elements:

    The scene (current reaction to the events of July 18th)
    The agent (the people of Massachusetts)
    The act (Kennedy's decision on whether to resign)
    The agency (statement of resignation)
    The purpose (to remove Kennedy from office)

Here, again, Kennedy described himself as having little control over the situation. However, it was not the scene that was controlling, but rather it was agents other than Kennedy. That is, Kennedy's decision on whether or not he will continue in the Senate was not to be based on the "whispers" and "innuendo" that constitute the scene. Rather his decision would be based on whether or not the people of Massachusetts believed those whispers.

Kennedy commented: "If at any time the citizens of Massachusetts should lack confidence in their senator's character or his ability, with or without justification, he could not, in my opinion, adequately perform his duties and should not continue in office." Thus, were Kennedy to decide not to remain in the Senate it would be because the people of

Massachusetts had lost confidence in him; responsibility in the situation rests with agents other than Kennedy.

This analysis suggests that Kennedy presented descriptions of reality which, if accepted, would lead the audience to two conclusions:

1. Kennedy was a tragic victim of a scene he could not control.
2. His future depended, not on his own decision, but on whether or not the people of Massachusetts accepted the whispers and innuendo that constituted the immediate scene.

Acceptance of the first conclusion would, in essence, constitute a rejection of any real guilt on the part of Kennedy. Acceptance of the second conclusion meant that responsibility for Kennedy's future was dependent on whether or not the people of Massachusetts believed Kennedy's description of what happened on the evening of July 18th, or if they would believe "whispers and innuendo."

Rhetorical Choice and Audience Response

If this analysis is correct, then it suggests some tentative implications concerning the effect of the speech. First, the positive response of the people of Massachusetts was virtually assured. During the next few days thousands of letters of support poured into Kennedy's office. The overwhelming endorsement was as much an act of purification for the people of that state as it was of Kennedy. That is, the citizenry was saying "We choose not to believe whispers and innuendo. Therefore, there is no reason for Ted Kennedy to resign." Support also indicated that the audience accepted his description of reality rather than his conclusion that he was responsible for his actions. Guilt has, therefore, shifted from Kennedy to the people of Massachusetts. Having presented a description of the events of July 18th which restricts his responsibility for those events, Kennedy suggested that the real "sin" would be for the people to believe that the "whispers and innuendoes" were true. As James Reston has commented, "What he [Kennedy] has really asked the people of Massachusetts is whether they want to kick a man when he is down, and clearly they are not going to do that to this doom-ridden and battered family."[7] The act of writing a letter of support becomes the means by which the people "absolve" themselves of guilt. The speech functioned to place responsibility for Kennedy's future as a Senator in the hands of the people and then provided a description that limited them to only one realistic alternative.

While the speech seemed to secure, at least temporarily, Kennedy's

---

[7] James Reston, "Senator Kennedy's Impossible Question," The New York Times, CXVII (July 27, 1969), section 4, p. 24.

Senate seat, its effect on his national future appeared negligible, if not detrimental. There are three reasons for this conclusion. First, Kennedy's description of the events of July 18th presented him as a normal agent who was overcome by an extraordinary scene. However, the myth that has always surrounded the office of the President is that it must be held by an agent who can make clear, rational decisions in an extraordinary scene. Kennedy, in this speech was, at least in part, conceding that he may not be able to handle such situations. This may explain why 57 per cent of those who responded to a CBS poll were still favorably impressed by Kennedy after his speech, but 87 per cent thought his chances of becoming President had been hurt by the incident.[8]

A second reason why the speech may not have had a positive influence on Kennedy's national future was the way in which the speech was prepared. Prior to the presentation of Kennedy's speech important Kennedy advisers were summoned to Hyannis Port, among them Robert McNamara and Theodore Sorensen. It was common knowledge that these advisers played an important role in the preparation of that presentation. Such an approach to the formulation was rhetorically inconsistent with the description of reality Kennedy presented. If Kennedy was the simple victim of the scene he could not control, then, in the minds of the audience that should be a simple matter to convey. However, the vision of professionals "manipulating" the speech, suggested in the minds of his audience that Kennedy may have been hiding his true role as agent. Here was an instance of an agent trying to control the scene. But given Kennedy's description of what occurred on July 18th such "manipulation" appeared unnecessary and inappropriate. The result was a credibility gap between Kennedy and his audience.

A third factor that may have mitigated against the success of this speech was the lack of detail in Kennedy's description. A number of questions relating to the incident were left unanswered: Why the wrong turn? What was the purpose of the trip, etc.? These were questions that had been voiced in the media and by the general public during the week preceding Senator Kennedy's address. Kennedy's failure to mention these details raised the speculation in the minds of some columnists and citizens that Kennedy may, in fact, have been responsible for the situation having occurred: the agent may have determined the scene. If this was not the case, then Kennedy's lack of important detail may have been a mistake rhetorically. Thus, while Kennedy's speech resulted in the kind of immediate and overt response necessary to secure his seat in the Senate, the speech and the conditions under

[8] "C.B.S. Evening News," C.B.S. Telecast, July 31, 1969.

which it was prepared appear to have done little to enhance Kennedy's chances for the Presidency.

Conclusion

Much of the analysis of the effect of this speech has been speculative. Judging the response of an audience to a speech is a difficult matter; judging the reasons for that response is even more precarious. The methodology employed here has suggested two conclusions. First, in spite of his statements to the contrary, Kennedy's presentation portrayed him, in the first instance, as a victim of the scene and in the second, the possible victim of other agents. Second, the pentad, in suggesting that only five elements exist in the description of a situation, indicated what alternative descriptions were available to Kennedy. Given those choices, an attempt was made to suggest some of the possible implications of the choices Kennedy made.

The Eagleton Affair: A Fantasy Theme Analysis
by Ernest G. Bormann

The 1972 presidential campaign was an exciting one for the rhetorical critic who wished to concentrate on the emotions and motives inherent in the symbolic action which was creating, no matter how momentary, a social reality for the American electorate. In a recent issue of the *Quarterly Journal of Speech* I described a fantasy theme approach to the discovery and analysis of rhetorical visions in the persuasion of campaigns and movements.[1] Examining the campaign of 1972 from that critical viewpoint reveals that the rhetoric provides an intriguing case study in the ways in which political unknowns become widely known persona.[2] In addition, the emotional evocation of dismay and frustration and the motivation commonly called *apathy* which characterized the chaining fantasies of those who earlier had been excited and impelled by the dramas of the New

From *The Quarterly Journal of Speech,* LIX, 2 (April 1973), 143–159. Used by permission of the author and the Speech Communication Association. Dr. Bormann is professor of speech-communication at the University of Minnesota.

[1] Ernest G. Bormann, *"Fantasy and Rhetorical Vision: The Rhetorical Criticism of Social Reality,"* 58 (December 1972), 396–407.

[2] *I am using the term* persona *in a relatively traditional way as the characters in a dramatic work, the speaker or voice of a poem or other literary work (although not necessarily the author), and the public personality or mask that an individual uses to meet a public situation. Since a fantasy theme analysis emphasizes the dramatizing aspects of rhetoric a critic needs a term to distinguish the public mask or personality of individuals from other aspects of their personality. The commonly used term* image *is unsatisfactory because it has been used for so many different concepts that it no longer communicates much of anything. Not only do professional persuaders tend to use the term* image *for such diverse purposes as to describe the overall general impression of a public figure, of institutions and of products, but scholarly commentators have also used the term to indicate a wide range of symbolic events. See for example, Daniel Boorstin,* The Image: A Guide to Pseudo-Events in America *(1961; rpt., New York: Harper and Row, 1964). See also*

Politics rhetorical vision are illuminated and clarified by a fantasy theme analysis of the campaign rhetoric of late summer and early fall. Finally, a critical analysis of the major fantasies that chained through the American electorate reveals the awesome power of the electronic media to provide, in the form of breaking news, the dramatizations that cause fantasies to chain through large sections of the American electorate and that thus provide the attitude reinforcement or change that results in voting behavior which elects a president and a vice president.[3]

No political campaign begins with a blank slate. Each party in a campaign has a well defined rhetorical vision which gives its members a sense of identity and which provides the basic assumptions upon which the party campaigns. On occasion a campaign will see the rise of a rhetorical vision that is either based upon elements from the older visions reshaped into a new pattern or one which rejects the older visions entirely. Often the emergence of a rhetorical vision is indexed by the term *new*. Such labels as the "New South," the "New Deal," and the "New Left" are shorthand ways of referring to rhetorical visions which have emerged clearly enough so people can refer to them and understand the basic elements of the vision when they are so characterized. As a new vision takes shape interested observers will often discuss and debate the meaning of a label. The rhetoric surrounding a new label when a vision is emerging is often couched in definitional terms but the real question at issue is essentially the character of the rhetorical vision indicated by the terms. A critic can often locate the period in history when a new rhetorical vision is emerging by searching for commentary relating to the meaning of labels such as "Black Power" and "New Left." Once the vision has clearly emerged and is well understood the discussion of definitions tends to die out. The campaign of 1972 is of particular interest because it saw the rise of and the demise of a rhetorical vision in the form of the "New Politics."

Kenneth Boulding. The Image *(Ann Arbor: University of Michigan Press, 1956).* Persona, *as I use the term, is restricted to the character a public person plays in a given dramatization. When the same persona acts in a series of fantasy themes that chain through the public, the cumulative dramatizations create a more generalized character or persona as part of the rhetorical visions of the various rhetorical communities. The concept of image also tends to be static whereas fantasy theme analysis requires a term which conveys the dynamic notion of action and also connotes the potential for change.*

[3] *There is a whole literature of "voting studies" which can be interpreted to prove that the electronic media do not influence voting behavior. The survey studies of voting behavior are apparently at odds with another large body of research literature which indicates that relatively short persuasive messages can change scores on attitude scales. For a summary of some of the conflicting studies see Carl I. Hovland, "Reconciling Conflicting Results Derived from Experimental and Survey Studies of Attitude Change," in Richard V. Wagner and John J. Sherwood, eds., The Study of Attitude Change (Belmont, California: Wadsworth Publishing, 1969), pp. 184–99. The problem with the voting studies is that the research designs tend to encourage the collection of data so gross that they miss the impact of television messages on the symbolic reality of the American electorate.*

What I propose to do in the brief confines of this essay is to concentrate on only one side of the campaign of 1972. I will begin with a capsule summary of the New Politics rhetorical vision of George McGovern and then move to a description and evaluation of one major fantasy that chained through the American electorate. My current estimate is that there were four major news events which provided the dramatization needed to start fantasies chaining through the communication system associated with the campaign of 1972. They were the Watergate Affair, the Eagleton Affair, the McGovern plan to give people 1000 dollars, and the peace negotiations of late October and early November. I will examine only the Eagleton Affair. The Eagleton fantasy theme was largely ignited and fueled by the mass media, particularly by television, and was an important factor in the dying out of the New Politics rhetorical vision.

Prior to the primary in California the McGovern character was a shadowy one in the fantasy themes of the general public. He was identified, if at all, as a dove, a stock antiwar persona. The pro-McGovern people, however, were deep into a rich rhetorical vision which contained powerful emotional evocations and compelling motives to action. The McGovern rhetorical vision had much in common with the over-reaching traditional Democratic Party rhetoric, particularly in its view of the Republicans as the party of the rich and the privileged oriented toward big business. Like the traditional Democratic vision, the New Politics rhetoric saw the persona of Richard Milhous Nixon as essentially that of Tricky Dick. The slogan that catches the persona in both visions is: Would you buy a used car from him? Despite the similarities, the McGovern vision has some crucial differences with the traditional Democratic Party rhetoric.

The rhetorical strategy which undergirded the McGovern vision was an emphasis upon the drama of character. The style and tone of the vision was that of high drama verging from melodrama to tragedy. The New Politics was more than politics according to its rhetoric; it was a movement that encompassed all of life from aesthetics to social style. Or, put another way, politics was elevated in the vision of the McGovernites into the fundamental and all important drama of life. The fantasy themes contained little humor, little irony, little satire. Potentially the scenario was one of tragedy or of glorious redemption in the mode of the mythic drama of the Christian religion. The rhetoric spoke of a turning point in history, of a "last chance," of no hope should the movement fail.[4]

[4] For a study of the New Politics rhetorical vision see Linda Putnam "The Rhetorical Vision and Fantasy Themes of McGovern Campaign Planners," Moments in Contemporary Rhetoric and Communication, 2 (Fall 1972), 13–20. The entire issue of Moments is devoted to the campaign.

The fantasy themes of the New Politics tended to be character sketches which stressed the moral superiority of the heroes and the evil nature of the villains. The vision had its roots back to the persona of clean Gene McCarthy and the 1968 campaign. The motives embedded in the rhetoric included a personal attachment to a persona of high ethical character for whom a participant would work and strong impulses to strive for such goals as ending the war, aiding the poor, the women, and the minorities. The emotional evocations of the vision were powerful and included admiration for a persona almost saintly in motivation and a hatred of the villainous devil figures. The McGovern rhetoric created a social reality which saw such villainous characters as Lyndon Johnson, Richard Daly, and Hubert Humphrey as the enemy. The vision saw both major parties as essentially corrupted by the war, both as racist and closed. The dream was of a purging of the Democratic party which would oust the bosses, the minions of the military-industrial complex, and the racist elements from all of society but particularly from the South.

As the McGovern Campaign grew more and more successful until its final triumph at the Miami convention, the vision solidified and the emphasis on villains became sharp and clear in the fantasy themes of the movement. The arch-enemy was Tricky Dick and his laughable hatchetman Spiro Agnew but these persona hovered in the background. The more tangible villains, the ones that were the main characters in the fantasy themes, were those symbolized by the Chicago convention of 1968 and these included the devil figures of Lyndon Johnson, Richard Daly, and Hubert Humphrey, all of whom stood for a closed convention, barricaded behind barbed wire, protected by police, a convention which barred the young, the poor, the blacks, the Chicanos, the Indians, and the women. Now the leadership of McGovern backed by the army of the formerly disenfranchised would defeat the old politicians.

The participants in the New Politics rhetorical vision saw themselves as a coalition of various liberation movements that would open the party and give power to the people. The style of the New Politics was openness, participation, community, and cooperation while the style of the old politics was closed, barricaded, unresponsive. The persona of McGovern in the vision of his followers before and during the Miami convention was that of St. George on a crusade. He was not really a politician. He was an honest, sincere, decent man who just happened to be in politics. The fantasy themes presented McGovern patiently working for party reform, opening it up to the people, standing courageously against the Vietnam war, and forging a dedicated and mighty army of hard-working volunteers who finally were to get their chance within the system. One salient scenario presented those who had been outside the walls in Chicago as on the floor in Miami.[5]

After Senator McGovern received the nomination the usual reconciliation of factions within the party in preparation for a campaign was made more difficult because of the collision of key elements of the old rhetorical vision of the Democratic Party with the rhetorical vision of the New Politics. The old vision saw labor at the core of the party; in the new vision, labor bosses such as George Meany were among the villains of the old politics. The labor movement was racist, conservative, and closed off from the poor and the minorities. In the old vision party regularity was a virtue. After all, the party was a coalition and the New Deal fantasy themes dramatized keeping the ethnic groups, the blacks, labor, and the South all under one umbrella. The new vision saw party regulars such as Mayor Daly of Chicago as the enemy. The new vision would sacrifice the racist South (symbolized in the persona of George Wallace) for the sake of the minorities. If the party was not purged the participants in the new vision were ready to leave the ranks.

Clearly, however, success at the polls required a new rhetoric which would transcend the two competing visions within the party. Unless the rhetoricians within both visions could find a strategy to fashion a coherent drama on the basis of the common materials within the two visions, one undergirded by the old mythic assumptions of the traditional rhetoric, the party had little possibility of winning the election in November.

The McGovern leadership group began the rhetorical effort at the convention itself. Fantasy themes began to chain through the McGovern delegations around the theme of *pragmatism.* Invoking the ultimate legitimizer of most political party visions, that is, winning an election, a move was made by the McGovern forces to create a unifying rhetoric.

How could a new vision be fashioned to transcend the competing visions within the party? The McGovern campaign strategy was to continue to emphasize *persona.* In an article entitled, "St. George Prepares to Face the Dragon," *Time* magazine noted, "The McGovern Campaign will be similar to the personality-oriented, almost evangelical appeal for faith in a candidate that was unsuccessful for Edmund Muskie,"[6] Why did the rhetoricians of the New Politics decide to emphasize fantasy themes based on persona? Certainly they knew that the Muskie candidacy has foundered and that the reports of Muskie's lashing out at a newspaper publisher and breaking down in tears had dramatized a fantasy theme which chained

[5] Time *reported this version: "Ted Pillow, 20, Iowa, vividly recalls the 1968 Democratic Convention in Chicago. He was one of the protesters outside the hall, taunting police, throwing rocks, breaking windows and fleeing down side streets. Last week in Miami Beach he was sitting inside the convention hall as a member of the Iowa delegation." (24 July 1972), p. 27.*
[6] *24 July 1972, p. 9.*

through the American electorate and severely damaged the Muskie persona. Emphasis on persona is a risky strategy unless the heroes can remain, in the words of presidential candidate Eisenhower when Richard Nixon was accused of double dealing in 1952, as "clean as a hound's tooth." What alternatives were open to the planners of the McGovern persuasion? They could have chosen to emphasize *scene*. The refrain of McGovern's acceptance speech was, after all, "Come home America." They could have emphasized *action* which was the strategy adopted by official Republican campaign rhetoricians.

In many respects the emphasis on persona is understandable. The rhetorical strategy had worked in the primaries and brought success at Miami. The nature of the opposition indicated that an emphasis on persona was a strong rhetorical ground. If the challenger selected action as a strategy he would be at a distinct disadvantage since the president is, by the nature of the office, where the action is. Then, too, the breaking news surrounding the Nixon persona during the 1970s presented the president in action scenarios. The Nixon persona had withdrawn troops from Vietnam, signed an arms limitation agreement with Russia, agreed to seating Red China in the United Nations, traveled to China, and traveled to Russia. In the campaign, many fantasy themes were available to dramatize the president as persona in action.[7] In addition, the scenarios in which the president was the leading actor were not all that unattractive. The persona of Nixon, on the other hand, seemed a good target for attack. Certainly those who participated in the New Politics vision and hated ·the persona would be tempted to frame rhetorical dramas in which Richard Milhous Nixon was the center of attack.

The unifying rhetoric at the Miami convention began first with the emphasis on a villainous persona. Bad as Mayor Daly might be, and bad as Hubert Humphrey might be, still, those deep in the New Politics vision ought to join forces with their old enemies within the party in order to defeat Nixon. As much as the old politicians disliked the new, would it be worth four more years of Nixon to carry on the internal battle? Senator McGovern developed the theme in his acceptance speech, "Now to anyone in this hall or beyond who doubts the ability of Democrats to join together in common cause I say never underestimate the power of Richard Nixon to bring harmony to Democratic ranks."[8]

The second rhetorical strategy which began at the convention was to find a new symbolic persona who could bridge the competing visions.

[7] *Which is precisely what many of the paid political announcements produced by the Committee to Reelect the President did do. Their persuasion on television tended to show montages of the President at work in the White House, walking along a beach with his wife, walking on the Great Wall of China, meeting with the Russian leaders, and so forth.*

[8] *CBS Network Coverage of the Convention, 14 July 1972.*

Traditionally the nomination of a vice president serves as a symbolic weld-ing of the disparate visions within a party. The McGovern team began its search with Theodore Kennedy who would have been ideal except the Kennedy persona was so potent it might have overshadowed the candi-date himself. When Kennedy would not accept, the McGovern forces turned to an attractive young senator with strong ties to the competing Democratic rhetorical vision, strong with labor, strong with the regulars, but also young and attractive, much in the mold of the Kennedy persona. Senator Thomas Eagleton seemed to provide a personality which could be fashioned into a transcending figure.

With the decision in Miami to select Senator McGovern the campaign for the votes of the electorate got under way in all seriousness. Now the fantasy themes that would chain out through the American public would carry with them the motives to go or not to go to the polls and, just as importantly, to vote for either the Nixon persona or the McGovern. For many the McGovern public figure was vague and shadowy at this stage; even the professionals of the media had not formed a clear rhetorical vision of that portion of the campaign dominated by McGovern. The tradi-tional rhetorical vision of the professional news person and political com-mentator was that of politicians as essentially ambitious people out to get elected, scrambling about for political advantage, generally hypocritical. Wise inside-dopesters such as professionals never were taken in by ap-pearances and never took a politician's words for anything more than smokescreen.[9]

The Miami convention provided the first big chance for newsmen to chain out on the dramatic action of events. One of the first fantasies to spread through the media was that of the McGovern machine. Some me-

[9] *The concept of inside-dopester is explained in detail in David Riesman, Nathan Glazer, and Reuel Denney,* The Lonely Crowd: A Study of the Changing American Character *(1950; rpt. Garden City, N.Y.: Doubleday Anchor Books, 1953), pp. 210– 17). Riesman, Glazer, and Denny note, "There are political newsmen and broad-casters who, after long training, have succeeded in eliminating all emotional re-sponses to politics and who pride themselves on achieving the inside-dopesters' goal: never to be taken in by any person, cause, or event" (p. 211). For further discussion of the media professionals' vision and its motive which causes them to seek out the dramatic, see David Berg,* "Rhetoric, Reality, and Mass Media," *Quar-terly* Journal of Speech, *58 (October 1972), 255–63. Richard Dougherty, McGov-ern's press secretary during the 1972 campaign, bitterly castigated the press be-cause they gave McGovern "a hell of a beating." He was referring to the Eagleton Affair. He concluded, "The man they offered up for the people to judge was a caricature of the real man, and most reporters knew it. I would guess that 90 percent of the news people who covered McGovern voted for him. Why, if that was their ultimate personal judgment of him, could they not pass that judgment on to the public? Hard news wouldn't let them. It wouldn't have been objective reporting. You can write about a candidate who is being sneaky and bumbling: that's objective reporting. But you can't write about a candidate who is being kind and forgiving: that's editorializing." "The Sneaky Bumbler,"* Newsweek, *8 January 1973, p. 7.*

dia reports dramatized the New Politics as just the Old Politics honed to a sharper than usual edge.[10] Larry Hart and Frank Mankiewicz emerged as characters in the drama; for some reporters, they were the able people who had harnessed the high idealism of a lot of students and new leftists and poor people to a volunteer organization that had outmachined Richard Daly himself.

In a sense the fantasy fit in well with the media vision where no politician is as virtuous as he or she maintains and the ultimate legitimatization for politics is winning. They had miscalculated McGovern's chances for many months. Now he had won. Now he was legitimatized. The fantasy accounted for their miscalculation and also put St. George the self-righteous in his place. They had miscalculated because they had not realized that the McGovern machine had such a thorough and effective grass roots organization. As the McGovern forces crushed all attempts to seat the contested delegates from the opposition and as it began to play down issues like women's liberation, abortion reform, and amnesty, the fantasy began to chain through the media that McGovern had worked a miracle and that he just might be ruthless enough and his machine might be well organized and disciplined enough to pull off a second miracle and unseat the President.

McGovern and the television cameras went to Sylvan Lake in the Black Hills of South Dakota to rest and plan for the campaign. The American public had every reason to pay more attention to the McGovern persona as it was portrayed by the media for he was now a potential president. The confident nominee had barely time to be seen on the television screens enjoying a well-earned rest in the serene mountains when a dramatic news story broke.

On Tuesday, July 25, 1972, Senators McGovern and Eagleton called a press conference in the Black Hills. That evening, Roger Mudd, sitting in for Walter Cronkite, asserted that an obviously "nervous" Eagleton had told the press of his mental health problems. The producers cut to a film clip of McGovern and Eagleton walking with a parade of supporters, workers, and newsmen to a building where the press conference was to be held. The film cut to Eagleton's statement which included the crucial phrase, "on three occasions in my life I have voluntarily gone into hospitals as a result of nervous exhaustion." As the press conference continued, the network producers cut to shots of Mrs. Eagleton and Mrs. McGovern, to Senator McGovern watching Senator Eagleton, and to the questions and answers of both senators. In answer to a question, Senator McGovern said, "I don't have the slightest doubt about the wisdom of my judgment in selecting him as my running mate nor would I have any hesitancy at all in

[10] Time magazine, for example, headlined its convention cover story: "Introducing . . . the McGovern Machine" (24 July 1972), p. 18.

trusting the United States Government in his hands." The producers cut back to Roger Mudd who said that the decision to hold a press conference "obviously followed a major crisis in the McGovern camp and apparently was precipitated by persistent rumors that Senator Eagleton had a possible drinking problem."[11]

The story of Senator Eagleton's nervous exhaustion was top priority news on all three major television networks. Key excerpts from the press conference were shown to the huge audiences that watch the dinner time and late evening news. David Brinkley on his journal on NBC mentioned electric shock therapy and noted that "it has been a long time since the office of the vice president got so much attention."

The story had the human interest required to chain out in all directions through the American electorate. Millions of people who had little impression of the McGovern persona and less of the Eagleton presence were suddenly attending to both. How far would the fantasy chaining process go? How compelling would the drama become for the majority of the American people? The answer to such questions depended partly upon new developments or, in dramatic terms, new complications and partly upon the rhetorical art with which the drama was presented.

Senator McGovern had expressed support of Senator Eagleton in the first press conference. In long film clips on all networks reporters questioned McGovern again and again about the nature and extent of his support for Senator Eagleton. ABC News on July 26th featured an interview between Harry Reasoner and George McGovern. They were pictured seated at a picnic table beside Sylvan Lake. Reasoner asked, "Can you flatly say that if you had known this before you selected him your decision would have been the same?" McGovern, "Absolutely. There would have been no difference." A bit later in the interview Reasoner asked, "Suppose Senator Eagleton in the face of whatever reaction there is to this announcement wanted to leave the ticket, what would you attitude be, sir?" McGovern answered, "I would . . . I would discourage that. I don't want him to leave the ticket. I think . . . uh . . . I think we're going to win the election. I think he's going to be a great vice president. If anything were to happen to me I think he would make a great president. I will do everything I can to discourage any move on his part to leave the ticket. He's not considering that, though, by the way." Later in the same newscast, Howard K. Smith asserted, "In the chat with reporters today McGovern escalated numerically his support of Eagleton. He was, he said, '1000 percent resolved to keep Eagleton as a running mate.' "

Where is the rhetorical dimension of the Eagleton Affair? Assuming, as I do, that rhetoric is an art, where is the artistry? Both the strategists for

[11] My reconstruction of the network newscasts is based upon videotape recordings of the broadcasts. I will identify the date and the network in the text.

McGovern and for Nixon made rhetorical choices affecting the dramatizations that were presented to the Amerian people. The media professionals also made rhetorical choices. Thus the dramatizations that appeared on the television network news programs on July 25, 26, 1972, were joint artistic efforts of the Nixon, McGovern, and media rhetoricians. (The same process was, of course, operating in radio, newspapers, and magazines.)

The age of mass communication has seen the rise of a unique mass rhetoric fashioned by groups of artists of strangely mixed objectives and approaches. Both McGovern and Nixon publicists had a clear persuasive objective and a general notion of how they would have liked to have their position presented on network television news. The two antagonistic groups had to make their rhetorical choices with an eye both to the symbolic responses of the other and to those of the "objective" media professionals. In one sense, if the Nixon forces gained, the McGovern forces would lose, and vice versa, but the essentially zero-sum game of the two campaigns was mediated by the electronic journalists with their own intent and the success or failure of each candidate's rhetoric was to some extent dependent upon the cooperation of the media professionals. The fact that the network news seldom dramatizes events as advocates wish they would accounts for some of the anger and disillusionment with the media.

McGovern's people made some of the more important early rhetorical choices. They decided to hold a press conference. Since their man was a newly nominated presidental candidate they could, if they were skillful in the way they planned and conducted the news briefing, assure themselves of free television time and of a very large audience.

The McGovern strategists certainly could select the scene for the drama. They might select, as they did, Sylvan Lake in the Black Hills of South Dakota; they could have chosen Washington, D.C., or Barnes Hospital in St. Louis. The strategists could also select the persona of the drama. Should, for instance, the McGovern persona take center stage with the Eagleton persona standing silently by? Should the McGovern persona be separated in space, for example, Senator Eagleton holding a press conference in Washington, D.C., with McGovern simply answering reporters' questions in the Black Hills? Should other persona be present? To indicate the extent of the rhetorical choices, one possible alternative for the McGovern rhetoricians could have been to have Senator Eagleton make his announcement from Barnes Hospital with a battery of doctors who would testify as to his medical record and to the present state of his mental health. The McGovern persona might then have stayed in South Dakota and expressed noncommital concern.

The contemporary stategist for mass audiences needs to be skilled at estimating the response of the mediating professionals and should draft messages, select time, scene, and persona with a view to getting the fantasy themes most likely to chain dramas persuasive to his position on prime-time evening television. In estimating the responses of the professionals and in their decisions as to persona, scene, and dialogue, the McGovern forces made some rhetorical errors of the first magnitude. They selected as the scene the Black Hills vacation retreat of Senator McGovern and they had the McGovern persona at the Eagleton press conference. Not only that, but McGovern made a strong statement supporting Senator Eagleton.

Everything about the setting, the persona, and the lines they spoke reinforced the support of McGovern for the Eagleton persona and his identification with it. In addition, no other major persona of the Democratic Party was on the scene to lend symbolic unity and support to the decisions.

On television the media reporters appeared delighted if a bit incredulous about the McGovern support and kept prodding for clear and unequivocal expresssions of such commitment. Clear expressions of positions in risky situations are rare in political campaigns but they are good news just because of that fact.

Having gotten the McGovern persona, epitome of the New Politics, to express unequivocal support, the rhetoricians of the media went to work to create a good news story. The media professionals evaluate a good story as one having the ability to hold the interest of the audience. Human interest stories dramatizing fantasies that chain out through the public raise television ratings.

When the McGovern forces called the news conference and staged the opening scenes of the Eagleton Affair they, of course, lost control of the story. They could affect future symbolic events but they could not completely control them as they could with the dramatizations they presented during the television time they purchased.

The stage was now set for dramatic action from the Nixon persona. In line with the overall Nixon rhetoric of playing down persona and emphasizing action, the Nixon decision came quickly and was delivered by the surrogate persona of MacGregor. On July 26th, film clips of MacGregor appeared on several network newscasts. On CBS MacGregor claimed that the Republicans knew about Eagleton's health record but, even before the announcement, had received "a mandate and directive from the President that no one connected with him in any way governmentally or politically would have any comment whatever to make."

The Nixon rhetoricians would keep the persona of the President out of the drama. By doing so they gained little but they also risked little. In a situation where the public opinion polls indicated that Nixon was ahead, the temptation to take a conservative position and not gamble was strong. The Nixon forces had, however, taken the same rhetorical stance in the much closer campaigns of 1960 in regard to the religion of his opponent,

John F. Kennedy. On that occasion the rhetoricians for Kennedy had set a scene in Houston, Texas, and provided the Kennedy persona with dramatic antagonists in the form of a group of protestant ministers. Kennedy made a strong direct defense of his religion and its role in his functioning as a president should he be elected. The fantasy theme of the Kennedy confrontation apparently chained out to the advantage of the Senator. His campaign organization subsequently bought time to show an artistic dramatization of the scene in the form of a documentary film on television stations throughout the country. In 1960 the low-risk decision nonetheless cost the campaign of Richard Nixon votes because of the artistry with which the skillful Kennedy rhetoricians presented the media and the public with further dramatizations.[12]

After the news conference announcing Eagleton's medical history the media rhetoricians had their turn. They operated under stringent time limitations. Their dramatic format was that of an "anchor man" with star status, the Walter Cronkite, Roger Mudd, David Brinkley, John Chancellor, Harry Reasoner, Howard K. Smith persona, playing the leading role and the lesser reporters serving as narrative voices, a mass media chorus, speaking from the scene of action. The narrator convention serves to tie the events that are dramatized into some sequence and fit them into an interpretative frame. The convention of narrator generally requires that the persona of the reporter be an "objective" voice.

The illusion of objectivity is created by the device of having the narrator attribute all editorial comments, unverified statements of fact, and opinion statements to others. Thus when the narrator chorus began to assert that pressure was building up on McGovern to dump Eagleton, the narrators always attributed the information to others. For instance, NBC reporter Bob Clark mentioned from South Dakota (July 26th) that the Democrats were keeping a clam public face but "off the record, a number of Democrats agree with most Republicans that the Eagleton disclosures have hurt the McGovern ticket." NBC reporter John Dancy asserted (July 27th) that "one of McGovern's top aides privately calls the disclosure a blow to their chances." ABC reporter Sam Donaldson maintained (July 28th) that the "Senator's top staff men are deeply worried about the Eagleton affair." Reporter Stephen Geer of ABC added, "McGovern's advisors are concerned because he has been on the defensive." Since the narrators present an objective voice they seem removed from partisanship and thus, in a political campaign, are often more credible sources than most of the partisan campaigners.

The dramatic structure of the network news in presenting an event such

[12] See for example Harold Barrett, "John F. Kennedy Before the Greater Houston Ministerial Association," Central States Speech Journal, 15 (November 1964), 259–66).

as the Eagleton developments consists of a lead-in by the star persona, a narrative commentary with short film clips of dramatic action presented either by the star or one of the lesser reporters, and transitional material usually provided by the anchor man. The media rhetoricians' artistry in selecting from the materials presented by the campaign rhetoricians and their skill in weaving new materials of their own manufacture into an interpretative frame has much to do with the way the story catches on and chains through the public (or fails to do so) and with the persuasive impact of the chaining fantasy. Whether the drama as it chains through the general public contains motives to vote for Nixon or for McGovern or for neither is of less importance to the media rhetoricians than that it does chain widely. The charge that the media are liberal or conservative or systematically biased in their dramatizations is too simple, in my estimation. The media rhetoricians are hard-headed dramatists more interested in success at the box office than in partisan political persuasion.

A drama to be compelling requires plausibility, action, suspense, and sympathetic characters. Developing audience interest in a drama which emphasizes character takes time and time is in short supply on the evening news (as contrasted, say, with daytime television dramas where time is in long supply and where the dramas tend to emphasize character at the expense of action). Because of the shortage of time on the evening news the skillful media professional tends to go for conflict and suspense. The McGovern rhetoricians thus were operating under a handicap because of their decision to emphasize character when it came to utilizing one of the most credible outlets of television, that of the network sponsored newscasts.

Now the professional news people began the artistic interpretation of the events. The day after the original press conference several networks interviewed a former alcoholic, Senator Hughes of Iowa, identified as Senator Muskie's vice presidential choice had the Maine Senator received the nomination. Hughes was supportive of Eagleton's staying on the ticket and asserted that the American people had "outgrown this immaturity" in regard to mental health. The Hughes persona was one of the few characters selected by the media rhetoricians which fit the fantasy that Eagleton's mental health problems were no drawback for the ticket and that, indeed, the American people would be sympathetic to him. Early in the breaking news the fantasy theme that Eagleton should stay on the ticket and demonstrate the maturity of the electorate appeared to be a viable one. For the most part, however, the professional journalists sought to dramatize the conflict.

CBS News on July 27th did an able and artistic job of finding and presenting the controversy. Roger Mudd began by listing all of the major newspapers which had come out for Eagleton's withdrawal. Reporter Duke interviewed Mankiewicz and Hart and both reiterated that the decision to keep Eagleton had been made and that it was irrevocable. Next CBS cut to an interview with Howard Metzenbaum, identified as a Cleveland attorney and millionaire fund raiser for McGovern. Metzenbaum was sought out to dramatize the story that the Eagleton disclosures were hurting fundraising for the McGovern campaign. Metzenbaum was of the opinion that Eagleton would do the right thing and resign. He said, "Unfortunately the American people don't comprehend the nature of psychiatric treatment." If Eagleton would resign, he felt, the election might still be won because, fortunately, "in time people do forget." Henry Kimmelman, identified as finance chairman, also appeared briefly, but took no firm stand.

Next the CBS News cut to a long interview with an articulate and attractive persona identified as Matthew Troy, Democratic leader in Queens, New York, and strong McGovern supporter. Troy asserted that people "are really scared that you're giving the power possibly to a man to . . . to . . . to destroy this world with a nuclear holocaust if he buckles under the pressure of the presidency." Troy had urged McGovern to drop Eagleton. What did McGovern reply? "He told me he was standing by Senator Eagleton and he would not walk away from him."

When a fantasy begins to catch on with a large group of people the evidence of public interest tends to draw outsiders into the social reality for self-serving reasons. Thus an unexpected outside complication is often a component of a major fantasy drama.

On July 27th an unexpected and dramatic complication entered the Eagleton affair when the crusading reporter persona, Jack Anderson, charged that Senator Eagleton had a record of arrests for drunken driving. Another press conference was arranged for Senator Eagleton and again he received extensive coverage on the three major networks. On ABC News Eagleton testified that he had no record of arrests for drunken driving. Eagleton said, "Mr. Anderson's statement to that effect is, in blunt but direct English, a damnable lie." The camera cut to a tight face shot catching the Senator from the hairline to just below the chin. He passed the test of the close-up lens. Clear-eyed, with jutting jaw, he reaffirmed his innocence and his firm resolve to stay in the race and vindicate himself and his record. "I have never been more determined in my life about any issue than I am today about remaining on this ticket. I'm not going to bow to Mr. Anderson. I'm not going to let a lie drive me from this ticket."

The Eagleton rhetoricians had responded brilliantly to the Anderson complication. The Senator's denial, his demeanor during the newscasts, his statements of resolve were appealing. The problem, or course, was the possibility that the crusading reporter was right. For the McGovern rhetoricians the new complication was probably extremely traumatic.

The media peoples' decisions to interview certain individuals (and not

others) and then feature these interviews as part of the dramatizations gave
them considerable control over the cast of the drama. Picking the cast gave
the electronic journalists some control over the action line and the conflict
and suspense that resulted and, thus, over the potential of the story to be a
big one—that is, to catch the attention of many people and remain in featured position on the evening news for a number of days. The media production people cast such individuals as Hart, Mankiewicz, Metzenbaum,
and Troy into the fantasy as it unfolded. Some of the breaking news was, of
course, beyond the control of media production crews. They were restricted
by the nature of the material presented by the McGovern and Nixon persuaders. They were also restricted by such intrusions as Jack Anderson's
charges. Nonetheless, the room for artistry and the options available are
very large and much larger than a rhetorically naive viewer watching the
hard news unfold at dinner time is likely to realize. They chose to feature the
Troy persona which emerged on television as an attractive, articulate, and
dramatic antagonist to keeping Eagleton on the ticket. The Metzenbaum
persona was less articulate and less attractive but presented the more
"pragmatic" and cynical political position most effectively.

Clearly the fantasies chaining through the media professionals, given
their rhetorical vision of politics, influenced their selection of persona. Although I do not have copies of all segments of all networks' newscasts
covering the Eagleton Affair, I do have the bulk of them. In none of the
segments that I have studied do the networks present a medical authority
on Senator Eagleton's health. His doctor never appeared on network
news. In many other dramatizations regarding the health of a president,
vice president, or candidate for those offices, the reporters often go to
medical men. When President Eisenhower had his heart attack medical
material was a prominent part of the news. When Lyndon Johnson was a
national leader his health was often discussed. In the instance of the
Eagleton candidacy, however, the networks featured the drama of pressure from within the Democratic Party for his resignation.

On July 28th the ABC News showed Eagleton saying, "I'm not quitting.
I'm not getting out . . . No, you're not going to get me out of this race . . .
never . . ." Howard K. Smith reported that Eagleton was considering taking
his case to the people on television as Richard Nixon had in 1952. On
NBC News an excerpt from Eagleton's press conference showed Eagleton
alluding to the fact that John Kennedy had taken the case of his Catholicism to the people and won and that maybe Eagleton would do something
to lay to rest the mental health issue.

By the 28th, fantasy themes which would be supportive and contain
sympathetic emotional evocations were beginning to chain out in the media in regard to Eagleton's candidacy. Like Richard Nixon in 1952, he
might take his case directly to the people. Like John Kennedy in 1960 he

might lay to rest another bigoted political prejudice. On his evening commentary, Howard K. Smith urged McGovern to keep Eagleton since he had expressed 1000 percent support for his running mate and "a switch now would give a wish-washy impression that would be bad for a presidential candidate." Smith noted that Abraham Lincoln and Winston Churchill had suffered from spells of melancholia which probably should have been treated professionally and yet one had been the greatest president ever and the other had been the greatest prime minister. Eagleton's colleagues in Washington found him to be, "outstandingly vigorous and easy to work with. Moreover, a couple more undocumented charges like Jack Anderson's yesterday and there is going to be a big backlash of sympathy for Eagleton. McGovern would look pretty bad disowning him just as the public may be about to turn for him."

Clearly, some media professionals were beginning to interpret the drama in ways which presented McGovern-Eagleton as heroic figures striking a blow for public understanding of mental problems. The blunder of the McGovern rhetoricians was one of timing in that they temporized and allowed the drama to unfold for too long in this age of electronic media. Here the symbolic role of money in a political campaign in the United States played an important part in the developing rhetoric. In the vision of many citizens, partisans, media professionals, and independents, the drama of politics is rife with monetary implications. In some visions elections can be bought but in most, campaigns require money. The election of 1972 saw a great preoccupation with campaign contributions and financing. The media decision to dramatize the impact of the Eagleton medical record on campaign contributions is indicative of the interpretive frames of the visions. Money symbolizes both the potential for success and for corruption; it symbolizes both the potential for the selling of a president and the selling out of a presidential candidate.

Now the McGovern rhetoricians had to accommodate to the fantasies chaining out from the media dramatization to the effect that their campaign was doomed because, already behind, they would find the sources of campaign funding drying up. At this juncture, I have no evidence of the extent to which the fantasy chained through those groups with the greatest likelihood of contributing to the campaign. Should the fantasy have chained out through those groups, however, it contained motives that would, indeed, shut off contributions. Thus fantasy theme analysis provides a clue to the mechanism by which the oftnoted phenomenon of the self-fulfilling prophecy comes about. The media, by dramatizing the possible impact of the Eagleton Affair on contributions, could trigger fantasy chains among potential contributors which would cause opinion leaders among potential contributors (such as Metzenbaum) to report to the McGovern headquarters that contributions would dry up.

Having allowed the drama to unfold to the point where the fantasies about monetary support were moving through the public, the potential loss of funds became a factor that the McGovern rhetoricians had to deal with on several levels. They had to estimate what, indeed, would happen to the flow of money if they decided to keep the Eagleton persona, which had by now been invested with great symbolic power, power to work either for or against their drive to persuade the American electorate to vote for McGovern. They also had to anticipate what would happen to American public opinion if they severed the powerful Eagleton persona from the ticket. Finally, if they removed Eagleton, could they find a suitable persona to replace him? Could they find a persona with the potential to repair the damage to their rhetoric of character? (Notice that I am phrasing all issues and options in rhetorical terms and such important questions as the ability of the candidate as administrator are bypassed. My analysis focuses on symbolic action. If rhetorical decisions clash with other considerations then a campaign organization might, of course, make a poor rhetorical decision in order to achieve other goals. For instance, if McGovern's forces had had evidence that Senator Eagleton's health was such that he could not assume the duties of president, they might decide to remove him from the ticket even if the Eagleton persona had become so attractive that the decision would have deleterious rhetorical effects.)[13]

The suspense continued to build up over the weekend. On July 30th, Jean Westwood said she thought Eagleton should resign. Eagleton continued to assert his decision to stay in the race. The news reporters intensified their reports of inside information and rumors of pressures and counterpressures.

On July 31st, CBS News reported that Senator McGovern would announce a final decision soon and that he would meet with Senator Eagleton. Bruce Morton of CBS asserted that Eagleton would argue to stay and McGovern would urge him to leave. The dramatization of CBS News on July 31st, however, clearly was based upon the theme that Eagleton would leave the ticket. CBS carried a feature on how the new vice presidential candidate would be chosen and reported rumors of who the new candidate might be. The commentator, Barry Serafin, narrated films of Eagleton in shirtsleeves on the telephone. Serafin reported that Eagleton was receiving many supportive letters. Eagleton said he had a good case to present but, according to Serafin, in McGovern he would have a difficult jury.

ABC News reported a poll of Democratic state chairmen and vice chairmen in which eighteen voted to keep Eagleton, seventeen voted to have him step down, and ten refused to comment. NBC News featured a three-

---

[13] *This is a purely hypothetical possibility; I have no information indicating this to be the case.*

way discussion with Chancellor asking questions of Fred Briggs who had been with Eagleton, and John Dancy who had been with McGovern. Chancellor asked Dancy why did not McGovern ask Eagleton to step down immediately? Why has it gone on this long? (Actually the first report came on the 25th so the Eagleton Affair had been before the public less than a week. Yet when one views the recordings of the television news shows for the week, the saturation coverage does give the impression that the drama has gone on for a long time.) Dancy answered that at first they were going to try to "tough it out" and, of course, that had not worked.

Howard K. Smith's commentary assumes that Eagleton will be dropped and Smith dramatizes a fantasy theme most damaging to McGovern's persona. Eagleton had hardened his resolve to stay. "McGovern, 1000 percent resolved to keep Eagleton, in his phrase, turned to marshmallow and let his national chairwoman tell the public Eagleton had to go," Smith said. He further asserted that McGovern's reputation for leadership had been "sullied by too much yielding to pressure. His 1000 dollar welfare plan went the way his 1000 percent support of Eagleton did."

Tuesday, August 1st, 1972, just a week after it had opened, the drama of the Eagleton Affair came to a close. John Chancellor opened the NBC Evening News with, "Good evening on a day that will make at least an important footnote in American history; for the first time ever, a vice presidential candidate has resigned." The CBS Morning News that day had featured an interview between Barry Serafin and Senator Eagleton. Eagleton said, "I've come out of it stronger than I went in. I'm . . . I'm at peace with myself. . . . This may be the most important week of my life. I did the job. I took the heat and I endured."

Tuesday was highlighted by a dramatic irony. CBS featured a news conference with Eagleton and Jack Anderson. The crusading reporter had checked and found his charges were unsubstantiated. He had done the Senator an injustice. "I owe him a great and humble apology." Eagleton made no comment on the film clip but the narrator asserted that Eagleton had said the books were closed on the matter.

Senator McGovern cancelled a talk he had scheduled to give the American people on television in regard to the matter of his decision to drop Eagleton.

David Brinkley, in his journal feature, delivered a bitter attack on politicians without mentioning any candidates by name. But straight out of the inside-dopester vision of the media professional, Brinkley asserted that most people do not believe politicians, that the public had turned sour on politics and politicians.

Eric Sevareid editorialized on CBS to the effect that Eagleton's career at the political summit had been one of the shortest on record but in the course of it he had become a household word and created thousands of friendly sympathizers. Sevareid used the term "Eagleton Affair" in his commentary. He asserted that Eagleton was burned by a fire started by the press and that a fire started by the press could be very hot indeed but that in the long run it was cleansing. Certainly, Sevareid concluded, the affair indicated that the press was not biased in a liberal direction as some had charged.

Sevareid was right. Much of the dramatization (the fire) was an artistic creation of the media. The impact of the media selection of characters and action lines upon the fantasy themes was considerable. When the announcement came of Eagleton's departure from the ticket the dramatic suggestion that McGovern had bowed to pressure for the crassest of political reasons, namely, loss of campaign financing from big contributors, was very strong. Certainly the emphasis on characters relating to financing and allusions to financing on NBC were most important.

The most sympathetic character in the drama turned out to be Tom Eagleton.[14] He came through the network news as an open, cleancut, if intense, young man. He recounted his medical problems in some detail. When he decided to stay in the race he was forthright and forceful in his statement about the American people being intelligent and sophisticated about mental health and ready to be understanding about his problem.

The Anderson charges which Eagleton denied put the characterization of Eagleton to the test. If Anderson had proved his charges then the Eagleton persona would have received a damaging blow to its credibility; then all of Eagleton's other testimony, no matter how convincingly portrayed on television, might be wrong also. With a discredited Eagleton persona in the drama, McGovern might not have appeared as the "heavy." When Anderson publicly admitted the charges were untrue, however, the Eagleton character increased its credibility and the halo effect of a man falsely accused increased the sympathy one felt about his earlier statements regarding his mental health.

Finally, as the pressure mounted, Eagleton remained adamant that he would stand firm and fight the charges through to ultimately win the election and thus justify his faith in the American people. A dramatic protagonist who has a clear and sympathetic goal and is willing to stand firm and fight for it, even at a personal sacrifice, is sympathetic. When the Eagleton persona was finally cut down, it was by the one force in the drama he could not fight, the presidential candidate himself.

The persona of Jack Anderson as presented in the Eagleton drama is important not only because it emerged as the antagonist but also because it was a key character in other fantasies relating to the campaign and to

[14] *On July 28, 1972, Howard K. Smith on ABC reported results of a poll showing 60% sympathetic to Eagleton although there was a 30% negative response to McGovern for being caught unaware of Eagleton's past medical history.*

the drama of corruption within the Nixon administration. Jack Anderson had been playing the role of the fearless investigative reporter discovering hidden deals and secret papers. The Anderson character was thus a kind of hero in the rhetorical vision of the New Politics. Now, he was playing the part of an antagonist. As the breaking news presented Anderson as an unethical opportunist trying to gain personal advantage by making unsupported charges, his persona was tarnished. Certainly, within the vision of the New Politics with its emphasis on high ethical standards for persona, the revelations were damaging to Anderson. The tension within the vision came from the role that Anderson was already playing in the fantasy themes related to other matters such as the I.T.T. Affair. If Anderson was lacking in credibility in the Eagleton Affair, could he be a hero in the I.T.T. Affair? How much the loss of credibility of the Anderson persona had to do with the apparent difficulty of the media and the McGovern campaign to make the Watergate Affair chain through the general public in a way that damaged Nixon is an interesting question beyond the scope of this essay. Certainly, however, the Watergate Affair deserves extended criticism from a fantasy theme frame of analysis.

The greatest damage of all the persona came, of course, to that of George McGovern. First there was his rather offhand response. The matter, he said, was really not very important but the decision was made to stop rumors. The persona asserted strong and unequivocal support for his vice president. The question, however, was never closed. The possibility apparently lingered. The continued rumors of possible "dumping" and then the indirect story that McGovern had signalled Eagleton that he would like a resignation persisted. Eagleton stood firm. Finally, after what seemed like pressure from his more unsavory supporters, the persona made his decision to remove Eagleton for apparently base political motivations.

What motives were embedded in the scenario for those who chained into it? For the New Politics vision the fantasy of Eagleton was more than the rhetoric could absorb in plausible fashion. The leading character in a rhetorical vision which had emphasized persona was revealed as a politician acting in expedient fashion. The motivational pivot went out of the vision. The only remaining spur to action was hatred for the villainous personae such as Nixon and Agnew, but that was much less impelling by itself than when coupled to admiration for a persona of high ethical power. Some continued to work for the candidacy of George McGovern, but for many with less inertia and momentum, the motivation was replaced with *apathy*. Thus the rising tide of apathy can partially be accounted for by the disillusionment of those who participated in the New Politics, responding after the Eagleton Affair. For those who had little impression of George McGovern before the Eagleton Affair became staple fare on television, the fantasy brought reactions of distrust and lack of confidence in the persona.[15]

The viewer who came to sympathize with Eagleton would have every reason to distrust the McGovern character. Eagleton had placed trust in McGovern in a situation of considerable personal risk. The McGovern persona had promised support in Eagleton's time of trial and then when the situation came to a dramatic climax, had "dumped" him. Inconsistency was a highlight of the dramatic action.

The one major piece of prepared campaign persuasion which tapped into the legacy of the Eagleton Affair was produced by the Democrats for Nixon and is, I believe, possibly the most skillful piece of persuasion produced during the campaign. Although the short spot announcement does not mention Eagleton by name, the suggestion connects very strongly with the residue of the Eagleton fantasy. McGovern's picture is presented on a weather vane-like stand. McGovern's position on a question is mentioned, the picture swings to face in the opposite direction and the narrator asserts that McGovern has shifted his position. Several shifts of the picture from left to right ensue until at the end of the announcement the picture is twirling in circles. The power of the announcement comes from its skillfully tapping into the rhetorical visions created by chaining fantasies such as the Eagleton Affair.

Coming at a strategic time in the campaign, capturing prime-time television for long film clips of the characters of the drama, the fantasy chained throughout the electorate and the role that the McGovern persona played in the fantasy as it was participated in by large segments of the American public was one of an inconsistent, inept, untrustworthy and politically expedient politician. Since the original dramatization was played out on the network evening news, on radio, and in the supposedly objective columns of the print media, the credibility of the presentation was high. The damage done to a rhetoric based on persona was considerable. Other breaking news events were subsequently interpreted along the same lines and the New Politics rhetorical vision lost its power to generate commitment and action and to attract new converts.

[15] *Columnists Evans and Novak reported a late October poll by interviews in three San Fernando Valley, California, precincts selected by elections analyst Richard Scammon. They interviewed 118 voters and found twenty-four registered Democrats decidedly for Nixon. The basic reasons given were the perception that McGovern was ideologically extreme and "habitual complaints about McGovern's inconsistency."* The Minneapolis Star, *1 November 1972, editorial page. The Harris Survey reported in early November to the effect that McGovern's credibility problem still plagued him. By 61 to 29 percent, a majority agreed with the statement that "he does not inspire confidence as a president should."* The Minneapolis Star, *6 November 1972, p. 1A.*

5
TWO META-CRITICAL APPROACHES

In describing and illustrating three perspectives for rhetorical criticism—traditional, experiential, and new rhetorics—we have shown that through the 1950s and 1960s the consensus for the traditional paradigm dissolved. During these decades numerous rhetorical theories and methods competed for acceptance, creating the pluralism of the 1960s and 1970s in which critics were free to use almost any method they deemed effective for the analysis of a given rhetorical act. Of course conflicts over rhetorical theories and methods were frequently aired; some of these seem especially symptomatic of the failure of any single rhetorical theory and method to gain a consensus as "the paradigm."

One such conflict erupted when a series of critics analyzed Richard M. Nixon's Vietnam Address of November 3, 1969, from three different perspectives. The various critiques are well worth study. Taken together they present an intriguing contrast of methods although we would caution against taking them as ultimate examples. Essays by Karlyn Kohrs Campbell, Robert P. Newman, and Hermann G. Stelzner[1] might be well classified as experiential; James W. Chesebro and Sandra E. Purnell reflect a Burkeian new rhetorics perspective.[2] Largely in response to Newman and especially to Campbell, Forbes I. Hill took the traditional neo-Aristotelian approach.[3] Needless to say, the critics evaluated Nixon's efforts very differently, and Campbell and Hill presented their differences in a journal debate. Campbell indicated that "Hill has invited controversy by attacking the methodologies of other critics," and she suggested "the conflict highlights certain important issues in rhetorical criticism."[4] One important issue in the debate was whether a neo-Aristotelian critic should "interpret the *Rhetoric* as if it were consistently amoral."[5] Here we would like to suggest

[1] Campbell, "Richard M. Nixon: 'Vietnamization: The President's Address on the War," in Critiques of Contemporary Rhetoric, Karlyn Kohrs Campbell (ed.), Belmont, California, Wadsworth Publishing Co., 1972, pp. 50–56; Newman, "Under the Veneer: Nixon's Vietnam Speech of November 3, 1969," The Quarterly Journal of Speech, LVI, 2 (April 1970), 168–78; and Stelzner, "The Quest Story and Nixon's November 3, 1969 Address, " The Quarterly Journal of Speech, LVII, 2 (April 1971), 163–72.

[2] Chesebro and Purnell, "The Rhetoric of Alignment: Can Nixon's Quest for Power Unite the Nation?" Speaker and Gavel, VII, 3 (March 1970), 77–84.

[3] "Conventional Wisdom—Traditional Form: The President's Message of November 3, 1969," The Quarterly Journal of Speech, LVIII, 4 (December 1972), 373–86.

[4] " 'Conventional Wisdom—Traditional Form': A Rejoinder," The Quarterly Journal of Speech, LVIII, 4 (December 1972), 451.

[5] "Reply to Professor Campbell," The Quarterly Journal of Speech, LVIII, 4 (December 1972), 459.

that Hill in supporting an amoral interpretation was reflecting the "objective" stance of the traditionalist and was, as we said earlier, "giving the speaker his purpose," while Campbell in supporting a moral stance was taking the more "subjective" position of the experientialist. We believe that various differences between the two parties in this controversy can best be explained in terms of the two different perspectives they accepted for rhetorical criticism. This more than anything else accounts for the varied interpretations of Aristotle.

Other journal debates reflected similar differences in perspective. Barbara Ann Harris responding to Robert L. Scott's, "Rhetoric That Postures: An Intrinsic Reading of Richard M. Nixon's Inaugural Address,"[6] argued that Scott's extremely negative evaluation of Nixon's Inaugural was not really limited to an "intrinsic" reading, and she implied Scott lacked the necessary objectivity for criticism.[7] In still another conflict, Parke G. Burgess objected to Jeanne Y. Fisher's "A Burkean Analysis of the Rhetorical Dimensions of a Multiple Murder and Suicide" in part because her analysis broadened the concept of rhetoric too much.[8] Again, in both of these controversies the major difference was that of perspective—Harris was more traditional, while Scott was experiential; and Burgess was experiential, while Fisher was a Burkeian new rhetorician.

These debates reflected what appeared to be an increasing concern for methodology within rhetorical criticism. Further evidence of this concern not only for method, but also for "fresh methods" was Judith S. Trent's "A Synthesis of Methodologies Used in Studying Political Communication." Trent reviewed fifty-four articles on political communication from national and regional speech-communication journals between 1967 and 1973. After classifying these articles into six categories: (1) candidates and their rhetoric; (2) message analysis; (3) media; (4) voter behavior; (5) over-all campaign setting and strategy; and (6) methodology, she then assessed the research within each category. Since many of these studies were rhetorical criticism, her conclusions should be of interest to us. Her analysis highlighted studies with "rigorous research methods" and "fresh forms" as examples scholars should use as models.[9] The result was a recommendation for non-traditional methods that were explicitly defined so that other researchers could either follow the analysis step by step or possibly replicate the study.

[6] "Rhetoric That Postures: An Intrinsic Reading of Richard M. Nixon's Inaugural Address," Western Speech, XXXIV, 1 (Winter 1970), 46–52.

[7] "The Inaugural of Richard Milhous Nixon: A Reply to Robert L. Scott," Western Speech, XXXIV, 3 (Summer 1970), 231–34. See also, Scott's "Response to Barbara Ann Harris," pp. 235–36.

[8] "Murder Will Out—But as Rhetoric?" The Quarterly Journal of Speech, LX, 2 (April 1974), 224–31.

[9] A Synthesis of Methodologies Used in Studying Political Communication," Central States Speech Journal, XXVI, 4 (Winter 1975), 287–97.

Finally, in response to the "proliferation of methods," David L. Swanson presented a "metatheory of rhetorical criticism" in two essays, "A Reflective View of the Epistemology of Critical Inquiry" and "The Requirements of Critical Justification." In a detailed epistemological analysis, Swanson identified critics as employing first or second order representational systems, that is, systems using concepts with invariant meanings, or systems using situationally constructed meanings for action. He also detailed two stances: the mundane stance, which takes the world as is, that is, as fundamentally unproblematic, and the critical stance, which takes the world as mediated interpretively. Using these variables, Swanson described and illustrated four forms that critical explanations may take. Swanson clearly saw his effort as an important first step in establishing order out of the confusion of methods in rhetorical criticism.[10]

We acknowledge Swanson's contribution to the literature of criticism, and we support his motive to make criticism more orderly. However we question whether his framework which was worked out deductively will be accepted by critics as the basis for evaluating rhetorical theories and methods. At this point there is little evidence that significant numbers of critics are willing to accept any rhetorical theory, method, or even metatheoretical framework. Commitments to theories and methods that could be perceived as inferior within Swanson's framework (traditional—first order and mundane) are too strong to be easily given up. Nor would critics be willing to accept the implied negative evaluation. Also, other theories and methods could be divided among two or more of his four forms making it unlikely that critics following these approaches would adopt his framework.

Consistent with but not identical to Swanson's concern for metatheory (theory about theory), we see critical methods that can cut across the three perspectives for criticism evolving at another level of abstraction. To label this supra-level we would like to borrow Ernest Bormann's term "meta-criticism." He employed this term to show "that the meta-critic stands above or beyond the first level of communication."[11] The "standing above" posture provides an overview that can potentially subsume other activities. Indeed, the subsuming of various sorts of methods to larger concerns has occurred in rhetorical criticism.

We see two strong tendencies that might well be called meta-critical views: searching for "genres" and seeking to typify the rhetoric of various "movements." The terms we indicate have been used by critics for years, but it is only comparatively recently that they have evolved to become

---

[10] "A Reflective View of the Epistemology of Critical Inquiry," Communication Monographs, XLIV, 3 (August 1977), 207–19; and "The Requirements of Critical Justifications," Communication Monographs, XLIV, 4 (November 1977), 306–20.
[11] "Rhetorical Criticism and Significant Form: A Humanistic Approach," in Form and Genre: Shaping Rhetorical Action, Karlyn Kohrs Campbell and Kathleen Hall Jamieson (eds.), Falls Church VA., The Speech Communication Association, p. 167.

general frames capable of containing critical work undertaken from the three perspectives we have discussed.

In dealing with these two meta-critical frames, we are not asserting that they are the only possible actualizations of a supra-level for rhetorical criticism. They are the two readily discernible and actively pursued at the present time. We shall discuss each in turn.

The Concern with Genre

The term "genre" is a classification traditionally associated with literary criticism. Since 1965, with the impetus of Edwin Black's influential book, *Rhetorical Criticism,* the term has gained a marked currency in the discipline of speech-communication.[12] Even though Black did not present a detailed definition of "genre" he used it to describe congregations of rhetorical discourses that share similar strategies, situations, and effects.[13] So generic criticism transcends a specific rhetorical act and establishes a type or class of rhetorical discourse. Black discussed the genres of exhortation and argumentation, but his concern was for these types of discourse themselves rather than for generic criticism itself.

Lawrence Rosenfield's "A Case Study in Speech Criticism: The Nixon-Truman Analog" (see chapter 3) carried generic criticism one step further. Still assuming rather than demonstrating the existence of genre, Rosenfield compared two speeches of the same type or genre. We should note that the classification of "mass-media apologia" is a contemporary adaptation of a traditional category.[14] This genre encouraged use of both traditional and contemporary forms as the basis for generic criticism. Further, critics quickly moved from a comparison of two specches to an analysis of numerous acts of a given type.[15]

Generic criticism received further impetus when one of the elements noted by Black, the situation, was defined rhetorically by Lloyd F. Bitzer as "a complex of persons, events, objects, and relations presenting an actual or potential exigence which can be completely or partially removed if discourse, introduced into the situation, can so constrain human decision or action as to bring about the significant modification of the exigence."[16] Bitzer's definition shifted critics' attention away from the traditional speaker orientation toward rhetoric as a response to a situation. Of course, other

---

[12] *Black discusses "the movement study" as a standard approach to criticism, and he introduces "generic" studies as a new frame, "An Alternate Frame of Reference" in* Rhetorical Criticism: A Study in Method, New York: Macmillan, 1965; and reprinted by the University of Wisconsin Press, Madison, Wisconsin, in 1978.

[13] Ibid., *pp. 132–35.*

[14] "A Case Study in Speech Criticism: The Nixon-Truman Analog," Speech Monographs, *XXXV, 4 (November 1968), 435–50.*

[15] *James W. Pratt, "An Analysis of Three Crisis Speeches," Western Speech, XXXIV, 3 (Summer 1970), 194–202.*

[16] *"The Rhetorical Situation," Philosophy and Rhetoric, I, 1 (January 1968), 6.*

theorists disagreed with Bitzer's definition of the rhetorical situation,[17] but the impact of his analysis was to ground generic criticism in the situation, influencing critics to define rhetorical forms based upon responses to various situations.

Bitzer's situational grounding of generic criticism was reinforced by Kathleen M. Hall Jamieson in her article "Generic Constraints and the Rhetorical Situation" when she extended situation to include "antecedent rhetorical forms."[18] Jamieson was the first critic to tie overtly Bitzer's "rhetorical situation" to generic criticism, but as she did she made "genre" the dominant term.

A major step in the evolution of generic criticism occurred in 1976 when the Speech Communication Association sponsored a conference on " 'Significant Form' in Rhetorical Criticism." The request for papers linked "form" and "genre" together: "The phrase 'significant form' is intended to refer to recurring patterns in discourse or action including, among others, the repeated use of images, metaphors, arguments, structural arrangements, configurations of language or a combination of such elements into what critics have termed 'genres' or 'rhetorics'."[19] The outcome of the conference was the book *Form and Genre: Shaping Rhetorical Action* edited by Karlyn Kohrs Campbell and Kathleen Hall Jamieson who in the introduction traced the evolution of generic criticism and established a general definition for genre—"a classification based on the fusion and interrelation of elements in such a way that a unique kind of rhetorical act is created."[20] *Form and Genre* reflects the diversity of generic criticism since it includes Herbert W. Simons' "scientific approach" as well as Ernest Bormann's "humanistic approach."[21]

The diversity of generic criticism is further reflected in the types of studies conducted in its name. Genres such as apology,[22] anti-aggressor rhetoric,[23] and radical strategies[24] have been studied. Also, in examining

[17] Richard E. Vatz, "The Myth of the Rhetorical Situation," Philosophy and Rhetoric, *VI, 3 (Summer 1973), 154–61; and Scott Consigny, "Rhetoric and Its Situations," Philosophy and Rhetoric, VII, 3 (Summer 1974), 175–86.*

[18] "Generic Constraints and the Rhetorical Situation," Philosophy and Rhetoric, *VI, 3 (Summer 1973), 162–70.*

[19] Form and Genre, p. 3.

[20] Ibid., p.25.

[21] " 'Genre-alizing' about Rhetoric: A Scientific Approach," and "Rhetorical Criticism and Significant Form: A Humanistic Approach," Form and Genre, pp. 35–50 and 165–87.

[22] Rosenfield's "Nixon-Truman Analog," (see chapter three) and Sherry Devereaux Butler, "The Apologia, 1971 Genre," Southern Speech Communication Journal, *XXXVII, 3 (Spring 1972), 281–89.*

[23] Lawrence W. Rosenfield, "George Wallace Plays Rosemary's Baby," The Quarterly Journal of Speech, *LV, 1 (February 1969), 36–44.*

[24] James W. Chesebro, "Rhetorical Strategies of Radicals," Today's Speech, *XXI, 2 (Winter 1972), 37–48.*

"rhetoric of" Black Power, desecration, confrontation, the new left, and the radical right[25] critics have highlighted important genres. Both the diverse and transcendent nature of generic criticism is reflected in the fact that generic studies have employed methods from all three of the perspectives we have previously discussed. Leff and Mohrmann who present a traditional neo-Aristotelian criticism of Lincoln's Cooper Union Address see genre theory as strengthening traditional criticism because it can serve "as a corrective to some defects in the neo-Aristotelian mode."[26] Two very different examples of experiential generic studies are Rosenfield's "Nixon-Truman Analog" and Hermann Stelzner's analysis of Richard Nixon's Vietnam Address as a "quest."[27] And a good example of a Burkeian new rhetorics study is Robert L. Ivie's "Presidential Motives For War."[28] Genre transcends the specific rhetorical act and critical perspective to establish a type of rhetoric.

We have chosen two essays to illustrate the theory and application of generic criticism. Jackson Harrell and Wil A. Linkugel in "On Rhetorical Genre: An Organizing Perspective" not only review the nature of genre but also attempt "to describe a methodology which can potentially aid in the systematization of research into rhetorical genres." They present this methodology so rhetorical scholars can "serve a theory-building function as well as a critical one." For an essay applying generic criticism, we have turned to the most common concern of generic study—speeches of apology. B. L. Ware and Wil A. Linkugel in "They Spoke in Defense of Themselves: On the Generic Criticism of Apologia" present and illustrate a psychological theory of self-defense as a "conceptualization of the apologetic genre into subgenres" that should aid critics in comparing rhetoric in various apologetic situations.

---

[25] Parke Burgess, "The Rhetoric of Black Power: A Moral Demand," The Quarterly Journal of Speech, LIV, 2 (April 1968), 122–33; Richard J. Goodman and William I. Gordon, "The Rhetoric of Desecration," The Quarterly Journal of Speech, LVII, 1 (February 1971), 23–31; Robert L. Scott and Donald K. Smith, "The Rhetoric of Confrontation," The Quarterly Journal of Speech, LV, 1 (February 1969), 1–8; Leland M. Griffin, "The Rhetorical Structure of the 'New Left' Movement: Part I," The Quarterly Journal of Speech, L, 2 (April 1964), 113–35; Barnet Baskerville, "The Cross and The Flag: Evangelists of the Far Right," Western Speech, XXVII, 4 (Fall 1963), 197–206; and Dale G. Leathers, "Fundamentalism of the Radical Right," Southern Speech Communication Journal, XXXIII, 4 (Summer 1968), 245–58.

[26] Michael C. Leff and G. P. Mohrmann, "Lincoln at Cooper Union: a Rhetorical Analysis of the Text," The Quarterly Journal of Speech, LX, 3 (October 1974), 346–58; and G. P. Mohrmann and Michael C. Leff, "Lincoln at Cooper Union: A Rationale for Neo-Classical Criticism," The Quarterly Journal of Speech, LX, 4 (December 1974), 459.

[27] See note 22 and note 1 above.

[28] "Presidential Motives For War," The Quarterly Journal of Speech, LX, 3 (October 1974), 337–45.

Movements Approach

The second meta-critical approach is "movements." Traditionally, critics studied a single speech or an individual orator, and at times this speaker orientation would be extended to include a group of speakers over a period of time. In such studies, the period of history was usually highly significant, so the historical approach usually was dominant with neo-Aristotelian language woven into the description at appropriate times. The first volume of *A History and Criticism of American Public Address* illustrates this tendency. As a context for a study of the "Leaders in American Public Address" five studies developed "The Historical Background of American Public Address." All were period studies in which the historical method dominated with one study, "Woman's Introduction to the American Platform,"[29] clustering a group of speakers together within a period.

Breaking from this traditional perspective, Leland M. Griffin launched movement studies with his article "The Rhetoric of Historical Movements." Raising and answering questions Griffin described the focus, scope, process of analysis, evaluation, and synthesis of reports on movements. Griffin indicated that the primary objective was "to discover . . . the rhetorical pattern inherent in the movement selected for investigation." But he also saw a larger purpose because he indicated that when movement studies become "a discrete field for research" broader rhetorical patterns may be identified.[30]

In establishing a new approach to rhetorical criticism, Griffin's departure—his rejection of a speaker orientation—was not radical because he maintained an historical orientation; he recommended isolating "the rhetorical movement within the matrix of the historical movement.[31] Yet his shift in emphasis to conceive histories "in terms of movements rather than of individuals" is significant and led to what has become a major effort of rhetorical criticism in the 1960s and 1970s.

Not only did Griffin initiate theoretical and methodological probes for movement studies, he also was the first to apply these methods. His two earliest studies, "The Rhetorical Structure of the Antimasonic Movement" and "The Rhetorical Structure of the 'New Left' Movement, Part I," for years served as models for movement studies. In tracing the Antimasonic Movement, Griffin was able to describe both *aggressor* and *defendant* rhetoricians through the periods of *inception, rhetorical crisis,* and *consummation,* so eventually he was able to arrive at a judgment about the movement.[32] In contrast, Griffin was only able to consider the inception

---

[29] W. Norwood Brigance (ed.), A History and Criticism of American Public Address, Vol. 1, New York, McGraw-Hill, 1943.

[30] "The Rhetoric of Historical Movements," The Quarterly Journal of Speech, XXXVIII, 2 (April 1952), 188.

[31] Ibid., 185.

[32] In The Rhetorical Idiom, ed. Donald C. Bryant, New York, Russell & Russell, 1966, pp. 145–60.

period for the "New Left" making it more difficult to perceive a pattern for the movement and draw conclusions about it.[33]

Leland Griffin's next contribution to movement studies, "A Dramatistic Theory of the Rhetoric of Movements," represented a more radical shift from the traditional perspective. Instead of an historical orientation, Griffin adopted a Burkeian new rhetorics approach in developing "a dramatistic model, or abstraction, of the structure of a movement's rhetoric."[34] Griffin's new model retained the important elements of his initial article but replaced the historical context with Burke's "dramatistic" process demonstrating how movement studies meta-critically transcend and often cut across the three perspectives we have discussed.

Acknowledging Griffin's contribution to movement studies and attempting to provide a direction for future studies, Herbert W. Simons drew upon sociological theory to present a "broad framework within which persuasion in social movements, particularly reformist and revolutionary movements, may be analyzed."[35] Simons's framework took a leader-centered approach toward rhetorical requirements, problems, and strategies. It is interesting that Simons recommended a return to a focus upon individuals (leaders) even though the orientation would be sociological rather than neo-Aristotelian or historical.

After Griffin separated movement studies from the traditional perspective and after Simons recommended the use of sociological theory, it was not surprising that other critics attempted to bring movements back into the traditional mode again. Dan F. Hahn and Ruth M. Gonchar in "Studying Social Movements: A Rhetorical Methodology" described how the Aristotelian concepts of ethos, logos, pathos, and style could be adapted to study movements.[36]

Finally, Robert S. Cathcart, also responding to the variety of approaches to the study of movements, argued that a rhetorical, not an historical or social-psychological definition of movements was required because the definition would determine the theory and methods for studying movements. Referring to Griffin's presentation of a Burkeian "dramatistic" approach to movements, Cathcart identified the essential attribute of a movement—"*a dialectical tension growing out of moral conflict* [emphasis in original]."[37] This attribute, then, was his starting point for a definition, "It is

---

[33] "The Rhetorical Structure of the 'New Left' Movement: Part I," The Quarterly Journal of Speech, L, 2 (April 1964), 113–35.

[34] "A Dramatistic Theory of the Rhetoric of Movements," in Critical Responses to Kenneth Burke, ed. William H. Rueckert, Minneapolis, University of Minnesota Press, 1969, p. 456.

[35] "Requirements, Problems, and Strategies: A Theory of Persuasion for Social Movements," The Quarterly Journal of Speech, LVI, 1 (February 1970), 11.

[36] "Studying Social Movements: A Rhetorical Methodology," The Speech Teacher, XX, 1 (January 1971), 44–52.

[37] "New Approaches to the Study of Movements: Defining Movements Rhetorically," Western Speech, XXXVI, 2 (Spring 1972), 87.

this *reciprocity or dialectical enjoinment in the moral arena* which defines movements and distinguishes them from other dramatistic forms."[38]

Having seen the evolution of theory and methods for movement studies, we would like to underscore some of the diverse applications throughout the 1960s and 1970s. A review of movement studies will quickly reveal an overlap with the "generic" approach because a number of the types of rhetoric were established by social movements. This overlap simply highlights our discussion in the experiential perspective that category systems are not discrete but arbitrarily establish classifications by emphasizing some characteristics and omitting others. The turmoil of the 1960s resulted in numerous studies focusing on the goals of movements—civil rights, Black Power, student rights, antiwar, women's liberation, and sexual liberation.[39] Most of these movements are in some way related to the "New Left." In contrast, other critics studied what might be called right wing rhetoric in groups like the Nazis, the radical right, and militant deism.[40] Other critics approached movements by studying the strategies used to attain their ends.[41]

The diversity of movement studies can be demonstrated in another way. In a meta-critical approach, studies can be found that represent all three critical perspectives. We have already mentioned that Griffin's model maintained a traditional historical approach even as it rejected a speaker orientation and that Hahn and Gonchar recommended a return to neo-

[38] Ibid.

[39] *David M. Jabusch, "The Rhetoric of Civil Rights,"* Western Speech, XXX, 3 (Summer 1966), 176–84; and Philip C. Wander, "The Savage Child: The Image of the Negro in the Pro-Slavery Movement," Southern Speech Communication Journal, XXXVII, 4 (Summer 1972), 335–60; Burgess, "Black Power"; Robert L. Scott and Wayne Brockriede, The Rhetoric of Black Power, New York, Harper & Row, 1969; and Arthur L. Smith, The Rhetoric of Black Revolution, Boston, Allyn & Bacon, 1969; James R. Andrews, "Confrontation at Columbia: A Case Study in Coercive Rhetoric," The Quarterly Journal of Speech, LV, 1 (February 1969), 9–16; and James F. Klumpp, "Challenge of Radical Rhetoric: Radicalization at Columbia," Western Speech, XXXVII, 3 (Summer 1973), 146–56; J. Robert Cox, "Perspectives on Rhetorical Criticism of Movements: Antiwar Dissent, 1964–1970," Western Speech, XXXVIII, 4 (Fall 1974), 254–68; Brenda Robinson Hancock, "Affirmation by Negation in the Women's Liberation Movement," The Quarterly Journal of Speech, LVIII, 3 (October 1972), 264-71; and Karlyn Kohrs Campbell, "The Rhetoric of Women's Liberation: An Oxymoron," The Quarterly Journal of Speech, LIX, 1 (February 1973), 74–86; and James W. Chesebro and Caroline D. Hamsher, "Orientations to Public Communication," in Modules in Speech Communication, eds. Ronald L. Applbaum and Roderick P. Hart, Chicago, Science Research Associates, Inc., 1976, pp. 17–29.

[40] Bruce T. Zortman, "The Theater of Ideology in Nazi Germany," The Quarterly Journal of Speech, LVII, 2 (April 1971), 153–61; and Michael McGuire, "Mythic Rhetoric in Mein Kampf: A Structuralist Critique," The Quarterly Journal of Speech, LXIII, 1 (February 1977), 1–13; Barnet Baskerville (see footnote 25); and Dale G. Leathers (see footnote 25); and Richard S. Rogers, "The Rhetoric of Militant Deism," The Quarterly Journal of Speech, LIV, 3 (October 1968), 247–51.

[41] Franklyn S. Haiman, "The Rhetoric of the Streets: Some Legal and Ethical Considerations," The Quarterly Journal of Speech, LIII, 2 (April 1967), 99–114.

Aristotelian methods of criticism. Then the experiential perspective was applied by Black, Burgess, Campbell, and Scott.[42] Finally, Griffin in his second model adopted a Burkeian new rhetorics approach. So the movements approach transcends a specific rhetorical act and critical perspective as it focuses on *dialectical enjoinment* or *confrontation* over a period of time.

Again, we have chosen two essays to illustrate the theory and application of movements criticism. Robert S. Cathcart in "Movements: Confrontation as Rhetorical Form" extends his article defining movements rhetorically and argues "that movements are a kind of ritual conflict whose most distinguishing form is confrontation." The concern for confrontation is clearly embodied in Brenda Robinson Hancock's "Affirmation by Negation in the Women's Liberation Movement" as she considers the inception period of contemporary feminist rhetoric.

Guidelines For Meta-Critical Approaches

In our discussion of the three perspectives on criticism we presented an orientation, assumptions, and a consensus for each one. Because "generic" and "movements" approaches are still evolving and because they do cut across the three major critical perspectives, an orientation, assumptions, and a consensus have not as yet emerged. So instead we will list a series of guidelines critics may follow in using these meta-critical approaches.

1. Critics must select a focus for criticism that transcends the first level of communication. Generic and movement critics are interested in specific first level rhetorical acts, so they will need to describe, interpret, and evaluate them. But more important to them is how these acts manifest a type of rhetoric or a rhetorical pattern developing over time. This concern for pattern shifts the critics' attention from the event itself to relationships. Questions which critics stressing genre might ask are, "How do a group of rhetorical acts form a genre?" Or possibly, "How does a given act fit into an established genre?" And movement critics might ask, "What pattern do a series of rhetorical acts form?" Or, "How does a specific act or a series of acts relate to an established pattern?" So these meta-critical approaches are directly concerned with concepts such as "rhetorics," "strategies," "metaphors," and "interactions."

2. Critics must clearly establish either a classification or boundaries for study. After critics select a focus they can not possibly deal with all first-level communication that relates to the relationship they have selected. It

---

[42] Edwin Black, "The Second Persona," The Quarterly Journal of Speech, *LVI, 2 (April 1970),* 109–19; Burgess, "Black Power"; Campbell, "Women's Liberation"; Robert L. Scott and Donald K. Smith, "The Rhetoric of Confrontation," The Quarterly Journal of Speech, *LV, 1 (February 1969),* 1–8.

is necessary to limit study to a sufficient number of rhetorical acts to understand the relationship, but not so many that critics are overwhelmed with data. This decision is easier for the generic critics who are asking how a specific act fits an established genre, but it is very difficult for critics who are inductively attempting to develop a genre. How many specific acts are necessary to establish a genre or a specific strategy within a genre? Likewise for movement critics, how many acts within a movement must be studied to establish a pattern, and what period of time is necessary to develop a pattern? We cannot provide answers, but critics must present arguments that respond to these questions in generic and movement studies.

3. Critics must select a perspective for describing, interpreting, and evaluating the first level of communication. Since generic and movement studies must in some way deal with specific rhetorical acts, critics are forced to select some perspective. Critics need to decide what perspective best approaches the focus and relationships inherent to the study.

4. Critics must be sure the focus and perspective they select are appropriate for previous research conducted within the classification or boundaries. Many critics have adopted meta-critical approaches so they can draw conclusions beyond a single rhetorical act. They are interested in inductively developing rhetorical theory. But to generalize from a number of rhetorical acts critics must employ the same critical perspective and methods.

Having described the evolution of rhetorical criticism as a rejection of a traditional paradigm followed by the establishment of two critical perspectives, experiential and new rhetorics, and two meta-critical approaches, generic and movements, we are still impressed by the variety of creative methods available to rhetorical critics. In spite of the concern in recent years for being more explicit about methods that has led to increased use of meta-critical approaches, we as yet do not see the acceptance of a single method as a paradigm in the near future.

THE GENERIC APPROACH

On Rhetorical Genre: An Organizing Perspective
by Jackson Harrell and Wil A. Linkugel

From antiquity rhetoricians have sought to classify discourse. Whether writers used the Aristotelian species of address or the Ciceronian ends of rhetoric,[1] behind the development of such schema have been presumptions that examples of discourse can be clustered, that discourse of one kind differs in important ways from discourse of other kinds, and that it is instructive to observe the similarities and differences among them. So, in 1965 Edwin Black created categories for classifying instances of rhetorical criticism.[2] In the time since Black added the term "generic criticism" to the vocabulary of the rhetorical critic, scholars of the field have produced a variety of seemingly unlike "generic" critiques. Taken together, these studies offer no clear picture of what genre is or what methods should be employed by the generic critic. Black's initial studies of the exhortative and argumentative genres,[3] as well as the later study by Raum and Measell on polarization,[4] classify the type and intensity of language employed by the rhetor. Zyskind, in his very early study of the Gettysburg Address,[5] and Mohrmann and Leff, in their recent study of Lincoln's Cooper Union Address,[6] use Aristotle's classical genres of forensic, deliberative, and epideictic speaking. Osborn, on the other hand, suggests critical study of

From *Philosophy and Rhetoric*, II, 4 (Fall 1978), 262–281. Used by permission of Jackson Harrell and Wil A. Linkugel. Dr. Harrell was professor of communication at the University of Texas at Arlington and is currently a Communication Planner for Texas Electric Service Company. Dr. Linkugel is professor of speech at the University of Kansas.

[1] *Aristotle, of course, noted three species of types of discourse in his* Art of Rhetoric: *forensic, deliberative, and epideictic. The Ciceronian ends of oratory were to instruct, to move, and to please.*

[2] *Edwin Black*, Rhetorical Criticism, A Study in Method *(New York: Macmillan, 1965).*

[3] *Ibid. Ironically, when this book was first published most readers saw as its strength its analysis of neo-Aristotelian criticism, and criticized it for presenting no real alternative; in the long run, however, it has been the alternative section of the book that has seemingly been of greatest benefit to the field of rhetorical criticism, because it stimulated the development of generic studies.*

[4] *Richard D. Raum and James S. Measell, "Wallace and His Ways: A Study of the Rhetorical Genre of Polarization," Central States Speech Journal (Spring 1974), 28–35.*

[5] *Harold Zyskind, "A Rhetorical Analysis of the Gettysburg Address," Journal of General Education (April 1950), 202–12.*

[6] *Michael C. Leff and G. P. Mohrmann, "Lincoln at Cooper Union: A Rhetorical Analysis of the Text," Quarterly Journal of Speech, (October 1974), 346–58; G. P. Mohrmann and Michael G. Leff, "Lincoln at Cooper Union: A Rationale for Neo-Classical Criticism," Quarterly Journal of Speech (December 1974), 459–67. Mohrmann and Leff begin with the Aristotelian classification of rhetoric but find that Lincoln's address does not fit cleanly in any one of Aristotle's categories and label it campaign oratory.*

public discourse through investigation of the archetypal metaphor;[7] Stelzner's assessment of Nixon's Cambodia Address serves as an example of archetypal criticism,[8] although he does not link his method to Osborn's analysis. Ivie employs motivational analysis to investigate the war messages of presidents.[9] Finally, Ware and Linkugel,[10] and Harrell, Ware, and Linkugel[11] approach generic criticism of apology from a situational basis. In short, "generic" seems to be loosely taken to mean "classificatory," and little has yet emerged to organize and systematize the development of generic criticism.[12] We believe that without a clear organizing perspective such a loose concept may suggest a confusing methodological weakness in the conduct of generic criticism.

The time has come to attempt a systematic development of theory and procedures for generic criticism. to this end, we hope (1) to offer a definition of generic criticism which will discriminate effectively among different approaches to the classificatory study of public rhetoric; (2) to focus on one approach to generic criticism which centers on the situational nature of rhetoric, providing a method for that approach; and (3) to identify the three operations for the study of rhetorical genre.

The Nature of Genre

Given the wide range of studies to which rhetorical scholars apply the term generic, it seems most appropriate to scrutinize the meaning of the term, for if generic criticism is to proceed in any systematic manner definition seems essential. At base, genre means class. A genus is a class or group of things. The decision to classify a particular group of things as a genus rests on recorded observations which indicate that one group of entities shares some important characteristic which differentiates it from all

[7] Michael Osborn, "Archetypal Metaphor in Rhetoric: The Light-Dark Family," Quarterly Journal of Speech, (April 1967), 115–25. Osborn does not claim this study falls under the rubric of generic criticism, but the classificatory principle is employed and, therefore, the study is included here.

[8] Hermann G. Stelzner, "The Quest Story and Nixon's November 3, 1969 Address," Quarterly Journal of Speech (April 1971), 163–72.

[9] Robert L. Ivie, "Presidential Motives for War," Quarterly Journal of Speech (October 1974), 337–45.

[10] B. L. Ware and Wil A. Linkugel, "They Spoke in Defense of Themselves, On the Generic Criticism of Apologia," Quarterly Journal of Speech (October 1973), 273–83. Noreen W. Kruse, "Motivational Factors in Non-Denial Apologia," Central States Speech Journal (Spring 1977), 13–23, has subsequently dealt with "non-denial" apologia from the perspective of the needs motivating the speaker.

[11] Jackson Harrell, B. L. Ware, and Wil A. Linkugel, "Failure of Apology in American Politics: Nixon on Watergate," Speech Monographs (November 1975), 245–61. See also Richard A. Katula, "The Apology of Richard M. Nixon," Today's Speech (Fall 1975), 1–5.

[12] Of note is the fact that Professor Karlyn Kohrs Campbell of the University of Kansas hosted a Speech Communication Association-sponsored conference on "Significant Form" in June, 1976.

other entities. A dog, for example, is like an aardvark in that they are both warm-blooded animals. They differ from snakes, which are not warm-blooded, and from junipers, which are not animal life. It is important to note, however, that the characteristics of more than one classification may be predicated of any entity. A dog is warm-blooded, is quadrupedal, and is non-symbolic. We may analyze it in relation to any of these groupings. And both dog and juniper are life forms, so while we may classify them separately for one purpose, we may also classify them together for quite another. In sum, the classification and analysis of an entity in one genus does not prevent its inclusion in other appropriate groupings.

The symbolic world of rhetoric, unfortunately, is not so apparently arranged in an ordered hierarchical fashion as is the world of natural science. One initial task of generic critics, therefore, is to discover a compensatory schema which will allow the systematic classification of rhetorical discourse. Preliminary to such a schema is an understanding of rhetorical genre. We think that rhetorical genres stem from *organizing principles* found in *recurring situations* that generate discourse characterized by a family of *common factors*. By organizing principles we mean a set of assumptions that crystalize the central features of a(any) type of discourse. Such principles involve a *root term,* representing an idea, which serves a canopy-like function—enveloping through implied association all which falls within its authority.

One can organize an inquiry into groupings of discourse from a number of methodological perspectives. Specifically, we later justify the identification of four root terms derived from different organizing principles, but we introduce them here to illustrate briefly the concept of an organizing principle. The first of these is *de facto classification,* in that its organizing principle is common-sense perception. For example, common-sense perception may suggest calling one group of speeches "inaugurals" simply because they occur when a new official takes office. Another group of speeches may be called Fourth of July orations because of the date on which they were given. Alternately, we can group speeches by *structural classification,* using characteristic patterns of language as the organizing principle. We might, for example, bring together an inaugural address and a Fourth of July oration based upon similar structural qualities. Likewise, *motivational classification* draws its organizing principle from the motive state of the rhetor. For example, "compromise" might be the controlling motive in a variety of recurring speech situations. Finally, *archetypal classification* may follow from organizing principles based upon persuasive images deeply imbedded in the audience's psyche. One could, for instance, productively explore the persuasiveness of the pioneer image as employed in speeches by political figures. In all four cases, generic classification begins with a clear notion of an organizing principle, and may be capsulized with reference to a root term.

We envision the notion of recurring situation in much the same way as Bitzer´ described the recurring nature of rhetorical situations: "a natural context of persons, events, objects, relations, and an exigence which strongly invites utterance . . ."[13] Regardless of the particular organizing principle employed by the critic, certain situational patterns tend to engender relatively limited types of rhetorical responses. Two examples should suffice as illustration. Quite obviously, when parishioners gather in church for worship, they expect to hear a religious homily from the minister. The situation is characterized by an exigency which in most cases can be productively altered only by a sermon. On the other hand, the role of situation in structural classification is illustrated by Jamieson's analysis of calcification in the Papal encyclical.[14] When an exigency becomes strong enough to demand a doctrinal edict from the Pope, the response is limited by audience expectations to a prescribed structural schema. Failure to employ this schema might well result in an inadequate alteration of the exigency.

Factors, in the sense we employ the term, are hypothetical variables which may account for variations in human behavior. Such factors are categorically derived from the linguistic strategies present in discourse which share a common generic root.[15] As a hypothetical example within archetypal classification, politicians often cast themselves in the image of a modern-day Cincinnatus who has left the plow to lead the nation out of a dire crisis. Development of such an archetypal image might well involve at least four common factors; demonstrating altruistic motives, projecting charismatic leadership qualities, expressing self-sacrifice, and voicing a desire to return to the simple life. In some cases, one may expect to find all factors present in all speeches of a given type. Howard Martin's analysis of the factors present in resignation speeches illustrates this approach.[16] In other cases, as with Ware and Linkugel's description of the factors of apology, different situations may be predictive of emphasis upon some factors at the expense of others.[17] Factors, in other words, are strategic variations which consistently appear within a given genre of discourse.

Root Terms and the Classification of Discourse

Rhetorical discourse, at first glance, occurs in a seemingly endless variety of potential classifications. The practitioner of generic criticism, by

---

[13] *Lloyd F. Bitzer, "The Rhetorical Situation," Philosophy and Rhetoric, I (1968), 5. The manner in which recurrent situations are revealed in controlling motives is illustrated below in our discussion of the motivational genres of discourse.*

[14] *Kathleen M. Hall Jamieson, "Generic Constraints and the Rhetorical Situation,"* Philosophy and Rhetoric, 6 (1973), 162–70.

[15] *The development of such factors is more fully explained and illustrated below in our discussion of generic description.*

[16] *Howard Martin, "A Generic Exploration: Staged Withdrawal, The Rhetoric of Resignation,"* The Central States Speech Journal (Winter 1976).

[17] *Ware and Linkugel, "They Spoke in Defense of Themselves" (n. 10).*

the nature of his art, faces the task of locating and describing groupings of discourse which differ from each other in important ways. Suffice it to say that if theoretically sound studies are to be derived from generic criticism, a systematic approach to identifying and describing such genres seems imperative.

All classification is, of course, a product of human thought. We may instructively contrast two primary modes of thinking which can form the basis for a systematic schema to be used in classifying rhetorical discourse: immanent classification and transcendent classification.

Immanent classification derives from a system of thinking based upon what Stephen C. Pepper terms "the simple common-sense perception of similar things."[18] In such classification, the investigator relies primarily upon direct, "face-value" observation and inference as his primary means of classification. In Pepper's explanation, "The world is full of things that seem to be just alike: blades of grass, leaves on a tree, a set of spoons, newspapers under a newsboy's arm, sheets of a single ream of paper."[19] Immanent classification, then, consists of a descriptive grouping of objects which common-sense perception tells us look alike, even though they may not be entirely the same.

Transcendent classification, on the other hand, inheres in the concept of normative participation. Norms represent central tendencies which are analytically derived, not inferred from surface observation. The concept of norm is illustrated by Pepper: "The norm of the oak is rarely or never fully present in any particular oak. Particular oaks merely approximate the form. Thus the character or characters of a class draw a circle, so to speak, about the particular objects which fully participate in them. But a norm is a center of rather vague intensity, claiming as exemplification objects which closely approximate it and making lesser and lesser claims toward the periphery and scarcely claiming at all so-called sports or freaks."[20]

The difference between these two systems of classification is a difference in methodology. The critic using immanent classification looks for and observes similarities which common sense tells him are there. Appearance rather than analysis is central to his method. Use of transcendent classification, alternately, derives norms from the analytic study of a certain type of object. His work in discovering norms transcends the individual objects under consideration.

These two systems of classification may be used to observe important relationships among various types of classificatory criticism. These rela-

---

[18] *Stephen C. Pepper,* World Hypotheses, *Berkeley and Los Angeles, University of California Press, 1942, p. 151. We are indebted to Pepper not only for the terms "immanent" and "transcendent," but also for the investigative perspectives which they imply.*
[19] Ibid.
[20] Ibid., *164.*

Figure 1
The Root Terms of Rhetorical Genres

Immanence	A	B	C	D	Transcendence
	d	s	m	a	
	e	t	o	r	
	f	r	t	c	
	a	u	i	h	
	c	c	v	e	
	t	t	a	t	
	o	u	t	y	
		r	i	p	
		a	o	a	
		l	n	l	
			a		
			l		

tionships, we believe, have not been sufficiently explored in previous literature.[21] Specifically, we imagine a continuum, the extreme ends of which are exemplified by relatively pure forms of immanent and transcendent classification. Clustered at various points along the continuum are types of "generic" studies employing methodologies which vary according to the degree of "common-sense perception" and "normative" analysis employed by the investigator. We have previously identified four primary types of generic classification: (A) de facto, (B) structural, (C) motivational, and (D) archetypal.

Works of rhetoric classified in a de facto manner do not require that the investigator even see the speech to be able to classify it. We call some speeches commencement addresses purely because they were given on the occasion of a graduation ceremony. Classifying discourse as a sermon because it is delivered from a church pulpit during church services is certainly an example of common-sense perception of similar things. Likewise, placing the president's address delivered at his inauguration into a category of "inaugural addresses" classifies rhetoric in a de facto manner. In each of these examples we find the "full appearance" of those qualities that make these discourses "seem to be just alike." We thus find that the use of "common-sense perception" to cluster rhetorical discourses clearly places them on the near end of our continuum labeled "immanence." The classification decision is derived from apparent association, not from analytically derived association.

[21] We shall later argue that differences between such extant type of criticism as archetypal criticism as described by Osborn (see n. 7) and the argumentative and exhortative genres as described by Black (see n. 2) can largely be accounted for by the type of analysis employed. Both of these, along with other extant types of classificatory criticism, fit well within our definition of rhetorical genre.

The root metaphor for *structural classification* is derived from character-istic patterns of language use. Two types of studies serve to illustrate structural classification. The first of these, language use as an organiza-tional pattern, is exemplified by New England Puritan sermons. Puritan sermons were presumed to have five major stages of development: the text was set forth, the doctrine of the text was classified into its constitu-tional elements, the text was set forth again in the form of a proposition, an analytic discussion of the scriptural proposition was presented, and the doctrine was applied to the congregation through a practical appeal.[22] The pattern was so commonplace, or in Jamieson's terms so "calcified,"[23] that failure to include all steps in the presentation of a sermon to a Puritan congregation could lead to a rejection of the message itself. A critic inves-tigating a sermon delivered to a Puritan audience might well declare such a sermon deficient if it failed to follow the anticipated form.

Black's description of the genre of exhortation illustrates a structural approach to generic classification at a much more sophisticated level. Black constitutively defined exhortation as "a congregation of discourses that may be found toward the end of a hypothetical scale of linguistic emotionalism."[24] Operationally, he loosely defined that genre as "the ex-tensive use of concrete description," and "the frequent substitution of *is* or *will be* for *should* or *should be*."[25]

We place structural studies farther to the right on the continuum than *de facto* studies because of their greater potential for the analytic derivation of normative descriptions. The norm of the Puritan sermon is a five-step organizational sequence; the norm of the exhortation is a preponderance of concrete description and heavy use of the copula. However, structural classification limits itself to investigation of the message characteristics of instances of discourse, not necessarily looking beyond the message itself in the construction or application of norms. This, in turn, provides a clear point of distinction between structural classification and our next category.

One factor potentially limiting the heuristic value of classification in the previous two systems is their failure to take situationally derived motives into account in the development of generic categories. *Motivational classi-fication,* on the other hand, draws its organizing principle from interaction between the rhetor and situational factors. Such interaction can aptly be termed motive.[26] Featured in this type of generic criticism are studies

---

[22] *See Jonathan Edwards' classic sermon, "Sinners in the Hands of an Angry God," for a good example of this form.*

[23] *Jamieson, 162–70.*

[24] *Black, p. 137.*

[25] Ibid., *143.*

[26] *Kenneth Burke has observed a similarly close correspondence between situa-tion and motive. See, e.g.,* Permanence and Change, *Indianapolis, Bobbs-Merrill, 1965, pp. 220–21, and* A Grammar of Motives, *1945, reissued, Berkeley, University of California Press, 1969, pp. 101–8.*

which derive their basic categories from the situation in which a speaker finds himself and in the goals he chooses to extricate himself from it. In several important ways, Windt's study of the diatribe[27] illustrates this type of investigation. Windt does not limit his investigation to a cataloging of the linguistic and/or organizational features of the diatribe, but rather focuses on the protester's view of society and his reasons for both rejecting traditional modes of appeal and affirming the more unique approach of the diatribe. It is within this context that he notes the symbolic choices of the rhetor. The metaphor of the diatribe is motivationally based. Likewise, studies of the apology begin with a motivationally derived definition of that type of rhetoric: the speaker, having come under attack, seeks to justify his personal worth. Only within this situational-motivational constraint is the symbolic strategy of the apology investigated and evaluated.

We have placed motivational studies farther to the right on the continuum than structural studies because of their tendency to employ multiple sources for the development of normative descriptions. Structural classification does not place primary emphasis upon motivation of the rhetor. Although Black, for example, exhibits a sensitivity to situational elements in rhetoric, his definition of exhortation is not situationally grounded. Extensive use of the copula and of concrete terms denotes exhortation regardless of the situation in which a given exhortative address occurs. On the other hand, an apology is made in a limited type of situation; additionally, a normal apology draws upon a limited number of linguistic factors in framing a strategic symbolic response. Even closer to the pure transcendent end of the continuum is the generic grouping we call archetypal.

Names for *archetypal* organizing principles are images which are commonly recognized and which carry inherent persuasive connotations, images which may have developed in the aesthetic realm of literature, or in myth, rather than in previous rhetoric. For example, the heroic metaphor implied in Stelzner's analysis of the Nixon quest[28] is derived from literature and is relatively unaffected by situational grounding. One may choose, as a persuader, to cast himself in the heroic image regardless of whether he is seeking to develop support for a war, clear himself of charges, act as the catalyst in a protest movement, or gain re-election. Similar to the heroic image is the concept of the rhetorical persona. Ware and Linkugel cast Marcus Garvey in the Black Moses persona.[29] They argue that orators oftentimes fulfill the vital factors of certain rhetorical personae and that these speakers acquire many of their leadership traits from this phenome-

---

[27] Theodore Otto Windt, Jr., "The Diatribe: Last Resort for Protest," Quarterly Journal of Speech (February 1972), 1–14.

[28] Stelzner, "The Quest Story" (see n. 8).

[29] B. L. Ware, Jr., and Wil A. Linkugel, "Marcus Garvey: Black Moses Persona" (in preparation).

non. Such rhetorical personae are archetypes in the truest sense of the word. It can appropriately be noted that Osborn's explication of the nature of the archetype in rhetoric suggests that its purpose is to achieve association with prominent features of experience and with basic human motivation in order to achieve universal appeal.[30] Archetypal classification is placed on the far right of the continuum because in its reliance on universal images it entirely transcends the literal nature of the object. The condensed image results from an analytic investigation resulting in a high level of critical abstraction.

Motivational Genres of Discourse

Initially we argued that the field of generic criticism suffers from a lack of systematic development. To this point we have been concerned with offering a theoretically derived schema for organizing *types* of generic groupings. We now wish to center attention upon a seemingly productive organizational schema for the study of motivational generic groupings of discourse.

Whether we define rhetoric as "the rationale of informative and suasory discourse,"[31] as "the faculty of discovering in the particular case what are the available means of persuasion,"[32] or as "pragmatically oriented discourse,,"[33] we derive a clear notion that rhetoric's function is to achieve substantive goals which the rhetor has designated as important. Such goals, of course, evolve from the interaction of a rhetor's motive state and elements of the rhetorical situation. In this sense, motivational generic criticism of rhetoric will search to investigate the ways in which speakers strategically pursue their goals. Judgments must be based on sets of norms which exist independent of individual instances of goal-seeking discourse. Presumably, by establishing normative standards for judgment, we can more clearly and consistently identify the ways in which individual rhetors pursue their goals, and by establishing such norms within generic groupings, we can develop tighter theoretical perspectives for testing the work of these speakers.

It can be productive to think of the nature of exigencies as motive states within the rhetor. According to Bitzer, "Any exigence is an imperfection marked by urgency; it is a defect, an obstacle, something waiting to be done, a thing which is other than it should be."[34] The impetus to rhetoric

[30] Osborn, "Archetypal Metaphor" (n. 7).

[31] Donald C. Bryant, "Rhetoric: Its Function and Its Scope," Quarterly Journal of Speech, (December 1953), 404.

[32] The Rhetoric of Aristotle, trans. Lane Cooper (New York: Appleton-Century-Crofts, 1960), p. 7.

[33] James Richard McNally, "Toward a Definition of Rhetoric," Philosophy and Rhetoric, 3 (1970), 76–77.

[34] Bitzer, 6.

provided by such imperfections is a desire on the part of the rhetor to bring about change, to remove or reduce the imperfection. In seeking to initiate and perhaps manage the alteration of the exigency, the speaker is acting through the lens of his motives—he is motivated to attempt an alteration of the exigency.

Additionally, Bitzer notes that situations, broadly conceived, do recur.[35] The specific, contextual conditions which give rise to a judgment of imperfection differ markedly, but the motivational characteristics of these conditions factor into recurrent controlling motives. Given that the decision to respond to the exigency in a rhetorical manner results from the interaction of perceived situation and motive state, and appropriate formula for organizing the motivational genres seems to be a schema derived from the study of human motives.

Walter Fisher has provided such a formulation.[36] In Fisher's view, communicators perceive "a rhetorical situation in terms of a motive . . . his perception determines the characteristics of his discourse and his presentation. Rhetorical communication is as much grounded in motives as it is in situation, given that motives are names . . . [for situations]."[37] Noting this interdependence between situation and motive, Fisher developed a scheme of four primary motive states which broadly encompass the characterization of "rhetorical situations in terms of motive," and which seem to offer a relatively complete description of the motivational states from which one can treat a substantive idea in rhetoric. The terms with which Fisher encompassed these primary motives are: "*affirmation,* concerned with giving birth to an image; *reaffirmation,* concerned with revitalizing an image; *purification,* concerned with correcting an image; and *subversion,* concerned with undermining an image."[38]

We offer these terms for controlling motives intended to guide the development of major motivational generic groupings. In the following discussion, we do not intend to indicate specific sets of generic names and descriptions that may evolve within these clusters; we view that as the next appropriate task for systematic generic research, and we view current generic research as too unsystematic to allow definitive statements regarding subgroups at this time. Rather, in the discussion which follows we intend only to illustrate the types of mapping decisions which might be made.

---

[35] *Bitzer, 12–13. Bitzer quite aptly observes that because some rhetorical situations persist "it is possible to have a body of truly rhetorical literature."*
[36] *Walter R. Fisher, "A Motive View of Communication," Quarterly Journal of Speech (April 1970), 131–39. As will soon be apparent, we are extensively employing the schema developed by Fisher and are indebted to him for his work in classifying substantive motives in communication.*
[37] Ibid., *132.*
[38] Ibid.

The nature of exigencies which might call forth discourse aimed at *affirmation* are those "situations when a communicator addresses potential believers in an effort to get them to adopt a 'new concept.' "[39] As examples of affirmation rhetoric in support of new ideologies, Fisher lists such speeches as Benjamin Franklin on behalf of the Constitution and Woodrow Wilson on behalf of the League of Nations. He notes Ralph Waldo Emerson's American Scholar address as an example of the affirmation of a new identity. Similarly, we might consider the introduction of a new candidate, a new corporate entity, or a new religious or social movement as examples of the rhetoric of affirmation.[40]

The basic form of exigencies which might call forth discourse aimed at *reaffirmation* are those situations in which a speaker attempts to revitalize an image or concept already held by the audience.[41] Fisher includes in the rhetoric of reaffirmation such speeches as Lincoln's Gettysburg Address and Martin Luther King's "I Have A Dream." Rhetorical situations which we normally think of as "sermonizing" might also fall into this category, since the speaker is attempting in these instances to intensify the listener's identification with a central action-guiding principle. It might also include such exigencies as the need to revitalize the spirit and commitment of workers in a faltering, lackluster campaign.[42]

The central feature of exigencies which produce discourse aimed at *purification* are those "situations in which a communicator seeks to refine an idea, image, or concept." It is in this generic grouping that much of the generic description (mapping) with which we are familiar has taken place. Subcategories of the controlling motive which have found their way into journals and convention halls include, for example, apology and ideological purification.[43] The differentia between this classification of exigency and the rhetoric of reaffirmation is that purification implies a previously established image or ideology has somehow become tarnished through attack or through some sort of redefinition.

Exigencies within the *subversion* cluster share a core definition of "situations in which a communicator attempts to weaken or destroy an ideology."[44] In Aristotle's duality of praise and blame, speeches of blame

---

[39] Ibid., *132–34.*

[40] *An example of a generic study that relates to the motive of affirmation is Robert L. Ivie, "Presidential Motives for War,"* Quarterly Journal of Speech *(October 1974), 337–45.*

[41] *Fisher, 134–36*

[42] *For a good example of a generic study relating to the motive of reaffirmation see James O. Payne, The American Eulogy: A Study in Generic Criticism (Master's Thesis, University of Kansas, 1975).*

[43] *Examples of generic studies concerned with the motive of purification are Ware and Linkugel, "They Spoke in Defense of Themselves," and a paper delivered at the Speech Communication Association Convention, December 1976, by Wil A. Linkugel, "The Rhetoric of Ideological Purification."*

[44] *Fisher, 136–37.*

might fall into this category. John Dean's opening statement before the Senate Watergate Committee might serve as a specific example, as might Senator Joseph McCarthy's attacks on presumed communists, and as might many of the documents produced by rhetors like Ralph Nader in his attacks on established American industrial production systems.[45]

We believe that these four controlling motives encompass relatively well the types of things that can rhetorically "happen" to a concept brought to a listener's consciousness. An idea can be introduced so as to generate initial belief. It can be reaffirmed as a means of intensifying the belief. It can be attacked and an attempt may be made to purify it. Because of their encompassing potentiality, we believe that they can serve well as organizing schema for developmental and applied research in motivational generic forms.

Basic Operations in Generic Research

Because of our concern for the systematic development and operation of generic criticism, we believe it is important to consider the methodological requisites of generic criticism. We intend the following methodological recommendations to apply specifically to research within the motivational genres just described, but many of these comments seem initially to be instructive for research into all types of genres. At base, we see generic research as involving at least three distinct operations: generic description, generic participation, and generic application.

Generic description involves at least two basic operations: identification of motivational precedents of the genre and mapping of the characteristic (i.e., normative) factors within the genre. Identification of motivational precedents should presumably focus upon the various exigency-clusters within the major root terms. Mapping operations should result from a study of representative examples of rhetorical artifacts flowing from exigency-clusters, and should result in a description of the major strategic factors which characterize the genre. The result of these operations should be a set of contitutive and operational definitions which can guide the work of other researchers wishing to work within the same genres. The clarity and precision of these definitions is especially important in generic criticism because of the potentially disorganizing effect of conceptually isolated studies.

Richard Hofstadter's essay. "The Paranoid Style in American Politics," illustrates these operations. Hofstadter scanned the style of right-wing politics in American political life and found distinct factors that characterize their rhetoric. The central image of the "paranoid style"—as Hofstadter labels it—is that of "a vast and sinister conspiracy, a gigantic and yet

---

[45] *A good example of a generic study concerned with subversion is Karlyn Kohrs Campbell, "The Rhetoric of Women's Liberation,"* The Quarterly Journal of Speech 59 *(February 1973), 74–86.*

subtle machinery of influence set in motion to undermine and destroy a way of life."[46] A second recurring aspect of the paranoid style is that the enemy is clearly delineated: "He is a perfect model of malice, a kind of amoral superman: sinister, ubiquitous, powerful, cruel, sensual, luxury-loving."[47] A third aspect is "the special significance that attaches to the figure of the renegade from the enemy cause."[48] Hofstadter suggests, for example, that the anti-Masonic movement seemed at times to be the creation of ex-Masons. The renegade is living proof that not all conversions are made by the wrong side and he brings with him "the promise of redemption and victory."[49] Finally, because of the fantastic character of the conclusions of the paranoid politician, he engages in "heroic strivings for 'evidence' to prove that the unbelievable is the only thing that can be believed."[50] Thus the paranoid style involves an accumulation of facts, or apparent facts, and a marshalling of these "facts" toward "an overwhelming 'proof' of the particular conspiracy that is to be established."[51]

Ware and Linkugel's essay on the apology, "They Spoke in Defense of Themselves," also illustrates these operations. After viewing a variety of speeches that resembled one another sufficiently to warrant investigation, a common motivational core was identified: In each case an accused person (the apologist) chose to face his accusers and to purify his personal image. These speeches were then carefully investigated; recurrent clusters or factors of language strategy were discovered which indicated the normative expectations for the apologetic genre. Finally, the authors sought to discover how the language strategies related to the types of discourses, or postures for personal defense, within the genre. Such generic description is, in the final analysis, not criticism itself but the precursor of criticism. It strives to generate theoretical constructs that assist the critic in making his assessment of specific instances of discourse.

Generic participation is not a complex process. It consists of determining what speeches participate in which genres. Procedurally, this involves the testing of an instance of discourse in question against the generic description. Harold Zyskind's article on Lincoln's Gettysburg Address provides one illustration. Zyskind raises the question whether Lincoln's address is "primarily epideictic or primarily deliberative, or some combination of the two."[52] He then proceeds to lay out the "usual characteristic by

---

[46] *Richard Hofstadter,* The Paranoid Style in American Politics and Other Essays *(New York, Knopf, 1965), p. 29.*

[47] Ibid., *pp. 31–32.*

[48] Ibid., *p. 34.*

[49] Ibid., *p. 35.*

[50] Ibid., *p. 36.*

[51] Ibid., *Roderick P. Hart, "The Rhetoric of the True Believer,"* Speech Monographs *(November 1971), quite similarly scans doctrinaire rhetoric to establish the common factors of the rhetoric of the "true believer."*

[52] *Zyskind, 206.*

which a speech is recognized as deliberative."[53] This testing procedure leads him to the conclusion that the Gettysburg Address can quite properly be placed in the category of deliberative rhetoric, despite the fact that casual observation would lead one to think of it as epideictic, since it was delivered on a ceremonial occasion.

Generic application entails what we normally think of as criticism, employing the stages of analysis detailed by Campbell.[54] Basically, it consists of the application of factors derived from generic description to specific discourses which have been defined as participating in a given genre. However, it is important for the critic to recall that the practice of generic criticism may alter the types of standards which may be applied in drawing critical judgments. It seems reasonable that the critic might expect to draw standards from sources within the genre (standards or norms derived from generic description) and from sources external to the genre itself. Instances of the latter might include the utilization of principles derived from attitude research or the use of principles derived from the field in which the instance of rhetoric is most "at home" (as, for example, exemplified in the use of political systems theory to derive standards for judging Nixon's Watergate apologia by Harrell, Ware, and Linkugel in their essay, "Failure of Apology in American Politics: Nixon on Watergate").

Richard A. Katula's article, "The Apology of Richard M. Nixon," demonstrates the principles of generic application. Katula employs generic description of apologia detailed by Ware and Linkugel for purposes of making a critical assessment of Nixon's resignation speech. To assist him in his analysis, he draws upon "an audience's need for closure."[55] Through this process he arrives at the conclusion that Nixon's "strategies of denial of intent and transcendence to a large context were largely unsuccessful in securing closure with his audience."[56]

Gerald L. Wilson, in his article on Nixon's resignation address, likewise applies generic description to a specific instance of discourse. He draws on the writings of Rosenfield, Butler, and Ware and Linkugel to demonstrate that Nixon's explanative apology failed to meet two critical requirements of the circumstances calling forth the speech: "the gravity of the misdeed and the congruity of the statements with reality."[57] Because of

[53] Ibid., *208.*

[54] *Karlyn Kohrs Campbell,* Critiques of Contemporary Rhetoric *(Belmont, California, Wadsworth, 1972), pp. 13–23.*

[55] *Katula, 4 (see n. 11).*

[56] Ibid., *1.*

[57] *Gerald L. Wilson, "A Strategy of Explanation: Richard M. Nixon's August 8, 1974, Resignation Address,"* Communication Quarterly *(Summer 1976), 20. Wilson in this paragraph is referring to L. W. Rosenfield, "A Case Study in Speech Criticism: The Nixon-Truman Analog,"* Speech Monographs, *35 (1968), 435–42; and Sherry Deveraux Butler, "The Apologia: 1971 Genre,"* Southern Speech Communication Journal *(Spring 1972), 281–89.*

this failure, Nixon's explanation "could only be well received by those who continued to follow the President with blind faith . . ."[58]

One potentially serious problem in generic application is the potential for conceptual slippage in the development and application of generic definitions. For example, Chesebro and Hamshir [sic] develop the conceptual framework of "concession" speeches and, in our opinion, in an otherwise insightful article, experience slippage in applying their conceptualization to MacArthur's address to Congress. They suggest: "The concession speech constitutes a formal conceding or yieldig in a conflict after the issues have been resolved in fact."[59] And they conclude: "Any situation involving a conflict in which one side wins and the other loses is the preliminary for a speech of concession, whether the issue be decided by the vote, by the scoreboard, by military supremacy, by economic pressure."[60] They find good examples for their genre in the formal concession of the losing candidate in a political election and in post-game interviews with losing athletic coaches. But whether MacArthur's address participates in this genre of speeches is at best problematic. In classifying the MacArthur address, Chesebro and Hamshir [sic] rely upon a situational definition which did provide a "preliminary" for a speech of concession, but their decision appears to have been made without sufficient regard to the motives of MacArthur as revealed in the speech. The stage, indeed, was set for a concession speech, but the actor did not appear in that role. Instead, he chose to play the role of the apologist.[61] To the best of our knowledge, MacArthur never did concede anything concerning his stance on Southeast Asia, even unto the end of his life. The potential for this type of conceptual slippage in the application of generic factors to specific discourse is always lurking, and thus, we think, warrants mention as a potential problem in generic criticism. This problem points to the need for rigorous application of generic descriptions.

Summary

To date, individual examples of the generic criticism of rhetoric attest to its potential. Taken as a unit, however, the method seems to be variously applied by individual researchers. The field has yet to develop a coordinated perspective for generic methodology. Unlike some other types of critical research, generic inquiry does offer the potential for a coordinated

---

[58] *Wilson, p. 20.*

[59] *James W. Chesebro and Caroline D. Hamshir [sic], "The Concession Speech: The MacArthur-Agnew Analog," Speaker and Gavel (January 1974), 39.*

[60] Ibid.

[61] *See Ware and Linkugel, "They Spoke in Defense of Themselves" (n. 10), for amplification of this thought. MacArthur went before Congress and told his audience, by implication at least, that he was right and Truman was wrong. His argument "justified" the position he took in relation to the President.*

investigation into the nature of applied rhetorical theory. Such coordination can assist scholars who wish their work to serve a theory-building function as well as a critical one. Scholars who use disparate methods can and do make significant contributions to the literature of the field. But we believe it is important for critics to be able to operate also in a more integrated manner. Generic criticism can allow them this option. It is for this reason that we argue for organizing an approach to this type of research.

Likewise, by its very nature, generic research investigates rhetorical activity within designated categories. If one researcher is to be able to investigate the "same" genre that another scholar has detailed, it seems imperative that he be able to identify the genre in the same way as his colleague. Otherwise, there is a risk of conceptual slippage in the development and application of generic descriptions.

In line with these assumptions, we have attempted to describe a methodology which can potentially aid in the systematization of research into rhetorical genres. Because generic research can be no better than the accuracy and consistency of classifications made by individual researchers separated in time and space, we believe it is especially important that such research proceed according to some workable and theoretically based schema. The issues we have confronted seem to us to be central to the systematization and future development of generic criticism. Our suggestions for identifying types of generic studies along an immanent—transcendent continuum and our conceptual and procedural suggestions for research into motivationally classified genres need, finally, to be put in perspective. We do not intend to "tie the hands" of practicing rhetorical theorists and critics. For this reason, we have avoided all but the broadest procedural and classificatory suggestions. Rather, we hope to initiate a needed organizing perspective for the work of generic critics. To this end we will be encouraged if our formulations, in some important way, contribute to the next appropriate task of generic researchers: discovery of the recurring, distinctive clusters of discourse in the various classification systems and mapping of the characteristics of these clusters.

They Spoke in Defense of Themselves:
On the Generic Criticism of Apologia
by B. L. Ware and Wil A. Linkugel

Within the last three decades, Richard Nixon, Adlai Stevenson, Harry Truman, and Edward Kennedy stood trial before the bar of public opinion

From *The Quarterly Journal of Speech*, LIX, 3 (April 1973), 273–283. Used by permission of the authors and the Speech Communication Association. Dr. Linkugel is professor of speech-communication and human relations at the University of Kansas. Dr. B. Lee Ware is adjunct professor of Law at the University of Houston.

regarding the propriety of some public or private action; each chose to take his case to the people in the form of an apologia, the speech of self-defense. In so doing, they followed a custom of Occidental culture firmly established by Socrates, Martin Luther, Robert Emmet, and thousands of lesser men. These events, separated by time and differing in particulars, are alike in that in each case the accused chose to face his accusers and to speak in defense of himself. That there are rhetorical genres and that one such may be the family of apologetic discourse occuring in situations such as those mentioned above are hardly revelations in the study of public address.[1] Yet, although most critics assent to the existence of genres, few engage in anything which even resembles what might appropriately be called *generic* criticism. Edwin Black, whose own *Rhetorical Criticism: A Study in Method* is one of the few lengthy considerations of speech genres, contends that "critics can probably do their work better by seeing and disclosing the elements common to many discourses rather than the singularities of a few"; but he is quick to add that the history of speech criticism to date is primarily one of attempts to "gauge the effects of the single discourse on its immediate audience." In the end, however, Black is critical of his own study of a genre, the argumentative, and characterizes his work as being too "gross" in the sense that it does not discriminate "among the types of discourses within the genre."[2] His self-criticism is valid, as well as of considerable import to the topic of this study, in that he leaves open the question of whether the argumentative genre subsumes apologia, as Black implies,[3] or whether apologetics is a genre in its own right, as others insist.[4]

We believe that apological discourses constitute a distinct *form* of public address, a family of speeches with sufficient elements in common so as to warrant legitimately generic status. The recurrent theme of accusation followed by apology is so prevalent in our record of public address as to be, in the words of Kenneth Burke, one of those "situations typical and recurrent enough for men to feel the need of having a name for

[1] *Examples of criticism in the apologetic genre include James H. Jackson, "Plea in Defense of Himself," Western Speech, 20 (Fall 1956), 185–95; L. W. Rosenfield, "A Case Study in Speech Criticism: The Nixon-Truman Analog," Speech Monographs, 35 (November 1968), 435–50; Wil A. Linkugel and Nancy Razak, "Sam Houston's Speech of Self-Defense in the House of Representatives," Southern Speech Journal, 43 (Summer 1969), 263–75; Bower Aly, "The Gallows Speech: A Lost Genre," Southern Speech Journal, 34 (Spring 1969), 204–13; David A. Ling, "A Pentadic Analysis of Senator Edward Kennedy's Address 'To the People of Massachusetts,' July 25, 1969," Central States Speech Journal, 21 (Summer 1970), 81–86; and Sherry Devereaux Butler, "The Apologia, 1971 Genre," Southern Speech Communication Journal, 36 (Spring 1972), 281–89.*

[2] *(New York: Macmillan, 1965), pp. 176–77.*

[3] *Ibid., pp. 150–61. Black considers John Henry Newman's Apologia pro Vita sua as a constituent of the argumentative genre.*

[4] *See Rosenfield, p. 435.*

them."[5] In life, an attack upon a person's character, upon his worth as a human being, does seem to demand a direct response. The questioning of a man's *moral nature, motives,* or *reputation* is qualitatively different from the challenging of his policies. Witnesses to such a personal charge seem completely and most easily satisfied only by the most personal of responses by the accused. In the case of men and women of position, this response is usually a public speech of self-defense, the apology.[6] Apologia appears to be as important in contemporary society as in years past, despite today's emphasis upon the legal representative and the public relations expert.

Our task in this paper is to examine a portion of the genre of speeches resulting from those occasions when men have spoken in self-defense. In the end, we hope to accomplish two goals. First, we attempt to discover those *factors* which characterize the apologetic form. Our choice of the term *factor* is problematic and requires some explanation. Factors are hypothetical variables which in various combinations account for or explain the variations in a particular kind of human behavior.[7] They are not found within the speech; they are merely classificatory instruments that the critic brings to the speech as a means of grouping like rhetorical strategies for ease in study. The use of the term *factor* as a means for classifying conglomerates of like strategies that are relatively invariant across apologia is not an attempt on our part to introduce scientific rigor into the critical act; it is likewise not intended to confuse, frighten, or threaten the speech critic of a traditional bent. Factor analytic theory as it is known in the social sciences serves merely as a source for a new departure in thought with regard to the criticism of public address.[8] For those who might find the use of the term objectionable on the grounds that it confuses "action," intended behavior on the part of sentient beings, with "motion," non-purposeful movement on the part of objects, we would remind them that no less of a humanist than Burke insists that "statistical" is another name for "symbolic," as "equations" is for "clusters" of terms, and that he speaks of the relationships among the terms of the dramatistic pentad as "ratios."[9]

[5] The Philosophy of Literary Form, 2d ed. (Baton Rouge: Louisiana State University Press, 1967), p. 3.

[6] In recent years, only Senator Thomas Eagleton among men of national prominence has eschewed delivery of an apologia when one seemed advantageous.

[7] See Paul Horst, Factor Analysis of Data Matrices (New York: Holt, Rinehart, 1965), p. 3.

[8] Such a use of scientific literature is at least implied by Wayne Brockriede, "Trends in the Study of Rhetoric: Towards a Blending of Criticism and Science," The Prospect of Rhetoric, ed. Lloyd F. Bitzer and Edwin Black (Englewood Cliffs, New Jersey: Prentice-Hall, 1971), pp. 123–39.

[9] The Philosophy of Literary Form, pp. 18–27; A Grammar of Motives (New York: Prentice-Hall, 1945), pp. 15–16.

Second, we hope to discover the sub-genres, the "types of discourses within the genre" of which Black speaks, by noting the *combinations* of factors found in speeches of self-defense. People speak in defense of themselves against diverse charges, in varied situations, and through the use of many different strategies. Each apology, therefore, is in some sense unique. The subgenres of the apologetic form, which we refer to as the *postures* of rhetorical self-defense, must not be viewed as a classification of speeches in the Aristotelian sense of *genus and differentia*.[10] Our determination of the apologetic postures is a mapping of the genre, a matter of detailed comparisons of differences and resemblances, which leaves open the possibility of finding intermediate cases.[11] Just as the genre itself is a rough grouping of speeches on the basis of occurrence in a situation of attack and defense of character, our divisions of the genre are merely working subcategorizations of apologetic discourses.

The Factors of Verbal Self-Defense

The nature of the resolution process occurring when a rhetor attempts to reconcile a derogatory charge with a favorable view of his character is the subject of an extensive body of psychological literature.[12] We feel, however, that the theory developed by Robert P. Abelson pertaining to the resolution of belief dilemmas is the most fruitful source of factors pertinent to the body of apologetic rhetoric.[13] We note at the outset that we take Abelson's theory as a starting point only. We borrow certain concepts and terminology from his work, but we often adapt the meanings of those terms for better usage in speech criticism. Much of his theory is discarded, not because it does not adequately describe psychological processes or interpersonal interaction, but because it implies a degree of predictive

[10] *The possibility of such definition of linguistic contexts is even to be doubted given Ludwig Wittgenstein's denial of the general form of propositions. See* Philosophical Investigations, *trans. G. E. M. Anscombe, 3d ed. (New York: Macmillan, 1971), No. 67.*

[11] *This discursive function of criticism is explained in detail in John Casey,* The Language of Criticism *(London: Methuen, 1966), pp. 16–17.*

[12] *For example, see T. M. Newcomb, "An Approach to the Study of Communicative Acts,"* Psychological Review, *60 (November 1953), 393–404; C. E. Osgood and Ph. H. Tannenbaum, "The Principle of Congruity in the Prediction of Attitude Change,"* Psychological Review, *62 (January 1955), 42–55; Leon Festinger, A Theory of Cognitive Dissonance (Stanford, California: Stanford University Press, 1957); R. P. Abelson and M. J. Rosenberg, "Symbolic Psychologic: A Model of Attitudinal Cognition,"* Behavioral Science, *3 (January 1958), 1–13; and Bernard Kaplan and Walter H. Crockett, "Developmental Analysis of Modes of Resolution," in* Theories of Cognitive Consistency: A Sourcebook, *ed. Robert P. Abelson et al. (Chicago: Rand McNally, 1968), pp. 661–69.*

[13] *"Modes of Resolution of Belief Dilemmas,"* Journal of Conflict Resolution, *3 (December 1959), 343–52.*

power which is not yet available to the critic. Abelson identifies four "modes of resolution": (1) denial, (2) bolstering, (3) differentiation, and (4) transcendence. Each of these is hereafter considered a factor commonly found in speeches of self-defense, and each is illustrated from at least one of the apologetic speeches from which we shall draw our examples for this article.[14]

The first factor, that of denial, is easily imagined to be important to speeches of self-defense. One may deny alleged facts, sentiments, objects, or relationships. Strategies of denial are obviously useful to the speaker only to the extent that such negations do not constitute a known distortion of reality or to the point that they conflict with other beliefs held by the audience. Denial is *reformative* in the sense that such strategies do not attempt to change the audience's meaning or affect for whatever is in question.[15] Denial consists of the simple disavowal by the speaker of any participation in, relationship to, or positive sentiment toward whatever it is that repeals the audience.[16] The use of such strategies has lent considerable psychological impact to a number of famous self-defense speeches.

Many apologia rely upon the denial of *intent* to achieve persuasiveness. Naive psychology dictates that people respond differently to the actions of others when they perceive those actions to be intended than when they perceive them to be merely "a part of the sequence of events."[17] The person who is charged with some despicable action often finds a disclaimer of *intent* as an attractive means of escaping stigma if the denial of the existence of the action itself is too great a reformation of reality to gain acceptance. Marcus Garvey's "Address to the Jury" in the 1923 trial concerning fraud in the activities of the Universal Negro Improvement Associa-

[14] *Speeches examined but not used as examples for this article include: Socrates's "Apology"; Isocrates's "On the Antidosis"; Demosthenes's "On the Crown"; Sir Thomas More's "Remarks at His Trial"; Martin Luther's "Speech at the Diet of Worms"; Thomas Cranmer's "Speech at the Stake"; Thomas Harrison's "Speech from the Scaffold"; The Earl of Strafford's (Thomas Wentworth) "Speech When Impeached for High Treason"; Sir Robert Walpole's "Address to the King for His Removal"; Edmund Burke's "Bristol Election Speech Upon Certain Charges Regarding His Parliamentary Conduct"; Mirabeau's "Against the Charge of Treason"; Marat's "Defense Against the Charges"; Robespierre's "Facing the Guillotine"; John Brown's "Courtroom Speech"; Susan B. Anthony's "Is It a Crime for a United States Citizen to Vote?"; Bartolomeo Vanzetti's "I Would Live Again"; Douglas MacArthur's "Address to Congress"; Harry S. Truman's "Television Address on Harry Dexter White"; Adlai Stevenson's "The Hiss Case"; and Thomas Dodd's "Address to the Senate Concerning Charges of Irregular Financial Dealings, June 14, 1967."*

[15] *The classification of strategies as "reformative" does not involve an ethical judgment on the part of the critic of the speaker's choices. Reformative strategies are those which simply review or amend the cognitions of the audience.*

[16] *See Abelson, pp. 344–45.*

[17] *See Fritz Heider,* The Psychology of Interpersonal Relations *(New York: Wiley, 1958), p. 100. In the naive analysis of action, "intent" merely implies the perception of "trying."*

tion is illustrative.[18] Garvey does not deny that people were defrauded of their investments in the Black Star Line. He does insist that he believed the steamship company to be a good investment and that, therefore, he had not intended to mislead investors.[19] However, the accused does not stop at this level of denial. Near the end of the speech, Garvey talks at some length concerning his race. Suddenly speaking of himself in the first instead of in the third person, as is his practice to this point, Garvey says: "I know there are certain people who do not like me because I am black; they don't like me because I am not born here, through no fault of my own."[20] Having established that neither his foreign birth nor his race is through his own intent, Garvey notes: "I didn't bring myself into this western world. You know the history of my race. I was brought here; I was sold to some slave master in the island of Jamaica."[21] Finally, he denies any purpose in working with the Black Star Line other than "to redeem Africa and build up a country" for the Negro.[22] Garvey cleverly uses stylistic strategies in his denials of intent to present himself as a *tragic* figure. Speaking of himself in the third person, he assumes the stance of one who is acted upon rather than one who acts with intent. Only at the end of the speech does he become an "I," but it proves to be to his own detriment when he does act, despite his good intent. The theme of the man who causes his own downfall in attempting great pain is common to tragedy, and by employing denial on several levels, Garvey manages to introduce an element of tragedy with all its implicit pathos into a speech of self-defense.[23]

We should conclude, therefore, that strategies of denial are not simplistic matters to be lightly passed over by the critic. To begin with, they compose an important element of many speeches of self-defense. Though only one lengthy illustration is presented here, many others would be equally suitable examples. Clarence Darrow's "They Tried to Get Me" is noteworthy in part because of his excellent use of strategies of denial.[24] Richard Nixon's "Checkers" speech contains such strategies: Sam Houston's "Address to the House of Representatives" results in a tragic pose

[18] *Text taken from* Philosophy and Opinion of Marcus Garvey, ed. Amy Jacques-Garvey, 2d ed. (London: Cass, 1967), pp. 184–216. Though not a lawyer, Garvey represented himself during the trail.

[19] Ibid., p. 186. In 1919, Garvey had started the Black Star Line to provide employment opportunities for the Black community. Stock in the company was sold through the mails. See Edmund David Cronon, Black Moses (Madison: University of Wisconsin Press, 1955), pp. 112–18.

[20] "Address to the Jury," p. 213.

[21] Ibid. Here, Garvey uses "I" to refer to his race; he was never personally a slave. He was, in fact, possibly a descendant of the Jamaican Maroons, runaway slaves who won their freedom and independence from England in 1939. See Cronon, p. 5.

[22] "Address to the Jury," pp. 213–14.

[23] For a discussion of the psychological aspects of tragedy, see Heider, p. 100.

[24] See Attorney for the Damned, ed. Arthur Weinberg (New York: Simon and Schuster, 1957), pp. 494–531.

based upon denial in much the same way Garvey accomplished this end.[25] Nor should we conclude that the examples here are exhaustive of all the possible uses of denial strategies, for such is certainly not the case. Due to considerations of space, however, we must now focus our attention upon the second reformative factor of apologia, that of bolstering.

The bolstering factor is best thought of as being the obverse of denial.[26] Bolstering refers to any rhetorical strategy which reinforces the existence of a fact, sentiment, object, or relationship. When he bolsters, a speaker attempts to identify himself with something viewed favorably by the audience. Bolstering, like denial, is reformative in the sense that the speaker does not totally invent the identification, nor does he try to change the audience's affect toward those things with which he can identify himself. In the case of bolstering strategies, the accused is limited to some extent by the reality the audience already perceives. Even so, this factor is an important component of the apologetic form.

Our examination of apologetic speeches disclosed a number of famous persons who have made effective use of bolstering strategies when speaking on their own behalf; few, however, proved as skillful as Senator Edward Kennedy in this respect. A careful reading of his "Chappaquiddick" address discloses the Senator's attempts to reinforce a "unit relationship," a feeling of belonging, between the public and the Kennedy family.[27] This is particularly true with regard to the people of Massachusetts, the group with which the Senator most closely identifies his family. This theme emerges early in the address. "In the weekend of July 18th," Kennedy observes, "I was on Martha's Vineyard Island participating with my nephew, Joe Kennedy, as for thirty years my family had participated, in the annual Edgartown sailing regatta." Referring to the party for Senator Robert Kennedy's campaign staff, special notice is taken of the efforts to make Mary Joe Kopechne "feel that she still had a home with the Kennedy family." The Senator refers to the weekend of her death as "an agonizing one for me, and for the members of my family"; it is the "most recent tragedy" in the family's history, a cause for speculation "whether some awful curse did actually hang over all the Kennedy's." The death of Mary Jo Kopechne becomes identified with the tragedy of the Kennedy family. The Kennedy family, in turn, is inseparably linked with the people of Massachusetts. Speaking directly to those citizens, Kennedy recalls: "You and I share many memories, some of them glorious, some have been very

[25] See "My Side of the Story," Vital Speeches of the Day, 19 (October 15, 1952), 11–15. The text for Houston's speech is in Gales and Seaton's Register of Debates in Congress, Vol. 8, part 2, 1st session, 22nd Congress, pp. 2810–22.
[26] See Abelson, p. 345.
[27] We take the text from "Kennedy Asks Voter Advice," Kansas City Times, 26 July 1969, p. 8A. For a discussion of the psychological processes involved in a sense of belonging, see Heider, p. 200ff.

sad." He then requests the "advice and opinion" of the people, much as one would ask a family member "to think this through with me," regarding whether he should keep his Senate seat or resign from Congress. The Senator through the use of bolstering strategies turns the entire affair into a family matter, a decision to be made by himself with the counsel of the many Americans who can identify with the tragedy of one of the first families of Massachusetts and of the United States.

Bolstering and denial, then, are factors vital to the apologetic form of public address. We should conclude that both subsume a number of diverse, lesser rhetorical forms which represent stylistic and strategic choices by speakers. They differ in the treatment they provide of the speaker's place in the audience's preception of reality. Denial is an instrument of negation; bolstering is a source of identification. Finally, strategies of bolstering and denial are reformative in the sense that they do not alter the audience's meaning for the cognitive elements involved. The two factors of apologetic discourse remaining to be discussed, differentiation and transcendence, are both, on the other hand, transformative.[28]

Differentiation subsumes those strategies which serve the purpose of separating some fact, sentiment, object, or relationship from some larger context within which the audience presently views that attribute. The division of the old context into two or more new constructions of reality is accompanied by a change in the audience's meanings. At least one of the new constructs takes on a meaning distinctively different from that it possessed when viewed as a part of the old, homogeneous context. In other words, any strategy which is cognitively *divisive* and concomitantly transformative is differentiation. The differentiation factor, therefore, consists of those strategies which represent a particularization of the charge at hand; the psychological movement on the part of the audience is toward the less abstract. Such strategies are useful in apologia only to the extent that the new meaning and the old lend themselves to radically different interpretations by the audience.[29] Quibbling over meanings of definitions is not likely to aid the accused, but strategies which place whatever it is about him that repels the audience into a new perspective can often benefit him in his self-defense. Indeed, this latter case has proven useful in numerous apologia.

The presence of differentiation as an important factor in apologia is often signaled by the accused's request for a suspension of judgment until his actions can be viewed from a different temporal perspective. Such is the case in Robert Emmet's speech from the dock delivered on September 19, 1803, prior to his sentencing to death for treason against Ireland. As a result of his secret dealings with the French, Emmet faces the charge

[28] *See Abelson, pp. 345–46.*
[29] Ibid., *p. 351.*

of desiring to supplant British rule of Ireland with domination by Napoleon. Early in his speech, Emmet makes the observation that he sought "a guarantee to Ireland similar to that which Franklin obtained for America."[30] He then explains why "treason" is an inappropriate definition of his intrigues with the French. "Were the French to come *as invaders or enemies uninvited by the wishes of the people,*" Emmet assures the court, "I should oppose them to the utmost of my strength."[31] He completes the differentiation in a phrase by suggesting that his actions are best termed "moral and patriotic,"[32] a conclusion that he is sure others will accept when his behavior is viewed from a future date as an attempt "to make Ireland totally independent of Great Britain, but not to let her become a dependent of France."[33] Hence, his strategies of differentiation permit him to make a final plea for the postponement of any judgment concerning his value as a human being:

Let no man write my epitaph; for, as no man who knows my motives dares now vindicate them,—let not prejudice or ignorance asperse them. Let them rest in obscurity and peace; my memory be left in oblivion, and my tomb remain uninscribed, until other times and other men can do justice to my character. When my country takes her place among the nations of the earth, then and not 'till then, let my epitaph be written—I have done.[34]

In his "Chappaquiddick" speech, Edward Kennedy employs differential strategies for his own defense in a manner quite different from that of Emmet. The Senator notes that he "felt morally obligated to plead guilty to the charge of leaving the scene of an accident" and that he feels the need to "talk to the people of Massachusetts about the tragedy." With a plea of guilty already entered, he resorts to a lengthy differentiation of his normal self from the Edward Kennedy who barely escaped drowning that night at Chappaquiddick. After commenting upon his exhausted state following repeated efforts to rescue Miss Kopechne from the water, Kennedy discourses: "My conduct and conversation during the next several hours, to the extent that I can remember them, make no sense to me. My doctors informed me that I suffered a cerebral concussion as well as shock." He describes his thoughts during that period at some length as:

[30] *We take the text from Thomas Addis Emmet,* The Emmet Family *(New York: Privately printed, 1898), pp. 161–64. For this citation, see p. 161.*

[31] Ibid.

[32] Ibid., *p. 164.*

[33] Ibid., *p. 162.*

[34] Ibid., *p. 164. Marcus Garvey employs differentiation in much the same manner as does Emmet when he urged the jury to judge his actions with regards to the Black Star Line from an imagined perspective a hundred years in the future when there would be a "terrible race problem in America." See Garvey's "Address to the Jury," pp. 213–14.*

All kinds of scrambled thought, all of them confused, some of them irra-
tional, many of them which I cannot recall, and some of which I would not
have seriously entertained under normal circumstances, went through my
mind during this period.

They were reflected in the various inexplicable, inconsistent and incon-
clusive things I said and did, including such question [sic] as whether the
girl might still be alive somewhere out of that immediate area . . . whether
there was some justifiable reason for me to doubt what had happened and
to delay my report, whether somehow the awful weight of this incredible
incident might in some way pass from my shoulders. I was overcome—I
am frank to say, by a jumble of emotion—grief, fear, doubt, torture, panic,
confusion, exhaustion, and shock.

Kennedy clearly does not expect to excuse his actions through this differentiation. "I do not seek," he says, "to escape responsibility for my actions
by placing the blame on the physical, emotional trauma brought on by the
accident or on anybody else." However, he is careful to complete the
differentiation by noting that he finally took the proper action the next
morning when his mind became "somewhat more lucid."[35] We can now
see the differentiation factor permits the Senator to assume a *palliative*
pose in his explanation of his behavior. Seemingly introducing new information about the accident, he is actually emphasizing the extenuating
circumstances that surrounded those events. In so doing, the stance of
palliation enables him to mitigate successfully the blame he feels he must
assume.[36]

The fourth and final major factor of self-defense, transcendence, is the
obverse of differentiation. This factor takes in any strategy which cognitively joins some fact, sentiment, object, or relationship with some larger
context within which the audience does not presently view that attribute.
As is the case with differentiation, transcendence is transformative in the
sense that any such strategy affects the meaning which the audience
attaches to the manipulated attribute.[37] In sum, those strategies which

[35] *All quotations taken from "Kennedy Asks Voter Advice," p. 8A.*
[36] *An easily identifiable use of differentiation occurs when a speaker employs*
regenerative strategies in an apology. Regeneration is the assertion that one is now
somehow fundamentally different and worthy of increased valuation than at some
previous time. Typically, therefore, a speaker employing these strategies will differ-
entiate his present self from the old, a self guilty of wrongdoing. An excellent
example of regeneration in a gallows speech is that of one John Whittington before
his execution at Forth Smith, Arkansas, on September 3, 1875. See Fred Harvey
Harrington, Hanging Judge (Caldwell, Idaho: Caxton, 1951), p. 35. Whittington
claimed that "good instruction" in prison had led him to realize that liquor was the
cause of his ruin and to wish that he could go free with his new lesson to live as a
"good and happy man." Also, see Aly, 212.
[37] *See Abelson, p. 346.*

involve a change in cognitive *identification* and in *meaning* factor together as transcendence. Transcendental strategies, therefore, psychologically move the audience away from the particulars of the charge at hand in a direction toward some more abstract, general view of his character. Such strategies are useful in apologetic discourse to the extent that the manipulated attribute(s) proves to be congruent with the new context in the minds of the audience. Several speeches of self-defense exemplify the transcendence factor as it results either from complex combinations of strategies or from relatively straight-forward attempts by speakers to identify attributes with new contexts.

Speeches by Eugene V. Debs[38] and Clarence Darrow illustrate usage of transcendental strategies. Although charged with allegedly inciting "insubordination, mutiny, disloyalty and refusal of duty within the military,"[39] Debs claims that the important issue of the Cleveland trial is not his guilt or innocence. He readily admits responsibility for the inflammatory speech delivered at Canton, Ohio, on June 15, 1918, the address which led to his indictment for violation of the Espionage Law. He obviously wants to transcend the particulars of his own case when he links World War I with the profit incentive of the capitalist class[40] and maintains: "I know that it is ruling classes that make war upon one another, and not the people. In all the history of this world the people have never yet declared a war. Not one."[41] Consequently, the Socialist leader is able to argue that his trial really does not concern his opposition to the war. He concludes:

> Gentlemen, I am the smallest part of this trial. I have lived long enough to appreciate my own personal insignificance in relation to a great issue, that involves the welfare of the whole people. What you may choose to do to me will be of small consequence after all. I am not on trial here. There is an infinitely greater issue that is being tried today in this court, though you may not be conscious of it. American institutions are on trial here before a court of American citizens.[42]

As Debs presents his case, the real issue becomes the First Amendment to the Constitution: freedom of speech, of the press, and of assembly.[43] He wisely attempts to justify his opposition to the war by identifying the attacks against himself with opposition to the people and to the people's Constitution. In such a manner, he places his actions into a context much

[38] The text is taken from "Debs' Speech to the Jury," The Debs White Book (Girard, Kansas: Appeal to Reason, n.d.), pp. 37–57.
[39] Ibid., p. 38. These are only the most important charges against Debs.
[40] Ibid., p. 53.
[41] Ibid., p. 42.
[42] Ibid., p. 57.
[43] Ibid., pp. 48–49.

more favorable to a public currently immersed in a patriotic fervor surrounding a massive war effort than would otherwise have been possible if
he had dealt solely with the indictment and evidence presented in court.
Transcendence strategies assist Debs in this speech by placing his reputation above the simple question concerning whether or not he opposes
the war in Europe.

Clarence Darrow was apparently more assured than was Debs that his
audience would see the broader context within which he cast his own trial.
He began employing strategies of transcendence very early in his "They
Tried to Get Me" speech.

*I am not on trial for having sought to bribe a man named Lockwood. . . . I
am on trial because I have been a lover of the poor, a friend of the
oppressed, because I have stood by labor for all these years, and have
brought down upon my head the wrath of the criminal interests in this
country. Whether guilty or innocent of the crime charged in the indictment,
that is the reason I am here, and that is the reason that I have been
pursued by as cruel a gang as ever followed a man.*[44]

The exact nature of the new context into which the trial was to be placed
did not, however, become apparent until Darrow began describing those
who desired his conviction. In brief summary of the opposition, the Chicago attorney exclaimed: "Oh, you wild, insane members of the Steel
Trust and Erectors' Association! Oh, you mad hounds of detectives who
are willing to do your master's will! Oh, you district attorneys."[45] Having
found such a diverse group of opponents, Darrow could then quite believ-
ably introduce a motive of conspiracy to his enemies, a theme which
carried with it a certain sinister aura to Darrow's new perspective of the
trial. "These men are interested," insisted Darrow, "in getting me. They
have concocted all sorts of schemes for the sake of getting me out of the
way."[46] Hence, the accused utilized one set of transcendental strategies
to represent himself as a hero of the downtrodden and another set to
shade his accusors as wicked plotters whose own evil deeds overshadowed any crimes charged against Darrow.[47] The persuasive impact of
such an archetypal motive was made possible by the judicious use of
transcendence strategies.

Transcendence and the other three major factors illustrated previously
account for most of the strategies people find useful in speaking in their own

[44] Darrow, *p. 495.*
[45] Ibid., *p. 497.*
[46] Ibid., *p. 496.*
[47] *The conspiracy theme is one common to many speeches of self-defense. For
another example of the use of transcendental strategies to introduce the conspiratorial motif, see Garvey, p. 210.*

defense. Two factors, denial and bolstering, are psychologically reformative and obversely related; the remaining two, differentiation and transcendence, are psychologically transformative and also represent an obverse relationship. Denial and differentiation are essentially divisive in that they result in a splitting apart, a particularization, of cognitive elements in the minds of the listeners. Bolstering and transcendence, on the other hand, end in a joining of cognitive elements, a newly realized identification on the part of the audience. Between the four, these factors subsume the many and varied strategies people invent in speaking in their own defense.

The critical value of the factor terminology, however, is not solely one of classification. The terms we employ as names for the various categories of strategies are dialectically related; each term, like the strategies they name, is a function of the others. A dialectic relationship among terms is a sign of ambiguity, and certainly, there are no objective means by which a critic can assign a given strategy to one factor as opposed to another. No two strategies are exactly alike. Therefore, the terms used to classify strategies are necessarily ambiguous, as ambiguous as the subject strategies are differing. Such ambiguity in classificatory terminology meets the needs of the critic, for as Burke notes, the student needs "not terms that avoid ambiguity, but terms that clearly reveal the strategic spots at which ambiguities necessarily arise."[48] The factor terminology does exactly that; it focuses the attention of the critic upon what language does for the apologetic rhetor when he deals with the charge of his character attributes, the strategic points in any speech of self-defense. By employing the factor terminology, the student must necessarily determine whether the rhetor is denying, bolstering, differentiating, or transcending through the strategic use of language, for these are the only rhetorical choices available to him in the apologetic situation. As the examples indicate, a speaker may employ reformative strategies; he may choose either to deny the charge directly or to ignore the charge through bolstering his character. On the other hand, he may opt for transformative strategies and move the audience's attention away from the charge through transcendental abstraction or through differential particularization. The factor terminology forces the critic to discern which choices a given strategy represents. The total import of these factors of apologetic discourse, however, become apparent only after we consider the ways in which speakers usually combine them to produce that human behavior we term the speech of self-defense.

The Postures of Verbal Self-Defense

Speakers usually assume one of four major rhetorical postures when speaking in defense of their characters: absolution, vindication, explana-

[48] A Grammar of Motives, p. xviii.

tion, or justification. Each of these postures results from a heavy reliance upon two of the factors described above, and we consider each to constitute a subgenre of the apologetic form.[49] We are not surprised to find that each of the four stances involves the combination of a transformative with a reformative factor. In a rhetorical situation as complex as that of accusation and response, a speaker would be expected to attempt to change the meaning of some, but not all, cognitive elements in the minds of the audience. Nor are we surprised to learn that only four of the possible combinations of factors have found widespread usage. Each combination represents a locus within the form around which similar, not identical, apologic tend to cluster; the four subgenres represent those postures which Western culture, customs, and institutions seem to dictate as being most acceptable in dismissing charges against a rhetor's character. The assignment of speeches to the postures is problematic, for our terms naming the subgenres are dialectic and ambiguous for the same reasons we note in discussing the factor terminology.[50] Each of the postures is a recognizable category of addresses into which the critic may group speeches on the basis of dominant strategies found in the discourses; the postures, like the factors, are not completely distinct classifications void of intermediate cases.

An *absolutive* address, resulting from the union of primarily the differentiation and denial factors, is one in which the speaker seeks acquittal. This posture is in no way limited to legal proceedings; the accused may seek acquittal from an extra-judicial body or even by public opinion. The absolutive speech is one in which the accused denies any wrong and in which he differentiates any personal attribute in question from whatever it is that the audience finds reprehensible. In this self-defense stance, the speaker is primarily concerned with "clearing his name: through focusing audience attention upon the particulars or specifics of the charge, just as Robert Emmet considered the nature of treason in great depth in "My Country Was My Idol."[51] The absolutive speech differs from the vindicative address in that it is more specific than the latter. The *vindicative* address, due to the reliance upon transcendental strategies, permits the accused greater ease in going beyond the specifics of a given charge. Such an

---

[49] *Any speech of self-defense is likely to contain all four of the factors of self-defense. We do not mean to imply that each of the apologetic postures contains only two of the factors. Rather, we contend that speeches of self-defense usually rely most heavily for their persuasive impact upon two of the factors. The determination of which two are most important in a given speech is, in this study at least, a subjective decision based only partly upon frequency of appearance of a given factor.*

[50] *See Burke, A Grammar of Motives, p. xix.*

[51] *Other examples of absolutive addresses would include Sam Houston's "Address to the House of Representatives"; Marcus Garvey's "Address to the Jury"; and Richard Nixon's "My Side of the Story."*

apology aims not only at the preservation of the accused's reputation, but also at the recognition of his greater worth as a human being relative to the worth of his accusers. A good example of the vindicative subgenre results from Clarence Darrow's use of transcendence strategies to formulate an implicit comparison between his own character and that of his prosecutors in his "They Tried to Get Me."[52]

A similar distinction is possible between the explanative and the justificative postures. The former, as a combination of bolstering and differentiation, is somewhat more defensive than is the latter, a category of discourse relying upon the use of bolstering and transcendence strategies. In the *explanative* address, the speaker assumes that if the audience understands his motives, actions, beliefs, or whatever, they will be unable to condemn him. This seems to have been the hope of Edward Kennedy in his "Chappaquiddick Address."[53] The *justificative* address, on the other hand, asks not only for understanding, but also for approval. Hence, Eugene V. Debs in his "Speech to the Jury" sought to establish the basis for his own actions in a concern with human dignity and fundamental rights such as freedom of speech.[54]

This conceptualization of the apologetic genre into subgenres should assist the critic in comparing the rhetorical uses of language occurring across somewhat different apologetic situations. The act is not, in and of itself, criticism, just as the categorizing of strategies into factors does not complete the critical act. Such classification taken alone lacks an evaluative dimension. However, the dialectic and ambiguous nature of the posture terminology focuses the critic's attention upon the strategic decision a speaker makes whenever he chooses a culturally acceptable stance from which to speak on his own behalf. Herein lies the critical advantage of mapping the apologetic genre, and as we argued in the beginning, the explication of the genre should precede the criticism proper of the apologetic form. We offer this conceptualization of the subgenres and the factor terminology as "experimental incursions into the field with which they deal; assays or examinations of specimen concepts drawn rather arbitrarily from a larger class; and finally *ballons d'essai,* trial balloons designed to draw the fire of others."[55]

---

[52] *Two further examples of vindicative discourses are Socrates's "Apology" and Harry S. Truman's "Television Address on Harry Dexter White."*

[53] *Other famous explanative addresses are Martin Luther's "Speech at the Diet of Worms" and Adlai Stevenson's "The Hiss Case."*

[54] *Susan B. Anthony's "Is It a Crime for a United States Citizen to Vote?" and Douglas MacArthur's "Address to Congress" are also well-known examples of justificative addresses.*

[55] The Uses of Argument *(Cambridge, England: Cambridge University Press, 1957), p. 1.*

THE MOVEMENTS APPROACH

Movements: Confrontation as Rhetorical Form
by Robert S. Cathcart

The author of this essay argues the thesis that the true movement is a kind of "agonistic ritual" whose most distinguishing form is confrontation.

"Every movement . . . has form. It is a progress from *pathema* through *poiema* to *mathema:* from a 'suffering, misfortune, passive condition, state of mind,' through 'a deed, doing, action, act,' to an 'adequate idea; the thing learned.' . . . To study a movement is to study a drama, an act of transformation, an act that ends in transcendence, the achievement of salvation. . . . And hence to study a movement is to study its form."[1]

This statement will serve as a beginning point for the contentions I advance. I assume that few would quarrel with the notion that a movement has form, and most rhetorical scholars accept the idea that a movement is primarily a symbolic or rhetorical act.[2] But, having said that movements are rhetorical acts, I have not said much more than the sociologists who say that movements are collective acts seeking social change. To understand movements as rhetorical acts constrained by a particular rhetorical form requires that we know something about how this form is exhibited, what are the forces that shape it and in turn are shaped by it, how it does its work, and the reasons for its existence as form.

In an earlier essay I argued that "Movements are carried forward through language, both verbal and non-verbal, in strategic [ways] that bring about identification of the individual with the movement. . . . [M]ovement is a form related to a rationale and a purpose . . . one which gives substance to its rationale and purpose."[3]

From *The Southern Speech Communication Journal*, XLIII, 3 (Spring 1978), 233–47. Used by permission of the Southern Speech Communication Association and Robert S. Cathcart. Dr. Cathcart is professor of speech at Queens College, New York.

[1] *Leland M. Griffin, "A Dramatistic Theory of the Rhetoric of Movements," Critical Responses to Kenneth Burke, ed. William H. Rueckert (Minneapolis: University of Minnesota Press, 1969), 461–62. Within this statement Griffin is quoting from Kenneth Burke's* A Grammar of Motives, *pp. x–xvi, 38–43, 376; Counter Statement, pp. 48, 128, 213–14; and* The Philosophy of Literary Form, *p. 76.*

[2] *See Leland M. Griffin, "The Rhetoric of Historical Movements," Quarterly Journal of Speech, 38 (1952), 181–85; Edwin Black, Rhetorical Criticism (New York: The Macmillan Co., 1965); Herbert Simons, "Requirements, Problems and Strategies: A Theory of Persuasion for Social Movements," Quarterly Journal of Speech, 56 (1970), 1–11; Dan F. Hahn and Ruth Gonchar, "Studying Social Movements: A Rhetorical Methodology," The Speech Teacher, 20 (1971), 44–52; Charles A. Wilkinson, "A Rhetorical Definition of Movements," The Central States Speech Journal, 27 (1976), 88–94; Ralph R. Smith and Russell R. Windes, "The Rhetoric of Mobilization: Implications for the Study of Movements," The Southern Speech Communication Journal, 42 (1976), 1–19.*

[3] *Robert S. Cathcart, "New Approaches to the Study of Movements: Defining Movements Rhetorically," Western Speech, 36 (Spring 1972), 86. This point is supported in part by William Bruce Cameron,* Modern Social Movements (New York: Random House, 1966), p. 174.

It was my purpose then to establish the notion that movements are essentially rhetorical transactions of a *special type*, distinguishable by the peculiar reciprocal rhetorical acts set off between the movement on the one hand and the established system or controlling agency on the other. I argued, "It is this *reciprocity* or *dialectical enjoinment in the moral arena* which defines movements and distinguishes them from other dramatistic forms."[4] I concluded, this "particular dialectic . . . becomes the *necessary ingredient* which produces the rhetorical form that we have come to recognize as a political or social movement."[5]

Since the appearance of that essay a number of articles on the rhetoric of movements have expressed disagreement with my position. The disagreements have centered mainly around the contentions that either my definition was incomplete, or too narrow and restrictive to be of practical use to rhetoricians studying movements.[6] That it was incomplete must be granted. That it was too narrow depends on whether one seeks definitions which will cast the widest net, allowing a multitude of acts to be claimed as movements, or definitions that will so focus our vision that we can more exactly distinguish amongst various similar appearing rhetorical acts. I for one think there is much merit in pursuing definitions which allow us to sort out rhetorical transactions that in the general socio-political milieu appear to be quite similar but which have at base a particular rhetorical form which brings forth a unique set of rhetorical strategies.

With that in mind, I will argue that a movement can be identified by its *confrontational form*. More specifically, I will argue that movements are a kind of ritual conflict whose most distinguishing form is *confrontation*. Unfortunately, the word "confrontation" is loosely applied to a wide variety of acts and enactments such as "confronting the morning newspaper" or "confronting the elements," as well as "confronting the police" or "confronting the system." Also, when applied in socio-political conflict it carries the notion of violence and the negation of reason. Despite such common usage and mis-usage, I find the concept, *confrontation*, to have a symbolic significance which, when traced to its conceptual underpinnings, is quite revealing of those collective behaviors referred to as "movements."

---

[4] Cathcart, "New Approaches to the Study of Movements: Defining Movements Rhetorically," p. 87.

[5] Cathcart, "New Approaches to the Study of Movements: Defining Movements Rhetorically, p. 88.

[6] Wilkinson (p. 90) states, "Unfortunately, Cathcart's article, though quite intentionally, ends where it should begin." And, Smith and Windes (p. 142) observe, "Change to a more restricted usage can have negative consequences." Also, Ralph R. Smith and Russel R. Windes in "The Innovational Movement: A Rhetorical Theory," Quarterly Journal of Speech, 61 (1975), 142, state, "While Cathcart properly limits the definition of rhetorical movements to the features of discourse, his approach does not distinguish between movements and other classes of rhetorical acts."

In this essay I will use confrontation to mean that form of human behavior labeled "agonistics," i.e., pertaining to ritual conflicts. Confrontation is symbolic display acted out when one is in the throes of agon. It is a highly dramatistic form; for every ritual has a moral aspect, expressing, mobilizing social relationships, confining or altering relationships, maintaining a reciprocal and mutual balancing system. Agonistic ritual is redressive. It is a means of reaffirming loyalties, testing and changing them or offering new ones to replace old loyalties, always expressed in a kind of muted symbolic display designed to elicit a symbolic response which changes attitudes and values without major and unlimited conflict. Confrontation as an agonistic ritual is not a prelude to revolution or warfare but is a ritual enactment that dramatizes the symbolic separation of the individual from the existing order.[7]

I note that others in the field of rhetoric like Scott, Burgess, Simons, Andrews, and Bailey have found "confrontation" to be worthy of examination in its own right, or at least as an adjunct to communication.[8] They have pointed out that, contrary to popular notions, confrontation is not anti-communication but rather is an extension of communication in situations where confronters have exhausted the normal (i.e., accepted) means of communication with those in power.[9] Further, they consider confrontation to be a communicative form directly associated with movements. Their examination of confrontation has, however, been limited to its *instrumental role*—to its use as a tactic for gaining an audience or opening channels to carry the primary message.[10] In addition, some of these studies have implied

---

[7] H. L. Nieburg, "Agonistics—Rituals of Conflict," The Annals of the American Academy of Political and Social Science, 391 (1970), 56–73.

[8] Robert L. Scott and Donald K. Smith, "The Rhetoric of Confrontation," Quarterly Journal of Speech, 55 (1969), 1–8; James R. Andrews, "Confrontation at Columbia: A Case Study in Coercive Rhetoric," Quarterly Journal of Speech, 55 (1969), 9–16; Herbert W. Simons, "Confrontation as a Pattern of Persuasion in University Settings" (Unpublished paper, Temple University, 1969); Harry A. Bailey, Jr., "Confrontation as an Extension of Communication," Militancy and Anti-Communication, ed. Donn W. Parson and Wil A. Linkugel (Lawrence, Kansas: House of Usher, 1969), pp. 11–26; and Parke G. Burgess, "The Rhetoric of Moral Conflict: Two Critical Dimensions," Quarterly Journal of Speech, 56 (1970), 120–30.

[9] See, for example, Bailey, "Confrontation as an Extension of Communication" (p. 24): "It [confrontation] is generally a signal that the usual and established methods of securing policy are not sufficient."

[10] See Bailey (p. 24): "Confrontation . . . is that which is designed to bring about not non-negotiable demands." See also, Andrews (p. 16): "It may be that in an examination of the means of protest and not necessarily in an inherent worthiness of their goals . . . the rhetorical critic could reach judgments concerning the essential nature of confrontation." Scott and Smith (p. 7), however, treat confrontation as both instrumental and consummatory: "One should observe the possible use of confrontation as a tactic for achieving attention and an importance not readily attainable through decorum." And, "Without doubt, for many the act of confrontation itself, the march, the sit-in, or altercation with police is enough. It is consummatory."

that confrontation is a somewhat questionable or exceedingly desperate form of communication.[11]

Without denying confrontation's widespread and important instrumental function, I wish to present confrontation as a *consummatory form essential to a movement*. To do so it is necessary first to re-examine the question, What is it we are seeing and describing when we talk about *a movement?* Most rhetorical scholars have answered this in part by using sociological descriptions; for example, the object referred to as a movement is "an uninstitutionalized collectivity that mobilizes for action to implement a program for the reconstitution of social norms and values."[12] In addition, there has been a general acceptance of the idea that there are various or distinctive types of movements such as reform movements, radical movements, etc. This view of movements as types has also been drawn from the literature of the sociologists of collective behavior. Accordingly, what we seem to be seeing when we observe a movement is a group of people, not identified by institutional membership, who act together to produce change; and this "acting together" can be distinguished by how militantly or aggressively the group performs, and by whether the goal of the group is change in social norms, hierarchical change, or a reordering of values. It generally is argued that, depending on the group's goals and methods, there will be produced a distinctive *form* of rhetoric.

I find it difficult to accept such a construct or definition of movements, not because I want to be a purist about the word "movement" but because such a definition fails, in my opinion, to help us distinguish between two fundamentally different forms of rhetoric—one which I shall call *managerial* and the other I shall call *confrontational*. To put it another way, it can be very useful to our understanding of socio-political activities if we can distinguish between those rhetorical acts which by their form uphold and re-enforce the established order or system and those which reject the system, its hierarchy and its values. Needless to say, the great bulk of communication in any society must of necessity fall into the former category. As Scott, Bevilacqua and others have pointed out, almost all Aristotelian rhetorics are *managerial* in form.[13] They are designed to keep the existing system viable: they do not question underlying epistemology and group ethic. On the other hand, *confrontational* rhetoric occurs only in

---

[11] *An example is the statement by William Bruce Cameron, "Some Causes and Effects of Campus Confrontations," in* Militancy and Anti-Communication *(p. 35): "Confrontation precludes disproof because it does not permit a rational examination of the issues. Often the very people who claim to be most concerned about examining the issues stage confrontations in such a way that no serious examination could possibly take place."*

[12] *Simons, p. 3.*

[13] *Robert L. Scott, "A Synoptic View of Systems of Western Rhetoric,"* Quarterly Journal of Speech, *61 (1975), 445–46; Vincent Bevilacqua, "Philosophical Origins of George Campbell's Philosophy of Rhetoric,"* Speech Monographs, *32 (1965), 7.*

special and limited circumstances, such as periods of societal breakdown or when moral underpinnings are called into question.

It is this confrontational aspect—the questioning of the basic values and societal norms—that makes true movements a real threat that cannot be explained away as a temporary malfunction of the system or as the conspiratorial work of a handful of fanatics. Though some individuals may have felt threatened when former Black Panther leader Bobby Seale ran for the office of Mayor of Oakland, California, many more felt a great sense of relief. And, rightly so, because no matter how radical his campaign platform, the form of his rhetoric as *office seeker* was supportive of the system. It was an overt act of faith in the legitimacy of the established order. On the other hand, no member of the established order could mistake the threat to the whole system when Seale and other Black Panthers confronted the Oakland police and the California State Assembly with rifles and shotguns in hand, for the Panthers were saying symbolically that they rejected the laws and codes of the "white establishment" and were placing themselves outside or apart from the existing white racist hierarchy. To know that the latter was confrontational and not managerial communication, one has only to examine the reciprocating rhetorical acts which came forth from all levels of the existing system. Almost all, including many blacks, condemned the act as a step toward anarchy or toward a suicidal racial war perpetuated by black devils of destruction. In other words, almost all perceived of it as a rhetorical act emanating from *outside the system.*

Using this notion of confrontational rhetoric as the counterpart of managerial rhetoric, I find that many of the so-called "types" of movements described in recent literature do not appear to be movements at all, but rather adjustments to the existing order. A closer look at those activities labeled "reform" movements reveals a rhetorical form which is managerial rather than confrontational. Their rhetoric is primarily concerned with adjusting the existing order, not rejecting it. The reformist campaign stays inside the value structures of its existing order and speaks with the same vocabularies of motive as do the conservative elements in the order. The reform must not seem to be a threat to the very existence of the established order, or the reformers may be forced out of the common value system. The reform movement uses a managerial rhetoric because to some degree it must have a *modus vivendi* with those in power if it is to exist.

To place reform movements on a continuum with radical movements by the claim that they are inherently the same kind of act—just less militant or aggressive—is to misconstrue the uses of "identification" and "consubstantiation" in a rhetorical setting.[14] I find Griffin to be instructive on how to

---

[14] *For an explanation of "identification" and "consubstantiation" as ingratiation see Kenneth Burke,* A Rhetoric of Motives *(New York: George Braziller, Inc., 1955), pp. 19–29, and Kenneth Burke, "Rhetoric—Old and New,"* The Journal of General Education, *5 (1951), 203.*

recognize the managerial form of identification and consubstantiation underlying reform movement rhetoric: "Though men, in any system, are inevitably divided, 'identification is compensatory to division.' And through identification with a common condition or 'substance,' men achieve an understanding (a sense of unity, identity, or consubstantiality). Any system that endures implies an adequate understanding, a dynamic understanding. . . . It is the understanding essential to the ultimate achievement of integration. . . . For it provides the basis for communication. . . . Men agree on meaning, value, and desire; and hence they gladly submit to a code of control, obey the commandments."[15] What we see when a "reform" movement or "status" movement, etc., is viewed through the Burkean prism is a rhetorical form which recognizes the division but accepts "the common substance." Such movements produce a rhetoric that embraces the values of the system, accepts that the order has a code of control which must not be destroyed, while at the same time striving to gain acceptance of that which will perfect (or restore to perfection) the system. Such a rhetoric is essentially managerial.

Furthermore, I believe that those who would have an activity that seeks corrective change in the system labeled "a movement" make the mistake of assuming that either there will be no alienation or agitation within a well-ordered system, or that movements are the only means of redress or alteration in the established order. As I pointed out in my earlier essay,

We must be aware that when we talk of society, or the establishment, or the system, we are talking about a dynamic, everchanging collection of groups. In one sense every group activity within society is a movement but in another and more important sense the ever-evolving, changing society is the status quo. What the rhetorical critic of movements must be concerned with then is not definitions [of movements] . . . which describe the dynamic status quo, i.e., the [activities] which give it its dynamism, but definitions which describe those collective behaviors which cannot be accommodated within the normal [motion] of the status quo.[16]

What most so-called reform movements have in common is the basic acceptance of the system as *the* system, along with its moral imperatives and ethical code. The rhetorical form produced by such groups is characterized by consubstantiating motives which are ground for the strategies for improving or perfecting the order. Examples of this are the Populist call for more direct representation in government and more control over (and therefore more rightful rewards for) one's own labors, and the Civil Rights call of the 1960s for "Freedom Now," meaning the wider distribution and

---

[15] *Griffin*, Critical Responses to Kenneth Burke, *p. 458.*
[16] *Cathcart, pp. 85–86.*

more even application of the justice and equality basic to the established system. Even so-called "status" or "transcendent" movements, with their striving for the moral improvement of individuals, are at base claiming that more perfect individuals will improve the existing order and make it function better morally.

Further, I believe that a careful examination of the rhetoric of such collectives, reform movements and the like, will reveal that their strategies of identification and consubstantiation are formed out of what Burke calls "the mystery" or the "keeping of the secret." It is Burke's position that "mystery arises at that point where different kinds of beings are in communication."[17] In any good rightful system men accept the mystery and strive to keep the secret; that is, preserve the hierarchy.[18] Within such rhetoric, identification with agency and purpose is always present. It is necessarily so because what we have is the rhetoric of piety, the essence of which is to establish what properly goes with what. To Burke, the rhetoric of piety is "a system builder, a desire to round things out, to fit experiences together as a unified whole."[19] It is the rhetoric of piety—the keeping of the secret—that is characteristic of most reform activities, and it is that which keeps the rhetoric in bounds—that which limits its agitation and dictates it strategies. This keeping of the secret governs also the *counter rhetoric* produced, which *defines the acts of the group seeking change as "reforms" rather than revolution.*

There is, I believe, another kind of collective behavior which is perceived of (or reacted to) as "radical" or "revolutionary." Its form is *confrontational.* It contains the rhetoric of "corrosion" and "impiety."[20] The dramatic enactment of this rhetoric reveals persons who have become so alienated that they reject "the mystery" and cease to identify with the prevailing hierarchy. They find themselves in a scene of confrontation where they stand alone, divided from the existing order; and inevitably they dream of a new order where there will be salvation and redemption. Once again, Griffin's description of this act is informative. He says such persons are "moved by an impious dream of a mythic new Order—inspired with a new purpose . . . they are moved to act: moved . . . to rise up and cry *No* to the existing order—and prophesy the coming of the new. And thus movements begin."[21]

This confrontation I consider to be "consummatory"—the essential form of a movement, *because up to the point of confrontation it is impossible to*

[17] *Burke,* A Rhetoric of Motives, *p. 115.*
[18] *Griffin,* Critical Responses to Kenneth Burke, *p. 458.*
[19] *Burke,* Permanence and Change *(Rev. ed., Los Altos, California: Hermes Publications, 1954), 69–75.*
[20] *Burke,* The Rhetoric of Religion *(Berkeley: University of California Press, 1970), pp. 215–22.*
[21] *Griffin,* Critical Responses to Kenneth Burke, *p. 460.*

know that a radical or true movement exists. That is, without confrontation the movement rhetoric cannot be distinguished from the rhetoric of the collective seeking change and improvement, but not replacement of the existing order. It is the confrontation form that *produces dialectial enjoinment in the moral area.* For, in every political order there are those who are alienated and who seek change within the hierarchy, and there will always be those who seek power and control over events and groups—those who want a greater "share of the pie" and those who want to improve the existing order for its own sake. Inevitably these persons will form collectives and utilize a rhetoric that petitions, that recruits, that even threatens dire consequences. What distinguishes these collectives from radical or true movements is that *they do not confront the system.* Rather, they maintain the mystery; i.e., keep the secret that the existing order is a true order, one that is in continual movement toward perfection and in which communication through identification and consubstantiation is possible. No matter how contentious the change seekers may become, there is an understood code of control—an identity, a consubstantiality which places limits on the kinds of rhetorical acts that may be performed. In short, there is a dramatization at this level that is rhetorically different from the dramatic enactment of those who confront the system.

For a movement to be perceived as something other than the evolving status quo or the legitimate action of system change agents there must be created a drama or agonistic ritual which forces a response from the establishment commensurate with the moral evil perceived by movement members. The confrontation ritual is enacted by the juxtaposing of two human forces or two agents, one standing for the erroneous or evil system and the other upholding the new or perfect order. These two agents must be brought into ritual conflict through confrontation in order for both to recognize that this is no ordinary reform or realignment of the established order.

The rhetoric of a movement is a rhetoric of re-ordering rather than of re-forming. As Burke points out, every order implies hierarchy—what goes with what, what is more, what is less, what is necessary, etc. Hierarchy includes what is *not* proper, *not* useful, *not* valuable; thus, "the negative." Man, the seeker after perfection, recognizes the negative and becomes aware of his own guilt. And to remove guilt he must seek redemption either through striving to perfect the hierarchy (i.e., established order) or by recognizing the evil of the erroneous system, confessing to his own victimage (mortification) and confronting the evil system with a new, more perfect order (redemption).

Through confrontation the seekers of change (the victims) experience a conversion wherein they recognize their own guilt, transcend the faulty order and acquire a new perspective. This "symbolic rejection of the existing order is a purgative act of transformation and transcendence. It affirms the commitment of the converted to the movement—to the new understanding . . . and hence it endows them with a new condition 'substance'—with a new identity, a new unity, a new motive."[22]

The enactment of confrontation gives a movement its identity, its substance and its form. No movement for radical change can be taken seriously without acts of confrontation. The system co-opts all actions which do not question the basic order, and transforms them into system messages. Confrontational rhetoric shouts "Stop!" at the system, saying, "You cannot go on assuming you are the true and correct order; you must see yourself as the evil thing you are."

An excellent example of the rhetoric of confrontation can be found in the act of the "Catonsville 9" wherein nine Catholic priests and lay workers used napalm to burn the selective service files at Catonsville, Maryland, in 1968. According to Charles Wilkinson, who has made a rhetorical study of this incident as part of the Catholic Anti-War Movement in the United States,[23] "The rhetoric of guilt is employed by nine 'American Citizens' and 'Catholic Christians' burdened with a collective sense of guilt for their country as a war-waging empire and for the church as an accomplice in those wars. Here, the rhetoric is clearly directed to themselves as well as to the masses which comprise the status quo of both church and state. . . . Most immediately it addressed the Nine themselves since they also required the rhetorics of its languaging process to enable them to act as they did."[24] The words of the Nine in their mimeographed press release reveal the nature of the confrontation—the rejection of the mystery, the victimage, and the dream of a new order:

We, American citizens, have worked with the poor in the ghetto and abroad. In the course of our Christian ministry we have watched our country produce more victims than an army of us could console or restore. . . . All of us identify with the victims of American oppression all over the world. We use napalm on these records because napalm has burned people to death in Vietnam, Guatemala and Peru; and because it may be used on America's ghettos. We destroy these draft records not only because they exploit our young men, but because these records represent misplaced power, concentrated in the ruling class of America. . . . We are Catholic Christians who take the Gospel of our Faith seriously. . . . We confront the

[22] Griffin, Critical Responses to Kenneth Burke, p. 465.
[23] Charles Wilkinson, "The Rhetoric of Movements: Definition and Methodological Approach, Applied to the Catholic Anti-War Movement in the United States," Dissertation, Northwestern University, 1974.
[24] Charles Wilkinson, "The Rhetorical Criticism of Movements: A Process Analysis of the Catonsville Nine Incident" (Unpublished paper, Northwestern University, 1977), p. 9.

Catholic Church, other Christian bodies and the synagogues of America with their silence and cowardice in the face of our country's crimes.[25]

The incident at Catonsville was a confrontation, and as such it forced a dialectical enjoinment in the moral arena between the perpetrators and the established order.

No individual can be *of* the movement without an act which recognizes one's own guilt or complicity with the system and which commits the individual to the *new* order. As Scott and Smith point out in their study of the rhetoric of confrontation, confrontation symbolizes the rite of the kill: "The situation [confrontation] shrieks kill-or-be-killed. . . . The blighted self must be killed in striking the enemy. By the act of overcoming his enemy, he who supplants demonstrates his own worthiness, effacing the mark, whatever it may be—immaturity, weakness, sub-humanity—that his enemy has set upon his brow. . . . To satisfy the rite that destroys the evil self in the act of destroying the enemy that has made the self evil, the radical may work out the rite of the kill symbolically."[26]

Brenda Hancock Robinson demonstrates how this act of confrontation as guilt and redemption is essential to the Women's Liberation Movement. In her article, "Affirmation by Negation in the Women's Liberation Movement," she points out that, "Lashing out at the enemy can serve to release women's own guilt feelings in a liberating catharsis. A frequent refrain in feminist rhetoric is that no revolution can occur unless women recognize their oppressed status; such recognition implies they have somehow participated in the oppression, at least by submitting to it. Many women have actually prided themselves on their duplicity—their ability to play at ignorance and helplessness, for example. Guilt from recognizing one's own acquiescent role in the oppression must be turned outward toward the oppressor."[27]

Robinson provides an analysis of an essay by Robin Morgan, "Goodbye to All That," which she considers exemplary of this aspect of the movement, and she finds that "Morgan's statement rings with the eloquence of all the previous no's combined, with a spirit not tentative but angry and final. The enemy is established. The victimage is complete. There is no entreaty to denounce male chauvinism; she rejects it outright." She concludes: "Morgan's essay illustrates that the process of negating the existing order and naming the enemy is important not only in isolating the

---

[25] Charles Wilkinson, "The Rhetorical Criticism of Movements: A Process Analysis of the Catonsville Nine Incident," p. 16.

[26] Scott and Smith, p. 4. In this passage the authors draw upon the ideas of Franz Fanon as expressed in The Wretched of the Earth.

[27] Brenda Robinson Hancock, "Affirmation by Negation in the Women's Liberation Movement," Quarterly Journal of Speech, 58 (1972), 266.

movement's victim, but also in giving women identity as the *antithesis* of men."[28]

Here we see the use of confrontational rhetoric as a "totalistic strategy," to use the words of Scott and Smith.[29] The members of the movement through confrontation draw the line that excludes themselves from the existing order and creates their total dependence on the movement. It is the point from which there is no turning back. Confrontation is a proclamation. It proclaims through the movement, "We are already dead but we are reborn." It says, "We are united in the movement and we understand you for what you are, and you know that we understand."

Confrontation as rhetoric is not an act of violence per se; nor is it a method of warfare. Rather, it is a symbolic enactment which dramatizes the complete alienation of the confronter. As a rhetorical act it is more consummatory than instrumental. It takes a form which prevents the receiver from construing its meaning as an expression of personal dissatisfaction or as a prod toward more rapid response to grievances. Confrontation demands a response that goes beyond the actions of the confrontation itself. It is a dramatization created by the forced juxtaposing of two agents, one standing for the evil, erroneous system and the other upholding the new or "perfect" order. These two agents must be brought into conflict through confrontation in order for both to recognize that what is called for is a moral response appropriate to the moral accusation communicated by the act of confrontation.

It is the act of confrontation that causes the establishment to reveal itself for what it is. The establishment, when confronted, must respond not to the particular enactment but to the challenge to its legitimacy. If it responds with full fury and might to crush the confronters, it violates the mystery and reveals the secret that it maintains power, not through moral righteousness but through its power to kill, actually or symbolically, those who challenge it. Invariably, the response of the establishment spokesmen will reveal whether or not there has been an actual confrontation. The response to confrontation is always characterized by polarization and radical division. Grievances are not recognized as such in confrontation; they are portrayed as trumped-up charges to fool the public and hide the conspiracy. The leadership of the movement is not recognized, for it has no legitimacy, and to confer with it would be tantamount to doing business with the devil. The response of the establishment to confronters is to treat them as moral lepers: to isolate them and pin the anarchist label on them. Such response fuels the confrontation and points the way for the movement. Now the secret has been revealed—the mystery violated—and the struggle can be

---

[28] *Hancock, p. 267.*
[29] *Scott and Smith, p. 6.*

seen as a true moral battle for power and for the legitimate right to define the true order.

Confrontation serves, also, to identify the membership of the movement. Movements are rag-tag organizations at best, continually plagued by problems of organization, recruitment and mobilization. Acts of confrontation demand a personal commitment beyond simply agreeing with the goals of the movement or recognizing that there are wrongs to be righted. To engage in confrontation requires that the individual admit complicity with the oppressors and to publicly confess guilt, while at the same time redeeming oneself. Many a follower of a movement stops short of confrontation, hoping to keep up a protest without either denying the system or the self. Witness, for example, the role of many liberals during the Vietnam antiwar movement. Acts of confrontation, however, are acts of acting together. They are public statements of conversion which, when coupled with the establishment response, formally commit the individual to the movement, making such individuals dependent on the movement for whatever legitimacy they are to have. Without the act of confrontation a movement would not be able to identify its true believers.

There remains much to be discovered about confrontation and the rhetoric of movements. Confrontation as a rhetorical act may be as important in its own way as the rhetorical act of identification. I believe a Burkean philosophy of rhetoric allows for, even requires, a rhetoric of confrontation if we are to fully understand the role of man as symbol maker and user.

Affirmation by Negation in the Women's Liberation Movement
by Brenda Robinson Hancock

Sisterhood is Powerful! Men are the Enemy! These two phrases capture much of the early rhetoric of the current radical Women's Liberation Movement. The two themes, dealt with here as the naming of the enemy and the pro-woman line, are congruent within the movement. Radical feminist rhetoric has created feelings of sisterhood and a new identity for women, by angrily negating or rejecting the identity of males.

Leland Griffin characterizes a social movement in Burkeian terms as a religious drama, with a conflict, a killing of the victim, and striving for salvation of the perfect order.[1] The rhetoric of Women's Liberation has

From The Quarterly Journal of Speech, LVIII, 3 (October 1972), 264–271. Used by permission of the author and the Speech-Communication Association. Dr. Robinson Hancock is professor of speech-communication at the University of Utah.

[1] Leland M. Griffin, "A Dramatistic Theory of the Rhetoric of Movements," in Critical Responses to Kenneth Burke, ed. William H. Rueckert (Minneapolis: University of Minnesota Press, 1969), pp. 456–78. See also Griffin, "The Rhetoric of Historical Movements," Quarterly Journal of Speech, 38 (April 1952), 184–88.

often demonstrated a religious fervor. By rejecting a male-dominated social ordér, women have been able not only to release their frustration with
the present order, but to define themselves in contrast to the male characteristics they criticized. Verbal killing of the victim, men, has allowed
women to discover strengths within themselves, and to unite in a strong
and separate revolutionary movement. The words with which radical feminists have affirmed their own identity by negating male standards will be
the focus of this analysis. The inception phase of the movement will be
emphasized.

The present American radical feminist movement began in late 1967
and early 1968. Somewhat earlier the "reformist" group NOW (National
Organization for Women) had been formed, for the most part by professional women who wanted equal employment opportunities. The radical or
revolutionary groups, on the other hand, were students and social activists
involved in the New Left, or "the Movement." These women had found that
in the "male-dominated" New Left, they were expected to cook, type, and
have sexual relations on demand—back to the kitchen and the bedroom—
despite their political knowledge and years of service and sacrifice to
social causes.[2]

Movements begin, according to Griffin, "when some pivotal individual or
group—suffering attitudes of alienation in a given social system, and
drawn (consciously or unconsciously) by the impious dream of a mythic
Order—enacts, gives voice to, a *No*."[3] Some radical women began to cry
No. Small independent groups started meeting to discuss their treatment
within the New Left and American society. Women began to voice their
rejection of male attitudes of superiority:

*Over the past few months, small groups have been coming together in
various cities to meet around the realization that as women radicals we are
not radical women—that we are unfree within the Movement and in personal relationships, as in the society at large. We realize that women are
organized into the Movement by men and continue to relate to it through
men. We find that the difficulty women have in taking initiative and in
acting and speaking in a political context is the consequence of internaliz-
ing the view that men define reality and women are defined in terms of
men.[4]*

In these barely structured beginnings women were groping for an ideology based on their own experiences as women. The term "consciousness-

[2] *Jo Freeman, "The New Feminists," Nation, 208 (February 24, 1969), 241–44.*
[3] *Griffin, "A Dramatistic Theory," p. 462.*
[4] *Naomi Jaffe and Bernardine Dohrn, "The Look Is You,"* New Left Notes *(March
18, 1968), in* The New Left: A Documentary History, *ed. Massimo Teodori (Indianapolis: Bobbs-Merrill, 1969), pp. 355–56.*

raising" was coined to describe their sharing of experiences and searching for causes of their frustrated sense of inferiority, indeed of exploitation.

Naming the Enemy

In their analysis, these groups of women found the first significant question was, "Who is the Enemy?" As Griffin notes, an enemy or victim is important in the development of a social movement.[5] In the case of Women's Liberation, the naming of the enemy was crucial. So long as women's enemy was the "capitalist system," they would be more effective working in a united front with men to bring about a revolution based on socialist principles. As such they would be simply another faction in the New Left, in which they had discovered feelings of alienation and helplessness.

Many women began their analysis with the New Left's economic viewpoint: capitalism exploits women as lowpaid or unpaid workers, and treats them as property.[6] Others, however, questioned a strictly economic interpretation. Ellen Willis expressed the then emerging view: "The basic misperception is the facile identification of 'the system' with 'capitalism.' In reality, the American system consists of two interdependent but distinct parts—the capitalistic state, and the patriarchal family."[7] Willis and other women observed that male-directed socialism had not freed the women of Russia, China, and Cuba. Similarly, men were making the revolution in the United States; men considered their female associates inferior; there was little hope they would later accept women as equals.

Consequently, to negate society or capitalism was not enough; the negation of men became imperative. Such negation was pronounced in several feminist manifestos. The first widely circulated statement negating the existing "male" order was a pamphlet of essays by Beverly Jones and Judith Brown, *Toward a Female Liberation Movement,* advocating female liberation as the *first* social cause for women. Brown's influential essay recognized the importance of naming the enemy in the struggle: "In the life of each woman, the most immediate oppressor, however unwilling he may be in theory to play that role, is 'the man.' Even if we prefer to view him as merely a pawn in the game, he's still the foreman on the big plantation of maleville."[8]

A lively debate in underground newspapers, pamphlets, and manifestos

[5] Griffin, "A Dramatistic Theory," p. 464.

[6] For the socialist analysis, see Evelyn Reed, Problems of Women's Liberation: A Marxist Approach (New York: Pathfinder Press, 1971).

[7] Ellen Willis, "Letter to a Critic," in Notes from the Second Year, eds. Shulamith Firestone and Ann Koedt (New York: Radical Feminists, 1970), p. 57.

[8] Beverly Jones and Judith Brown, Toward a Female Liberation Movement, pamphlet (Boston: 1968), in Voices from Women's Liberation, ed. Leslie B. Tanner (New York: Signet, 1970), p. 411.

ensued. The emerging conclusion was expressed in "The Redstocking Manifesto," written by one of the earliest and most influential groups in New York: "We identify the agents of our oppression as men."[9] Men were particularly seen as the enemy within the patriarchal family structure. Men had the power, and women were an oppressed class within the patriarchy.

The naming of the enemy often reached great heights of rage and invective, causing many to associate Women's Liberation with man-hating. An extreme example of invective is the SCUM (Society for Cutting up Men) Manifesto by Valerie Solanas.[10] The strategic value of such anger is signifi- cant. As the authors of Black Rage suggest, if such anger is not turned outward upon the oppressor, it is turned inward upon the self.[11] Self-hatred and hatred of others like oneself prevent unity and positive identity. Psy- chologist Richard Farson, in a speech to NOW, observed that self-hatred and hatred of other women "is the most prevalent way women have of dealing with their rage and it's the most important to overcome. That's why it's so difficult to organize women in their own behalf. . . . They don't be- lieve that they want to spend time with other women trying to work for the improvement of their condition."[12] Feminist Marlene Dixon called for women to release their anger: "Women must learn the meaning of rage, the violence that liberates the human spirit. The rhetoric of invective is an equally essential stage, for in discovering and venting their rage against the enemy—and the enemy in everyday life is men—women also experi- ence the justice of their own violence."[13]

Lashing out at the enemy can serve to release women's own guilt feelings in a liberating catharsis. A frequent refrain in feminist rhetoric is that no revolution can occur unless women recognize their oppressed status; such recognition implies they have somehow participated in the oppression, at least by submitting to it. Many women have actually prided themselves on their duplicity—their ability to play at ignorance and helplessness, for example. Guilt from recognizing one's own acqui- escent role in the oppression must be turned outward toward the oppres- sor. As Scott and Smith note, the act of striking at the enemy can be a way of asserting one's worth at last: "The blighted self must be killed in striking the enemy."[14]

[9] "Redstocking Manifesto," mimeographed, July 7, 1969, in Tanner, p. 109.
[10] Valerie Solanas, SCUM Manifesto [Society for Cutting Up Men], (New York: Olympia Press, 1968).
[11] William H. Grier and Price M. Cobbs, Black Rage (New York: Basic Books, 1968), pp. 208–13.
[12] Reported in Los Angeles Free Press, August 28, 1970, p. 52.
[13] Marlene Dixon, "The Rise of Women's Liberation," Ramparts, 8 (December 1969), 63.
[14] Robert L. Scott and Donald K. Smith, "The Rhetoric of Confrontation," Quarterly Journal of Speech, 55 (February 1969), 4.

It should be emphasized that rage and violence have been largely verbal in the Women's Liberation Movement. Many feminists have associated physical violence with male power tactics and rejected such violence as a feminist strategy. For example, Robin Morgan, in a particularly angry and vituperative essay, criticized the women among the violent Weatherman faction "for claiming that the *machismo* style and the gratuitous violence is their own style by 'free choice' and for believing that this is the way for a woman to make her revolution."[15]

Morgan's essay, "Goodbye to All That," is an excellent example of the anger in the movement, as well as of the negation and naming of the enemy. Her statement illustrates several key rhetorical strategies and themes.

The essay is built around negation, for which Morgan's term is "goodbye," which appears thirty times and introduces nine of the twenty-four paragraphs. She rejects the violence of the male revolutionaries, as well as their ego-tripping ambition, "bringing their hang-ups about power-dominance and manipulation to everything they touch." She rejects the New Left's treatment of women as sex objects and work horses, in "a microcosm of capitalist economy, with men competing for power and status at the top, and women doing all the work at the bottom (and functioning as objectified prizes or 'coin' as well)." She rejects new sexual freedom as an excuse to use women physically and symbolically (in pornography).[16]

She denies that socialism is the only solution to women's problems: "The hell with the simplistic notion that automatic freedom for women—or non-white peoples—will come about ZAP! with the advent of a socialist revolution. Bullshit." She rejects white males as potential leaders of the revolution: "To become a true revolutionary one must first become one of the oppressed (not organize or educate or manipulate them)."[17]

Morgan's statement rings with the eloquence of all the previous no's combined, with a spirit not tentative but angry and final. The enemy is established. The victimage is complete. There is no entreaty to denounce male chauvinism; she rejects it outright.

She increases the impact and breadth of her negation by encompassing all men, including "real nice guys we all know and like." She uses the terms male and men in deprecation, usually as subjects acting upon objects—oppressing women. She creates "devil words" by word combination, the most frequent of which is "male-dominated." For example, she speaks of social standards as "male-created, male-dominated, male-

[15] *Robin Morgan, "Goodbye to All That,"* Rat: Subterranean News, *February 6, 1970, p. 6. A complete text appears in Tanner, pp. 268–76.*
[16] Ibid.
[17] Ibid., *p. 7.*

fucked-up, and in male self-interest."[18] The male-pejorative is a common tactic in the rhetoric of Women's Liberation.

Morgan also employs vilification of specific male leaders in the New Left, to illustrate by concrete example her generalized indictment of men. Her use of such name-calling closely parallels Arthur Smith's description of black radicals' use of vilification, or "caustic and bitter language" against a person well known to the audience.[19] For example, Morgan attacks Abbie Hoffman: "Good-bye to the notion that good ol' Abbie is any different from any other up and coming movie star . . . who ditches the first wife and kids, good enough for the old days but awkward once you're Making It."[20] Like other feminists she singles out Hugh Hefner, but her attacks on radical leaders are more meaningful in showing that even radical men oppress women.

Morgan's essay illustrates that the process of negating the existing order and naming the enemy is important not only in isolating the movement's victim, but also in giving women identity as the *antithesis* of men. Women, then, are oppressed rather than oppressor, cooperative rather than manipulative and competitive, capable of love rather than sexual exploitation. Thus, although her essay—and much of feminist rhetoric—is what Griffin terms *anti rhetoric*,[21] and Walter Fisher calls "rhetoric of subversion,"[22] it goes beyond negation. As Fisher notes, to subvert an old image is to affirm a new one.[23]

The Pro-Woman Line

The process of naming men as the enemy thus led to the development of a rhetorical strategy known as the pro-woman line. Women affirmed their own identity by negating the identity of men, and in the process found reasons for strength and a positive self-image.[24] The pro-woman line attempted to identify women's positive characteristics, as contrasted to the negative characteristics of males, and to create a feeling of sisterhood among women.

Rhetoric using the pro-woman line emphasized that women were not only

[18] Ibid.
[19] *Arthur L. Smith,* Rhetoric of Black Revolution *(Boston: Allyn & Bacon, 1969),* pp. 26–27.
[20] *Morgan, p. 6.*
[21] *Griffin, "The Rhetoric of Historical Movements."*
[22] *Walter R. Fisher, "A Motive View of Communication,"* Quarterly Journal of Speech, *56 (April 1970), 131–39. Professor Fisher also gave personal advice in the preparation of this analysis, and his assistance is gratefully acknowledged.*
[23] Ibid.
[24] *Richard Gregg reached a similar conclusion, and suggests that defining oneself in contrast to the enemy may be a common strategy in protest rhetoric. See "The Ego-Function of the Rhetoric of Protest,"* Philosophy and Rhetoric, *4 (Spring 1971), 82.*

useful but vital to the structuring of a new society. Feminists rejected male attitudes as antithetical to the goals of a true revolution, and thereby defined their own attitudes and roles more clearly. For example, like Morgan, many feminists criticized the aggressive, capitalistic attitudes among white men in the New Left, characterizing them as domineering, highly verbal, manipulative, and hypercompetitive.[25] These characteristics, based on male power politics, were used as standards against which to measure women's positive attributes. Since women had been oppressed and had therefore been unable to develop the skills needed to gain and exercise power, they could in their "innocence" play an important part in restructuring a society not based on power and dominance. Judith Brown explained, "In our oppression—being forced to learn to care for others—we have gained valuable skills that we need to teach the male order."[26] Traits conditioned into women, especially nurturance, were advanced as morally superior to the male traits of power and dominance, particularly in the modern, depersonalized nuclear age. Feminists stressed that their movement did not want to wrest power from men and attain dominance over them but to restructure society so that power relationships would be minimal or non-existent. In such a restructured society women would have to lead the way. Thus, as Roxanne Dunbar avowed, "Women and other oppressed people must lead and structure the revolutionary movement and the new society."[27]

By outlining women in bold relief from males, by emphasizing areas of superiority, the pro-woman line was important in creating a feeling of sisterhood. A much-needed rise in self-esteem was effected. Effort was made to say nothing critical of women, to elevate the image of women, to reject condescension toward women of other classes or races. Programs and people were evaluated in terms of whether they were pro-woman or anti-woman.

The importance of this rhetorical strategy lay in its impact on self-esteem. Feelings of inferiority and self-hatred prevented women from uniting to change society. According to Marlene Dixon, "The greatest obstacle facing those who would organize women remains women's belief in their own inferiority."[28] Only through realizing their own worth could women gain a sense of political identity and strength.

Emphasizing the validity of women's ideas and experiences led to political strength through separation. Radical feminists saw the need to make

[25] See for example, Marge Piercy, "The Grand Coolie Damn," Leviathan, 1 (November 1969), 16–22.

[26] Judith Brown, "Introduction," in Joan Robins, Handbook of Women's Liberation (Hollywood: Now Library Press, 1970), p. 9.

[27] Roxanne Dunbar, "Female Liberation as the Basis for Social Revolution," in Sisterhood is Powerful, ed. Robin Morgan (New York: Random House, 1970), pp. 490–91.

[28] Dixon, p. 59.

their own analyses of social problems, untainted by male perspective, with consciousness-raising as their vehicle. They would develop conclusions from their own experiences rather than from books written by men or from the rhetoric of the New Left. As in the Black Power movement, from which Women's Liberation draws many ideas, women insisted that people get radicalized fighting their own battles, and that only the oppressed can decide how to solve their own problems.[29] They insisted on separatism from men in their small groups in order to avoid male domination and female vying for male attention and approval, to develop feelings of sisterhood and cohesiveness among female members.

Aside from their individual experiences, these women turned to other women's views in the development of their ideology. Several underground newspapers and journals appeared: *Aphra; Notes from the First Year; Notes from the Second Year; It Ain't Me, Babe; Off Our Backs.*[30] Anthologies were published, bringing together statements from mimeographed papers, underground journal articles, and historical documents on early feminism. There was a proliferation of new channels of communication, through the printed word and newly formed small groups, converting new members to the faith and unifying the dedicated feminists. These channels of communication, largely underground, were the unifying force in the movement during its inception. Members knew of each other and influenced one another nationally, without the existence of any national structure or organization. Despite a few regional and national conferences, at this time there was little emphasis on public speaking to large groups. Such speaking carried dangers of developing "stars," antithetical to feelings of sisterhood and ideals of non-manipulative equality.[31] The channels chosen for the emerging rhetoric were well suited to the need for purity of ideology and the avoidance of hierarchical power relationships associated with masculine politics. Thus, communication patterns developed as a reaction to negating male patterns, and in the spirit of the pro-woman line.

It should be emphasized that the pro-woman line *emerged* during the inception period of Women's Liberation. Its basis was the negation of "masculine" characteristics. Its effect was sisterhood and unity.

But despite its unifying power, the strategy of total rejection of men and elevation of women involved some dangers for the success of the move-

---

[29] *See for example, Jones and Brown, p. 364.*
[30] *Robin Morgan provides a list of radical women's publication in Sisterhood is Powerful, pp. 580–82.*
[31] *The present (1972) movement, perhaps with more sense of strength, is expanding its rhetoric into the broader public. But such "stars" as Gloria Steinem and Germaine Greer are still subject to much criticism from radical feminists for their "elitist" activities. See for example Claudia Dreifus, "The Selling of a Feminist," in Notes From the Third Year, eds. Anne Koedt and Shulamith Firestone (New York: Radical Feminists, 1971), pp. 100–2.*

ment. Radical feminists were faced with no easy task: to raise women's self-image, without doing violence to the principles of humanism and egalitarianism on which their fundamental case was based. Some feminists were careful to point out that women's superior attributes were due not to natural endowments but to conditioning. For example, Gloria Steinem said, "We are not more moral than men; we are only uncorrupted by power so far."[32] But with others the qualifiers were lost, and the rhetoric has been in danger of perpetuating the very sex role stereotypes against which the movement ultimately struggles. A historical clue about the danger of such a strategy is provided by Betty and Theodore Roszak, who concluded that early feminists in America failed to alter radically their position in society because the advocates clung to the feminine mystique for themselves, instead of emphasizing that charity, mercy, and tenderness were good *human* traits.[33] The strategy of total rejection of men and absolute superiority of women, encouraged by the pro-woman line, may lead the movement to distort not only equality but its own conception of legitimate power. The most successful use of the pro-woman line may be that stressing any superiority as due to conditioning, with no implication that women should gain power over men. That is, the two rhetorical themes of praising women and condemning power relationships can amplify each other when used in conjunction.

Reaction

What was the male reaction, particularly within the New Left, to their rejection by radical femininsts? Many men in the New Left dismissed the feminists as "just chicks with personal hangups."[34] Many labeled them as counter-revolutionary. The women's cause was seen as personal rather than political, self-serving rather than self-sacrificing. Their consciousness-raising sessions were seen at best as personal therapy, at worst as just more women getting together to gossip. Men in the New Left had seen women's issues only as radicalizing tools to recruit women into the revolutionary movement,[35] and women who spoke for their rights as a first cause rather than a tool were often greeted with hisses, boos, and ridicule.[36]

As the radical feminists increased their efforts at conversion, males in the New Left escalated the counter-revolutionary accusations and their efforts to retain female members. Women's caucuses were organized, in

[32] Time, *August 31, 1970, p. 22.*
[33] *Betty Roszak and Theodore Roszak, eds.,* Masculine/Feminine *(New York: Harper and Row, 1969), pp. 100–2.*
[34] *Willis, p. 57.*
[35] *Shulamith Firestone,* The Dialectic of Sex, *1970; rpt. (New York: Bantam, 1970), p. 34.*
[36] *For example, Shulamith Firestone was hissed and booed at a peace march in 1968, according to Brown,* Handbook of Women's Liberation, *p. 7.*

which women's issues, such as abortion, were dealt with. But these cau- cuses, were still under the influence of the males, stressed capitalism as the first cause of problems, and were careful not to blame men (one SDS women's resolution ended with, "Freedom now! We love you!"[37]).

Some women chose to remain within New Left groups. These women, no longer in the mainstream of radical feminism, were labeled by Shula- mith Firestone as "politicos" rather than "feminists" and the "Ladies Auxili- aries of the Left."[38] In keeping with the pro-woman line, however, most feminists did not attack the women who stayed, but the male counter- movement which attempted to entrap them. For example, Robin Morgan asserted, "It is the job of revolutionary feminists to build an ever stronger independent Women's Liberation Movement, so that the Sisters in counter- left captivity will have somewhere to turn, to use their power and rage and beauty and coolness in their own behalf for once. . . . Not for us in Women's Liberation to hassle them and confront them the way their men do, nor to blame them—or ourselves—for what any of us are: an op- pressed people."[39]

Reactions of New Left males are particularly significant in light of their politics. Political observers have pointed out that the American New Left is not socialist, *per se,* since "values of human liberty prevail over the eco- nomic aspects."[40] These radical women activists, then, had learned in the New Left to look beyond economics. That the males could not in this instance do so but insisted that capitalism was the cause of any problems women might have, probably says much about the strength of traditional sexual patterns in our society.

Inadvertently these attacks by New Left males, like condescending criti- cism of "bra-burners" by the media, served the cause of Women's Libera- tion. As Griffin indicates, the development of a counter-movement is vital in the growth of a social movement. A counter-movement provides the needed dialectic, as well as a more clearly outlined victim as a target for rhetorical attack.[41] New Left men, by the intensity of their reaction, proved that "all" men, even revolutionaries, are the enemy. The struggle would be painted in absolute terms: all men oppress women.

Conclusion

This study of the rhetoric of Women's Liberation has revealed strategies developed in the modern inception period of feminism. Radical feminist rhetoric, primarily addressed to women, emphasizing what they term con-

[37] *Jones and Brown, p. 364.*
[38] *Firestone, p. 33.*
[39] *Morgan, "Goodbye to All That," p. 7.*
[40] *Teodori, p. 80.*
[41] *Griffin, "A Dramatistic Theory," p. 464.*

sciousness-raising rather than verbal manipulation, has been adapted to the group's goals. Although the rhetoric has often appeared to consist only of rejection and negation, the present analysis suggests affirmation can be achieved by such negation—by defining women as the antithesis of traditional masculinity. Attacking the enemy can serve to direct guilt and anger outward in a liberating catharsis. Separation from men, the enemy, can also serve to give women an identity in their own revolutionary movement. Attacking the enemy and battling the counter-movement can unify women in a common cause. The task of future rhetoric must be to go beyond man-hating and unification, however, to the restructuring of society—the building of the perfect order. There is danger that feminists will hate individual men rather than seek to change the society which produced them. More recent feminist rhetoric, beyond the scope of this analysis, suggests that the Women's Liberation Movement, having gained strength from the rhetorical strategies discussed here, is now stressing action programs and social change.

6
DECISIONS IN
RHETORICAL CRITICISM

Fundamentally, critics must decide what they are trying to do when dealing with material that interests them; in making these decisions they assume a perspective toward their work. The consciousness of a perspective, like the consciousness of anything else, may wax and wane. Since critics work from assumptions that affect the shape of their final materials, they must be aware of their points of view.

This book is based on the contentions that various perspectives can be differentiated from one another, and that distinguishing them will aid those interested in criticism to see its potentialities more clearly.

Characteristics of the Perspectives

We would like to review the characteristics of the various perspectives in outline form. We do so to enable one to compare and contrast them quickly. Furthermore, we hope that presenting them in this form will stress a general truth: that generalizations are possible only at the expense of omitting detail. The characteristics we attribute are abstracted from a large collection of unique writing about rhetoric and rhetorical criticism. Therefore, like any set of labels, ours will have considerable variety, and some theoretical and critical works will be difficult to classify, given our headings.

The Traditional Perspective

1. Orientation. The critic concentrates on the speaker (or the apparent source of discourse). His purpose is to consider the speaker's response to the rhetorical problems that the speaking situation poses.

2. Assumptions.

a. Society is stable; people, circumstances, and rhetorical principles are fundamentally the same throughout history.

b. Rhetoricians have discovered the essential principles of public discourse.

c. Rhetorical concepts are reasonably discrete and can be studied apart form one another in the process of analyzing rhetorical discourse.

d. A reasonably close word-thought-thing relationship exists. Rhetorical concepts accurately describe an assumed reality.

3. Consensus. Rhetoricians generally agree that Aristotle has identified the ideal rhetorical process.

The Experiential Perspective

1. Orientation. No single element or rhetorical principle can be assumed as the starting point for criticism. Thus, the critic, depending on his or her sensitivity and knowledge, must make the fundamental choice or emphasis.

2. Assumptions.

a. Society is in a continual state of process.

b. An infinite combination of concepts, strategies, and postures are available for the study of public discourse.

c. Any system of categorizing is arbitrary and does not accurately reflect an assumed external reality for extended periods of time.

3. Consensus. No special pattern exists for the study of public discourse. Therefore, discourse must continually be studied afresh.

The Perspective of the "New Rhetorics"

1. Orientation. The critic must find stable relationships in understanding the interaction of people and their social environment.

2. Assumptions.

a. Society is in process, but fairly stable relationships can be found that govern human interaction with the environment.

b. A flexible framework may be constructed for the study of public discourse.

c. A symbol system influences one's perception of reality.

3. Consensus. A unified rhetorical framework is necessary for the productive study of rhetoric and criticism.

Two Meta-Critical Approaches

Since "generic" and "movements" approaches transcend the conventional perspectives, we will list a series of guidelines appropriate for these approaches:

1. Critics should select a focus for criticism that transcends the first level of communication.

2. Critics should establish either a classification or clear boundaries for study.

3. Critics should select a perspective for describing, interpreting, and evaluating the first level of communication.

4. Critics should be sure their focus and perspective are appropriate for previous research conducted within the classification or boundaries.

We have taken the position that rhetorical criticism reflects a perspective. However, at a time when rhetorical criticism is pre-paradigmatic and many theories are competing for acceptance, we discover that critics frequently make choices that seem to combine elements of what we have purported to be distinct perspectives. For example, an essay may exhibit a criticial orientation that is typical of an experiential perspective, but the vocabulary employed may be neo-Aristotelian or dramatistic. It is not difficult to imagine that a critic might use a basically language-action approach but take a speaker orientation, or a critical orientation with descriptive-historical development of the subject matter, or a number of other possible combinations.

We believe that in most cases of mixed forms the assumptions made by the critic will line up substantially with one perspective or another. However, what seems to us to be a hybrid form may prove to be one of a number of instances that demonstrate a fresh perspective. Regardless of the classificatory system, a crossing and overlapping will always reflect a process reality and the arbitrary and ambiguous nature of language.

Basic Choices in Rhetorical Criticism

In the introduction we indicated that this is not a handbook on writing rhetorical criticism, but we also indicated that we have included applications for each method because we wanted to maintain a link with the actual writing of rhetorical criticism. For this reason we would like to discuss some of the basic decisions critics make in executing criticism.

Some writers believe that criticism is an intuitive process for which one has or has not the necessary instinct and experience. Although they recognize that critics implicitly make numerous choices as they engage in the act of criticism, these writers are apt to assert that making these choices explicit tears the process of criticism apart. There is certainly an element of truth to their position; but if we are to think about and teach criticism, we must attempt to delineate at least in general terms some of the decisions that rhetorical critics make implicitly or explicitly each time they engage in criticism. We suggest five centers of interest. We do not suggest the order given as an ideal sequence through which the critic should move, nor do we imply that these centers of interest will always be distinct or that they exhaust the possibilities.

1. Focus. Critics should find a focus for their work that will unify all the necessary elements of the critical act. Their interest will probably be aroused by some specific public discourse, but they should keep it general for a time, asking: "Just what is it that attracts me? What is it that puzzles me?" Obviously, the *it* is vague. Probably the critic's focal point will gradually take the form of a thesis statement.

Any number of specific concepts could serve as the focus for criticism. Focal points in the traditional perspective tended to be speakers, their ideas and purposes, or their effectiveness in moving audiences. Today critics often give focal attention to larger patterns of discourse which are seen as arising from a multiplicity of sources, and also to strategies for communicating within on-going, interactive social groups. Actually, any element or relationship involved in the rhetorical act has the potential of serving to focus criticism.

Quite possibly two critics examining the same rhetorical act may select different aspects on which to focus. In analyzing the "confrontation at Columbia University" in the spring of 1968, James R. Andrews focused on the "distinction between persuasion and coercion,"[1] while James F. Klumpp focused "on the interaction of rhetoric and action."[2] Different focal points contributed heavily to quite different conclusions about the events of the student strike and occupation of several university buildings. Andrews strongly argued that the abandoning of persuasion for coercion was not justified, while Klumpp constructed the term "polar-rejective identification" to explain how the Students for a Democratic Society (the SDS) was successful in gaining acceptance without compromise for many of their aims.

In a sense, the critic shapes the event. What we mean by this statement is that our idea of "an event" is always a simplification of a dizzying complex of actions on which we impose boundaries in order to give a sense of singularity: We focus on some aspects and ignore others in perceiving "an event." For example, a presidential campaign is an event that is so complex that it will invite a wide array of foci. Thus in studying the 1972 campaign, Edwin Black highlighted the theme of time; David L. Swanson started with voter reports on political information; Ernest G. Bormann emphasized the fantasy surrounding George McGovern's decision about Thomas Eagleton's vice-presidential candidacy; Walter R. Fisher considered two views of the American dream; and Herbert W. Simons, James W. Chesebro, and C. Jack Orr studied McGovern's tie to the "New Left."[3]

Critics need to find a focus for their work. When they do they will discover that their decisions have implications for other critical decisions that they will need to make.

2. Vocabulary. In describing, interpreting, and evaluating a speech, a career, a movement, a dominant strategy, and so forth, writers need a critical vocabulary that is instrumental to the sort of interest they are trying to develop. They may look toward established theories for their terms; they may select among them or they may develop them for their particular

---

[1] "Confrontation at Columbia: A Case Study in Coercive Rhetoric," The Quarterly Journal of Speech, LV, 1 (February 1969), 15.
[2] "Challenge of Radical Rhetoric: Radicalization at Columbia," Western Speech, XXXVII, 3 (Summer 1973), 156.
[3] "Electing Time"; "Political Information, Influence, and Judgment in the Presidential Campaign"; "The Eagleton Affair: A Fantasy Theme Analysis"; "Reaffirmation and Subversion of the American Dream"; and "A Movement Perspective on the 1972 Presidential Campaign," The Quarterly Journal of Speech, LIX, 2 (April 1973), 125–79.

tasks. Two important influences on their choices of vocabulary will be critics' past experiences and the necessities imposed by the nature of the materials with which they are dealing.

In discussing the "generic" approach we referred to six critics who chose to analyze Nixon's Vietnam Address from three different perspectives. These criticisms reflected an even greater variety of choices of vocabulary. The first criticism published by James W. Chesebro and Sandra E. Purnell suggested the "dramatistic" theory of Kenneth Burke as they talked about "strategies," "views of reality," and "alienation."[4] Next, Robert P. Newman allowed his vocabulary to evolve from the speech itself as well as from argumentation theory. He evaluated the speech in terms of "truth," "evidence," "argument," "audiences," "strategy," and "style."[5] Then, Hermann G. Stelzner chose the archetypal quest story as a basis for criticism and selection of vocabulary. So the important elements were "a precious Object and/or Person," "a long journey," "a Hero," "Guardians of the Object," and "Helpers."[6] Karlyn Kohrs Campbell did not turn to an external theory, but considered criteria suggested by the speech itself. She arrived at four criteria influential in her selection of vocabulary— "truth," "credibility," "unity," and "ethical principles."[7] Finally, Forbes I. Hill intentionally drew upon Aristotelian rhetoric because he wanted to demonstrate its usefulness in criticism. Hill's important terms were "situation," "disposition," "logos," "pathos," "ethos," and "style."[8]

These articles show how critics necessarily make a choice of vocabulary and that there are an infinite number of rhetorical and non-rhetorical theories available. The choice of vocabulary is usually the result of some other basic decision the critic must make.

3. Perspective. Any criticism will automatically have a starting point even though critics do not consciously make such decisions. However, if these decisions are consciously made (which in some cases will mean that critics seek to uncover their perspectives), they can be more certain that the decisions are consistent with their materials, their purposes, and the sorts of judgments they intend to make. Consciously selecting perspectives from which to approach their work will probably enable critics to make their writing more consistent internally. The premise of this book is

[4] *"The Rhetoric of Alignment: Can Nixon's Quest for Power Unite the Nation?"* Speaker and Gavel, VII, 3 (March 1970), 77–84.
[5] *"Under the Veneer: Nixon's Vietnam Speech of November 3, 1969,"* The Quarterly Journal of Speech, LVI, 2 (April 1970), 168–78.
[6] *"The Quest Story and Nixon's November 3, 1969 Address,"* The Quarterly Journal of Speech, LVII, 2 (April 1971), 163–72.
[7] *"Richard M. Nixon: 'Vietnamization: The President's Address on the War,"* in Critiques of Contemporary Rhetoric, Karlyn Kohrs Campbell (ed.), Belmont, California: Wadsworth Publishing Co., 1972, pp. 50–56.
[8] *"Conventional Wisdom–Traditional Form: The President's Message of November 3, 1969,"* The Quarterly Journal of Speech, LVIII, 4 (December 1972), 373–86.

the importance of the critical perspective, so we would refer you to the characteristics of the perspectives we have outlined and the many examples we have used throughout our discussion of the three perspectives and two meta-critical approaches.

4. Judgment. Critics should determine the sorts of judgments they wish to make. We have already indicated that a given criticism may be descriptive, interpretive, or evaluative. Traditional criticism tends to be primarily descriptive, and the criticism typifying the new rhetorics tends to be primarily interpretive. In general, rhetorical critics have backed away from the evaluative, but experiential critics are the most likely to accept that responsibility of judgment. Too often, however, we believe that critics have failed to think through the implications of their choices of purpose. Critics must be certain that their purposes are consistent with their theses and the ends they wish to achieve through their work.

An example where critics coming from the same experiential perspective arrived at significantly different judgments was Andrews's and Klumpp's analyses of the "confrontation at Columbia." Remember, the two critics had selected different starting points—Andrews focused on the "distinction between persuasion and coercion," while Klumpp considered "the interaction of rhetoric and action." This difference, along with what were probably different general attitudes toward the event, led them to very different judgments. Andrews was strongly negative as he talked about the "rape of the university" when the Students for a Democratic Society abandoned persuasion in favor of coercion.[9] Klumpp's judgment was more interpretive in that his term "polar-rejective identification" explained what occurred in the confrontation, but Klumpp also implied a positive, not a negative, judgment in concluding that the SDS had discovered a way to broaden the base of the movement without compromising the purity of its ideology.[10] The nature and strength of judgment is an important decision in rhetorical criticism, but it is intimately related to the other decisions critics must make.

5. End. Critics must conceive carefully the end they wish to achieve through their work. Do they wish to provide insight into a given body of public discourse as achieved by Ling's analysis of Edward Kennedy's Address (see chapter 4) and Burgess's criticism of the rhetoric of "Black Power."[11] And, if so, what sort of insight will suffice? Should critics not provide a point of view that most people in being exposed to the rhetoric would miss?

Or are critics primarily interested in building rhetorical theory or in influ-

[9] Andrews, "Confrontation at Columbia," 9–16.
[10] Klumpp, "Challenge of Radical Rhetoric," 146–56.
[11] "The Rhetoric of Black Power: A Moral Demand," The Quarterly Journal of Speech, LIV, 2 (April 1968), 122–33.

encing society? Klumpp's introduction of the concept "polar-rejective identification" was an attempt at building rhetorical theory that other critics could utilize. Andrew's judgment about the use of coercion surely was an attempt to influence society's attitude toward the confrontation.

The final result that critics wish to achieve is the underlying motive that influences all their decisions. If critics are concerned with applying or building theory, their critical vocabulary and probably their perspective will have been determined for them. If they are interested in influencing society, they will almost certainly be required to convey an evaluative judgment. On the other hand, so intimately related are these basic choices in writing criticism that selecting a critical vocabulary, perspective, and type of judgment may determine the ultimate end critics can serve.

Whether criticism is an intuitive process or whether choices such as these briefly outlined are made explicitly, they must be made because they are inherent in the critical act. In our opinion, critics will profit in terms of the clarity and insight of their work by striving to become aware of the basic choices they make and of the implications of these choices.

A fully formed, coherent piece of criticism is an ideal that may always be just beyond the grasp of the critic. But the impulse to criticize is a human one. Developing the capacity to strive carefully and conscientiously toward the ideal is humanizing.

Future of Rhetorical Criticism: Paradigmatic or Pluralistic?

In the first edition of this book we made a statement concerning the future of rhetorical criticism. We present it here unchanged; fundamentally we believe that it still holds: rhetorical criticism has continued to be pluralistic. We are adding to what was, and still is, a predictive statement, a short postscript.

1971 Statement.

The twentieth century has witnessed tremendous scientific advances. These advances have been accompanied by and perhaps even made possible by a strong sense of the reality of science and the efficacy of its method. On a strong scientific basis the world, or at least the economically advantaged portion of it, has become increasingly re-formed on a technological basis. So complete have these changes been that some social critics have been referring to the United States, Western Europe, and the Soviet Union as "technocracies."[1]

More recently, however, increasing portions of the citizens of these

---

[1] For a review of technocratic forces and references to some literature, see Theodore Roszak, The Making of a Counter Culture: Reflections on the Technocratic Society and Its Youthful Opposition, Garden City, N.Y., Anchor Books, 1969, chap. 1.

nations have become convinced that their technical proficiencies have so deeply affected their societies that not only economic means but social existences have been technologized. One concomitant of the technical advances has been a plundering of the natural environment to the degree that life itself is threatened. More and more voices have been raised against the seeming consequences of technical sufficiency and spiritual poverty. Part of the outcry, of course, has arisen because, in spite of the plenty produced by bureaucratized industry, education, and government, economic poverty still exists in pockets in the advanced nations and in large segments of the disadvantaged world. These pockets of poverty are often attributed more to a lack of will than to a lack of ability.

Although it seems foolhardy to us to assert that the blame for these conditions should be laid at the door of science, we are confident that one result has been and will continue to be a resurgence of humanistic scholarship. Humane traditions are even making themselves felt in the philosophy of science. Thomas S. Kuhn's work, on which we have depended heavily, placed science in a much different light than that typical earlier in this century and is still the most prevalent viewpoint. Such thinkers as Michael Polanyi and J. Bronowski stress the humane values of science itself.[2]

We believe that there will be an increasing ability in academia and in public interchange to tolerate the pluralistic tendencies that seem endemic in humane studies, and we believe that rhetorical criticism is and will remain consistent with this trend. Within a humane tradition rhetorical criticism will be fundamentally subjective, leaving the field open for numerous approaches.

Increasingly, rhetorical criticism is becoming much broader, as interest and research in communication become more complex. Within the broad scope of that criticism, individual critics are finding and will need to find particular focuses if their work is to be productive. Methods will develop from the variety of questions asked and the public communicative processes that are probed.

In his review of the theoretical writing on rhetorical criticism, Barnet Baskerville concluded that "alone among recent writings, Mouat's 'An Approach to Rhetorical Criticism'[3] rejects pluralism and seeks for a uniform

[2] See Michael Polanyi, Personal Knowledge: Toward a Post Critical Philosophy, New York, Harper Torchbooks, 1964; and J. Bronowski, The Identity of Man, Garden City, N.Y., American Museum Science Books, 1965, and Science and Human Values, New York, Harper Torchbooks, 1965; Stephen Toulmin, Foresight and Understanding, New York, Harper Torchbooks, 1963 is also relevant, as is, of course, Thomas S. Kuhn, The Structure of Scientific Revolutions, Chicago, University of Chicago Press, 1962.

[3] Lawrence H. Mouat, in The Rhetorical Idiom, Donald C. Bryant (ed.), Ithaca, N.Y., Cornell University Press, 1958, pp. 161–77.

approach."[4] We believe that this criticism is even more valid today than it was in 1967. The forces that brought about the general acceptance of pluralism have, if anything, become stronger since Baskerville surveyed the literature.

We conclude then that no paradigm will soon arise to gain the adherence that neo-Aristotelianism had in the 1930s and 1940s. If a pluralistic attitude becomes generally recognized and understood, we should see a lessening of interest in theorizing about criticism and a revitalized concern with criticizing public discourse.

At the very least we should expect a lessening of interest in traditional methods of theorizing. It seems fair to say of academic speech criticism during the first part of the twentieth century that a unified theory was rather well accepted before it was applied to the reality of discourse. The process was deductive. Even when faith in the paradigm began to break down, theorists persisted in the deductive mode. In the future rhetorical theory will probably be developed more inductively, as abstractions from the study of discourse. In a sense, this development will mean less distinction between theory and criticism.

A productive "closeness" of theory and criticism will result if the abstractions from critical practice take on the character of tentative principles, which are held tentatively, applied, confirmed (to some degree), and modified by further criticism of public discourse. If theory is to be descriptive of the process of public discourse in a rapidly changing society, then rhetoric must be a constantly growing and changing body of knowledge.

Accompanying the pluralism, tentativeness, and change that we predict, we see a shift from the traditional critical interest in speakers (or the sources of discourse) to the interactions that make communication a process. Thus, rhetoric as such will be closer to the center of critical interest. Critics are now assuming that rhetoric is not something added to the deliberation of a set of issues by spokesmen but rather something integrally associated with the reality of whatever those issues are.[5] Although critics will be interested in what speakers, writers, or demonstrators have to say, they will be more concerned with the forces that seem to permeate public discourse, issues, campaigns, or movements.

These generalizations about the future may not be completely accurate,

[4] Barnet Baskerville, "Selected Writings on the Criticism of Public Address, Addendum, 1967," in Thomas R. Nilsen (ed.), Essays on Rhetorical Criticism, New York, Random House, 1968, p. 189.

[5] On this point see Robert L. Scott, "On Viewing Rhetoric as Epistemic," Central States Speech Journal, XVIII, 1 (February 1967), 9–17. Excellent examples of well-integrated criticism of the sort we suggest are Edwin Black, "The Second Persona," The Quarterly Journal of Speech, LVI, 2 (April 1970), 109–19; and Parke G. Burgess, "The Rhetoric of Moral Conflict: Two Critical Dimensions," The Quarterly Journal of Speech, LVI, 2 (April 1970), 120–30.

of course, but they are based on what present practice appears to indicate. In concluding, we would like to stress one more potentiality. In the future critics are apt to find themselves dealing rhetorically with rhetorical materials, that is, they are likely to enter the arena of social influence, at least to the extent that the manner in which messages are received and made meaningful will be determined in some part by the general critical sensibilities of audiences. If the critic finds the persuasive implications of his own messages, then he should be willing to take responsibility for the evaluations that he will inevitably make.

1980 Postscript.

Interests in building rhetorical theory on the one hand and concentrating on concrete events that seem to exhibit specific rhetorical interactions on the other are scarcely mutually exclusive. In fact one can argue that both impulses are interdependent. Nonetheless, there seems to be an ebb and flow between these activities as if between two magnetic poles.

The past decade of work in rhetorical scholarship has been dominated by the former tendency rather than the latter, more by the theoretical than the critical (if one considers the latter as digging into specific events). If we are correct in noting an ebb and flow, then we can expect more emphasis on specific critical studies in the next decade.

Another tendency may be even more important. Echoing the ideal we stated as the interdependency of theory and criticism, Caroline D. Hamsher and James W. Chesebro argue that the relationship is so demonstrably close that it constitutes a single distinct field of study.[6] Although we are not as sanguine about the actualizing of the ideal, we believe that the growing trend for writers when arguing for theoretical constructs to illustrate those with concrete pieces of criticism is healthy.[7]

More and more the perspectives on criticism seem to be taking the shape of tools for interpretation. The implication is that in general the critic's role is best seen as enhancing understanding, recognizing that understanding is a joint product of the environment—including the social and communicative environment—and the actors within that environment. This sort of thrust subordinates both description and evaluation as purposes of criticism. Seeing both rhetorical theory and rhetorical as interpre-

---

[6] "Contemporary Rhetorical Theory and Criticism: Dimensions of the New Rhetoric," Speech Monographs, XLII, 4 (November 1975), 311–34.

[7] Good example of an article introducing a new theory with an application is "Language-Action: A Paradigm for Communication" by Thomas S. Frentz and Thomas B. Farrell, The Quarterly Journal of Speech, LXII, 4.

In addition we have printed here the pair of essays by Thomas Frentz and Janet Hocker Rushing in this book. Many other examples could be cited including the pair of essays by G. P. Mohrmann and Michael Leff which we have cited repeatedly (see the bibliography at the end of this book).

tive may help connect the two more closely and encourage an already active pluralism by shifting concern from what is right or wrong to what is helpful *given a point of view* in understanding events.

When critics do serve the urge to evaluate, an interpretive frame should encourage (1) a declaration of a particular frame within which the evaluation is relevant and (2) a recognition that varied evaluations will inevitably result given different frames and even that these often need not be taken as inconsistent with one another.

A spirit of toleration may well relieve rhetorical critics of a feeling that a paradigm in the sense of a single, favored model is not at all necessary for vigorous scholarship that may at once satisfy our need to understand the flow of rhetorical communication that is formative of society and our need to refine critical theory. In short, pluralism may be a viable ideal for humanistic learning and teaching.

SELECTED
BIBLIOGRAPHY

Books

Aly, Bower. *The Rhetoric of Alexander Hamilton*. New York: Columbia University Press, 1941.

Andrews, James R. *A Choice of Worlds*. New York: Harper and Row, 1973.

Arnold, Caroll C. *Criticism of Oral Rhetoric*. Columbus, Ohio: Merrill, 1974.

Auer, J. Jeffrey, ed. *Antislavery and Disunion, 1858–1861: Studies in the Rhetoric of Compromise and Conflict*. New York and Evanston: Harper and Row, 1963.

Bitzer, Lloyd F., and Black, Edwin, eds. *The Prospect of Rhetoric*. New York: Prentice-Hall, 1971.

Black, Edwin B. *Rhetorical Criticism: A Study in Method*. New York: Macmillan, 1965.

Bormann, Ernest G. *Theory and Research in the Communicative Arts*. New York: Holt, Rinehart and Winston, 1965.

Braden, Waldo W., ed. *Oratory in the Old South, 1828–1860*. Baton Rouge: Louisiana State University Press, 1970.

Brigance, William N. *A History of American Public Address*. 2 vols. New York: McGraw-Hill, 1943.

Brockriede, Wayne, and Scott, Robert L. *Moments in the Rhetoric of the Cold War*. New York: Random House, 1970.

Bryant, Donald C., ed. *Papers in Rhetoric and Poetic*. Iowa City: University of Iowa Press, 1965.

———. *Rhetorical Dimensions in Criticism*. Baton Rouge, Louisiana: Louisiana State University Press, 1973.

Burke, Kenneth. *Counter-Statement*. New York: Harcourt, Brace, 1931.

———. *Permanence and Change*. New York: New Republic, 1935.

———. *The Philosophy of Literary Form*. Baton Rouge, Louisiana: Louisiana State University Press, 1941.

———. *A Grammar of Motives*. Englewood Cliffs, N.J.: Prentice-Hall, 1946.

———. *A Rhetoric of Motives*. Englewood Cliffs, N.J.: Prentice-Hall, 1950.

———. *The Rhetoric of Religion*. Boston: Beacon Press, 1961.

———. *Language as Symbolic Action*. Berkeley: University of California Press, 1966.

Campbell, Karlyn Kohrs. *Critiques of Contemporary Rhetoric*. Belmont, California: Wadsworth, 1972.

Campbell, Karlyn Kohrs, and Jamieson, Kathleen Hall, eds. *Form and Genre: Shaping Rhetorical Action*. Falls Church, Va.: Speech Communication Association, 1978.

Cathcart, Robert. *Post Communication: Critical Analysis and Evaluation.* Indianapolis: Bobbs-Merrill, 1966.

Fogarty, Daniel. *Roots for a New Rhetoric.* New York: Teachers College Press, 1959.

Golden, James, and Rieke, Richard. *The Rhetoric of Black Americans.* Columbus, Ohio: Charles E. Merrill, 1971.

Goodrich, Chauncey A. *Select British Eloquence (1859).* Indianapolis: Bobbs-Merrill, 1963.

Graham, John, ed. *Great American Speeches of the Twentieth Century, Texts and Studies.* New York: Appleton-Century-Crofts, 1970.

Grover, David H. *Debaters and Dynamiters.* Corvallis: Oregon State University Press, 1964.

———, ed. *Landmarks in Western Oratory.* Laramie: University of Wyoming Press, 1968.

Hart, Roderick P. *The Political Pulpit.* West Lafayette, Indiana: Purdue University Press, 1977.

Hillbruner, Anthony. *Critical Dimensions: The Art of Public Address Criticism.* New York: Random House, 1966.

Holland, De Witte, ed. *Preaching in American History.* Nashville, Tenn.: Abingdon Press, 1969.

Howes, Raymond F., ed. *Historical Studies of Rhetoric and Rhetoricians.* Ithaca, N.Y.: Cornell University Press, 1961.

Linsley, William A., ed. *Speech Criticism: Methods and Materials.* Dubuque, Iowa: William C. Brown, 1968.

Lomas, Charles W. *The Agitator in American Society.* Englewood Cliffs, N.J.: Prentice-Hall, 1968.

Nichols, Marie Hochmuth, ed. *A History and Criticism of American Public Address.* vol. 3. London: Longmans, Green, 1955.

———. *Rhetoric and Criticism.* Baton Rouge: Louisiana State University Press, 1963.

Reid, Loren, ed. *American Public Address, Essays in Honor of Albert Craig Baird.* Columbia: University of Missouri Press, 1961.

———. *Charles James Fox: A Man for the People.* Columbia: University of Missouri Press, 1969.

Richards, I. A. *The Philosophy of Rhetoric.* New York: Oxford University Press, 1936.

Rueckert, William H. *Kenneth Burke and the Drama of Human Relations.* Minneapolis: University of Minnesota Press, 1963.

———, ed. *Critical Responses to Kenneth Burke.* Minneapolis: University of Minnesota Press, 1969.

Scott, Robert L., and Brockriede, Wayne. *The Rhetoric of Black Power.* New York: Harper and Row, 1969.

Smith, Arthur L. *The Rhetoric of Black Revolution.* Boston: Allyn and Bacon, 1969.

Thonssen, Lester, and Baird, A. Craig. *Speech Criticism: The Development of Standards for Rhetorical Appraisal.* New York: Ronald Press, 1948. 2d ed., 1970, with Waldo W. Braden.

Wallace, Karl R., ed. *A History of Speech Education in America.* New York: Appleton-Century-Crofts, 1954.

Weaver, Richard M. *The Ethics of Rhetoric.* Chicago: Henry Regnery, 1953.

Wrage, Ernest J., and Baskerville, Barnet, eds. *American Forum: Speeches on Historic Issues, 1788–1900.* New York: Harper and Row, 1960.

————, eds. *Contemporary Forum: American Speeches on Twentieth-Century Issues.* New York: Harper and Row, 1962.

Articles on Theory

Anderson, Robert O. "The Characterization Model for Rhetorical Criticism of Political Image Campaigns." *Western Speech* 37 (1973): 75–86.

Andrews, James R. "The Rhetoric of Coercion and Persuasion." *The Quarterly Journal of Speech* 56 (1970): 187–95.

Backes, James G. "Rhetorical Criticism: Yet Another Emphasis." *Western Speech* 26 (1962): 164–67.

Baird, A. Craig. "The Study of Speeches." *American Public Addresses, 1740–1952* New York: McGraw-Hill, 1956.

Bashford, Bruce. "The Rhetorical Method in Literary Criticism." *Philosophy and Rhetoric* 9 (1976): 133–46.

Baskerville, Barnet. "Principal Themes of Nineteenth-Century Critics of Oratory." *Speech Monographs* 19 (1952): 11–26.

————. "The Critical Method in Speech." *Central States Speech Journal* 4 (1953): 1–5.

————. "The Dramatic Criticism of Oratory." *The Quarterly Journal of Speech* 45 (1959): 39–45.

————. "Rhetorical Criticism, 1971: Retrospect, Prospect, Introspect." *Southern Speech Journal* 37 (1971): 113–24.

————. "Must We All Be 'Rhetorical Critics?' " *The Quarterly Journal of Speech* 63 (1977): 107–16.

Bennett, W. Lance. "The Ritualistic and Pragmatic Bases of Political Campaign Discourse." *The Quarterly Journal of Speech* 63 (1977): 219–38.

Berthold, Carol A. "Kenneth Burke's Cluster-Agon Method: Its Development and an Application." *Central States Speech Journal* 27 (1976): 302–9.

Black, Edwin. "The Second Persona." *The Quarterly Journal of Speech* 56 (1970): 109–19.

Bormann, Ernest G. "Fantasy and Rhetorical Vision: The Rhetorical Criticism of Social Reality." *The Quarterly Journal of Speech* 58 (1972): 396–407.

Breen, Myles P. "Rhetorical Criticism and Media." *Central States Speech Journal* 27 (1976): 15–21.

Brockriede, Wayne. "Toward a Contemporary Aristotelian Theory of Rhetoric." *The Quarterly Journal of Speech* 52 (1966): 33–40.

———. "Dimensions of the Concept of Rhetoric." *The Quarterly Journal of Speech* 54 (1968): 1–12.

———. "Rhetorical Criticism as Argument." *The Quarterly Journal of Speech* 60 (1974): 165–74.

Brummett, Barry. "Some Implications of 'Process' or 'Intersubjectivity': Postmodern Rhetoric." *Philosophy and Rhetoric* 9 (1976): 21–51.

Bryant, Donald C. "Some Problems of Scope and Method in Rhetorical Scholarship." *The Quarterly Journal of Speech* 23 (1937): 182–89.

———. "Aspects of the Rhetorical Tradition." *The Quarterly Journal of Speech* 36 (1950): 169–176; 326–32.

———. "Rhetoric: Its Function and Scope." *The Quarterly Journal of Speech* 39 (1953): 401–24.

———. "Rhetorical Criticism in The Middlesex Journal, 1774." *The Quarterly Journal of Speech* 50 (1964): 45–52.

Burgess, Parke G. "The Rhetoric of Moral Conflict: Two Critical Dimensions." *The Quarterly Journal of Speech* 56 (1970): 120–30.

———. "Crisis Rhetoric: Coercion vs. Force." *The Quarterly Journal of Speech* 59 (1973): 61–73.

Burke, Kenneth. "Rhetoric—Old and New." *The Journal of General Education* 5 (1951): 202–9.

———. "A Dramatistic View of the Origins of Language." *The Quarterly Journal of Speech*. Part 1. 38 (1952): 251–64; Part II. 38 (1952): 446–60; Part III. 39 (1953): 79–92.

Byrne, Richard B. "Stylistic Analysis of the Film: Notes on a Methodology." *Speech Monographs* 32 (1965): 74–78.

Cain, Earl R. "A Method for Rhetorical Analysis of Congressional Debate." *Western Speech* 18 (1954): 91–95.

Campbell, Karlyn Kohrs. "Criticism: Ephemeral and Enduring." *Speech Teacher* 23 (1974): 9–14.

Cathcart, Robert S. "New Approaches to the Study of Movements: Defining Movements Rhetorically." *Western Speech* 36 (1972): 82–87.

———. "Movements: Confrontation as Rhetorical Form." *Southern Speech Communication Journal* 43 (1978): 233–47.

Chapel, Gage William. "Television Criticism: A Rhetorical Perspective." *Western Speech Communication Journal* 39 (1975): 81–91.

Chesebro, James W., and Hamsher, Caroline D. "Rhetorical Criticism: A Message-Centered Procedure." *Speech Teacher* 22 (1973): 282–90.

———. "Contemporary Rhetorical Theory and Criticism: Dimensions of a New Rhetoric." *Speech Monographs* 42 (1975): 311–34.

Clark, Robert D. "Lesson from the Literary Critics." *Western Speech* 21 (1957): 83–89.

———. "Biography and Rhetorical Criticism" (review essay). *The Quarterly Journal of Speech* 44 (1958): 182–86.

Conville, Richard. "Northrup Frye and Speech Criticism: An Introduction." *Quarterly Journal of Speech* 44 (1970): 417–25.

Cragan, John F. "Rhetorical Strategy: A Dramatistic Interpretation and Application." *Central States Speech Journal* 24 (1975): 4–11.

Croft, Albert J. "The Functions of Rhetorical Criticism." *The Quarterly Journal of Speech* 42 (1956): 283–91.

Dell, George W. "Philosophic Judgments in Contemporary Rhetorical Criticism." *Western Speech* 30 (1966): 81–89.

De Vito, Joseph A. "Style and Stylistics: An Attempt at Definition." *The Quarterly Journal of Speech* 53 (1967), 248–55.

Duhamel, P. Albert. "The Concept of Rhetoric as Effective Presentation." *Journal of the History of Ideas* 10 (1949): 344–56.

Ehninger, Douglas. "On Rhetoric and Rhetorics." *Western Speech* 31 (1967): 242–49.

Ellingsworth, Huber W. "Anthropology and Rhetoric: Toward a Culture-Related Methodology of Speech Criticism." *Southern Speech Journal* 28 (1963):307–12.

Ericson, Jon M. "A Critique of Rhetorical Criticism." *The Quarterly Journal of Speech* 50 (1964): 313–15.

Ewbank, Barbara H., and Ewbank, Henry L. "The Critical Statement." *Central States Speech Journal* 27 (1976): 285–94.

Fisher, Walter. "Method in Rhetorical Criticism." *Southern Speech Journal* 35 (1969): 101–9.

———. "Rhetorical Criticism as Criticism." *Western Speech* 38 (1974): 75–80.

Gregg, Richard B. "A Phenomenologically Oriented Approach to Rhetorical Criticism." *Central States Speech Journal* 17 (1966): 83–90.

Griffin, Leland M. "The Rhetoric of Historical Movements." *The Quarterly Journal of Speech* 38 (1952): 184–88.

———. "The Edifice Metaphor in Rhetorical Theory." *Speech Monographs* 27 (1960): 279–92.

Gronbeck, Bruce E. "Rhetorical History and Rhetorical Criticism." *Speech Teacher* 24 (1975): 309–20.

Hagan, Michael R. "Kenneth Burke and Generative Criticism of Speeches." *Central States Speech Journal* 22 (1971): 252–56.

Hahn, Dan F., and Gonchar, Ruth M. "Rhetorical Biography: A Methodology for the Citizen-Critic." *Speech Teacher* 22 (1973): 48–53.

———. "Studying Social Movements: A Rhetorical Methodology." *Speech Teacher* 20 (1971): 44–52.

Haiman, Franklyn S. "Rhetoric of the Streets: Some Legal and Ethical Considerations." *The Quarterly Journal of Speech* 53 (1967): 99–115.

Hance, Kenneth G. "The Historical-Critical Type of Research: A Re-examination." *Central States Speech Journal* 13 (1962): 165–70.

Hendrix, J. A. "In Defense of Neo-Aristotelian Rhetorical Criticism." *Western Speech* 32 (1968): 246–51.

———, et al. "Rhetorical Criticism: Prognoses for the Seventies—a Symposium." *Southern Speech Journal* 36 (1970): 101–64.

———, and Wood, James A. "The Rhetoric of Film: Toward Critical Methodology." *Southern Speech Communication Journal* 39 (1973): 105–22.

Hillbruner, Anthony. "The Rhetorical Critic's Role in Society." *The Quarterly Journal of Speech* 44 (1958): 100–102.

———. "Creativity and Contemporary Criticism." *Western Speech* 24 (1960): 5–11.

———. "Criticism as Persuasion." *Southern Speech Journal* 28 (1963): 260–67.

———. "Speech Criticism and American Culture." *Western Speech* 32 (1968): 162–67.

———. "The Moral Imperative of Criticism." *Southern Speech Communication Journal* 40 (1975): 228–47.

———. "Rhetoric, Region and Social Science." *Central States Speech Journal* 21 (1970): 167–74.

Holland, L. Virginia. "Rhetorical Criticism: A Burkeian Method." *The Quarterly Journal of Speech* 39 (1953): 444–50.

———. "Kenneth Burke's Dramatistic Approach to Speech Criticism." *The Quarterly Journal of Speech* 41 (1955): 352–58.

Hunsaker, David M., and Smith, Craig R. "Rhetorical Distance: A Critical Dimension." *Western Speech* 37 (1973): 241–52.

Hunt, Everett Lee. "Rhetoric and Literary Criticism." *The Quarterly Journal of Speech* 21 (1935): 564–68.

———. "Rhetoric as a Humane Study." *The Quarterly Journal of Speech* 41 (1955): 114–17.

———. "Thoughts on a History and Criticism of American Public Address." *The Quarterly Journal of Speech* 42 (1956): 187–90.

Jamieson, Kathleen. "Antecedent Genre as Rhetorical Constraint." *The Quarterly Journal of Speech* 61 (1975): 406–15.

Johannesen, Richard J. "Richard Weaver's View of Rhetoric and Criticism." *Southern Speech Journal* 32 (1966): 133–53.

———. "Attitude of Speaker Toward Audience: A Significant Concept for Contemporary Rhetorical Theory and Criticism." *Central States Speech Journal* 25 (1974): 95–104.

Karstetter, Allan B. "Toward a Theory of Rhetorical Irony." *Speech Monographs* 31 (1964): 162–78.

Kruse, Noreen W. "Motivational Factors in Non-Denial Apologia." *Central States Speech Journal* 28 (1977): 13–23.

Larson, Barbara A. "Method in Rhetorical Criticism: A Pedagogical Approach and Proposal." *Central States Speech Journal* 27 (1976): 295–301.

Lee, Irving J. "Four Ways of Looking at a Speech." *The Quarterly Journal of Speech* 28 (1942): 148–55.

Lomas, Charles W. "Rhetorical Criticism and Historical Perspective." *Western Speech* 32 (1968): 191–203.

Macksoud, John S. "Kenneth Burke on Perspective and Rhetoric." *Western Speech* 33 (1969): 167–76.

Maloney, Martin. "Some New Directions in Rhetorical Criticism." *Central States Speech Journal* 4 (1953): 1–5.

Mohrmann, G. R., and Leff, Michael C. "Lincoln at Cooper Union: A Rationale for Neo-Classical Criticism." *The Quarterly Journal of Speech* 40 (1974): 459–67.

Mouat, L. H. "An Approach to Rhetorical Criticism." In *The Rhetorical Idiom,* edited by Donald C. Bryant. Ithaca, N.Y.: Cornell University Press, 1958.

Munshaw, Joe A. "The Structures of History: Dividing Phenomena for Rhetorical Understanding." *Central States Speech Journal* 24 (1973): 29–42.

Murphy, Richard. "The Speech as Literary Genre." *The Quarterly Journal of Speech* 44 (1958): 117–27.

Nichols, Marie Hochmuth. "Lincoln's First Inaugural." In *American Speeches,* edited by Wayland Maxwell Parrish and Marie Hochmuth Nichols. London: Longmans, Green, 1954.

Nilsen, Thomas. "Criticism and Social Consequences." *The Quarterly Journal of Speech* 42 (1956): 173–78.

North, Helen F. "Rhetoric and Historiography." *The Quarterly Journal of Speech* 42 (1956): 234–42.

Olian, J. Robert. "The Intended Use of Aristotle's Rhetoric." *Speech Monographs* 35 (1968): 137–48.

Osborn, Michael M. "Archetypal Metaphor in Rhetoric: The Light-Dark Family." *The Quarterly Journal of Speech* 53 (1967): 115–26.

————. "The Evolution of the Theory of Metaphor in Rhetoric." *Western Speech* 31 (1967): 121–30.

————, and Ehninger, Douglas. "The Metaphor in Public Address." *Speech Monographs* 29 (1962): 223–34.

Parrish, Wayland M. "The Study of Speeches." In *American Speeches*, edited by Wayland M. Parrish and Marie Hochmuth Nichols. New York: Longmans Green, 1954.

Rasmussen, Karen. "An Interaction Analysis of Justificatory Rhetoric." *Western Speech* 37 (1973): 111–17.

Redding, Charles. "Extrinsic and Intrinsic Criticism." *Western Speech* 21 (1957): 96–102.

Reid, Loren D. "The Perils of Rhetorical Criticism." *The Quarterly Journal of Speech* 30 (1944): 416–22.

Rosenfield, Lawrence B. "Set Theory: Key to the Understanding of Kenneth Burke's Use of the Term 'Identification.' " *Western Speech* 32 (1969): 178–83.

Rosenfield, Lawrence W. "Rhetorical Criticism and An Aristotelian Notion of Process." *Speech Monographs* 33 (1966): 1–16.

————. "The Anatomy of Critical Discourse." *Speech Monographs* 25 (1968): 50–69.

————. "The Experience of Criticism." *The Quarterly Journal of Speech* 60 (1974): 489–96.

Scott, Robert L. "Dialogue and Rhetoric." In *Rhetoric and Communication*, edited by Jane Blankenship and Hermann Stelzner, pp. 99–109. Urbana, Illinois: University of Illinois Press, 1976.

————. "On *Not* Defining 'Rhetoric.' " *Philosophy and Rhetoric* 6 (1973): 81–96.

————, and Smith, Donald K. "The Rhetoric of Confrontation." *The Quarterly Journal of Speech* 55 (1969): 1–8.

Sillars, Malcolm O. "Persistent Problems in Rhetorical Criticism." In *Rhetoric and Communication*, edited by Jane Blankenship and Hermann Stelzner, pp. 69–88. Urbana, Illinois: University of Illinois Press, 1976.

Simons, Herbert W. "Confrontation as a Pattern of Persuasion in University Settings." *Central States Speech Journal* 20 (1969): 163–69.

————. "Requirements, Problems and Strategies: A Theory of Persuasion of Social Movements." *The Quarterly Journal of Speech* 56 (1970): 1–11.

Smith, Craig R. and Streifford, Howard. "An Axiological Adjunct to Rhetorical Criticism." *Central States Speech Journal* 27 (1976): 22–30.

Smith, Ralph R., and Windes, Russel R. "The Rhetoric of Mobilization: Implications for the Study of Movements." *Southern Speech Communication Journal* 41 (1976): 1–19.

————. "Collective Action and the Single Text." *Southern Speech Communication Journal* 43 (1978): 110–28.

Smith, Robert W. "The Textual Critic: Hung up on Trivia?" *Southern Speech Communication Journal* 38 (1972): 424–36.

Steele, Edward D. "Social Values, the Enthymeme, and Speech Criticism." *Western Speech* 26 (1962): 70–75.

Swanson, David L. "A Reflective View of the Epistemology of Critical Inquiry." *Communication Monographs* 44 (1977): 207–19.

———. "The Requirements of Criticial Justifications." *Communication Monographs* 44 (1977): 306–20.

Thompson, Wayne. "Contemporary Public Address: A Problem in Criticism." *The Quarterly Journal of Speech* 40 (1954): 24–30.

Tompkins, Phillip K. "Rhetorical Criticism: Wrong Medium?" *Central States Speech Journal* 13 (1962): 90–95.

———. "The Rhetorical Criticism of Non-Oratorical Works." *The Quarterly Journal of Speech* 55 (1969): 431–39.

Trent, Judith. "A Synthesis of Methodologies Used in Studying Political Communication." *Central States Speech Journal* 26 (1975): 287–97.

Turner, Kathleen J. "Comic Strips: A Rhetorical Perspective." *Central States Speech Journal* 28 (1977): 24–35.

Wallace, Karl R. "The Substance of Rhetoric: Good Reasons." *The Quarterly Journal of Speech* 49 (1963): 239–49.

Wander, Philip, and Jenkins, Steven. "Rhetoric, Society, and the Critical Response." *The Quarterly Journal of Speech* 58 (1972): 441–50.

Ware, B. L., and Linkugel, Wil A. "They Spoke in Defense of Themselves: On The Generic Criticism of Apologia." *The Quarterly Journal of Speech* 59 (1973): 273–83.

Wichelns, Herbert. "The Literary Criticism of Oratory." In *Studies in Rhetoric and Public Speaking in Honor of James A. Winans,* edited by A. M. Drummond. New York: Century, 1925.

Wilkinson, Charles A. "A Rhetorical Definition of Movements." *Central States Speech Journal* 27 (1976): 88–94.

Wrage, Ernest J. "Public Address: A Study in Social and Intellectual History." *The Quarterly Journal of Speech* 33 (1947): 451–57.

———. "The Ideal Critic." *Central States Speech Journal* 8 (1957): 20–23.

Wright, Warren E. "Judicial Rhetoric: A Field for Research." *Speech Monographs* 31 (1964): 64–72.

Criticism

Anderson, Ray Lynn. "Rhetoric and Science Journalism." *The Quarterly Journal of Speech* 56 (1972): 358–68.

———. "The Rhetoric of the Report from Iron Mountain." *Speech Monographs* 37 (1970): 219–31.

Andrews, James R. "Confrontation at Columbia." *The Quarterly Journal of Speech* 55 (1969): 9–16.

————. "The Passionate Negation: The Chartist Movement in Rhetorical Perspective." *The Quarterly Journal of Speech* 59 (1973): 196–208.

————. "Reflections of the National Character in American Rhetoric." *The Quarterly Journal of Speech* 57 (1971): 316–24.

————. "Spindles vs. Acres: Rhetorical Perceptions on the British Free Trade Movement." *Western Speech* 38 (1974): 41–52.

————. "Coercive Rhetorical Strategy in Political Conflict: A Case Study of the *Trent* Affair." *Central States Speech Journal* 24 (1973): 253–61.

Auer, J. Jeffrey. "Tom Corwin: 'King of the Stump.' " *The Quarterly Journal of Speech* 30 (1944): 47–55.

Baird, John E. "The Rhetoric of Youth in Controversy Against the Religious Establishment." *Western Speech* 34 (1970): 53–61.

Barton, Stephen Nye, and O'Leary, John B. "The Rhetoric of Rural Physician Procurement Campaigns: An Application of Tavistock." *The Quarterly Journal of Speech* 60 (1974): 144–54.

Baskerville, Barnet. "Joe McCarthy, Brief Case Demagogue." *Today's Speech* 2 (1954): 8–15.

Baudhin, E. Scott. "From Campaign to Watergate: Nixon's Communication Image." *Western Speech* 38 (1974): 182–89.

Becker, Samuel L., and Kraus, Sidney, (eds.) "Campaign '76: Communication Studies of the Presidential Campaign." A Special Issue of *Communication Monographs* 45 (1978).

Bennett, W. Lance; Harris, Patricia Dempsey; Laskey, Janet K.; Levitch, Alan H., and Monrad, Sarah E. "Deep and Surface Issues in the Construction of Political Issues: The Case of Amnesty." *The Quarterly Journal of Speech* 62 (1976): 109–26.

Benson, Thomas W. "Rhetoric and Autobiography: The Case of Malcolm X." *The Quarterly Journal of Speech* 60 (1974): 1–13.

Berens, John F. " 'Like a Prophetic Spirit': Samuel Davies, American Eulogists, and the Deification of George Washington." *The Quarterly Journal of Speech* 63 (1977): 290–97.

Berg, David M. "Rhetoric, Reality and Mass Media." *The Quarterly Journal of Speech* 58 (1972): 255–63.

Betz, Brian R. "Eric Fromm and the Rhetoric of Prophecy." *Central States Speech Journal* 26 (1975): 310–15.

Black, Edwin. "Electing Time." *The Quarterly Journal of Speech* 59 (1973): 125–29.

Blankenship, Jane. "The Search for the 1972 Democratic Nomination: A Metaphorical Perspective." In *Rhetoric and Communication,* edited by Jane Blankenship and Hermann Stelzner, pp. 236–60. Urbana, Illinois: University of Illinois Press, 1976.

Bloodworth, John David. "Communication in the Youth Counter Culture: Music as Expression." *Central States Speech Journal* 26 (1975): 304–9.

Bormann, Ernest G. "The Eagleton Affair: A Fantasy Theme Analysis." *The Quarterly Journal of Speech* 59 (1973): 143–59.

———. "Fetching Good Out of Evil: A Rhetorical Use of Calamity." *The Quarterly Journal of Speech* 63 (1977): 130–39.

Bosmajian, Haig A. "Nazi Persuasion and the Crown Mentality." *Western Speech* 24 (1965): 68–78.

Bostrom, Robert N. "I Give You a Man–Kennedy's Speech for Adlai Stevenson." *Speech Monographs* 35 (1968): 129–36.

Braden, Waldo W., and Brandenburg, Earnest. "Roosevelt's Fireside Chats." *Speech Monographs* 22 (1955): 290–302.

Brandenburg, Earnest. "The Preparation of Franklin D. Roosevelt's Speeches." *The Quarterly Journal of Speech* 35 (1949): 214–21.

———. "Franklin D. Roosevelt's International Speeches: 1939–1941." *Speech Monographs* 16 (1949): 21–40.

Briggs, Nancy E. "Rhetorical Dimensions of the Nursery Rhyme." *Speech Teacher* 22 (1973): 215–19.

Brock, Bernard L. "1968 Democratic Campaign: A Political Upheaval." *The Quarterly Journal of Speech* 55 (1969): 26–35.

Brockriede, Wayne E., and Scott, Robert L. "Stokely Carmichael: Two Speeches on Black Power." *Central States Speech Journal* 19 (1968): 3–13.

Brooks, Paul D. "A Field Study of the Johnson and Goldwater Campaign Speeches in Pittsburgh." *Southern Speech Journal* 32 (1967): 273–81.

Brown, Janet. "Kenneth Burke and the *Mod Donna:* The Dramatistic Method Applied to Feminist Criticism." *Central States Speech Journal* 29 (1978): 138–44.

Brown, William R., and Crable, Richard E. "Industry, Mass Magazines, and the Ecology Issue." *The Quarterly Journal of Speech* 59 (1973): 259–72.

Brownlow, Paul C., and Davis, Beth. "A Certainty of Honor: The Eulogies of Adlai Stevenson." *Central States Speech Journal* 25 (1974): 217–24.

Brummett, Barry. "Presidential Substance: The Address of August 15, 1973." *Western Speech Communication* 39 (1975): 249–59.

———. "Gary Gilmore, Power, and the Rhetoric of Symbolic Forms." *Western Journal of Speech Communication* 43 (1979): 3–13.

Burdich, Norman R. "The 'Coatesville Address': Crossroad of Rhetoric and Poetry." *Western Speech Communication* 41 (1978): 73–82.

Burgess, Parke G. "The Rhetoric of Black Power: A Moral Demand?" *The Quarterly Journal of Speech* 54 (1968): 122–33.

Bytwerk, Randall L. "The Rhetoric of Defeat: Nazi Propaganda in 1945." *Central States Speech Journal* 29 (1978): 44–52.

Campbell, Finley C. "Voices of Thunder, Voices of Rage: A Symbolic Analysis of a Selection from Malcolm X's Speech, 'Message to the Grass Roots.' " *The Speech Teacher* 19 (1970): 101–10.

Campbell, John Angus. "Darwin and The Origin of the Species: The Rhetorical Ancestory of an Idea." *Speech Monographs* 37 (1970): 1–14.

———. "Charles Darwin and the Crisis of Ecology: A Rhetorical Perspective." *The Quarterly Journal of Speech* 60 (1974): 442–49.

———. "The Polemical Mr. Darwin." *The Quarterly Journal of Speech* 61 (1975): 375–90.

Campbell, Karlyn Kohrs. "The Rhetoric of Radical Black Nationalism: A Case Study of Self-Conscious Criticism." *Central States Speech Journal* 22 (1971): 151–60.

———. "The Rhetoric of Women's Liberation: An Oxymoron." *The Quarterly Journal of Speech* 59 (1973): 74–86.

Carpenter, Ronald H. "The Rhetorical Genesis of Style in the Frontier Thesis of Frederick Jackson Turner." *Southern Speech Journal* 37 (1972): 233–48.

———. "Frederick Jackson Turner and the Rhetorical Impact of the Frontier Thesis." *The Quarterly Journal of Speech* 63 (1977): 117–29.

Casmir, Fred L. "An Analysis of Hitler's January 30, 1941, Speech." *Western Speech* 30 (1966): 96–105.

Cherwitz, Richard A. "Lyndon Johnson and the 'Crisis' of Tonkin Gulf: A President's Justification of War." *Western Journal of Speech Communication* 41 (1978): 93–104.

Chesebro, James W. "Rhetorical Strategies of Radicals." *Today's Speech* 20 (1972): 37–48.

Clark, Thomas D. "An Exploration of Generic Aspects of Contemporary American Christian Sermons." *The Quarterly Journal of Speech* 63 (1977): 384–94.

Collins, Catherine Ann. "Kissinger's Press Conferences, 1972–1974: An Exploration of Form and Role Relationship of News Management." *Central States Speech Journal* 28 (1977): 185–93.

Corder, Jim W. "Efficient Ethos in *Shane,* with a Proposal for Discriminating Among Kinds of Ethos." *Communication Quarterly* 25 (1977): 28–31.

Cox, J. Robert. "Perspectives on Rhetorical Criticism of Movements: Antiwar Dissent, 1964–1970." *Western Speech* 38 (1974): 254–68.

———. "The Rhetoric of Child Labor Reform: An Efficacy-Utility Analysis." *The Quarterly Journal of Speech* 60 (1974): 359–70.

Cragan, John F. "Foreign Policy Communication Dramas: How Mediated Rhetoric Played in Peoria in Campaign '76." *The Quarterly Journal of Speech* 63 (1977): 274–89.

Crocker, James W. "A Rhetoric of Encounter Following the May 4th, 1970, Disturbance at Kent State University." *Communication Quarterly* 25 (1977): 44–55.

Crowell, Laura. "Franklin D. Roosevelt's Audience Persuasion in the 1936 Campaign." *Speech Monographs* 17 (1950): 48–64.

————. "Three Sheers for Kenneth Burke." *The Quarterly Journal of Speech* 63 (1977): 152–67.

deSpain, Jerry Lynn. "A Rhetorical View of J. R. R. Tolkien's The Lord of the Rings Trilogy." *Western Speech* 35 (1971): 88–97.

Devin, Lee. "Lincoln's Ethos: Viewed and Practiced." *Central States Speech Journal* 16 (1965): 99–105.

Devlin, L. Patrick. "Contrasts in Presidential Campaign Commercials of 1976." *Central States Speech Journal* 28 (1977): 238–49.

Duncan, Rodger Dean. "Rhetoric of the Kidvid Movement: Ideology, Strategy, and Tactics." *Central States Speech Journal* 27 (1976): 129–35.

Eich, Ritch K., and Goodman, Donald. "Communication, Confrontation and Coercion: Agitation at Michigan." *Central States Speech Journal* 27 (1976): 120–28.

Erlich, Howard S. " '. . . And by Opposing, End Them': The Genre of Moral Justification for Legal Transgressions." *Today's Speech* 23 (1975): 13–16.

————. "Populist Rhetoric Reassessed: A Paradox." *The Quarterly Journal of Speech* 63 (1977): 140–51.

Faries, Clyde J. "Private Allen's Strategy of Reconciliation." *The Quarterly Journal of Speech* 52 (1966): 358–63.

Fisher, Jeanne Y. "A Burkean Analysis of the Rhetorical Dimensions of a Multiple Murder and Suicide." *The Quarterly Journal of Speech* 60 (1974): 175–89.

Fisher, Walter R. "Reaffirmation and Subversion of the American Dream." *The Quarterly Journal of Speech* 59 (1973): 160–67.

Fletcher, Winona L. "Knight-Errant or Screaming Eagle? E. L. Godkin's Criticism of Wendell Phillips." *Southern Speech Journal* 29 (1964): 214–23.

Frentz, Thomas S., and Rushing, Janet Hocker. "The Rhetoric of 'Rocky': Part Two." *Western Journal of Speech Communication* 42 (1978): 231–40.

Golden, James A. "John F. Kennedy and the 'Ghosts.' " *The Quarterly Journal of Speech* 52 (1966): 348–57.

Gravlee, G. Jack. "Franklin D. Roosevelt's Speech Preparation During His First National Campaign." *Speech Monographs* 21 (1964): 437–60.

Gregg, Richard B. "A Rhetorical Re-Examination of Arthur Vandenberg's 'Dramatic Conversion,' January 10, 1945." *The Quarterly Journal of Speech* 61 (1975): 154–68.

————. "The Rhetoric of Political Newscasting." *Central States Speech Journal* 27 (1977): 221–37.

————, and Hauser, Gerald A. "Richard Nixon's April 30, 1970 Address on Cambodia: The Ceremony of Confrontation." *Speech Monographs* 40 (1973): 167–81.

Gribbin, William. "The Juggernaut Metaphor in American Rhetoric." *The Quarterly Journal of Speech* 59 (1973): 297–303.

Griffin, Leland M. "The Rhetorical Structure of the 'New Left' Movement: Part I." *The Quarterly Journal of Speech* 50 (1964): 113–35.

Gronbeck, Bruce E. "Government's Stance in Crisis: A Case Study of Pitt the Younger." *Western Speech* 34 (1970): 250–61.

———. "John Morley and the Irish Question: Chart-Prayer-Dream." *Speech Monographs* 40 (1973): 287–95.

———. "Rhetorical Invention in the Regency Crisis Pamphlets." *The Quarterly Journal of Speech* 58 (1972): 418–30.

Haberman, Frederick W. "General MacArthur's Speech: A Symposium of Critical Comment." *The Quarterly Journal of Speech* 37 (1951): 321–31.

Hagan, Michael. "Roe V. Ward: The Rhetoric of Fetal Life." *Central States Speech Journal* 27 (1976): 192–99.

Hancock, Brenda Robinson. "Affirmation by Negation in the Women's Liberation Movement." *The Quarterly Journal of Speech* 58 (1972): 264–71.

Harrell, Jackson, Ware, B. L., and Linkugel, Wil A. "Failure of Apology in American Politics: Nixon on Watergate." *Speech Monographs* 42 (1975): 245–61.

Hart, Roderick P. "The Rhetoric of the True Believer." *Speech Monographs* 38 (1971): 249–61.

———. "An Unquiet Desperation: Rhetorical Aspects of 'Popular' Atheism in the United States." *The Quarterly Journal of Speech* 64 (1978): 33–46.

Hayes, Merwyn A. "William L. Yancey Presents the Southern Case to the North; 1860." *Southern Speech Journal* 29 (1964): 194–208.

Heath, Robert L. "Common Cause and Nonpartisan Influence in Political Campaigns: A Case Study." *Central States Speech Journal* 25 (1974): 182–89.

———. "A Time for Silence: Booker T. Washington in Atlanta." *The Quarterly Journal of Speech* 64 (1978): 385–99.

Heisey, D. Ray. "The Rhetoric of the Arab-Israeli Conflict." *The Quarterly Journal of Speech* 56 (1970): 12–21.

Henderlider, Clair R. "Woodrow Wilson's Speeches on the League of Nations, September 4–25, 1919." *Speech Monographs* 12 (1946): 23–34.

Hensley, Carl Wayne. "Rhetorical Vision and the Persuasion of a Historical Movement: The Disciples of Christian Nineteenth Century American Culture." *The Quarterly Journal of Speech* 61 (1975): 250–64.

Hill, Forbes I. "Conventional Wisdom—Traditional Form: The President's Message of November 3, 1969." *The Quarterly Journal of Speech* 58 (1972): 373–86. (See also *Forum*, same issue. Hill and K. K. Campbell.)

Hillbruner, Anthony. "Rhetoric and Politics: The Making of the President, 1960." *Western Speech* 29 (1965): 91–101.

Hope, Dianne S. "Redefinition of Self: A Comparison of The Rhetoric of

The Women's Liberation and Black Liberation Movements." *Today's Speech* 23 (1975): 17–26.

Hunsaker, David M. "The Rhetoric of Brown v. Board of Education: Paradigm for Contemporary Social Protest." *Southern Speech Communication Journal* 43 (1978): 91–109.

Hunter, Charles F. "Thomas Hart Benton: An Evaluation." *The Quarterly Journal of Speech* 30 (1944): 279–85.

Ilkka, Richard J. "Rhetorical Dramatization in the Development of American Communication." *The Quarterly Journal of Speech* 63 (1977): 413–27.

Ivie, Robert L. "Presidential Motives for War." *The Quarterly Journal of Speech* 60 (1974): 337–45.

Jamieson, Kathleen. "Interpretation of Natural Law in the Conflict Over Humanae Vitae." *The Quarterly Journal of Speech* 60 (1974): 201–11.

Jensen, J. Vernon. "The Rhetorical Strategy of Thomas H. Huxley and Robert G. Ingersoll: Agnostics and Roadblock Removers." *Speech Monographs* 32 (1965): 59–68.

———. "British Voices on the Eve of the American Revolution: Trapped by the Family Metaphor." *The Quarterly Journal of Speech* 63 (1977): 43–50.

Jensen, Richard J., and Jensen, Carol L. "Labor's Appeal to the Past: The 1972 Election in the United Mine Workers." *Central States Speech Journal* 28 (1977): 173–84.

Johnstone, Christopher L. "Thoreau and Civil Disobedience: A Rhetorical Paradox." *The Quarterly Journal of Speech* 60 (1974): 313–22.

Kane, Peter E. "Evaluating the 'Great Debates.'" *Western Speech* 30 (1966): 89–95.

Katula, Richard A. "The Apology of Richard M. Nixon." *Today's Speech* 23 (1975): 7–12.

Kennedy, George. "Anthony's Speech at Caesar's Funeral." *The Quarterly Journal of Speech* 54 (1968): 99–106.

Kennicott, Patrick C. "Black Persuaders in the Antislavery Movement." *Speech Monographs* 37 (1970): 15–24.

———, and Pace, Wayne E. "H. Rap Brown: The Cambridge Incident." *The Quarterly Journal of Speech* 57 (1971): 325–34.

Kerr, Henry P. "The Election Sermon: Primer for Revolutionaries." *Speech Monographs* 29 (1962): 13–22.

Kidd, Virginia. "Happily Ever After and Other Relationship Styles: Advice on Interpersonal Relations in Popular Magazines, 1951–1973." *The Quarterly Journal of Speech* 61 (1975): 31–39.

King, Andrew A. "Booker T. Washington and the Myth of Heroic Materialism." *The Quarterly Journal of Speech* 60 (1974): 323–27.

———. "The Rhetoric of Power Maintenance: Elites at the Precipice." *The Quarterly Journal of Speech* 62 (1976): 127–34.

————, and Anderson, Floyd Douglas. "Nixon, Agnew, and the Silent Majority: A Case Study in the Rhetoric of Polarization." *Western Speech* 35 (1971): 243–55.

————. "Power: The Rhetoric of Mobilization." *Central States Speech Journal* 29 (1978): 147–54.

Klumpp, James F. "Challenge of Radical Rhetoric: Radicalization at Columbia." *Western Speech* 37 (1973): 146–56.

————, and Lukehart, Jeffrey K. "The Pardoning of Richard Nixon: A Failure in Motivational Strategy." *Western Journal of Speech Communication* 41 (1978): 116–23.

Lanigan, Richard L. "Urban Crisis: Polarization and Communication." *Central States Speech Journal* 21 (1970): 108–16.

Larson, Barbara A. "The Election Eve Address of Edmund Muskie: A Case Study of the Televised Public Address." *Central States Speech Journal* 23 (1972): 78–85.

————. "Samuel Davies, and the Rhetoric of the New Light." *Speech Monographs* 38 (1971): 207–16.

Lazenby, Walter. "Exhortation as Exorcism: Cotton Mather's Sermons to Murderers." *The Quarterly Journal of Speech* 57 (1971): 50–56.

Leathers, Dale G. "Fundamentalism of the Radical Right." *Southern Speech Journal* 33 (1968): 245–58.

Leff, Michael C., and Mohrmann, G. P. "Lincoln at Cooper Union: A Rhetorical Analysis of the Text." *The Quarterly Journal of Speech* 60 (1974): 346–58.

Ling, David A. "A Pentadic Analysis of Senator Edward Kennedy's Address to the People of Massachusetts, July 25, 1969." *Central States Speech Journal* 21 (1970): 81–86.

Linkugel, Wil A. "Lincoln, Kansas, and Cooper Union." *Speech Monographs* 37 (1970): 172–79.

Litfin, A. Duane. "Eisenhower on the Military-Industrial Complex: Critique of a Rhetorical Strategy." *Central States Speech Journal* 25 (1974): 198–209.

————. "Senator Edmund Muskie's 'Five Smooth Stones': An Analysis of Rhetorical Strategies and Tactics in His 1970 Election Eve Speech." *Central States Speech Journal* 23 (1972): 5–10.

Logue, Cal M. "Rhetorical Ridicule of Reconstruction Blacks." *The Quarterly Journal of Speech* 62 (1976): 400–409.

————. "The Rhetorical Appeals of Whites to Blacks During Reconstruction." *Communication Monographs* 44 (1977): 241–51.

Lucas, Stephen E. "The Man with the Muck Rake: A Reinterpretation." *The Quarterly Journal of Speech* 59 (1973): 452–62.

Martin, Howard H. "The Rhetoric of Academic Protest." *Central States Speech Journal* 17 (1966): 244–50.

McBath, James H., and Fisher, Walter R. "Persuasion in Presidential Campaign Communication." *The Quarterly Journal of Speech* 55 (1969): 17–25.

McGee, Michael. "The Fall of Wellington: A Case Study of the Relationship Between Theory, Practice and Rhetoric in History." *Quarterly Journal of Speech* 63 (1977): 28–42.

McGuckin, Henry E., Jr. "A Value Analysis of Richard Nixon's 1952 Campaign-Fund Speech." *Southern Speech Journal* 33 (1968): 259–69.

McGuire, Michael. "Mythic Rhetoric in Mein Kampf: A Structuralist Critique." *The Quarterly Journal of Speech* 63 (1977): 1–13.

———, and Patton, John H. "Preaching in the Mystic Mode: The Rhetorical Art of Meister Eckhart." *Communication Monographs* 44 (1977): 263–72.

McKerrow, Ray E. "Truman and Korea: Rhetoric in the Pursuit of Victory." *Central States Speech Journal* 28 (1977): 1–12.

McPherson, Louise. "Communication Techniques of the Women's Liberation Front." *Today's Speech* 21 (1973): 33–36.

Medhurst, Martin J. "McGovern at Wheaton: A Quest for Redemption." *Communication Quarterly* 25 (1977): 32–39.

———. "Image and Ambiguity: A Rhetorical Approach to THE EXORCIST." *Southern Speech Communication Journal* 44 (1978): 73–92.

Mowe, Gregory, and Nobles, W. Scott. "James Baldwin's Message for White America." *Quarterly Journal of Speech* 58 (1972): 142–51.

Murray, Michael D. "Persuasive Dimensions of See It Now's 'Report on Senator Joseph R. McCarthy.' " *Today's Speech* 23 (1975): 13–20.

Nelson, Paul. E. "The Fugal Form of Charles James Fox's Rejection of Bonaparte's Overtures." *Western Speech* 36 (1972): 9–14.

Newman, Robert P. "Under the Veneer: Nixon's Vietnam Speech of November 3, 1969." *The Quarterly Journal of Speech* 56 (1970): 168–78.

Nichel, W. Sandra. "The Rhetoric of Union: A Stylized Utterance." *Central States Speech Journal* 24 (1973): 137–42.

Norton, Robert Wayne. "The Rhetorical Situation Is The Message: Muskie's Election Eve Television Broadcast." *Central States Speech Journal* 22 (1971): 171–78.

Oliver, Robert T. "Wilson's Rapport with His Audience." *The Quarterly Journal of Speech* 27 (1941): 79–90.

Patton, John H. "The Eagleton Phenomenon in the 1972 Presidential Campaign: A Case Study in the Rhetoric of Paradox." *Central States Speech Journal* 24 (1973): 278–87.

———. "Rhetoric at Catonsville: Daniel Berrigan, Conscience, and Image Alteration." *Today's Speech* 23 (1975): 3–12.

———. "A Government as Good as Its People: Jimmy Carter and the Restoration of Transcendence to Policies." *The Quarterly Journal of Speech* 63 (1977): 249–57.

Quimby, Rollin W. "Agnew, the Press and The Rhetorical Critic." *Western Speech* 39 (1975): 146–54.

Rassmussen, Karen. "Nixon and the Strategy of Avoidance." *Central States Speech Journal* 24 (1973): 193–202.

Raum, Richard D., and Measell, James S. "Wallace and His Ways: A Study of the Rhetorical Genre of Polarization." *Central States Speech Journal* 25 (1974): 28–35.

Reed, Robert Michael. "The Case of Missionary Smith: A Crucial Incident in the Rhetoric of the British Anti-Slavery Movement." *Central States Speech Journal* 29 (1978): 61–71.

Reid, Ronald F. "New England Rhetoric and the French War, 1754–1760: A Case Study in the Rhetoric of War." *Communication Monographs* 43 (1976): 259–86.

Rickert, William E. "Winston Churchill's Archetypal Metaphors: A Mythopoetic Translation of World War II." *Central States Speech Journal* 28 (1977): 106–113.

Ritter, Kurt R. "Ronald Reagan and 'The Speech': The Rhetoric of Public Relations Politics." *Western Speech* 32 (1968): 50–58.

Rosenfield, Lawrence W. "A Case Study in Speech Criticism: The Nixon-Truman Analog." *Speech Monographs* 35 (1968): 435–50.

———. "Politics and Pornography." *The Quarterly Journal of Speech* 59 (1973): 413–22.

———. "August 9, 1974: The Victimage of Richard Nixon." *Communication Quarterly* 24 (1976): 19–23.

Rosenthal, Paul I. "The Concept of the Paramessage in Persuasive Communication." *The Quarterly Journal of Speech* 58 (1972): 15–30.

Rosenwasser, Marie J. "Movement Rhetoric on Women's Liberation." *Today's Speech* 20 (1972): 45–56.

Rushing, Janice Hocking, and Frentz, Thomas S. "The Rhetoric of 'Rocky': A Social Value Model of Criticism." *Western Journal of Speech Communication* 41 (1978): 63–72.

Sanbonmatsu, Akira. "Darrow and Rorke's Use of Burkeian Identification Strategies in New York vs. Gitlow (1920)." *Speech Monongraphs* 38 (1971): 36–48.

Schmidt, Patricia L. "The Role of Moral Idealism in Social Change: Lord Ashley and the Ten Hours Factory Act." *The Quarterly Journal of Speech* 63 (1977): 14–28.

Schuetz, Janice. " 'The Exorcist': Images of Good and Evil." *Western Speech Communication* 39 (1975): 92–101.

Scott, Robert L. "A Rhetoric of Facts: Arthur Larson's Stance as a Persuader." *Speech Monographs* 35 (1968): 109–21.

———. "Justifying Violence—The Rhetoric of Black Power." *Central States Speech Journal* 19 (1968): 96–104.

————. "Rhetoric That Postures: An Intrinsic Reading of Richard M. Nixon's Inaugural Address." *Western Speech* 34 (1970): 46–52.

————. "The Conservative Voice in Radical Rhetoric: A Common Response to Division." *Speech Monographs* 40 (1973): 123–35.

————. "Diego Rivera at Rockefeller Center: Fresco Painting and Rhetoric." *Western Journal of Speech Communication* 41 (1977): 70–82.

Shields, Evelyn. "The Rhetoric of Emerging Nationalism: A Case Study in Irish Rhetorical Failure." *Central States Speech Journal* 25 (1974): 225–32.

Sillars, Malcolm O. "The Rhetoric of the Petition in Boots." *Speech Monographs* 39 (1972): 92–104.

Sloan, Thomas O. "A Rhetorical Analysis of John Donne's 'The Prohibition.'" *The Quarterly Journal of Speech* 48 (1962): 38–45.

————. "Persona as Rhetor: An Interpretation of Donne's Satyre III." *The Quarterly Journal of Speech* 51 (1965): 14–27.

Smith, Craig. "The Republican Keynote Address of 1968: Adaptive Rhetoric for the Multiple Audience." *Western Speech* 39 (1975): 32–39.

————. "Television News as Rhetoric." *Western Journal of Speech Communication* 41 (1977): 147–59.

Smith, F. Michael. "Rhetorical Implications of the Aggression Thesis in the Johnson Administration's Vietnam Argumentation." *Central States Speech Journal* 23 (1972): 217–24.

Smith, Robert W. "Rhetoric in Crisis: The Abdication Address of Edward VIII." *Speech Monographs* 30 (1963): 335–39.

Solomon, Martha. "Jimmy Carter and *Playboy:* A Sociolinguistic Perspective on Style." *The Quarterly Journal of Speech* 64 (1978): 173–82.

————. "The Rhetoric of STOP ERA: Fatalistic Reaffirmation." *Southern Speech Communication Journal* 44 (1978): 42–59.

Stelzner, Hermann G. "The British Orators, VII: John Morley's Speech-Making." *The Quarterly Journal of Speech* 45 (1959): 171–81.

————. "Speech Criticism by Journalists." *Southern Speech Journal* 28 (1962): 17–26.

————. "'War Message' December 8, 1941, An Approach to Language." *Speech Monographs* 33 (1966): 419–37.

————. "Humphrey and Kennedy Court West Virginia, May 3, 1960." *Southern Speech Journal* 37 (1971): 21–33.

————. "John F. Kennedy at Houston, Texas, September 12, 1960." In *Rhetoric and Communication,* edited by Jane Blankenship and Hermann Stelzner, pp. 223–35. Urbana, Illinois: University of Illinois Press, 1976.

————. "Ford's War on Inflation: A Metaphor that Did Not Cross." *Communication Monographs* 44 (1977): 284–97.

Strine, Mary S. "*The Confessions of Nat Turner:* Styron's 'Meditation on

History' as Rhetorical Act." *The Quarterly Journal of Speech* 64 (1978): 246–66.

Stuart, Charlotte L. "Mary Wollenstonecraft's 'A Vindication of the Rights of Women': A Rhetorical Assessment." *Western Journal of Speech Communication* 41 (1978): 83–92.

Swanson, David L. "The New Politics Meets the Old Rhetoric: New Direction in Campaign Communication Research." *The Quarterly Journal of Speech* 58 (1972): 31–40.

––––––. "Political Information, Influence, and Judgment in the 1972 Presidential Campaigns." *The Quarterly Journal of Speech* 59 (1973): 130–42.

––––––. "And That's the Way It Was? Television Covers the 1976 Presidential Campaign." *The Quarterly Journal of Speech* 63 (1977): 239–48.

Thomas, Cheryl Irwin. " 'Look What They've Done to My Song, Ma': The Persuasiveness of Song." *Southern Speech Communication Journal* 39 (1974): 260–68.

Tompkins, Phillip K. "The Rhetoric of James Joyce." *The Quarterly Journal of Speech* 54 (1968): 107–14.

––––––. "On 'Paradoxes' in the Rhetoric of the New England Transcendentalists." *The Quarterly Journal of Speech* 67 (1976): 40–48.

Trent, Judith S., and Trent, Jimmie D. "The Rhetoric of the Challenger: George Stanley McGovern." *Central States Speech Journal* 25 (1974): 11–18.

Vasilew, Eugene. "Norman Thomas at the Townsend Convention of 1936." *Speech Monographs* 24 (1957): 233–43.

Wallace, Karl. "On the Criticism of the MacArthur Speech." *The Quarterly Journal of Speech* 39 (1953): 69–74.

Wander, Philip C. "The John Birch and Martin Luther King Symbols in the Radical Right." *Western Speech* 35 (1971): 4–14.

Warnick, Barbara. "The Rhetoric of Conservative Resistance." *Southern Speech Communication Journal* 42 (1977): 256–73.

Wiethoff, William. "Rhetorical Enterprise in the Ministry of 'Reverend Ike.' " *Communication Monographs* 44 (1977): 52–59.

––––––. "Rhetorical Strategies in Birmingham Political Union, 1830–1832." *Central States Speech Journal* 29 (1978): 53–60.

Williams, Donald E. "Andrew D. White: Spokesman for the Free University." *The Quarterly Journal of Speech* 47 (1961): 133–42.

Wilson, Gerald L. "A Strategy of Explanation: Richard M. Nixon's August 8, 1974, Resignation Address." *Communication Quarterly* 24 (1976): 14–20.

Windes, Russel, Jr. "A Study in Effective and Ineffective Presidential Campaign Speaking." *Speech Monographs* 27 (1961): 39–49.

––––––, and Robinson, James A. "Public Address in the Career of Adlai E. Stevenson." *The Quarterly Journal of Speech* 42 (1956): 225–33.

Windt, Theodore Otto, Jr. "The Diatribe: Last Resort for Protest." *The Quarterly Journal of Speech* 58 (1972): 1–14.

———. "The Rhetoric of Peaceful Co-existence: Krushchev in America, 1959." *The Quarterly Journal of Speech* 57 (1971): 11–22.

Woodward, Gary C. "Mystifications in the Rhetoric of Cultural Dominance and Colonial Control." *Central States Speech Journal* 26 (1975): 298–303.

Wrage, Ernest J. "E. L. Godkin and the Nation: Critics of Public Address." *Southern Speech Journal* 15 (1949): 100–111.

———. "The Little World of Barry Goldwater." *Western Speech* 27 (1963): 207–15.

Wylie, Phillip. "Medievalism and the MacArthurian Legend." *The Quarterly Journal of Speech* 37 (1951): 473–78.

Zarefsky, David. "President Johnson's War on Poverty: The Rhetoric of Three 'Establishment' Movements." *Communication Monographs* 44 (1977): 352–73.

INDEX

Bernard L. Brock is professor of speech-communication at Wayne State University, and has taught speech at the University of Minnesota. He received his B.A. from Illinois State University (1954), and his M.A. and Ph.D. from Northwestern University (1961, 1965).

Robert L. Scott is professor and chairman of the department of speech-communication at the University of Minnesota, and has taught speech at the University of Houston. He received his A.B. from the University of Northern Colorado (1950), his M.A. from the University of Nebraska (1951), and his Ph.D. from the University of Illinois (1955).

The manuscript was prepared for publication by Jacqueline Nash. The book was designed by Mary Primeau. The typeface for the text is Helvetica, designed by Max Miedinger.

The text is printed on S. D. Warren's 1854 text paper and the book is bound in Holliston Mills Roxite Vellum over binder's boards. Manufactured in the United States of America.